SYSTAT ® 9

Statistics II

For more information about SYSTAT® software products, please visit our WWW site at *http://www.spss.com* or contact

SPSS Science Marketing Department
SPSS Inc.
233 South Wacker Drive, 11th Floor
Chicago, IL 60606-6307
Tel: (312) 651-3000
Fax: (312) 651-3668

SYSTAT is a registered trademark and the other product names are the trademarks of SPSS Inc. for its proprietary computer software. No material describing such software may be produced or distributed without the written permission of the owners of the trademark and license rights in the software and the copyrights in the published materials.

The SOFTWARE and documentation are provided with RESTRICTED RIGHTS. Use, duplication, or disclosure by the Government is subject to restrictions as set forth in subdivision (c)(1)(ii) of The Rights in Technical Data and Computer Software clause at 52.227-7013. Contractor/manufacturer is SPSS Inc., 233 South Wacker Drive, 11th Floor, Chicago, IL 60606-6307.

General notice: Other product names mentioned herein are used for identification purposes only and may be trademarks of their respective companies.

Windows is a registered trademark of Microsoft Corporation.
ImageStream® Graphics & Presentation Filters, copyright © 1991-1997 by INSO Corporation. All Rights Reserved.
ImageStream Graphics Filters is a registered trademark and ImageStream is a trademark of INSO Corporation.

For using GSLIB:
Copyright © 1996, The Board of Trustees of the Leland Stanford Junior University. All rights reserved.
The programs in GSLIB are distributed in the hope that they will be useful, but WITHOUT ANY WARRANTY. No author or distributor accepts responsibility to anyone for the consequences of using them or for whether they serve any particular purpose or work at all, unless he says so in writing. Everyone is granted permission to copy, modify and redistribute the programs in GSLIB, but only under the condition that this notice and the above copyright notice remain intact.

For using Kernel statistics code:
Ken Clarkson wrote this. Copyright © 1995 by AT&T.
Permission to use, copy, modify, and distribute this software for any purpose without fee is hereby granted, provided that this entire notice is included in all copies of any software which is or includes a copy or modification of this software and in all copies of the supporting documentation for such software.
THIS SOFTWARE IS BEING PROVIDED "AS IS," WITHOUT ANY EXPRESS OR IMPLIED WARRANTY. IN PARTICULAR, NEITHER THE AUTHORS NOR AT&T MAKE ANY REPRESENTATION OR WARRANTY OF ANY KIND CONCERNING THE MERCHANTABILITY OF THIS SOFTWARE OR ITS FITNESS FOR ANY PARTICULAR PURPOSE.

SYSTAT ® 9 Statistics II
Copyright © 1999 by SPSS Inc.
All rights reserved.
Printed in the United States of America.

No part of this publication may be reproduced, stored in a retrieval system, or transmitted, in any form or by any means, electronic, mechanical, photocopying, recording, or otherwise, without the prior written permission of the publisher.

1 2 3 4 5 6 7 8 9 0   04 03 02 01 00 99

ISBN 1-13-026158-0

Table of Contents

1 Missing Value Analysis   II-1

Statistical Background II-1
    Techniques for Handling Missing Values II-3
    Randomness and Missing Data II-9
    A Final Caution II-12
Missing Value Analysis in SYSTAT II-12
    Missing Main Dialog II-12
    Using Commands II-14
    Usage Considerations II-15
Examples II-15
    Example 1
    Missing Values: Preliminary Examinations II-15
    Example 2
    Casewise Pattern Table II-20
    Example 3
    Correlation Estimation II-25
    Example 4
    Comparing Correlation Estimation Methods II-33
    Example 5
    Missing Value Imputation II-42
Computation II-46
    Algorithms II-46
References II-46

2 Multidimensional Scaling   II-47

Statistical Background II-48
    Assumptions II-48
    Collecting Dissimilarity Data II-49
    Scaling Dissimilarities II-50

Multidimensional Scaling in SYSTAT II-51
    Multidimensional Scaling Main Dialog Box II-51
    Using Commands II-55
    Usage Considerations II-55
Examples II-56
    Example 1
    Kruskal Method II-56
    Example 2
    Guttman Loss Function II-58
    Example 3
    Individual Differences Multidimensional Scaling II-60
    Example 4
    Nonmetric Unfolding II-64
    Example 5
    Power Scaling Ratio Data II-68
Computation II-70
    Algorithms II-70
    Missing Data II-72
References II-73

3 *Nonlinear Models*   *II-75*

Statistical Background II-76
    Modeling the Dose-Response Function II-76
    Loss Functions II-79
    Model Estimation II-83
    Problems II-83
Nonlinear Models in SYSTAT II-84
    Nonlinear Model Specification II-84
    Loss Functions for Analytic Function Minimization II-92
    Using Commands II-93
    Usage Considerations II-93
Examples II-94
    Example 1
    Nonlinear Model with Three Parameters II-94

Example 2
Confidence Curves and Regions II-97
Example 3
Fixing Parameters and Evaluating Fit II-100
Example 4
Functions of Parameters II-102
Example 5
Contouring the Loss Function II-105
Example 6
Maximum Likelihood Estimation II-107
Example 7
Iteratively Reweighted Least Squares for Logistic Models. . . .II-108
Example 8
Robust Estimation (Measures of Location) II-110
Example 9
Regression II-113
Example 10
Piecewise Regression. II-118
Example 11
Kinetic Models II-120
Example 12
Minimizing an Analytic Function II-121
Computation II-122
   Algorithms II-122
   Missing Data II-123
References. II-124

4 *Nonparametric Statistics*   *II-125*

Statistical Background II-126
   Rank (Ordinal) Data II-126
   Categorical (Nominal) Data. .II-127
   Robustness II-127
Nonparametric Statistics for Independent Samples in SYSTAT. . . .II-127
   Kruskal-Wallis Main Dialog Box II-127
   Two-Sample Kolmogorov-Smirnov Main Dialog Box II-128
   Using Commands II-129

Nonparametric Statistics for Related Variables in SYSTAT II-129
    Sign Tests Main Dialog Box II-129
    Wilcoxon Signed-Rank Test Main Dialog Box II-130
    Friedman Tests Main Dialog Box II-130
    Using Commands II-131
Nonparametric Statistics for Single Samples in SYSTAT II-131
    One-Sample Kolmogorov-Smirnov Main Dialog Box II-131
    Wald-Wolfowitz Runs Main Dialog Box II-133
    Using Commands II-133
Usage Considerations II-134
Examples II-134
    Example 1
    Kruskal-Wallis Test II-134
    Example 2
    Mann-Whitney Test II-136
    Example 3
    Two-Sample Kolmogorov-Smirnov Test II-137
    Example 4
    Sign Test II-137
    Example 5
    Wilcoxon Test II-139
    Example 6
    Sign and Wilcoxon Tests for Multiple Variables II-139
    Example 7
    Friedman Test II-140
    Example 8
    One-Sample Kolmogorov-Smirnov Test II-142
    Example 9
    Wald-Wolfowitz Runs Test II-144
Computation II-145
    Algorithms II-145
References II-146

5 Partially Ordered Scalogram Analysis with Coordinates II-147

Statistical Background II-147
    Coordinates. II-149
POSAC in SYSTAT. II-150
    POSAC Main Dialog Box II-150
    Using Commands II-150
    Usage Considerations. II-151
Examples. II-151
    Example 1
    Scalogram Analysis—A Perfect Fit II-152
    Example 2
    Binary Profiles II-153
    Example 3
    Multiple Categories II-156
Computation II-160
    Algorithms II-160
    Missing Data II-160
References. II-160

6 Path Analysis (RAMONA) II-161

Statistical Background II-161
    The Path Diagram II-161
    RAMONA's Model. II-169

Path Analysis in SYSTAT II-171
    RAMONA Model Main Dialog Box II-171
    Using Commands II-177
    Usage Considerations II-177
Examples II-178
    Example 1
    Path Analysis Basics II-178
    Example 2
    Path Analysis with a Restart File II-183
    Example 3
    Path Analysis Using Rectangular Input II-196
    Example 4
    Path Analysis and Standard Errors II-202
Computation II-212
    Algorithms II-212
References II-218
Acknowledgments II-219

7 Perceptual Mapping   II-221

Statistical Background II-221
    Preference Mapping II-222
    Biplots and MDPREF II-226
    Procrustes Rotations II-226
Perceptual Mapping in SYSTAT II-227
    Perceptual Mapping Main Dialog Box II-227
    Using Commands II-229
    Usage Consideration II-229
Examples II-230
    Example 1
    Vector Model II-230
    Example 2
    Circle Model II-231
    Example 3
    Internal Model II-232

         Example 4
            Procrustes Rotation II-234
         Computation II-236
            Algorithms II-236
            Missing data II-236
         References II-237

8 Probit Analysis   II-239

         Statistical Background II-239
            Interpreting the Results II-240
         Probit Analysis in SYSTAT II-240
            Probit Analysis Main Dialog Box II-240
            Using Commands II-242
            Usage Considerations II-243
         Examples II-243
            Example 1
               Probit Analysis (Simple Model) II-243
            Example 2
               Probit Analysis with Interactions II-245
         Computation II-246
            Algorithms II-246
            Missing Data II-246
         References II-247

9 Set and Canonical Correlation   II-249

         Statistical Background II-249
            Sets II-250
            Partialing II-250
            Notation II-251
            Measures of Association Between Sets II-251
            $R^2_{Y,X}$ Proportion of Generalized Variance II-251

$T^2_{Y,X}$ and $P^2_{Y,X}$ Proportions of Additive Variance II-252
Interpretations II-253
Types of Association between Sets II-254
Testing the Null Hypothesis II-255
Estimates of the Population $R^2_{Y,X}$, $T^2_{Y,X}$, and $P^2_{Y,X}$ II-256
Set and Canonical Correlations in SYSTAT II-257
Set and Canonical Correlations Main Dialog Box II-257
Using Commands II-259
Usage Considerations II-259
Examples II-260
Example 1
Canonical Correlations—Simple Model II-260
Example 2
Partial Set Correlation Model II-263
Example 3
Contingency Table Analysis II-267
Computation II-270
Algorithms II-270
Missing Data II-271
References II-271

10 Signal Detection Analysis II-273

Statistical Background II-273
Detection Parameters II-274
Signal Detection Analysis in SYSTAT II-275
Signal Detection Analysis Main Dialog Box II-275
Using Commands II-278
Usage Considerations II-279
Examples II-282
Example 1
Normal Distribution Model for Signal Detection II-282
Example 2
Nonparametric Model for Signal Detection II-287

Example 3
Logistic Model for Signal Detection II-288
Example 4
Negative Exponential Model for Signal Detection II-289
Example 5
Chi-Square Model for Signal Detection II-292
Example 6
Poisson Model for Signal Detection II-295
Example 7
Gamma Model for Signal Detection II-296
Computation II-298
  Algorithms II-298
  Missing Data II-299
References II-299

11 Smoothing   II-301

Statistical Background II-302
  The Three Ingredients of Nonparametric Smoothers II-302
  A Sample Dataset II-303
  Kernels II-304
  Bandwidth II-307
  Smoothing Functions II-310
  Smoothness II-311
  Interpolation and Extrapolation II-312
  Close Relatives (Roses by Other Names) II-312
Smoothing in SYSTAT II-314
  Smooth Main Dialog II-314
  Using Commands II-316
  Usage Considerations II-317
Examples II-318
  Example 1
  Smoothing: Saving and Plotting Results II-318
  Example 2
  Confidence Intervals for Smoothers II-319
  Example 3
  Polynomial Regression and Smoothing II-322

Example 4
    Smoothing Binary Data in Three Dimensions II-331
References II-333

12 Spatial Statistics   *II-335*

Statistical Background II-335
    The Basic Spatial Model. II-335
    The Geostatistical Model II-337
    Variogram II-338
    Variogram Models II-339
    Anisotropy. II-342
    Simple Kriging. II-343
    Ordinary Kriging. II-343
    Universal Kriging II-343
    Simulation II-344
    Point Processes. II-344
Spatial Statistics in SYSTAT II-348
    Spatial Statistics Main Dialog Box II-348
    Using Commands II-355
    Usage Considerations II-357
Examples II-357
    Example 1
    Kriging (Ordinary) II-357
    Example 2
    Simulation II-364
    Example 3
    Point Statistics II-365
    Example 4
    Unusual Distances II-370
Computation II-372
    Missing Data II-372
    Algorithms II-372
References II-373

13 Survival Analysis

Statistical Background	II-375
Graphics	II-377
Parametric Modeling	II-380
Survival Analysis in SYSTAT	II-383
Survival Analysis Main Dialog Box	II-383
Using Commands	II-389
Usage Considerations	II-390
Examples	II-391
Example 1 Life Tables: The Kaplan-Meier Estimator	II-391
Example 2 Actuarial Life Tables	II-394
Example 3 Stratified Kaplan-Meier Estimation	II-395
Example 4 Turnbull Estimation: K-M for Interval-Censored Data	II-399
Example 5 Cox Regression	II-402
Example 6 Stratified Cox Regression	II-404
Example 7 Stepwise Regression	II-409
Example 8 The Weibull Model for Fully Parametric Analysis	II-411
Computation	II-414
Algorithms	II-414
Missing Data	II-415
References	II-422

14 T Tests   II-425

Statistical Background II-425
    Degrees of Freedom II-428
    The T Test II-428
    Pooling II-430
    Assumptions II-430
T Tests in SYSTAT II-431
    Two-Sample T Test Main Dialog Box II-431
    Paired T Test Main Dialog Box II-432
    One-Sample T Test Main Dialog Box II-432
    Using Commands II-434
    Usage Considerations II-434
Examples II-435
    Example 1
    Two-Sample T Test II-435
    Example 2
    Bonferroni and Dunn-Sidak Adjustments II-437
    Example 3
    T Test Assumptions II-439
    Example 4
    Paired T Test II-441
    Example 5
    One-Sample T Test II-443
References II-444

15 Test Item Analysis   II-445

Statistical Background II-446
    Classical Model II-447
    Latent Trait Model II-448
Test Item Analysis in SYSTAT II-449
    Classical Test Item Analysis Main Dialog Box II-449
    Logistic Test Item Analysis Main Dialog Box II-450

Using Commands	II-451
Usage Considerations	II-451
Examples	II-455
Example 1 Classical Test Analysis	II-455
Example 2 Logistic Model (One Parameter)	II-456
Example 3 Logistic Model (Two Parameter)	II-459
Computation	II-461
Algorithms	II-462
Missing Data	II-463
References	II-463

16 Time Series   II-465

Statistical Background	II-466
Smoothing	II-466
ARIMA Modeling and Forecasting	II-469
Seasonal Decomposition and Adjustment	II-479
Exponential Smoothing	II-480
Fourier Analysis	II-481
Graphical Displays for Time Series in SYSTAT	II-482
T-Plot Main Dialog Box	II-482
Time Main Dialog Box	II-483
ACF Plot Main Dialog Box	II-484
PACF Plot Main Dialog Box	II-484
CCF Plot Main Dialog Box	II-485
Using Commands	II-486
Transformations of Time Series in SYSTAT	II-486
Transformations Main Dialog Box	II-486
Clear Series	II-487
Using Commands	II-488

Smoothing a Time Series in SYSTAT II-488
    Smooth Main Dialog Box II-488
    LOWESS Main Dialog Box II-489
    Exponential Smoothing Main Dialog Box II-490
    Using Commands II-491
Seasonal Adjustments in SYSTAT II-491
    Seasonal Adjustment Main Dialog Box II-491
    Using Commands II-492
ARIMA Models in SYSTAT II-492
    ARIMA Main Dialog Box II-492
    Using Commands II-493
Fourier Models in SYSTAT II-494
    Fourier Main Dialog Box II-494
    Using Commands II-495
Usage Considerations II-495
Examples II-496
    Example 1
    Time Series Plot II-496
    Example 2
    Autocorrelation Plot II-497
    Example 3
    Partial Autocorrelation Plot II-498
    Example 4
    Cross-Correlation Plot II-498
    Example 5
    Differencing II-500
    Example 6
    Moving Averages II-503
    Example 7
    Smoothing (A 4253H Filter) II-504
    Example 8
    LOWESS Smoothing II-505
    Example 9
    Multiplicative Seasonal Factor II-507
    Example 10
    Multiplicative Seasonality with a Linear Trend II-508
    Example 11
    ARIMA Models II-512
    Example 12
    Fourier Modeling of Temperature II-518

Computation	II-520
Algorithms	II-520
References	II-521

17 Two-Stage Least Squares   II-523

Statistical Background	II-523
Two-Stage Least Squares Estimation	II-523
Heteroskedasticity	II-524
Two-Stage Least Squares in SYSTAT	II-525
Two-Stage Least Squares Main Dialog Box	II-525
Using Commands	II-527
Usage Considerations	II-527
Examples	II-528
Example 1 Heteroskedasticity-Consistent Standard Errors	II-528
Example 2 Two-Stage Least Squares	II-530
Example 3 Two-Stage Instrumental Variables	II-532
Example 4 Polynomially Distributed Lags	II-533
Computation	II-534
Algorithms	II-534
Missing Data	II-534
References	II-535

Index   537

List of Examples

Actuarial Life Tables	II-394
ARIMA Models	II-512
AutocorrelationPlot	II-497
Binary Profiles	II-153
Bonferroni and Dunn-Sidak Adjustments	II-437
Canonical Correlations—Simple Model	II-260
Casewise Pattern Table	II-20
Chi-Square Model for Signal Detection	II-292
Circle Model	II-231
Classical Test Analysis	II-455
Comparing Correlation Estimation Methods	II-33
Confidence Curves and Regions	II-97
Confidence Intervals for Smoothers	II-319
Contingency Table Analysis	II-267
Contouring the Loss Function	II-105
Correlation Estimation	II-25
Cox Regression	II-402
Cross-Correlation Plot	II-498
Differencing	II-500
Fixing Parameters and Evaluating Fit	II-100
Fourier Modeling of Temperature	II-518
Friedman Test	II-140
Functions of Parameters	II-102
Gamma Model for Signal Detection	II-296
Guttman Loss Function	II-58
Heteroskedasticity-Consistent Standard Errors	II-528
Individual Differences Multidimensional Scaling	II-60

Internal Model	II-232
Iteratively Reweighted Least Squares for Logistic Models	II-108
Kinetic Models	II-120
Kriging (Ordinary)	II-357
Kruskal Method	II-56
Kruskal-Wallis Test	II-134
Life Tables: The Kaplan-Meier Estimator	II-391
Logistic Model (One Parameter)	II-456
Logistic Model (Two Parameter)	II-459
Logistic Model for Signal Detection	II-288
LOWESS Smoothing	II-505
Mann-Whitney Test	II-136
Maximum Likelihood Estimation	II-107
Minimizing an Analytic Function	II-121
Missing Value Imputation	II-42
Missing Values: Preliminary Examinations	II-15
Moving Averages	II-503
Multiple Categories	II-156
Multiplicative Seasonal Factor	II-507
Multiplicative Seasonality with a Linear Trend	II-508
Negative Exponential Model for Signal Detection	II-289
Nonlinear Model with Three Parameters	II-94
Nonmetric Unfolding	II-64
Nonparametric Model for Signal Detection	II-287
Normal Distribution Model for Signal Detection	II-282
One-Sample Kolmogorov-Smirnov Test	II-142
One-Sample T Test	II-443
Paired T Test	II-441
Partial Autocorrelation Plot	II-498
Partial Set Correlation Model	II-263
Path Analysis and Standard Errors	II-202

Path Analysis Basics	II-178
Path Analysis Using Rectangular Input	II-196
Path Analysis with a Restart File	II-183
Piecewise Regression	II-118
Point Statistics	II-365
Poisson Model for Signal Detection	II-295
Polynomial Regression and Smoothing	II-322
Polynomially Distributed Lags	II-533
Power Scaling Ratio Data	II-68
Probit Analysis (Simple Model)	II-243
Probit Analysis with Interactions	II-245
Procrustes Rotation	II-234
Regression	II-113
Robust Estimation (Measures of Location)	II-110
Scalogram Analysis—A Perfect Fit	II-152
Sign and Wilcoxon Tests for Multiple Variables	II-139
Sign Test	II-137
Simulation	II-364
Smoothing (A 4253H Filter)	II-504
Smoothing Binary Data in Three Dimensions	II-331
Smoothing: Saving and Plotting Results	II-318
Stepwise Regression	II-409
Stratified Cox Regression	II-404
Stratified Kaplan-Meier Estimation	II-395
T Test Assumptions	II-439
The Weibull Model for Fully Parametric Analysis	II-411
Time Series Plot	II-496
Turnbull Estimation: K-M for Interval-Censored Data	II-399
Two-Sample Kolmogorov-Smirnov Test	II-137
Two-Sample T Test	II-435
Two-Stage Instrumental Variables	II-532

Two-Stage Least Squares. II-530
Unusual Distances. II-370
Vector Model II-230
Wald-Wolfowitz Runs Test II-144
Wilcoxon Test II-139

Chapter 1

Missing Value Analysis

Rick Marcantonio and Michael Pechnyo

Missing value analysis helps address several concerns caused by incomplete data. Cases with missing values that are systematically different from cases without missing values can obscure the results. Also, missing data may reduce the precision of calculated statistics because there is less information than originally planned. Another concern is that the assumptions behind many statistical procedures are based on complete cases, and missing values can complicate the theory required.

The MISSING module displays and analyzes missing value patterns in data. The procedure computes maximum likelihood estimates of correlation, covariance, and cross-products of deviations matrices using either linear regression or an EM algorithm. You can downweight outliers using a normal or a t distribution.

Statistics computed include missing value patterns, means, correlations, variances and covariances, cross-products of deviations, and a pairwise frequency table. In addition, for EM estimation, SYSTAT reports Little's MCAR test. The correlation, covariance, or SSCP matrix can be saved to a data file for further analyses. Alternatively, you can save imputed estimates in place of missing values.

Statistical Background

Even in the best designed and monitored study, observations can be missing—a subject inadvertently skips a question, a blood sample is ruined, or the recording equipment malfunctions. Because many classical statistical analyses require complete cases (no missing values), when data are incomplete it may be hard "to get off the ground." That is, if the analyst wants to explore a new data set by, say, using a factor analysis to identify redundant variables or sets of related variables, a cluster analysis to check for distinct subpopulations, or a stepwise discriminant analysis to see which variables differ among subgroups, there may be too few complete cases for an analysis. Alternatively, the complete cases may not fully represent the total sample, leading to biased results.

Analysis of missing values focuses on three issues:

- **Description of patterns.** How many missing values are there? Where are they located (specific cases and/or variables)? Are values missing randomly? For each variable, the word *pattern* indicates the dichotomized version of the variable—that is, a binary distribution where each value is *missing* or *present*. Also, when the same variables are missing for several cases, cases are said to have the same *pattern*.
- **Estimation of parameters, including means, covariances, and correlations.** Statistics are computed using either the EM (expectation maximization) algorithm or linear regression.
- **Imputation of values.** EM and regression methods are provided for estimating replacement values for the missing data.

Often it is necessary to run the MISSING procedure several times. You should:

- First, see the extent and pattern of missing values, and determine if values are missing randomly. At this point, you may want to delete cases and variables with large numbers of missing data and, most importantly, screen variables with skewed distributions for symmetrizing transformations before proceeding to the estimation or imputation phases.
- Next, study various estimates of descriptive statistics, possibly making a side step to check relations graphically when differences in estimates are found.
- Finally, impute values (estimate replacement values) and use graphics to assess the suitability of the filled-in values.

The use of a data matrix with imputed values may not be acceptable for a final report of results, but by using the approaches and methods described here, you may be able to find a subset of variables with enough complete cases for a meaningful analysis. You may omit variables simply because a large proportion of their values are missing; or, by making exploratory runs using the imputed data matrix, you may learn that some variables are redundant or have little relation to the outcome variables of interest. For example:

- In a stepwise regression, you may find that some variables have no relation to your outcome variable. Try rerunning the analysis with a smaller subset of candidate variables that has many more complete cases.
- In a factor analysis, you may identify one or more redundant variables. You might also learn this by examining an estimate of the correlation matrix in the MISSING procedure.

Techniques for Handling Missing Values

Over the years, many software users approached the missing data problem by using a pairwise complete method to compute a covariance or correlation matrix and then using this matrix as input for, say, a factor analysis. However, such a matrix may have eigenvalues less than 0, and some correlations may be computed from substantially different subsets of the cases. Other analysts use EM (expectation-maximization) or regression methods to estimate statistics or to impute data. Simulation studies indicate that pairwise estimates are often more distorted than estimates obtained via the EM method. In most algorithms, they are simply the first iteration of the EM method. A few analysts use multiple imputation, a computationally complex method that is not commonly available.

Deletion Methods

The two most common deletion methods are listwise and pairwise deletion. In listwise deletion, the analysis uses complete cases only. That is, the procedure removes from computations any observation with a value missing on any variable included in the analysis.

Pairwise deletion is listwise deletion done separately for every pair of selected variables. In other words, counts, sums of squares, and sums of cross-products are computed separately for every pair of variables in the file. With pairwise deletion, you get the same correlation (covariance, etc.) for two variables containing missing data if you select them alone or with other variables containing missing data. With listwise deletion, correlations under these two circumstances may differ, depending on the pattern of missing data among the other variables in the file.

Because it makes better use of the data than listwise deletion, pairwise deletion is a popular method for computing correlations on matrices with missing data. Many regression programs include it as a standard method for computing regression estimates from a covariance or correlation matrix.

Ironically, pairwise deletion is one of the worst ways to handle missing values. If as few as 20% of the values in a data matrix are missing, it is not difficult to find two correlations that were computed using substantially different subsets of the cases. In such cases, it is common to encounter error messages that the matrix is singular in regression programs and to get eigenvalues less than 0 in factor analysis.

But, more importantly, *classical statistical analyses require complete cases*. For exploration, this restriction can be circumvented by identifying one or more variables that are not needed, deleting them, and requesting the desired analysis—there should be more complete cases for this smaller set of variables.

If you have missing values, you may want to compare results from pairwise deletion with those from the EM method. Or, you may want to take the time to replace the missing values in the raw data by examining similar cases or variables with nonmissing values.

Imputation Methods

Deletion methods attempt to restrict computations to complete cases by eliminating cases or variables that are incomplete. Imputation methods, on the other hand, replace missing data with hypothesized values, resulting in a "complete" data set consisting of observed and imputed values. Analyses that require complete cases can then be applied to the resulting data.

Unconditional Mean Imputation

One common imputation technique replaces all missing values for a variable with the mean of the observed values for that variable. Although it is highly unlikely that the missing values, if actually observed, would all lie at the center of the distribution for the variable, the most likely value for each missing point is the mean. Placing all missing values at the center of the distribution, however, underestimates the variances and covariances for the variables.

Let's look at a simple case. Consider two variables, X and Y, having a perfect positive correlation of 1. X has a mean of 5 and a variance of 1. Y has a mean of 13.5

and a variance of 3.25. The covariance between X and Y equals 1.80. The data in the X and Y columns of the following table represent ten observations on these variables.

Case	X	Y	X'	Y'
1	4.65	13.85	4.67	13.86
2	6.21	16.41	6.21	15.22*
3	6.63	15.68	6.64	15.68
4	4.94	15.76	4.95	15.77
5	7.21	17.70	4.98*	17.70
6	5.09	13.44	5.09	15.22*
7	6.08	15.64	4.98*	15.64
8	4.19	12.94	4.20	12.95
9	3.09	10.67	3.09	15.22*
10	5.19	14.95	4.98*	14.96
Sample Mean	5.33	14.71	4.98	15.22
Sample Variance	1.51	4.06	.95	1.55
Sample Covariance	2.29		.33	

Suppose that the Y values for cases 2, 6, and 9 and the X values for 5, 7, and 10 could not be observed. Simple mean imputation yields the data in columns X' and Y' (imputed values are marked with an asterisk). Notice:

- For X' and Y', the mean for the ten cases equals the mean for the seven observed cases.
- The variances for X' and Y' underestimate the corresponding true variances.
- The covariance between X' and Y' underestimates the true covariance between X and Y.

The systematic underestimation of the variances and covariances suggests that any conclusions drawn from analyses using the imputed data are suspect.

Regression Imputation

Buck (1960) suggested an alternative procedure for imputation using conditional means. In Buck's method, the sample means and covariance matrix for the complete cases are used as estimates for the corresponding population parameters. These estimates are subsequently used to compute linear regressions of the variables with missing values on the variables without missing values *for each case*. The resulting regression equations allow you to predict the missing values from the observed values.

The following plot illustrates the technique for the ten cases presented above. Cases with missing Y values could be placed at any Y value for the corresponding observed X value; cases with missing X values could be placed at any X value for the corresponding observed Y value. In this display, we place missing values at points corresponding to the complete sample (if we had been able to observe it). The solid line represents the regression of Y on X and should be used to impute values for cases lacking Y values. The dashed line indicates the regression of X on Y and is used to impute values when the X value is missing.

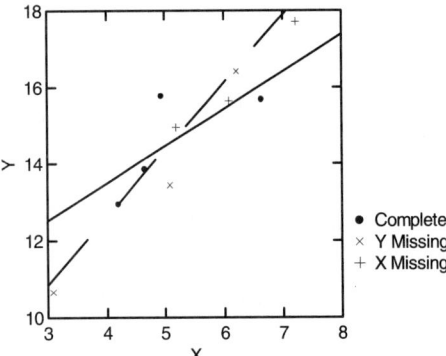

The two regression lines result in the following imputed estimates appearing in columns X'' and Y'':

Case	X'	Y'	X''	Y''
1	4.67	13.86	4.67	13.86
2	6.21	15.22*	6.21	15.64*
3	6.64	15.68	6.64	15.68
4	4.95	15.77	4.95	15.77
5	4.98*	17.70	6.90*	17.70
6	5.09	15.22*	5.09	14.55*
7	4.98	15.64	5.72*	15.64
8	4.20	12.95	4.20	12.95
9	3.09	15.22*	3.09	12.60*
10	4.98*	14.96	5.33*	14.96
Mean	4.98	15.22	5.27	14.93
Variance	.95	1.55	1.34	2.29
Covariance	.33		1.57	

Compare the mean, variance, and covariance estimates with those obtained using unconditional mean imputation (columns X' and Y'). The variance for Y and the covariance still underestimate the true values, but to a lesser extent than found previously.

Other Imputation Methods

Replacing missing values by means (unconditional or conditional) is one approach to imputation. Other techniques found in the literature include:

- replacing missing data with values selected randomly from a distribution for each missing value.
- replacing missing data with values selected from cases not included in the analysis.
- adding a random residual to the conditional mean estimates.
- imputating multiple values for each missing item.

None of these methods, however, should be used as a panacea for solving the missing data problem. For a complete discussion of these methods, see Little and Rubin.

EM Method

Instead of pairwise deletion, many data analysts prefer to use an EM algorithm when estimating correlations, covariances, or an SSCP matrix. EM uses the maximum likelihood method to compute the estimates. This procedure defines a model for the partially missing data and bases inferences on the likelihood under that model. Each iteration consists of an E step and an M step. The E step finds the conditional expectation of the "missing" data given the observed values and current estimates of the parameters. These expectations are then substituted for the "missing" data. For the M step, maximum likelihood estimation is performed as though the missing data had been filled in. "Missing" is enclosed in quotation marks because the missing values are not being directly filled but, rather, functions of them are used in the log-likelihood. Estimation iterates between these two steps until the parameters converge.

Returning to the previous data set, the EM imputed values appear in the final two columns of the following table:

Case	X"	Y"	X'''	Y'''
1	4.67	13.86	4.67	13.86
2	6.21	15.64*	6.21	16.00*
3	6.64	15.68	6.64	15.68
4	4.95	15.77	4.95	15.77
5	6.90*	17.70	6.86*	17.70
6	5.09	14.55*	5.09	14.86*
7	5.72*	15.64	5.62*	15.64
8	4.20	12.95	4.20	12.95
9	3.09	12.60*	3.09	12.83*
10	5.33*	14.96	5.21*	14.96
Mean	5.27	14.93	5.25	15.02
Variance	1.34	2.29	1.51	2.55
Covariance	1.57		1.54	

For this simple example, the regression and EM results are very similar. However, when data are missing for several variables across cases, the EM method generally outperforms regression imputation. The latter technique cannot capture covariances between jointly missing data.

If you compute the covariance matrix for the imputed data, the estimates will differ from the variances shown above. The EM algorithm estimates two sets of parameters (the means and covariances) with corresponding sufficient statistics (the sums of values, and the sums of cross-products). In the M step, the first set of statistics yields the EM mean estimates and the second set yields the EM covariance estimates. Using the imputed data to estimate the covariances and variances ignores any relationships between the presence or absence of data across variables. In effect, one set of sufficient statistics is being used to estimate both sets of parameters. As a result, the variances estimated from the imputed data always underestimate the variances produced by the EM algorithm. See Little and Rubin for details.

By default for the EM method, the Missing Value procedure assumes that the data follow a normal distribution. If you know that the tails of the distributions are longer than those of a normal distribution, you can request that a t distribution with n degrees of freedom be used in constructing the likelihood function (n is specified by the user). A second option also provides a distribution with longer tails. You specify the ratio of standard deviations of a mixed normal distribution and the mixture proportion of the two distributions. This assumes that only the standard deviations of the distributions differ, not the means.

Randomness and Missing Data

You should take care in assessing the pattern of how the values are missing. For simplicity in graphic presentation, we consider a bivariate situation with incomplete data for one of the variables. Given variables X and Y (education and income, for example), is the probability of a response:

- Independent of the values of X and Y? That is, is the probability that income is recorded the same for all people regardless of their education or incomes? The recorded or observed values of income form a random subsample of the true incomes for all of the people in the sample. Little and Rubin call this pattern MCAR (Missing Completely At Random).

- Dependent on X but not on Y? In this case, the probability that income is recorded depends on the subject's education, so the probability varies by education but not by income *within that education group*. This pattern is called MAR (Missing At Random).

- Dependent on Y and possibly X also? In this case, the probability that income is present varies by the value of income within each education group. This is not an unusual pattern for real-world applications.

The following figure illustrates these missing data situations. In the upper left plot, the data contain no missing values. The remaining three plots depict show the relationship between X and Y when approximately 30% of the data are missing. The border plots display the approximate distribution of cases for each situation.

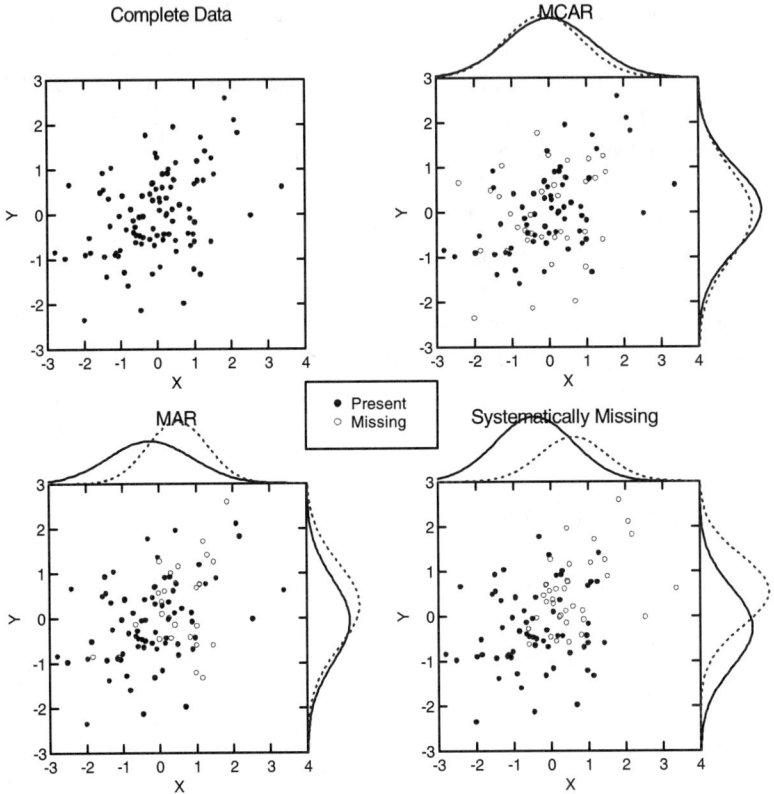

In the MCAR plot, notice the random scatter of missing and present data. Missing observations occur for both low and high values of both variables. The distribution of the missing values is indistinguishable form the distribution of observed values for both variables. If data follow this pattern, the pairwise deletion, EM, and regression methods give consistent and unbiased estimates of correlations and covariances.

In the MAR plot, the missing values tend to occur for large values of X. However, the unobserved values are spread throughout the range of Y. The distributions for the missing and complete groups are practically identical when focusing on Y. In other words, the probability of nonresponse is independent of Y. However, two distributions emerge along the X variable. The missing value distribution (shown with a dashed line) shifts toward higher values. The probability of observing nonresponse increases as X increases.

The pairwise, EM, and regression methods may still provide good estimates if the data are missing at random. For example, in a study of education and income, the subjects with low education may have more missing income values. If education is MCAR and if, for a given level of education, income is MCAR, pairwise, EM, and regression methods may still yield good estimates.

If the data are MAR and the assumption that the distributions are normal, mixed normal, or t with specific degrees of freedom is met, the EM method yields maximum likelihood estimates of means, standard deviations, covariances, and correlations. Be sure to check the data for outliers and to determine whether symmetrizing transformations are required before applying the technique, however.

In the final plot, the missing values appear in the upper right area of the plot. In contrast to the MAR plot, the value of Y influences the probability of nonresponse; the higher the Y value, the more likely the value will be missing. The distributions along both axes have much less overlap, with unique centers appearing for each group of cases. This situation is not an unusual pattern for real-world applications, but no current estimation methods are appropriate for data of this type.

Testing for Randomness

The Little (1988) chi-square statistic for testing whether values are missing completely at random is printed with EM matrices. The test computes the Mahalanobis distance between parameter estimates based on listwise complete data and parameter estimates resulting from the EM algorithm. The resulting sum is referred to a chi-square distribution with degrees of freedom based on the number of patterns of missing data in the dataset. If the test is rejected, the EM and listwise estimates are sufficiently "far" enough apart to warrant further examination, and certainly tells one that analysis based on listwise estimates MAY be biased.

Another method for testing for randomness involves dividing a variable into two groups based on whether data is missing or present for another variable. The means for the two groups can be compared using a t-statistic; if the values are not missing randomly, the test statistic will be large. However, be aware that while a sizable t statistic does indicate a departure from randomness, a small t may be no confirmation that values are missing randomly. Sadly, there is no magic test for MAR.

A Final Caution

Imputed data are not complete. Although missing values do not occur in imputed data, imputation does not replace them with values that would have been observed had all data been available. If you use imputed data in analyses, you should control for the imputation. For example, if you use the EM estimates in a regression, the degrees of freedom for the error term should be adjusted back down to either the listwise complete value or some other reasonable estimate.

To us, none of the approaches to estimation and imputation should be viewed as a magic black box. While the EM and regression methods allow a specific way in which the values of one variable may be related to another, a good data analyst will want to ferret out possible problems in how the data are sampled, recorded, or otherwise fail to conform to the study protocol—for example, which regions of a multivariate space are sparse because data are missing? It is hard to separate the selection of an appropriate method for estimation or imputation from the basic data screening process.

Missing Value Analysis in SYSTAT

Missing Main Dialog

To analyze missing values, from the menus choose:

Statistics
  Missing Values…

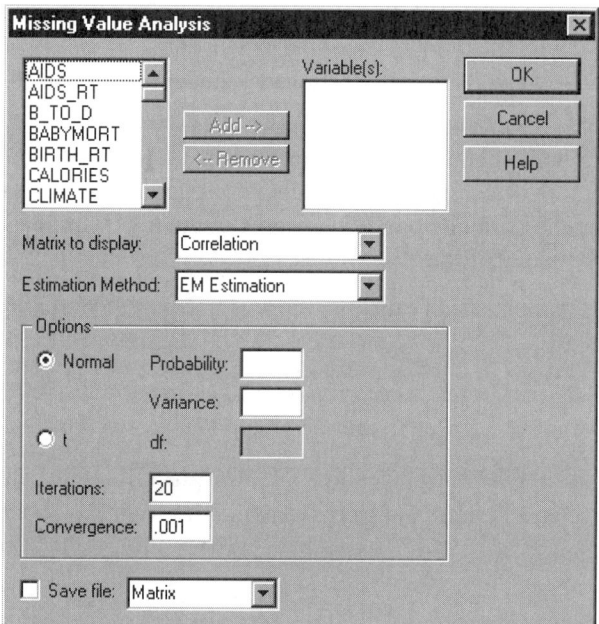

SYSTAT treats all selected variables as continuous (numeric) data. Select a matrix to compute and a method for handling missing data.

Matrix to display. SYSTAT computes the correlation, covariance, or SSCP matrix.

Estimation Method. Two estimation methods are available:

- **Regression Substitution.** Uses multiple linear regression to impute estimates for missing values. For each case, SYSTAT uses linear regression on the observed variables to predict values for the missing variables.
- **EM Estimation.** Requests the EM algorithm to estimate Pearson correlation, covariance, or SSCP matrices. Little's MCAR test is shown with a display of the pattern of missing values.

You can downweight outliers using a Normal or t distribution. The following options are available:

- Normal produces maximum likelihood estimates for a contaminated multivariate normal sample. For the contaminated normal, SYSTAT assumes that the distribution is a mixture of two normal distributions (same mean, different variances) with a specified probability of contamination. The Probability value is the probability of contamination (for example, 0.10), and Variance is the variance of contamination. Downweighting for the normal model tends to be concentrated in a few outlying cases.

- t produces maximum likelihood estimates for a *t* distribution, where df is the degrees of freedom. Downweighting for the multivariate *t* model tends to be more spread out than for the normal model. The degree of downweighting is inversely related to the degrees of freedom.

Iterations. For EM estimation, specify the maximum number of iterations for computing the estimates.

Convergence. Define the convergence criterion for EM estimation. If the relative change of covariance entries is less than the specified value, convergence is assumed.

Save file. Saves the matrix being displayed to a SYSTAT data file. You can also save the raw data with imputed estimates in place of any missing values.

Using Commands

Select your data by typing USE filename. Continue with:

```
MISSING
MODEL varlist
SAVE outfile / DATA
ESTIMATE / MATRIX = CORRELATION
                   COVARIANCE
                   SSCP,
           NORMAL = n1,n2,
           T = df,
           ITER = n,
           CONV = n,
           REGRESSION
```

Omitting the DATA option from SAVE results in the current matrix being saved to *outfile*.

Missing Value Analysis

Usage Considerations

Types of data. Data for missing value analysis must be rectangular and all variables must be numerical. This procedure should not be used to estimate missing categorical values, but categorical variables can be used to estimate values for missing continuous data. In this case, dummy code the categories and use the resulting indicator variables in the analysis.

Print options. With PRINT=LONG, SYSTAT prints the mean of each variable. In addition, for EM estimation, SYSTAT prints an iteration history, missing value patterns, Little's MCAR test, and mean estimates.

Quick Graphs. Missing value analysis produces a cases-by-variables plot similar to a shaded data matrix.

Saving files. You can save the correlation, covariance, or SSCP matrix, or save a rectangular file of the raw data with missing values replaced by imputed estimates. SYSTAT automatically defines the type of file as CORR, COVA, SSCP, or RECT.

BY groups. Missing value analysis produces separate analyses for each level of any BY variables.

Bootstrapping. Bootstrapping is available in this procedure.

Case frequencies. FREQ=var increases the number of cases by the FREQ variable.

Case weights. WEIGHT is available in missing value analysis.

Examples

Example 1
Missing Values: Preliminary Examinations

Where are the missing values located? How extensive are they? If a value is missing for one variable, does it tend to be missing for one or more other variables? Conversely, if a value is present for one variable, do values tend to be missing for other specific variables? Is the pattern of missing values related to values of another variable?

You may need to uncover patterns of incomplete data in order to:

- select enough complete cases for a meaningful analysis. If you omit a few variables, or even just one, does the sample size of complete cases increase dramatically?

- select a method of estimation or imputation. If, for example, you plan to use complete cases for a final analysis, you need to verify that values are missing *completely* at random, missing at random, or missing nonrandomly.
- understand how results may be biased or distorted because of a failure to meet necessary assumptions about randomness of the missing values.

In this example, we explore the *world95m* data for patterns of how values are missing. We focus on descriptive statistics to explore variable distributions and reveal the amount of missing data. The input is:

```
USE world95m
STATS
STATISTICS POPULATN DENSITY URBAN LIFEEXPF LIFEEXPM,
          LITERACY POP_INCR BABYMORT GDP_CAP CALORIES,
          BIRTH_RT DEATH_RT B_TO_D FERTILTY LIT_MALE,
          LIT_FEMA /  Mean Median SD SES Skewness N
```

The resulting statistics follow:

	POPULATN	DENSITY	URBAN	LIFEEXPF	LIFEEXPM
N of cases	109	109	108	109	109
Median	10400.00	64.00	60.00	74.00	67.00
Mean	47723.88	203.41	56.53	70.16	64.92
Standard Dev	146726.36	675.71	24.20	10.57	9.27
Skewness(G1)	6.59	6.89	-0.31	-1.11	-1.08
SE Skewness	0.23	0.23	0.23	0.23	0.23

	LITERACY	POP_INCR	BABYMORT	GDP_CAP	CALORIES
N of cases	107	109	109	109	75
Median	88.00	1.80	27.70	2995.00	2653.00
Mean	78.34	1.68	42.31	5859.98	2753.83
Standard Dev	22.88	1.20	38.08	6479.84	567.83
Skewness(G1)	-0.99	0.32	1.09	1.15	0.17
SE Skewness	0.23	0.23	0.23	0.23	0.28

	BIRTH_RT	DEATH_RT	B_TO_D	FERTILTY	LIT_MALE
N of cases	109	108	108	107	85
Median	25.00	9.00	2.67	3.05	87.00
Mean	25.92	9.56	3.20	3.56	78.73
Standard Dev	12.36	4.25	2.12	1.90	20.45
Skewness(G1)	0.45	1.31	1.83	0.66	-0.85
SE Skewness	0.23	0.23	0.23	0.23	0.26

```
                   LIT_FEMA
N of cases               85
Median                71.00
Mean                  67.26
Standard Dev          28.61
Skewness(G1)          -0.50
SE Skewness            0.26
```

This output provides your first look, variable by variable, at the extent of incomplete data. Because means and standard deviations are computed using all available data for each variable, the sample sizes vary from variable to variable. The total number of observations is 109. The number of values present for each variable is reported as 'N of cases'. For calories, 75 countries (cases) report a value, so 109 – 75, or 34, do not. That is, calories is missing for 34 / 109 = 31.2% of the cases. The female and male literacy rates (*lit_fema* and *lit_male*) are each missing for 22% of the cases. Eight variables have no missing values, and five others have from 0.9% to 1.8% missing values.

Use the skewness statistic to identify nonsymmetric distributions. Symmetry is important if one's goal is to estimate means, standard deviations, covariances, or correlations. Both *POPULATN* and *DENSITY* are highly positively skewed. Transformations should be considered to make the distributions of these variables more symmetric.

Boxplots and Transformations

Boxplots and stem-and-leaf plots provide a visual display of distributions and assist in identifying outliers. To generate boxplots for the *WORLD95m* data:

```
USE world95m
STATS
 DENSITY POPULATN DENSITY URBAN LIFEEXPF LIFEEXPM,
         LITERACY POP_INCR BABYMORT GDP_CAP CALORIES,
         BIRTH_RT DEATH_RT B_TO_D FERTILTY LIT_MALE,
         LIT_FEMA / BOX
```

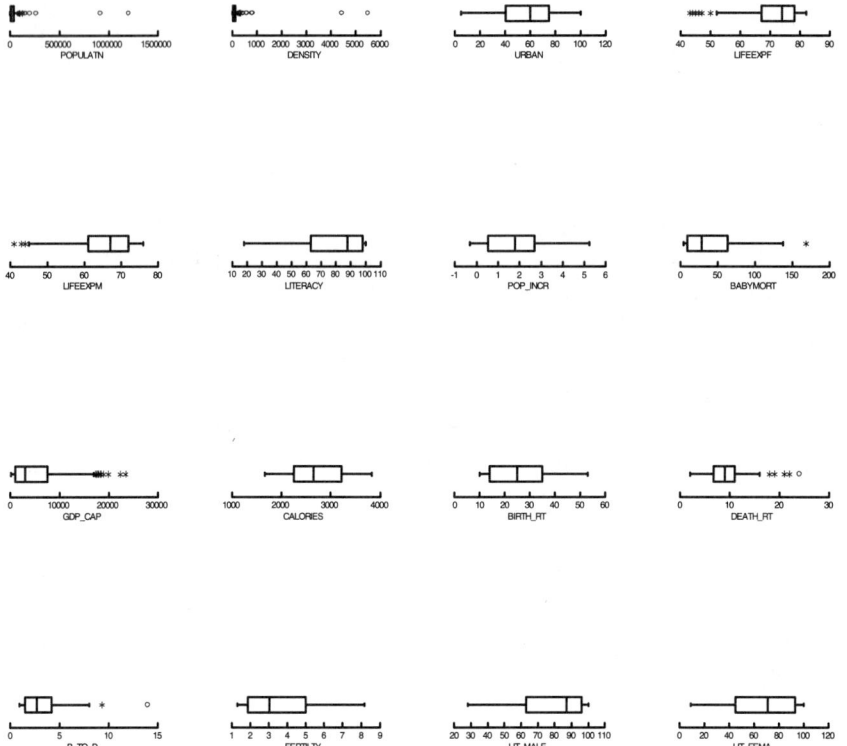

POPULATN, *DENSITY*, *GDP_CAP* and *DEATH_RT* all contain many extreme cases and outliers. Transforming these variables may eliminate these problematic cases and improve the symmetry of the distributions. Use the Dynamic Explorer to find this transformation.

The log transformation (X-power = 0 and Y-power = 0 in the Dynamic Explorer) improves the distributions of these variables considerably. Here we plot the boxplots for the original data next to the boxplots for the log-transformed data. In order to display the four distributions within each plot, we standardize the variables before plotting.

Missing Value Analysis

```
USE world95m
LET zpop = POPULATN
LET zdens = DENSITY
LET zgdp = GDP_CAP
LET zdeath = DEATH_RT
LET zlog_pop = L10(POPULATN)
LET zlog_den = L10(DENSITY)
LET zlog_gdp = L10(GDP_CAP)
LET zlog_dea = L10(DEATH_RT)
STANDARDIZE ZPOP ZDENS ZGDP ZDEATH,
    ZLOG_POP ZLOG_DEN ZLOG_GDP ZLOG_DEA
BEGIN
DENSITY ZPOP ZDENS ZGDP ZDEATH / REPEAT BOX XLAB='',
                    TITLE='Raw Data' LOC=-3IN,0IN
DENSITY ZLOG_POP ZLOG_DEN ZLOG_GDP ZLOG_DEA / REPEAT BOX,
                    XLAB='' TITLE='Transformed Data',
                    YMIN=-5 YMAX=10 LOC=3IN,0IN
END 'Boxplots'
```

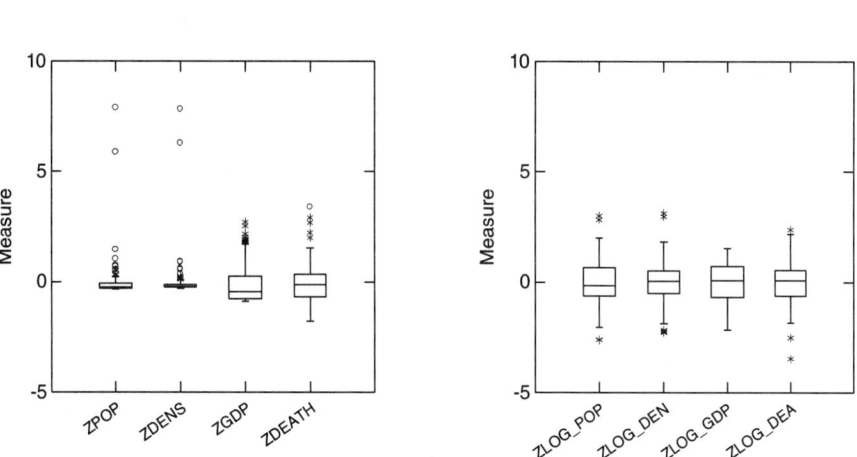

For each variable, the number of extreme cases decreases after applying the transformation. In addition, cases identified as extreme occur at both ends of the distribution for the transformed data. In contrast, extreme cases for the raw data correspond only to the high end of the distributions. The improvement in the distributions suggests transforming these variables to logarithms before applying any missing value analysis.

Example 2
Casewise Pattern Table

A casewise pattern table is a picture of the data file that highlights the location of missing observations. Each column in the display represents the values of a variable; each row represents the data for one case. This display is used to see if particular cases and/or variables have too little complete data to use and also to see if variables (or groups of variables) have values missing nonrandomly.

In this example, we create this layout using the MIS function. In addition, we recode the variables as (0,1) indicator variables, in which a 1 indicates a missing value and a 0 indicates an observed value. To save space, the Eastern European, African, and Latin American countries are omitted. The input is:

```
USE world95m
LET NUMMISS=MIS(POPULATN DENSITY URBAN LIFEEXPF LIFEEXPM,
     LITERACY POP_INCR BABYMORT GDP_CAP CALORIES,
     BIRTH_RT DEATH_RT B_TO_D FERTILTY LIT_MALE,
     LIT_FEMA)
LET PERCENTM = NUMMISS/(NUMMISS+NUM(POPULATN DENSITY URBAN,
     LIFEEXPF LIFEEXPM LITERACY POP_INCR BABYMORT GDP_CAP,
     CALORIES BIRTH_RT DEATH_RT B_TO_D FERTILTY LIT_MALE,
     LIT_FEMA))*100
LET (POPULATN DENSITY URBAN LIFEEXPF LIFEEXPM,
     LITERACY POP_INCR BABYMORT GDP_CAP CALORIES,
     BIRTH_RT DEATH_RT B_TO_D FERTILTY LIT_MALE,
     LIT_FEMA) = @ = .
SORT REGION2 COUNTRY$
SELECT REGION2=. OR REGION2=1 OR REGION2=3 OR REGION2=5
REM 'In the following table, a 1 indicates a missing value.'
REM 'A 0 indicates an observed value.'
LIST COUNTRY$ NUMMISS PERCENTM POPULATN DENSITY URBAN LIFEEXPF,
     LIFEEXPM LITERACY POP_INCR BABYMORT GDP_CAP CALORIES,
     BIRTH_RT DEATH_RT B_TO_D FERTILTY LIT_MALE LIT_FEMA / ,
     FORMAT='########### ## ##.## || # # # # # # # # # # # # # # # #'
```

Because USA and Canada have missing values for *REGION2*, we select cases where *REGION2* is missing to include these countries in the table. We also sort the cases by

Missing Value Analysis

geographical region and by country name, yielding an alphabetical listing of countries within each region. The output follows:

```
              C            P       P           L  L  L  P  B        C  B  D        F  L  L
              O    N       E       O    D      I  I  I  O  A        A  I  E        E  I  I
              U    U       R       P    E      F  F  T  P  B   D    L  R  A   B    R  T  T
              N    M       C       U    N      E  E  E  _  Y   P    O  T  T   _    T  _  _
              T    M       E       L    S   R  E  E  R  I  M   _    R  H  H   T    I  M  F
              R    I       N       A    I   B  X  X  A  N  O   C    I  _  _   O    L  A  E
              Y    S       T       T    T   A  P  P  C  R  A   E    R  R  _   T    L  M
              $    S       M       N    Y   N  F  M  Y  R  T   P    S  T  T   D    Y  E  A
   ----------    --    -----      -    -   -  -  -  -  -  -   -    -  -  -   -    -  -  -
       Canada    2     12.50  ||   0    0   0  0  0  0  0  0   0    0  0  0   0    0  1  1
          USA    0      0.00  ||   0    0   0  0  0  0  0  0   0    0  0  0   0    0  0  0
      Austria    2     12.50  ||   0    0   0  0  0  0  0  0   0    0  0  0   0    0  1  1
      Belgium    3     18.75  ||   0    0   0  0  0  0  0  0   0    1  0  0   0    0  1  1
      Denmark    2     12.50  ||   0    0   0  0  0  0  0  0   0    0  0 .0   0    0  1  1
      Finland    2     12.50  ||   0    0   0  0  0  0  0  0   0    0  0  0   0    0  1  1
       France    2     12.50  ||   0    0   0  0  0  0  0  0   0    0  0  0   0    0  1  1
      Germany    2     12.50  ||   0    0   0  0  0  0  0  0   0    0  0  0   0    0  1  1
       Greece    0      0.00  ||   0    0   0  0  0  0  0  0   0    0  0  0   0    0  0  0
      Iceland    3     18.75  ||   0    0   0  0  0  0  0  0   0    1  0  0   0    0  1  1
      Ireland    2     12.50  ||   0    0   0  0  0  0  0  0   0    0  0  0   0    0  1  1
        Italy    0      0.00  ||   0    0   0  0  0  0  0  0   0    0  0  0   0    0  0  0
  Netherlands    2     12.50  ||   0    0   0  0  0  0  0  0   0    0  0  0   0    0  1  1
       Norway    2     12.50  ||   0    0   0  0  0  0  0  0   0    0  0  0   0    0  1  1
     Portugal    1      6.25  ||   0    0   0  0  0  0  0  0   0    1  0  0   0    0  0  0
        Spain    0      0.00  ||   0    0   0  0  0  0  0  0   0    0  0  0   0    0  0  0
       Sweden    2     12.50  ||   0    0   0  0  0  0  0  0   0    0  0  0   0    0  1  1
  Switzerland    2     12.50  ||   0    0   0  0  0  0  0  0   0    0  0  0   0    0  1  1
           UK    2     12.50  ||   0    0   0  0  0  0  0  0   0    0  0  0   0    0  1  1
  Afghanistan    1      6.25  ||   0    0   0  0  0  0  0  0   0    1  0  0   0    0  0  0
    Australia    0      0.00  ||   0    0   0  0  0  0  0  0   0    0  0  0   0    0  0  0
   Bangladesh    0      0.00  ||   0    0   0  0  0  0  0  0   0    0  0  0   0    0  0  0
     Cambodia    0      0.00  ||   0    0   0  0  0  0  0  0   0    0  0  0   0    0  0  0
        China    0      0.00  ||   0    0   0  0  0  0  0  0   0    0  0  0   0    0  0  0
    Hong Kong    1      6.25  ||   0    0   0  0  0  0  0  0   0    1  0  0   0    0  0  0
        India    0      0.00  ||   0    0   0  0  0  0  0  0   0    0  0  0   0    0  0  0
    Indonesia    0      0.00  ||   0    0   0  0  0  0  0  0   0    0  0  0   0    0  0  0
        Japan    2     12.50  ||   0    0   0  0  0  0  0  0   0    0  0  0   0    0  1  1
     Malaysia    0      0.00  ||   0    0   0  0  0  0  0  0   0    0  0  0   0    0  0  0
     N. Korea    1      6.25  ||   0    0   0  0  0  0  0  0   0    1  0  0   0    0  0  0
  New Zealand    2     12.50  ||   0    0   0  0  0  0  0  0   0    0  0  0   0    0  1  1
     Pakistan    1      6.25  ||   0    0   0  0  0  0  0  0   0    1  0  0   0    0  0  0
```

```
                    C          P       P          L  L  L  P  B    C  B  D     F  L  L
                    O     N    E       O    D     I  I  I  O  A    G  A  I  E     E  I  I
                    U     U    R       P    E     F  F  T  P  B    D  L  R  A  B   R  T  T
                    N     M    C       U    N  U  E  E  E  _  Y    P  O  T  T  _   T  _  _
                    T     M    E       L    S  R  E  E  R  I  M  _ R  H  H  T  I   M  F
                    R     I    N       A    I  B  X  X  A  N  O  C I  _  _  O  L   A  E
                    Y     S    T       T    A  P  P  C  C  R  A  E R  R  _  T  L   _  M
                    $     S    M       N    Y  N  F  M  Y  R  T  P S  T  T  D  Y   E  A
               ------------   -----    -    -  -  -  -  -  -  -  -  - -  -  -  -   -  -
           Philippines    0    0.00 || 0    0  0  0  0  0  0  0  0  0 0  0  0  0   0  0
              S. Korea    1    6.25 || 0    0  0  0  0  0  0  0  0  1 0  0  0  0   0  0
             Singapore    0    0.00 || 0    0  0  0  0  0  0  0  0  0 0  0  0  0   0  0
                Taiwan    6   37.50 || 0    0  0  0  0  0  0  0  0  1 0  1  1  1   1  1
              Thailand    0    0.00 || 0    0  0  0  0  0  0  0  0  0 0  0  0  0   0  0
               Vietnam    0    0.00 || 0    0  0  0  0  0  0  0  0  0 0  0  0  0   0  0
               Armenia    1    6.25 || 0    0  0  0  0  0  0  0  0  1 0  0  0  0   0  0
            Azerbaijan    1    6.25 || 0    0  0  0  0  0  0  0  0  1 0  0  0  0   0  0
               Bahrain    1    6.25 || 0    0  0  0  0  0  0  0  0  1 0  0  0  0   0  0
                 Egypt    0    0.00 || 0    0  0  0  0  0  0  0  0  0 0  0  0  0   0  0
                  Iran    0    0.00 || 0    0  0  0  0  0  0  0  0  0 0  0  0  0   0  0
                  Iraq    0    0.00 || 0    0  0  0  0  0  0  0  0  0 0  0  0  0   0  0
                Israel    1    6.25 || 0    0  0  0  0  0  0  0  0  1 0  0  0  0   0  0
                Jordan    0    0.00 || 0    0  0  0  0  0  0  0  0  0 0  0  0  0   0  0
                Kuwait    0    0.00 || 0    0  0  0  0  0  0  0  0  0 0  0  0  0   0  0
               Lebanon    1    6.25 || 0    0  0  0  0  0  0  0  0  1 0  0  0  0   0  0
                 Libya    0    0.00 || 0    0  0  0  0  0  0  0  0  0 0  0  0  0   0  0
                  Oman    4   25.00 || 0    0  0  0  0  1  0  0  0  1 0  0  0  0   1  1
          Saudi Arabia    0    0.00 || 0    0  0  0  0  0  0  0  0  0 0  0  0  0   0  0
                 Syria    1    6.25 || 0    0  0  0  0  0  0  0  0  1 0  0  0  0   0  0
                Turkey    0    0.00 || 0    0  0  0  0  0  0  0  0  0 0  0  0  0   0  0
            U.Arab Em.    1    6.25 || 0    0  0  0  0  0  0  0  0  1 0  0  0  0   0  0
            Uzbekistan    1    6.25 || 0    0  0  0  0  0  0  0  0  1 0  0  0  0   0  0
```

The 1's show that when female literacy is missing, male literacy is missing too (see the final two columns). *LIT_MALE* and *LIT_FEMA* are missing frequently for European countries, but calories is missing more often for Middle Eastern countries. In the complete sample, 37.5% of Taiwan's data are missing, 25% of Oman's data are missing, and so forth.

Sorted Pattern Table

In a sorted pattern table, cases and variables are sorted by the patterns of the missing data. Complete cases are not included. The input is:

```
USE world95m
LET NUMMISS=MIS(POPULATN DENSITY URBAN LIFEEXPF LIFEEXPM,
    LITERACY POP_INCR BABYMORT GDP_CAP CALORIES,
    BIRTH_RT DEATH_RT B_TO_D FERTILTY LIT_MALE,
    LIT_FEMA)
LET PERCENTM = NUMMISS/(NUMMISS+NUM(POPULATN DENSITY,
    URBAN LIFEEXPF LIFEEXPM LITERACY POP_INCR BABYMORT,
    GDP_CAP CALORIES BIRTH_RT DEATH_RT B_TO_D FERTILTY,
    LIT_MALE LIT_FEMA))*100
ESAVE world95n
TRANSPOSE POPULATN DENSITY URBAN LIFEEXPF LIFEEXPM,
    LITERACY POP_INCR BABYMORT GDP_CAP CALORIES,
    BIRTH_RT DEATH_RT B_TO_D FERTILTY LIT_MALE,
    LIT_FEMA NUMMISS PERCENTM
LET NUMMISS=MIS(COL(1)..COL(109))
SORT NUMMISS
TRANSPOSE
ESAVE recode

MERGE world95n (COUNTRY$ NUMMISS PERCENTM)  recode
DELETE 110
DROP LABEL$

LET (POPULATN DENSITY URBAN LIFEEXPF LIFEEXPM,
    LITERACY POP_INCR BABYMORT GDP_CAP CALORIES,
    BIRTH_RT DEATH_RT B_TO_D FERTILTY LIT_MALE,
    LIT_FEMA) = @ = .
SORT NUMMISS
SELECT NUMMISS>1
REM 'In the following table, a 1 indicates a missing value.'
REM 'A 0 indicates an observed value.'
LIST / FORMAT='########### ## ##.## || # # # # # # # # # # # # # # #'
```

To shorten the output, we omit countries with one missing value. *CALORIES* is missing for most of the omitted cases.

```
                     C              P       P  B       B P L L         D    F L L L C
                     O       N      E       O  A  G    I O I I D       E    E I I I A
                     U       U      R       P  B  D    R P F F E B A   R    T T T L
                     N       M      C       U  Y  P    T _ E E N _ T U T    E _ _ O
                     T       M      E       L  M  _    H I E E S T H R I    R M F R
                     R       I      N       A  O  C    _ N X X I O _ B L    A A E I
                     Y       S      T       T  R  A    R C P P T _ R A T    C L M E
                     $       S      M       N  T  P    T R M F Y D T N Y    Y E A S
     ------------    --    -----    -       -  -  -    - - - - - - - - -    - - - -
          Ireland    2     12.50   ||       0  0  0    0 0 0 0 0 0 0 0 0    0 1 1 0
          Romania    2     12.50   ||       0  0  0    0 0 0 0 0 0 0 0 0    0 1 1 0
          Germany    2     12.50   ||       0  0  0    0 0 0 0 0 0 0 0 0    0 1 1 0
          Denmark    2     12.50   ||       0  0  0    0 0 0 0 0 0 0 0 0    0 1 1 0
            Japan    2     12.50   ||       0  0  0    0 0 0 0 0 0 0 0 0    0 1 1 0
           France    2     12.50   ||       0  0  0    0 0 0 0 0 0 0 0 0    0 1 1 0
          Finland    2     12.50   ||       0  0  0    0 0 0 0 0 0 0 0 0    0 1 1 0
           Sweden    2     12.50   ||       0  0  0    0 0 0 0 0 0 0 0 0    0 1 1 0
      Switzerland    2     12.50   ||       0  0  0    0 0 0 0 0 0 0 0 0    0 1 1 0
      Netherlands    2     12.50   ||       0  0  0    0 0 0 0 0 0 0 0 0    0 1 1 0
           Canada    2     12.50   ||       0  0  0    0 0 0 0 0 0 0 0 0    0 1 1 0
      New Zealand    2     12.50   ||       0  0  0    0 0 0 0 0 0 0 0 0    0 1 1 0
               UK    2     12.50   ||       0  0  0    0 0 0 0 0 0 0 0 0    0 1 1 0
           Norway    2     12.50   ||       0  0  0    0 0 0 0 0 0 0 0 0    0 1 1 0
          Austria    2     12.50   ||       0  0  0    0 0 0 0 0 0 0 0 0    0 1 1 0
     South Africa    3     18.75   ||       0  0  0    0 0 0 0 0 0 0 0 0    0 1 1 1
          Croatia    3     18.75   ||       0  0  0    0 0 0 0 0 0 0 0 0    0 1 1 1
         Bulgaria    3     18.75   ||       0  0  0    0 0 0 0 0 0 0 0 0    0 1 1 1
          Iceland    3     18.75   ||       0  0  0    0 0 0 0 0 0 0 0 0    0 1 1 1
          Belgium    3     18.75   ||       0  0  0    0 0 0 0 0 0 0 0 0    0 1 1 1
             Oman    4     25.00   ||       0  0  0    0 0 0 0 0 0 0 0 0    1 1 1 1
           Bosnia    4     25.00   ||       0  0  0    0 0 0 0 0 0 0 0 1    0 1 1 1
       Czech Rep.    4     25.00   ||       0  0  0    0 0 0 0 0 0 0 1 0    1 1 1 0
           Taiwan    6     37.50   ||       0  0  0    0 0 0 0 1 1 0 1 0    1 1 1 1
```

The last three columns are *LIT_MALE*, *LIT_FEMA*, and *CALORIES*, and the four last cases are Oman, Bosnia, Czech Rep., and Taiwan, because they have the most values missing. Recalling that cases with one missing value are not included and that this missing value is usually *CALORIES*, it is easy to see that when *CALORIES* is missing, the literacy rates for females and males tend to be present. For larger data files, the most common patterns may be less apparent

Example 3
Correlation Estimation

In this example, we continue to use the *world95m* data used in the "Preliminary Examinations" example, now requesting estimates of correlations. Even though we established that values are nonrandomly missing, we request listwise estimates so that they can be compared later with estimates obtained by the pairwise, and EM.

```
USE world95m
LET log_dea = L10(DEATH_RT)
FORMAT 6,3
CORR
NOTE 'Listwise Deletion'
PEARSON LOG_POP LOG_DEN LIFEEXPF LIFEEXPM POP_INCR,
    BABYMORT LOG_GDP BIRTH_RT LOG_DEA B_TO_D,
    FERTILTY URBAN LITERACY LIT_FEMA,
    LIT_MALE CALORIES / LISTWISE
```

The output follows:

```
                         Listwise Deletion
    Means
            LOG_PO LOG_DE LIFEEX LIFEEX POP_IN BABYMO LOG_GD BIRTH_ LOG_DE
             4.237  1.660 65.831 61.339  2.214 57.729  3.129 31.492  0.945


            B_TO_D FERTIL  URBAN LITERA LIT_FE LIT_MA CALORI
             3.776  4.303 49.763 69.576 62.119 75.356 2.59E3


Pearson correlation matrix
            LOG_PO LOG_DE LIFEEX LIFEEX POP_IN BABYMO LOG_GD BIRTH_ LOG_DE
   LOG_POP   1.000
   LOG_DEN   0.282  1.000
  LIFEEXPF   0.038  0.004  1.000
  LIFEEXPM   0.059  0.023  0.987  1.000
   POP_INCR -0.299 -0.206 -0.392 -0.325  1.000
   BABYMORT -0.009 -0.037 -0.951 -0.931  0.420  1.000
   LOG_GDP  -0.139 -0.216  0.766  0.736 -0.363 -0.745  1.000
   BIRTH_RT -0.223 -0.136 -0.817 -0.773  0.776  0.809 -0.674  1.000
   LOG_DEA   0.029 -0.015 -0.801 -0.823 -0.102  0.742 -0.478  0.468  1.000
   B_TO_D   -0.269 -0.072  0.270  0.318  0.692 -0.231  0.083  0.188 -0.731
   FERTILTY -0.240 -0.142 -0.790 -0.747  0.755  0.784 -0.586  0.968  0.503
   URBAN    -0.141 -0.226  0.741  0.717 -0.192 -0.705  0.786 -0.566 -0.583
   LITERACY  0.082  0.004  0.827  0.785 -0.567 -0.891  0.642 -0.822 -0.589
   LIT_FEMA  0.109  0.072  0.815  0.773 -0.580 -0.856  0.602 -0.811 -0.570
   LIT_MALE  0.176  0.097  0.754  0.727 -0.542 -0.805  0.580 -0.756 -0.529
   CALORIES  0.142 -0.012  0.716  0.711 -0.393 -0.701  0.803 -0.658 -0.407
```

```
                B_TO_D FERTIL  URBAN LITERA LIT_FE LIT_MA CALORI
     B_TO_D      1.000
     FERTILTY    0.152  1.000
     URBAN       0.261 -0.533  1.000
     LITERACY    0.043 -0.814  0.614  1.000
     LIT_FEMA    0.032 -0.819  0.634  0.963  1.000
     LIT_MALE    0.029 -0.759  0.595  0.939  0.960  1.000
     CALORIES    0.040 -0.581  0.674  0.575  0.548  0.576  1.000


Number of observations: 59
```

Of the 109 cases in the file, 50 have missing data. All statistics reported here are based on the remaining 59 cases. If you compute the means for these variables using STATS, the values will differ. The latter procedure deletes cases on a variable-by-variable basis, instead of deleting a case if it has a missing value on any variable.

Pairwise Deletion

A table of frequency counts for each pair of variables provides a picture of the pattern of incomplete data. SYSTAT displays this table when using pairwise deletion in CORR or when using PRINT = MEDIUM in MISSING.

```
USE world95m
LET log_dea = L10(DEATH_RT)
FORMAT 6,3
CORR
NOTE 'Pairwise Deletion'
PEARSON LOG_POP LOG_DEN LIFEEXPF LIFEEXPM POP_INCR,
     BABYMORT LOG_GDP BIRTH_RT LOG_DEA B_TO_D,
     FERTILTY URBAN LITERACY LIT_FEMA,
     LIT_MALE CALORIES / PAIRWISE
```

Missing Value Analysis

The output follows:

```
                           Pairwise Deletion

Means
         LOG_PO LOG_DE LIFEEX LIFEEX POP_IN BABYMO LOG_GD BIRTH_ LOG_DE
          4.114  1.784 70.156 64.917  1.682 42.313  3.422 25.923  0.941


         B_TO_D FERTIL  URBAN LITERA LIT_FE LIT_MA CALORI
          3.204  3.563 56.528 78.336 67.259 78.729 2.75E3


Pearson correlation matrix

         LOG_PO LOG_DE LIFEEX LIFEEX POP_IN BABYMO LOG_GD BIRTH_ LOG_DE
LOG_POP   1.000
LOG_DEN   0.143  1.000
LIFEEXPF -0.088  0.126  1.000
LIFEEXPM -0.082  0.153  0.982  1.000
POP_INCR -0.078 -0.252 -0.579 -0.502  1.000
BABYMORT  0.109 -0.152 -0.962 -0.936  0.602  1.000
LOG_GDP  -0.217  0.004  0.831  0.805 -0.557 -0.824  1.000
BIRTH_RT -0.027 -0.216 -0.862 -0.805  0.861  0.865 -0.769  1.000
LOG_DEA   0.089 -0.064 -0.587 -0.640 -0.206  0.534 -0.322  0.230  1.000
B_TO_D   -0.153 -0.111 -0.087 -0.011  0.800  0.118 -0.209  0.483 -0.690
FERTILTY -0.060 -0.223 -0.838 -0.783  0.840  0.833 -0.693  0.975  0.268
URBAN    -0.138  0.015  0.743  0.730 -0.375 -0.718  0.754 -0.629 -0.431
LITERACY -0.050  0.084  0.865  0.809 -0.699 -0.900  0.732 -0.869 -0.385
LIT_FEMA  0.005  0.113  0.819  0.745 -0.638 -0.843  0.632 -0.835 -0.442
LIT_MALE  0.076  0.138  0.777  0.717 -0.619 -0.809  0.611 -0.794 -0.414
CALORIES  0.046  0.050  0.775  0.765 -0.609 -0.777  0.847 -0.762 -0.267


         B_TO_D FERTIL  URBAN LITERA LIT_FE LIT_MA CALORI
B_TO_D    1.000
FERTILTY  0.452  1.000
URBAN    -0.032 -0.619  1.000
LITERACY -0.271 -0.866  0.650  1.000
LIT_FEMA -0.148 -0.839  0.612  0.973  1.000
LIT_MALE -0.153 -0.796  0.587  0.948  0.964  1.000
CALORIES -0.240 -0.696  0.692  0.682  0.548  0.576  1.000
```

```
Pairwise frequency table

         LOG_PO LOG_DE LIFEEX LIFEEX POP_IN BABYMO LOG_GD BIRTH_ LOG_DE
LOG_POP     109
LOG_DEN     109    109
LIFEEXPF    109    109    109
LIFEEXPM    109    109    109    109
POP_INCR    109    109    109    109    109
BABYMORT    109    109    109    109    109    109
LOG_GDP     109    109    109    109    109    109    109
BIRTH_RT    109    109    109    109    109    109    109    109
LOG_DEA     108    108    108    108    108    108    108    108    108
B_TO_D      108    108    108    108    108    108    108    108
FERTILTY    107    107    107    107    107    107    107    107    107
URBAN       108    108    108    108    108    108    108    108    107
LITERACY    107    107    107    107    107    107    107    107    106
LIT_FEMA     85     85     85     85     85     85     85     85     85
LIT_MALE     85     85     85     85     85     85     85     85     85
CALORIES     75     75     75     75     75     75     75     75     75

         B_TO_D FERTIL URBAN  LITERA LIT_FE LIT_MA CALORI
B_TO_D      108
FERTILTY    107    107
URBAN       107    106    108
LITERACY    106    105    107    107
LIT_FEMA     85     85     85     85     85
LIT_MALE     85     85     85     85     85     85
CALORIES     75     75     74     74     59     59     75
```

In contrast to listwise deletion, the number of cases used to compute each correlation and mean varies with the variable(s) involved. The mean computations use all observed cases for each variable. The correlation computations involve all cases that have observed values for both variables. The pairwise frequency table displays the number of cases used to calculate each correlation.

The sample size for each variable is reported on the diagonal of the table; sample sizes for complete pairs of cases, off the diagonal. *CALORIES* alone has 75 values, but when paired with male or female literacy, the count of cases with both values drops to 59. If you need a set of variables for a multivariate analysis, it would be wise to omit *CALORIES* or the male and female literacy rates. Otherwise, if these variables are essential to your analysis, be concerned that results may be biased due to the fact they are not missing randomly.

Regression Method

We now use the regression method for estimating the correlation matrix.

```
USE world95m
LET log_dea = L10(DEATH_RT)
FORMAT 6,3
MISSING
NOTE 'Regression Method'
MODEL LOG_POP LOG_DEN LIFEEXPF LIFEEXPM POP_INCR,
      BABYMORT LOG_GDP BIRTH_RT LOG_DEA B_TO_D,
      FERTILTY URBAN LITERACY LIT_FEMA,
      LIT_MALE CALORIES
ESTIMATE / MATRIX=CORRELATION REGRESSION
```

The output follows:

```
                        Regression Method


 No.of  Missing value patterns
 Cases  (X=nonmissing; .=missing)
   26   XXXXXXXXXXXXXXX.
   59   XXXXXXXXXXXXXXXX
   15   XXXXXXXXXXXXX..X
    5   XXXXXXXXXXXXX...
    1   XXXXXXXXX.XX...
    1   XXXXXXXXXXX....X
    1   XXXXXXXXXXXX....
    1   XXXXXXX...XX...


Regression Substitution estimate of means
          LOG_PO LOG_DE LIFEEX LIFEEX POP_IN BABYMO LOG_GD BIRTH_ LOG_DE
           4.114  1.784 70.156 64.917  1.682 42.313  3.422 25.923  0.941

          B_TO_D FERTIL  URBAN LITERA LIT_FE LIT_MA CALORI
           3.200  3.527 56.664 78.472 72.954 82.657  2.80E3
```

```
Regression Substitution estimated correlation matrix

          LOG_PO LOG_DE LIFEEX LIFEEX POP_IN BABYMO LOG_GD BIRTH_ LOG_DE
LOG_POP    1.000
LOG_DEN    0.143  1.000
LIFEEXPF  -0.088  0.126  1.000
LIFEEXPM  -0.082  0.153  0.982  1.000
POP_INCR  -0.078 -0.252 -0.579 -0.502  1.000
BABYMORT   0.109 -0.152 -0.962 -0.936  0.602  1.000
LOG_GDP   -0.217  0.004  0.831  0.805 -0.557 -0.824  1.000
BIRTH_RT  -0.027 -0.216 -0.862 -0.805  0.861  0.865 -0.769  1.000
LOG_DEA    0.087 -0.069 -0.587 -0.640 -0.203  0.535 -0.323  0.232  1.000
B_TO_D    -0.153 -0.113 -0.088 -0.012  0.799  0.119 -0.209  0.483 -0.689
FERTILTY  -0.054 -0.234 -0.839 -0.785  0.841  0.835 -0.691  0.975  0.276
URBAN     -0.138  0.018  0.743  0.729 -0.378 -0.718  0.754 -0.630 -0.426
LITERACY  -0.047  0.091  0.865  0.807 -0.698 -0.899  0.729 -0.866 -0.372
LIT_FEMA   0.005  0.144  0.838  0.777 -0.707 -0.857  0.689 -0.857 -0.319
LIT_MALE   0.070  0.171  0.797  0.748 -0.682 -0.823  0.669 -0.816 -0.297
CALORIES   0.018  0.114  0.748  0.731 -0.591 -0.748  0.811 -0.734 -0.200

          B_TO_D FERTIL URBAN  LITERA LIT_FE LIT_MA CALORI
B_TO_D     1.000
FERTILTY   0.454  1.000
URBAN     -0.039 -0.605  1.000
LITERACY  -0.276 -0.857  0.643  1.000
LIT_FEMA  -0.311 -0.857  0.657  0.968  1.000
LIT_MALE  -0.306 -0.813  0.633  0.942  0.965  1.000
CALORIES  -0.274 -0.668  0.661  0.644  0.611  0.641  1.000
```

In the Missing Value Patterns display, the patterns of missing values across variables are tabulated. An X indicates an observed value for a variable; a . represents a missing value for a variable. The ordering of the variables corresponds to the order of the variables in the analysis. The first row in the display represents the pattern for 26 cases and has X's for all variables but the last (*CALORIES*); for 26 cases, *CALORIES* is the only missing value. Fifty-nine cases have no missing values. *LIT_FEMA* and *LIT_MALE* are the only missing values for 15 cases and five cases are missing *CALORIES, LIT_FEMA,* and *LIT_MALE*. The remaining four cases exhibit unique missing value patterns.

EM Method

Here we employ the EM algorithm to iteratively arrive at final correlation estimates. This method often performs better than the other methods when data are jointly missing.

```
USE world95m
LET log_dea = L10(DEATH_RT)
FORMAT 6,3
MISSING
NOTE 'EM Method'
MODEL LOG_POP LOG_DEN LIFEEXPF LIFEEXPM POP_INCR,
      BABYMORT LOG_GDP BIRTH_RT LOG_DEA B_TO_D,
      FERTILTY URBAN LITERACY LIT_FEMA,
      LIT_MALE CALORIES
ESTIMATE / MATRIX=CORRELATION ITER=200
```

The output follows:

```
                              EM Method

NOTE: Case          7 is an outlier. Mahalanobis D^2=38.457898   z=3.150632
NOTE: Case         14 is an outlier. Mahalanobis D^2=67.356520   z=5.333587
NOTE: Case         47 is an outlier. Mahalanobis D^2=37.977113   z=3.103577
NOTE: Case         60 is an outlier. Mahalanobis D^2=69.504934   z=5.477735
NOTE: Case        100 is an outlier. Mahalanobis D^2=38.732621   z=3.177344
NOTE: Case        109 is an outlier. Mahalanobis D^2=39.694367   z=3.119462


 No.of  Missing value patterns
 Cases  (X=nonmissing; .=missing)
   26   XXXXXXXXXXXXXX.
   59   XXXXXXXXXXXXXXX
   15   XXXXXXXXXXXX..X
    5   XXXXXXXXXXXX...
    1   XXXXXXXXX.XX...
    1   XXXXXXXXXXX....X
    1   XXXXXXXXXXX....
    1   XXXXXXX...XX...
```

```
Little MCAR test statistic:      133.476  df =     88  prob = 0.001


EM estimate of means
         LOG_PO LOG_DE LIFEEX LIFEEX POP_IN BABYMO LOG_GD BIRTH_ LOG_DE
          4.114  1.784 70.156 64.917  1.682 42.313  3.422 25.923  0.941


         B_TO_D FERTIL  URBAN LITERA LIT_FE LIT_MA CALORI
          3.200  3.530 56.641 78.408 72.735 82.710  2.79E3


EM estimated correlation matrix

         LOG_PO LOG_DE LIFEEX LIFEEX POP_IN BABYMO LOG_GD BIRTH_ LOG_DE
LOG_POP   1.000
LOG_DEN   0.143  1.000
LIFEEXPF -0.088  0.126  1.000
LIFEEXPM -0.082  0.153  0.982  1.000
POP_INCR -0.078 -0.252 -0.579 -0.502  1.000
BABYMORT  0.109 -0.152 -0.962 -0.936  0.602  1.000
LOG_GDP  -0.217  0.004  0.831  0.805 -0.557 -0.824  1.000
BIRTH_RT -0.027 -0.216 -0.862 -0.805  0.861  0.865 -0.769  1.000
LOG_DEA   0.087 -0.070 -0.588 -0.640 -0.202  0.535 -0.323  0.233  1.000
B_TO_D   -0.153 -0.112 -0.088 -0.012  0.799  0.119 -0.209  0.483 -0.689
FERTILTY -0.055 -0.233 -0.839 -0.785  0.841  0.835 -0.692  0.975  0.275
URBAN    -0.138  0.018  0.743  0.729 -0.377 -0.718  0.754 -0.629 -0.427
LITERACY -0.045  0.094  0.864  0.807 -0.700 -0.898  0.727 -0.868 -0.370
LIT_FEMA  0.006  0.139  0.838  0.776 -0.703 -0.856  0.686 -0.855 -0.325
LIT_MALE  0.070  0.167  0.799  0.748 -0.686 -0.824  0.669 -0.819 -0.295
CALORIES  0.009  0.095  0.748  0.732 -0.582 -0.749  0.809 -0.730 -0.213


         B_TO_D FERTIL  URBAN LITERA LIT_FE LIT_MA CALORI
B_TO_D    1.000
FERTILTY  0.454  1.000
URBAN    -0.037 -0.606  1.000
LITERACY -0.280 -0.860  0.646  1.000
LIT_FEMA -0.307 -0.858  0.653  0.970  1.000
LIT_MALE -0.311 -0.818  0.630  0.944  0.965  1.000
CALORIES -0.261 -0.664  0.646  0.637  0.600  0.634  1.000
```

Roderick J. A. Little's chi-square statistic for testing whether values are missing completely at random accompanies EM matrices. This statistic has an asymptotic chi-square distribution with degrees of freedom equal to the sum of the number of observed variables across missing value patterns minus the number of variables. In this example, the degrees of freedom equal 15 + 16 + 14 + 13 + 12 + 12 + 12 + 10 − 16, or 88. For a chi-square distribution with 88 degrees of freedom, the obtained value of 133.476 has a p-value of .001. This small p-value suggests that the missing values are not missing completely at random, but instead depend on the variables in the analysis.

SYSTAT identifies six cases as outliers. Outliers have undue influence on the estimates and you should examine these cases for possible omission from the analysis.

Example 4
Comparing Correlation Estimation Methods

In a large study, it is difficult to compare two correlation matrices for differences (or to determine whether they differ at all). Here, we save three correlation matrices and use MATRIX to compute the differences between elements in each pair of matrices.

```
USE world95m
LET log_dea = L10(DEATH_RT)
FORMAT 6,3
CORR
SAVE lcorr
PEARSON LOG_POP LOG_DEN LIFEEXPF LIFEEXPM POP_INCR,
        BABYMORT LOG_GDP BIRTH_RT LOG_DEA B_TO_D,
        FERTILTY URBAN LITERACY LIT_FEMA,
        LIT_MALE CALORIES / LISTWISE
SAVE pcorr
PEARSON LOG_POP LOG_DEN LIFEEXPF LIFEEXPM POP_INCR,
        BABYMORT LOG_GDP BIRTH_RT LOG_DEA B_TO_D,
        FERTILTY URBAN LITERACY LIT_FEMA,
        LIT_MALE CALORIES / PAIRWISE
MISSING
MODEL LOG_POP LOG_DEN LIFEEXPF LIFEEXPM POP_INCR,
      BABYMORT LOG_GDP BIRTH_RT LOG_DEA B_TO_D,
      FERTILTY URBAN LITERACY LIT_FEMA,
      LIT_MALE CALORIES
SAVE emcorr
ESTIMATE / MATRIX=CORRELATION ITER=200

MATRIX
USE emcorr
```

```
              ROWNAME emcorr = LOG_POP LOG_DEN LIFEEXPF LIFEEXPM POP_INCR,
                   BABYMORT LOG_GDP BIRTH_RT LOG_DEA B_TO_D,
                   FERTILTY URBAN LITERACY LIT_FEMA,
                   LIT_MALE CALORIES
              USE pcorr
              ROWNAME pcorr = LOG_POP LOG_DEN LIFEEXPF LIFEEXPM POP_INCR,
                   BABYMORT LOG_GDP BIRTH_RT LOG_DEA B_TO_D,
                   FERTILTY URBAN LITERACY LIT_FEMA,
                   LIT_MALE CALORIES
              USE lcorr
              MAT diff_lp=lcorr-pcorr
              MAT diff_le=lcorr-emcorr
              MAT diff_pe=pcorr-emcorr
              SHOW diff_lp diff_le diff_pe
```

The differences between the listwise and pairwise estimates follow:

```
Matrix: DIFF_LP
              LOG_PO LOG_DE LIFEEX LIFEEX POP_IN BABYMO LOG_GD BIRTH_ LOG_DE
   LOG_POP     0.000    .      .      .      .      .      .      .      .
   LOG_DEN     0.139  0.000    .      .      .      .      .      .      .
   LIFEEXPF    0.126 -0.122  0.000    .      .      .      .      .      .
   LIFEEXPM    0.141 -0.129  0.005  0.000    .      .      .      .      .
   POP_INCR   -0.221  0.046  0.188  0.177  0.000    .      .      .      .
   BABYMORT   -0.118  0.115  0.011  0.005 -0.182  0.000    .      .      .
   LOG_GDP     0.078 -0.220 -0.066 -0.069  0.194  0.079  0.000    .      .
   BIRTH_RT   -0.196  0.080  0.045  0.032 -0.086 -0.057  0.095  0.000    .
   LOG_DEA    -0.059  0.050 -0.214 -0.183  0.104  0.208 -0.156  0.238  0.000
   B_TO_D     -0.116  0.039  0.357  0.329 -0.108 -0.349  0.291 -0.295 -0.041
   FERTILTY   -0.180  0.081  0.048  0.035 -0.085 -0.049  0.108 -0.007  0.235
   URBAN      -0.003 -0.241 -0.003 -0.013  0.183  0.013  0.032  0.063 -0.153
   LITERACY    0.132 -0.081 -0.039 -0.024  0.132  0.010 -0.090  0.047 -0.205
   LIT_FEMA    0.104 -0.042 -0.004  0.029  0.059 -0.013 -0.030  0.024 -0.128
   LIT_MALE    0.100 -0.042 -0.023  0.010  0.077  0.004 -0.031  0.037 -0.116
   CALORIES    0.097 -0.062 -0.059 -0.054  0.216  0.076 -0.045  0.104 -0.140

              B_TO_D FERTIL URBAN  LITERA LIT_FE LIT_MA CALORI
   B_TO_D      0.000    .      .      .      .      .      .
   FERTILTY   -0.300  0.000    .      .      .      .      .
   URBAN       0.293  0.086  0.000    .      .      .      .
   LITERACY    0.314  0.052 -0.035  0.000    .      .      .
   LIT_FEMA    0.180  0.020  0.022 -0.010  0.000    .      .
   LIT_MALE    0.182  0.036  0.008 -0.009 -0.005  0.000    .
   CALORIES    0.279  0.115 -0.018 -0.106  0.000  0.000  0.000
```

Missing Value Analysis

We find many large differences between the correlations estimated by the two deletion methods. The differences are particularly large for *B_TO_D*.

To assist in identifying the large differences, we use MATRIX to create a rectangular data file of correlation differences. We then create a bar chart of these differences. Anchoring the bars at 0 allows rapid discrimination between positive and negative differences. We also use blue bars for positive differences and red bars for negative differences.

```
MATRIX
USE pcorr
USE lcorr
MAT diff_lp=lcorr-pcorr
CLEAR pcorr lcorr
MAT cix=[1 2 3 4 5 6 7 8 9 10 11 12 13 14 15 16]
MAT cix=cix//cix//cix//cix//cix//cix//cix//cix//cix//cix//cix//cix//cix//cix//cix//cix
MAT rix=TRP(cix)
MAT rix=SHAPE(rix,256,1)
MAT cix=SHAPE(cix,256,1)
MAT diff_lp=FOLD(diff_lp)
MAT col_lp=SHAPE(diff_lp,256,1)
MAT col_lp=col_lp||rix||cix
SHOW col_lp
SAVE col_lp
EXIT

USE col_lp
IF v(1)<0 THEN LET sign=0
IF v(1)=>0 THEN LET sign=1
```

```
LABEL v(2) / 1=LOG_POP 2=LOG_DEN 3=LIFEEXPF 4=LIFEEXPM,
              5=POP_INCR 6=BABYMORT 7=LOG_GDP 8=BIRTH_RT,
              9=LOG_DEA 10=B_TO_D 11=FERTILTY 12=URBAN,
              13=LITERACY 14=LIT_FEMA 15=LIT_MALE,
              16=CALORIES
LABEL v(3) / 1=LOG_POP 2=LOG_DEN 3=LIFEEXPF 4=LIFEEXPM,
              5=POP_INCR 6=BABYMORT 7=LOG_GDP 8=BIRTH_RT,
              9=LOG_DEA 10=B_TO_D 11=FERTILTY 12=URBAN,
              13=LITERACY 14=LIT_FEMA 15=LIT_MALE,
              16=CALORIES
CATEGORY V(2) V(3)
BAR V(1)*V(3)*V(2) / GROUP=sign OVERLAY COLOR=RED,BLUE,
              BASE=0 BTHICK= 0.80 LEGEND=NONE,
              XLAB='' YLAB='' ZMIN=-.5 ZMAX=.5,
              ZLAB='Correlation Difference'
```

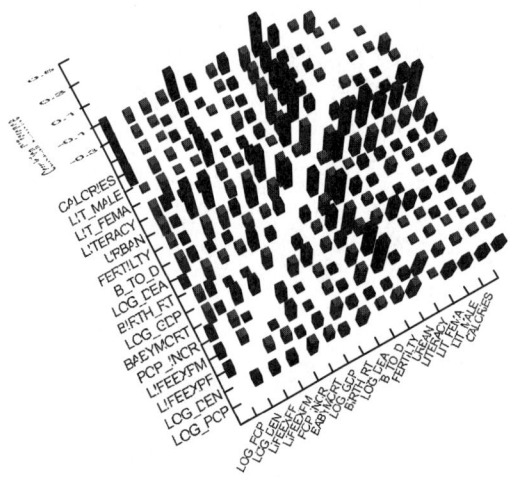

The order of the variables along an axis corresponds to variables with little or no missing data at the left end (*LOG_POP*) and variables with the most missing data at the right end (*CALORIES*). The bar graph reveals that *LOG_DEA* pairwise correlation estimates tend to be larger than listwise estimates when the variable being correlated with *LOG_DEA* contains many missing values. The reverse pattern occurs for *B_TO_D*. These patterns suggest that the data are not missing completely at random.

Listwise Deletion vs EM Method

The differences between the listwise and EM correlation estimates follow:

```
Matrix: DIFF_LE
            LOG_PO LOG_DE LIFEEX LIFEEX POP_IN BABYMO LOG_GD BIRTH_ LOG_DE
  LOG_POP    0.000    .      .      .      .      .      .      .      .
  LOG_DEN    0.139  0.000    .      .      .      .      .      .      .
  LIFEEXPF   0.126 -0.122  0.000    .      .      .      .      .      .
  LIFEEXPM   0.141 -0.129  0.005  0.000    .      .      .      .      .
  POP_INCR  -0.221  0.046  0.188  0.177  0.000    .      .      .      .
  BABYMORT  -0.118  0.115  0.011  0.005 -0.182  0.000    .      .      .
  LOG_GDP    0.078 -0.220 -0.066 -0.069  0.194  0.079  0.000    .      .
  BIRTH_RT  -0.196  0.080  0.045  0.032 -0.086 -0.057  0.095  0.000    .
  LOG_DEA   -0.058  0.055 -0.214 -0.183  0.101  0.207 -0.155  0.236  0.000
  B_TO_D    -0.116  0.040  0.358  0.330 -0.107 -0.350  0.292 -0.295 -0.043
  FERTILTY  -0.185  0.090  0.049  0.038 -0.086 -0.051  0.106 -0.007  0.228
  URBAN     -0.003 -0.243 -0.002 -0.012  0.185  0.013  0.033  0.063 -0.156
  LITERACY   0.126 -0.090 -0.038 -0.022  0.133  0.008 -0.085  0.046 -0.220
  LIT_FEMA   0.103 -0.068 -0.023 -0.002  0.123  0.000 -0.084  0.045 -0.245
  LIT_MALE   0.106 -0.070 -0.045 -0.021  0.144  0.019 -0.089  0.063 -0.234
  CALORIES   0.134 -0.107 -0.032 -0.022  0.189  0.048 -0.007  0.072 -0.194

            B_TO_D FERTIL URBAN  LITERA LIT_FE LIT_MA CALORI
  B_TO_D     0.000    .      .      .      .      .      .
  FERTILTY  -0.301  0.000    .      .      .      .      .
  URBAN      0.299  0.073  0.000    .      .      .      .
  LITERACY   0.323  0.046 -0.031  0.000    .      .      .
  LIT_FEMA   0.339  0.039 -0.019 -0.007  0.000    .      .
  LIT_MALE   0.339  0.059 -0.035 -0.005 -0.005  0.000    .
  CALORIES   0.301  0.083  0.028 -0.062 -0.052 -0.059  0.000
```

Again, we find large differences between many correlations involving *B_TO_D*. The EM estimates tend to be larger when values are not missing. *LOG_DEA* also exhibits large differences, but not to the degree of *B_TO_D*.

Chapter 1

As done for listwise/pairwise comparison, here we create a bar chart of the correlation differences between the listwise and EM estimates.

```
MATRIX
USE lcorr
USE emcorr
MAT diff_le=lcorr-emcorr
CLEAR lcorr emcorr
MAT cix=[1 2 3 4 5 6 7 8 9 10 11 12 13 14 15 16]
MAT cix=cix//cix//cix//cix//cix//cix//cix//cix//cix//cix//cix//cix//cix//cix//cix//cix
MAT rix=TRP(cix)
MAT rix=SHAPE(rix,256,1)
MAT cix=SHAPE(cix,256,1)
MAT diff_le=FOLD(diff_le)
MAT col_le=SHAPE(diff_le,256,1)
MAT col_le=col_le||rix||cix
SHOW col_le
SAVE col_le
EXIT

USE col_le
IF v(1)<0 THEN LET sign=0
IF v(1)=>0 THEN LET sign=1
LABEL v(2)  / 1=LOG_POP 2=LOG_DEN 3=LIFEEXPF 4=LIFEEXPM,
              5=POP_INCR 6=BABYMORT 7=LOG_GDP 8=BIRTH_RT,
              9=LOG_DEA 10=B_TO_D 11=FERTILTY 12=URBAN,
              13=LITERACY 14=LIT_FEMA 15=LIT_MALE,
              16=CALORIES
LABEL v(3)  / 1=LOG_POP 2=LOG_DEN 3=LIFEEXPF 4=LIFEEXPM,
              5=POP_INCR 6=BABYMORT 7=LOG_GDP 8=BIRTH_RT,
              9=LOG_DEA 10=B_TO_D 11=FERTILTY 12=URBAN,
              13=LITERACY 14=LIT_FEMA 15=LIT_MALE,
              16=CALORIES
CATEGORY V(2) V(3)
BAR V(1)*V(3)*V(2)  / GROUP=sign OVERLAY COLOR=RED,BLUE,
                      BASE=0 BTHICK= 0.80 LEGEND=NONE,
                      XLAB='' YLAB='' ZMIN=-.5 ZMAX=.5,
                      ZLAB='Correlation Difference'
```

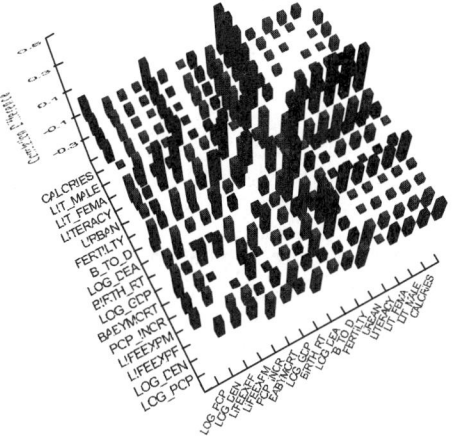

As found elsewhere for pairwise estimates, this bar graph reveals that *LOG_DEA* EM correlation estimates tend to be larger than listwise estimates when the variable being correlated with *LOG_DEA* contains many missing values. *B_TO_D* exhibits the opposite pattern. For a given pair of variables, the difference between EM and listwise estimates tends to be larger than the difference between pairwise and listwise estimates.

Pairwise Deletion vs EM Method

The differences between the pairwise and EM correlation estimates follow:

```
Matrix: DIFF_PE
            LOG_PO LOG_DE LIFEEX LIFEEX POP_IN BABYMO LOG_GD BIRTH_ LOG_DE
   LOG_POP   0.000      .      .      .      .      .      .      .      .
   LOG_DEN   0.000  0.000      .      .      .      .      .      .      .
  LIFEEXPF   0.000  0.000  0.000      .      .      .      .      .      .
  LIFEEXPM   0.000  0.000  0.000  0.000      .      .      .      .      .
  POP_INCR   0.000  0.000  0.000  0.000  0.000      .      .      .      .
   BABYMORT  0.000  0.000  0.000  0.000  0.000  0.000      .      .      .
   LOG_GDP   0.000  0.000  0.000  0.000  0.000  0.000  0.000      .      .
   BIRTH_RT  0.000  0.000  0.000  0.000  0.000  0.000  0.000  0.000      .
   LOG_DEA   0.001  0.005  0.001  0.000 -0.003 -0.001  0.001 -0.002  0.000
   B_TO_D    0.000  0.001  0.001  0.001  0.001 -0.001  0.000  0.001 -0.001
  FERTILTY  -0.005  0.009  0.001  0.002 -0.001 -0.002 -0.001 -0.000 -0.007
     URBAN   0.000 -0.002  0.001  0.001  0.002 -0.000  0.001 -0.000 -0.004
  LITERACY  -0.005 -0.009  0.001  0.002  0.000 -0.002  0.005 -0.001 -0.015
  LIT_FEMA  -0.001 -0.026 -0.019 -0.031  0.065  0.013 -0.054  0.020 -0.117
  LIT_MALE   0.006 -0.028 -0.022 -0.031  0.067  0.015 -0.058  0.025 -0.118
   CALORIES  0.037 -0.045  0.027  0.033 -0.026 -0.028  0.038 -0.032 -0.054
```

	B_TO_D	FERTIL	URBAN	LITERA	LIT_FE	LIT_MA	CALORI
B_TO_D	0.000	.	.	.	.	.	.
FERTILTY	-0.001	0.000	.	.	.	.	.
URBAN	0.005	-0.013	0.000	.	.	.	.
LITERACY	0.009	-0.006	0.004	0.000	.	.	.
LIT_FEMA	0.159	0.019	-0.041	0.004	0.000	.	.
LIT_MALE	0.157	0.023	-0.043	0.004	-0.000	0.000	.
CALORIES	0.022	-0.031	0.046	0.044	-0.052	-0.059	0.000

The differences between these two sets of correlation estimates are very small. The largest differences appear for variables missing 22% of the data, *LIT_FEMA* and *LIT_MALE*.

As done for the other method comparisons, here we create a bar chart of the correlation differences between the pairwise and EM estimates.

```
MATRIX
USE pcorr
USE emcorr
MAT diff_pe=pcorr-emcorr
CLEAR pcorr emcorr
MAT cix=[1 2 3 4 5 6 7 8 9 10 11 12 13 14 15 16]
MAT cix=cix//cix//cix//cix//cix//cix//cix//cix//cix//cix//cix//cix//cix//cix//cix//cix
MAT rix=TRP(cix)
MAT rix=SHAPE(rix,256,1)
MAT cix=SHAPE(cix,256,1)
MAT diff_pe=FOLD(diff_pe)
MAT col_pe=SHAPE(diff_pe,256,1)
MAT col_pe=col_pe||rix||cix
SHOW col_pe
SAVE col_pe
EXIT

USE col_pe
IF v(1)<0 THEN LET sign=0
IF v(1)=>0 THEN LET sign=1
```

```
LABEL v(2) / 1=LOG_POP 2=LOG_DEN 3=LIFEEXPF 4=LIFEEXPM,
              5=POP_INCR 6=BABYMORT 7=LOG_GDP 8=BIRTH_RT,
              9=LOG_DEA 10=B_TO_D 11=FERTILTY 12=URBAN,
              13=LITERACY 14=LIT_FEMA 15=LIT_MALE,
              16=CALORIES
LABEL v(3) / 1=LOG_POP 2=LOG_DEN 3=LIFEEXPF 4=LIFEEXPM,
              5=POP_INCR 6=BABYMORT 7=LOG_GDP 8=BIRTH_RT,
              9=LOG_DEA 10=B_TO_D 11=FERTILTY 12=URBAN,
              13=LITERACY 14=LIT_FEMA 15=LIT_MALE,
              16=CALORIES
CATEGORY V(2) V(3)
BAR V(1)*V(3)*V(2) / GROUP=sign OVERLAY COLOR=RED,BLUE,
                     BASE=0 BTHICK= 0.80 LEGEND=NONE,
                     XLAB='' YLAB='' ZMIN=-.5 ZMAX=.5,
                     ZLAB='Correlation Difference'
```

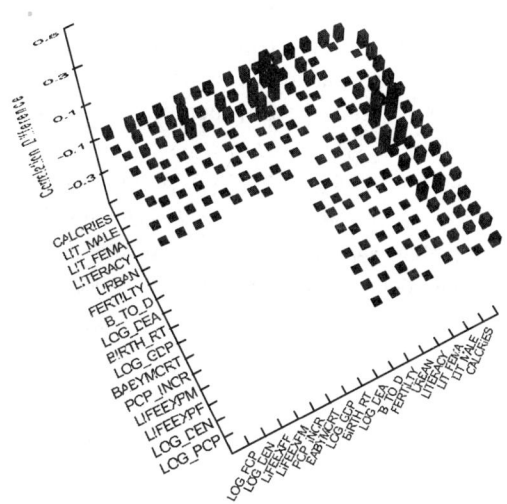

Notice the large empty area in the lower left of the plot. This area corresponds to variables with no missing data; pairwise deletion and EM estimation behave identically in this region. For variables with missing data, the differences between the two estimates are small. The largest differences occur for *LIT_FEMA* and *LIT_MALE*.

Example 5
Missing Value Imputation

MISSING provides EM and regression methods for estimating (imputing) replacement values, but this should not be done until the data have been screened for recording errors and variables in need of a symmetrizing transformation.

Values in the *world95m* data are not randomly missing (we're sure that they are not missing *completely* at random and also have doubts about satisfying the MAR condition). So, how good are the imputed values? In this section, we display some plots that you might create when evaluating your own filled-in data. You can:

- Display the variables with the most values missing in a pair of bivariate scatterplots with the same plot scales—one using the observed data only and the other using the imputed values. For our example, we use *calories* and *lit_fema*.

- For the same variable, plot the imputed values from one method against those from another. For female literacy, we plot imputed values from the regression method with random residuals against those from the EM method.

Generating pattern variables. When evaluating imputation estimates, pattern variables are used as case selection variables to group and identify observed and imputed values. Use the original data to generate pattern variables and merge the pattern variables with the imputed data. Here, we compute pattern variables for calories and female literacy.

```
USE world95m
LET pat_cal = calories
LET pat_litf = lit_fema
LET (pat_cal, pat_litf) = @ = .
LET pat_both = 10*pat_cal + pat_litf
```

PAT_CAL and *PAT_LITF* are binary variables. A 1 indicates a missing value and a 0 indicates an observed value. We also generate a third pattern variable (*PAT_BOTH*) that combines the missing/present information for calories and female literacy. The result of this transformation is four codes: 0, 1, 10, and 11. For example, if, for a case, both values are missing (*PAT_CAL* and *PAT_LITF* are both 1), the value of the new variable *PAT_BOTH* is 10*1 + 1 or 11. When only female literacy is missing, the code for *PAT_BOTH* is 1; when only calories is missing, the code is 10; and when values of both variables are present, the code is 0.

Scatterplots of Observed and Imputed Values

Comparing estimates for variables with many missing values assists in evaluating the performance of the imputation methods. We create pattern variables for *CALORIES* and *LIT_FEMA* and use them to look for trends in the estimates.

```
USE world95m
LET pat_cal = calories
LET pat_litf = lit_fema
LET (pat_cal, pat_litf) = @ = .
LET pat_both = 10*pat_cal + pat_litf
LET log_dea = L10(DEATH_RT)
ESAVE world95p
MISSING
MODEL LOG_POP LOG_DEN LIFEEXPF LIFEEXPM POP_INCR,
      BABYMORT LOG_GDP BIRTH_RT LOG_DEA B_TO_D,
      FERTILTY URBAN LITERACY LIT_FEMA,
      LIT_MALE CALORIES
SAVE regest / DATA
ESTIMATE / MATRIX=CORRELATION REGRESSION
MODEL LOG_POP LOG_DEN LIFEEXPF LIFEEXPM POP_INCR,
      BABYMORT LOG_GDP BIRTH_RT LOG_DEA B_TO_D,
      FERTILTY URBAN LITERACY LIT_FEMA,
      LIT_MALE CALORIES
SAVE emest / DATA
ESTIMATE / MATRIX=CORRELATION ITER=200
MERGE world95p (pat_cal,pat_litf,pat_both,country$) regest
BEGIN
USE emest
PLOT LIT_FEMA*CALORIES / OVERLAY GROUP=PAT_BOTH YLIMIT=100,
                        COLOR=2,1,3,10 sym=1,4,5,8,
                        FILL=1,0,0,0 LEGEND=NONE,
                        TITLE='EM Imputed Values',
                        LOC=-3in,0in
USE regest
PLOT LIT_FEMA*CALORIES / OVERLAY GROUP=PAT_BOTH YLIMIT=100,
                        COLOR=2,1,3,10 sym=1,4,5,8,
                        FILL=1,0,0,0 LTITLE='Missing Patterns',
                        LLABEL='Both present','LIT missing',
                        'CAL missing','Both missing',
                        TITLE='Regression Imputed Values',
                        LOC=3in,0in
END
```

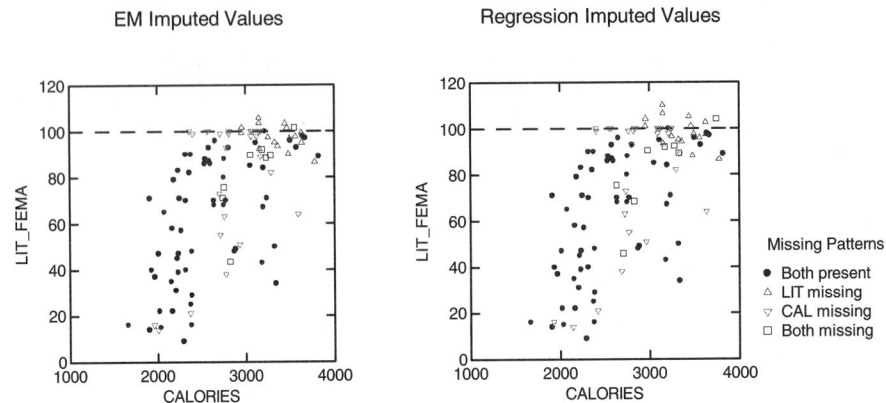

Some of the imputed values for both EM and regression lie above 100%. However, the regression estimates tend to be higher. Furthermore, when female literacy is missing, both methods impute values that tend to be high.

EM vs Regression Imputation

In this example, values imputed by the EM method are compared with those imputed by the regression method. The EM results must be merged with the regression results. To prevent overwriting, we create two new variables in the EM file and merge them with the regression values.

```
USE emest
LET emlitf=lit_fema
LET emcal=calories
ESAVE emest
MERGE emest(EMCAL EMLITF) regest
ESAVE regest
BEGIN
SELECT PAT_BOTH>0
PLOT LIT_FEMA*EMLITF / OVERLAY GROUP=PAT_BOTH COLOR=2,1,3,
                      SYM=4,5,8 FILL=0,0,0 XGRID YGRID,
                      LEGEND=NONE LOC=-3IN,0IN XMAX=120,
                      XLAB='Female Literacy via EM',
                      YLAB='Female Literacy via Regression'
SELECT EMLITF>80 AND PAT_BOTH>0
```

```
PLOT LIT_FEMA*EMLITF / OVERLAY GROUP=PAT_BOTH COLOR=2,1,3,
                SYM=4,5,8 FILL=0,0,0 XGRID YGRID,
                LEGEND=-1.6IN,-1.8IN,
                LTITLE='Missing Patterns',
                LLABEL='LIT missing','CAL missing',
                'Both missing' LABEL=COUNTRY$,
                LOC=3IN,0IN XMAX=120,
                XLAB='Female Literacy via EM',
                YLAB='Female Literacy via Regression'
END

SELECT PAT_BOTH>0
PLOT CALORIES*EMCAL / OVERLAY GROUP=PAT_BOTH COLOR=2,1,3,
                SYM=4,5,8 FILL=0,0,0 XGRID YGRID,
                LTITLE='Missing Patterns',
                LLABEL='LIT missing','CAL missing',
                'Both missing' XMAX=4000 YMIN=1500,
                YMAX=4000 XLAB='Calories via EM',
                YLAB='Calories via Regression'
```

Ideally, the points should fall along a line connecting the intersection of grid lines for the same percentage (for example, 80% for EM with 80% for regression). When both calories and female literacy are estimated, the regression estimates tend to be higher than the EM estimates. The points with estimated literacy values are clustered together, making it difficult to identify them in the left plot. On the right side, we zoom in on the area containing the imputed *LIT_FEMA* values.

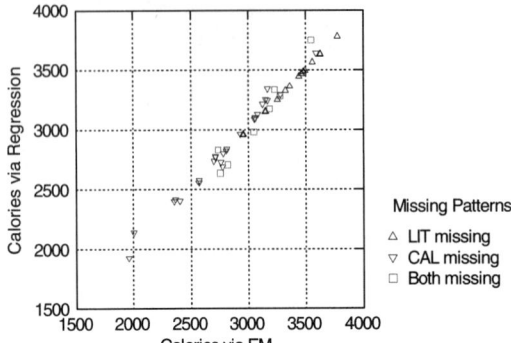

In this plot, we compare imputed values for *CALORIES*. In general, when there is a difference, the regression estimates tend to be higher more often than they are lower.

Computation

All computations are implemented in double precision.

Algorithms

The computational algorithms use provisional means, sums of squares, and cross-products (Spicer, 1972). Starting values for the EM algorithm use all available values (see Little and Rubin, 1987, p. 42).

References

Buck, S.F. (1960). A method of estimation of missing values in multivariate data suitable for use with an electronic computer. *Journal of the Royal Statistical Society*, B22, 302-306.

Little, R.J.A. (1988). Robust estimation of the mean and covariance matrix from data with missing values. *Applied Statistics*, 37, 23-28.

Little, R. J. A. and Rubin, D. B. (1987). *Statistical analyses with missing data*. New York: John Wiley & Sons, Inc.

Rubin, D.B. (1976). Inference and missing data. *Biometrika*, 63, 581-592.

Chapter 2

Multidimensional Scaling

Leland Wilkinson

Multidimensional scaling offers nonmetric multidimensional scaling of a similarity or dissimilarity matrix in one to five dimensions. Multidimensional scaling is a powerful data reduction procedure that can be used on a direct similarity or dissimilarity matrix or on one derived from rectangular data with Correlations. SYSTAT provides three MDS loss functions (Kruskal, Guttman, and Young) that produce results comparable to those from three of the major MDS packages (KYST, SSA, and ALSCAL). All three methods perform a similar function: to compute coordinates for a set of points in a space such that the distances between pairs of these points fit as closely as possible to measured dissimilarities between a corresponding set of objects.

The family of procedures called principal components or factor analysis is related to multidimensional scaling in function, but multidimensional scaling differs from this family in important respects. Usually, but not necessarily, multidimensional scaling can fit an appropriate model in fewer dimensions than can these other procedures. Furthermore, if it is implausible to assume a linear relationship between distances and dissimilarities, multidimensional scaling nevertheless provides a simple dimensional model.

MDS also computes the INDSCAL (individual differences multidimensional scaling) model (Carroll and Chang, 1970). The INDSCAL model fits dissimilarity/similarity matrices for multiple subjects into one common space, with jointly estimated weight parameters for each subject (that is, a dissimilarity matrix is input for each subject and separate (monotonic) regression functions are computed). MDS can fit the INDSCAL model using any of the three loss functions, although we recommend using Kruskal's STRESS for this purpose.

Finally, MDS can fit the nonmetric unfolding model. This allows one to analyze rank-order preference data.

Statistical Background

Multidimensional scaling (MDS) is a procedure for fitting a set of points in a space such that the distances between points correspond as closely as possible to a given set of dissimilarities between a set of objects. Dissimilarities may be measured directly, as in psychological judgments, or derived indirectly, as in correlation matrices computed on rectangular data.

Assumptions

Because MDS, like cluster analysis, operates directly on dissimilarities, no statistical distribution assumptions are necessary. There are, however, other important assumptions. First, multidimensional scaling is a spatial model. To fit points in the kinds of spaces that MDS covers, you assume that your data satisfy *metric* conditions:

- The distance from an object to itself is 0.
- The distance from object A to object B is the same as that from B to A.
- The distance from object A to C is less than or equal to the distance from A to B plus B to C. This is sometimes called the **triangle inequality**.

You may think these conditions are obvious, but there are numerous counter-examples in psychological perception and elsewhere. For example, commuters often view the distance from home to the city as closer than the distance from the city to home because of traffic patterns, terrain, and psychological expectations related to time of day. Framing or context effects can also disrupt the metric axioms, as Amos Tversky has shown. For example, Miami is similar to Havana. Havana is similar to Moscow. Is Miami similar to Moscow? If your data (objects) are not consistent with these three axioms, do not use MDS.

Second, there are ways of deriving distances from rectangular data that do not satisfy the metric axioms. The ones available in Correlations do, but if you are thinking of using some other derived measure of similarity, check it carefully.

Finally, it is assumed that all of your objects will fit in the same metric space. It is best if they diffuse somewhat evenly through this space as well. Don't expect to get interpretable results for 25 nearly indistinguishable objects and one that is radically different.

Collecting Dissimilarity Data

You can collect dissimilarities directly or compute them indirectly.

Direct Methods

Examples of direct dissimilarities are:

Distances. Take distances between objects (for example, cities) directly off a map. If the scale is local, MDS will reproduce the map nicely. If the scale is global, you will need three dimensions for an MDS fit. Two- or three-dimensional spatial distances can be measured directly. Direct measures of social distance might include spatial propinquity or the number of times or amount of time one individual interacts with another.

Judgments. Ask subjects to give a numerical rating of the dissimilarity (for example, 0 to 10) between all pairs of objects.

Clusters. Ask people to sort objects into piles; or examine naturally occurring aggregates, such as paragraphs, communities, and associations. Record 0 if two objects occur in the same group and 1 if they do not. Sum these counts over replications or judges.

Triads. Ask subjects to compare three objects at a time and report which two are most similar (or which is the odd one out). Do this over all possible triads of objects. To compute dissimilarities, sum over all triads, as for the clustering method. There are usually many more triads than pairs of objects, so this method is more tedious; however, it allows you to assess independently possible violations of the triangle inequality.

Indirect Methods

Indirect dissimilarities are computed over a rectangular matrix whose columns are objects and rows are attributes. You can transpose this matrix if you want to scale rows instead. Possible indirect dissimilarities include:

Computed Euclidean distances. These are the square root of the sum-of-squared discrepancies between columns of the rectangular matrix.

Negatives of correlations. For standardized data (mean of 0 and standard deviation of 1), Pearson correlations are proportional to Euclidean distances. For unstandardized data, Pearson correlations are comparable to computing Euclidean distances after standardizing. MDS automatically negates correlations if you do not. Other types of correlations—for example, Spearman and gamma—are analogous to standardized distances, but only approximately. Also, be aware that large negative correlations will be treated as large distances and large positive correlations, as small distances. Make sure that all variables are scored in the same direction before computing correlations. If you find that a whole row of a correlation matrix is negative, reverse the variable by multiplying by –1, and recompute the correlations.

Counts of discrepancies. Counting discrepancies between columns or using some of the binary association measures in Correlations is closely related to computing the Euclidean distance. These methods are also related to the clustering distance calculations mentioned above for direct distances.

Scaling Dissimilarities

Once you have dissimilarities (or similarities, correlations, etc., which MDS automatically transforms to dissimilarities), you may scale them. You do not need to know how the computer does the calculations in order to use the program intelligently as long as you pay attention to the following:

Stress and Iterations

Stress is the goodness-of-fit statistic that MDS tries to minimize. It consists of the square root of the normalized squared discrepancies between interpoint distances in the MDS plot and the smoothed distances predicted from the dissimilarities. Stress varies between 0 and 1, with values near 0 indicating better fit. It is printed for each *iteration*, which is one movement of all of the points in the plot toward a better solution. Make sure that iterations proceed smoothly to a minimum. This is true for the examples in this chapter. If you find that the stress values increase or decrease in uneven steps, you should be suspicious.

The Shepard Diagram

The Shepard diagram is a scatterplot of the distances between points in the MDS plot against the observed dissimilarities (or similarities). The points in the plot should adhere cleanly to a curve or straight line (which would be the smoothed distances). In other words, you should look at a good Shepard plot and think it resembles the outcome of a well-designed experiment. Check the examples in this chapter.

If the Shepard diagram resembles a stepwise or *L*-shaped function, beware. You may have achieved a degenerate solution. Publish it and you will be excoriated by the clergy.

The MDS Plot

The plot of points is what you seek. The points should be scattered fairly evenly through the space. The orientation of axes is arbitrary—remember we are scaling distances, not axes. Feel free to reverse axes or rotate the solution. MDS rotates it to the largest dimensions of variation, but these don't necessarily mean anything for your data.

You may interpret the axes as in principal components or factor analysis. More often, however, you should look for clusters of objects or regular patterns among the objects, such as circles, curved manifolds, and other structures. See the Guttman loss function example for a good view of a circle.

Multidimensional Scaling in SYSTAT

Multidimensional Scaling Main Dialog Box

To open the Multidimensional Scaling dialog box, from the menus choose:
Statistics
  Data Reduction
    Multidimensional Scaling (MDS)...

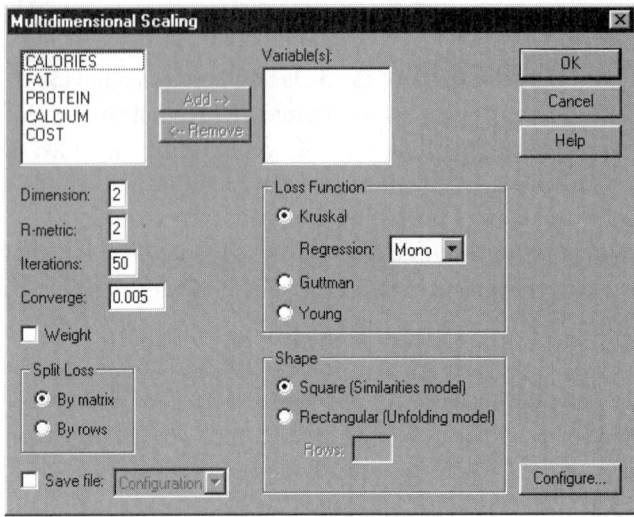

The following options are available:

Variable(s). Select the variables that contain the matrix of data to be analyzed.

Dimension. Number of dimensions in which to scale. The number of dimensions must be a positive integer less than or equal to the number of variables that you scale.

R-metric. Constant for the Minkowski power metric for computing distances. For ordinary Euclidean distance, enter 2. For city-block distance, enter 1. For values other than 1 or 2, computation is slower because logarithms and exponentials are used.

The general formula for calculating distances is:

$$d_{jk} = \left[\sum_{i=1}^{p} |x_{ij} - x_{ik}|^r \right]^{\frac{1}{r}}$$

where r is the specified power and p is the number of dimensions.

Iterations. Limit for the number of iterations.

Converge. Iterations terminate when the maximum absolute difference between any coordinate in the solution at iteration i versus iteration $i - 1$ is less than the specified convergence criterion. Because the configuration is standardized to unit variance on every iteration, iteration stops when no coordinate moves more than the specified convergence criterion (0.005 by default) from its value on the previous iteration.

Most MDS programs terminate when stress reaches a predetermined value or changes by less than a small amount. These programs can terminate prematurely, however, because comparable stress values can result from different configurations. The SYSTAT convergence criterion allows you to stop iterating when the configuration ceases to change.

Weight. Adds weights for each dimension and each matrix (subject) into the calculation of separate distances that are used in the minimization. For an individual differences model, select Weight.

Split Loss. For an individual differences of unfolding model, split the calculation of the loss function by rows of the matrix or by matrices. Splitting by rows is possible only for a rectangular matrix.

Loss Function. MDS scales similarity and dissimilarity matrices using three loss functions:

- Kruskal uses Kruskal's STRESS formula 1 scaling method.
- Guttman uses Guttman's coefficient of alienation scaling method.
- Young uses Young's S-STRESS scaling method, which allows you to scale using the loss function featured in ALSCAL.

Iterations with Kruskal's method are faster but usually take longer to converge to a minimum value than those with the Guttman method. The procedure used in the latter has been found in simulations to be less susceptible to local minima than that used in the Kruskal method (Lingoes and Roskam, 1973). We do not recommend Young's S-STRESS loss function. Because it weights squares of distances, large distances have more influence than smaller ones. Weinberg and Menil (1993) summarized why this is a problem: "...error variances of dissimilarities tend to be positively correlated with their means. If this is the case, large distances should be, if anything, *down*-weighted relative to small distances."

When using the Kruskal loss function, choose the form of the function relating distances to similarities (or dissimilarities):

- Mono specifies nonmetric scaling.
- Linear specifies metric scaling.
- Log specifies a log function, allowing a smooth curvilinear relation between dissimilarities and distances.
- Power specifies a power function.

Shape. Specify the type of matrix input. For a similarities model, select **Square**. For an unfolding model, select **Rectangular** and enter the number of rows in your matrix.

Save file. You can save three sets of output to a data file:

- **Configuration** saves the final configuration.
- **Distances** saves the matrix of distances between points in the final scaled configuration.
- **Residuals** saves the data, distances, estimated distances, residuals, and the row and column number of the original distance in the rectangular SYSTAT file.

With the residuals, MDS displays the root-mean-squared residuals for each point in its output. Because STRESS is a function of the sum-of-squared residuals, the root-mean-squared residuals are a measure of the influence of each point on the STRESS statistic. This can help you identify ill-fitting points.

Multidimensional Scaling Configuration

SYSTAT offers several alternative initial configurations.

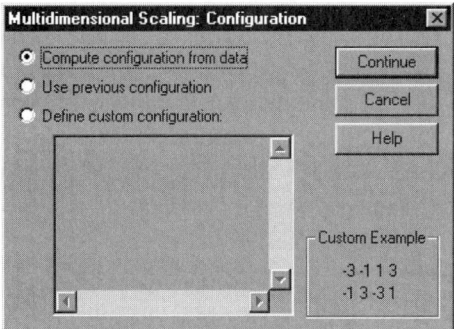

Compute configuration from data. By default, the configuration is computed from the data. The method used depends on the loss function.

Use previous configuration. Uses the configuration from the previous scaling.

Define custom configuration. You can specify a custom starting configuration for the scaling. There must be as many rows as items and columns as dimensions. When you type a matrix, SYSTAT reads as many numbers in each row as you specify. It reads as many rows as there are points to scale.

Multidimensional Scaling

You can specify a configuration for confirmatory analysis. Enter a hypothesized configuration and let the program iterate only once. Then look at the stress.

Using Commands

First, specify your data with USE filename. Continue with:

```
MDS
     MODEL varlist / ROWS=n  SHAPE=SQUARE or RECT
     CONFIG = LAST
        or
     CONFIG [matrix]
     ESTIMATE / DIM=n  R=n  ITER=n  WEIGHT  CONVERGE=n ,
               LOSS=GUTTMAN or KRUSKAL or YOUNG ,
               REGRESS=MONO or LINEAR or LOG or POWER ,
               SPLIT=ROW or MATRIX
     SAVE filename / CONFIG or DIST or RESID
```

Usage Considerations

Types of data. MDS uses a data file that contains an SSCP, covariance, correlation, or dissimilarity matrix. When you open the data file, MDS automatically recognizes its type.

Print options. The output is standard for all PRINT lengths.

Quick Graphs. MDS produces a Shepard diagram for each matrix analyzed and a plot of the final configuration. For solutions containing four or more dimensions, the final configuration appears as a scatterplot matrix of all dimension pairs.

Saving files. You can save the final configuration, matrix of distances between points in the final scaled configuration, distances, estimated distances, residuals, and the row and column number of the original distance in SYSTAT data files.

BY groups. MDS produces separate analyses for each level of a BY variable.

Bootstrapping. Bootstrapping is available in this procedure.

Case frequencies. FREQ variables are not available in MDS.

Case weights. WEIGHT is not available in MDS.

Examples

Example 1
Kruskal Method

The data in the *ROTHKOPF* file are adapted from an experiment by Rothkopf (1957). They were originally obtained from 598 subjects who judged whether or not pairs of Morse code signals presented in succession were the same. Morse code signals for letters and digits were used in the experiment, and all pairs were tested in each of two possible sequences. For multidimensional scaling, the data for letter signals have been averaged across sequence, and the diagonal (pairs of the same signal) has been omitted. The data in this form were first scaled by Shepard.

The input is:

```
MDS
    USE ROTHKPF1
    MODEL a .. z
    IDVAR = code$
    ESTIMATE / LOSS=KRUSKAL
```

Use the shortcut notation (..) in **MODEL** for listing consecutive variables in the file (otherwise, simply list each variable name separated by a space).

The program begins by generating an initial configuration of points whose interpoint distances are a linear function of the input data. For this estimation, MDS uses a metric multidimensional scaling. To do this, missing values in the input matrix are replaced by mean values for the whole matrix. Then the values are converted to distances by adding a constant.

The output is:

```
Monotonic Multidimensional Scaling
The data are analyzed as similarities
Minimizing Kruskal STRESS (form 1) in 2 dimensions

Iteration     STRESS
---------     ------
     0        0.263538
     1        0.237909
     2        0.218821
     3        0.202184
     4        0.190513
     5        0.184340
     6        0.181176
     7        0.179394
     8        0.178271
Stress of final configuration is: 0.17827
Proportion of variance (RSQ) is: 0.84502
```

```
Coordinates in 2 dimensions
Variable         Dimension
--------         ---------
                    1      2
   .-           -1.21   -.31
   -...           .59   -.45
   -.-.           .67    .05
   -..            .06   -.44
   .            -1.54    .89
   ..-.           .48   -.57
   --.            .22    .65
   ....           .03  -1.05
   ..           -1.45   -.38
   .---           .78    .77
   -.-            .22    .02
   .-..           .60   -.27
   --            -.62    .76
   -.           -1.15   -.04
   ---            .47   1.02
   .--.           .63    .31
   --.-           .90    .56
   .-.           -.28   -.34
   ...           -.66  -1.04
   -            -1.47    .95
   ..-           -.31   -.75
   ...-           .37   -.87
   .--            .04    .13
   -..-           .83   -.15
   -.--           .87    .38
   --..           .94    .18
```

Shepard Diagram

Configuration

The solution required eight iterations. Notice that STRESS reduces at each iteration. Final STRESS values near zero may indicate the presence of a degenerate solution.

The Shepard diagram is a scatterplot of distances between points in the MDS plot against the observed dissimilarities or similarities. In monotonic scaling, the regression function has steps at various points. For most solutions, the function in this plot should be relatively smooth (without large steps). If the function looks like one or two large steps, you should consider setting REGRESSION to LOG or LINEAR under ESTIMATE.

Notice that large values of the data tend to have small distances in the configuration. The diagram displays an overall decreasing trend because we are using similarities (large data values indicate similar objects). For dissimilarities, the Shepard diagram displays an increasing trend.

In the configuration plot, the points should be scattered fairly evenly through the space. If you are scaling in more than two dimensions, you should examine plots of pairs of axes or rotate the solution in three dimensions. The solution has been rotated to principal axes (that is, the major variation is on the first dimension). This rotation is not performed unless the scaling is in Euclidean space, as in the present example.

The two-dimensional solution clearly distinguishes short signals from long and dots from dashes. Dashes tend to appear in the upper right and dots in the lower left. Long codes tend to appear in the lower right and short in the upper left.

Regression Function

If you use the Kruskal or Young loss function, you can fit a MONOTONIC, LINEAR, or LOG function of distances onto input dissimilarities. The standard option is MONOTONIC multidimensional scaling. To avoid degenerate solutions, however, log or linear scaling is sometimes handy. Log scaling is recommended for this purpose because it allows a smooth curvilinear relation between dissimilarities and distances.

Example 2
Guttman Loss Function

To illustrate the Guttman loss function, this example uses judged similarities among 14 spectral colors (from Ekman, 1954). Nanometer wavelengths (W434, ..., W674) are used to name the variables for each color. Blue-violets are in the 400's; reds are in the 600's. The judgments are averaged across 31 subjects; the larger the number for a pair of colors, the more similar the two colors are. The file (*EKMAN*) has no diagonal elements, and its type is SIMILARITY.

The Guttman method is used to scale these judgments in two dimensions to determine whether the data fit a perceptual color wheel. The Kruskal loss function will give you a similar result. The input is:

```
MDS
   USE ekman
   MODEL w434 .. w674
   ESTIMATE / LOSS=GUTTMAN
```

Multidimensional Scaling

The output is:

```
Monotonic Multidimensional Scaling
The data are analyzed as similarities
Minimizing Guttman/Lingoes Coefficient of Alienation in 2 dimensions

Iteration    Alienation
---------    ----------
     0        0.070826
     1        0.042069
     2        0.037770
     3        0.036155
     4        0.035069
Alienation of final configuration is: 0.03507
Proportion of variance (RSQ) is: 0.99623


Coordinates in 2 dimensions
Variable             Dimension
--------             ---------
                       1      2
W434                 .31    -.91
W445                 .40    -.84
W465                 .89    -.57
W472                 .95    -.48
W490                 .98     .11
W504                 .81     .64
W537                 .55     .89
W555                 .33     .97
W584                -.54     .73
W600                -.83     .38
W610               -1.01     .06
W628               -1.01    -.18
W651                -.94    -.33
W674                -.90    -.47
```

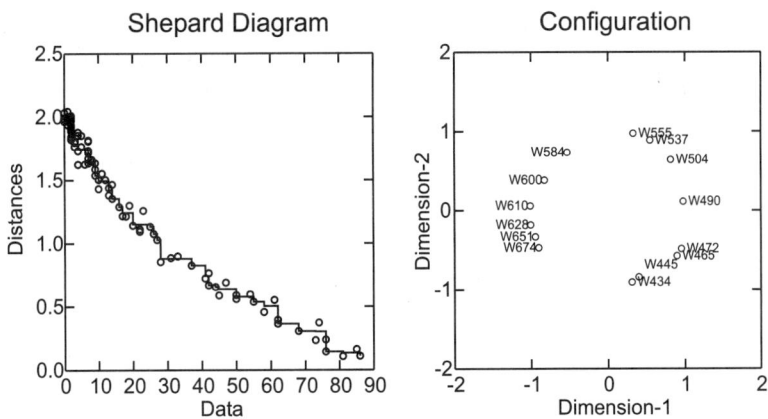

The fit of configuration distances to original data is extremely close, as evidenced by the low coefficient of alienation and clean Shepard diagram.

The resulting configuration is almost circular, denoting a "circumplex" by Guttman (1954). There is a large gap at the bottom of the figure, however, because the perceptual color between deep red and dark purple is not a spectral color.

Example 3
Individual Differences Multidimensional Scaling

The data in the *COLAS* file are taken from Schiffman, Reynolds, and Young (1981). The data in this file have an unusual structure. The file consists of 10 dissimilarity matrices stacked on top of each other. They are judgments by 10 subjects of the dissimilarity (0–100) between pairs of colas. The example will fit the INDSCAL (individual differences scaling) model to these data, seeking a common group space for the 10 different colas and a parallel weight space for the 10 different judges.

The input follows:

```
MDS
    USE colas
    MODEL dietpeps .. dietrite
    ESTIMATE / LOSS=KRUSKAL  WEIGHT  SPLIT=MATRIX  DIM=3
```

The WEIGHT option tells SYSTAT to weight each matrix separately. Without this option, all matrices would be weighted equally, and you would have a single pooled solution. You want to use weighting so that you can see which subjects favor one dimension over the others in their judgments. The MATRIX option of SPLIT tells SYSTAT to compute separate (monotonic) regression functions for each subject (matrix). Finally, scale the result in three dimensions, as did Schiffman et al. (1981).

The output is:

```
Monotonic Multidimensional Scaling
The data are analyzed as dissimilarities
There are 10 replicated data matrices
Dimensions are weighted separately for each matrix
Fitting is split between data matrices
Minimizing Kruskal STRESS (form 1) in 3 dimensions

Iteration      STRESS
---------      ------
    0         0.220899
    1         0.184422
    0         0.221307
    1         0.184508
Stress of final configuration is: 0.18451
Proportion of variance (RSQ) is: 0.53501


Coordinates in 3 dimensions
Variable           Dimension
--------           ---------
                    1      2      3
 DIETPEPS         -.61    .20    .78
 RC                .52    .05    .76
 YUKON             .42   -.09   -.87
 PEPPER            .27  -1.27    .06
 SHASTA            .80    .02   -.14
 COKE              .39    .84   -.35
 DIETPEPR         -.75   -.84   -.17
 TAB              -.79    .44   -.61
 PEPSI             .57    .22    .38
 DIETRITE         -.82    .43    .17

Matrix Weights
Matrix    Stress    RSQ      Dimension
------    ------    ---      ---------
                              1     2     3
   1       .188    .548     .70   .43   .53
   2       .200    .416     .45   .47   .72
   3       .196    .468     .35   .52   .74
   4       .171    .564     .59   .49   .61
   5       .178    .594     .70   .37   .56
   6       .172    .621     .70   .37   .57
   7       .181    .552     .42   .58   .66
   8       .180    .560     .48   .60   .61
   9       .163    .625     .56   .50   .63
  10       .212    .402     .44   .61   .62
```

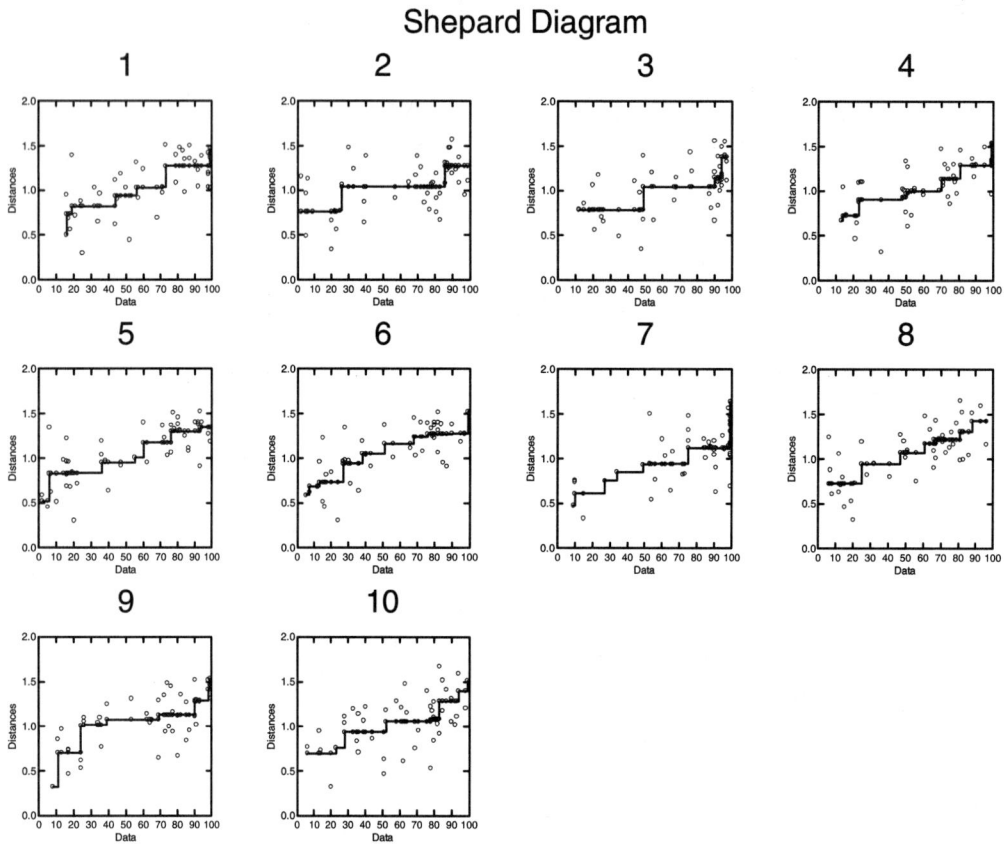

Multidimensional Scaling

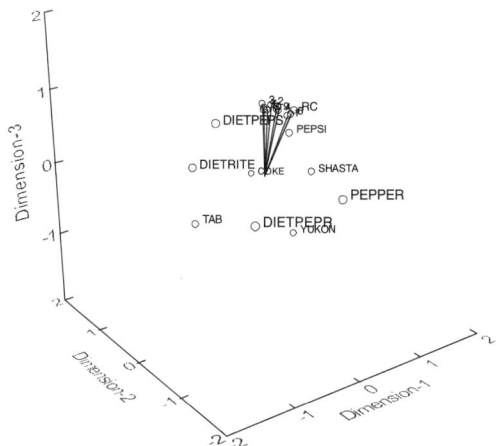

Configuration

The solution required four iterations. Notice that the second two iterations appear to be a restart. That is exactly what they are. Because the fourth matrix has a missing value, SYSTAT uses the EM algorithm to reestimate this value, compute a new metric solution, and iterate two more times until convergence. This extra set of iterations did not do much for you in this example because the stress is insignificantly higher than it would have been had you stopped at only two iterations. With many missing values, however, the EM algorithm will improve MDS solutions substantially.

For the INDSCAL model, you have a set of coordinates for the colas and one for the subjects. In the three-dimensional graph of the coordinates, the colas are represented by symbols and the subjects by vectors. The first dimension separates the diet colas from the others. The second dimension differentiates between Dr. Pepper/diet Dr. Pepper and the remaining colas.

For each subject, you have a contribution to overall stress and a separate squared correlation (RSQ) between the predicted and obtained distances in the configuration. Notice that subject 10 is fit worst (STRESS = 0.212) and subject 9 best (STRESS = 0.163). Furthermore, subjects 1, 5, and 6 have a high loading on the first dimension, indicating that they place a higher emphasis on diet/nondiet differences than on cherry cola/cola differences. Subjects 7, 8, and 10, on the other hand, emphasize the second dimension more.

Example 4
Nonmetric Unfolding

The *COLRPREF* data set contains color preferences among 15 SYSTAT employees for five primary colors. This example uses the MDS unfolding model to scale the people and the colors in two dimensions, such that each person's coordinate is near his or her favorite color's coordinate and far from his or her least favorite color's coordinate. For this example, use ROWS to specify the number of rows for a rectangular matrix and SHAPE to specify the type of matrix input to use. When you enter these data for the first time, you must remember to specify their type as DISSIMILARITY so that small numbers are understood as meaning most similar (preferred).

To scale these with the unfolding model, specify:

```
MDS
    USE colrpref
    MODEL red .. blue / SHAPE=RECT
    IDVAR=name$
    ESTIMATE / SPLIT=ROWS
```

Notice that you are using the Kruskal loss function as the default. The output is shown below:

```
Monotonic Multidimensional Scaling
The data are analyzed as dissimilarities
The data are rectangular (lower corner matrix)
Fitting is split between rows of data matrix
Minimizing Kruskal STRESS (form 1) in 2 dimensions

Iteration       STRESS
---------       ------
    0          0.148374
    1          0.135423
    2          0.125152
    3          0.117255
    4          0.111131
    5          0.106394
    6          0.102623
    7          0.099539
    8          0.096883
    9          0.094497
    0          0.107456
    1          0.100496
    2          0.096038
    3          0.092748
    4          0.090087
Stress of final configuration is: 0.09009
Proportion of variance (RSQ) is: 0.94001
```

```
Coordinates in 2 dimensions
Variable         Dimension
--------         ---------
                   1     2
RED              .25  -.49
ORANGE           .53 -1.70
YELLOW         -1.31  -.56
GREEN           1.39   .26
BLUE            -.55   .79
Patrick          .56   .78
Laszlo          -.73  -.13
Mary           -1.01   .11
Jenna            .19  -.25
Julie           -.70  -.22
Steve           1.18  -.76
Phil             .61   .61
Mike            -.80  -.02
Keith            .27   .76
Kathy            .05   .76
Leah            -.72   .00
Stephanie        .50   .58
Lisa             .78   .21
Mark            -.57   .50
John             .06 -1.24
Row Fit Measures
   Row      Stress    RSQ
   ---      ------    ---
Patrick       .000  1.000
Laszlo        .068   .970
Mary          .004  1.000
Jenna         .048   .983
Julie         .272   .508
Steve         .033   .993
Phil          .061   .972
Mike          .083   .958
Keith         .172   .774
Kathy         .000  1.000
Leah          .067   .971
Stephanie     .029   .994
Lisa          .055   .981
Mark          .000  1.000
John          .025   .996
```

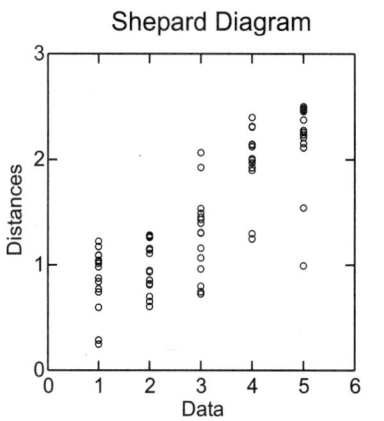

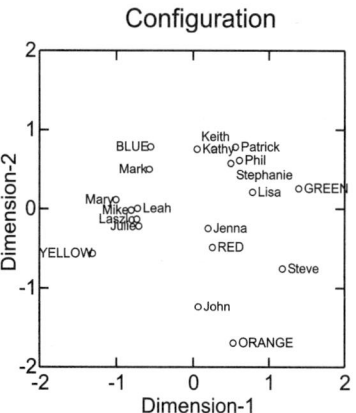

Nonmetric Unfolding and the EM Algorithm

The nonmetric unfolding model has often presented problems to MDS programs because so much data are missing. If you think of the unfolding matrix as the lower corner matrix in a larger triangular matrix of subjects + objects, you can visualize how much data (namely, all of the subject-object comparisons) are missing. Since SYSTAT uses the EM algorithm for missing values, unfolding models do not degenerate as frequently. SYSTAT does a complete MDS using all available data and then estimates missing dissimilarities/similarities using the distances in the solution. These estimated values are then used to get a starting configuration for another complete iteration cycle. This process continues until there are no changes between EM cycles.

The following example, from Borg and Lingoes (1987) adapted from Green and Carmone (1970), shows how this works. This unfolding data set contains dissimilarities only between the points delineating A and M, and these dissimilarities are treated only as rank orders. Borg and Lingoes discuss the problems in fitting an unfolding model to these data.

The input follows:

```
MDS
    USE am
    IDVAR = row$
    MODEL / SHAPE=RECT
    ESTIMATE / LOSS=GUTTMAN  SPLIT=ROWS
```

Notice that the example uses the Guttman loss function, but the others provide similar results. The output is shown below:

```
Monotonic Multidimensional Scaling
The data are analyzed as dissimilarities
The data are rectangular (lower corner matrix)
Fitting is split between rows of data matrix
Minimizing Guttman/Lingoes Coefficient of Alienation in 2 dimensions

Iteration  Alienation
---------  ----------
    0        0.076135
    1        0.037826
    2        0.023540
    3        0.017736
    4        0.013277
    5        0.009962
Alienation of final configuration is: 0.00996
Proportion of variance (RSQ) is: 0.99925
```

```
Coordinates in 2 dimensions
Variable          Dimension
--------          ---------
                    1      2
 A1              -.94  -1.02
 A2              -.89   -.98
 A3             -1.09   -.41
 A4             -1.07   -.40
 A5             -1.19    .15
 A6             -1.23    .34
 A7             -1.54    .67
 A8             -1.00    .55
 A9               -.69    .47
 A10              -.31    .36
 A11               .01    .10
 A12               .10    .10
 A13               .13    .09
 A14              -.85    .09
 A15              -.74    .14
 A16              -.57    .13
 M1                .74  -1.08
 M2                .43   -.52
 M3                .20   -.56
 M4                .01   -.43
 M5               -.15   -.33
 M6               -.21   -.18
 M7               -.17    .12
 M8               -.06    .22
 M9                .18    .27
 M10               .56    .24
 M11               .59    .22
 M12               .59    .22
 M13               .83    .87
 M14               .89    .66
 M15              1.04    .21
 M16              1.24    .16
 M17              1.50    .23
 M18              1.70   -.21
 M19              1.94   -.49
Row Fit Measures
    Row      Stress     RSQ
    ---      ------     ---
    M1        .000     1.000
    M2        .000     1.000
    M3        .000     1.000
    M4        .000     1.000
    M5        .027      .993
    M6        .022      .996
    M7        .024      .997
    M8        .016      .999
    M9        .000     1.000
    M10       .000     1.000
    M11       .000     1.000
    M12       .000     1.000
    M13       .002     1.000
    M14       .000     1.000
    M15       .000     1.000
    M16       .000     1.000
    M17       .000     1.000
    M18       .000     1.000
    M19       .000     1.000
```

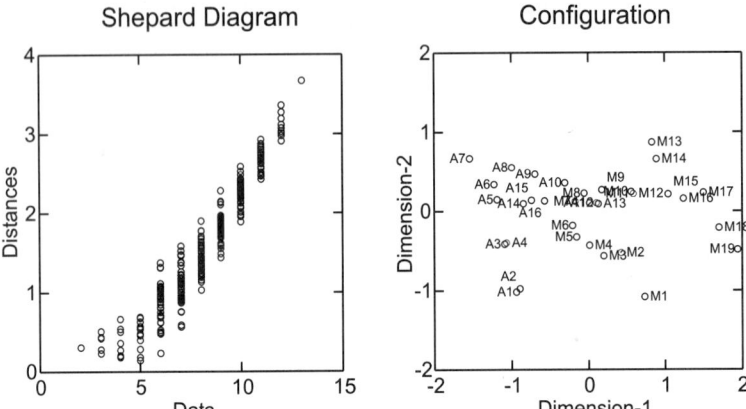

Example 5
Power Scaling Ratio Data

Because similarities or dissimilarities are often collected as rank-order data, the nonmetric MDS model has to work "backward" in order to solve for a configuration fitting the data. As J. D. Carroll has pointed out, the MDS model should really express observed data as a function of distances between points in a configuration rather than the other way around. If your data are direct or derived distances, however, you should try setting REGRESSION = POWER with LOSS = FUNCTION. This way, you can fit a Stevens power function to the data using distances between points in the configuration. The results may not always differ much from nonmetric or linear or log MDS, but SYSTAT will also tell you the exponent of the power function in the Shepard diagram. Notice with this model that the data and distances are transposed in the Shepard diagram because loss is being computed from errors in the data rather than the distances. SYSTAT calls the loss for the power model PSTRESS to distinguish it from Kruskal's STRESS. In PSTRESS, you use DATA and its DHAT instead of DIST and its DHAT to compute the loss.

The *HELM* data set contains highly accurate estimates of distance between color pairs by one experimental subject (CB). These are from Helm (1959) and reprinted by Borg and Lingoes (1987). To scale these with power model, specify:

```
MDS
    USE helm
    MODEL a .. s
    ESTIMATE / REGRESS=POWER
```

The output is shown below:

```
Power regression function, where Dissimilarities=a*Distances^p
The data are analyzed as dissimilarities
Minimizing PSTRESS (STRESS with DIST and DATA exchanged) in 2 dimensions

Iteration      PSTRESS
---------      -------
    0          0.142060
    1          0.131422
    2          0.127135
    3          0.125206
Stress of final configuration is: 0.12521
Estimated exponent for power regression is: 0.85154
Proportion of variance (RSQ) is: 0.91039


Coordinates in 2 dimensions
Variable          Dimension
--------          ---------
                    1      2
A                 -.83   -.79
C                  .40  -1.09
E                 1.13   -.50
G                  .98    .10
I                  .79    .48
K                  .33    .68
M                 -.21    .80
O                 -.73    .58
Q                -1.00    .05
S                 -.87   -.32
```

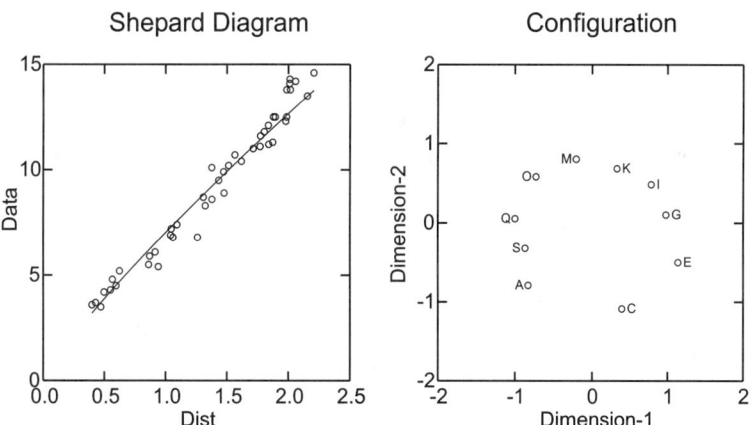

SYSTAT estimated the power exponent for the function, fitting distances to dissimilarities as 0.85. Color and many other visual judgments show similar power exponents less than 1.0.

Computation

This section summarizes algorithms separately for the Kruskal and Guttman methods. The algorithms in these options substantially follow those of Kruskal (1964ab) and Guttman (1968). MDS output should agree with other nonmetric multidimensional scaling except for rotation, dilation, and translation of the configuration. Secondary documentation can be found in Schiffman, Reynolds, and Young (1981) and the other multidimensional scaling references. The summary assumes that dissimilarities are input. If similarities are input, MDS inverts them.

Algorithms

Kruskal Method

The program begins by generating a configuration of points whose interpoint distances are a linear function of the input data. For this estimation, MDS uses a metric multidimensional scaling. Missing values in the input dissimilarities matrix are replaced by mean values for the whole matrix. Then the values are converted to distances by adding a constant. A scalar products matrix B is then calculated following the procedures described in Torgerson (1958). The initial configuration matrix X in p dimensions is computed from the first p eigenvectors of B using the Young-Householder procedure (Torgerson, 1958)

After an initial configuration is computed by the metric method, nonmetric optimization begins (there are no metric pre-iterations). At the beginning of each iteration, the configuration is normalized to have zero centroid and unit dispersion. Next, Kruskal's DHAT (fitted) distance values are computed by a monotonic regression of distances onto data. Tied data values are ordered according to their corresponding distances in the configuration.

Stress (formula 1) is calculated from fitted distances, observed distances, and input data values. If the stress is less than 0.001 or has decreased in the last five iterations less than 0.001 per iteration, or the number of iterations equals the number specified by the user (default is 50), iterations terminate (that is, go to the next paragraph). Otherwise, the negative gradient is computed for each point in the configuration by taking the partial derivatives of stress with respect to each dimension. Points in the configuration are moved along their gradients with a step size chosen as a function of the rate of descent; the steeper the descent, the smaller the step size. This completes an iteration.

After the last iteration, the configuration is shifted so that the origin lies in the centroid. Thus, the point coordinates sum to 0 on each dimension. Moreover, the configuration is normalized to unit size so that the sum of squares of its coordinates is 1. If the Minkowski constant is 2 (Euclidean scaling, which is the standard option), the final configuration is rotated to its principal axis.

Guttman Method

The initial configuration for the Guttman option is computed according to Lingoes and Roskam (1973). Principal components are computed on a matrix **C**,

$$c_{ij} = 1 - \frac{r_{ij}}{\frac{n(n-1)}{2}}$$

where r_{ij} are the ranks of the input dissimilarities (smallest rank corresponding to smallest dissimilarity), and n is the number of points. The diagonal elements of **C** are

$$c_{ij} = 1 - \Sigma r_{ij}$$

where the sum is taken over the entire row of the dissimilarity matrix.

For the iteration stage, the initial configuration is normalized as in the Kruskal method. Then rank images corresponding to each distance in the configuration are computed by permuting the configuration distances so that they mirror the rank order of the original input dissimilarities. Ties in the data are handled as in the Kruskal method. These rank images are used to compute the Guttman/Lingoes coefficient of alienation. Iterations are terminated if this coefficient becomes arbitrarily small, if the number of iterations exceeds the maximum, or if the change in its value becomes small. Otherwise, the points in the configuration are moved five times using the same rank images but different interpoint distances each time to compute a new negative gradient. These five cycles within each iteration are what lengthens the calculations in the Guttman method. This completes an iteration.

The final configuration is rotated and scaled as with the Kruskal method. Guttman/Lingoes programs normalize the extreme values of the configuration to unity and thus do not plot the configuration with a zero centroid, so MDS output corresponds to their output within rigid motion and configuration size.

Missing Data

Missing values in a similarity/dissimilarity matrix are ignored in the computation of the loss function that determines how points in the configuration are moved. For information on how this function is computed, see the discussion of algorithms.

If you compute a similarity matrix with Correlations for input to MDS, the matrix will have no missing values unless all of your cases in the raw data have a constant or missing value on one or more variables.

References

Borg, I. and Lingoes, J. (1981). *Multidimensional data representations: When and why?* Ann Arbor: Mathesis Press.

Borg, I. and Lingoes, J. (1987). *Multidimensional similarity structure analysis.* New York: Springer Verlag.

Carroll, J. D. and Arabie, P. (1980). Multidimensional scaling. M. R. Rosenzweig and L. W. Porter, eds. *Annual Review of Psychology*, 31, 607–649.

Carroll, J. D. and Chang, J. J. (1970). Analysis of individual differences in multidimensional scaling via an N-way generalization of Eckart-Young decomposition. *Psychometrika*, 35, 283–319.

Carroll, J. D. and Wish, M. (1974). Models and methods for three-way multidimensional scaling. D. H. Krantz, R. C. Atkinson, R. D. Luce, and P. Suppes, eds. *Contemporary Developments in Mathematical Psychology, Vol. II: Measurement, Psychophysics, and Neural Information Processing.* San Francisco: W. H. Freeman and Company.

Coombs, C. H. (1964). *A theory of data.* New York: John Wiley & Sons, Inc.

Davison, M. L. (1983). *Multidimensional scaling.* New York: John Wiley & Sons, Inc.

Ekman, G. (1954). Dimensions of color vision. *Journal of Psychology*, 38, 467–474.

Green, P. E. and Carmone, F. J. (1970). *Multidimensional scaling and related techniques.* Boston: Allyn and Bacon.

Green, P. E. and Rao, V. R. (1972). *Applied multidimensional scaling.* New York: Holt, Rinehart, and Winston.

Guttman, L. (1954). A new approach to factor analysis: The radex. P. F. Lazarsfeld, ed. *Mathematical Thinking in the Social Sciences.* New York: Free Press.

Guttman, L. (1968). A general nonmetric technique for finding the smallest coordinate space for a configuration of points. *Psychometrika*, 33, 469–506.

Helm, C. E. (1959). A multidimensional ratio scaling analysis of color relations. *Technical Report*, Princeton University and Educational Testing Service, June 1959.

Kruskal, J. B. (1964). Multidimensional scaling by optimizing goodness of fit to a nonmetric hypothesis. *Psychometrika*, 29, 1–27.

Kruskal, J. B. (1964). Nonmetric multidimensional scaling: A numerical method. *Psychometrika*, 29, 115–129.

Kruskal, J. B. and Wish, M. (1978). *Multidimensional scaling.* Beverly Hills, Calif.: Sage Publications.

Lingoes, J. C. and Roskam, E. E. (1973). A mathematical and empirical study of two multidimensional scaling algorithms. *Psychometrika Monograph Supplement*, 19.

Rothkopf, E. Z. (1957). A measure of stimulus similarity and errors in some paired-associate learning tasks. *Journal of Experimental Psychology*, 53, 94–101.

Schiffman, S. S., Reynolds, M. L., and Young, F. W. (1981). *Introduction to multidimensional scaling: Theory, methods, and applications.* New York: Academic Press.

Shepard, R. N. (1963). Analysis of proximities as a study of information processing in man. *Human Factors*, 5, 33–48.

Shepard, R. N., Romney, A. K., and Nerlove, S., eds. (1972). *Multidimensional scaling: Theory and application in the behavioral sciences.* New York: Academic Press.

Takane, Y., Young, F. W., and de Leeuw, J. (1977). Nonmetric individual differences scaling: An alternating least squares method with optimal scaling features. *Psychometrika*, 42, 3–27.

Torgerson, W. S. (1958). *Theory and methods of scaling.* New York: John Wiley & Sons, Inc.

Weinberg, S. L. and Menil, V. C. (1993). The recovery of structure in linear and ordinal data: INDSCAL and ALSCAL. *Multivariate Behavioral Research*, 28:2, 215–233.

Chapter 3

Nonlinear Models

Laszlo Engelman

Nonlinear modeling estimates parameters for a variety of nonlinear models using a Gauss-Newton (SYSTAT computes exact derivatives), Quasi-Newton, or Simplex algorithm. In addition, you can specify a loss function other than least squares, so maximum likelihood estimates can be computed. You can set lower and upper limits on individual parameters. When the parameters are highly intercorrelated, and there is concern about overfitting, you can fix the value of one or more parameters, and Nonlinear Model will test the result against the full model. If the estimates have trouble converging, or if they converge to a local minimum, Marquardting is available.

For assessing the certainty of the parameter estimates, Nonlinear Model offers Wald confidence regions and Cook-Weisberg graphical confidence curves. The latter are useful when it is unreasonable to assume that the estimates follow a normal distribution. You can also save values of the loss function for plotting contours in a bivariate display of the parameter space. This allows you to study the combinations of parameter estimates with approximately the same loss function values.

When your response contains outliers, you may want to downweight their residuals using one of Nonlinear Model's robust ψ functions: median, Huber, Hampel, bisquare, t, trim, or the pth power of the absolute value of the residuals.

You can specify functions of parameters (like LD50 for a logistic model). SYSTAT evaluates the function at each iteration, and prints the standard error and the Wald interval for the estimate after the last iteration.

Statistical Background

The following data are from a toxicity study for a drug designed to combat tumors. The table shows the proportion of laboratory rats dying (*Response*) at each dose level (*Dose*) of the drug. Clinical studies usually scale dose in natural logarithm units, which are listed in the center column (*Log Dose*). We arbitrarily set the *Log Dose* to –4 for zero *Dose* for the purpose of plotting and fitting with a linear model.

Dose	Log Dose	Response
0.00	–4.000	0.026
0.10	–2.303	0.120
0.25	–1.386	0.088
0.50	–0.693	0.169
1.00	0.000	0.281
2.50	0.916	0.443
5.00	1.609	0.632
10.00	2.303	0.718
25.00	3.219	0.820
50.00	3.912	0.852
100.00	4.605	0.879

Modeling the Dose-Response Function

The plot of *Response* against *Log Dose* is clearly curvilinear.

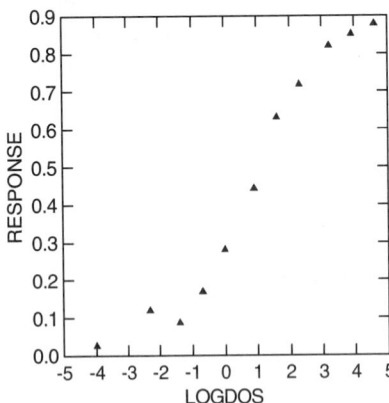

Nonlinear Models

The *S*-shaped function suggests that we could use a linear model with linear, quadratic, and cubic terms (that is, a polynomial function) to fit a curved line to the data. Here are the results:

```
Dep Var: RESPONSE   N: 11    Multiple R: 0.993    Squared multiple R: 0.986
Adjusted squared multiple R: 0.980    Standard error of estimate: 0.047

Effect          Coefficient   Std Error    Std Coef  Tolerance    t      P(2 Tail)
CONSTANT          0.314         0.021        0.0         .       15.241    0.000
LOGDOS            0.166         0.013        1.344     0.168     12.418    0.000
LOGDOS
*LOGDOS           0.009         0.002        0.202     0.771      3.995    0.005
LOGDOS
*LOGDOS
*LOGDOS          -0.004         0.001       -0.492     0.152     -4.322    0.003
```

Notice that all the coefficients are highly significant and the overall fit is excellent ($R^2 = 0.986$). Even the tolerances are relatively large, so we need not worry about collinearity. The residual plots for this function are reasonably well behaved. There is no significant autocorrelation in the residuals.

The following figure shows the observed data and the fitted curve.

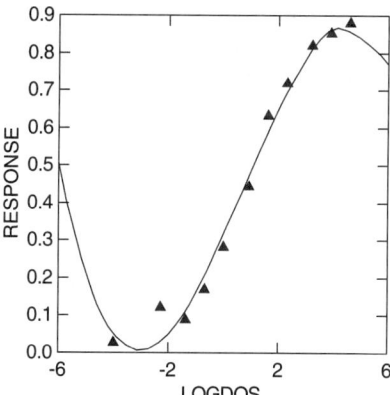

How do the researchers interpret this plot? First of all, the curve is consistent with the printed output; it fits extremely well in the range of the data. Putting the fitted curve into ordinary language, we can say that fewer animals die at lower dosages and more at higher. At the extremes, however, more animals die with extremely low dosages and fewer animals die at extremely high dosages.

This is nonsense. While it is possible to imagine some drugs (arsenic, for example) for which dose-response functions are nonmonotonic, the model we fit makes no sense for a clinical drug of this sort. Second, the cubic function we fit extrapolates beyond the 0–1 response interval. It implies that there is something beyond dying and something less than living. Third, the parameters of the model we fit have no theoretical interpretation.

Clinical researchers usually prefer to fit quantal response data like these with a bounded monotonic response function of the following form:

$$\text{proportion dying} = \alpha + \frac{1-\alpha}{1 + e^{[\beta - \gamma \log(\text{dose})]}}$$

where α is the background response, or rate of dying, β is a location parameter for the curve, and γ is a slope parameter for the curve.

Estimating a quantity called LD50 is the usual purpose of this type of study. LD50 is the dose at which 50 percent of the animals are expected to die. LD50 is:

$$e^{\beta/\gamma}(1 - 2\alpha)^{1/\gamma}$$

Notice how the parameters of this model make theoretical sense. We have a problem, however. We cannot fit an intrinsically nonlinear model like this with a linear regression program. We cannot even transform this equation, using logs or other mathematical operators, to a linear form. The cubic linear model we fit before was nonlinear in the data but linear in the parameters. Linear models involve additive combinations of parameters. The model we want to fit now is nonlinear in the data *and* nonlinear in the parameters.

We need a program that fits this type of model iteratively. NONLIN begins with initial estimates of parameter values and modifies them in small steps until the fit of the curve to the data is as close as possible.

Here is the result:

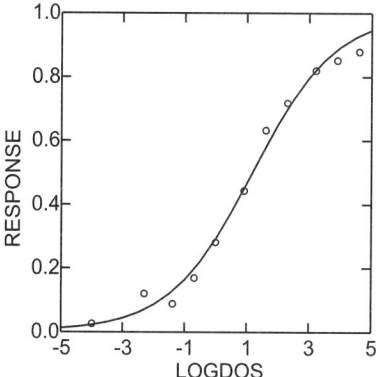

Notice how the curve tapers at the ends so that it is bounded by 0 and 1 on the *Response* scale. This behavior fits our theoretical ideas about the effect of this drug. The value for LD50 is 3.295, which is in raw dose units.

Interestingly, this model does not fit significantly better than the cubic polynomial. Both have comparable sums of squared residuals. True, the cubic model has four parameters and we have used only three. Nevertheless, this example should convince you that blind searching for models that produce good fits is not good science. It is even possible that a model with a poorer fit can be the true model generating data and one with a better fit can be bogus.

Loss Functions

Nonlinear estimation includes a broad variety of statistical procedures. We have performed nonlinear least squares, which is analogous to ordinary least squares. Both methods minimize squared deviations of the dependent variable data values from values estimated by the function at the same independent variable data points. In these cases, loss is the sum of least squares.

Other types of loss functions can be defined which produce different estimates of parameters in the same functions. The most widely used loss is negative log likelihood. This loss is used for maximum likelihood estimation. Other loss functions are used for robust estimators and nonparametric procedures.

Maximum Likelihood

A maximum likelihood estimate of a parameter is a value of that parameter in a given distribution that has the highest probability of generating the observed sample data. Sometimes maximum likelihood and least squares estimators coincide (as in fixed effects, fully crossed, balanced factorial ANOVA), and at other times they diverge. In our quantal response data example, the maximum likelihood estimates are different. They can be computed in NONLIN by using the loss function.

In general, maximum likelihood estimates are found by maximizing the likelihood function L with respect to the parameter vector θ:

$$L = \prod_{i=1}^{n} d(x_i, \theta)$$

where $d(x_i, \theta)$ is the density of the response at each value of x. Equivalently, the negative of the log of the likelihood function can be minimized:

$$-\log L = \sum_{i=1}^{n} \ln(d(x_i, \theta))$$

Here we outline four methods for computing maximum likelihood estimates in NONLIN. To define them, we use a specific model and a specific density. The model is the sum of two exponentials:

$$\hat{y} = p_1 e^{p_2 x} + p_3 e^{p_4 x}$$

and the distribution of y at each x is Poisson:

$$d(x_i, \lambda) = \frac{e^{-\lambda} \lambda^y}{y!}$$

In our definitions, we also use the log of the density:

$$\ln d = -\lambda + y \ln \lambda - \text{LGM}(y + 1)$$

where LGM is the log gamma function for computing $y!$.

Method 1. Set the LOSS function to –ln(density). In NONLIN, you can specify your own loss function. Here we specify the negative of the log of the density function:

$$\text{LOSS} = \lambda - y\ln\lambda + \text{LGM}(y + 1)$$

For the estimate of lambda, we use $\hat{y}$, or **estimate**, as it is known to Nonlinear Model. Using commands, we type:

```
MODEL Y = p1*EXP(p2*x) + p3*EXP(p4*x)
   LOSS = estimate - y*LOG(estimate) + LGM(y+1)
   ESTIMATE
```

Note that for this method, you need to specify only the loss function. This method can be used for any distribution; however, the estimated standard errors may not be correct.

Method 2. Iteratively reweighted least squares. This method is appropriate for distributions belonging to the exponential family (for example, normal, binomial, multinomial, Poisson, and gamma). It provides meaningful standard errors for the parameter estimates and useful residuals. For this method, you define a case weight that is recomputed at each iteration:

$$\text{weight} = \frac{1}{\text{variance}(y_i)}$$

For our Poisson distribution, the mean and variance are equal, so lambda is the variance, and our estimate of the variance is *estimate*. Thus, the weight is:

$$\text{weight} = \frac{1}{\text{estimate}}$$

Here's how to specify this method using NONLIN commands:

```
LET wt=1
   WEIGHT = wt
   MODEL y = p1*EXP(p2*x) + p2*EXP(p4*x)
   RESET wt = 1 / estimate
   ESTIMATE / SCALE
```

The standard deviation of the resulting estimates are the usual information theory standard errors.

Method 3. Estimate ln(density) and reset the predicted value to y + 1. For this method, the data may follow any distribution and the standard errors are correct, but the method does not yield correct residuals. You define a dummy outcome variable and estimate the log of the density, and then reset the outcome variable to $\hat{y} + 1$ at each iteration. For our example, with commands:

```
LET dummy = 0
   MODEL dummy = -p1*EXP(p2*x) - p3*EXP(p4*x),
                 + y*LOG(p1*EXP(p2*x) + p3*EXP(p4*x)),
                 -LGM(y + 1)
   RESET dummy = estimate + 1
   ESTIMATE / SCALE
```

Method 4. Set the predicted value to zero and define the function as the square root of the negative log density. This method is a variation of method 1, so it is appropriate for data from any distribution and provides estimates of the parameters only. Here we trick NONLIN by setting $y=0$ for all cases:

$$f = \sqrt{-\ln d(x, \theta)}, \text{ so } \Sigma(y-f)^2 \text{ becomes}$$

$$\Sigma(0 - \sqrt{-\ln d(x, q)})^2 = \Sigma -\ln d(x, \theta)$$

For our example, with commands:

```
LET dummy = 0
   MODEL dummy = SQR(p1*EXP(p2*x) + p3*EXP(p4*x),
                 - y*LOG(p1*EXP(p2*x) + p3*EXP(p4*x)),
                 + LGM(y + 1)
   ESTIMATE
```

Least Absolute Deviations

As an example of other types of loss functions, consider minimizing least absolute values of deviations of the dependent variable data values from values estimated by the function at the same independent variable data points. This procedure produces estimates which, on average, are influenced less by outliers than the least squares estimates. This is because squaring a large value increases its impact. While there are more sophisticated robust procedures, least absolute values estimates are easy to compute in NONLIN and fun to compare with least squares estimates.

Model Estimation

SYSTAT provides three algorithms for estimating your model: Gauss-Newton, Quasi-Newton, and Simplex. The Gauss-Newton method with its exact derivatives produces more accurate estimates of the asymptotic standard errors and covariances and can converge in fewer iterations and more quickly than the other two algorithms.

Both GN and the Quasi-Newton method do not work if the derivatives are undefined in the region in which you are seeking minimum values. Specifically, the first and second derivatives must exist at all points for which the algorithm computes values. However, the algorithms cannot identify situations where the derivatives do not exist. Also, Quasi-Newton cannot detect when derivatives fluctuate rapidly—thus, Gauss-Newton can be more accurate.

The Simplex algorithm does not have this requirement. It calculates a value for your loss function at some point, looks to see if this value is less than values elsewhere, and steps to a new point to try again. When the steps become small, iterations stop.

GN is the fastest method. Simplex is generally slower than the others, particularly for least squares, because Simplex cannot make use of the information in the derivatives to find how far to move its estimates at each step.

How Nonlinear Modeling Works

The estimation works as follows: the starting values of the parameters are selected by the program or by you. Then the model (if stated) is evaluated for the first case in double precision. The result of this function is called the **estimate**. Then the loss function is evaluated for the first case, using the estimate from the model. If you did not include a loss function, then loss is computed by squaring the residual for the first case.

This procedure is repeated for all cases in the file and the loss is summed over cases. The summed loss is then minimized using the Gauss-Newton, Quasi-Newton, or Simplex algorithms. Iterations continue until both convergence criteria are met or the maximum number of iterations is reached.

Problems

You may encounter numerous pitfalls (for example, dependencies, discontinuities, local minima, and so on). Nonlinear Model offers several possibilities to overcome these pitfalls, but in some instances, even your best efforts may be futile.

- Find reasonable starting values by considering approximately what the values should be. Try plotting the data. For example in the contouring example, you could let DAYS $\to \infty$ and estimate θ_1 to be approximately 20.
- Try Marquardting.
- Use several different starting values for each method before you feel comfortable with the final estimates. This can help you expose local minima. The Simplex method is most robust against local minima. There is a trade-off, however, because it is considerably slower.
- Try switching back and forth between Gauss-Newton, Quasi-Newton, and Simplex without changing the starting values. That way, one may help you out of a convergence or local minimum problem.
- If you get illegal function values for starting values, try some other estimates. For some functions with many parameters, you may need high quality starting values to get an estimable function at all.
- Never trust the output of an iterative nonlinear estimation procedure until you have plotted estimates against predictors and you have tried several different starting values. SYSTAT is designed so that you can quickly save estimates, residuals, and model variables and plot them. All of the examples in this chapter were tested this way. Although most began with default starting values for the parameters, they were checked with other starting values.

Nonlinear Models in SYSTAT

Nonlinear Model Specification

To open the Nonlinear Model dialog box, from the menus choose:

Statistics
  Regression
    Nonlinear
      Model/Loss...

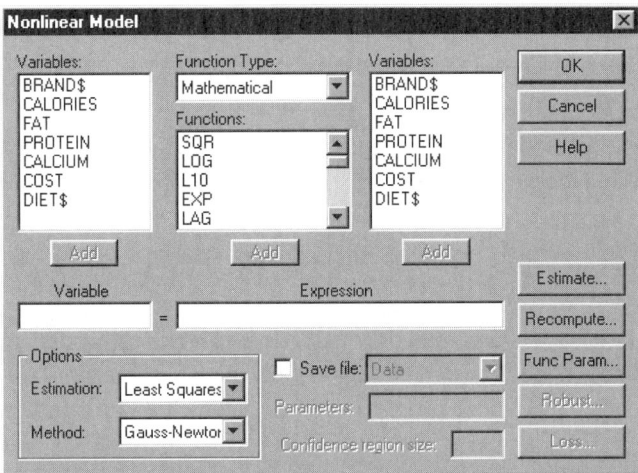

Model specification. Specify a general algebraic equation model to be estimated. Terms that are not variables are assumed to be parameters. If you want to use a function in the model, choose a Function Type from the drop-down list, select the function in the Functions list, and click Add.

Nonlinear modeling uses models resembling those for General Linear Model (GLM). There is one critical difference, however. The Nonlinear Model statement is a literal algebraic expression of variables and parameters. Choose any name you want for these parameters. Any names you specify that are not variable names in your file are assumed to be parameter names. Suppose you specify the following model for the *USSTATES* data:

 liver = b0 + b1 * wine

Since b0 and b1 are not variables (they are parameters), the following model is the same:

 liver = constant + beta * wine

Parameter names can be any names that meet the requirements for SYSTAT numeric variable names (twelve characters beginning with a letter). However, unlike variable names, parameter names may not have subscripts.

Any legal SYSTAT expression can be used in a model statement, including trigonometric and other functions, plus the special variables *CASE* and *COMPLETE*. The only restriction is that the dependent variable must be a variable in your file. Here is a more complicated example:

cardio = (division < 5) * mu1 + (division ≥ 5) * mu2

This model has two parameters (mu1 and mu2). Their values are conditional on the value of division. Notice that the remaining parts of this expression involve relational operations (division ≥ 5). SYSTAT evaluates these to 1 (true) or 0 (false).

You can perform piecewise regression by fitting different curves to different subsets of your data:

y = (x ≤ 0) * 10 + (x > 0 AND x < 1)* beta * x + (x ≥ 1) * 20

In this model, y is 10 if x is less than or equal to 0, y is BETA*x if x is greater than 0 and less than 1, and y is 20 if x is greater than or equal to 1. These types of constraints are useful for specifying bounded probability functions such as the cumulative uniform distribution.

Estimation. You can specify a loss function other than least squares. From the drop-down list, select Loss Function to perform loss analysis. When your response contains outliers, you may want to downweight their residuals using a robust ψ function by selecting Robust.

Method. Three model estimation methods are available.

- **Gauss-Newton.** Computes exact derivatives.
- **Quasi-Newton.** Uses numeric estimates of the first and second derivatives.
- **Simplex.** Uses a direct search procedure.

Save file. You can save seven sets of statistics to a file.

- **Data.** The data, estimated values, and residuals.
- **Residuals.** The estimated values, residuals, and variables in the model.
- **Residuals/Data.** All of the above.
- **Response Surface.** Five levels of contours of the loss function surrounding the converged minimum (like a response surface for the loss function in a 2-D parameter space).
- **Confidence Interval.** Cook-Weisberg graphical confidence curves. These are useful when it is unreasonable to assume that the estimates follow a normal distribution.
- **Confidence Region.** A closed curve that defines the *n%* confidence region for a pair of parameters surrounding the converged minimum. Type a number, *n*, between 0 and 0.99 in the Confidence Region field to specify the size of the confidence region.
- **Parameters.** Parameter estimates.

Parameters. For Response Surface and Confidence Region, you must specify names of two parameters. For Confidence Interval, you must specify the names of the parameters. Use a comma between each parameter name.

Estimate

Click Estimate in the Nonlinear Model dialog box to open the Estimate dialog box.

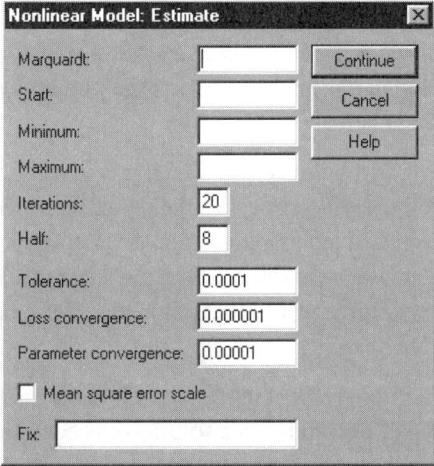

SYSTAT offers several options for controlling model computation.

Marquardt. Marquardt method of inflating the diagonal of the (Jacobian'Jacobian) matrix by *n*. This speeds convergence when initial values are far from the estimates and when the estimates of the parameters are highly intercorrelated. This method is similar to "ridging," except that the inflation factor *n* is omitted from final iterations.

Start. Starting values for model parameters. Specify values for each parameter in the order the parameters appear in your model (or loss statement if no model is specified). Separate the values with commas or blanks. You can specify starting values for some of the parameters and leave blanks for others.

SYSTAT chooses starting values if you do not. Specify starting values that give the general shape of the function you expect as a result. For example, if you expect that the function is a negative exponential function, then specify initial values that yield a negative exponential function. Also, make sure that the starting values are in a reasonable range. For example, if the function contains EXP(P*TIME) and TIME ranges from 10,000 to 20,000, then the initial value of P should be around 1/10,000. If you specified an initial value such as 0.1, the function would have extremely large values, such as e^{1000}.

Minimum. Lower limits for the parameters, one number per parameter.

Maximum. Upper limits for the parameters, one number per parameter.

Iterations. Maximum number of iteration for fitting your model.

Half. Maximum number of step halvings. If the loss increases between two iterations, Nonlinear Model halves the increment size, computes the loss at the midpoint, and compares it to the residual sum of squares at the previous iteration. This process continues until the residual sum of squares is less than that at the previous iteration or until the maximum number of halvings is reached.

Tolerance. A check for near singularity. In order for SYSTAT to invert the matrix of sums of cross-products of the derivatives with respect to the parameters, the matrix cannot be singular. Use Tolerance to guard against this singularity problem. A parameter estimate is not changed at an iteration if more than 1 − TOL proportion of the sum of squares of partial derivatives with respect to that parameter can be expressed with partial derivatives of other parameters.

Loss convergence. When the relative improvement in the loss function for an iteration is less than the specified value, SYSTAT declares that a solution has been found. Note, for convergence, both loss convergence and parameter convergence must be satisfied.

Parameter convergence. When the largest relative improvement of parameters for an iteration is less than the specified value, SYSTAT considers that the estimates of the parameters have converged. Each parameter estimate must satisfy this criterion.

Mean square error scale. Rescales the mean square error to 1 at the end of the iterations.

Fix. Specify names of parameters to be held fixed at a constant value. SYSTAT estimates the remaining parameters and tests whether the result differs from that for the full model. An example is p3 = 1.0.

Recompute

The dependent variable or the weight variable can be recomputed after each iteration, using the current values of the parameters.

You can open the Recompute dialog box by clicking **Recompute** in the Nonlinear Model dialog box.

Nonlinear Models

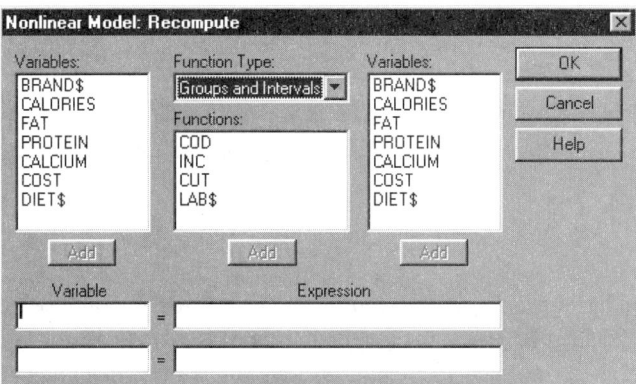

Type the name of the dependent variable or the weight variable in the Variable field or select the appropriate variable in the Variables list and click Add. If you want to use a function in your expression, choose a Function Type from the drop-down list, select the function in the Functions list, and click Add.

Functions of Parameters

Click Func Param in the Nonlinear Model dialog box to open the Functions of Parameters dialog box.

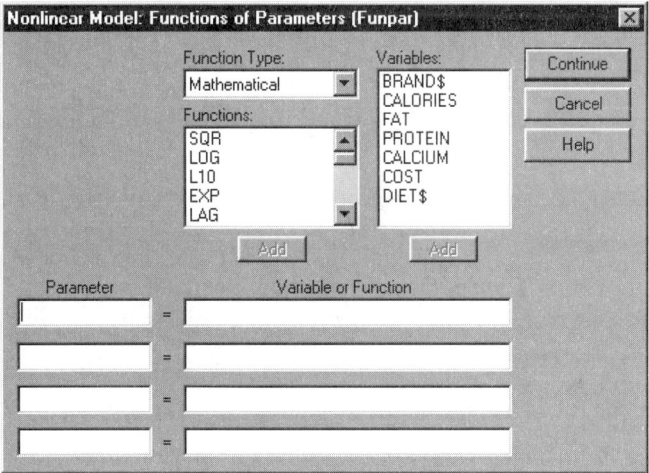

SYSTAT allows you to estimate functions of parameters. Assign a name to each function in the Parameter field. You can state up to four functions in this dialog box. SYSTAT estimates each function and reports related statistics.

If you want to use a built-in function in the expression, choose a Function Type from the drop-down list, select the function in the Functions list, and click **Add**.

Robust Analysis

When your dependent variable contains outliers, a robust regression procedure can downweight their influence on the parameter estimates. Thus, the resulting estimates reflect the great bulk of the data and are not sensitive to the value of a few unusual cases.

To specify a robust analysis, select **Robust** under Estimation in the Nonlinear Model dialog box and click **Robust**.

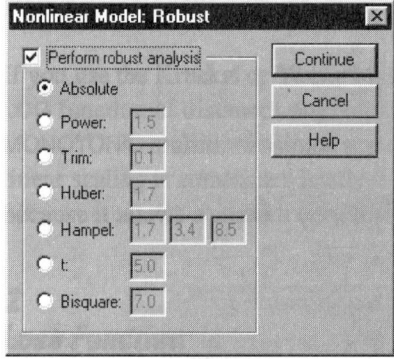

You must select **Perform robust analysis** to specify a robust estimation procedure. Available methods include:

- **Absolute.** The sum of absolute values of residuals.
- **Power.** The sum of the nth power of absolute values of residuals.
- **Trim.** Trims the n proportion of the residuals (those with the largest absolute values) and minimizes the sum of squares of the remaining residuals.
- **Huber.** The sum of MAD standardized residuals weighted by Huber.
- **Hampel.** The sum of MAD standardized residuals weighted by Hampel.
- **T.** A t distribution with df degrees of freedom.
- **Bisquare.** The sum of MAD standardized residuals weighted by Bisquare.

Nonlinear Models

The parameters for Huber, Hampel, *t*, and Bisquare are defined in MAD units (median absolute deviations from the median of the residuals).

Each procedure has a ψ function that is used to construct a weight for each residual (that is recomputed at each iteration). Here is the weighting scheme for the Hampel procedure (the heavy line is the Hampel ψ function):

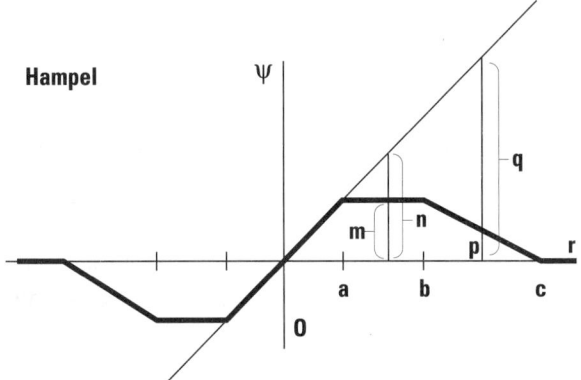

for | residual | < a   the weight ((residual)/residual) is 1.0
        a < | residual | < b   the weight is m/n
        b < | residual | < c   the weight is p/q
        c < | residual | the weight is 0.0

Nonlinear Model's default values for a, b, and c are 1.7, 3.4, and 8.5, respectively. So, if the size of the residual is less than 1.7, the weight is one; if it is over 8.5, the weight is zero. As the residual increases in absolute value, the weight decreases.

Loss Functions for Nonlinear Model Estimation

As an alternative to least squares and robust regression, you can specify a custom loss function to apply in model estimation. The default (least squares) loss function is $(\text{depvar} - \text{estimate})^2$. The word "estimate" in the function is the fitted value from your model. It is a special Nonlinear Model word, so you should not name a variable *ESTIMATE*. The model defines the parameters (that is, new parameters cannot be introduced in the loss function).

To specify a loss function for a model, select **Loss Function** under Estimation in the Nonlinear Model dialog box, and click **Loss**.

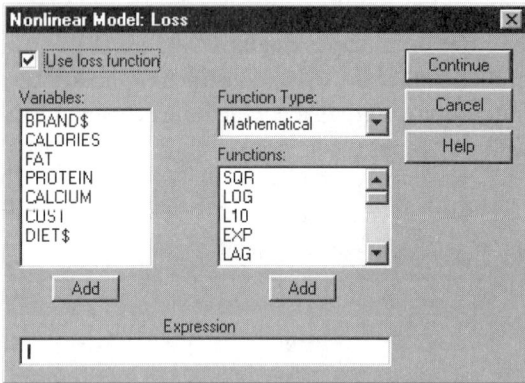

Expression. Enter the desired loss function. If you want to use a function in the expression, choose a Function Type from the drop-down list, select the function in the Functions list, and click Add.

Loss Functions for Analytic Function Minimization

You can also use nonlinear estimation to minimize an algebraic function. Such a function requires no model specification. As a result, the loss function defines the parameters and SYSTAT computes no *estimate*s for a dependent variable.

To open the Loss dialog box, from the menus choose:

Statistics
  Regression
    Nonlinear
      Loss...

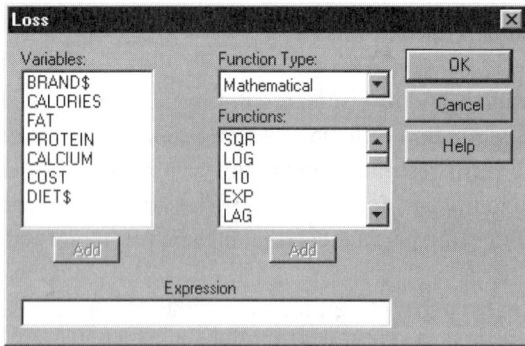

Nonlinear Models

Expression. Enter the desired loss function. If you want to use a function in the expression, choose a Function Type from the drop-down list, select the function in the Functions list, and click **Add**.

If estimation problems arise, use an alternative estimation method. The Simplex method generally does better with algebraic expressions that incur roundoff error.

Using Commands

First, specify your data with **USE filename**. Continue with:

```
NONLIN
     MODEL var = function
     LOSS function
     RESET depvar = expression or weightvar = expression
     ROBUST argument / ABSOLUTE  or  POWER=n  or  TRIM=n  or  HUBER=n ,
                or  HAMPEL=n1,n2,n3  or  T=df  or  BISQUARE=n
     FUNPAR name1=function1, name2=function2, …
     SAVE filename / DATA  RESID  RS=p1,p2  CI=p1,p2  CR=p1,p2  CONFI=n
     ESTIMATE / GN or QUASI or SIMPLEX
               MARQUADT=n  START=n1,n2,…  MIN=n1,n2,…  MAX=n1,n2,…,
               ITER=n  HALF=n  TOL=n  LCONV=n  CONV=n  SCALE
     FIX p1=n1, p2=n2, …
     ESTIMATE
```

Usage Considerations

Types of data. NONLIN uses rectangular data only.

Print options. If you specify LONG output, casewise predictions and the asymptotic correlation matrix of parameters are printed in addition to the default output.

Quick Graphs. NONLIN produces a scatterplot of the dependent variable against the variables in the model expression. The fitted function appears as either a line or a surface. If the model expression contains three or more variables, only the first two appear in the plot.

Saving files. In nonlinear modeling, you can save residuals, estimated values, and variables from your model statement, loss function values surrounding the converged minimum, or data for plotting the Cook-Weisberg confidence intervals or two-parameter confidence region.

BY groups. NONLIN produces separate results for each level of any BY variables.

Chapter 3

Bootstrapping. Bootstrapping is available in this procedure.

Case frequencies. NONLIN uses a FREQUENCY variable, if present, to duplicate cases.

Case weights. You can weight cases in NONLIN by specifying a WEIGHT variable.

Examples

Example 1
Nonlinear Model with Three Parameters

For this first example, we do not specify any options specific to NONLIN; we simply specify the model using the operators and functions available for SYSTAT's transformations. Here, we use the default Gauss-Newton algorithm that computes exact derivatives.

The Pattison data are from a 1987 JASA article by C. P. Y. Clarke (Clarke took the data from an unpublished thesis by N. B. Pattinson). For 13 grass samples collected in a pasture, Pattinson recorded the number of weeks since grazing began in the pasture (*TIME*) and the weight of grass (*GRASS*) cut from 10 randomly sited quadrants. He then fit the Mitcherlitz equation. Here is the model with the Quick Graph from its fit:

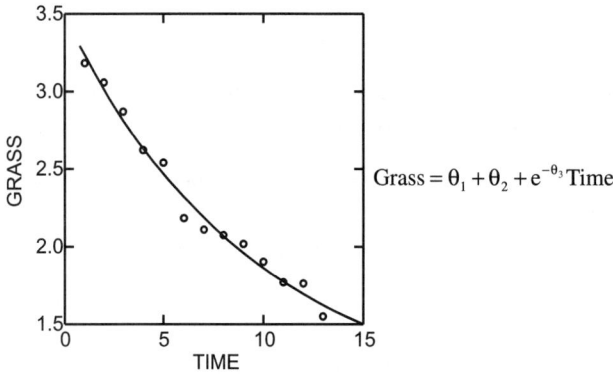

$$\text{Grass} = \theta_1 + \theta_2 + e^{-\theta_3}\text{Time}$$

The input is:

```
USE pattison
NONLIN
    PRINT=LONG
    MODEL grass = p1 + p2*EXP(-p3*time)
    ESTIMATE
```

Nonlinear Models

The output follows:

```
Iteration
No.      Loss         P1            P2             P3
  0 .220818D+02 .101000D+01  .102000D+01   .103000D+01
  1 .120609D+02 .117014D+01  .182736D+00  -.152631D+00
  2 .112473D+02 .172163D+01 -.530281D-01  -.212060D+00
  3 .530076D+01 .272740D+01 -.314883D+00   .112491D+00
  4 .281714D+01 .971285D+00  .251024D+01   .186373D+00
  5 .127700D+00 .120930D+01  .223520D+01   .109079D+00
  6 .540618D-01 .966518D+00  .251532D+01   .102374D+00
  7 .534536D-01 .963226D+00  .251890D+01   .103061D+00
  8 .534536D-01 .963120D+00  .251900D+01   .103055D+00
  9 .534536D-01 .963121D+00  .251900D+01   .103055D+00


Dependent variable is GRASS

     Source   Sum-of-Squares   df   Mean-Square
 Regression       70.871        3      23.624
   Residual        0.053       10       0.005

      Total       70.925       13
Mean corrected     3.309       12

           Raw R-square (1-Residual/Total)            =    0.999
  Mean corrected R-square (1-Residual/Corrected)     =    0.984
              R(observed vs predicted) square        =    0.984

                                                  Wald Confidence Interval
Parameter    Estimate    A.S.E.   Param/ASE      Lower < 95%> Upper
   P1          0.963     0.322      2.995         0.247       1.680
   P2          2.519     0.266      9.478         1.927       3.111
   P3          0.103     0.026      4.041         0.046       0.160

            GRASS       GRASS
   Case    Observed   Predicted    Residual
     1       3.183       3.235      -0.052
     2       3.059       3.013       0.046
     3       2.871       2.812       0.059
     4       2.622       2.631      -0.009
     5       2.541       2.468       0.073
     6       2.184       2.320      -0.136
     7       2.110       2.188      -0.078
     8       2.075       2.068       0.007
     9       2.018       1.959       0.059
    10       1.903       1.862       0.041
    11       1.770       1.774      -0.004
    12       1.762       1.695       0.067
    13       1.550       1.623      -0.073

Asymptotic Correlation Matrix of Parameters
                 P1          P2          P3
    P1        1.000
    P2       -0.972       1.000
    P3        0.984      -0.923       1.000
```

The estimates of parameters converged in nine iterations. At each iteration, Nonlinear Model prints the number of the iteration, the loss, or the residual sum of squares (RSS), and the estimates of the parameters. At step 0, the estimates of the parameters are the starting values chosen by SYSTAT or specified by the user with the START option of ESTIMATE. The residual sum of squares is

$$RSS = \sum \{w*(y-f)^2\}$$

where y is the observed value, f is the estimated value, and w is the value of the case weight (its default is 1.0).

Sums of squares (SS) appearing in the output include:

Regression: $\sum wy^2 - \sum (y-f)^2$
Residual: $\sum w(y-f)^2$
Total: $\sum wy^2$
Mean corrected: $\sum w(y-\bar{y})^2$

The Raw R^2 (*Regression SS / Total SS*) is the proportion of the variation in y that is explained by the sum of squares due to regression. Some researchers object to this measure because the means are not removed. The Mean corrected R^2 tries to adjust for this. Many researchers prefer the last measure of R^2 (*R(observed vs. predicted) squared*). It is the correlation squared between the observed values and the predicted values.

A period (there is none here) for the asymptotic standard error indicates a problem with the estimate (the correlations among the estimated parameters may be very high, or the value of the function may not be affected if the estimate is changed). Read Param/ASE, the estimate of each parameter divided by its asymptotic standard error, roughly as a t statistic.

The Wald Confidence Intervals for the estimates are defined as EST ± t*A.S.E for the t distribution with residual degrees of freedom (df = 10 in this example). SYSTAT prints the 95% confidence intervals. Use CONFI=n to specify a different confidence level.

SYSTAT computes asymptotic standard errors and correlations by estimating the INV(J'J) matrix after iterations have terminated. The matrix is computed from the asymptotic covariance matrix that inverts INV(J'J) * RMS, where J is the Jacobian and RMS is the residual mean squared. You should examine your model for redundant parameters. If the J'J matrix is singular (parameters are very highly intercorrelated), SYSTAT prints a period to mark parameters with problems. In this example, the parameters are highly intercorrelated; the model may be overparameterized.

Example 2
Confidence Curves and Regions

Confidence curves and regions provide information about the certainty of your parameter estimates. The usual Wald confidence intervals can be misleading when intercorrelations among the parameters are high.

Confidence curves. Cook and Weisberg construct confidence curves by plotting an assortment of potential estimates of a specific parameter on the y axis against the absolute value of a t statistic derived from the residual sum of squares (RSS) associated with each parameter estimate. To obtain the values for the x axis, SYSTAT:

- Computes the model as usual and saves RSS.
- Fixes the value of the parameter of interest of (for example, the estimate plus half the standard error of the estimate), recomputes the model, and saves RSS*.
- Computes the t statistic:

$$t = \sqrt{\frac{\frac{RSS*-RSS}{1}}{\frac{RSS}{n-p}}}$$

- Repeats the above steps for other estimates of the parameter.

Now SYSTAT plots each parameter estimate against the absolute value of its associated t^* statistic. Vertical lines at the 90, 95, and 99 percentage points of the t distribution with $(n-p)$ degrees of freedom provide a useful frequentist calibration of the plot.

To illustrate the usefulness of confidence curves, we again use the Pattison data used in the three-parameter nonlinear model example. Recall that the parameter estimates were:

p1 = 0.93
p2 = 2.519
p3 = 0.103

Chapter 3

To produce the Cook-Weisberg confidence curves for the model:

```
USE pattison
NONLIN
    MODEL grass = p1 + p2*EXP(-p3*time)
    SAVE pattci / CI=p1 p2 p3
    ESTIMATE
SUBMIT pattci
```

Here are the results:

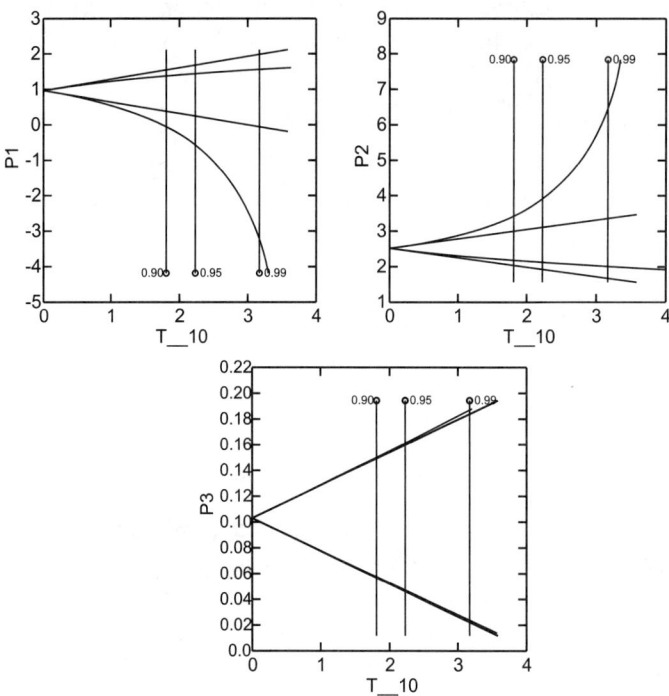

The nonvertical straight lines (blue on a computer monitor) are the Wald 95% confidence intervals and the solid curves are the Cook-Weisberg confidence curves. The vertical lines show the 90th, 95th, and 99th percentiles of the t distribution with $n - p = 10$ degrees of freedom.

For *P1* and *P2*, the coverage of the Wald intervals differs makedly from that of the Cook-Weisberg (C-W) curves. The 95% interval for *P1* on the C-W curve is approximately from –0.58 to 1.45; the Wald interval extends from 0.247 to 1.68. The steeply descending lower C-W curve indicates greater uncertainty for smaller estimates of *P1*. For *P2*, the C-W interval ranges from 2.12 to 3.92; the Wald interval ranges from 1.9 to 3.1. The agreement between the two methods is better for *P3*. The C-W curves show that the distributions of estimates for *P1* and *P2* are quite asymmetric.

Confidence region. SYSTAT also provides the CR option for confidence regions. When there are more than two parameters in the model, this feature causes Nonlinear Model to search for the best values of the additional parameters for each combination of estimates for the first two parameters. Type:

```
USE pattison
NONLIN
    MODEL grass = p1 + p2*EXP(-p3*time)
    SAVE pattcr / CR=p1 p2
    ESTIMATE
SUBMIT pattcr
```

The plot follows:

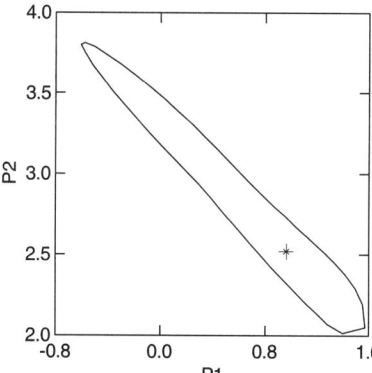

You can also specify the level of confidence. For example,

```
SAVE pattcr / CR=p1 p2 CONFI=.90
```

Example 3
Fixing Parameters and Evaluating Fit

In the three-parameter nonlinear model example, the R^2 between the observed and predicted values is 0.984, indicating good agreement between the data and fitted values. However, there may be consecutive points across time where the fitted values are consistently overestimated or underestimated. We can look for trends in the residuals by plotting them versus *TIME* and connecting the points with a line. A stem-and-leaf plot will tell us if extreme values are identified as outliers (outside values or far outside values). The input is:

```
USE pattison
NONLIN
    MODEL grass = p1 + p2*EXP(-p3*time)
    SAVE myresids / DATA
    ESTIMATE
USE myresids
PLOT RESIDUAL*TIME / LINE YLIMIT=0
STATISTICS
    STEM RESIDUAL
```

The output is:

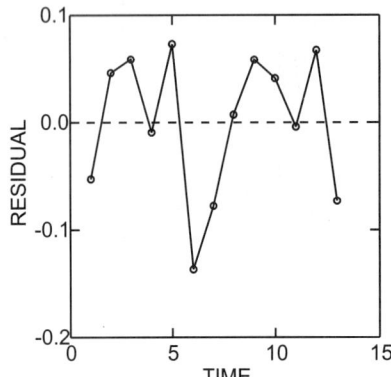

```
Stem and Leaf Plot of variable:      RESIDUAL, N = 13
    Minimum:         -0.136
    Lower hinge:           -0.052
    Median:           0.007
    Upper hinge:            0.059
    Maximum:          0.073
         -1    3
         -0 H  775
         -0 H  00
          0 M  044
          0 H  5567
```

The results of a runs test would not be significant here. The large negative residual in the center of the plot, –0.137, is not identified as an outlier in the stem-and-leaf plot.

We should probably be more concerned about the fact that the parameters are highly intercorrelated: The correlation between *P1* and *P2* is –0.972, and the correlation between *P1* and *P3* is 0.984. This might indicate that our model has too many parameters. You can fix one or more parameters and let SYSTAT estimate the remaining parameters. Suppose, for example, that similar studies report a value of *P1* close to 1.0. You can fix *P1* at 1.0 and then test whether the results differ from the results for the full model.

To do this, first specify the full model. Use FIX to specify the parameter as *P1* with a value of 1. Then initiate the estimation process with ESTIMATE:

```
USE pattison
NONLIN
    MODEL grass = p1 + p2*EXP(-p3*time)
    ESTIMATE
    FIX p1=1
    SAVE pattci / CI=p2 p3
    ESTIMATE
SUBMIT pattci
```

Here are selections from the output:

```
Parameter           Estimate        A.S.E.     Param/ASE       Lower < 95%> Upper
P1                  1.000           0.0              .               .         .
P2                  2.490           0.060         41.662          2.358     2.621
P3                  0.106           0.004         23.728          0.096     0.116

Analysis of the effect of fixing parameter(s)
Source       Sum-of-squares    df   Mean-square    F-value    p(F-value)
Parameter fix        0.000      1         0.000      0.014         0.908
 Residual            0.053     10         0.005
```

The analysis of the effect of fixing parameter(s) *F* test tests the hypothesis that *P1*=1.0. In our output, $F = 0.014$ ($p = 0.908$), indicating that there is no significant difference between the two models. This is not surprising, considering the similarity of the results:

	Three parameters	P1 fixed at 1.0
P1	0.963	1.000
P2	2.519	2.490
P3	0.103	0.106
RSS	0.053	0.054
R^2	0.984	0.984

There are some differences between the two models. The correlation between *P2* and *P3* is 0.923 for the full model and 0.810 when *P1* is fixed. The most striking difference is in the Wald intervals for *P2* and *P3*. When *P1* is fixed, the Wald interval for *P2* is less than one-fourth of the interval for the full model. The interval for *P3* is less than one-fifth the interval for the full model. Let's see what information the C-W curves provide about the uncertainty of the estimates. Here are the curves for the model with *P1* fixed:

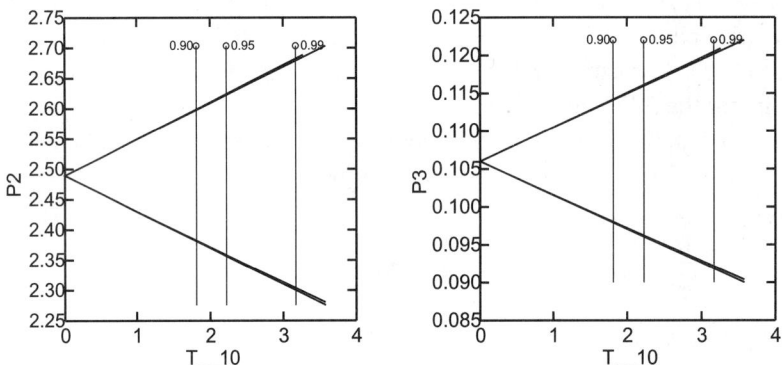

Compare these curves with the curves for the full model. The C-W curve for *P2* has straightened out and is very close to the Wald interval. If we were to plot the *P2* C-W curve for both models on the same axes, the wedge for the fixed *P1* model would be only a small slice of the wedge for the full model.

Example 4
Functions of Parameters

Frequently, researchers are not interested in the estimates of the parameters themselves, but instead want to make statements about functions of parameters. For example, in a logistic model, they may want to estimate *LD50* and *LD90* and determine the variability of these estimates. You can specify functions of parameters in Nonlinear Model. SYSTAT evaluates the function at each iteration and prints the standard error and the Wald interval for the estimate after the last iteration.

We look at a quadratic function described by Cook and Weisberg. Here is the Quick Graph that results from fitting the model:

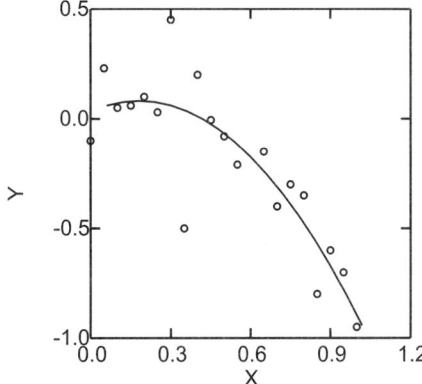

This function reaches its maximum at $-b/2c$. However, for the data given by Cook and Weisberg, this maximum is close to the smallest x. That is, to the left of the maximum, there is little of the response curve.

In SYSTAT, you can estimate the maximum (and get Wald intervals) directly from the original quadratic by using FUNPAR. The input is:

```
USE quad
NONLIN
   MODEL y = a + b*x + c*x^2
   FUNPAR max = -b/(2*c)
   ESTIMATE
```

The parameter estimates are:

Parameter	Estimate	A.S.E.	Param/ASE	Lower < 95%> Upper	
A	0.034	0.117	0.292	-0.213	0.282
B	0.524	0.555	0.944	-0.647	1.694
C	-1.452	0.534	-2.718	-2.579	-0.325
MAX	0.180	0.128	1.409	-0.090	0.450

Using the Wald interval, we estimate that the maximum response occurs for an x value between –0.09 and 0.45.

C-W Curves

To obtain the C-W confidence curves for *MAX*, we have to re-express the model so that *MAX* is a parameter of the model:

$$b = -2c\text{Max}$$

so

$$y = a - (2c\text{Max})x + cx^2$$

The original model is easy to compute because it is linear. The reparameterized model is not as well-behaved, so we use estimates from the first run as starting values and request C-W confidence curves:

```
MODEL y=a - (2*c*max)*x + c*x^2
SAVE quadcw / CI=max
ESTIMATE / START=0.034,-1.452, 0.180
SUBMIT quadcw
```

The C-W confidence curves describe our uncertainty about the *x* value at which the expected response is maximized much better than the Wald interval does.

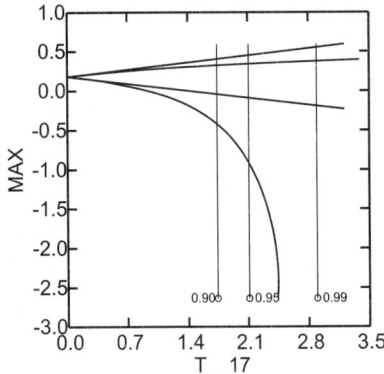

The picture provides clear information about the *MAX* response in the positive direction. We can be confident that the value is less than 0.4 because the C-W curve is lower than the Wald interval on the 95th percentile line. The lower bound is much less clear; it could certainly be lower than the Wald interval indicates.

Example 5
Contouring the Loss Function

You can save loss function values along contour curves and then plot the loss function. For this example, we use the *BOD* data (Bates and Watts, 1988). These data were taken from stream samples in 1967 by Marske. Each sample bottle was inoculated with a mixed culture of microorganisms, sealed, incubated, and opened periodically for analysis of dissolved oxygen concentration.

The data are:

DAYS	BOD
1.0	8.3
2.0	10.3
3.0	19.0
4.0	16.0
5.0	15.0
7	19.8

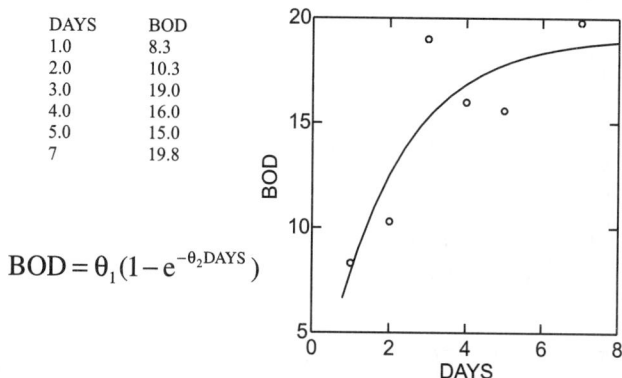

$$BOD = \theta_1 (1 - e^{-\theta_2 DAYS})$$

where *DAYS* is time in days and *BOD* is the biochemical oxygen demand. The six *BOD* values are averages of two analyses on each bottle. An exponential decay model with a fixed rate constant was estimated to predict biochemical oxygen demand.

Let's look at the contours of the parameter space defined by *THETA_2* with *THETA_1*. We use loss function data values stored in the *BODRS* data file. Here's how we created the file:

```
USE bod
NONLIN
   MODEL bod = theta_1*(1-EXP(-theta_2*days))
   PRINT=LONG
   SAVE bodrs / RS
   ESTIMATE
SUBMIT bodrs
```

The output follows:

```
Dependent variable is BOD

     Source    Sum-of-Squares   df   Mean-Square
 Regression         1401.390     2      700.695
   Residual           25.990     4        6.498

      Total         1427.380     6
Mean corrected       107.213     5

          Raw  R-square (1-Residual/Total)       =    0.982
Mean corrected R-square (1-Residual/Corrected)   =    0.758
        R(observed vs predicted) square          =    0.758

                                                      Wald Confidence Interval
Parameter       Estimate    A.S.E.    Param/ASE       Lower < 95%> Upper
 THETA_1         19.143      2.496      7.670         12.213       26.072
 THETA_2          0.531      0.203      2.615         -0.033        1.095

             BOD        BOD
 Case     Observed   Predicted    Residual
   1         8.300       7.887       0.413
   2        10.300      12.525      -2.225
   3        19.000      15.252       3.748
   4        16.000      16.855      -0.855
   5        15.600      17.797      -2.197
   6        19.800      18.678       1.122

Asymptotic Correlation Matrix of Parameters
              THETA_1     THETA_2
 THETA_1        1.000
 THETA_2       -0.853       1.000
```

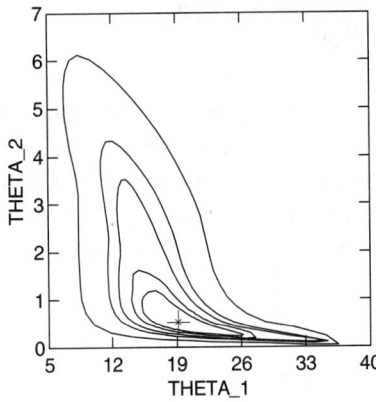

The kidney-shaped area near the center of the plot is the region where the loss function is minimized. Any parameter value combination (that is, any point inside the kidney) produces approximately the same loss function.

Example 6
Maximum Likelihood Estimation

Because NONLIN includes a loss function, you can maximize the likelihood of a function in the model equation. The way to do this is to minimize the negative of the log-likelihood.

Here is an example using the *IRIS* data. Let's compute the maximum likelihood estimates of the mean and variance of *SEPALWID* assuming a normal distribution for the first species in the *IRIS* data. For a sample of n independent normal random variables, the log-likelihood function is:

$$L(\mu, \sigma^2) = -\frac{n}{2}\ln(2\pi) - \frac{n}{2}\ln(\sigma^2) - \frac{1}{2\sigma^2}\sum(X-\mu)^2$$

However, we can use the ZDF function as a shortcut. In this example, we minimize the negative of the log-likelihood with LOSS and thus maximize the likelihood. SYSTAT's small default starting values for *MEAN* and *SIGMA* (0.101 and 0.100) will produce very large z scores ((x – mean) / sigma) and values of the density close to 0, so we arbitrarily select larger starting values. We use the *IRIS* data. Under SELECT, we specify SPECIES = 1. Then, we type in our LOSS statement. Finally, we use ESTIMATE's START option to specify start values (2,2):

```
USE iris
NONLIN
    SELECT species=1
    LOSS = -log(zdf(sepalwid,mean,sigma))
    ESTIMATE / START=2,2
```

The estimates are:

Parameter	Estimate	A.S.E.	Param/ASE	Wald Confidence Interval Lower < 95%> Upper	
MEAN	3.428	0.053	65.255	3.322	3.534
SIGMA	0.375	0.037	10.102	0.301	0.450

Note that the least squares estimate of sigma (0.379) computed using STATISTICS is larger than the biased maximum likelihood estimate here (0.375).

Example 7
Iteratively Reweighted Least Squares for Logistic Models

Cox (1970) reports the following data on tests among objects for failures after certain times. These data are in the *COX* data file—*FAILURE* is the number of failures and *COUNT* is the total number of tests.

Cox uses a logistic model to fit the failures:

$$\text{estimate} = (\text{count}) \frac{e^{\beta_0 + \beta_1 \text{time}}}{1 + e^{\beta_0 + \beta_1 \text{time}}}$$

The log-likelihood function for the logit model is:

$$L(\beta_0, \beta_1) = \sum \left[p \ln(\text{estimate}) + (1-p) \ln(1 - \text{estimate}) \right]$$

where the sum is over all observations. Because the counts differ at each time, the variances of the failures also differ. If *FAILURE* is randomly sampled from a binomial, then.

$$\text{VAR}(\text{failure}) = \text{estimate} * (\text{count} - \text{estimate}) / \text{count}$$

Therefore, the weight is $1/\text{variance}$:

$$w_i = \text{count} / (\text{estimate} * (\text{count} - \text{estimate}))$$

We use these variances to weight each case in the estimation. On each iteration, the variances are recalculated from the new estimates and used anew in computing the weighted loss function.

In the following commands, we use RESET to recompute the weight after each iteration. The SCALE option of ESTIMATE rescales the mean square error to 1 at the end of the iterations. The commands are:

```
USE COX
NONLIN
   PRINT = LONG
   LET w = 1
   WEIGHT = w
   MODEL failure = count*EXP(-b0 - b1*time)/,
                   (1 + EXP(-b0 - b1*time))
   RESET w = count / (estimate*(count-estimate))
   ESTIMATE / SCALE
```

The output follows:

```
Iteration
  No.      Loss         B0             B1
   0   .162222D+03  .101000D+00  .102000D+00
   1   .161785D+02  .272314D+01 -.109931D-01
   2   .325354D+01  .419599D+01 -.509510D-01
   3   .754172D+00  .510574D+01 -.736890D-01
   4   .665897D+00  .539079D+01 -.801623D-01
   5   .674806D+00  .541501D+01 -.806924D-01
   6   .674876D+00  .541518D+01 -.806960D-01

Dependent variable is FAILURE

     Source    Sum-of-Squares   df   Mean-Square
 Regression        13.038        2      6.519
   Residual         0.675        2      0.337

      Total        13.712        4
Mean corrected     10.539        3

           Raw  R-square (1-Residual/Total)         =    0.951
Mean corrected R-square (1-Residual/Corrected)      =    0.936
           R(observed vs predicted) square          =    0.988
Standard Errors of Parameters are rescaled

                                                    Wald Confidence Interval
Parameter      Estimate    A.S.E.    Param/ASE      Lower < 95%> Upper
   B0             5.415     0.728      7.443         3.989       6.841
   B1            -0.081     0.022     -3.610        -0.125      -0.037

          FAILURE    FAILURE
  Case    Observed   Predicted   Residual    Case Weight
    1       0.0        0.427      -0.427       2.360
    2       2.000      2.132      -0.132       0.475
    3       7.000      6.013       0.987       0.173
    4       3.000      3.427      -0.427       0.371
```

Jennrich and Moore (1975) show that this method can be used for maximum likelihood estimation of parameters from a distribution in the exponential family.

Example 8
Robust Estimation (Measures of Location)

Robust estimators provide methods other than the mean, median, or mode to estimate the center of a distribution. The sample mean is the least squares estimate of location; that is, it is the point at which the squared deviations of the sample values are at a minimum. (The sample medians minimize absolute deviations instead of squared deviations.) In terms of ψ weights, the usual mean assigns a weight of 1.0 to each observation, while the robust methods assign smaller weights to residuals far from the center.

In this example, we use sepal width of the Setosa iris flowers and SELECT SPECIES = 1. We request the usual sample mean and then ask for a 10% trimmed mean, a Hampel estimator, and the median. But first, let's view the distribution graphically. Here are a box-and-whisker display and a dit plot of the data.

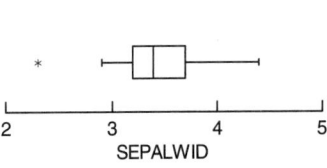 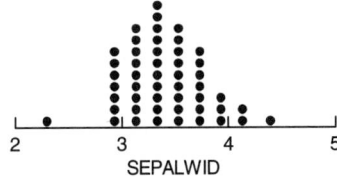

Except for the outlier at the left, the distribution of *SEPALWID* is slightly right-skewed.

Mean

In the maximum likelihood example, we requested maximum likelihood estimates of the mean and standard deviation. Here is the least squares estimate:

```
USE iris
NONLIN
   SELECT species = 1
   MODEL sepalwid = mean
   ESTIMATE
```

Nonlinear Models

The output is:

```
Iteration
   No.       Loss         MEAN
    0    .299377D+03  .101000D+01
    1    .704080D+01  .342800D+01
    2    .704080D+01  .342800D+01
    3    .704080D+01  .342800D+01

Dependent variable is SEPALWID

       Source    Sum-of-Squares     df    Mean-Square
   Regression        587.559         1       587.559
     Residual          7.041        49         0.144

        Total         594.600       50
Mean corrected          7.041       49

          Raw  R-square (1-Residual/Total)           =    0.988
Mean corrected R-square (1-Residual/Corrected)       =    0.0
           R(observed vs predicted) square           =    0.0

                                                        Wald Confidence Interval
Parameter       Estimate      A.S.E.     Param/ASE     Lower < 95%> Upper
MEAN               3.428       0.054        63.946     3.320        3.536
```

Trimmed Mean

We enter the following commands after viewing the results for the mean. Note that SYSTAT resets the starting values to their defaults when a new model is specified. If MODEL is not given, SYSTAT uses the final values from the last calculation as starting values for the current task.

For this trimmed mean estimate, SYSTAT deletes the five cases (0.1 * 50 = 5) with the most extreme residuals. The input is:

```
MODEL sepalwid = trimmean
ROBUST TRIM = 0.1
ESTIMATE
```

The output follows:

```
Iteration
   No.       Loss        TRIMMEAN
    0    .560487D+03  .101000D+00
    1    .704080D+01  .342800D+01
    2    .344888D+01  .342800D+01
    3    .337200D+01  .338667D+01
    4    .337200D+01  .338667D+01
    5    .337200D+01  .338667D+01

TRIM robust regression:    45 cases have positive psi-weights
                              The average psi-weight is 1.00000

Dependent variable is SEPALWID
```

```
Zero weights, missing data or estimates reduced degrees of freedom
    Source    Sum-of-Squares    df    Mean-Square
  Regression      587.474        1      587.474
   Residual         7.126       44        0.162

    Total         594.600       45
Mean corrected      7.041       44

         Raw  R-square (1-Residual/Total)         =    0.988
Mean corrected R-square (1-Residual/Corrected)    =    0.0
         R(observed vs predicted) square          =    0.0

                                                    Wald Confidence Interval
Parameter         Estimate    A.S.E.    Param/ASE    Lower < 95%> Upper
TRIMMEAN           3.387       0.060      56.451      3.266      3.508
```

The trimmed estimate deletes the outlier, plus the four flowers on the right side of the distribution with width equal to or greater than 4.0 (if you select the LONG mode of output, you would see that these flowers have the largest residuals).

Hampel

We now request a Hampel estimator using the default values for its parameters.

```
MODEL sepalwid = hamp_est
ROBUST HAMPEL
ESTIMATE
```

The output is:

```
Iteration
  No.     Loss         HAMP_EST
   0   .560487D+03    .101000D+00
   1   .704080D+01    .342800D+01
   2   .509172D+01    .342800D+01
   3   .507163D+01    .341620D+01
   4   .506858D+01    .341450D+01
   5   .506825D+01    .341431D+01
   6   .506822D+01    .341429D+01
   7   .506821D+01    .341429D+01
   8   .506821D+01    .341429D+01

HAMPEL robust regression:   50 cases have positive psi-weights
                         The average psi-weight is 0.94551
Dependent variable is SEPALWID

    Source    Sum-of-Squares    df    Mean-Square
  Regression      587.550        1      587.550
   Residual         7.050       49        0.144

    Total         594.600       50
Mean corrected      7.041       49

         Raw  R-square (1-Residual/Total)         =    0.988
Mean corrected R-square (1-Residual/Corrected)    =    0.0
         R(observed vs predicted) square          =    0.0

                                                    Wald Confidence Interval
Parameter         Estimate    A.S.E.    Param/ASE    Lower < 95%> Upper
HAMP_EST           3.414       0.054      63.648      3.306      3.522
```

Median

We let NONLIN minimize the absolute value of the residuals for an estimate of the median.

```
MODEL sepalwid = median
ROBUST ABSOLUTE
ESTIMATE
```

The output is:

```
Iteration
  No.      Loss         MEDIAN
    0  .299377D+03  .101000D+01
    1  .143680D+02  .342800D+01
    2  .142988D+02  .341647D+01
    3  .142499D+02  .340831D+01
    4  .142214D+02  .340357D+01
    5  .142081D+02  .340135D+01
    6  .142028D+02  .340047D+01
    7  .142010D+02  .340016D+01
    8  .142003D+02  .340005D+01
    9  .142001D+02  .340002D+01
   10  .142000D+02  .340001D+01
   11  .142000D+02  .340000D+01
   12  .142000D+02  .340000D+01
   13  .142000D+02  .340000D+01

ABSOLUTE robust regression:    50 cases have positive psi-weights
                               The average psi-weight is 2418627.93032

Dependent variable is SEPALWID

      Source    Sum-of-Squares    df    Mean-Square
  Regression       587.520         1       587.520
    Residual         7.080        49         0.144

       Total       594.600        50
Mean corrected       7.041        49

         Raw R-square (1-Residual/Total)          =    0.988
Mean corrected R-square (1-Residual/Corrected)    =    0.0
         R(observed vs predicted) square          =    0.0

                                                     Wald Confidence Interval
Parameter       Estimate      A.S.E.     Param/ASE     Lower < 95%> Upper
MEDIAN            3.400          .            .             .          .
```

If you request the median for these data in the Basic Statistics procedure, the value is 3.4.

Example 9
Regression

Usually, you would not use NONLIN for linear regression because other procedures are available. If, however, you are concerned about the influence of outliers on the estimates of the coefficients, you should try one of Nonlinear Model's robust procedures

The example uses the *OURWORLD* data file and we model the relation of military expenditures to gross domestic product using information reported by 57 countries to the United Nations. Each country is a case in our file and *MIL* and *GDP_CAP* are our two variables. In the transformation example for linear regression, we discovered that both variables require a log transformation, and that Iraq and Libya are outliers.

Here is a scatterplot of the data. The solid line is the least squares line of best fit for the complete sample (with its corresponding confidence band); the dotted line (and its confidence band) is the regression line after deleting Iraq and Libya from the sample. How do robust lines fit within original confidence bands?

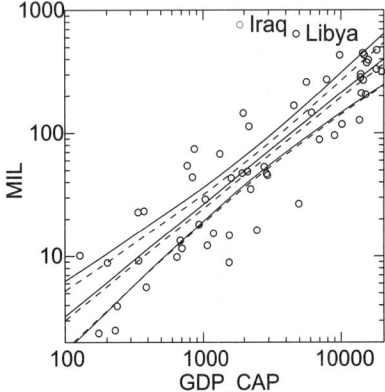

Visually, we see the dotted line-of-best fit falls slightly below the solid line for the complete sample. More striking, however, is the upper curve for the confidence band—the dotted line is considerably lower than the solid one.

We can use NONLIN to fit a least squares regression line with the following input:

```
USE ourworld
NONLIN
   LET log_mil = L10(mil)
   LET log_gdp = L10(gdp_cap)
   MODEL log_mil = intercept + slope*log_gdp
   ESTIMATE
```

Nonlinear Models

The output is:

```
Dependent variable is LOG_MIL

Zero weights, missing data or estimates reduced degrees of freedom
    Source    Sum-of-Squares    df   Mean-Square
Regression       194.332         2      97.166
  Residual         6.481        54       0.120

     Total       200.813        56
Mean corrected    24.349        55

      Raw  R-square (1-Residual/Total)         =    0.968
Mean corrected R-square (1-Residual/Corrected) =    0.734
      R(observed vs predicted) square          =    0.734

                                              Wald Confidence Interval
Parameter       Estimate    A.S.E.   Param/ASE    Lower < 95%> Upper
INTERCEPT        -1.308     0.257     -5.091      -1.822     -0.793
SLOPE             0.909     0.075     12.201       0.760      1.058
```

The estimate of the intercept (−1.308) and the slope (0.909) are the same as those produced by GLM. The residual for Iraq (1.216) is identified as an outlier—its Studentized value is 4.004. Libya's residual is 0.77.

1st Power

We now estimate the model using a least absolute values loss function (first power regression). We do not respecify the model, so by default, SYSTAT uses our last estimates as starting values. To avoid this, we specify START without an argument.

```
ROBUST ABSOLUTE
ESTIMATE / START
```

The output follows:

```
Iteration
  No.     Loss        INTERCEPT      SLOPE
   0  .119361D+03   .101000D+00   .102000D+00
   1  .147084D+02  -.130751D+01   .909014D+00
   2  .146579D+02  -.135163D+01   .919628D+00
   3  .146302D+02  -.138083D+01   .926673D+00
   4  .146142D+02  -.140215D+01   .931814D+00
   5  .146139D+02  -.140402D+01   .932266D+00
   6  .146135D+02  -.140636D+01   .932831D+00
   7  .146130D+02  -.140918D+01   .933513D+00
   8  .146125D+02  -.141248D+01   .934310D+00
   9  .146118D+02  -.141622D+01   .935214D+00
  10  .146111D+02  -.142033D+01   .936207D+00
  11  .146104D+02  -.142471D+01   .937267D+00
  12  .146096D+02  -.142924D+01   .938362D+00
  13  .146089D+02  -.143375D+01   .939451D+00
  14  .146082D+02  -.143801D+01   .940481D+00
  15  .146075D+02  -.144174D+01   .941383D+00
  16  .146070D+02  -.144461D+01   .942075D+00
  17  .146068D+02  -.144633D+01   .942491D+00
  18  .146066D+02  -.144701D+01   .942656D+00
  19  .146066D+02  -.144717D+01   .942695D+00
  20  .146066D+02  -.144720D+01   .942701D+00
  21  .146066D+02  -.144720D+01   .942702D+00
```

```
ABSOLUTE robust regression:    56 cases have positive psi-weights
                               The average psi-weight is 40210712082202.71000

Dependent variable is LOG_MIL

Zero weights, missing data or estimates reduced degrees of freedom
    Source    Sum-of-Squares     df    Mean-Square
 Regression       194.271         2       97.136
   Residual         6.542        54        0.121

     Total         200.813       56
Mean corrected      24.349       55

           Raw  R-square (1-Residual/Total)      =     0.967
 Mean corrected R-square (1-Residual/Corrected)  =     0.731
           R(observed vs predicted) square       =     0.734

                                                       Wald Confidence Interval
Parameter         Estimate     A.S.E.     Param/ASE    Lower < 95%> Upper
INTERCEPT          -1.447         .           .           .           .
SLOPE               0.943         .           .           .           .
```

Huber

For the Hampel estimator, the weights begin to be less than 1.0 after the value of the first parameter (1.7). For this Huber estimate, we let the weight taper off sooner by setting the parameter at 1.5.

```
ROBUST HUBER = 1.5
ESTIMATE / START
```

The output is:

```
Iteration
   No.      Loss        INTERCEPT      SLOPE
    0   .119361D+03   .101000D+00   .102000D+00
    1   .648115D+01  -.130751D+01   .909014D+00
    2   .428867D+01  -.130751D+01   .909014D+00
    3   .426728D+01  -.133847D+01   .913898D+00
    4   .417969D+01  -.135733D+01   .918472D+00
    5   .418018D+01  -.136897D+01   .921389D+00
    6   .418202D+01  -.137260D+01   .922285D+00
    7   .418261D+01  -.137367D+01   .922546D+00
    8   .418278D+01  -.137398D+01   .922623D+00
    9   .418283D+01  -.137407D+01   .922646D+00
   10   .418285D+01  -.137410D+01   .922653D+00
   11   .418285D+01  -.137411D+01   .922655D+00
   12   .418285D+01  -.137411D+01   .922655D+00
   13   .418285D+01  -.137411D+01   .922656D+00

HUBER robust regression:    56 cases have positive psi-weights
                            The average psi-weight is 0.92050

Dependent variable is LOG_MIL
```

Nonlinear Models

```
Zero weights, missing data or estimates reduced degrees of freedom
    Source    Sum-of-Squares    df    Mean-Square
    Regression     194.305       2       97.153
     Residual       6.508       54        0.121

       Total      200.813      56
Mean corrected     24.349      55

        Raw  R-square (1-Residual/Total)         =    0.968
Mean corrected R-square (1-Residual/Corrected)   =    0.733
        R(observed vs predicted) square          =    0.734

                                                   Wald Confidence Interval
Parameter       Estimate      A.S.E.    Param/ASE   Lower < 95%> Upper
INTERCEPT        -1.374        0.255      -5.398    -1.885      -0.864
SLOPE             0.923        0.073      12.567     0.775       1.070
```

5% Trim

In the linear regression version of this example, we removed Iraq from the sample by specifying:

```
SELECT mil < 700 or SELECT country$ <> 'Iraq'
```

Here, we ask for 5% trimming (0.05*56=2.8 or 2 cases):

```
ROBUST TRIM = .05
ESTIMATE / START
```

The output is:

```
Iteration
  No.    Loss          INTERCEPT      SLOPE
    0  .119361D+03   .101000D+00   .102000D+00
    1  .648115D+01  -.130751D+01   .909014D+00
    2  .440626D+01  -.130751D+01   .909014D+00
    3  .433275D+01  -.133192D+01   .905350D+00
    4  .433275D+01  -.133192D+01   .905350D+00
    5  .433275D+01  -.133192D+01   .905350D+00

TRIM robust regression:   54 cases have positive psi-weights
                          The average psi-weight is 1.00000

Dependent variable is LOG_MIL

Zero weights, missing data or estimates reduced degrees of freedom
    Source    Sum-of-Squares    df    Mean-Square
    Regression     194.256       2       97.128
     Residual       6.557       52        0.126

       Total      200.813      54
Mean corrected     24.349      53

        Raw  R-square (1-Residual/Total)         =    0.967
Mean corrected R-square (1-Residual/Corrected)   =    0.731
        R(observed vs predicted) square          =    0.734

                                                   Wald Confidence Interval
Parameter       Estimate      A.S.E.    Param/ASE   Lower < 95%> Upper
INTERCEPT        -1.332        0.264      -5.049    -1.861      -0.803
SLOPE             0.905        0.077      11.829     0.752       1.059
```

Example 10
Piecewise Regression

Sometimes we need to fit two different regression functions to the same data. For example, sales of a certain product might be strongly related to quality when advertising budgets are below a certain level—that is, when sales are generated by "word of mouth." Above this advertising budget level, sales may be less strongly related to quality of goods and more by marketing and advertising factors. In these cases, we can fit different sections of the data with different models. It is easier to combine these into a single model, however.

Here is an example of a quadratic function with a ceiling using data from Gilfoil (1982). This particular study is one of several that show that dialog menu interfaces are preferred by inexperienced computer users and that command based interfaces are preferred by experienced users. The data for one subject are in the file *LEARN*. The variable *SESSION* is the session number and *TASKS* is the number of user-controlled tasks (as opposed to dialog) chosen by the subject during a session.

We fit these data with a quadratic model for earlier sessions and a ceiling for later sessions. We use NONLIN to estimate the point where the learning hits this ceiling (at six tasks). The input is:

```
USE learn
NONLIN
   PRINT = LONG
   MODEL tasks = b*session^2*(session<known) +,
                 b*known^2*(session>=known)
   ESTIMATE
```

Note that the expressions (SESSION<KNOWN and SESSION>=KNOWN) control which function is to be used—the quadratic or the horizontal line. The output follows:

```
Iteration
 No.     Loss          B             KNOWN
   0  .313871D+03  .101000D+01   .102000D+01
   1  .207272D+03  .505000D+00   .204177D+01
   2  .175758D+03  .252500D+00   .311938D+01
   3  .152604D+03  .126250D+00   .461304D+01
   4  .122355D+03  .451977D-01   .802625D+01
   5  .270318D+02  .552896D-01   .112719D+02
   6  .161372D+02  .544354D-01   .105367D+02
   7  .145557D+02  .620140D-01   .967811D+01
   8  .144181D+02  .633275D-01   .965934D+01
   9  .144181D+02  .633275D-01   .965971D+01
  10  .144181D+02  .633275D-01   .965971D+01
```

Nonlinear Models

```
Dependent variable is TASKS

    Source   Sum-of-Squares    df   Mean-Square
Regression         445.582      2       222.791
  Residual          14.418     18         0.801

     Total         460.000     20
Mean corrected     140.000     19

        Raw  R-square (1-Residual/Total)        =    0.969
Mean corrected R-square (1-Residual/Corrected)  =    0.897
        R(observed vs predicted) square         =    0.912

                                                 Wald Confidence Interval
Parameter       Estimate     A.S.E.    Param/ASE    Lower < 95%> Upper
B                  0.063      0.007        8.762    0.048       0.079
KNOWN              9.660      0.594       16.269    8.412      10.907

              TASKS      TASKS
  Case      Observed    Predicted    Residual
     1         0.0         0.063      -0.063
     2         0.0         0.253      -0.253
     3         0.0         0.570      -0.570
     4       1.000         1.013      -0.013
     5         0.0         1.583      -1.583
     6       1.000         2.280      -1.280
     7       1.000         3.103      -2.103
     8       6.000         4.053       1.947
     9       6.000         5.130       0.870
    10       6.000         5.909       0.091
    11       5.000         5.909      -0.909
    12       6.000         5.909       0.091
    13       6.000         5.909       0.091
    14       6.000         5.909       0.091
    15       6.000         5.909       0.091
    16       6.000         5.909       0.091
    17       6.000         5.909       0.091
    18       6.000         5.909       0.091
    19       6.000         5.909       0.091
    20       6.000         5.909       0.091

Asymptotic Correlation Matrix of Parameters
                       B           KNOWN
B                    1.000
KNOWN               -0.928         1.000
```

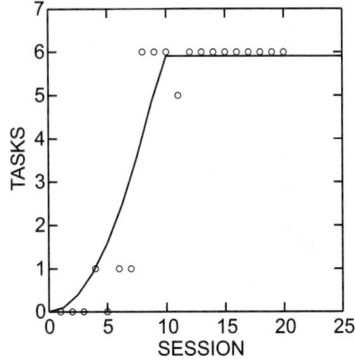

Chapter 3

From the Quick Graph, we see that the fit at the lower end is not impressive. We might want to fit a truncated logistic model instead of a quadratic because learning is more often represented with this type of function. This model would have a logistic curve at the lower values of *SESSION* and a flat ceiling line at the upper end. We should use a LOSS also to make the fit maximum likelihood.

Piecewise linear regression models with known breakpoints can be fitted similarly. These models look like this:

y = b0 + b1*x + b2*(x–break)*(x>break)

If the break point is known, then you could also use GLM to do ordinary regression to fit the separate pieces. See Neter, Wasserman, and Kutner (1985) for an example.

Example 11
Kinetic Models

You can also use NONLIN to test kinetic models. The following analysis models competitive inhibition for an enzyme inhibitor. The data are adapted from a conference session on statistical computing with microcomputers (Greco, et al., 1982). We will fit three variables: initial enzyme velocity (*V*), concentration of the substrate (*S*), and concentration of the inhibitor (*I*). The parameters of the model are the maximum velocity (*VMAX*), the Michaelis constant (*KM*) and the dissociation constant of the enzyme-inhibitor complex (*KIS*). The input is:

```
USE ENZYME
NONLIN
   PRINT = LONG
   MODEL V = VMAX*S / (KM*(1 + I/KIS) + S)
   ESTIMATE / MIN = 0,0,0
```

The output follows:

```
Iteration
  No.    Loss        VMAX         KM           KIS
    0 .356767D+01 .101000D+01 .102000D+01 .103000D+01
    1 .228856D+01 .100833D+01 .932638D+00 .122786D-06
    2 .228607D+01 .100847D+01 .932573D+00 .124013D-04
    3 .204340D+01 .102226D+01 .925997D+00 .125254D-02
    4 .269664D-01 .125640D+01 .818472D+00 .227823D-01
    5 .137491D-01 .125852D+01 .844568D+00 .268902D-01
    6 .136979D-01 .125946D+01 .846743D+00 .271757D-01
    7 .136979D-01 .125952D+01 .846854D+00 .271759D-01
    8 .136979D-01 .125952D+01 .846857D+00 .271760D-01
```

```
Dependent variable is V

    Source    Sum-of-Squares    df    Mean-Square
Regression         15.404        3        5.135
  Residual          0.014       43        0.000

     Total         15.418       46
Mean corrected      5.763       45

        Raw  R-square (1-Residual/Total)          =    0.999
Mean corrected R-square (1-Residual/Corrected)   =    0.998
        R(observed vs predicted) square          =    0.998

                                              Wald Confidence Interval
Parameter      Estimate    A.S.E.   Param/ASE    Lower < 95%> Upper
VMAX             1.260     0.012     104.191     1.235       1.284
KM               0.847     0.027      31.876     0.793       0.900
KIS              0.027     0.001      31.033     0.025       0.029
```

You could try alternative models for these data such as one for uncompetitive inhibition,

```
MODEL V = VMAX*S / (KM + S + S*I/KII)
```

or one for noncompetitive inhibition,

```
MODEL V = VMAX*S / (KM + KM/KIS + S + S*I/KII)
```

where *KII* is the dissociation constant of the enzyme-inhibitor-substrate complex.

Example 12
Minimizing an Analytic Function

You can also use NONLIN to find the minimum of an algebraic function. Since this requires no data, you need a trick. Use any data file. We do not use any of the variables in this file, but SYSTAT requires a data file to be open to do a nonlinear estimation. The minimization input is:

```
USE dose
NONLIN
LOSS=100*(U-V^2)^2+(1-V)^2
ESTIMATE / SIMPLEX
```

This particular function is from Rosenbrock (1960). We are using **SIMPLEX** to save space and because it generally does better with algebraic expressions which incur roundoff error. Here is the result:

```
Iteration
    No.     Loss          U           V
     0  .102098D+01    .1010D+01   .1020D+01
     1  .931215D+00    .1262D+01   .1126D+01
     2  .216987D-02    .1005D+01   .1003D+01
     3  .593092D-05    .9992D+00   .9996D+00
     4  .689847D-08    .1000D+01   .1000D+01
     5  .162557D-10    .1000D+01   .1000D+01
     6  .793924D-13    .1000D+01   .1000D+01
     7  .264812D-15    .1000D+01   .1000D+01
     8  .140037D-17    .1000D+01   .1000D+01
     9  .110445D-20    .1000D+01   .1000D+01
    10  .165203D-23    .1000D+01   .1000D+01
Final value of loss function is        0.000

                                              Wald Confidence Interval
Parameter       Estimate    A.S.E.  Param/ASE   Lower < 95%> Upper
U                 1.000        .         .         .         .
V                 1.000        .         .         .         .
```

Computation

Algorithms

The Quasi-Newton method is described in Fletcher (1972) and is sometimes called modified Fletcher/Powell. Modifications include the LDL' Cholesky factorization of the updated Hessian matrix. It is the same algorithm employed in **SERIES** for ARIMA estimation. The Simplex method is adapted from O'Neill (1971), with several revisions noted in Griffiths and Hill (1985).

The loss function is computed in two steps. First, the model statement is evaluated for a case using current values of the parameters and data. Second, the **LOSS** statement is evaluated using **ESTIMATE** (computed as the result of the model statement evaluation) and other parameter and data values. These two steps are repeated for all cases, over which the result of the loss function is summed. The summed **LOSS** is then minimized by the Quasi-Newton or Simplex procedure. Step halvings are used in the minimizations when model or loss statement evaluations overflow or result in illegal values. If repeated step halvings down to machine epsilon (error limit) fail to remedy this situation, iterations cease with an "Illegal values" message.

Asymptotic standard errors are computed by the central differencing finite approximation of the Hessian matrix. Some nonlinear regression programs compute standard errors by squaring the Jacobian matrix of first derivatives. Others use different methods altogether. For linear models, all valid methods produce identical results. For some nonlinear models, however, the results may differ. The Hessian approach, which works well for nonlinear regression, is also ideally suited for NONLIN's maximum likelihood estimation.

Missing Data

Missing values are handled according to the conventions of SYSTAT BASIC. That is, missing values propagate in algebraic expressions. For example, "X + ." is a missing value. The expression "X = ." is not missing, however. It is 1 if X is missing and 0 if not. Thus, you can use logical expressions to put conditions on model or loss functions; consider the following loss function:

(X<>.)*(Y - ESTIMATE)^2 + (X=.)*(Z - ESTIMATE)^2

Illegal expressions (such as division by 0 and negative square roots) are set to missing values. If this happens when computing the loss statement for a particular case, the loss function is set to an extremely large value (10^{35}). This way, parameter estimates are forced to move away from regions of the parameter space that yield illegal function evaluations.

Overflows (such as a positive number with an extremely large exponent) are set to machine overflow (10^{35}). Negative overflows are set to the negative of this value. Overflows usually cause the loss function to be large, so the program is forced to move away from estimates that produce overflows.

These features mean that NONLIN tends to "crash" less frequently than most other nonlinear estimation programs. It will continue for several iterations to try parameter values that lower the loss value, even when some of these lead to a seemingly hopeless result. It is your responsibility to check whether final estimates are reasonable, however, by using both estimation methods, different starting values, and other options.

References

Bates, D. M. and Watts, D. G. (1988). *Nonlinear regression and its applications*. New York: John Wiley & Sons, Inc.

Clark, G. P. Y. (1987). Approximate confidence limits for a parameter function in nonlinear regression, *Journal of the American Statistical Association*, 82, 221–230.

Cook, R. D. and Weisberg, S. (1990). Confidence curves in nonlinear regression, *Journal of the American Statistical Association*, 85, 544–551.

Cox, D. R. (1970). *The analysis of binary data*. New York: Halsted Press.

Fletcher, R. (1972). *FORTRAN subroutines for minimization by Quasi-Newton methods*. AERE R. 7125.

Griffiths, P. and Hill, I. D. (1985). *Applied statistics algorithms*. Chichester: Ellis Horwood Limited.

Gilfoil, D. M. (1982). Warming up to computers: A study of cognitive and affective interaction over time. In *Proceedings: Human factors in computer systems*. Washington, D.C.: Association for Computing Machinery.

Greco, W. R., et al. (1982). ROSFIT: An enzyme kinetics nonlinear regression curve fitting package for a microcomputer. *Computers and Biomedical Research*, 15, 39–45.

Hill, M. A. and Engelman, L. (1992). Graphical aids for nonlinear regression and discriminant analysis. *Computational Statistics,* vol. 2, Y. Dodge and J. Whittaker, eds. Proceedings of the 10th Symposium on Computational Statistics Physica-Verlag, 111–126.

Jennrich, R. I. and Moore, R. H. (1975). Maximum likelihood estimation by means of nonlinear least squares. *Proceedings of the Statistical Computing Section*, American Statistical Association, 57–65.

Neter, J., and Wasserman, W., and Kutner, M. (1985). *Applied linear statistical models*, 2nd ed. Homewood, Ill.: Richard D. Irwin, Inc.

O'Neill, R. (1971). Functions minimization usign a simplex procedure. Algorithms AS 47. *Applied Statistics*, 338.

Rousseeuw, P. J. and Leroy, A. M. (1987). *Robust regression and outlier detection*. New York: John Wiley & Sons, Inc.

Chapter

4

Nonparametric Statistics

Leland Wilkinson

Nonparametric tests compute nonparametric statistics for groups of cases and pairs of variables. Tests are available for two or more independent groups of cases, two or more dependent variables, and for the distribution of a single variable.

Nonparametric tests do not assume that the data conform to a particular probability distribution. Nonparametric models are often appropriate when the usual parameters, such as mean and standard deviation based on normal theory, do not apply. Usually, however, some other assumptions about shape and continuity are made. Note that if you can find normalizing transformations for your data that allow you to use parametric tests, you will usually be better off doing so.

Several nonparametric tests are available. The Kruskal-Wallis test and the two-sample Kolmogorov-Smirnov test measure differences of a single variable across two or more independent groups of cases. The sign test, the Wilcoxon signed-rank test, and the Friedman test measure differences among related samples. The one-sample Kolmogorov-Smirnov test and the Wald-Wolfowitz runs test examine the distribution of a single variable.

Many nonparametric statistics are computed elsewhere in SYSTAT. Correlations calculates matrices of coefficients, such as Spearman's rho, Kendall's tau-*b*, Guttman's mu2, and Goodman-Kruskal gamma. Descriptive Statistics offers stem-and-leaf plots, and Box Plot offers box plots with medians and quartiles. Time Series can perform nonmetric smoothing. Crosstabs can be used for chi-square tests of independence. Multidimensional Scaling (MDS) and Cluster Analysis work with nonmetric data matrices. Finally, you can use Rank to compute a variety of rank-order statistics.

Note: Beware of using nonparametric procedures to rescue bad data. In most cases, these procedures were designed to apply to categorical or ranked data, such as rank judgments and binary data. If you have data that violate distributional assumptions for linear models, you should consider transformations or robust models before retreating to nonparametrics.

Statistical Background

Nonparametric statistics is a misnomer. The term is ordinarily used to describe a heterogeneous group of procedures that require relatively minimal assumptions about the shape of distributions underlying an analysis. Frequently, however, nonparametric models include parameters. These parameters are not necessarily ones like μ and σ, which we see in typical parametric tests based on normal theory, but they are parameters in a class of mathematical functions nonetheless.

In this context, a better term for nonparametric is **distribution-free**. That is, the data for this class of statistical tests are not assumed to follow a specific probability distribution. This does not mean, however, that we make *no* assumptions about distributions in nonparametric methods. For example, in the Mann-Whitney and Kruskal-Wallis tests, we assume that the underlying populations are continuous and have the same shape.

Rank (Ordinal) Data

An aspect of many nonparametric tests is that they are invariant under *rank-order* transformations of the data values. In other words, we may change actual data values as long as we preserve relative ranks, and the results of our hypothesis tests will not change. Data that can be replaced by rank-order values without losing information are often called **rank** or **ordinal data**. For example, if we believe that the list (–25, 54, 107.6, 3400) contains only ordinal information, then we can replace it with the list (1, 2, 3, 4) without loss of information.

Categorical (Nominal) Data

Some nonparametric methods are invariant under *permutation* transformations. That is, we can interchange data values and get the same results, provided we keep all cases with one value before transformation single valued after transformation. Data that can be treated like this are often called **categorical** or **nominal**. For example, if we believe the list (1, 1, 5, 5, 10, 10, 10) contains only nominal information, then we can replace it with the list (red, red, green, green, blue, blue, blue) without loss of information.

Robustness

Sometimes, we may think our data contain more than nominal or ordinal information, but we want to be extremely conservative. For example, our data may contain extreme outliers. We could eliminate these outliers, downweight them, or apply some nonlinear transformation to reduce their influence. An alternative, however, would be to use a nonparametric test based on ranks. If we can afford to lose some power by using a nonparametric test, we can gain robustness. If we find significant results with a nonparametric test, no skeptic can challenge us on the basis of scale artifacts or outliers. This is not to say that you should retreat to nonparametric methods every time you find a histogram that does not look normal. If you can find a simple normalizing transformation that works, such as logging the data, you will almost always be better off using normal parametric methods.

Nonparametric Statistics for Independent Samples in SYSTAT

Kruskal-Wallis Main Dialog Box

For the Kruskal-Wallis test, the values of a variable are transformed to ranks (ignoring group membership) to test that there is no shift in the center of the groups (that is, the centers do not differ). This is the nonparametric analog of a one-way analysis of variance. When there are only two groups, this procedure reduces to the Mann-Whitney test, the nonparametric analog of the two-sample *t* test.

Chapter 4

To open the Kruskal-Wallis dialog box, from the menus choose:

Statistics
  Nonparametric Tests
    Kruskal-Wallis...

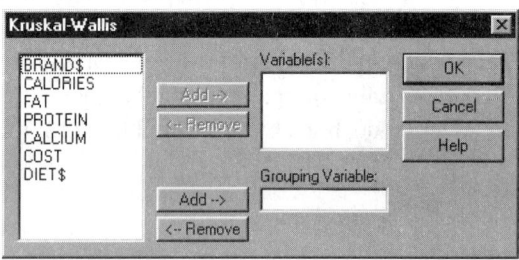

Variables(s). SYSTAT computes a separate test for each variable in the Variable(s) list.

Grouping Variable. The grouping variable can be string or numeric.

Two-Sample Kolmogorov-Smirnov Main Dialog Box

The two-sample Kolmogorov-Smirnov test tests whether two independent samples come from the same distribution by comparing the two-sample cumulative distribution functions. The test assumes that both samples come from exactly the same distribution. The distributions can be organized as two variables (two columns) or as a single variable (column) with a second variable that identifies group membership. The latter layout is necessary when sample sizes differ.

To open the Two-Sample Kolmogorov-Smirnov dialog box, from the menus choose:

Statistics
  Nonparametric Tests
    Two sample KS...

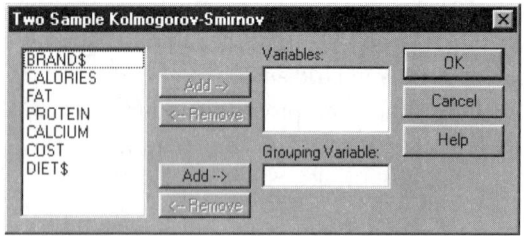

Nonparametric Statistics

Variable(s). If each sample is a separate variable, both variables must be selected. Selecting three or more variables yields a separate test for each pair of variables. If you select only one variable, you must identify the grouping variable.

Grouping Variable. If the grouping variable has three or more levels, separate tests of each pair of levels result. Selecting multiple variables and a grouping variable yields a test comparing the groups for the first variable only.

Using Commands

First, specify your data with USE filename. Continue with:

```
NPAR
    KRUSKAL varlist*grpvar
    KS varlist*grpvar
```

Nonparametric Statistics for Related Variables in SYSTAT

A need for comparing variables frequently arises in before and after studies, where each subject is measured before and after a treatment. Here your goal is to determine if any difference in response can be attributed to chance alone. As a test, researchers often use the sign test or the Wilcoxon signed-rank test. For these tests, the measurements need not be collected at different points in time; they simply can be two measures on the same scale for which you want to test differences. If you have more than two measures for each subject, the Friedman test can be used.

Sign Tests Main Dialog Box

The sign test compares two related samples and is analogous to the paired t test for parametric data. For each case, the sign test computes the sign of the difference between two variables. This test is attractive because of its simplicity and the fact that the variance of the first measure in each pair may differ from that of the second. However, you may be losing information since the magnitude of each difference is ignored.

To open the Sign Tests dialog box, from the menus choose:

Statistics
  Nonparametric Tests
    Sign…

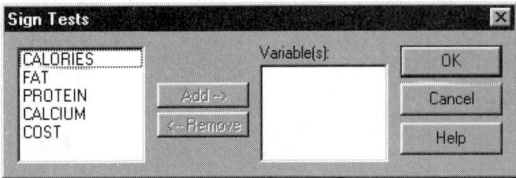

Selecting three or more variables yields separate tests for each pair of variables.

Wilcoxon Signed-Rank Test Main Dialog Box

To open the Wilcoxon Tests dialog box, from the menus choose:

Statistics
  Nonparametric Tests
    Wilcoxon…

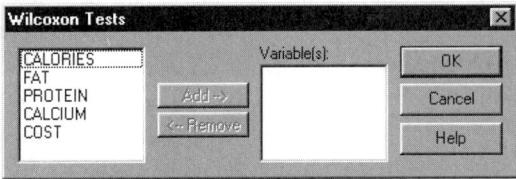

The Wilcoxon test compares the rank values of the variables you select, pair by pair, and displays the count of positive and negative differences. For ties, the average rank is assigned. It then computes the sum of ranks associated with positive differences and the sum of ranks associated with negative differences. The test statistic is the lesser of the two sums of ranks.

Friedman Tests Main Dialog Box

To open the Friedman Tests dialog box, from the menus choose:

Statistics
  Nonparametric Tests
    Friedman…

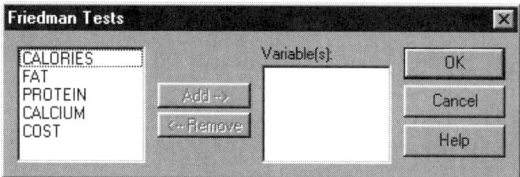

The Friedman test computes a Friedman two-way analysis of variance on selected variables. This test is a nonparametric extension of the paired t test, where, instead of two measures, each subject has n measures ($n > 2$). In other terms, it is a nonparametric analog of a repeated measures analyses of variance with one group. The Friedman test is often used for analyzing ranks of three or more objects by multiple judges. That is, there is one case for each judge and the variables are the judges' ratings of several types of wine, consumer products, or even how a set of mothers relate to their children. The Friedman statistic is used to test the hypothesis that there is no systematic response or pattern across the variables (ratings).

Using Commands

First, specify your data with USE filename. Continue with:

```
NPAR
    SIGN varlist
    WILCOXON varlist
    FRIEDMAN varlist
```

Nonparametric Statistics for Single Samples in SYSTAT

One-Sample Kolmogorov-Smirnov Main Dialog Box

The one-sample Kolmogorov-Smirnov test is used to compare the shape and location of a sample distribution to a specified distribution. The Kolmogorov-Smirnov test and its generalizations are among the handiest of distribution-free tests. The test statistic is based on the maximum difference between two cumulative distribution functions (CDF). In the one-sample test, one of the CDF's is continuous and the other is discrete. Thus, it is a companion test to a probability plot.

To open the One-Sample Kolmogorov-Smirnov dialog box, from the menus choose:

Statistics
  Nonparametric Tests
    One sample KS...

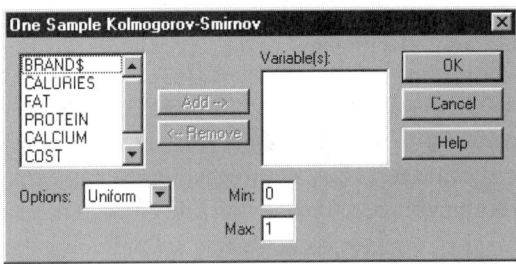

Options. Allows you to choose the test distribution. Many options allow you to specify parameters of the hypothesized distribution. For example, if you choose a Uniform distribution, you can specify values for Min and Max. Distributions include:

- **Uniform.** Compares the data to the uniform(a,b) distribution.
- **Normal.** Compares the data to the normal distribution with the specified mean and standard deviation.
- **t.** Compares the data to the *t* distribution with the specified degrees of freedom.
- **F.** Compares the data to the *F* distribution with the specified degrees of freedom.
- **ChiSQ.** Compares the data to the chi-square distribution with the specified degrees of freedom.
- **Gamma.** Compares the data to the gamma(a) distribution.
- **Beta.** Compares the data to the beta(a,b) distribution.
- **Exp.** Compares the data to the exponential distribution with mean equaling the location parameter and sd equaling the scale parameter.
- **Logistic.** Compares the data to logistic distribution with the specified location parameter (mean) and scale parameter (sd).
- **Range.** Compares the data to the Studentized range(n,p) distribution.
- **Weibull.** Compares the data to the Weibull(n,p) distribution.
- **Binomial.** Compares the data to the binomial(n,p) distribution.

Nonparametric Statistics

- **Poisson.** Compares the data to the Poisson distribution with mean=lambda.
- **Lilliefors.** The Lilliefors test uses the standard normal distribution. The variables you select are automatically standardized, and the test determines whether the standardized versions are normally distributed.

Wald-Wolfowitz Runs Main Dialog Box

The Wald-Wolfowitz runs test detects serial patterns in a run of numbers (for example, runs of heads or tails in a series of coin tosses). The runs test measures such behavior for dichotomous (or binary) variables.

To open the Wald-Wolfowitz Runs dialog box, from the menus choose:

Statistics
  Nonparametric Tests
    Wald-Wolfowitz Runs...

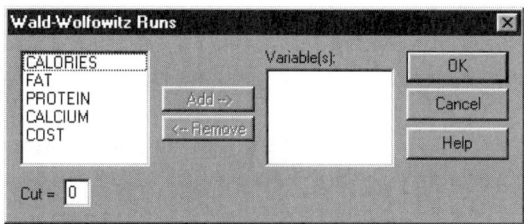

For continuous variables, use Cut to define a cutpoint to determine whether values fluctuate in patterns above and below this cutpoint. This feature is useful for studying trends in residuals from a regression analysis.

Using Commands

First, specify your data with USE filename. Continue with:

```
NPAR
    RUNS varlist / CUT=n
    KS varlist / distribution=parameters
```

Possible distributions for the Kolmogorov-Smirnov test include:

Distribution	Parameters	Distribution	Parameters
UNIFORM	min, max	NORMAL	mean, SD
T	df	F	df1, df2
CHISQ	df	GAMMA	a
BETA	a, b	EXP	mean, SD
LOGISTIC	mean, SD	RANGE	n, p
WEIBULL	n, p	BINOMIAL	n, p
POISSON	lambda	LILLIEFORS	

Usage Considerations

Types of data. NPAR uses rectangular data only.

Print options. The output is standard for all PRINT lengths.

Quick Graphs. NPAR produces no Quick Graphs.

Saving files. NPAR saves no statistics.

BY groups. You can perform tests using a BY variable. The output includes separate tests for each level of the BY variable.

Bootstrapping. Bootstrapping is available in this procedure.

Case frequencies. NPAR uses a FREQUENCY variable (if present) to increase the number of cases in the analysis.

Case weights. WEIGHT variables have no effect in NPAR.

Examples

Example 1
Kruskal-Wallis Test

For two or more independent groups, the Kruskal-Wallis test statistic tests whether the k samples come from identically distributed populations. If the grouping variable has only two levels, the Mann-Whitney (Wilcoxon) statistic is reported. For two groups,

Nonparametric Statistics

the Kruskal-Wallis test and the Mann-Whitney *U* statistic are analogous to the independent groups *t* test.

In this example, we compare the percentage of people who live in cities (*URBAN*) for three groups of countries: European, Islamic, and New World. We use the *OURWORLD* data file that has one record for each of 57 countries with the variables *URBAN* and *GROUP$*. We include a box plot of *URBAN* grouped by *GROUP$* to illustrate the test. The input is:

```
NPAR
    USE ourworld
    DENSITY urban * group$ / BOX   TRANS
    KRUSKAL urban * group$
```

The output follows:

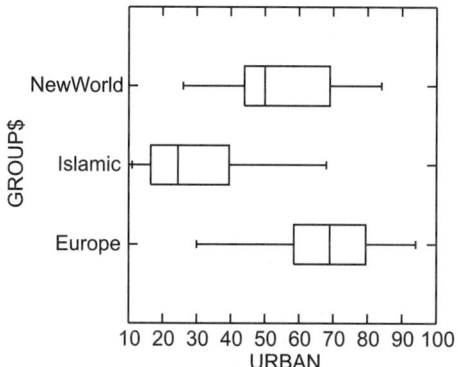

```
Categorical values encountered during processing are:
GROUP$ (3 levels)
   Europe, Islamic, NewWorld

Kruskal-Wallis One-Way Analysis of Variance for 56 cases
Dependent variable is URBAN
 Grouping variable is GROUP$

       Group      Count    Rank Sum

       Europe        19     765.000
       Islamic       16     198.000
       NewWorld      21     633.000

Kruskal-Wallis Test Statistic =      25.759
Probability is              0.000 assuming Chi-square distribution with 2 df
```

In the box plot, the median of each distribution is marked by the vertical bar inside the box: the median for European countries is 69%; for Islamic countries, 24.5%; and for New World countries, 50%. We ask, "Is there a difference in typical values of *URBAN* among these groups of countries?"

Looking at the Kruskal-Wallis results, we find a p value < 0.0005. We conclude that urbanization differs markedly across the three groups of countries.

Example 2
Mann-Whitney Test

When there are only two groups, Kruskal-Wallis provides the Mann-Whitney test. Note that your grouping variable must contain exactly two values. Here we modify the Kruskal-Wallis example by deleting the Islamic group. We ask, "Do European nations tend to be more urban than New World countries?" The input is:

```
NPAR
    USE ourworld
    SELECT group$ <> 'Islamic'
    KRUSKAL urban * group$
```

The output follows:

```
Categorical values encountered during processing are:
GROUP$ (2 levels)
   Europe, NewWorld

Kruskal-Wallis One-Way Analysis of Variance for 40 cases
Dependent variable is URBAN
 Grouping variable is GROUP$

      Group         Count    Rank Sum

      Europe          19       475.000
      NewWorld        21       345.000
Mann-Whitney U test statistic =        285.000
Probability is         0.020
Chi-square approximation =             5.370 with 1 df
```

The percentage of population living in urban areas is significantly greater for European countries than for New World countries (p value = 0.02).

Example 3
Two-Sample Kolmogorov-Smirnov Test

The two-sample Kolmogorov-Smirnov test measures the discrepancy between two-sample cumulative distribution functions.

In this example, we test if the distributions of *URBAN*, the proportion of people living in cities, for European and New World countries have the same mean, standard deviation, and shape. The input is:

```
NPAR
    USE ourworld
    SELECT group$ <> 'Islamic'
    KS urban * group$
```

The output follows:

```
Kolmogorov-Smirnov Two Sample Test results
  Maximum differences for pairs of groups
              Europe      NewWorld
      Europe    0.0
    NewWorld    0.520       0.0
  Two-sided probabilities
              Europe      NewWorld
      Europe    .
    NewWorld    0.009       .
```

The two distributions differ significantly (p value = 0.009).

Example 4
Sign Test

Here, for a sample of countries (not subjects), we ask, "Does life expectancy differ for males and females?" Using the *OURWORLD* data, we compare *LIFEEXPF* and *LIFEEXPM*, using stem-and-leaf plots to illustrate the distributions. The sign test counts the number of times male life expectancy is greater than that for females and vice versa.

The input is:

```
STATISTICS
    USE ourworld
    STEM lifeexpf lifeexpm / LINES=10
NPAR
    SIGN lifeexpf lifeexpm
```

The output follows:

```
Stem and Leaf Plot of variable:          Stem and Leaf Plot of variable:
LIFEEXPF, N = 57                         LIFEEXPM, N = 57
        Minimum:         44.000                  Minimum:         40.000
        Lower hinge:     65.000                  Lower hinge:     61.000
        Median:          75.000                  Median:          68.000
        Upper hinge:     79.000                  Upper hinge:     73.000
        Maximum:         83.000                  Maximum:         75.000

        4   4                                    4   0
        4   679                                  * * * Outside Values * * *
        5   0234                                 4   56789
        5   55667                                5   122334
        6   4                                    5   6
        6 H 567788889                            6 H 01222444
        7   01344                                6 M 5556778899
        7 M 5666777778889999                     7 H 001111223333333334444
        8   0000111111223                        7   55555


Sign test results
   Counts of differences (row variable greater than column)
                 LIFEEXPM        LIFEEXPF
   LIFEEXPM            0               2
   LIFEEXPF           55               0


   Two-sided probabilities for each pair of variables
                 LIFEEXPM        LIFEEXPF
   LIFEEXPM        1.000
   LIFEEXPF        0.000           1.000
```

For each case, SYSTAT first reports the number of differences that were positive and the number that were negative. In two countries (Afghanistan and Bangladesh), the males live longer than the females; the reverse is true for the other 55 countries. Note that the layout of this output allows reports for many pairs of variables.

In the two-sided probabilities panel, the smaller count of differences (positive or negative) is compared to the total number of nonzero differences. SYSTAT computes a sign test on all possible pairs of specified variables. For each pair, the difference between values on each case is calculated, and the number of positive and negative differences is printed. The lesser of the two types of difference (positive or negative) is then compared to the total number of nonzero differences. From this comparison, the probability is computed according to the binomial (for a total less than or equal to 25) or a normal approximation to the binomial (for a total greater than 25). A correction for continuity (0.5) is added to the normal approximation's numerator, and the denominator is computed from the null value of 0.5. The large sample test is thus equivalent to a chi-square test for an underlying proportion of 0.5. The probability for our test is 0.000 (or < 0.0005). We conclude that there is a significant difference in life expectancy; females tend to live longer.

Example 5
Wilcoxon Test

Here, as in the sign test example, we ask, "Does life expectancy differ for males and females?" The input is:

```
USE ourworld
NPAR
    WILCOXON lifeexpf lifeexpm
```

The output is:

```
Wilcoxon Signed Ranks Test Results

  Counts of differences (row variable greater than column)
              LIFEEXPM      LIFEEXPF
LIFEEXPM           0             2
LIFEEXPF          55             0


  Z = (Sum of signed ranks)/square root(sum of squared ranks)
              LIFEEXPM      LIFEEXPF
LIFEEXPM         0.0
LIFEEXPF         6.535         0.0


  Two-sided probabilities using normal approximation
              LIFEEXPM      LIFEEXPF
LIFEEXPM         1.000
LIFEEXPF         0.000         1.000
```

Two-sided probabilities are computed from an approximate normal variate (Z in the output) constructed from the lesser of the sum of the positive ranks and the sum of the negative ranks (for example, Marascuilo and McSweeney, 1977, p. 338). The Z for our test is 6.535 with a probability less than 0.0005. As with the sign test, we conclude that females tend to live longer.

Example 6
Sign and Wilcoxon Tests for Multiple Variables

SYSTAT can compute a sign or Wilcoxon test on all pairs of specified variables (or all numeric variables in your file). To illustrate the layout of the output, we add two more variables to our request for a sign test: the birth-to-death ratios in 1982 and 1990. The input follows:

```
NPAR
    USE ourworld
    SIGN b_to_d82 b_to_d lifeexpm lifeexpf
```

The resulting output is:

```
Sign test results

  Counts of differences (row variable greater than column)
                B_TO_D82       LIFEEXPM       LIFEEXPF       B_TO_D
  B_TO_D82          0              0              0             17
  LIFEEXPM         57              0              2             57
  LIFEEXPF         57             55              0             57
  B_TO_D           36              0              0              0


  Two-sided probabilities for each pair of variables
                B_TO_D82       LIFEEXPM       LIFEEXPF       B_TO_D
  B_TO_D82       1.000
  LIFEEXPM       0.000          1.000
  LIFEEXPF       0.000          0.000          1.000
  B_TO_D         0.013          0.000          0.000          1.000
```

The results contain some meaningless data. SYSTAT has ordered the variables as they appear in the data file. When you specify more than two variables, there may be just a few numbers of interest. In the first column, the birth-to-death ratio in 1982 is compared with the birth-to-death ratio in 1990—and with male and female life expectancy! Only the last entry is relevant—36 countries have larger ratios in 1990 than they did in 1982. In the last column, you see that 17 countries have smaller ratios in 1990. The life expectancy comparisons you saw in the last example are in the middle of this table. In the two-sided probabilities panel, the probability for the birth-to-death ratio comparison (0.013) is at the bottom of the first column. We conclude that the ratio is significantly larger in 1990 than it was in 1982. Does this mean that the number of births is increasing or that the number of deaths is decreasing?

Example 7
Friedman Test

In this example, we study dollars that each country spends per person for education, health, and the military. We ask, "Do the typical values for the three expenditures differ significantly?" We stratify our analysis and look within each type of country separately. Here are the median expenditures:

	EDUCATION	HEALTH	MILITARY
Europe	496.28	502.01	271.15
Islamic	13.67	4.28	22.80
New World	57.39	22.73	29.02

Nonparametric Statistics

The input is:

```
NPAR
USE ourworld
BY group$
FRIEDMAN educ health mil
```

The output is:

```
The following results are for:
   GROUP$       = Europe

Friedman Two-Way Analysis of Variance Results for 20 cases.

     Variable        Rank Sum

     EDUC            43.000
     HEALTH          52.000
     MIL             25.000


Friedman Test Statistic =      18.900
Kendall Coefficient of Concordance =       0.472
Probability is         0.000 assuming Chi-square distribution with 2 df

The following results are for:
   GROUP$       = Islamic

Friedman Two-Way Analysis of Variance Results for 15 cases.

     Variable        Rank Sum

     EDUC            37.500
     HEALTH          17.000
     MIL             35.500


Friedman Test Statistic =      17.033
Kendall Coefficient of Concordance =       0.568
Probability is         0.000 assuming Chi-square distribution with 2 df

The following results are for:
   GROUP$       = NewWorld

Friedman Two-Way Analysis of Variance Results for 21 cases.

     Variable        Rank Sum

     EDUC            56.000
     HEALTH          31.500
     MIL             38.500


Friedman Test Statistic =      15.167
Kendall Coefficient of Concordance =       0.361
Probability is         0.001 assuming Chi-square distribution with 2 df
```

The Friedman test transforms the data for each country to ranks (1 for the smallest value, 2 for the next, and 3 for the largest) and then sums the ranks for each variable.

Thus, if each country spent the least on the military, the rank rum for *MIL* would be 20. The largest the rank sum could be is 60 (20 * 3). For these three countries, no expenditure is always the smallest or largest. In addition to the rank sums, SYSTAT reports the Kendall coefficient of concordance, an estimate of the average correlation among the expenditures.

For all three countries, we reject the hypothesis that the expenditures are equal.

Example 8
One-Sample Kolmogorov-Smirnov Test

In this example, we use SYSTAT's random number generator to make a normally distributed random number and then test it for normality. We use the variable *Z* as our normal random number and the variable *ZS* as a standardized copy of *Z*. This may seem strange because normal random numbers are expected to have a mean of 0 and a standard deviation of 1. This is not exactly true in a sample, however, so we standardize the observed values to make a variable that has exactly a mean of 0 and a standard deviation of 1. The input follows:

```
BASIC
    NEW
    REPEAT 50
    LET z=zrn
    LET zs=z
    RUN
    SAVE NORM
    STAND ZS/SD
USE norm
STATISTICS
STATS
NPAR
KS z zs / NORMAL
```

We use STATISTICS to examine the mean and standard deviation of our two variables. Remember, if you correlated these two variables, the Pearson correlation would be 1. Only their mean and standard deviations differ. Finally, we test *Z* for normality.

The output is:

```
                            Z            ZS
N of cases                 50            50
Minimum                -2.194        -2.271
Maximum                 1.832         1.932
Mean                   -0.018         0.000
Standard Dev            0.958         1.000

Kolmogorov-Smirnov One Sample Test using Normal(0.00,1.00) distribution

   Variable       N-of-Cases      MaxDif   Probability (2-tail)

   Z                  50.000       0.069          0.969
   ZS                 50.000       0.065          0.983
```

Why are the probabilities different? The one-sample Kolmogorov-Smirnov test pays attention to the shape, location, and scale of the sample distribution. Z and ZS have the same shape in the population (they are both normal). Because ZS has been standardized, however, it has a different location.

Thus, you should never use the Kolmogorov-Smirnov test with the normal distribution on a variable you have standardized. The probability printed for ZS (0.983) is misleading. If you select ChiSq, Normal, or Uniform, you are assuming that the variable you are testing has been randomly sampled from a standard normal, uniform (0 to 1), or chi-square (with stated degrees of freedom) population.

Lilliefors Test

Here we perform a Lilliefors test using the data generated for the one-sample Kolmogorov-Smirnov example. Note that Lilliefors automatically standardizes the variables you list and tests whether the standardized versions are normally distributed. The input is:

```
USE norm
    KS z zs / LILLIEFORS
```

The output is:

```
Kolmogorov-Smirnov One Sample Test using Normal(0.00,1.00) distribution

   Variable       N-of-Cases      MaxDif   Lilliefors Probability (2-tail)

   Z                  50.000       0.065          0.895
   ZS                 50.000       0.065          0.895
```

Notice that the probabilities are smaller this time even though *MaxDif* is the same as before. The probability values for Z and ZS (0.895) are the same because this test pays attention only to the shape of the distribution and not to the location or scale. Neither significantly differs from normal.

This example was constructed to contrast Normal and Lilliefors. Many statistical package users do a Kolmogorov-Smirnov test for normality on their standardized data without realizing that they should instead do a Lilliefors test.

One last point: The Lilliefors test can be used for residual analysis in regression. Just standardize your residuals and use Nonparametric Tests to test them for normality. If you do this, you should always look at the corresponding normal probability plot.

Example 9
Wald-Wolfowitz Runs Test

We use the *OURWORLD* file and cut *MIL* (dollars per person each country spends on the military) at its median and see whether countries with higher military expenditures are grouped together in the file. (Be careful when you use a cutpoint on a continuous variable, however. Your conclusions can change depending on the cutpoint you use.) We include a scatterplot of the military expenditures against the case number (order of each country in the file), adding a dotted line at the cutpoint of 53.889. The input is:

```
NPAR
   USE ourworld
   RUNS mil / CUT=53.889
   IF (country$='Iraq' or country$='Libya' or country$='Canada'),
      THEN LET country2$=country$
   PLOT mil / LINE DASH=11 YLIM=53.9 LABEL=country2$ SYMBOL=2
```

Following is the output:

```
Wald-Wolfowitz runs test using cutpoint =        53.889
                                                                Probability
   Variable    Cases LE Cut   Cases GT Cut   Runs       Z        (2-tail)

   MIL              28             28         17     -3.237        0.001
```

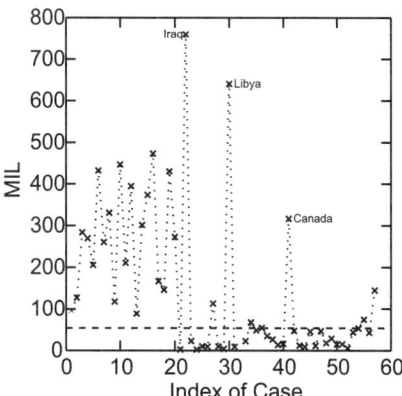

The test is significant (*p* value = 0.001). The military expenditures are not ordered randomly in the file.

The European countries are first in the file, followed by Islamic and New World. Looking at the plot, notice that the first 20 cases exceed the median. The remaining cases are for the most part below the median. Iraq, Libya, and Canada stand apart from the other countries in their group. When the line joining the *MIL* values crosses the median line, a new run begins. Thus, the plot illustrates the 17 runs.

Computation

Algorithms

Probabilities for the Kolmogorov-Smirnov statistic for $n < 25$ are computed with an asymptotic negative exponential approximation.

Lilliefors probabilities are computed by a nonlinear approximation to Lilliefors' table. Dallal and Wilkinson (1986) recomputed Lilliefors' study using up to a million replications for estimating critical values. They found a number of Lilliefors' value to be incorrect. Consequently, the SYSTAT approximation uses the corrected values. The approximation discussed in Dallal and Wilkinson and used in SYSTAT differs from the tabled values by less than 0.01 and by less than 0.001 for $p < 0.05$.

References

Conover, W. J. (1980). *Practical nonparametric statistics.* 2nd ed. New York: John Wiley & Sons, Inc.

Hollander, M. and Wolfe, D. A. (1973). *Nonparametric statistical methods.* New York: John Wiley & Sons, Inc.

Lehmann, E. L. (1975). *Nonparametrics.* San Francisco: Holden-Day, Inc.

Marascuilo, L. A. and McSweeney, M. (1977). *Nonparametric and distribution-free methods for the social sciences.* Belmont, Calif.: Wadsworth Publishing.

Mosteller, F. and Rourke, R. E. K. (1973). *Sturdy statistics.* Reading, Mass.: Addison-Wesley.

Siegel, S. (1956). *Nonparametric statistics for the behavioral sciences.* New York: McGraw-Hill.

Chapter 5

Partially Ordered Scalogram Analysis with Coordinates

Leland Wilkinson, Samuel Shye, Reuben Amar, and Louis Guttman

The POSAC module calculates a partial order scalogram analysis on a set of multicategory items. It consolidates duplicate data profiles, computes profile similarity coefficients, and iteratively computes a configuration of points in a two-dimensional space according to the partial order model. POSAC produces Quick Graphs of the configuration, labeled by either profile values or an ID variable. Shye (1985) is the authoritative reference on POSAC. See also Borg's review (1987) for more information. The best approach to setting up a study for POSAC analysis is to use facet theory (see Canter, 1985).

Statistical Background

The figure below shows a pattern of bits in two dimensions, an instance of a partially ordered set (POSET). There are several interesting things about this pattern.

- The vertical dimension of the pattern runs from four 1's on the top to no 1's on the bottom.
- The horizontal dimension runs from 1's on the left to 1's in the center to 1's on the right.
- Except for the bottom row, each bit pattern is the result of an OR operation of the two bit patterns below itself, as denoted by the arrows in the figure. For example, (1111) = (1110) or (0111).
- There are $2^4 = 16$ possible patterns for four bits. Only 11 patterns meet the above requirements in two dimensions. The remaining patterns are: (1011), (1101), (1010), (0101), and (1001).

- This structure is a *lattice*. We can move things around and still represent the POSET geometrically as long as none of the arrows cross or head down instead of up.

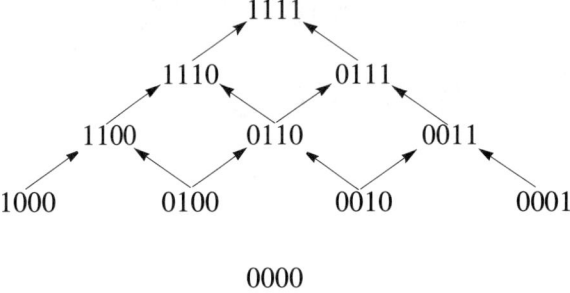

Suppose we had real binary data involving presence or absence of attributes and wanted to determine whether our data fit a POSET structure. We would have to do the following:

- Order the attributes from left to right so that the horizontal dimension would show 1's moving from left to right in the plotted profile, as in the figure above.
- Sort the profiles of attributes from top to bottom.
- Sort the profiles from left to right.
- Locate any profiles not fitting the pattern and make sure the overall solution was not influenced by them.

The fourth requirement is somewhat elusive and depends on the first. That is, if we had patterns (1010) and (0101), exchanging the second and third bits would yield (1100) and (0011), which would give us two extreme profiles in the third row rather than two ill-fitting profiles. If we exchange bits for one profile, we must exchange them for all, however. Thus, the global solution depends on the order of the bits as well as their positioning.

POSAC stands for partially ordered scalogram analysis with coordinates. The algorithm underlying POSAC computes the ordering and the lattice for cases-by-attributes data. Developed originally by Louis Guttman and Shmuel Shye, POSAC fits not only binary, but also multivalued data, into a two-dimensional space according to the constraints we have discussed.

The following figure (a multivalue POSET) shows a partial ordering on some multivalue profiles. Again, we see that the marginal values increase on the vertical dimension (from 0 to 1 to 2 to 4 to 8) and the horizontal dimension distinguishes left and right skew.

Partially Ordered Scalogram Analysis with Coordinates

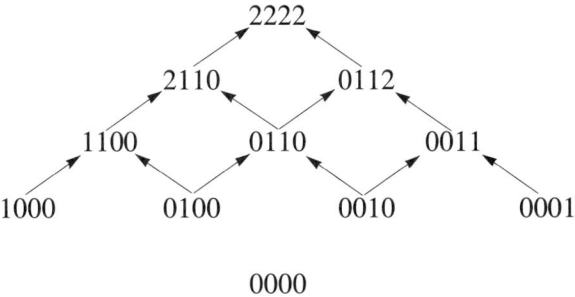

The following figure shows this distributional positioning more generally. For ordered profiles with many values on each attribute, we expect the central profiles in the POSAC to be symmetrically distributed, profiles to the left to be right-skewed, and profiles to the right to be left-skewed.

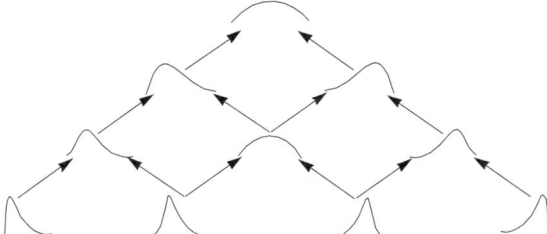

Coordinates

There are two standard coordinate systems for displaying profiles. The first uses joint and lateral dimensions to display the profiles as in the figures above. Profiles that have similar sum scores fall at approximately the same latitude in this coordinate system. Comparable profiles differing in their sum scores (for example, 112211 and 223322) fall above and below each other at the same longitude.

The second coordinate display, the one printed in the SYSTAT plots, is a 45-degree rotation of this set. These base coordinates have the joint dimension running from southwest to northeast and the lateral dimension running from northwest to southeast. The diamond pattern is transformed into a square.

POSAC in SYSTAT

POSAC Main Dialog Box

To open the POSAC dialog box, from the menus choose:

Statistics
  Data Reduction
    POSAC...

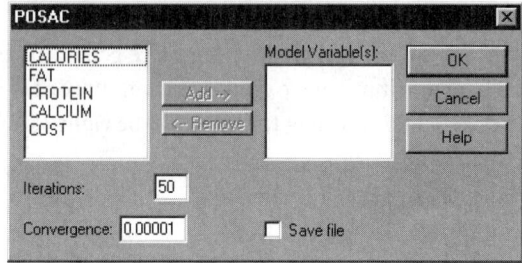

Model Variable(s). Specify the items to be scaled.

Iterations. Enter the maximum number of iterations that you wish to allow the program to perform in order to estimate the parameters.

Convergence. Enter the convergence criterion. This is the largest relative change in any coordinate before iterations terminate.

Using Commands

After selecting a file with USE filename, continue with:

```
POSAC
     MODEL varlist
     ESTIMATE / ITER=n,CONVERGE=d
```

The FREQ command is useful when data are aggregated and there is a variable in the file representing frequency of profiles.

Usage Considerations

Types of data. POSAC uses rectangular data only. It is most suited for data with up to nine categories per item. If your data have more than nine categories, the profile labels will not be informative, since each item is displayed with a single digit in the profile labels. If your data have many more categories in an item, the program may refuse the computation. Similarly, POSAC can handle many items, but its interpretability and usefulness as an analytical tool declines after 10 or 20 items. These practical limitations are comparable to those for loglinear modeling and analysis of contingency tables, which become complex and problematic for multiway tables.

Print options. The output is the same for all PRINT options.

Quick Graphs. POSAC produces a Quick Graph of the coordinates labeled either with value profiles or an ID variable.

Saving files. POSAC saves the configuration into a SYSTAT file.

BY groups. POSAC analyzes data by groups. Your file need not be sorted on the BY variable(s).

Bootstrapping. Bootstrapping is available in this procedure.

Case frequencies. FREQ=<variable> increases the number of cases by the FREQ variable.

Case weights. WEIGHT is not available in POSAC.

Examples

The following examples illustrate the features of the POSAC module. The first example involves binary profiles that fit the POSAC model perfectly. The second example shows an analysis for real binary data. The third example shows how POSAC works for multicategory data.

Chapter 5

Example 1
Scalogram Analysis—A Perfect Fit

The file *BIT5* contains five-item binary profiles fitting a two-dimensional structure perfectly. The input is:

```
USE BIT5
POSAC
MODEL X(1)..X(5)
ESTIMATE
```

The resulting output is:

```
Variables in the SYSTAT Rectangular file are:
  X(1..5)

Reordered item weak monotonicity coefficients

                    X(5)        X(4)        X(3)        X(2)        X(1)

       X(5)        1.000
       X(4)        0.750       1.000
       X(3)        0.111       0.667       1.000
       X(2)       -0.286       0.0         0.667       1.000
       X(1)       -0.391      -0.286       0.111       0.750       1.000


Iteration  Loss
---------------
     1     0.019009
     2     0.005559
     3     0.000291
     4     0.000000

Final loss value:         0.000
Proportion of profile pairs correctly represented:        1.000
Score-distance weighted coefficient:        1.000
              Label       DIM 1       DIM 2       Joint       Lateral      Fit
              11111       1.000       1.000       1.000       0.500        0.0
              01111       0.933       0.667       0.800       0.633        0.0
              11110       0.667       0.933       0.800       0.367        0.0
              01110       0.600       0.600       0.600       0.500        0.0
              00111       0.867       0.400       0.633       0.733        0.0
              11100       0.400       0.867       0.633       0.267        0.0
              01100       0.333       0.533       0.433       0.400        0.0
              00011       0.800       0.200       0.500       0.800        0.0
              11000       0.200       0.800       0.500       0.200        0.0
              00110       0.533       0.333       0.433       0.600        0.0
              00100       0.267       0.267       0.267       0.500        0.0
              10000       0.067       0.733       0.400       0.167        0.0
              00010       0.467       0.133       0.300       0.667        0.0
              00001       0.733       0.067       0.400       0.833        0.0
              01000       0.133       0.467       0.300       0.333        0.0
              00000       0.000       0.000       0.000       0.500        0.0
EXPORT successfully completed.
```

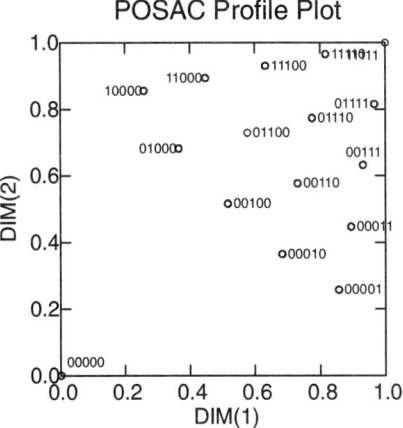

POSAC first computes Guttman monotonicity coefficients and orders the matrix of them using an SSA (multidimensional scaling) algorithm. These monotonicity coefficients, which Shye (1985) discusses in detail, are similar to the MU2 coefficients in the SYSTAT CORR module.

The next section of the output shows the iteration history and computed coordinates. SYSTAT's POSAC module calculates the square roots of the coordinates before display and plotting. This is done in order to make the lateral direction linear rather than curvilinear. Notice that for the perfect data in this example, the profiles are confined to the upper right triangle of the plot, as in the theoretical examples in Shye (1985). If you are comparing output with the earlier Jerusulem program, remember to include this transformation. Notice that the profiles are ordered in both the joint and lateral directions.

Example 2
Binary Profiles

The following data are reports of fear symptoms by selected United States soldiers after being withdrawn from World War II combat. The data were originally reported by Suchman in Stouffer et al. (1950). Notice that we use FREQ to represent duplicate profiles.

Chapter 5

The input is:

```
USE COMBAT
FREQ=COUNT
POSAC
MODEL POUNDING..URINE
ESTIMATE
```

The resulting output is:

```
Variables in the SYSTAT Rectangular file are:
 POUNDING    SINKING     SHAKING     NAUSEOUS    STIFF       FAINT
 VOMIT       BOWELS      URINE       COUNT

  Case frequencies determined by value of variable COUNT.

Reordered item weak monotonicity coefficients
```

	STIFF	VOMIT	NAUSEOUS	FAINT	SINKING
STIFF	1.000				
VOMIT	0.682	1.000			
NAUSEOUS	0.728	0.815	1.000		
FAINT	0.716	0.665	0.844	1.000	
SINKING	0.583	0.381	0.706	0.644	1.000
SHAKING	0.829	0.495	0.661	0.729	0.705
BOWELS	0.751	0.780	0.780	0.761	0.513
URINE	0.782	0.589	1.000	0.846	1.000
POUNDING	0.290	0.443	0.615	0.569	0.449

	SHAKING	BOWELS	URINE	POUNDING
SHAKING	1.000			
BOWELS	0.617	1.000		
URINE	0.763	0.960	1.000	
POUNDING	0.709	1.000	1.000	1.000

```
Iteration  Loss
---------------
   1       4.611967
   2       2.260031
   3       1.193905
   4       0.877537
   5       0.898418

Final loss value:         0.878
Proportion of profile pairs correctly represented:      0.810
Score-distance weighted coefficient:          0.977
```

Label	DIM 1	DIM 2	Joint	Lateral	Fit
111111111	1.000	1.000	1.000	0.500	0.0
111111101	0.918	0.980	0.949	0.469	2.577
101111111	0.939	0.878	0.908	0.531	10.242
111111001	0.857	0.898	0.878	0.480	11.973
111110101	0.694	0.755	0.724	0.469	13.251
101111101	0.816	0.837	0.827	0.490	7.571
101111011	0.878	0.816	0.847	0.531	9.357
111101001	0.306	0.939	0.622	0.184	8.880
011111001	0.959	0.510	0.735	0.724	6.641
101111001	0.714	0.653	0.684	0.531	10.411
111011001	0.653	0.796	0.724	0.429	11.101
110111001	0.551	0.714	0.633	0.418	8.689
011110001	0.796	0.388	0.592	0.704	7.238
001111001	0.776	0.490	0.633	0.643	4.255
100111001	0.490	0.673	0.582	0.408	6.911
111001001	0.265	0.918	0.592	0.173	12.063
011011001	0.837	0.347	0.592	0.745	9.030

```
111100001    0.245    0.857    0.551    0.194    10.225
111010001    0.469    0.694    0.582    0.388    13.307
011010101    0.898    0.245    0.571    0.827     5.937
001010111    0.980    0.184    0.582    0.898     1.793
101011001    0.531    0.612    0.571    0.459     8.332
101011000    0.061    0.735    0.398    0.163     8.936
111010000    0.041    0.959    0.500    0.041     9.716
001011001    0.633    0.306    0.469    0.663     4.639
100001101    0.286    0.776    0.531    0.255    18.117
101010001    0.408    0.551    0.480    0.429     6.088
011010001    0.755    0.224    0.490    0.765    10.334
001110001    0.673    0.327    0.500    0.673     7.902
110010001    0.388    0.633    0.510    0.378     9.413
000111001    0.612    0.286    0.449    0.663     6.454
101001001    0.224    0.592    0.408    0.316     6.892
100011001    0.429    0.531    0.480    0.449     7.752
001010001    0.449    0.082    0.265    0.684     7.128
000011001    0.510    0.265    0.388    0.622     8.843
000110001    0.592    0.163    0.378    0.714     7.337
000010001    0.327    0.122    0.224    0.602     1.155
100000001    0.082    0.449    0.265    0.316     5.579
001000001    0.367    0.143    0.255    0.612     7.827
000011000    0.204    0.367    0.286    0.418     9.295
001100000    0.184    0.469    0.327    0.357    10.533
100010000    0.020    0.571    0.296    0.224    10.084
000001001    0.347    0.204    0.276    0.571     8.718
000000101    0.735    0.041    0.388    0.847    15.543
010000001    0.571    0.102    0.337    0.735    18.115
000000001    0.163    0.020    0.092    0.571     6.259
000100000    0.122    0.408    0.265    0.357    10.401
010000000    0.143    0.429    0.286    0.357    13.698
000010000    0.102    0.061    0.082    0.520    11.087
000000000
EXPORT successfully completed.
```

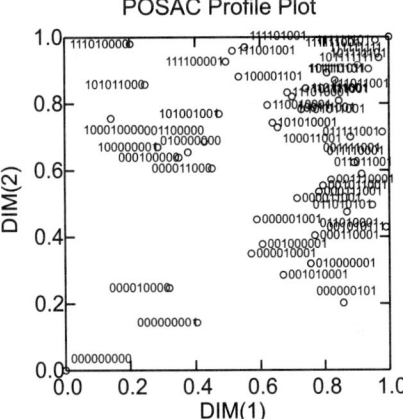

POSAC Profile Plot

The output shows an initial ordering of the symptoms that, according to the SSA, runs from stiffness to loss of urine and bowel control and a pounding heart. The lateral dimension follows this general ordering. Notice that the joint dimension runs from absence of symptoms to presence of all symptoms.

Example 3
Multiple Categories

This example uses the crime data to construct a 2D solution of crime patterns. We first recode the data into four categories for each item by using the CUT function. The cuts are made at each standard deviation and the mean. Then, POSAC computes the coordinates for these four category profiles. The input is:

```
USE CRIME
STANDARDIZE MURDER..AUTOTHFT
LET (MURDER..AUTOTHFT)=CUT(@,-1,0,1,4)
POSAC
MODEL MURDER..AUTOTHFT
ESTIMATE
```

The resulting output is:

```
Reordered item weak monotonicity coefficients

                LARCENY    AUTOTHFT    BURGLARY    ROBBERY    RAPE
    LARCENY     1.0000
    AUTOTHFT    0.8215     1.0000
    BURGLARY    0.9302     0.9497      1.0000
    ROBBERY     0.8058     0.9003      0.8677      1.0000
    RAPE        0.7858     0.7314      0.8504      0.9220     1.0000
    ASSAULT     0.5161     0.6669      0.7424      0.8788     0.9207
    MURDER      0.2802     0.4826      0.5793      0.6500     0.8230

                ASSAULT    MURDER
    ASSAULT     1.0000
    MURDER      0.9650     1.0000

Iteration  Loss
---------------
    1      0.451041
    2      0.332829
    3      0.130639
    4      0.101641
    5      0.085226
    6      0.091481

Final loss value:       0.0852
Proportion of profile pairs correctly represented:      0.8163
Score-distance weighted coefficient:         0.9939
        Label        DIM 1       DIM 2       Joint       Lateral         Fit
      4444444
      4444443       0.9242      0.9895      0.9569      0.4673        2.0147
      4343344       0.9574      0.8416      0.8995      0.5579        4.7697
      4344433       0.8292      0.9465      0.8878      0.4413        2.5764
      4343443       0.8165      0.9354      0.8760      0.4405        1.9954
      4443432       0.7071      0.9789      0.8430      0.3641        1.0454
      4443333       0.8539      0.9682      0.9111      0.4428        2.5587
      3444243       0.7638      0.9014      0.8326      0.4312        3.1705
      3334443       0.8660      0.8780      0.8720      0.4940        1.5690
      3334433       0.8416      0.8539      0.8478      0.4939        1.1482
      3333334       0.9354      0.8165      0.8760      0.5595        2.0266
      2323444       0.9895      0.6455      0.8175      0.6720        0.4374
      3333333       0.7773      0.8292      0.8032      0.4741        0.5635
```

Partially Ordered Scalogram Analysis with Coordinates

```
3324333    0.8036    0.8036    0.8036    0.5000    3.8324
3322434    0.8898    0.7071    0.7984    0.5913    4.1468
3332333    0.7360    0.7773    0.7566    0.4793    2.5768
4442212    0.3819    0.9574    0.6697    0.2122    2.1545
4233322    0.5951    0.9242    0.7597    0.3355    3.0452
2232334    0.9465    0.6292    0.7878    0.6587    0.6921
4242322    0.5774    0.9129    0.7451    0.3322    2.6240
2222244    0.9682    0.5590    0.7636    0.7046    2.3395
1222344    0.9789    0.3536    0.6662    0.8127    2.1700
3323322    0.6455    0.7906    0.7180    0.4275    1.7497
3432122    0.4330    0.8898    0.6614    0.2716    4.2661
2323322    0.6922    0.6614    0.6768    0.5154    2.6771
2333222    0.6614    0.7217    0.6916    0.4699    2.3523
2222234    0.9129    0.5774    0.7451    0.6678    1.9414
3222233    0.6770    0.7360    0.7065    0.4705    2.0523
2432222    0.7500    0.7638    0.7569    0.4931    6.8248
2332222    0.6292    0.6770    0.6531    0.4761    2.8814
4222222    0.5590    0.8660    0.7125    0.3465    0.9197
1122333    0.7906    0.4787    0.6346    0.6559    4.2385
3222222    0.5401    0.7500    0.6450    0.3950    1.7113
1222233    0.7217    0.4082    0.5650    0.6567    2.2306
1222224    0.9014    0.2887    0.5950    0.8064    1.8188
1223222    0.6124    0.6124    0.6124    0.5000    6.1082
1112234    0.8780    0.2041    0.5410    0.8369    1.2590
2222222    0.5204    0.5401    0.5302    0.4902    1.1929
3122222    0.3536    0.6922    0.5229    0.3307    5.8713
2222211    0.4564    0.5000    0.4782    0.4782    2.5150
2212221    0.5000    0.5204    0.5102    0.4898    2.9364
2112212    0.4787    0.4564    0.4676    0.5111    3.5318
2212111    0.2500    0.5951    0.4226    0.3274    2.8411
1112122    0.4082    0.2500    0.3291    0.5791    2.1351
1212111    0.3227    0.3819    0.3523    0.4704    2.9375
1121211    0.2887    0.3227    0.3057    0.4830    3.6207
2111111    0.1443    0.4330    0.2887    0.3557    3.4967
1112111    0.2041    0.1443    0.1742    0.5299    0.3086
1111111
```

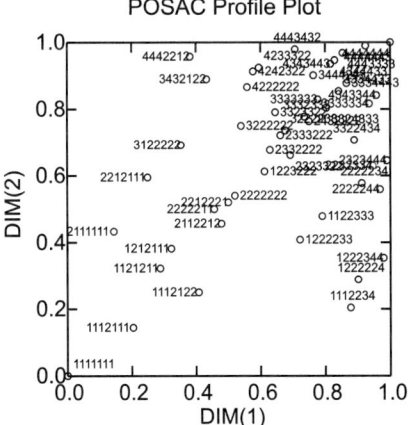

The configuration plot is labeled with the profile values. We can see that the larger values generally fall in the upper extreme of the joint (diagonal) dimension. The lateral dimension runs basically according to the ordering of the initial SSA, from property crimes at the left end of each profile to person crimes at the right end. POSAC thus has organized the states in two dimensions by frequency (low versus high) and by type of crime (person versus property).

If we add

    IDVAR=STATE$

before the ESTIMATE command, we can label the points with the state names. The result is shown in the following POSAC profile plot:

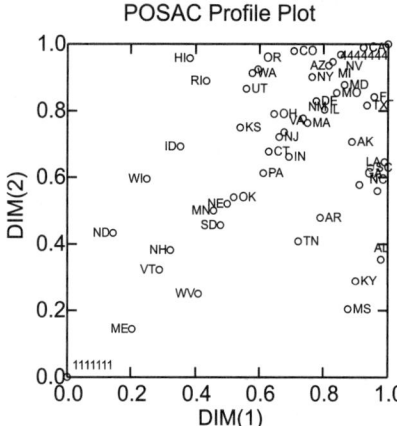

POSAC and MDS

To see how the POSAC compares to a multidimensional scaling, we ran an MDS on the transposed crime data. The following input program illustrates several important points about SYSTAT and data analyses in this context. Our goal is to run an MDS on the distances (differences) between states on crime incidence for the seven crimes. First, we standardize the variables so that all of the crimes have a comparable influence on the differences between states. This prevents a high-frequency crime, like auto theft, from unduly influencing the crime differences. Next, we add a *LABEL$* variable to the file because TRANSPOSE renames the variables with its values if a variable with this name is found in the source file. We save the transposed file into *TCRIME* and then use

CORR to compute Euclidean distances between the states. MDS then is used to analyze the matrix of pairwise distances of the states ranging from Maine to Hawaii (the two-letter state names are from the U.S. Post Office designations).

We save the MDS configuration instead of looking at the plot immediately because we want to do one more thing. We are going to make the symbol sizes proportional to the standardized level of the crimes (by summing them into a *TOTAL* crime variable). States with the highest value on this variable rank highest, in general, on all crimes. By merging *SCRIME* (produced by the original standardization) and *CONF* (produced by MDS), we retain the labels and the crime values and the configuration coordinates.

```
USE CRIME
STANDARDIZE MURDER..AUTOTHFT
SAVE SCRIME
RUN
CORR
USE SCRIME
LET LABEL$=STATE$
TRANSPOSE MURDER..AUTOTHFT
SAVE TCRIME
EUCLID ME..HI
MDS
USE TCRIME
MODEL ME..HI
SAVE CONF / CONFIG
ESTIMATE
MERGE CONF SCRIME
LET TOTAL=SUM(MURDER..AUTOTHFT)
PLOT DIM(2)*DIM(1)/SIZE=TOTAL,LAB=STATE$,LEGEND=NONE
```

The resulting graph follows:

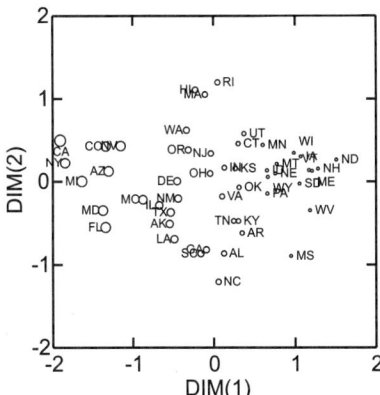

Notice that the first dimension comprises a frequency of crime factor since the size of the symbols is generally larger on the left. This dimension is not much different from the joint dimension in the POSAC configuration. The second dimension, however, is less interpretable than the POSAC lateral dimension. It is not clearly person versus property.

Computation

Calculations are in single precision for profile categories, with double precision variables used where needed in the minimization to ensure accuracy.

Algorithms

POSAC uses algorithms developed by Louis Guttman and Samuel Shye. The SYSTAT program is a recoding of the Hebrew University version using different minimization algorithms, an SSA procedure to reorder the profiles according to a suggestion of Guttman, and a memory model which allows large problems.

Missing Data

Profiles with missing data are excluded from the calculations.

References

Borg, I. (1987). Review of S. Shye, Multiple scaling. *Psychometrika,* 52, 304–307.
Borg, I. and Shye, S. (1995). *Facet theory: Form and content*. Thousand Oaks, Calif.: Sage Publications.
Canter, D., ed. (1985). *Facet theory approaches to social research*. New York: Springer Verlag.
Shye, S., ed. (1978). *Theory construction and data analysis in the behavioral sciences*. San Francisco, Calif.: Jossey-Bass.
Shye, S. (1985). *Multiple scaling: The theory and application of Partial Order Scalogram Analysis*. Amsterdam: North-Holland.
Stouffer, S. A., Guttman, L., Suchman, E. A., Lazarsfeld, P. F., Staf, S. A., and Clausen, J. A. (1950). *Measurement and Prediction*. Princeton, N.J.: Princeton University Press.

Chapter 6

Path Analysis (RAMONA)

Michael W. Browne and Gerhard Mels

RAMONA implements the McArdle and McDonald Reticular Action Model (RAM) for path analysis with manifest and latent variables. Input to the program is coded directly from a path diagram without reference to any matrices.

RAMONA stands for *RAM Or Near* Approximation. The deviation from RAM is minor—no distinction is made between residual variables and other latent variables. As in RAM, only two parameter matrices are involved in the model. One represents single-headed arrows in the path diagram (path coefficients) and the other, double-headed arrows (covariance relationships).

RAMONA can correctly fit path analysis models to correlation matrices, and it avoids the errors associated with treating a correlation matrix as if it were a covariance matrix (Cudeck, 1989). Furthermore, you can request that both exogenous and endogenous latent variable variances have unit variances. Consequently, estimates of standardized path coefficients, with the associated standard errors, can be obtained, and difficulties associated with the interpretation of unstandardized path coefficients (Bollen, 1989) can be avoided.

Statistical Background

The Path Diagram

The input file for RAMONA is coded directly from a path diagram. We first briefly review the main characteristics of path diagrams. More information can be found in texts dealing with structural equation modeling (Bollen, 1989; Everitt, 1984; and McDonald, 1985).

Chapter 6

Look at the path diagram on the following page. This is a model, adapted from Jöreskog (1977), for a study of the stability of attitudes over time conducted by Wheaton, Muthén, Alwin, and Summers (1977). Attitude scales measuring anomia (*ANOMIA*) and powerlessness (*POWRLS*) were regarded as indicators of the latent variable alienation (*ALNTN*) and administered to 932 persons in 1967 and 1971. A socioeconomic index (*SEI*) and years of school completed (*EDUCTN*) were regarded as indicators of the latent variable socioeconomic status (*SES*).

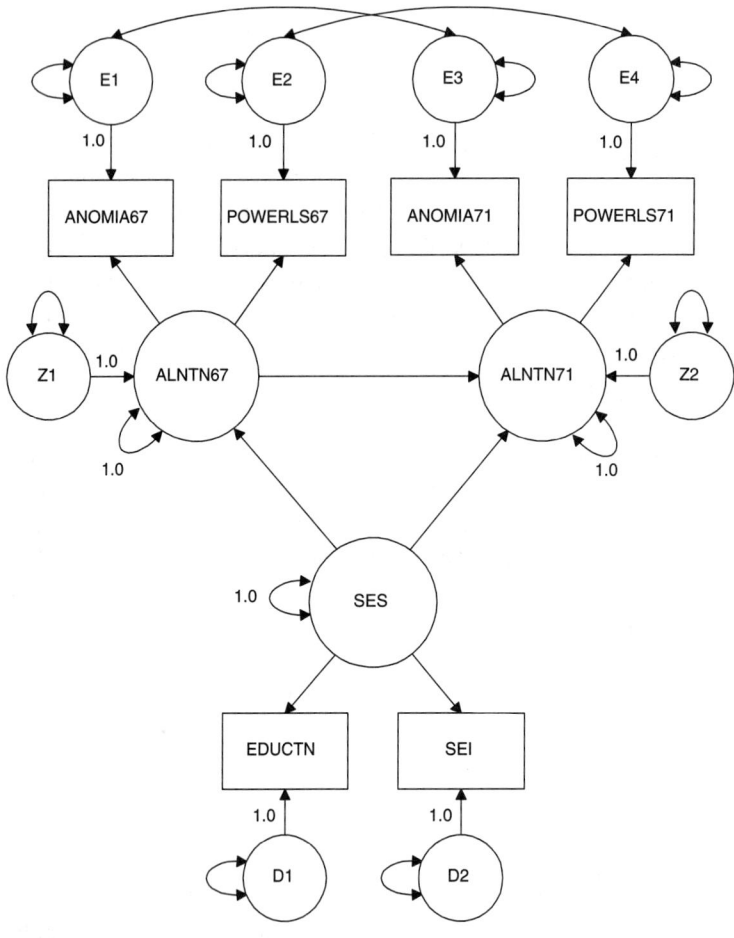

In the path diagram, a manifest (observed) variable is represented by a square or rectangular box:

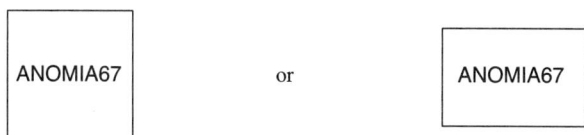

while a circle or ellipse signifies a latent (unobservable) variable:

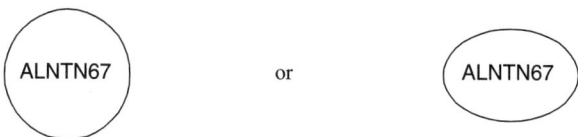

A **dependence path** is represented by a single-headed arrow emitted by the *explanatory* variable and received by the *dependent* variable:

while a **covariance path** is represented by a double-headed arrow:

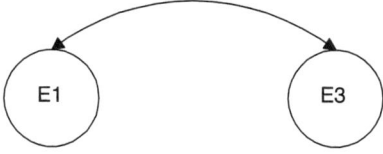

In many diagrams, **variance paths** are omitted. Because variances form an essential part of a model and must be specified for RAMONA, we represent them here explicitly by curved double-headed arrows (McArdle, 1988) with both heads touching the same circle or square:

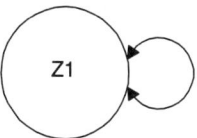

If a path coefficient, variance, or covariance is fixed (at a nonzero value), we attach the value to the single- or double-headed arrow:

A variable that acts as an explanatory variable in all of its dependence relationships (emits single-headed arrows but does not receive any) is **exogenous** (outside the system):

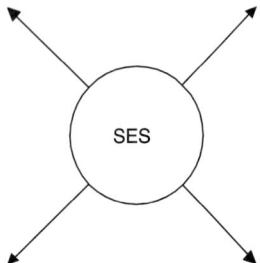

A variable that acts as a dependent variable in at least one dependence relationship (receives at least one single-headed arrow) is **endogenous** (inside the system), whether or not it ever acts as an explanatory variable (emits any arrows):

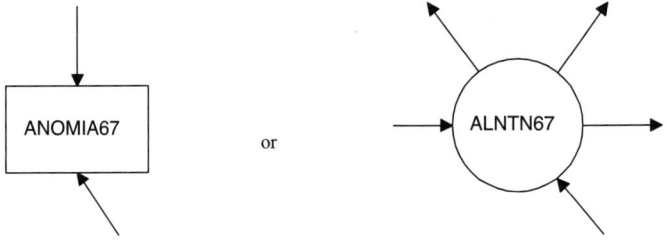

A parameter in RAMONA is associated with each dependence path and covariance path between two exogenous variables. Covariance paths are permitted only between exogenous variables. For example, the following covariance paths are permissible:

Permissible

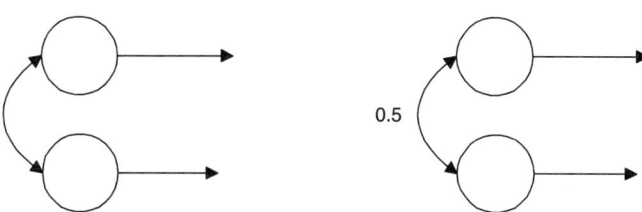

Variances and covariances of endogenous variables are implied by the corresponding explanatory variables and have no associated parameters in the model. Thus, an endogenous variable may not have a covariance path with any other variable. The covariance is a function of path coefficients and variances or covariances of exogenous variables and is not represented by a parameter in the model. The following covariance paths, for example, are not permissible:

Not permissible

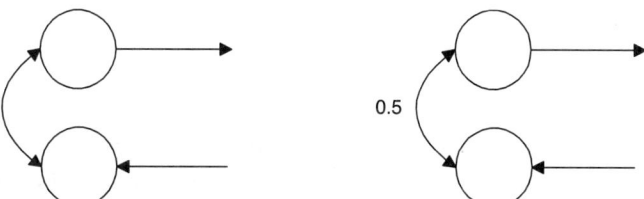

Also, an endogenous variable does not have a free parameter representing its variance. Its variance is a *function* of the path coefficients and variances of its explanatory variables. Therefore, it may not have an associated double-headed arrow with no fixed value:

Not permissible

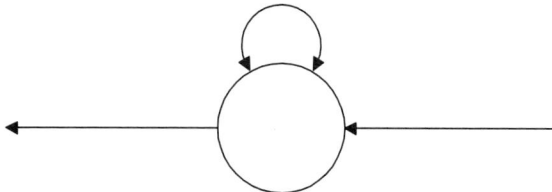

Exogenous variables alone may have free parameters representing their variances:

Permissible

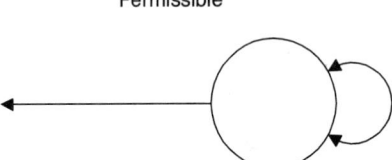

We do, however, allow *fixed* variances for both endogenous and exogenous variables. These two types of fixed variances are interpreted differently in the program:

- A fixed variance for an endogenous variable is treated as a nonlinear equality constraint on the parameters in the model:

Constraint

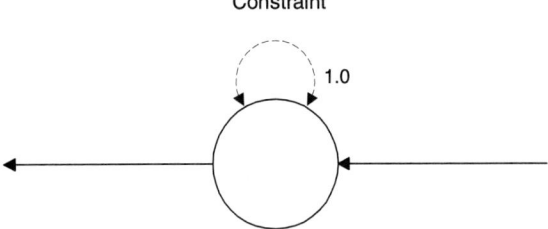

The fixed implied variance is represented by a dotted two-headed arrow instead of a solid two-headed arrow because it is a nonlinear constraint on several other parameters in the model and does not have a single fixed parameter associated with it.

- A fixed variance for an exogenous variable is treated as a model parameter with a fixed value:

Parameter

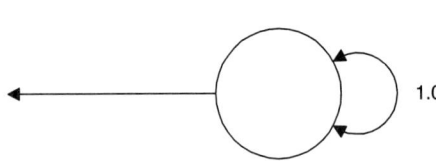

Every latent variable must emit at least one arrow. No latent variable can receive arrows without emitting any:

Not permissible

The scale of every latent variable (exogenous or endogenous) should be fixed to avoid indeterminate parameter values. Some ways for accomplishing this are:

- To fix one of the path coefficients, associated with an emitted arrow, to a nonzero value (usually 1.0):

- To fix both the variance and path coefficient of an associated error term, if the latent variable is endogenous (for example, Jöreskog and Goldberger, 1975):

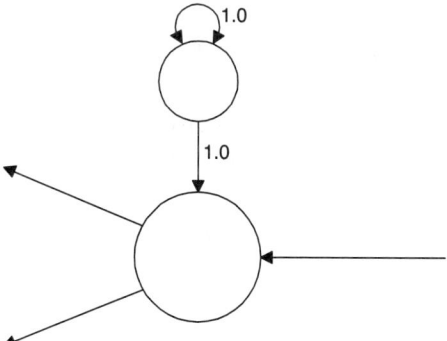

Chapter 6

- To fix the variance of the latent variable:

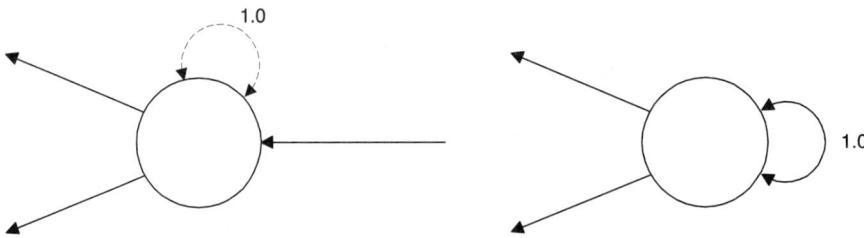

If a latent variable is endogenous and the third method is used, RAMONA fixes the implied variance by means of equality constraints. Programs that do not have this facility require the user to employ the first or second method to determine the scales of endogenous latent variables.

Consider *ALNTN67* in the path diagram. This latent variable is endogenous (it receives arrows from *SES* and *Z1*). It also emits arrows to *ANOMIA67* and *POWRLS67*. Consequently, it is necessary to fix either the variance of *ALNTN67*, the path coefficient from *ALNTN67* to *ANOMIA67*, the path coefficient from *ALNTN67* to *POWRLS67*, or the variance of *Z1*. It is conventional to use 1.0 as the fixed value. Our preference is to use the third method and fix the variance of *ALNTN67* rather than use the first or second method because we find standardized path coefficients easier to interpret (Bollen, 1989). The first two methods result in latent variables with non-unit variances. RAMONA does, however, allow the use of these methods.

The model shown in the path diagram is equivalent to Jöreskog's (1977) model but makes use of different identification conditions. We apply nonlinear equality constraints to fix the variances of the endogenous variables *ALNTN67* and *ALNTN71*, but treat the path coefficients from *ALNTN67* to *ANOMIA67* and from *ALNTN71* to *ANOMIA71* as free parameters. Jöreskog fixed the path coefficients from *ALNTN67* to *ANONMIA67* and from *ALNTN71* to *ANOMIA71* and did not apply any nonlinear equality constraints.

An error term is an exogenous latent variable that emits only one single-headed arrow and shares double-headed arrows only with other error terms. In the path diagram, the variables *E1*, *E2*, *E3*, *E4*, *D1*, *D2*, *Z1*, and *Z2* are error terms. RAMONA treats error terms in exactly the same manner as other latent variables.

RAMONA's Model

Let v_1 be a $p \times 1$ vector of manifest variables, v_2 be an $m \times 1$ vector of latent variables, and let

$$v = \begin{bmatrix} v_1 \\ v_2 \end{bmatrix} \qquad \text{Equation 6-1}$$

be the $t \times 1$ vector ($t = p + m$) representing all variables in the system, manifest and latent. Suppose that B is a $t \times t$ matrix of path coefficients. The path coefficient corresponding to the directed arrow from the jth element, v_j, of v to the ith element, v_i, will appear in the ith row and jth column of B. Let v_x be a $t \times 1$ vector formed from v by replacing all elements corresponding to non-null rows of B by zeros. Thus, v_x consists of exogenous variables with endogenous variables replaced by zeros. The system of directed paths represented in the path diagram is then given by:

$$v = Bv + v_x \qquad \text{Equation 6-2}$$

The formulation of the model given in Equation 6-1 differs only slightly from that of RAM (McArdle and McDonald, 1984). All non-null elements of v_x are also elements of v. Also, the non-null elements of v_x can, in some situations, be common factors rather than residuals. Let

$$\Phi = \text{Cov}(v_x, v_x')$$

be the $t \times t$ covariance matrix of v_x. Thus, the nonzero elements of Φ are parameters associated with two-headed arrows in the path diagram. Null rows and columns of Φ will be associated with endogenous variables in v.

Let $\Upsilon = \text{Cov}(v, v')$. It follows from Equation 6-2 that (McArdle and McDonald)

$$\Upsilon = (I - B)^{-1} \Phi (I - B')^{-1} \qquad \text{Equation 6-3}$$

The manifest variable covariance matrix $\Sigma = \text{Cov}(v_1, v_1')$ is the first $p \times p$ submatrix of Υ (see Equation 6-1). Specified values may be assigned to exogenous variable covariances by applying constraints to appropriate diagonal elements of Υ.

The structural model employed by RAMONA is given in Equation 6-3. Both B and Φ are large matrices with most of their elements equal to 0. Their nonzero elements alone are stored in RAMONA. Sparse matrix methods are used in the computation of $(I-B)^{-1}$ and Υ. Details can be found in Mels (1988).

The covariance structure in Equation 6-3 differs from a formulation of Bentler and Weeks (1980) in that there is a single matrix, B, for path coefficients instead of two.

Structural equation models are often fitted to sample correlation matrices. There are many published studies where this has been done incorrectly (Cudeck, 1989). RAMONA fits a correlation structure by introducing a duplicate standardized variable, v_i^*, with unit variance to correspond to each manifest variable v_i, $i \leq p$, and then taking

$$v_i = \sigma_i v_i^* \text{ for } i \leq p$$

where σ_i stands for the standard deviation of v_i. The duplicate variables are treated in the same way as latent variables—with variances constrained to unity if they are endogenous and fixed at unity if they are exogenous. Also, the standard deviation, σ_i, is treated in the same way as a path coefficient. This procedure is equivalent to expressing the manifest variable covariance matrix in the form

$$\Sigma = D_\sigma P D_\sigma$$

where D_σ is a diagonal matrix with the σ_i, $i \leq p$, as diagonal elements, and P is the manifest variable correlation matrix, which is treated as the covariance matrix of the standardized duplicate variables v_i^*, $i \leq p$. Fitting the model to a sample correlation matrix instead of a sample covariance matrix results in the estimates $\hat{\sigma}_i$ being replaced by $\hat{\sigma}_i/s_i$, where s_i is a sample standard deviation. These quantities are referred to as *Scaled Standard Deviations (nuisance parameters)* in the output. Other parameter estimates are not affected.

This approach involves the introduction of p additional parameters, σ_i, and p additional constraints on the variances of the v_i^*. The number of degrees of freedom is not affected (unless some parameters or constraints are redundant), but computation time is increased because of the additional parameters and additional constraints.

Path Analysis in SYSTAT

RAMONA Model Main Dialog Box

To open the RAMONA Model dialog box, from the menus choose:

Statistics
  Path Analysis (RAMONA)...

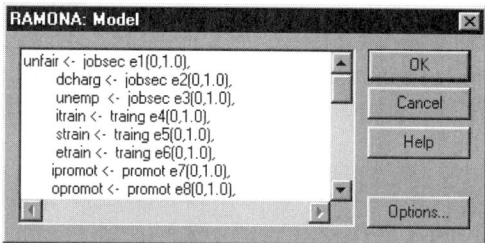

Specify the paths or relationships in the path diagram. Include a statement for each arrow. SYSTAT checks each variable to determine whether it is in the input file. (If it is in the file, SYSTAT considers it manifest; if not, it is considered latent).

The relationships represented in the path diagram are of two types: dependence and covariance. These relationships may be specified in any order. Parameter numbers and values, if not the default values, are specified in parentheses after the variable name.

Dependence Relationships

A dependence relationship is indicated by the symbol <-, which relates directly to a single-headed arrow in the path diagram. To code a dependence path, enter the descriptive name of the dependent variable followed by the symbol <-. Then name the explanatory variable, including the parameter number and the starting value for the parameter involved within parentheses. For example,

dependent <- explanatory(1, 0.6)

The parameter number is an integer used to indicate fixed parameters or parameters whose values are constrained to be equal. A fixed parameter must have a parameter number of 0. Any free parameters whose values are required to be equal are assigned the same parameter number. A free parameter that is not constrained to equality with any other parameter may be assigned the symbol * instead of a parameter number. Its parameter number is assigned within the program.

The starting value is a real number and is used to initialize the iterative process. Some rules for choosing starting values are given by Bollen (1989). If you have difficulty in deciding on a starting value, you can replace it with a *. The program then chooses a very rough starting value. If a parameter is fixed with a 0 as the parameter number, then the fixed value must replace the starting value. It is not permissible to use a * instead of the fixed value.

Inspection of the path diagram in the "Statistical Background" section shows that the endogenous manifest variable *POWRLS67* receives single-headed arrows from the latent variable *ALNTN67* and the measurement error *Z1*. These dependence relationships can be coded as:

powrls67 <- alntn67(*,*),
powrls67 <- e2(0,1.0)

In the first path, the parameter is free and not constrained to equality with any other parameter. The parameter number is replaced by a *. No starting value is specified and it is replaced by a *. The parameter in the second path is fixed at 1.0 so that the parameter number is 0 and the parameter value is 1.0.

The default is (*,*), so it is not necessary to type it:

powrls67 <- alntn67,
powrls67 <- e2(0,1.0)

It is not necessary to have a different statement for each path. Several paths with the same dependent (receiving) variable can be combined into one statement. Since the same endogenous variable, *POWRLS67*, is involved in two dependence relationships, the two paths can be coded in a single statement as:

powrls67 <- alntn67 e2(0,1.0)

If the statement continues to a second line, place a comma at the end of the first line.

Constraining parameters. If you want to constrain two or more free parameters to be equal, the parameters are assigned the same nonzero positive integer for the parameter number. Suppose you want to constrain the path coefficient from *SES* to *ALNTN67* and from *SES* to *ALNTN71* to be equal. You can specify:

alntn67 <- ses(7,*) z1(0,1.0),
alntn71 <- alntn67 ses(7,*) z2(0,1.0)

Providing starting values. You can provide starting values for free parameters. Suppose that it is known from a previous run that the path coefficient of *ALNTN67* to *ALNTN71* is approximately 0.6. In this case, you can specify the following:

alntn71 <- alntn67(*,0.6) ses(7,*) z2(0,1.0)

When specifying dependence relationships, bear in mind that:

- Dependence relationships can be specified in any order.
- A statement can specify several dependence paths involving the same dependent variable.
- Specified path numbers need not be sequential; for example, 5, 3, 9 can be used. Sequential path numbers will be reassigned by the program.

Covariance Relationships

A variance or a covariance relationship is indicated by the symbol <->, which relates directly to the double-headed arrow in the path diagram. To specify a covariance path, enter the name of one of the variables in the path, followed by the symbol <->. Then enter the name of the other variable, and include the path number and the starting value within parentheses. Unlike the dependence relationship, it does not matter which variable is given first. For example,

e2 <-> e2(10,*)

You can replace the number and/or the starting value of a free parameter with the symbol *. In this case, they are provided by the program. In the case of a fixed parameter, however, you must specify 0 as the number of the parameter and provide the fixed value of the parameter.

Inspection of the path diagram shows that double-headed arrows are used from the measurement error *E1* to itself to specify a variance and to *E3* to specify a covariance. These relationships are specified in the statement:

e1 <-> e1(*,*) e3(*,*)

or

e1 <-> e1 e3

Covariance paths can be constrained to be equal in the same manner as dependence paths. Suppose you want to specify that the variances of the measurement errors *E1*, *E2*, and *E3* must be equal:

e1 <-> e1(10,*) e3,
e2 <-> e2(10,*),
e3 <-> e3(10,*)

You can again provide starting values for free parameters:

e3 <-> e3(*,0.32)

Variances of both exogenous and endogenous variables can be required to have fixed values. Thus, both

ses <-> ses(0,1.0)

and

altntn67 <-> altntn67(0,1.0)

are acceptable. They are, however, treated differently within the program. The exogenous latent variable, *SES*, has a parameter associated with its variance and it is set equal to 1.0. There is no parameter representing the variance of the endogenous latent variable, *ALNTN67*. This variance is a function of the path coefficient, *ALNTN67 <- SES*, the variance of *SES*, and the variance of *Z1*. It is constrained to have a value of 1.0 by RAMONA.

When specifying covariance relationships, bear in mind that:

- Covariance paths can be specified in any order.
- Several covariance paths per statement can be specified. For example, the variance of an exogenous variable as well as its covariances with other exogenous variables can be specified in the same statement.
- Dependence paths and covariance paths must be specified in separate substatements. The dependence path subparagraph must precede the covariance path subparagraph.
- If every manifest endogenous variable has a corresponding measurement error with an unconstrained variance, the coding of these variances can be omitted. When all error path coefficients are fixed and no error variance paths are input for the measurement errors, the program will automatically provide the error variance paths.

- If there are exogenous manifest variables and if all of their variances and covariances are present in the system and are unrestricted, the coding of these variance and covariance paths can be omitted. When no variance and covariance paths for exogenous manifest variables are input, the program will automatically provide them.

RAMONA Options

To specify RAMONA options, click **Options** in the Model dialog box.

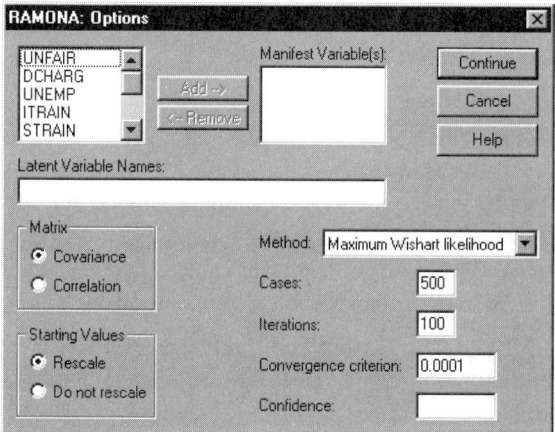

The following options can be specified:

Manifest Variable(s). Specify the manifest (observable) variables in the model.

Latent Variable Names. Specify the latent (unobservable) variables in the model. Decide upon descriptive names including errors. A systematic way of organizing names is to let the endogenous latent variables be followed by the exogenous latent variables and to include the error terms last. It is not, however, essential to do this.

You can specify the type of matrix to be analyzed.

- **Covariance.** If the input matrix is a correlation matrix (has unit diagonal elements), the analysis is performed, but RAMONA prints a warning in the output. This is the default.
- **Correlation.** If a covariance matrix is input, RAMONA rescales it to be a correlation matrix.

RAMONA offers five methods of estimation:

- **Maximum Wishart likelihood.** This is the default.
- **Generalized least squares.** Assumes a Wishart distribution for S.
- **Ordinary least squares.** No measures of fit and no standard errors of estimators are printed.
- **ADF Gramian.** Asymptotically distribution-free estimate that uses a biased but Gramian (non-negative definite) estimate of the asymptotic covariance matrix.
- **ADF Unbiased.** Asymptotically distribution-free estimate that uses an unbiased estimate of the asymptotic covariance matrix.

You can designate how starting values are to be scaled.

- **Rescale.** Rescales the starting values to satisfy the specified variance constraints. RAMONA applies ordinary least squares initially. After partial convergence, RAMONA switches to the method you specify. If starting values are poor, you are advised to rescale them. If you require MWL estimates and supply poor starting values or if you use the * alternative for the starting value, use this option. You should also rescale for ADFG and ADFU if starting values are poor because the time taken per iteration is less for GLS than for these two methods.
- **Do not rescale.** RAMONA uses the estimation procedure specified under Method from the beginning of the iterative procedure. This option should always be used with OLS.

Cases. Number of cases used to compute the matrix. The number of cases should exceed the number of p manifest variables if you use the maximum Wishart likelihood method or the generalized least squares method. If you use the ADF Gramian method or the ADF unbiased method the number of cases must exceed $0.5\,p(p + 1)$.

Iterations. Maximum number of iterations allowed for the iterative procedure.

Convergence criterion. Limit for the residual cosine employed as a convergence criterion.

Confidence. Confidence interval range.

Path Analysis (RAMONA)

Using Commands

First, specify your data with USE filename. Continue with:

```
RAMONA
    MANIFEST var1,var2,…
    LATENT var1,var2,…
    MODEL depvar1<-expvar1(i,n1), expvar2(j,n2),…
          e1<->e2,e3(k,n3)…
    ESTIMATE  / DISP= COVA or CORR
               METHOD = MWL or GLS or OLS or ADFG or ADFU
               START = ROUGH or CLOSE
               NCASES=n  ITER=n  CONVG=n  RESTART  CONFI=n
```

Usage Considerations

Types of data. RAMONA uses a correlation or covariance matrix either read from a file or computed from a rectangular file. When specifying ADFG or ADFU, a cases-by-variables input file must be used.

Print options. Three lengths of output are available. Results included for each include:

- SHORT. The sample covariance (correlation) matrix, path coefficient estimates, 90% confidence intervals, standard errors and *t* statistics, and variance/covariance or correlation estimates.
- MEDIUM. The panels listed for SHORT, plus details of the iterative procedure, the reproduced covariance or correlation matrix, the matrix of residuals, and information about equality constraints on variances (if applicable).
- LONG. The panels listed for MEDIUM, plus the asymptotic correlation matrix of the estimators.

Quick Graphs. RAMONA produces no Quick Graphs.

Saving files. You cannot save specific RAMONA results to a file.

BY groups. For a rectangular file, RAMONA produces separate results for each BY variable.

Bootstrapping. Bootstrapping is not available in this procedure.

Case frequencies. RAMONA uses a FREQUENCY variable, if present, to duplicate cases.

Case weights. RAMONA ignores WEIGHT variables.

Examples

Example 1
Path Analysis Basics

The covariance matrix of six manifest variables is shown below. These covariances and variances were computed from a sample of 932 respondents and are stored in the *EX1* data file.

	ANOMIA67	POWRLS67	ANOMIA71	POWRLS71	EDUCTN	SEI
ANOMIA67	11.834					
POWRLS67	6.947	9.364				
ANOMIA71	6.819	5.091	12.532			
POWRLS71	4.783	5.028	7.495	9.986		
EDUCTN	–3.839	–3.889	–3.841	–3.625	9.610	
SEI	–21.899	–18.831	–21.748	–18.755	35.522	450.288

In this example, we specify the model illustrated in "Statistical Background" on p. 161. The role of the manifest and latent variables is clear from the MODEL statement below. Manifest variables are in the SYSTAT file (latent variables are not). The input is:

```
USE ex1
RAMONA
  MODEL anomia67 <-  alntn67(*,*) e1(0,1.0),
        powrls67 <-  alntn67(*,*) e2(0,1.0),
        anomia71 <-  alntn71(*,*) e3(0,1.0),
        powrls71 <-  alntn71(*,*) e4(0,1.0),
          eductn <-  ses(*,*) d1(0,1.0),
             sei <-  ses(*,*) d2(0,1.0),
         alntn67 <-  ses(*,*) z1(0,1.0),
         alntn71 <-  alntn67(*,*) ses(*,*) z2(0,1.0),
             ses <-> ses(0,1.0),
              e1 <-> e1(*,*) e3(*,*),
              e2 <-> e2(*,*) e4(*,*),
              e3 <-> e3(*,*),
              e4 <-> e4(*,*),
              d1 <-> d1(*,*),
              d2 <-> d2(*,*),
              z1 <-> z1(*,*),
              z2 <-> z2(*,*),
         alntn71 <-> alntn71(0,1.0),
         alntn67 <-> alntn67(0,1.0)
  PRINT = MEDIUM
  ESTIMATE / TYPE=CORR   NCASES=932
```

Path Analysis (RAMONA)

If you were to specify explicitly the default values of the options for **ESTIMATE**, the last statement would read:

```
ESTIMATE / TYPE=CORR   METHOD=MWL   START=ROUGH,
           CONVG=0.0001 ITER=500
```

We use the default maximum Wishart likelihood method (METHOD = MWL) to analyze the correlation matrix. Our analysis differs from Jöreskog's analysis in that the model is treated as a correlation structure rather than a covariance structure. The display correlation option of **ESTIMATE** (TYPE = CORR) identifies that the input is a correlation matrix, and **NCASES** = 932 denotes the sample size used to compute it.

The output follows:

```
There are 6 manifest variables in the model. They are:
    ANOMIA67 POWRLS67 ANOMIA71 POWRLS71 EDUCTN SEI

There are 11 latent variables in the model. They are:
    ALNTN67 E1 E2 ALNTN71 E3 E4 SES D1 D2 Z1 Z2


RAMONA options in effect are:
    Display             Corr
    Method              MWL
    Start               Rough
    Convg               0.000100
    Maximum iterations  100
    Number of cases     932
    Restart             No
    Confidence Interval 90.000000

Number of manifest variables            =    6
Total number of variables in the system =   23.

                    Details of Iterations
    Iter    Method  Discr. Funct.  Max.R.Cos.   Max.Const.    NRP  NBD
    ------  ------  -------------  -----------  ------------  ---  ---
       0    OLS        2.990254                   0.000000
     1(0)   OLS     9363.179841    0.999315      87.020340     0    0
     1(1)   OLS       67.826312    0.974346       9.357014     0    0
     1(2)   OLS        1.861094    0.657239       1.221196     0    0
     2(0)   OLS        0.863526    0.644690       0.787367     0    0
     3(0)   OLS        0.020374    0.512199       0.131453     0    0
     4(0)   OLS        0.001137    0.301991       0.004030     0    0
     5(0)   OLS        0.001007    0.001247       0.000027     0    0
     5(0)   MWL        0.005313    0.034276       0.000027     0    0
     6(0)   MWL        0.005095    0.009493       0.000065     0    0
     7(0)   MWL        0.005090    0.000712       0.000003     0    0
     8(0)   MWL        0.005090    0.000172       0.000000     0    0
     9(0)   MWL        0.005090    0.000014       0.000000     0    0
    10(0)   MWL        0.005090    0.000003       0.000000     0    0

Iterative procedure complete.


Convergence limit for residual cosines = 0.000100 on 2 consecutive
iterations.

Convergence limit for variance constraint violations =   5.00000E-07
Value of the maximum variance constraint violation   =   1.29230E-11
```

Chapter 6

```
Sample Correlation Matrix :
            ANOMIA67    POWRLS67    ANOMIA71    POWRLS71    EDUCTN
ANOMIA67     1.000
POWRLS67     0.660       1.000
ANOMIA71     0.560       0.470       1.000
POWRLS71     0.440       0.520       0.670       1.000
EDUCTN      -0.360      -0.410      -0.350      -0.370       1.000
SEI         -0.300      -0.290      -0.290      -0.280       0.540
              SEI
SEI          1.000

Number of cases = 932.


Reproduced Correlation Matrix :
            ANOMIA67    POWRLS67    ANOMIA71    POWRLS71    EDUCTN
ANOMIA67     1.000
POWRLS67     0.660       1.000
ANOMIA71     0.560       0.469       1.000
POWRLS71     0.441       0.520       0.670       1.000
EDUCTN      -0.367      -0.404      -0.357      -0.369       1.000
SEI         -0.280      -0.308      -0.272      -0.281       0.540
              SEI
SEI          1.000

Residual Matrix (correlations) :
            ANOMIA67    POWRLS67    ANOMIA71    POWRLS71    EDUCTN
ANOMIA67     0.000
POWRLS67     0.000       0.000
ANOMIA71    -0.000       0.001       0.000
POWRLS71    -0.001       0.000      -0.000       0.000
EDUCTN       0.007      -0.006       0.007      -0.001       0.000
SEI         -0.020       0.018      -0.017       0.001       0.000
              SEI
SEI          0.000


Value of the maximum absolute residual =        0.020



               ML Estimates of Free Parameters in Dependence Relationships

                                   Point    90.00% Conf. Int.   Standard      T
               Path      Param #  Estimate   Lower      Upper     Error     Value
         --------------------------------  --------  -----------------  -------  -----
ANOMIA67    <- ALNTN67       1     0.774     0.733     0.816     0.025    30.73
POWRLS67    <- ALNTN67       2     0.852     0.810     0.894     0.026    33.06
ANOMIA71    <- ALNTN71       3     0.805     0.763     0.848     0.026    31.03
POWRLS71    <- ALNTN71       4     0.832     0.788     0.876     0.027    31.19
EDUCTN      <- SES           5     0.842     0.789     0.894     0.032    26.44
SEI         <- SES           6     0.642     0.592     0.691     0.030    21.30
ALNTN67     <- SES           7    -0.563    -0.620    -0.506     0.035   -16.26
ALNTN71     <- ALNTN67       8     0.567     0.500     0.634     0.041    13.88
ALNTN71     <- SES           9    -0.207    -0.281    -0.133     0.045    -4.60


Scaled Standard Deviations (nuisance parameters)

        Variable       Estimate
        ------------   ------------
        ANOMIA67        1.000
        POWRLS67        1.000
        ANOMIA71        1.000
        POWRLS71        1.000
        EDUCTN          1.000
        SEI             1.000
```

Path Analysis (RAMONA)

Values of Fixed Parameters in Dependence Relationships

Path			Value
ANOMIA67	<-	E1	1.000
POWRLS67	<-	E2	1.000
ANOMIA71	<-	E3	1.000
POWRLS71	<-	E4	1.000
EDUCTN	<-	D1	1.000
SEI	<-	D2	1.000
ALNTN67	<-	Z1	1.000
ALNTN71	<-	Z2	1.000

ML estimates of free parameters in variance/covariance relationships

	Path		Param #	Point Estimate	90.00% Conf. Int. Lower	Upper	Standard Error	T Value
E1	<->	E1	10	0.400	0.341	0.470	0.039	10.25
E1	<->	E3	11	0.133	0.091	0.175	0.026	5.22
E2	<->	E2	12	0.274	0.211	0.357	0.044	6.24
E2	<->	E4	13	0.035	-0.009	0.080	0.027	1.30
E3	<->	E3	14	0.351	0.289	0.427	0.042	8.40
E4	<->	E4	15	0.308	0.243	0.390	0.044	6.94
D1	<->	D1	16	0.292	0.216	0.395	0.054	5.44
D2	<->	D2	17	0.588	0.528	0.656	0.039	15.22
Z1	<->	Z1	18	0.683	0.616	0.743	0.039	17.52
Z2	<->	Z2	19	0.503	0.448	0.557	0.033	15.08

Values of Fixed Parameters in Variance/Covariance Relationships

	Path		Value
SES	<->	SES	1.000

Equality Constraints on Variances

	Constraint		Value	Lagrange Multiplier	Standard Error
ALNTN71	<->	ALNTN71	1.0000	0.000	0.000
ALNTN67	<->	ALNTN67	1.0000	0.000	0.000
ANOMIA67	<->	ANOMIA67	1.0000	0.000	0.000
POWRLS67	<->	POWRLS67	1.0000	0.000	0.000
ANOMIA71	<->	ANOMIA71	1.0000	0.000	-0.000
POWRLS71	<->	POWRLS71	1.0000	0.000	0.000
EDUCTN	<->	EDUCTN	1.0000	0.000	-0.000
SEI	<->	SEI	1.0000	0.000	0.000

Maximum Likelihood Discrepancy Function

Measures of fit of the model

Sample Discrepancy Function Value   : 0.005   (5.090285E-03)

Population discrepancy function value, Fo
Bias adjusted point estimate   : 0.001
90.000 percent confidence interval   :(0.0,0.011)

Root mean square error of approximation
Steiger-Lind : RMSEA = SQRT(Fo/df)
Point estimate   : 0.014
90.000 percent confidence interval   :(0.0,0.053)

Expected cross-validation index
Point estimate (modified aic)   : 0.042
90.000 percent confidence interval   :(0.041,0.052)
CVI (modified AIC) for the saturated model   : 0.045

```
Test statistic:                                       : 4.739
Exceedance probabilities:-
Ho: perfect fit (RMSEA = 0.0)                         : 0.315
Ho: close fit   (RMSEA <=      0.050)                 : 0.929

Multiplier for obtaining test statistic    =       931.000
Degrees of freedom                         =     4
Effective number of parameters             =    17
```

After a summary of the input specifications, SYSTAT produces details of the iteration process. The number of the step halving step, carried out to yield a reduction in the discrepancy function plus a penalty for constraint violations, is given in parentheses next to the iteration number. *Method* indicates the method of estimation. *Discr. Funct.* reports the discrepancy function value. *Max. R. Cos.* equals the absolute value of the maximum residual cosine used to indicate convergence. *Max. Const.* is the absolute value of the maximum violated variance constraint. This panel also includes the number of apparently redundant parameters (number of zero pivots of the coefficient matrix of the normal equations—*NRP*) and the number of active bounds on parameter values (*NBD*).

The values of *NRP* and *NBD* can change from iteration to iteration. If *NRP* has a constant nonzero value for several iterations prior to convergence, this suggests that the model could be overparameterized. The value of *NBD* indicates the number of variance or correlation estimates on bounds at any iteration.

Next, the output includes three matrices: the sample correlation (covariance) matrix, the correlation (covariance) matrix reproduced by the model, and the matrix of residuals. The residual matrix is the difference between the sample correlation (covariance) matrix and the reproduced correlation (covariance) matrix. If the input is a correlation matrix (TYPE = CORR), the residual matrix will have null diagonal elements.

For both the dependence and covariance relationships, SYSTAT prints estimates of the free-path coefficients and the values of all fixed-path coefficients involved in the model. The following values are reported for the free parameters:

- *Path*.
- *Param #*. The number of the parameter. This number need not be the same as the number in the input file. (It is the number assigned to the parameter name in the asymptotic covariance matrix of estimators given subsequently.)
- *Point Estimate*. The estimate of the path coefficient.
- *90.00% Conf. Int*. A 90% confidence interval for the path coefficient (the default). If you want to alter the confidence level, specify, for example, CONFI = 0.95.
- *Standard Error*. An estimate of the standard error of the estimator.
- *T value*. The value of the *t* statistic (ratio of estimate to standard error).

If the input is a correlation matrix, the scaled standard deviations (nuisance parameters) are reported with:

- The name of the manifest variable
- The ratio of the standard deviation reproduced from the model to the sample standard deviation

After the covariance relationship output, SYSTAT presents information about equality constraints on endogenous variable variances (if applicable):

- *Constraint.* The variance path that is constrained.
- *Value.* The value of the endogenous variable variance at convergence.
- *Lagrange Multiplier.* The value of the Lagrange multiplier at convergence.
- *Standard Error.* An estimate of the standard error of the Lagrange multiplier.

In most applications, the constraints on endogenous variable variances serve as identification conditions and all Lagrange multipliers and standard errors are 0.

Example 2
Path Analysis with a Restart File

This example is based on Jöreskog's (1977) path analysis model for the Duncan, Haller, and Portes (1971) data on peer influences on ambition. It illustrates a situation where some manifest variables are exogenous. It also illustrates the use of a restart file for creating a data file for a second run where some modifications have been made.

The example consists of two runs. Jöreskog's original model is used for the first run. The model is treated as a covariance structure—this is inappropriate because a correlation matrix is used as input. In the second run, we use a restart file that treats the model as a correlation structure.

The six manifest exogenous variables are:

RPARASP	Respondent's parental aspiration
RESOCIEC	Respondent's socioeconomic status
REINTGCE	Respondent's intelligence
BFINTGCE	Best friend's intelligence
BFSOCIEC	Best friend's socioeconomic status
BFPARASP	Best friend's parental aspiration

The four endogenous variables are:

REOCCASP	Respondent's occupational aspiration
BFEDASP	Best friend's educational aspiration
REEDASP	Respondent's educational aspiration
BFOCCASP	Best friend's occupational aspiration

The latent endogenous variables are:

REAMBITN	Respondent's ambition
BFAMBITN	Best friend's ambition

And the exogenous error variables are $E1$, $E4$, $E2$, $Z1$, $E3$, and $Z2$.

Path Analysis (RAMONA)

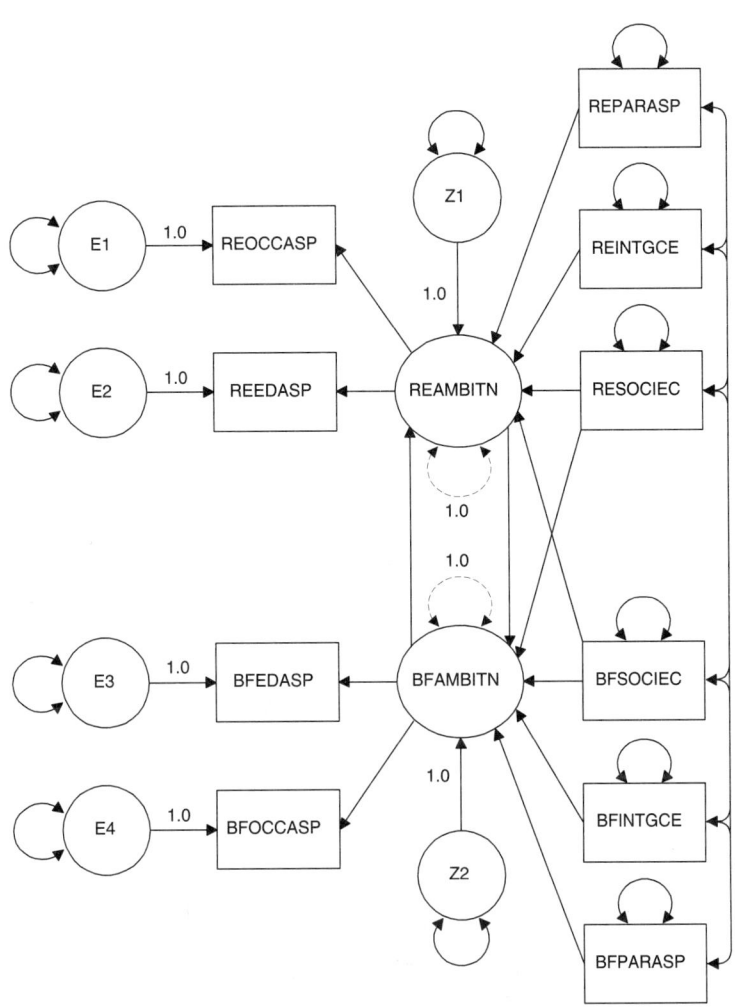

The correlation matrix for the manifest variables is stored in the file *EX2*. Following is the input file for the first run:

```
USE ex2
RAMONA
    MANIFEST = reintgce reparasp resociec reoccasp,
               reedasp bfintgce bfparasp bfsociec,
               bfoccasp bfedasp
    LATENT = reambitn bfambitn e1 e2 e3 e4 z1 z2
    MODEL reoccasp <-  reambitn(0,1.0) e1(0,1.0),
          reedasp  <-  reambitn e2(0,1.0),
          bfedasp  <-  bfambitn e3(0,1.0),
          bfoccasp <-  bfambitn(0,1.0) e4(0,1.0),
          reambitn <-  bfambitn z1(0,1.0) reparasp,
          reambitn <-  reintgce resociec bfsociec,
          bfambitn <-  reambitn z2(0,1.0) resociec,
          bfambitn <-  bfsociec bfintgce bfparasp,
          reparasp <-> reparasp reintgce resociec,
          reparasp <-> bfsociec bfintgce bfparasp,
          reintgce <-> reintgce resociec bfsociec,
          reintgce <-> bfintgce bfparasp,
          resociec <-> resociec bfsociec bfintgce,
          resociec <-> bfparasp,
          bfsociec <-> bfsociec bfintgce bfparasp,
          bfintgce <-> bfintgce bfparasp,
          bfparasp <-> bfparasp,
                e1 <-> e1,
                e2 <-> e2,
                e3 <-> e3,
                e4 <-> e4,
                z1 <-> z1,
                z2 <-> z2
    PRINT = MEDIUM
    OUTPUT BATCH = 'ex2b.syc'  / PROGRAM
    ESTIMATE / TYPE=COVA  NCASES=329  RESTART
```

You would specify the default values of other options for **ESTIMATE** as:

```
ESTIMATE / TYPE=COVA  METHOD=MWL  START=ROUGH  ITER=500,
           CONVG=0.0001  NCASES  RESTART
```

The **RESTART** option of **ESTIMATE** creates a restart command file, *EX2B.SYC*, that is submitted as input in the second run. RESTART tells RAMONA to take the estimated parameter values and insert them as starting values in the MODEL statement. Note that we must also type OUTPUT BATCH = filename to do this. Before the second run, we modify *EX2B.SYC* to treat the model as a correlation structure.

Following Jöreskog's model, the path coefficients REOCCASP <- REAMBITN and BFOCCASP <- BFAMBITN are set equal to 1 for identification purposes. The output follows.

Path Analysis (RAMONA)

```
There are 10 manifest variables in the model. They are:
    REINTGCE REPARASP RESOCIEC REOCCASP REEDASP BFINTGCE BFPARASP
    BFSOCIEC BFOCCASP BFEDASP

There are 8 latent variables in the model. They are:
    REAMBITN E1 E2 BFAMBITN E3 E4 Z1 Z2


RAMONA options in effect are:
    Display              Covar
    Method               MWL
    Start                Rough
    Convg                0.000100
    Maximum iterations   100
    Number of cases      329
    Restart              Yes
    Confidence Interval  90.000000

Number of manifest variables           =   10
Total number of variables in the system =   18.
***WARNING***
A correlation matrix was provided although DISP=COV fit measures and
standard errors may be inappropriate.


                    Details of Iterations
    Iter    Method  Discr. Funct.  Max.R.Cos.    Max.Const.   NRP   NBD
    --------  ------  -------------  ------------  ------------  ----------
       0      OLS     1.500570
       1(0)   OLS     0.325498       0.720392                     0     0
       2(0)   OLS     0.023128       0.191263                     0     0
       3(0)   OLS     0.019538       0.007112                     0     0
       3(0)   MWL     0.085416       0.059603                     0     0
       4(0)   MWL     0.082172       0.016527                     0     0
       5(0)   MWL     0.082003       0.003878                     0     0
       6(0)   MWL     0.081991       0.001141                     0     0
       7(0)   MWL     0.081990       0.000260                     0     0
       8(0)   MWL     0.081990       0.000081                     0     0
       9(0)   MWL     0.081990       0.000018                     0     0

Iterative procedure complete.


Convergence limit for residual cosines = 0.000100 on 2 consecutive
iterations.

Sample Covariance Matrix :
              REINTGCE   REPARASP   RESOCIEC   REOCCASP   REEDASP
    REINTGCE   1.000
    REPARASP   0.184      1.000
    RESOCIEC   0.222      0.049      1.000
    REOCCASP   0.410      0.214      0.324      1.000
    REEDASP    0.404      0.274      0.405      0.625      1.000
    BFINTGCE   0.336      0.078      0.230      0.299      0.286
    BFPARASP   0.102      0.115      0.093      0.076      0.070
    BFSOCIEC   0.186      0.019      0.271      0.293      0.241
    BFOCCASP   0.260      0.084      0.279      0.422      0.328
    BFEDASP    0.290      0.112      0.305      0.327      0.367
              BFINTGCE   BFPARASP   BFSOCIEC   BFOCCASP   BFEDASP
    BFINTGCE   1.000
    BFPARASP   0.209      1.000
    BFSOCIEC   0.295     -0.044      1.000
    BFOCCASP   0.501      0.199      0.361      1.000
    BFEDASP    0.519      0.278      0.410      0.640      1.000

Number of cases = 329.
```

Chapter 6

```
Reproduced Covariance Matrix :
            REINTGCE   REPARASP   RESOCIEC   REOCCASP   REEDASP
REINTGCE     1.000
REPARASP     0.184      1.000
RESOCIEC     0.222      0.049      1.000
REOCCASP     0.393      0.239      0.357      0.999
REEDASP      0.417      0.254      0.379      0.623      0.999
BFINTGCE     0.336      0.078      0.230      0.258      0.274
BFPARASP     0.102      0.115      0.093      0.103      0.110
BFSOCIEC     0.186      0.019      0.271      0.255      0.270
BFOCCASP     0.255      0.095      0.282      0.330      0.351
BFEDASP      0.273      0.102      0.303      0.354      0.376
            BFINTGCE   BFPARASP   BFSOCIEC   BFOCCASP   BFEDASP
BFINTGCE     1.000
BFPARASP     0.209      1.000
BFSOCIEC     0.295     -0.044      1.000
BFOCCASP     0.489      0.237      0.374      0.999
BFEDASP      0.525      0.254      0.401      0.639      0.999

Residual Matrix (covariances) :
            REINTGCE   REPARASP   RESOCIEC   REOCCASP   REEDASP
REINTGCE     0.0
REPARASP     0.0        0.0
RESOCIEC     0.0        0.000      0.0
REOCCASP     0.018     -0.026     -0.033      0.001
REEDASP     -0.013      0.020      0.026      0.001      0.001
BFINTGCE     0.0        0.0        0.0        0.042      0.013
BFPARASP     0.0        0.0        0.0       -0.027     -0.039
BFSOCIEC     0.0        0.0        0.0        0.038     -0.030
BFOCCASP     0.005     -0.011     -0.004      0.091     -0.023
BFEDASP      0.017      0.010      0.003     -0.027     -0.009
            BFINTGCE   BFPARASP   BFSOCIEC   BFOCCASP   BFEDASP
BFINTGCE     0.0
BFPARASP     0.0        0.0
BFSOCIEC     0.0        0.0        0.0
BFOCCASP     0.011     -0.038     -0.013      0.001
BFEDASP     -0.006      0.024      0.009      0.001      0.001

Value of the maximum absolute residual =     0.091
```

ML Estimates of Free Parameters in Dependence Relationships

```
                                        Point    90.00% Conf. Int.  Standard    T
               Path         Param #    Estimate    Lower    Upper     Error   Value
---------------------------------       --------  ------------------ -------- -----
REEDASP   <- REAMBITN          1         1.062    0.914    1.210     0.090   11.80
BFEDASP   <- BFAMBITN          2         1.073    0.940    1.206     0.081   13.23
REAMBITN  <- BFAMBITN          3         0.174    0.032    0.316     0.086    2.02
REAMBITN  <- REPARASP          4         0.164    0.100    0.228     0.039    4.23
REAMBITN  <- REINTGCE          5         0.255    0.185    0.324     0.043    5.99
REAMBITN  <- RESOCIEC          6         0.222    0.151    0.294     0.043    5.11
REAMBITN  <- BFSOCIEC          7         0.079    0.001    0.156     0.047    1.68
BFAMBITN  <- REAMBITN          8         0.185    0.054    0.317     0.080    2.33
BFAMBITN  <- RESOCIEC          9         0.067   -0.004    0.138     0.043    1.55
BFAMBITN  <- BFSOCIEC         10         0.218    0.151    0.284     0.040    5.38
BFAMBITN  <- BFINTGCE         11         0.330    0.262    0.398     0.041    7.97
BFAMBITN  <- BFPARASP         12         0.152    0.092    0.212     0.036    4.18
```

Path Analysis (RAMONA)

Values of Fixed Parameters in Dependence Relationships

Path			Value
REOCCASP	<-	REAMBITN	1.000
REOCCASP	<-	E1	1.000
REEDASP	<-	E2	1.000
BFEDASP	<-	E3	1.000
BFOCCASP	<-	BFAMBITN	1.000
BFOCCASP	<-	E4	1.000
REAMBITN	<-	Z1	1.000
BFAMBITN	<-	Z2	1.000

ML estimates of free parameters in variance/covariance relationships

	Path		Param #	Point Estimate	90.00% Conf. Int. Lower	90.00% Conf. Int. Upper	Standard Error	T Value
REPARASP	<->	REPARASP	13	1.000	0.879	1.137	0.078	12.81
REPARASP	<->	REINTGCE	14	0.184	0.092	0.276	0.056	3.28
REPARASP	<->	RESOCIEC	15	0.049	-0.042	0.140	0.055	0.88
REPARASP	<->	BFSOCIEC	16	0.019	-0.072	0.109	0.055	0.34
REPARASP	<->	BFINTGCE	17	0.078	-0.013	0.169	0.055	1.41
REPARASP	<->	BFPARASP	18	0.115	0.023	0.206	0.056	2.06
REINTGCE	<->	REINTGCE	19	1.000	0.879	1.137	0.078	12.81
REINTGCE	<->	RESOCIEC	20	0.222	0.129	0.315	0.057	3.93
REINTGCE	<->	BFSOCIEC	21	0.186	0.094	0.278	0.056	3.31
REINTGCE	<->	BFINTGCE	22	0.336	0.240	0.431	0.058	5.76
REINTGCE	<->	BFPARASP	23	0.102	0.011	0.193	0.056	1.84
RESOCIEC	<->	RESOCIEC	24	1.000	0.879	1.137	0.078	12.81
RESOCIEC	<->	BFSOCIEC	25	0.271	0.177	0.365	0.057	4.73
RESOCIEC	<->	BFINTGCE	26	0.230	0.137	0.323	0.057	4.06
RESOCIEC	<->	BFPARASP	27	0.093	0.002	0.184	0.055	1.68
BFSOCIEC	<->	BFSOCIEC	28	1.000	0.879	1.137	0.078	12.81
BFSOCIEC	<->	BFINTGCE	29	0.295	0.200	0.390	0.058	5.12
BFSOCIEC	<->	BFPARASP	30	-0.044	-0.135	0.047	0.055	-0.79
BFINTGCE	<->	BFINTGCE	31	1.000	0.879	1.137	0.078	12.81
BFINTGCE	<->	BFPARASP	32	0.209	0.116	0.301	0.056	3.70
BFPARASP	<->	BFPARASP	33	1.000	0.879	1.137	0.078	12.81
E1	<->	E1	34	0.412	0.336	0.506	0.051	8.07
E2	<->	E2	35	0.337	0.262	0.434	0.052	6.50
E3	<->	E3	36	0.313	0.246	0.399	0.046	6.84
E4	<->	E4	37	0.404	0.335	0.487	0.046	8.75
Z1	<->	Z1	38	0.281	0.214	0.370	0.047	6.03
Z2	<->	Z2	39	0.229	0.173	0.303	0.039	5.86

Maximum Likelihood Discrepancy Function

Measures of fit of the model

Sample Discrepancy Function Value   : 0.082 (8.199040E-02)

Population discrepancy function value, Fo
Bias adjusted point estimate   : 0.033
90.000 percent confidence interval   :(0.001,0.089)

Root mean square error of approximation
Steiger-Lind : RMSEA = SQRT(Fo/df)
Point estimate   : 0.046
90.000 percent confidence interval   :(0.008,0.075)

Expected cross-validation index
Point estimate (modified aic)   : 0.320
90.000 percent confidence interval   :(0.288,0.376)
CVI (modified AIC) for the saturated model   : 0.335

```
Test statistic:                                  : 26.893
Exceedance probabilities:-
Ho: perfect fit (RMSEA = 0.0)                    : 0.043
Ho: close fit   (RMSEA <=       0.050)           : 0.560

Multiplier for obtaining test statistic  =       328.000
Degrees of freedom                       =    16
Effective number of parameters           =    39
```

Using the Restart File

A restart file was created during the first run to form an input file that specifies the model represented in the path diagram. Now type the following modifications into the *EX2B* restart file and save the file:

- TYPE = COV is replaced by TYPE = CORR.
- START = ROUGH is replaced by START = CLOSE.
- REOCCASP <- REAMBTN(0,1.0) is replaced by REOCCASP <- REAMBITN(*,1.0), freeing a fixed-path coefficient.
- BFOCCASP <- BFAMBITN(0,1.0) is replaced by BFOCCASP <- BFAMBITN(*,1.0), freeing a fixed-path coefficient.
- REAMBITN <-> REAMBITN(0,1.0) is added, imposing a variance constraint on an endogenous latent variable.
- BFAMBITN <-> BFAMBITN(0,1.0) is added, imposing a variance constraint on an endogenous latent variable.

Path Analysis (RAMONA)

The modified restart file is shown below:

```
USE ex2
RAMONA
  MODEL reoccasp <-  reambitn(*,1.0) e1(0,1.0),
        reedasp <-  reambitn(1,1.062) e2(0,1.0),
         bfedasp <-  bfambitn(2,1.073) e3(0,1.0),
         bfoccasp <-  bfambitn(*,1.0) e4(0,1.0),
         reambitn <-  bfambitn(3,0.174) z1(0,1.0),
                     reparasp(4,0.164) reintgce(5,0.255),
                     resociec(6,0.222) bfsociec(7,0.079),
         bfambitn <-  reambitn(8,0.185) z2(0,1.0),
                     resociec(9,0.668),
                     bfsociec(10,0.218),
                     bfintgce(11,0.330),
                     bfparasp(12,0.152),
         reparasp <-> reparasp(13,1.0,),
                     reintgce(14,0.184),
                     resociec(15,0.049),
                     bfsociec(16,0.019),
                     bfintgce(17,0.078),
                     bfparasp(18,0.115),
         reintgce <-> reintgce(19,1.000),
                     resociec(20,0.222),
                     bfsociec(21,0.186),
                     bfintgce(22,0.336),
                     bfparasp(23,0.102),
         resociec <-> resociec(24,1.0),
                     bfsociec(25,0.271),
                     bfintgce(26,0.230),
                     bfparasp(27,0.093),
         bfsociec <-> bfsociec(28,1.0),
                     bfintgce(29,0.29),
                     bfparasp(30,-0.044),
         bfintgce <-> bfintgce(31,1.0),
                     bfparasp(32,0.209),
         bfparasp <-> bfparasp(33,1.0),
               e1 <-> e1(34,0.412),
               e2 <-> e2(35,0.337),
               e3 <-> e3(36,0.313),
               e4 <-> e4(37,0.404),
               z1 <-> z1(38,0.281),
               z2 <-> z2(39,0.229),
         reambitn <-> reambitn(0,1.0),
         bfambitn <-> bfambitn(0,1.0)
  PRINT = MEDIUM
  ESTIMATE / TYPE=CORR  START=CLOSE  NCASES=329
```

Note that we rounded some parameter values to shorten the commands. Also, the START setting, ROUGH, has been changed to CLOSE (under ESTIMATE) because a restart file is used.

Now execute this modified file (after you have edited it and saved it using FEDIT or another text editor). The input is:

```
SUBMIT ex2b
```

The output is:

```
There are 10 manifest variables in the model. They are:
      REINTGCE REPARASP RESOCIEC REOCCASP REEDASP BFINTGCE BFPARASP
      BFSOCIEC BFOCCASP BFEDASP

There are 8 latent variables in the model. They are:
      REAMBITN E1 E2 BFAMBITN E3 E4 Z1 Z2

RAMONA options in effect are:
    Display                  Corr
    Method                   MWL
    Start                    Close
    Convg                    0.000100
    Maximum iterations       100
    Number of cases          329
    Restart                  No
    Confidence Interval      90.000000

Number of manifest variables            =    10
Total number of variables in the system =    28.
Reading correlation matrix...

                        Details of Iterations
   Iter    Method  Discr. Funct.   Max.R.Cos.    Max.Const.    NRP    NBD
--------  -------  -------------  ------------  ------------  -----  -----
      0     MWL       0.081990                    0.000000
   1(0)     MWL       0.081990      0.000005      0.000000      0      0
   2(0)     MWL       0.081990      0.000001      0.000000      0      0

Iterative procedure complete.

Convergence limit for residual cosines = 0.000100 on 2 consecutive
iterations.

Convergence limit for variance constraint violations =  5.00000E-07
Value of the maximum variance constraint violation =    7.33524E-12


Sample Correlation Matrix :
               REINTGCE      REPARASP      RESOCIEC      REOCCASP      REEDASP
    REINTGCE    1.000
    REPARASP    0.184         1.000
    RESOCIEC    0.222         0.049         1.000
    REOCCASP    0.410         0.214         0.324         1.000
    REEDASP     0.404         0.274         0.405         0.625         1.000
    BFINTGCE    0.336         0.078         0.230         0.299         0.286
    BFPARASP    0.102         0.115         0.093         0.076         0.070
    BFSOCIEC    0.186         0.019         0.271         0.293         0.241
    BFOCCASP    0.260         0.084         0.279         0.422         0.328
    BFEDASP     0.290         0.112         0.305         0.327         0.367
               BFINTGCE      BFPARASP      BFSOCIEC      BFOCCASP      BFEDASP
    BFINTGCE    1.000
    BFPARASP    0.209         1.000
    BFSOCIEC    0.295        -0.044         1.000
    BFOCCASP    0.501         0.199         0.361         1.000
    BFEDASP     0.519         0.278         0.410         0.640         1.000

Number of cases = 329.
```

Path Analysis (RAMONA)

Reproduced Correlation Matrix :

	REINTGCE	REPARASP	RESOCIEC	REOCCASP	REEDASP
REINTGCE	1.000				
REPARASP	0.184	1.000			
RESOCIEC	0.222	0.049	1.000		
REOCCASP	0.393	0.240	0.357	1.000	
REEDASP	0.417	0.254	0.379	0.624	1.000
BFINTGCE	0.336	0.078	0.230	0.258	0.274
BFPARASP	0.102	0.115	0.093	0.103	0.110
BFSOCIEC	0.186	0.019	0.271	0.255	0.270
BFOCCASP	0.255	0.095	0.282	0.330	0.351
BFEDASP	0.273	0.102	0.303	0.355	0.376

	BFINTGCE	BFPARASP	BFSOCIEC	BFOCCASP	BFEDASP
BFINTGCE	1.000				
BFPARASP	0.209	1.000			
BFSOCIEC	0.295	-0.044	1.000		
BFOCCASP	0.489	0.237	0.374	1.000	
BFEDASP	0.525	0.254	0.401	0.640	1.000

Residual Matrix (correlations) :

	REINTGCE	REPARASP	RESOCIEC	REOCCASP	REEDASP
REINTGCE	0.0				
REPARASP	0.0	0.0			
RESOCIEC	0.0	0.0	0.0		
REOCCASP	0.017	-0.026	-0.033	0.000	
REEDASP	-0.013	0.020	0.025	0.001	0.000
BFINTGCE	0.0	0.0	0.0	0.042	0.012
BFPARASP	0.000	0.0	0.0	-0.027	-0.039
BFSOCIEC	0.0	0.0	0.0	0.038	-0.030
BFOCCASP	0.005	-0.011	-0.004	0.091	-0.023
BFEDASP	0.017	0.010	0.002	-0.028	-0.010

	BFINTGCE	BFPARASP	BFSOCIEC	BFOCCASP	BFEDASP
BFINTGCE	0.0				
BFPARASP	0.0	0.0			
BFSOCIEC	0.0	0.0	0.0		
BFOCCASP	0.011	-0.038	-0.013	0.000	
BFEDASP	-0.006	0.024	0.009	0.001	0.000

Value of the maximum absolute residual =   0.091

ML Estimates of Free Parameters in Dependence Relationships

	Path	Param #	Point Estimate	90.00% Conf. Int. Lower	Upper	Standard Error	T Value
REOCCASP	<- REAMBITN	1	0.766	0.710	0.823	0.034	22.21
REEDASP	<- REAMBITN	2	0.814	0.759	0.868	0.033	24.52
BFEDASP	<- BFAMBITN	3	0.828	0.781	0.876	0.029	28.49
BFOCCASP	<- BFAMBITN	4	0.772	0.721	0.823	0.031	24.75
REAMBITN	<- BFAMBITN	5	0.175	0.034	0.317	0.086	2.04
REAMBITN	<- REPARASP	6	0.214	0.133	0.294	0.049	4.36
REAMBITN	<- REINTGCE	7	0.332	0.248	0.417	0.051	6.47
REAMBITN	<- RESOCIEC	8	0.290	0.201	0.378	0.054	5.39
REAMBITN	<- BFSOCIEC	9	0.103	0.002	0.204	0.061	1.69
BFAMBITN	<- REAMBITN	10	0.184	0.055	0.313	0.078	2.35
BFAMBITN	<- RESOCIEC	11	0.087	-0.005	0.178	0.056	1.55
BFAMBITN	<- BFSOCIEC	12	0.282	0.200	0.365	0.050	5.62
BFAMBITN	<- BFINTGCE	13	0.428	0.349	0.506	0.048	9.00
BFAMBITN	<- BFPARASP	14	0.197	0.121	0.273	0.046	4.27

Chapter 6

Scaled Standard Deviations (nuisance parameters)

Variable	Estimate
REOCCASP	1.000
REEDASP	1.000
BFOCCASP	1.000
BFEDASP	1.000
REPARASP	1.000
BFINTGCE	1.000
BFPARASP	1.000
BFSOCIEC	1.000
RESOCIEC	1.000
REINTGCE	1.000

Values of Fixed Parameters in Dependence Relationships

Path			Value
REOCCASP	<-	E1	1.000
REEDASP	<-	E2	1.000
BFEDASP	<-	E3	1.000
BFOCCASP	<-	E4	1.000
REAMBITN	<-	Z1	1.000
BFAMBITN	<-	Z2	1.000

ML estimates of free parameters in variance/covariance relationships

Path			Param #	Point Estimate	90.00% Conf. Int. Lower	Upper	Standard Error	T Value
REPARASP	<->	REINTGCE	15	0.184	0.095	0.270	0.053	3.45
REPARASP	<->	RESOCIEC	16	0.049	-0.042	0.139	0.055	0.89
REPARASP	<->	BFSOCIEC	17	0.019	-0.072	0.109	0.055	0.34
REPARASP	<->	BFINTGCE	18	0.078	-0.012	0.168	0.055	1.42
REPARASP	<->	BFPARASP	19	0.115	0.024	0.203	0.054	2.10
REINTGCE	<->	RESOCIEC	20	0.222	0.134	0.306	0.052	4.23
REINTGCE	<->	BFSOCIEC	21	0.186	0.097	0.272	0.053	3.49
REINTGCE	<->	BFINTGCE	22	0.336	0.253	0.414	0.049	6.85
REINTGCE	<->	BFPARASP	23	0.102	0.012	0.191	0.055	1.87
RESOCIEC	<->	BFSOCIEC	24	0.271	0.185	0.353	0.051	5.29
RESOCIEC	<->	BFINTGCE	25	0.230	0.143	0.314	0.052	4.40
RESOCIEC	<->	BFPARASP	26	0.093	0.003	0.182	0.055	1.70
BFSOCIEC	<->	BFINTGCE	27	0.295	0.210	0.376	0.050	5.85
BFSOCIEC	<->	BFPARASP	28	-0.044	-0.134	0.047	0.055	-0.79
BFINTGCE	<->	BFPARASP	29	0.209	0.120	0.294	0.053	3.95
E1	<->	E1	30	0.413	0.334	0.509	0.053	7.80
E2	<->	E2	31	0.338	0.259	0.439	0.054	6.25
E3	<->	E3	32	0.314	0.244	0.404	0.048	6.51
E4	<->	E4	33	0.404	0.332	0.492	0.048	8.39
Z1	<->	Z1	34	0.479	0.390	0.570	0.055	8.64
Z2	<->	Z2	35	0.384	0.305	0.470	0.051	7.59

Values of Fixed Parameters in Variance/Covariance Relationships

Path			Value
REPARASP	<->	REPARASP	1.000
REINTGCE	<->	REINTGCE	1.000
RESOCIEC	<->	RESOCIEC	1.000
BFSOCIEC	<->	BFSOCIEC	1.000
BFINTGCE	<->	BFINTGCE	1.000
BFPARASP	<->	BFPARASP	1.000

Path Analysis (RAMONA)

Equality Constraints on Variances

Constraint			Value	Lagrange Multiplier	Standard Error
REAMBITN	<->	REAMBITN	1.0000	0.000	0.000
BFAMBITN	<->	BFAMBITN	1.0000	0.000	-0.000
REOCCASP	<->	REOCCASP	1.0000	0.000	-0.000
REEDASP	<->	REEDASP	1.0000	0.000	0.000
BFOCCASP	<->	BFOCCASP	1.0000	0.000	0.000
BFEDASP	<->	BFEDASP	1.0000	0.000	0.000

Maximum Likelihood Discrepancy Function

Measures of fit of the model

Sample Discrepancy Function Value   : 0.082   (8.199040E-02)

Population discrepancy function value, Fo
Bias adjusted point estimate   : 0.033
90.000 percent confidence interval   :(0.001,0.089)

Root mean square error of approximation
Steiger-Lind : RMSEA = SQRT(Fo/df)
Point estimate   : 0.046
90.000 percent confidence interval   :(0.008,0.075)

Expected cross-validation index
Point estimate (modified aic)   : 0.320
90.000 percent confidence interval   :(0.288,0.376)
CVI (modified AIC) for the saturated model   : 0.335

Test statistic: : 26.893
Exceedance probabilities:-
Ho: perfect fit (RMSEA = 0.0)   : 0.043
Ho: close fit   (RMSEA <=   0.050)   : 0.560

Multiplier for obtaining test statistic   =   328.000
Degrees of freedom   =   16
Effective number of parameters   =   39

The discrepancy function values and measures of fit of the model are the same in both runs, but the maximum likelihood estimates differ because of different identification conditions. The standard errors in the second run differ (those in the first run were incorrect). An appropriate warning has been output by RAMONA. Notice in the last run that the Lagrange multipliers and the corresponding standard errors are 0 because all equality constraints on endogenous variable variances act as identification conditions, not constraints on the model. This is the case in most, but not all, practical applications.

Example 3
Path Analysis Using Rectangular Input

This example (Mels and Koorts, 1989) illustrates how RAMONA uses the usual cases-by-variables SYSTAT data file. Asymptotically distribution-free estimates are obtained.

A questionnaire concerned with job satisfaction was completed by 213 nurses. There are 10 manifest variables that serve as indicators of 4 latent variables: job security (*JOBSEC*), attitude toward training (*TRAING*), opportunities for promotion (*PROMOT*), and relations with superiors (*RELSUP*). The path diagram shows a model to account for causal relationships between the three latent variables.

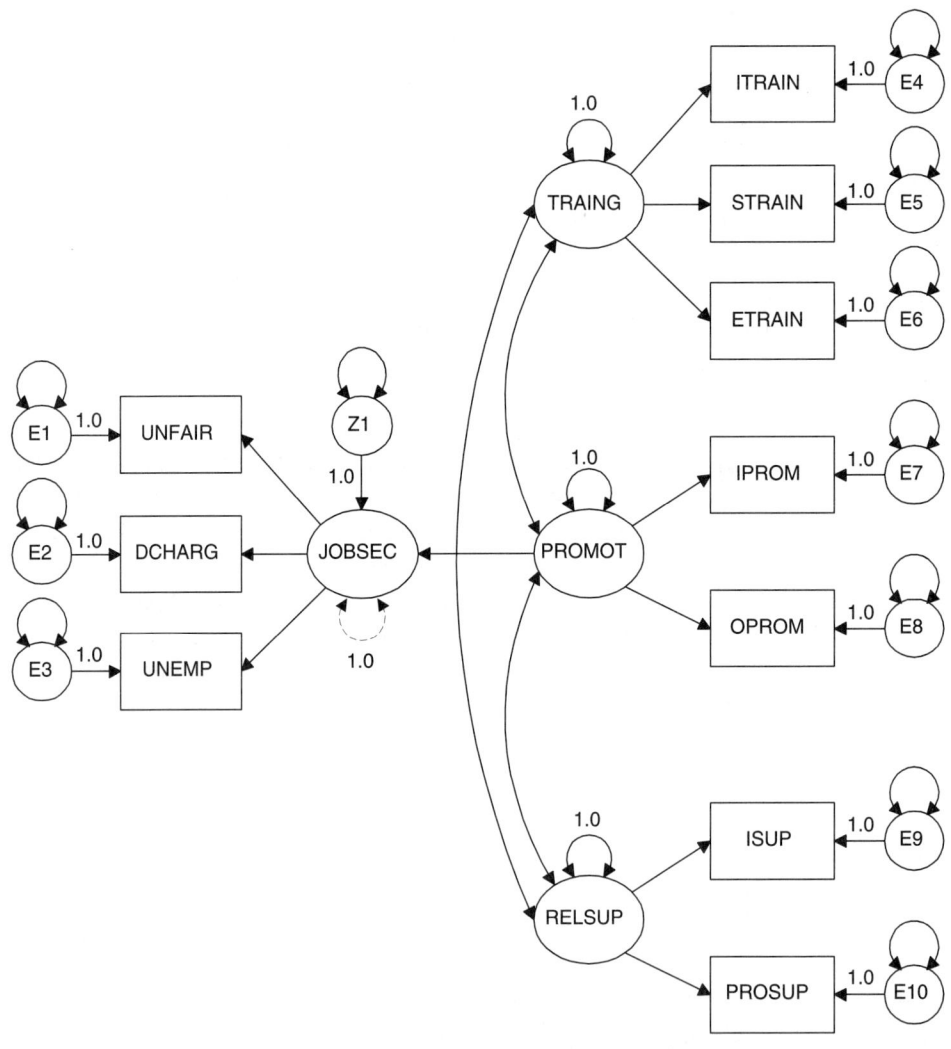

Path Analysis (RAMONA)

```
USE ex3
RAMONA
  MANIFEST = unfair dcharg unemp itrain strain etrain,
            ipromot opromot isup prosup
  LATENT = jobsec traing promot relsup e1 e2 e3 e4 e5,
           e6 e7 e8 e9 e10 z1
  MODEL unfair  <-  jobsec e1(0,1.0),
        dcharg  <-  jobsec e2(0,1.0),
         unemp  <-  jobsec e3(0,1.0),
        itrain  <-  traing e4(0,1.0),
        strain  <-  traing e5(0,1.0),
        etrain  <-  traing e6(0,1.0),
       ipromot  <-  promot e7(0,1.0),
       opromot  <-  promot e8(0,1.0),
          isup  <-  relsup e9(0,1.0),
        prosup  <-  relsup e10(0,1.0),
        jobsec  <-  traing promot relsup z1(0,1.0),
        traing  <-> traing (0,1.0),
        promot  <-> promot (0,1.0),
        relsup  <-> relsup (0,1.0),
        traing  <-> promot,
        traing  <-> relsup,
        promot  <-> relsup,
            e1  <-> e1,
            e2  <-> e2,
            e3  <-> e3,
            e4  <-> e4,
            e5  <-> e5,
            e6  <-> e6,
            e7  <-> e7,
            e8  <-> e8,
            e9  <-> e9,
           e10  <-> e10,
            z1  <-> z1,
        jobsec  <-> jobsec(0,1.0)
  PRINT = MEDIUM
  ESTIMATE / TYPE=CORR   METHOD=ADFU
```

The output is:

```
There are 10 manifest variables in the model. They are:
     UNFAIR DCHARG UNEMP ITRAIN STRAIN ETRAIN IPROMOT OPROMOT
     ISUP PROSUP

There are 15 latent variables in the model. They are:
     JOBSEC E1 E2 E3 TRAING E4 E5 E6 PROMOT E7 E8 RELSUP E9
     E10 Z1
```

Chapter 6

```
RAMONA options in effect are:
   Display              Corr
   Method               ADFU
   Start                Rough
   Convg                0.000100
   Maximum iterations   100
   Number of cases      determined when data are read
   Restart              No
   Confidence Interval  90.000000

Number of manifest variables            =   10
Total number of variables in the system =   35.
Computing mean vector...
Computing covariance matrix and fourth order moments...
Computing ADF weight matrix...

        Overall kurtosis =       19.754
              Normalised =        9.305
                Relative =        1.165
```

	Individual		
Variable	kurtoses	Normalised	Relative
UNFAIR	1.395	4.155	1.465
DCHARG	1.866	5.560	1.622
UNEMP	0.181	0.540	1.060
ITRAIN	-0.560	-1.669	0.813
STRAIN	-1.102	-3.282	0.633
ETRAIN	-0.730	-2.174	0.757
IPROMOT	-1.006	-2.997	0.665
OPROMOT	-0.757	-2.256	0.748
ISUP	-0.945	-2.815	0.685
PROSUP	-0.547	-1.628	0.818

Smallest relative pivot of covariance matrix of sample covariances = 0.149

Details of Iterations

Iter	Method	Discr. Funct.	Max.R.Cos.	Max.Const.	NRP	NBD
0	OLS	1.254639		0.000000		
1(0)	OLS	0.398537	0.556472	0.405283	0	0
2(0)	OLS	0.079200	0.115359	0.045912	0	0
3(0)	OLS	0.075227	0.010971	0.000398	0	0
4(0)	OLS	0.075196	0.002148	0.000018	0	0
4(0)	ADFU	0.393299	0.361351	0.000018	0	0
5(0)	ADFU	0.190011	0.084716	0.039737	0	0
6(0)	ADFU	0.184936	0.019973	0.004648	0	0
7(0)	ADFU	0.184639	0.003195	0.000205	0	0
8(0)	ADFU	0.184609	0.001973	0.000061	0	0
9(0)	ADFU	0.184606	0.000414	0.000002	0	0
10(0)	ADFU	0.184605	0.000219	0.000001	0	0
11(0)	ADFU	0.184605	0.000049	0.000000	0	0
12(0)	ADFU	0.184605	0.000025	0.000000	0	0

Iterative procedure complete.

Convergence limit for residual cosines = 0.000100 on 2 consecutive iterations.

Convergence limit for variance constraint violations = 5.00000E-07
Value of the maximum variance constraint violation = 1.13880E-08

Path Analysis (RAMONA)

```
Sample Correlation Matrix :
             UNFAIR      DCHARG      UNEMP       ITRAIN      STRAIN
   UNFAIR    1.000
   DCHARG    0.438       1.000
   UNEMP     0.249       0.455       1.000
   ITRAIN    0.150       0.110       0.056       1.000
   STRAIN    0.173       0.209       0.028       0.543       1.000
   ETRAIN    0.184       0.168      -0.006       0.544       0.694
   IPROMOT   0.134       0.210       0.169       0.082       0.240
   OPROMOT   0.099       0.179       0.159       0.115       0.184
   ISUP      0.154       0.177       0.140       0.284       0.456
   PROSUP    0.213       0.212       0.038       0.263       0.337
             ETRAIN      IPROMOT     OPROMOT     ISUP        PROSUP
   ETRAIN    1.000
   IPROMOT   0.237       1.000
   OPROMOT   0.208       0.683       1.000
   ISUP      0.348       0.389       0.319       1.000
   PROSUP    0.262       0.263       0.185       0.475       1.000

Number of cases = 213.


Reproduced Correlation Matrix :
             UNFAIR      DCHARG      UNEMP       ITRAIN      STRAIN
   UNFAIR    1.000
   DCHARG    0.481       1.000
   UNEMP     0.382       0.602       1.000
   ITRAIN    0.081       0.128       0.102       1.000
   STRAIN    0.093       0.146       0.116       0.638       1.000
   ETRAIN    0.089       0.140       0.111       0.609       0.695
   IPROMOT   0.140       0.221       0.176       0.171       0.195
   OPROMOT   0.121       0.192       0.152       0.148       0.169
   ISUP      0.124       0.196       0.156       0.364       0.415
   PROSUP    0.098       0.154       0.122       0.286       0.326
             ETRAIN      IPROMOT     OPROMOT     ISUP        PROSUP
   ETRAIN    1.000
   IPROMOT   0.186       1.000
   OPROMOT   0.161       0.743       1.000
   ISUP      0.396       0.377       0.327       1.000
   PROSUP    0.311       0.296       0.257       0.560       1.000

Residual Matrix (correlations) :
             UNFAIR      DCHARG      UNEMP       ITRAIN      STRAIN
   UNFAIR   -0.000
   DCHARG   -0.043      -0.000
   UNEMP    -0.133      -0.148      -0.000
   ITRAIN    0.068      -0.018      -0.045       0.000
   STRAIN    0.080       0.062      -0.088      -0.095       0.000
   ETRAIN    0.095       0.028      -0.117      -0.065      -0.000
   IPROMOT  -0.007      -0.011      -0.007      -0.089       0.045
   OPROMOT  -0.023      -0.013       0.007      -0.033       0.016
   ISUP      0.030      -0.020      -0.016      -0.080       0.042
   PROSUP    0.115       0.057      -0.084      -0.023       0.012
             ETRAIN      IPROMOT     OPROMOT     ISUP        PROSUP
   ETRAIN    0.000
   IPROMOT   0.051       0.000
   OPROMOT   0.047      -0.060       0.000
   ISUP     -0.047       0.011      -0.008      -0.000
   PROSUP   -0.049      -0.034      -0.072      -0.085       0.000

Value of the maximum absolute residual =      0.148
```

ADFU Estimates of Free Parameters in Dependence Relationships

	Path		Param #	Point Estimate	90.00% Conf. Int. Lower	Upper	Standard Error	T Value
UNFAIR	<-	JOBSEC	1	0.552	0.451	0.653	0.061	9.01
DCHARG	<-	JOBSEC	2	0.871	0.770	0.972	0.061	14.22
UNEMP	<-	JOBSEC	3	0.692	0.592	0.791	0.061	11.42
ITRAIN	<-	TRAING	4	0.748	0.670	0.826	0.047	15.78
STRAIN	<-	TRAING	5	0.853	0.808	0.899	0.028	30.81
ETRAIN	<-	TRAING	6	0.814	0.756	0.873	0.035	23.04
IPROMOT	<-	PROMOT	7	0.926	0.842	1.011	0.052	17.98
OPROMOT	<-	PROMOT	8	0.802	0.714	0.891	0.054	14.96
ISUP	<-	RELSUP	9	0.844	0.752	0.937	0.056	14.97
PROSUP	<-	RELSUP	10	0.663	0.568	0.758	0.058	11.48
JOBSEC	<-	TRAING	11	0.074	-0.129	0.277	0.123	0.60
JOBSEC	<-	PROMOT	12	0.192	0.075	0.310	0.071	2.70
JOBSEC	<-	RELSUP	13	0.132	-0.081	0.345	0.130	1.02

Scaled Standard Deviations (nuisance parameters)

Variable	Estimate
UNFAIR	1.008
DCHARG	0.962
UNEMP	0.974
ITRAIN	1.000
STRAIN	1.002
ETRAIN	0.983
IPROMOT	0.989
OPROMOT	1.001
ISUP	0.998
PROSUP	0.970

Values of Fixed Parameters in Dependence Relationships

	Path		Value
UNFAIR	<-	E1	1.000
DCHARG	<-	E2	1.000
UNEMP	<-	E3	1.000
ITRAIN	<-	E4	1.000
STRAIN	<-	E5	1.000
ETRAIN	<-	E6	1.000
IPROMOT	<-	E7	1.000
OPROMOT	<-	E8	1.000
ISUP	<-	E9	1.000
PROSUP	<-	E10	1.000
JOBSEC	<-	Z1	1.000

ADFU estimates of free parameters in variance/covariance relationships

	Path		Param #	Point Estimate	90.00% Conf. Int. Lower	Upper	Standard Error	T Value
TRAING	<->	PROMOT	14	0.246	0.120	0.364	0.075	3.30
TRAING	<->	RELSUP	15	0.576	0.452	0.677	0.069	8.40
PROMOT	<->	RELSUP	16	0.482	0.354	0.593	0.073	6.62
E1	<->	E1	17	0.695	0.593	0.816	0.068	10.28
E2	<->	E2	18	0.242	0.117	0.499	0.107	2.26
E3	<->	E3	19	0.522	0.400	0.679	0.084	6.22
E4	<->	E4	20	0.440	0.338	0.574	0.071	6.21
E5	<->	E5	21	0.272	0.204	0.362	0.047	5.75
E6	<->	E6	22	0.337	0.254	0.446	0.058	5.85
E7	<->	E7	23	0.142	0.047	0.429	0.095	1.48
E8	<->	E8	24	0.356	0.239	0.530	0.086	4.14
E9	<->	E9	25	0.287	0.166	0.495	0.095	3.01
E10	<->	E10	26	0.560	0.448	0.702	0.077	7.31
Z1	<->	Z1	27	0.898	0.818	0.945	0.037	24.06

Values of Fixed Parameters in Variance/Covariance Relationships

	Path		Value
TRAING	<->	TRAING	1.000
PROMOT	<->	PROMOT	1.000
RELSUP	<->	RELSUP	1.000

Equality Constraints on Variances

Constraint			Value	Lagrange Multiplier	Standard Error
JOBSEC	<->	JOBSEC	1.0000	0.000	-0.000
UNFAIR	<->	UNFAIR	1.0000	0.000	-0.000
DCHARG	<->	DCHARG	1.0000	0.000	-0.000
UNEMP	<->	UNEMP	1.0000	0.000	-0.000
ITRAIN	<->	ITRAIN	1.0000	0.000	0.000
STRAIN	<->	STRAIN	1.0000	0.000	0.000
ETRAIN	<->	ETRAIN	1.0000	0.000	-0.000
IPROMOT	<->	IPROMOT	1.0000	0.000	-0.000
OPROMOT	<->	OPROMOT	1.0000	0.000	0.000
ISUP	<->	ISUP	1.0000	0.000	0.000
PROSUP	<->	PROSUP	1.0000	0.000	-0.000

ADFU Discrepancy Function

Measures of fit of the model

Sample Discrepancy Function Value   : 0.185   (1.846051E-01)

Population discrepancy function value, Fo
Bias adjusted point estimate   : 0.048
90.000 percent confidence interval   :(0.0,0.144)

Root mean square error of approximation
Steiger-Lind : RMSEA = SQRT(Fo/df)
Point estimate   : 0.041
90.000 percent confidence interval   :(0.0,0.071)

Expected cross-validation index
Point estimate (modified aic)   : 0.430
90.000 percent confidence interval   :(0.382,0.526)
CVI (modified AIC) for the saturated model   : 0.519

Test statistic: : 39.136
Exceedance probabilities:-
Ho: perfect fit (RMSEA = 0.0)   : 0.099
Ho: close fit   (RMSEA <=   0.050)   : 0.662

Multiplier for obtaining test statistic   =   212.000
Degrees of freedom   =   29
Effective number of parameters   =   26

If the usual SYSTAT cases-by-variables file is used as input, then kurtosis estimates are printed before the iteration details. These can be used to judge the appropriateness of normality assumptions. They can also be used to apply corrections manually to test statistics and standard errors if the user is willing to accept that the assumption of an elliptical distribution is appropriate for the data (Shapiro and Browne, 1987).

Example 4
Path Analysis and Standard Errors

Lawley and Maxwell (1971) gave correct standard errors for maximum likelihood parameter estimates in a restricted factor analysis model for a correlation matrix. This example shows how RAMONA can produce these correct standard errors. The method used for calculating the standard errors differs from that of Lawley and Maxwell in that RAMONA makes use of constrained optimization and Lawley and Maxwell obtained their formula by applying the delta method to standardized estimates. It can be shown, however, that the two methods are equivalent and produce the same results. Lawley and Maxwell made use of a sample correlation matrix between nine ability tests administered to 72 children.

Path Analysis (RAMONA)

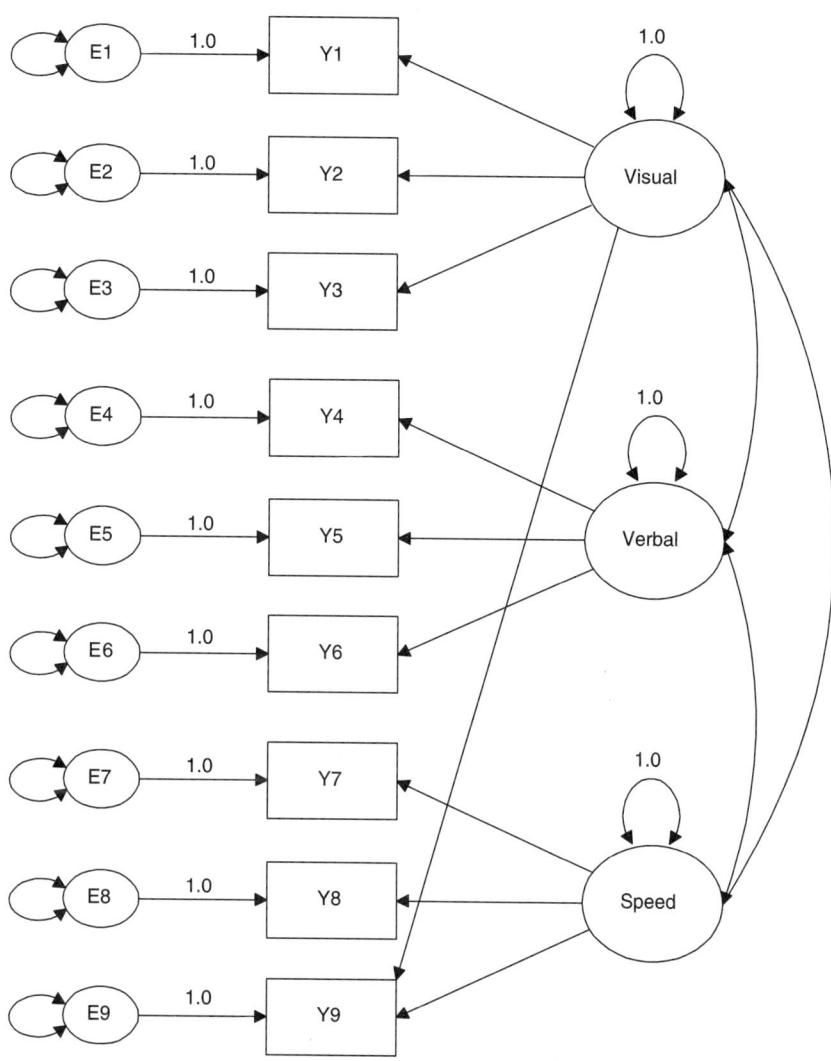

We analyze the relationships in the path diagram using the correlation matrix. The difference between the two runs is that we first treat the model (inappropriately) as a covariance structure and then as a correlation structure. We specify TYPE as COVA in the first run and CORR in the second.

Chapter 6

Following is the input file for the first run:

```
USE ex4a
RAMONA
   MANIFEST = y1 y2 y3 y4 y5 y6 y7 y8 y9
   LATENT = visual verbal speed e1 e2 e3 e4 e5 e6,
          e7 e8 e9
   MODEL y1 <- visual e1(0,1.0),
         y2 <- visual e2(0,1.0),
         y3 <- visual e3(0,1.0),
         y4 <- verbal e4(0,1.0),
         y5 <- verbal e5(0,1.0),
         y6 <- verbal e6(0,1.0),
         y7 <- speed e7(0,1.0),
         y8 <- speed e8 (0,1.0),
         y9 <- visual speed e9(0,1.0),
      visual <-> visual(0,1.0),
      verbal <-> verbal(0,1.0),
       speed <-> speed(0,1.0),
      visual <-> verbal,
      visual <-> speed,
      verbal <-> speed
   PRINT = MEDIUM
   ESTIMATE / TYPE=COVA   NCASES=72
```

The resulting output is:

```
There are 9 manifest variables in the model. They are:
    Y1 Y2 Y3 Y4 Y5 Y6 Y7 Y8 Y9


There are 12 latent variables in the model. They are:
    VISUAL E1 E2 E3 VERBAL E4 E5 E6 SPEED E7 E8 E9


RAMONA options in effect are:
    Display              Covar
    Method               MWL
    Start                Rough
    Convg                0.000100
    Maximum iterations   100
    Number of cases      72
    Restart              No
    Confidence Interval  90.000000
Variance paths for errors were omitted from the job specification
and have been added by RAMONA.

Number of manifest variables            =    9
Total number of variables in the system =   21
Reading correlation matrix...
***WARNING***
A correlation matrix was provided although DISP=COV fit measures and
standard errors may be inappropriate.
```

Path Analysis (RAMONA)

```
                   Details of Iterations
    Iter    Method  Discr. Funct.  Max.R.Cos.   Max.Const.   NRP   NBD
    ----    ------  -------------  ----------   ----------   ---   ---
       0    OLS     1.013354
    1(0)    OLS     0.437034       0.649686                    0     0
    2(0)    OLS     0.143538       0.092248                    0     0
    3(0)    OLS     0.135197       0.053602                    0     0
    4(0)    OLS     0.134714       0.004511                    0     0
    4(0)    MWL     0.472377       0.164664                    0     0
    5(0)    MWL     0.425693       0.031463                    0     0
    6(0)    MWL     0.421825       0.019794                    0     0
    7(0)    MWL     0.421170       0.006232                    0     0
    8(0)    MWL     0.421041       0.005613                    0     0
    9(0)    MWL     0.421014       0.001271                    0     0
   10(0)    MWL     0.421008       0.001616                    0     0
   11(0)    MWL     0.421006       0.000284                    0     0
   12(0)    MWL     0.421006       0.000478                    0     0
   13(0)    MWL     0.421006       0.000085                    0     0
   14(0)    MWL     0.421006       0.000144                    0     0
   15(0)    MWL     0.421006       0.000028                    0     0
   16(0)    MWL     0.421006       0.000044                    0     0
```

Iterative procedure complete.

Convergence limit for residual cosines = 0.000100 on 2 consecutive iterations.

```
Sample Covariance Matrix :
            Y1          Y2          Y3          Y4          Y5
  Y1     1.000
  Y2     0.245       1.000
  Y3     0.418       0.362       1.000
  Y4     0.282       0.217       0.425       1.000
  Y5     0.257       0.125       0.304       0.784       1.000
  Y6     0.239       0.131       0.330       0.743       0.730
  Y7     0.122       0.149       0.265       0.185       0.221
  Y8     0.253       0.183       0.329       0.021       0.139
  Y9     0.583       0.147       0.455       0.381       0.400
            Y6          Y7          Y8          Y9
  Y6     1.000
  Y7     0.118       1.000
  Y8    -0.027       0.601       1.000
  Y9     0.235       0.385       0.462       1.000
```

Number of cases = 72.

```
Reproduced Covariance Matrix :
            Y1          Y2          Y3          Y4          Y5
  Y1     1.000
  Y2     0.232       1.000
  Y3     0.448       0.225       1.000
  Y4     0.341       0.171       0.330       1.000
  Y5     0.325       0.163       0.315       0.788       1.000
  Y6     0.309       0.155       0.300       0.748       0.715
  Y7     0.210       0.105       0.203       0.052       0.050
  Y8     0.298       0.149       0.289       0.074       0.070
  Y9     0.517       0.260       0.501       0.351       0.336
            Y6          Y7          Y8          Y9
  Y6     1.000
  Y7     0.047       1.000
  Y8     0.067       0.601       1.000
  Y9     0.319       0.331       0.471       1.000
```

Chapter 6

```
Residual Matrix (covariances) :
              Y1          Y2          Y3          Y4          Y5
    Y1    -0.000
    Y2     0.013       0.000
    Y3    -0.030       0.137      -0.000
    Y4    -0.059       0.046       0.095       0.000
    Y5    -0.068      -0.038      -0.011      -0.004       0.000
    Y6    -0.070      -0.024       0.030      -0.005       0.015
    Y7    -0.088       0.044       0.062       0.133       0.171
    Y8    -0.045       0.034       0.040      -0.053       0.069
    Y9     0.066      -0.113      -0.046       0.030       0.064
              Y6          Y7          Y8          Y9
    Y6     0.000
    Y7     0.071      -0.000
    Y8    -0.094      -0.000      -0.000
    Y9    -0.084       0.054      -0.009      -0.000

Value of the maximum absolute residual =     0.171
```

ML Estimates of Free Parameters in Dependence Relationships

	Path	Param #	Point Estimate	90.00% Conf. Int. Lower	90.00% Conf. Int. Upper	Standard Error	T Value
Y1	<- VISUAL	1	0.679	0.483	0.876	0.119	5.70
Y2	<- VISUAL	2	0.341	0.128	0.554	0.130	2.63
Y3	<- VISUAL	3	0.659	0.462	0.856	0.120	5.50
Y4	<- VERBAL	4	0.908	0.751	1.065	0.095	9.51
Y5	<- VERBAL	5	0.867	0.707	1.028	0.098	8.87
Y6	<- VERBAL	6	0.824	0.659	0.989	0.100	8.23
Y7	<- SPEED	7	0.651	0.435	0.866	0.131	4.97
Y8	<- SPEED	8	0.924	0.691	1.158	0.142	6.51
Y9	<- VISUAL	9	0.670	0.449	0.892	0.135	4.98
Y9	<- SPEED	10	0.192	-0.023	0.406	0.130	1.47

Values of Fixed Parameters in Dependence Relationships

	Path	Value
Y1	<- E1	1.000
Y2	<- E2	1.000
Y3	<- E3	1.000
Y4	<- E4	1.000
Y5	<- E5	1.000
Y6	<- E6	1.000
Y7	<- E7	1.000
Y8	<- E8	1.000
Y9	<- E9	1.000

ML estimates of free parameters in variance/covariance relationships

	Path	Param #	Point Estimate	90.00% Conf. Int. Lower	90.00% Conf. Int. Upper	Standard Error	T Value
VISUAL	<-> VERBAL	11	0.552	0.369	0.735	0.111	4.97
VISUAL	<-> SPEED	12	0.474	0.239	0.708	0.143	3.32
VERBAL	<-> SPEED	13	0.088	-0.131	0.307	0.133	0.66
E1	<-> E1	14	0.538	0.373	0.777	0.120	4.49
E2	<-> E2	15	0.884	0.664	1.177	0.154	5.75
E3	<-> E3	16	0.566	0.398	0.806	0.122	4.65
E4	<-> E4	17	0.175	0.100	0.308	0.060	2.92
E5	<-> E5	18	0.248	0.162	0.378	0.064	3.88
E6	<-> E6	19	0.321	0.224	0.459	0.070	4.59
E7	<-> E7	20	0.577	0.387	0.859	0.140	4.13
E8	<-> E8	21	0.146	0.014	1.473	0.205	0.71
E9	<-> E9	22	0.392	0.255	0.604	0.103	3.81

```
Values of Fixed Parameters in Variance/Covariance Relationships

            Path                    Value
------------------------------  ------------
VISUAL      <-> VISUAL              1.000
VERBAL      <-> VERBAL              1.000
SPEED       <-> SPEED               1.000


Maximum Likelihood Discrepancy Function

 Measures of fit of the model
 ---------------------------
 Sample Discrepancy Function Value              : 0.421   (4.210057E-01)

 Population discrepancy function value, Fo
 Bias adjusted point estimate                   : 0.097
 90.000 percent confidence interval             :(0.0,0.354)

 Root mean square error of approximation
 Steiger-Lind : RMSEA = SQRT(Fo/df)
 Point estimate                                 : 0.065
 90.000 percent confidence interval             :(0.0,0.124)

 Expected cross-validation index
 Point estimate (modified aic)                  : 1.041
 90.000 percent confidence interval             :(0.944,1.298)
 CVI (modified AIC) for the saturated model     : 1.268

 Test statistic:                                : 29.891
 Exceedance probabilities:-
 Ho: perfect fit (RMSEA = 0.0)                  : 0.153
 Ho: close fit   (RMSEA <=        0.050)        : 0.330

 Multiplier for obtaining test statistic  =     71.000
 Degrees of freedom                       =     23
 Effective number of parameters           =     22
```

Analyzing the Correlation Structure

The maximum likelihood estimates and measures of t from the two jobs are the same; the standard errors differ. Those from the first job agree with the incorrect standard errors in Lawley and Maxwell; those from the second job agree with Lawley and Maxwell's correct standard errors. Comparison of iteration times in the two jobs shows that the introduction of additional (nuisance) parameters and Lagrange multipliers (TYPE = CORR) results in substantially slower iteration times. The second run differs from the first only in that we specified TYPE = CORR instead of TYPE = COVA.

Chapter 6

The input is:

```
USE ex4b
RAMONA
   MANIFEST = y1 y2 y3 y4 y5 y6 y7 y8 y9
   LATENT = visual verbal speed e1 e2 e3 e4 e5,
            e6 e7 e8 e9
   MODEL y1 <-  visual e1(0,1.0),
         y2 <-  visual e2(0,1.0),
         y3 <-  visual e3(0,1.0),
         y4 <-  verbal e4(0,1.0),
         y5 <-  verbal e5(0,1.0),
         y6 <-  verbal e6(0,1.0),
         y7 <-  speed e7(0,1.0),
         y8 <-  speed e8(0,1.0),
         y9 <-  visual speed e9(0,1.0),
      visual <-> visual(0,1.0),
      verbal <-> verbal(0,1.0),
       speed <-> speed(0,1.0),
      visual <-> verbal,
      visual <-> speed,
      verbal <-> speed
   PRINT = MEDIUM
   ESTIMATE / TYPE=CORR   NCASES=72
```

The output is:

```
There are 9 manifest variables in the model. They are:
     Y1 Y2 Y3 Y4 Y5 Y6 Y7 Y8 Y9


There are 12 latent variables in the model. They are:
     VISUAL E1 E2 E3 VERBAL E4 E5 E6 SPEED E7 E8 E9


RAMONA options in effect are:
    Display                Corr
    Method                 MWL
    Start                  Rough
    Convg                  0.000100
    Maximum iterations     100
    Number of cases        72
    Restart                No
    Confidence Interval    90.000000
Variance paths for errors were omitted from the job specification
and have been added by RAMONA.

Number of manifest variables              =    9
Total number of variables in the system   =   30.
Reading correlation matrix...
```

Path Analysis (RAMONA)

```
                     Details of Iterations
    Iter   Method  Discr. Funct.  Max.R.Cos.   Max.Const.   NRP    NBD
   --------  ------  -------------  -----------  -----------  ----------
       0     OLS      1.013354                    0.0
       1(0)  OLS      0.437034      0.649686      0.192907     0      0
       2(0)  OLS      0.143538      0.092248      0.017916     0      0
       3(0)  OLS      0.135197      0.053602      0.006726     0      0
       4(0)  OLS      0.134714      0.004511      0.000055     0      0
       4(0)  MWL      0.472377      0.164664      0.000055     0      0
       5(0)  MWL      0.425693      0.031463      0.003106     0      0
       6(0)  MWL      0.421825      0.019794      0.001177     0      0
       7(0)  MWL      0.421170      0.006232      0.000072     0      0
       8(0)  MWL      0.421041      0.005613      0.000050     0      0
       9(0)  MWL      0.421014      0.001271      0.000003     0      0
      10(0)  MWL      0.421008      0.001616      0.000003     0      0
      11(0)  MWL      0.421006      0.000284      0.000000     0      0
      12(0)  MWL      0.421006      0.000478      0.000000     0      0
      13(0)  MWL      0.421006      0.000085      0.000000     0      0
      14(0)  MWL      0.421006      0.000144      0.000000     0      0
      15(0)  MWL      0.421006      0.000028      0.000000     0      0
      16(0)  MWL      0.421006      0.000044      0.000000     0      0
```

Iterative procedure complete.

Convergence limit for residual cosines = 0.000100 on 2 consecutive iterations.

Convergence limit for variance constraint violations = 5.00000E-07
Value of the maximum variance constraint violation = 2.14295E-09

```
Sample Correlation Matrix :
            Y1          Y2          Y3          Y4          Y5
   Y1     1.000
   Y2     0.245       1.000
   Y3     0.418       0.362       1.000
   Y4     0.282       0.217       0.425       1.000
   Y5     0.257       0.125       0.304       0.784       1.000
   Y6     0.239       0.131       0.330       0.743       0.730
   Y7     0.122       0.149       0.265       0.185       0.221
   Y8     0.253       0.183       0.329       0.021       0.139
   Y9     0.583       0.147       0.455       0.381       0.400
            Y6          Y7          Y8          Y9
   Y6     1.000
   Y7     0.118       1.000
   Y8    -0.027       0.601       1.000
   Y9     0.235       0.385       0.462       1.000
```

Number of cases = 72.

```
Reproduced Correlation Matrix :
            Y1          Y2          Y3          Y4          Y5
   Y1     1.000
   Y2     0.232       1.000
   Y3     0.448       0.225       1.000
   Y4     0.341       0.171       0.330       1.000
   Y5     0.325       0.163       0.315       0.788       1.000
   Y6     0.309       0.155       0.300       0.748       0.715
   Y7     0.210       0.105       0.203       0.052       0.050
   Y8     0.298       0.149       0.289       0.074       0.070
   Y9     0.517       0.260       0.501       0.351       0.336
            Y6          Y7          Y8          Y9
   Y6     1.000
   Y7     0.047       1.000
   Y8     0.067       0.601       1.000
   Y9     0.319       0.331       0.471       1.000
```

```
Residual Matrix (correlations) :
              Y1          Y2          Y3          Y4          Y5
  Y1        -0.000
  Y2         0.013       0.000
  Y3        -0.030       0.137      -0.000
  Y4        -0.059       0.046       0.095       0.000
  Y5        -0.068      -0.038      -0.011      -0.004       0.000
  Y6        -0.070      -0.024       0.030      -0.005       0.015
  Y7        -0.088       0.044       0.062       0.133       0.171
  Y8        -0.045       0.034       0.040      -0.053       0.069
  Y9         0.066      -0.113      -0.046       0.030       0.064
              Y6          Y7          Y8          Y9
  Y6         0.000
  Y7         0.071      -0.000
  Y8        -0.094      -0.000      -0.000
  Y9        -0.084       0.054      -0.009      -0.000


Value of the maximum absolute residual =      0.171


          ML Estimates of Free Parameters in Dependence Relationships

                                    Point     90.00% Conf. Int.   Standard    T
           Path          Param #   Estimate    Lower     Upper      Error    Value
  -----------------------------------------------------------------------------
  Y1    <- VISUAL           1       0.679     0.537     0.822      0.086     7.87
  Y2    <- VISUAL           2       0.341     0.143     0.539      0.121     2.83
  Y3    <- VISUAL           3       0.659     0.513     0.804      0.089     7.44
  Y4    <- VERBAL           4       0.908     0.850     0.967      0.036    25.52
  Y5    <- VERBAL           5       0.867     0.801     0.934      0.041    21.41
  Y6    <- VERBAL           6       0.824     0.747     0.901      0.047    17.66
  Y7    <- SPEED            7       0.651     0.480     0.821      0.103     6.29
  Y8    <- SPEED            8       0.924     0.741     1.108      0.111     8.30
  Y9    <- VISUAL           9       0.670     0.485     0.856      0.113     5.96
  Y9    <- SPEED           10       0.192    -0.021     0.404      0.129     1.48


Scaled Standard Deviations (nuisance parameters)

       Variable     Estimate
       --------     --------
         Y1          1.000
         Y2          1.000
         Y3          1.000
         Y4          1.000
         Y5          1.000
         Y6          1.000
         Y7          1.000
         Y8          1.000
         Y9          1.000

        Values of Fixed Parameters in Dependence Relationships

               Path                  Value
        -----------------------     --------
         Y1     <- E1                1.000
         Y2     <- E2                1.000
         Y3     <- E3                1.000
         Y4     <- E4                1.000
         Y5     <- E5                1.000
         Y6     <- E6                1.000
         Y7     <- E7                1.000
         Y8     <- E8                1.000
         Y9     <- E9                1.000
```

Path Analysis (RAMONA)

ML estimates of free parameters in variance/covariance relationships

	Path		Param #	Point Estimate	90.00% Conf. Int. Lower	Upper	Standard Error	T Value
VISUAL	<->	VERBAL	11	0.552	0.344	0.708	0.111	4.97
VISUAL	<->	SPEED	12	0.474	0.210	0.674	0.143	3.32
VERBAL	<->	SPEED	13	0.088	-0.132	0.299	0.133	0.66
E1	<->	E1	14	0.538	0.376	0.771	0.117	4.59
E2	<->	E2	15	0.884	0.758	1.030	0.082	10.74
E3	<->	E3	16	0.566	0.403	0.794	0.117	4.85
E4	<->	E4	17	0.175	0.096	0.322	0.065	2.72
E5	<->	E5	18	0.248	0.155	0.395	0.070	3.52
E6	<->	E6	19	0.321	0.216	0.476	0.077	4.17
E7	<->	E7	20	0.577	0.393	0.847	0.135	4.29
E8	<->	E8	21	0.146	0.014	1.491	0.206	0.71
E9	<->	E9	22	0.392	0.250	0.615	0.107	3.66

Values of Fixed Parameters in Variance/Covariance Relationships

	Path		Value
VISUAL	<->	VISUAL	1.000
VERBAL	<->	VERBAL	1.000
SPEED	<->	SPEED	1.000

Equality Constraints on Variances

Constraint			Value	Lagrange Multiplier	Standard Error
Y1	<->	Y1	1.0000	0.000	-0.000
Y2	<->	Y2	1.0000	0.000	-0.000
Y3	<->	Y3	1.0000	0.000	0.000
Y4	<->	Y4	1.0000	0.000	0.000
Y5	<->	Y5	1.0000	0.000	-0.000
Y6	<->	Y6	1.0000	0.000	-0.000
Y7	<->	Y7	1.0000	0.000	-0.000
Y8	<->	Y8	1.0000	0.000	-0.000
Y9	<->	Y9	1.0000	0.000	0.000

Maximum Likelihood Discrepancy Function

Measures of fit of the model

Sample Discrepancy Function Value   : 0.421   (4.210057E-01)

Population discrepancy function value, Fo
Bias adjusted point estimate   : 0.097
90.000 percent confidence interval   :(0.0,0.354)

Root mean square error of approximation
Steiger-Lind : RMSEA = SQRT(Fo/df)
Point estimate   : 0.065
90.000 percent confidence interval   :(0.0,0.124)

Expected cross-validation index
Point estimate (modified aic)   : 1.041
90.000 percent confidence interval   :(0.944,1.298)
CVI (modified AIC) for the saturated model   : 1.268

Test statistic: : 29.891
Exceedance probabilities:-
Ho: perfect fit (RMSEA = 0.0)   : 0.153
Ho: close fit   (RMSEA <=   0.050)   : 0.330

Multiplier for obtaining test statistic = 71.000
Degrees of freedom   = 23
Effective number of parameters   = 22

Computation

Algorithms

Let γ be the parameter vector and $\Sigma = \Sigma(\gamma)$ the covariance structure. Parameter estimates are obtained by minimizing a discrepancy function, $F(\mathbf{S}, \Sigma(\gamma))$, specified using METHOD. Alternatives are:

MWL
Maximum Wishart likelihood.
$F(\mathbf{S}, \Sigma) = \ln|\Sigma| - \ln|\mathbf{S}| + \text{tr}[\mathbf{S}\,\Sigma^{-1}] - p$

GLS
Generalized least squares assuming a Wishart distribution for $\mathbf{S}$.
$F(\mathbf{S}, \Sigma) = \frac{1}{2}\,\text{tr}[S^{-1}(\mathbf{S} - \Sigma)]^2$

OLS
Ordinary least squares.
$F(\mathbf{S}, \Sigma) = \frac{1}{2}\,\text{tr}[(\mathbf{S} - \Sigma)]^2$

ADFU, ADFG
Asymptotically distribution-free methods
$F(\mathbf{S}, \Sigma) = (s - \sigma)'\,\hat{\Gamma}^{-1}(s - \sigma)$
where s and σ are column vectors with $p(p+1)/2$ elements formed from the distinct elements of $\mathbf{S}$ and Σ, respectively, and $\hat{\Gamma}$ is an estimate of the asymptotic covariance matrix of sample covariances. For ADFU, $\hat{\Gamma}$ is unbiased (Browne, 1982) but need not be positive definite. If $\hat{\Gamma}$ is indefinite, the program moves automatically from ADFU to ADFG. With ADFG, $\hat{\Gamma}$ is biased but Gramian (Browne, 1982).

An iterative Gauss-Newton computing procedure with constraints (Browne and Du Toit, 1992) is used to obtain parameter estimates. With MWL, the weight matrix is respecified on each iteration. The procedure is then equivalent to the Aitchison and Silvey (1960) adaptation of the Fisher scoring method to deal with equality constraints.

Some computer programs can yield negative estimates of variances. This does not happen with RAMONA. Bounds are imposed to ensure that variance estimates are non-negative and that all correlation estimates lie between −1 and +1. The imposition of these bounds can result in the convergence of RAMONA in situations where programs that do not impose them fail to converge. In some cases, a program that allows negative variance estimates and does converge will yield a smaller discrepancy function value than RAMONA.

Iteration is continued until the largest absolute residual cosine (Browne, 1982) falls below a tolerance, specified in CONVG, on two consecutive iterations.

Confidence Intervals

Approximate 90% confidence intervals are given for parameter estimates associated with dependence paths and with covariance paths. Confidence intervals for path coefficients and covariances (variances unrestricted) are provided under the assumption of a normal distribution for the estimator $\hat{\gamma}$ (Browne, 1974) and are symmetric about the parameter estimate. Confidence intervals for other parameters are nonsymmetric about the parameter estimate (Browne, 1974) and are obtained under the following assumptions:

- Correlation coefficients (covariances with both corresponding variances restricted to unity): a normal distribution is assumed for the z-transform, $\frac{1}{2}\ln[(1 + \hat{\gamma})/(1 - \hat{\gamma})]$, (Browne, 1974).

- Variances: a normal distribution is assumed for the natural logarithm, $\ln\hat{\gamma}$, (Browne, 1974).

- Error variances under a correlation structure (corresponding dependent variable variances are constrained to unity): a normal distribution is assumed for $-\ln(\hat{\gamma}^{-1} - 1)$ (Browne, 1974).

Measures of Fit of a Model

This section provides a brief description of the measures of fit output by RAMONA. Further information concerning these measures of fit can be found in Browne and Cudeck (1992).

Let $N = n + 1$ be the sample size; p, the number of manifest variables; and q, the number of free parameters in the model. Then the number of degrees of freedom is $d = \frac{1}{2} p(p + 1) - q$. The sample covariance matrix is denoted by S and the corresponding population covariance matrix by Σ_0.

The minimal sample discrepancy function value is

$$\hat{F} = \min_{\gamma} F(S, \sum(\gamma))$$

Now F_0 is bounded below by 0 and takes on a value of 0 if and only if Σ_0 satisfies the structural model exactly. Therefore, we can regard F_0 as a measure of badness-of-fit of the model, $\Sigma(\gamma)$, to the population covariance matrix, Σ_0.

We assume that the test statistic $n\hat{F}$ has an approximate noncentral chi-square distribution with d degrees of freedom and a noncentrality parameter $\sigma = nF_0$. This will be true if the discrepancy function is correctly specified for the distribution of the data, F_0 is small enough, and N is large enough (Steiger, Shapiro, and Browne, 1985). Then the expected value of $\hat{F}$ will be approximately $F_0 + d/n$, so that $\hat{F}$ is a biased estimator of F_0. As a less biased point estimator of F_0 we use:

$$\hat{F}_0 = \text{Max}\{\hat{F} - (d/n), 0\}$$

We also provide a 90% confidence interval on F_0 as suggested by Steiger and Lind (1980). Let $\Phi(x|\delta, d)$ be the cumulative distribution function of a noncentral chi-square distribution with noncentrality parameter δ and d degrees of freedom. Given $x = n \times \hat{F}$ and d, the lower limit, δ_L, of the 90% confidence interval on $n \times F_0$ is the solution for δ of the equation

$$\Phi(x|\delta, d) = 0.95$$

and the upper limit δ_U is the solution for δ of

$$\Phi(x|\delta, d) = 0.05$$

A 90% confidence interval on F_0 is then given by $(n^{-1}\delta_L; n^{-1}\delta_U)$.

Because F_0 cannot increase if additional parameters are added, it gives little guidance about when to stop adding parameters. It is preferable to use the root mean square error of approximation (Steiger and Lind, 1980):

$$\text{RMSEA} = \sqrt{\frac{\hat{F}_0}{d}}$$

as a measure of the fit per degree of freedom of the model. This population measure of badness-of-fit is also bounded below by 0 and will be 0 only if the model fits perfectly. It will decrease if the inclusion of additional parameters substantially reduces F_0 but will increase if the inclusion of additional parameters reduces F_0 only slightly. Consequently, it can give some guidance as to how many parameters to use. Practical experience has suggested that a value of the RMSEA of about 0.05 or less indicates a close fit of the model in relation to the degrees of freedom. A value of about 0.08 or less indicates a reasonable fit of the model in relation to the degrees of freedom.

A point estimate of the RMSEA is given by

$$\text{Estimate (RMSEA)} = \sqrt{\frac{\hat{F}_0}{d}}$$

and a 90% confidence interval by

$$\text{Interval Estimate (RMSEA)} = \left(\sqrt{\frac{\delta_L}{nd}}; \sqrt{\frac{\delta_U}{nd}}\right) \quad \text{Equation 6-4}$$

The RMSEA does not depend on sample size and therefore does not take into account the fact that it is unwise to fit a model with many parameters if N is small. A measure of fit that does this is the expected cross-validation index (ECVI). Consider two samples of size N—a calibration sample C and a validation sample V. Suppose that the model is fitted to the calibration sample yielding a reproduced covariance matrix $\hat{\Sigma}_C$. The discrepancy between $\hat{\Sigma}_C$ and the validation sample covariance matrix S_V is then measured with the discrepancy function yielding $F(S_V, \hat{\Sigma}_C)$ as a measure of stability under cross-validation. A difficulty with this approach is that two samples are required. One can avoid a second sample by estimating the expected value of $F(S_V, \hat{\Sigma}_C)$ from a single sample. Assume that the discrepancy function is correctly specified for the distribution of the data. Taking expectations over calibration samples and validation samples gives the expected cross-validation index:

$$\text{ECVI} = \underset{CV}{\xi\xi} F(SV, \hat{\Sigma}_C) \approx F_0 + (d + 2q)/n \quad \text{Equation 6-5}$$

A point estimate of the ECVI is given by (Browne and Cudeck, 1990):

$$\text{Estimate (ECVI)} = \hat{F} + 2q/n \quad \text{Equation 6-6}$$

If METHOD is set to MWL, this point estimate of the ECVI is related by a linear transformation to the Akaike Information Criterion (Akaike, 1973) and will lead to the same conclusions.

The point estimate in Equation 6-6 will decrease if an additional parameter reduces $\hat{F}$ sufficiently and increases otherwise. This will give some guidance as to the number of parameters to retain. However, the amount of reduction in $\hat{F}$ required before an increase in the point estimate occurs is affected by the sample size. If n is very large, increasing the number of parameters will tend to reduce the point estimate of the ECVI. One should also bear in mind that sampling variability affects the point estimates.

An approximate 90% confidence interval on the ECVI may be obtained from:

$$\text{Interval Estimate (ECVI)} = \left(\frac{\delta_L + d + 2q}{n}; \frac{\delta_U + d + 2q}{n}\right) \quad \text{Equation 6-7}$$

It can happen that $(\hat{F} - d) < \delta_L$, so that the point estimate in Equation 6-6 is smaller than the lower limit of the confidence interval in Equation 6-7. In particular, this will be true if the (approximately unbiased) point estimate in Equation 6-6 is less than the lower bound $(d + 2q)/n$ for the approximation to the ECVI given in Equation 6-5.

For comparative purposes, RAMONA also provides the ECVI of the saturated model where no structure is imposed on Σ:

$$\text{ECVI (Saturated Model)} = \frac{2 \times (d + q)}{n}$$

The test statistic $n \times \hat{F}$ is also output by RAMONA. We follow convention in providing the exceedance probability, $1 - \Phi(n\hat{F} \mid 0, d)$, for a test of the point hypothesis

$$H_0: F_0 = 0 \quad \text{Equation 6-8}$$

which implies that the model holds exactly. Our opinion, however, is that this null hypothesis is implausible and that it does not much help to know whether or not the statistical test has been able to detect that it is false. More relevant is the exceedance probability for an interval hypothesis of close fit, which we define by

$$H_0: \text{RMSEA} \leq 0.05 \quad \text{Equation 6-9}$$

and which implies that $\delta \leq \delta^* = n \times d \times 0.05^2$.

The exceedance probability output by RAMONA is given by $1 - \Phi(n\hat{F} \mid \delta^*, d)$.

Note that the null hypothesis of perfect fit in Equation 6-8 is not rejected at the 5% level if $\delta_L = 0$ or, equivalently, the lower limit of the confidence interval in Equation

6-4 is 0. The null hypothesis of close fit in Equation 6-9 is not rejected at the 5% level if the lower limit of the confidence interval in Equation 6-4 is not greater than 0.05.

When METHOD is set to MWL, two sets of measures of fit are output. One is based on the maximum likelihood discrepancy function value

$$\hat{F} = \ln|\hat{\Sigma}| - \ln|S| + \text{tr}[S\hat{\Sigma}^{-1}] - p$$

and the other on the generalized least squares discrepancy function value

$$\hat{F} = \frac{1}{2}\text{tr}[\hat{\Sigma}^{-1}(S - \hat{\Sigma})]$$

When the model fits well, the differences between the two sets of fit measures should be small (Browne, 1974).

References

Aitchison, J. and Silvey, S. D. (1960). Maximum likelihood estimation procedures and associated tests of significance. *Journal of the Royal Statistical Society*, Series B, 22, 154–171.

Akaike, H. (1973). Information theory and an extension of the maximum likelihood principle. *Second International Symposium on Information Theory,* B. N. Petrov and F. Csaki, eds. Budapest: Akademiai Kiado.

Bentler, P. M. and Weeks, D. G. (1980). Linear structural equations with latent variables. *Psychometrika*, 45, 289–308.

Bollen, K. A. (1989). *Structural equations with latent variables.* New York: John Wiley & Sons, Inc.

Browne, M. W. (1974). Generalized least squares estimators in the analysis of covariance structures. *South African Statistical Journal*, 8, 1–24. (Reprinted in *Latent Variables in Socioeconomic Models*, D. J. Aigner and A. S. Goldberger, eds. 205–226. Amsterdam: North Holland.)

Browne, M. W. (1982). Covariance structures. In *Topics in Applied Multivariate Analysis*, D. M. Hawkins, ed. 72–141. Cambridge: Cambridge University Press.

Browne, M. W. and Cudeck, R. (1990). Single sample cross-validation indices for covariance structures. *Multivariate Behavioral Research*, 24, 445–455.

Browne, M. W. and Cudeck, R. (1992). Alternative ways of assessing model fit. *Testing Structural Equation Models,* K. A. Bollen and J. S. Long, eds. Beverly Hills, Calif.: Sage.

Browne, M. W. and Du Toit, S. H. C. (1992). Automated fitting of nonstandard models. *Multivariate Behavioral Research.*

Cudeck, R. (1989). Analysis of correlation matrices using covariance structure models. *Psychological Bulletin,* 105, 317–327.

Duncan, O. D., Haller, A. O., and Portes, A. (1971). Peer influence on aspirations, a reinterpretation. *Causal Models in the Social Sciences*, H. M. Blalock, ed. 219–244. Aldine-Atherstone.

Everitt, B. S. (1984). *An introduction to latent variable models.* New York: Chapman and Hall.

Guttman, L. (1954). A new approach to factor analysis: The radex. *Mathematical Thinking in the Social Sciences*, P. F. Lazarsfeld, ed. 258–348. Glencoe: The Free Press.

Jöreskog, K. G. (1977). Structural equation models in the social sciences: Specification estimation and testing. *Applications of Statistics*, P. R. Krishnaiah, ed. 265–287. Amsterdam: North Holland.

Lawley, D. N. and Maxwell, A. E. (1971). *Factor analysis as a statistical method.* 2nd ed. New York: American Elsevier.

McArdle J. J. (1988). Dynamic but structural equation modeling of repeated measures data.

Handbook of Multivariate Experimental Psychology, J. R. Nesselroade and R. B. Cattell, eds. 2nd ed. 561–614. New York: Plenum.

McArdle, J. J., and McDonald, R. P. (1984). Some algebraic properties of the Reticular Action Model for moment structures. *British Journal of Mathematical and Statistical Psychology,* 37, 234–251.

McDonald, R. P. (1985). *Factor analysis and related methods.* Hillsdale: Erlbaum.

Mels, G. (1988). *A general system for path analysis with latent variables.* M. Sc. thesis, University of South Africa.

Mels, G. and Koorts, A. S. (1989). *Causal Models for various job aspects. SAIPA,* 24, 144–156.

Shapiro, A. and Browne, M. W. (1987). Analysis of covariance structures under elliptical distributions. *Journal of the American Statistical Association,* 82, 1092–1097.

Steiger, J. H. and Lind, J. (1980). *Statistically based tests for the number of common factors.* Paper presented at the annual meeting of the Psychometric Society: Iowa City.

Steiger, J. H., Shapiro, A., and Browne, M. W. (1985). On the asymptotic distribution of sequential chi-square statistics. *Psychometrika,* 50, 253–264.

Wheaton, B., Muthén, B., Alwin, D. F., and Summers, G. F. (1977). Assessing reliability and stability in panel models. *Sociological Methodology 1977,* D. R. Heise, ed. 84–136. San Francisco: Jossey-Bass.

Acknowledgments

The development of this program was partially supported by the Institute of Statistical Research of the South African Human Sciences Research Council, the South African Foundation for Research Development, and the University of South Africa.

The authors are indebted to Professor S.H.C. du Toit and to Mrs. Yvette Seymore for a number of subroutines used in the program.

Chapter 7

Perceptual Mapping

Leland Wilkinson

PERMAP offers two types of tools. The first is a group of procedures for fitting subjects and objects in a common space. This group includes Carroll's (1972) internal and external unfolding models, MDPREF and PREFMAP, as well as Gabriel's (1971) BIPLOT, which is a minor modification of MDPREF. The second is a set of procedures for relating one dimensional configuration to another, generally called a Procrustes rotation. Both the orthogonal Procrustes and the more general canonical rotations are available.

PERMAP is a misnomer. Although most of the techniques it incorporates have been used for perceptual mapping, they have applications outside of market research or psychology and, like the biplot technique, may even have their origins elsewhere. Furthermore, classical perceptual mapping techniques, such as multidimensional scaling, correspondence analysis, and principal components, are found elsewhere in SYSTAT. In the end, since almost all of the methods in this module involve a singular value decomposition and are not bulky enough to deserve their own modules, they have been collected into a single grab bag.

Statistical Background

Perceptual mapping involves a variety of techniques for displaying the judgments of a set of objects by a group of subjects. Most of these techniques were developed in the 1970's by psychometricians, but they were soon adopted by market researchers and scientists for analyzing a variety of preference and similarity data.

In applied usage, especially among market researchers, perceptual mapping is an even more general term. Some commercial perceptual mapping programs are based on classical statistical or psychometric models. Some of these methods include Fisher's linear discriminant function, correspondence analysis, factor analysis, and multidimensional scaling. Indeed, any procedure that produces a set of coordinates in a q dimensional space from an $n \times p$ matrix, $q \leq \min(n, p)$, can be considered perceptual mapping in the broad, applied sense. Quantitative theoretical market researchers (for example, Green and Tull, 1975, and Lilien, Kotler, and Moorthy, 1992) use the term in this more general sense as well.

The origin of the term can be found in classical psychometrics (see Cliff, 1973, for a review). Soon after the development of psychometric spatial models, some psychologists thought scaling methods could be used to derive "cognitive maps" from subjects' ratings of stimuli. These maps would be "pictures" of the mental structures used to perceive and integrate information. Following the classic linguistic studies of Osgood, Suci, and Tannenbaum (1957), researchers produced intriguing cognitive maps of stimuli such as countries, cities, adjectives, colors, and consumer products (for example, Wish, Deutsch, and Biener, 1972, and Milgram and Jodelet, 1976).

Not long afterwards, perceptual and memory psychologists abandoned the cognitive map model and developed theories based on information processing, problem solving, and associative memory. Research by Shepard and Cooper (1982) and Kosslyn (1981), for example, focused specifically on the storage and processing of mental images rather than inferring spatial structure among nonspatial stimuli from associations between responses to attributes. Shepard's psychometric findings on mental rotations, for example, were subsequently confirmed at the physiological level (Dow, 1990).

While no longer an active theoretical model, perceptual mapping *can* be useful as a general collection of procedures for presenting statistical analyses to nontechnical clients. Like classification trees, perceptual maps can show complex relations relatively simply without algebra or statistical parameters. It is easier for many clients to judge a distance on a map than to evaluate a conditional probability. Thus, perceptual mapping techniques can be useful for data that have nothing to do with perception.

Preference Mapping

A variety of algebraic and geometric models of preferences have been developed over the last century. The unidimensional preference model (Coombs, 1950) is presented in the following figure. Imagine that three subjects have expressed their preferences for each of five objects (A,B,C,D,E). If their preferences can be represented by a single dimension, the following figure is one of several possible models. Each subject's preference strength on the single attribute dimension is represented by a normal distribution. In this model, the farther an object is from the mean of the subject's preference distribution, the less that object is preferred. Following this rule, in the following figure, the ordering of preferences for the five objects shows above each subject's curve. Thus, the leftmost subject prefers object *B* most and *E* least, while the rightmost subject prefers *E* most and *A* least. The following figure is the unidimensional preference model for normal curves.

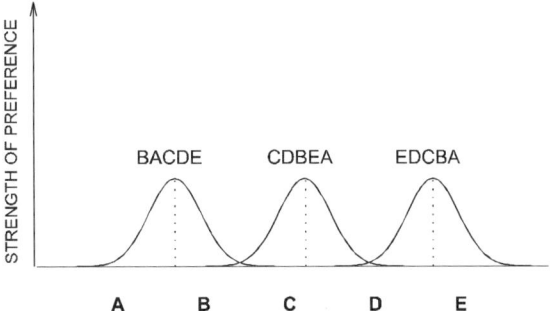

Coombs devised a method for recovering a unidimensional preference scale from the subjects' rankings of the objects. His procedure is called *unfolding*. If we assume that the distances to objects from a subject's ideal point on the scale are all positive and follow the usual distance axioms (see Chapter 2), then direction doesn't enter into the calculation of preference. We can therefore imagine folding the scale about the subject's ideal point to see the point of view of that subject. Coombs discovered that if there are enough subjects and objects, we can *unfold* the scale from the given orderings of the subjects' preferences without knowing the strengths of the preferences. In general, the more subjects and objects, the less room there is to represent the preference orderings correctly by moving the locations of the preference curves. Like MDS itself, the system becomes highly constrained to allow only one solution. The MDS procedure in SYSTAT can be used to compute Coomb's solution for unidimensional data.

Students of Coombs (Bennet and Hays, 1960) extended the unfolding model to higher dimensions. The multidimensional preference model for normal curves shows how this works. As in the unidimensional preference model for normal curves, there are three subjects and five objects. The closest subject's preference curve leads to preferences of *BCEAD*, in left-to-right order. The other two subjects have preference curves nearest object *E* in the center of the configuration. Consequently, their most preferred object is *E*. In the multidimensional model, distance is calculated in all directions from the center of the subject's preference curve. Again, the SYSTAT MDS module can be used to find solutions for multidimensional unfolding problems. The following figure is the multidimensional preference model for normal curves.

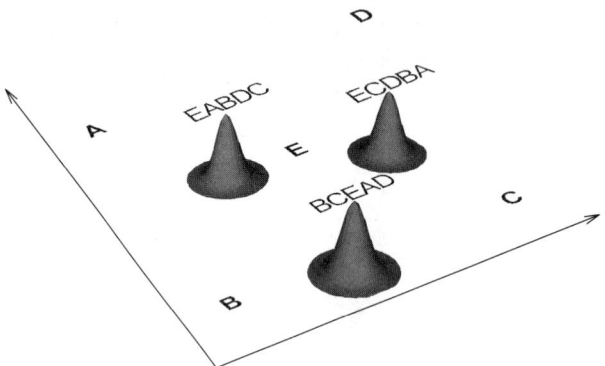

Preference curves do not have to be normal, symmetric, or even probability distributions. Carroll (1972) devised an unfolding procedure based on a quadratic preference curve model. He called the procedure "external" because it relied on quantitative ratings of the subject's preferences *and* a previously determined fixed configuration of objects in a space. While ordinary unfolding begins with an $n \times p$ matrix of n subjects' rank orderings of p objects, external unfolding begins with a $p \times q$ matrix of p objects' coordinates in q dimensions and a $p \times n$ matrix of n subjects' ratings of their preferences for the p objects.

The unidimensional preference model for quadratic curves shows Carroll's model in one dimension. Unlike the normal curve model, the quadratic preference curves involve negative preferences. The subject on the left in the unidimensional preference model for normal curves, for example, is indifferent about object E (or more indifferent than she is about object D). The subject on the left in the unidimensional preference model for quadratic curves, on the other hand, likes object E least. Carroll's model is therefore appropriate for data following a bipolar (approach-avoidance) preference model. The following is the unidimensional preference model for quadratic curves.

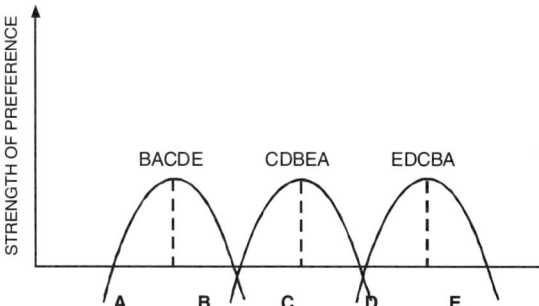

Carroll fits each subject's vector of preferences to a configuration of objects via ordinary least squares. In fact, the preference curves in the previous unidimensional preference model for quadratic curves are really inverted (negative) quadratic loss for each subject when Carroll's least squares fitting method is used to fit her vector of preferences to the coordinates of the objects.

Carroll offers four fitting methods, three of which appear in SYSTAT. The first, called the VECTOR model in SYSTAT, is simply a multiple regression of the preference vector on the coordinates themselves:

$$s_{ij} = \sum_{k=1}^{q} a_{ik} x_{jk} + b_i + e_{ij}$$

where s_{ij} is the preference scale value of the jth stimulus for the ith subject. The coefficients a_{ik} are estimated from regressing $\mathbf{y}$ (the vector of preferences) on $\mathbf{X}$ (the $p \times q$ matrix of coordinates) and then transforming the coefficients.

This is called a vector model because the resulting fit is displayed as a vector superimposed on the object configuration. Preferences are predicted from the perpendicular projections of the objects' coordinates onto each vector.

The second model, called the CIRCLE model in SYSTAT, is the one in the figures above. It is fit by regressing each subject's preferences on the coordinates and squared coordinates of the object configuration. From the coefficients in this regression, the ideal points are established in the coordinate space of the object configuration. In two dimensions, the intersection of each preference surface with the zero preference plane is a circle. The basic algebraic model is

$$s_{ij} = a_i d_{ij}^2 + b_i + e_{ij}$$

where

$$d_{ij}^2 = \sum_{k=1}^{q} (x_{jk} - y_{ik})^2$$

The third model, called the ELLIPSE model in SYSTAT, allows for differential weighting of preference dimensions. It uses weights in computing the distances instead of the ordinary regression in the circular model. As a result, each preference curve may be elliptical at the zero preference plane. The model is

$$s_{ij} = a_i d_{ij}^2 + b_i + e_{ij}$$

where

$$d_{ij}^2 = \sum_{k=1}^{q} w_{ik}(x_{jk} - y_{ik})^2$$

Biplots and MDPREF

The CORAN procedure in SYSTAT performs a correspondence analysis on a tabular matrix. The singular value decomposition is used to compute row and column coordinates in a single configuration. These coordinates are popularly represented as a set of vectors for the columns and a set of points for the rows.

Biplots (Gabriel, 1971) are a singular value decomposition of a general $n \times p$ matrix. MDPREF (Carroll, 1972) is the same model except that the vectors (column coordinates) are standardized to have equal length. This is because Carroll developed the procedure for representing preferences with the vector model based on n subjects' preferences for p objects.

Procrustes Rotations

Procrustes rotations involve matching a source configuration to a target. SYSTAT offers two types of rotations. The first is a **classical orthogonal Procrustes rotation** (Schönemann, 1966). This produces a fit by rotating and transposing axes and is especially suited for principal components and factor analyses.

The second method, called **canonical rotation** in SYSTAT, is a general translation, rotation, reflection, and uniform dilation transformation that is ideally suited for multidimensional scaling and any procedure where location, scale, and orientation are arbitrary. This method is documented in Borg and Groenen (1997).

Perceptual Mapping in SYSTAT

Perceptual Mapping Main Dialog Box

To open the Perceptual Mapping dialog box, from the menus choose:

Statistics
  Data Reduction
    Perceptual Mapping...

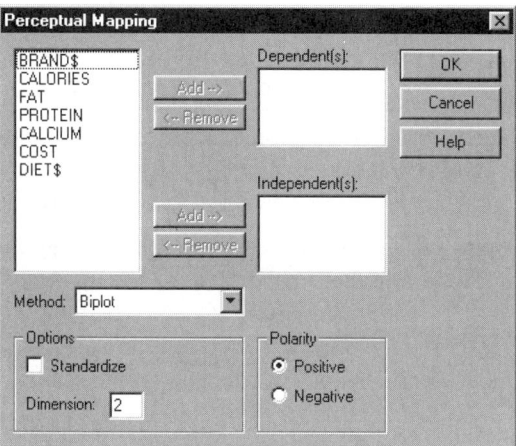

Dependent(s). The dependent variables should be continuous or categorical numeric variables (for example, *income*).

Independent(s). The independent variables should be continuous or categorical variables (grouping variables).

Method. The following methods are available.

- **Biplot.** Requires only a dependent variable. Biplots are a singular value decomposition of a general matrix.
- **Canonical rotations.** Requires both a dependent and independent variable. Relates a one-dimensional configuration to another. Canonical rotation is a general translation, rotation, reflection, and uniform dilation transformation that is ideally suited for multidimensional scaling and any procedure where location, scale, and orientation are arbitrary.
- **Circle.** Requires both a dependent and an independent variable. The columns of the first set are fit to the configuration in the second.
- **Ellipse.** Requires both a dependent and an independent variable. The columns of the first set are fit to the configuration in the second.
- **MDPREF.** Requires only a dependent variable. MDPREF is a biplot except that the vectors (column coordinates) are the same unit length.
- **Procrustes.** Requires both a dependent and an independent variable. Procrustes rotation relates a one-dimensional configuration to another and involves matching a source configuration to a target. It produces a fit by rotating and transposing axes and is especially suited for principal components and factor analyses.
- **Vector.** Requires both a dependent and an independent variable. The columns of the first set are fit to the configuration in the second.

Standardize. Standardizes the data before fitting.

Dimension. Specifies the number of dimensions in which to do the scaling.

Polarity. Specifies the polarity of the preferences when doing preference mapping. If the smaller number indicates the least and the higher number the most, select **Positive**. For example, a questionnaire may include the question, "Rate a list of movies where one star is the worst and five stars is the best." If the higher number indicates a lower ranking and the lower number indicates a higher ranking, select **Negative**. For example, a questionnaire may include the question, "Rank your favorite sports team where 1 is the best and 10 is the worst."

Using Commands

After selecting a file with USE filename, continue with:

```
PERMAP
     MODEL varlist or depvarlist = indvarlist
     ESTIMATE / METHOD = BIPLOT
                         MDPREF
                         VECTOR
                         CIRCLE
                         ELLIPSE
                         PROCRUSTES
                         CANONICAL ,
                STANDARDIZE ,
                DIMENSION = n ,
                POLARITY= POSITIVE
                         NEGATIVE
```

Usage Considerations

Types of data. PERMAP uses only rectangular data.

Print options. The output is standard for all PRINT options.

Quick Graphs. PERMAP produces Quick Graphs for every analysis. You can turn these off with GRAPH=NONE.

Saving files. PERMAP does not save coordinates.

BY groups. PERMAP analyzes data by groups.

Bootstrapping. Bootstrapping is available in this procedure.

Case frequencies. PERMAP uses the FREQ variable, if present, to duplicate cases. This inflates the total degrees of freedom to be the sum of the number of frequencies. Using a FREQ variable does not require more memory, however.

Case weights. PERMAP does not use WEIGHT.

Examples

Example 1
Vector Model

The PREFMAP procedure of Carroll is implemented through a model that regresses a set of subjects (the left side of the model equation) onto the coordinates of a set of objects (the right side of the model equation). The file *SYMP* contains coordinates from a multidimensional scaling of disease symptoms from Wilkinson, Blank, and Gruber (1996). It also contains, for a selected set of diseases, indicators for the presence or absence of a symptom. These are informal ratings.

The input for fitting the vector model to the data is:

```
USE SYMP
IDVAR=SYMPTOM$
PERMAP
     MODEL LYME MALARIA YELLOW RABIES FLU = DIM1 DIM2
     ESTIMATE / METHOD=VECTOR
```

Following is the output:

```
Variables in the SYSTAT Rectangular file are:
SYMPTOM$    DIM1         DIM2          LYME        MALARIA      YELLOW      RABIES       FLU
Configuration has been centered prior to fitting.
External unfolding via vector model.
Goodness of fit for subjects
 Subject    R-square      F-ratio       df          "p"
    1        0.007         0.056       2  15       0.946
    2        0.029         0.226       2  15       0.800
    3        0.173         1.574       2  15       0.240
    4        0.059         0.474       2  15       0.632
    5        0.079         0.642       2  15       0.540

Regression coefficients for subjects
                           1            2            3
             1            0.0          0.057       -0.002
             2            0.0          0.096       -0.070
             3            0.0          0.170        0.177
             4            0.0         -0.073        0.161
             5            0.0         -0.084        0.147

Subject coordinates
                           1            2
             1           0.999       -0.032
             2           0.806       -0.592
             3           0.692        0.722
             4          -0.415        0.910
             5          -0.496        0.869

EXPORT successfully completed.
```

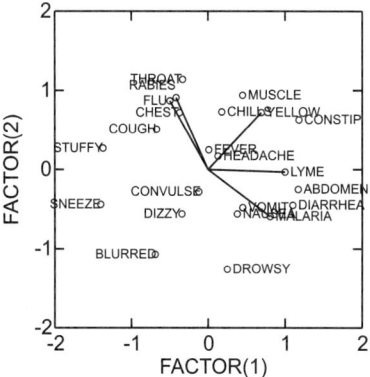

External Unfolding Vector Model

Example 2
Circle Model

The circular model places the diseases near the symptoms they most involve. The input for fitting the circle model to the data is:

```
USE SYMP
IDVAR=SYMPTOM$
PERMAP
    MODEL LYME MALARIA YELLOW RABIES FLU = DIM1 DIM2
    ESTIMATE / METHOD=CIRCLE
```

Following is the output:

```
Variables in the SYSTAT Rectangular file are:
 SYMPTOM$    DIM1         DIM2         LYME         MALARIA      YELLOW       RABIES       FLU
Configuration has been centered prior to fitting.
External unfolding via circular ideal point model.
Goodness of fit for subjects
 Subject    R-square     F-ratio      df           "p"
      1       0.271        1.735      3   14       0.206
      2       0.385        2.926      3   14       0.071
      3       0.265        1.685      3   14       0.216
      4       0.257        1.615      3   14       0.231
      5       0.079        0.401      3   14       0.755 Anti-Ideal

Regression coefficients for subjects
                           1            2            3            4
      1        0.379        0.001       -0.046       -0.380
      2        0.449        0.029       -0.123       -0.450
      3        0.191        0.142        0.155       -0.191
      4        0.334       -0.123        0.122       -0.335
      5       -0.009       -0.083        0.148        0.009
```

Chapter 7

```
Subject coordinates
                    1         2
         1        0.017    -1.000
         2        0.232    -0.973
         3        0.675     0.738
         4       -0.710     0.704
         5        0.487    -0.874

EXPORT successfully completed.
```

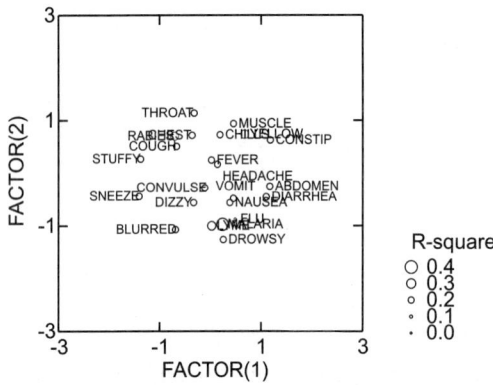

External Unfolding Circular Model

Example 3
Internal Model

The *DIVORCE* file includes grounds for divorce in the United States in 1971. It is adapted from Wilkinson, Blank, and Gruber (1996), and originally from Long (1971). We will do an *MDPREF* analysis on these data to plot the rows and columns in a common space. The input is:

```
USE DIVORCE
IDVAR STATE$
PERMAP
     MODEL ADULTERY..SEPARATE
     ESTIMATE / METHOD=MDPREF
```

Following is the output:

```
Variables in the SYSTAT Rectangular file are:
  ADULTERY     CRUELTY      DESERT       SUPPORT      FELONY       IMPOTENT
  PREGNANT     DRUGS        CONTRACT     INSANE       BIGAMY       SEPARATE
  STATE$
Configuration has been centered prior to fitting.
MDPREF (Biplot) Analysis
Eigenvalues
    1            2            3            4            5            6            7            8            9
   19.196       18.277        9.792        9.132        8.035        6.483        4.825        3.595        2.278
   10           11           12
    0.866        0.581        0.000

Vector coordinates
                          1            2
              1         0.657        0.754
              2         0.540        0.842
              3         0.661        0.751
              4         0.078        0.997
              5         0.746        0.666
              6         0.969       -0.248
              7         0.793       -0.610
              8         0.626        0.780
              9         0.694       -0.720
             10        -0.657       -0.754
             11         0.851       -0.525
             12        -0.982        0.191

Object coordinates
                          1            2
              1         0.102        0.117
              2         0.048        0.092
              3        -0.032        0.088
              :            :            :
             49        -0.165        0.007
             50         0.176        0.057

EXPORT successfully completed.
```

Following is a graph of the output:

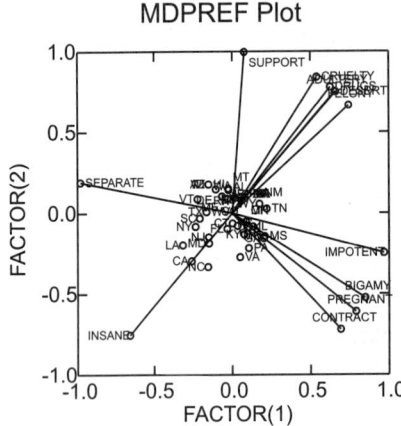

The biplot looks similar, with all of the grounds for divorce vectors approximately equal in length because the original data have comparable variances on these variables.

Example 4
Procrustes Rotation

In a profound but seldom-cited dissertation, Wilkinson (1975) scaled perceptions of cars and dogs among car club and dog club members. The file *CARDOG* contains the INDSCAL configurations of the scalings of cars and dogs. Wilkinson paired cars and dogs by using subjects' responses on additional rating scales of attributes. INDSCAL dimensions, on the other hand, are claimed to have an intrinsic canonical orientation that ordinarily precludes rotation (see the references in "Multidimensional Scaling"). The question here, then, is whether a Procrustes rotation guided by the extrinsically based pairings will change the original INDSCAL configurations. We will rotate cars to dogs. The input is:

```
USE CARDOG
PERMAP
    MODEL C1,C2 = D1,D2
    ESTIMATE/METHOD=PROCRUSTES
```

Perceptual Mapping

Following is the output:

```
Orthogonal Procrustes Rotation
Rotation matrix T
                            1           2

              1           0.98        0.21
              2          -0.21        0.98

Target (X) coordinates
                            1           2

              1          21.00       -1.00
              2          13.00       -6.00
              3          -4.00       26.00
              4          -9.00       20.00
              5           3.00       15.00
              6          -2.00       14.00
              7         -20.00        1.00
              8          -8.00      -16.00
              9          -1.00      -26.00
             10           4.00      -20.00
             11           6.00      -15.00
             12           8.00        6.00

Rotated (Y) coordinates
                            1           2

              1          20.19        1.17
              2          16.53       -5.73
              3         -14.92       22.41
              4          -9.00       18.55
              5           9.69       12.25
              6          -2.05        9.79
              7         -12.15       -0.51
              8         -15.47      -23.68
              9          -4.65      -26.52
             10           3.44      -11.54
             11          -6.65       -2.42
             12          11.95        1.49
```

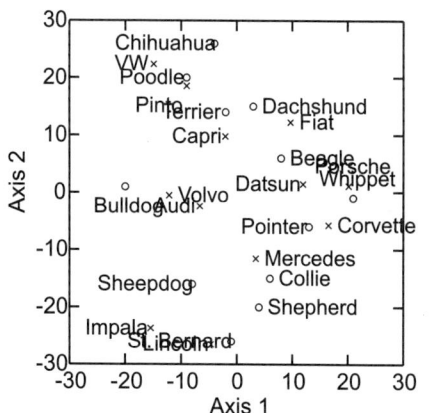

The rotation matrix in the output is nearly an identity matrix. Unlike the nonmetric multidimensional scalings in Wilkinson's dissertation, which required rotation to common orientation, the INDSCAL analyses recovered the apparently canonical dimensions. These were agile-clumsy (horizontal) and big-small (vertical).

In place of the Procrustes output, which is normally separate scatterplots of the two sets, we present a plot of the superimposed configurations.

Computation

All computations are in double precision.

Algorithms

The algorithms are documented in the Statistical Background section above. Most involve a singular value decomposition computed in the standard manner.

Missing data

Cases and variables with missing data are omitted from the calculations.

References

Bennet, J. F. and Hays, W. L. (1960). Multidimensional unfolding: Determining the dimensionality of ranked preference data. *Psychometrika,* 25, 27–43.

Borg, I. and Groenen, P. J. F. (1997). *Modern multidimensional scaling: Theory and applications.* New York: Springer Verlag.

Carroll, J. D. (1972). Individual differences in multidimensional scaling. In R. N. Shepard, A. K. Romney, S. B. Nerlove (eds.), *Multidimensional scaling: Theory and applications in the behavioral sciences,* Vol. 1, 105–155. New York: Seminar Press.

Cliff, N. (1973). Scaling. *Annual Review of Psychology,* 24, 473–506.

Coombs, C. H. (1950). Psychological scaling without a unit of measurement. *Psychological Review,* 57, 148–158.

Dow, B. M. (1990). Nested maps in macaque monkey visual cortex. In K. N. Leibovic (ed.), *Science of vision,* 84–124. New York: Springer Verlag.

Gabriel, K. R. (1971). The biplot graphic display of matrices with application to principal component analysis. *Biometrika,* 58, 453–467.

Green, P. E. and Tull, D. S. (1975). *Research for marketing decisions,* 3rd ed. Englewood Cliffs, N. J.: Prentice Hall.

Kosslyn, S. M. (1981). *Image and mind.* Cambridge: Harvard University Press.

Lilien, G. L., Kotler, P., and Moorthy, K. S. (1992). *Marketing models.* Englewood Cliffs, N.J.: Prentice Hall.

Long, L. H. (ed.) (1971). *The world almanac.* New York: Doubleday.

Milgram, S. and Jodelet, D. (1976). Psychological maps of Paris. In H. M. Proshansky, W. H. Itelson, and L. G. Revlin (eds.), *Environmental Psychology.* New York: Holt, Rinehart, and Winston.

Osgood, C. E., Suci, G. J., and Tannenbaum, P. H. (1957). *The measurement of meaning.* Urbana, Ill.: University of Illinois Press.

Schönemann, P. H. (1966). The generalized solution of the orthogonal Procrustes problem. *Psychometrika,* 31, 1–16.

Schwartz, E. J. (1981). Computational anatomy and functional architecture of striate cortex: A spatial mapping approach to perceptual coding. *Visual Research,* 20, 645–669.

Wilkinson, L. (1975). The effect of involvement on similarity and preference structures. Unpublished dissertation, Yale University.

Wilkinson, L., Blank, G., and Gruber, C. (1996). *Desktop Data Analysis with SYSTAT.* Upper Saddle River, N.J.: Prentice-Hall.

Wish, M., Deutsch, M., and Biener, L. (1972). Differences in perceived similarity of nations. In R. N. Shepard, A. K. Romney, S. B. Nerlove (eds.), *Multidimensional scaling: Theory and applications in the behavioral sciences,* Vol. 2, 289–313. New York: Seminar Press.

Chapter 8

Probit Analysis

Dan Steinberg

The PROBIT module calculates maximum likelihood estimates of the parameters of the PROBIT general linear model. A modified Gauss-Newton algorithm is used to compute the estimates. Conventionally, the dependent variable is coded as 0 or 1, although the PROBIT module will automatically recode values of the dependent variable because it assumes that it is categorical. Models may include categorical predictors (dummy coded), as well as interaction terms.

Statistical Background

The PROBIT model provides an appropriate method for estimating a multiple regression or analysis of variance or covariance when the dependent variable is categorical and can take only one of two values. PROBIT analyzes models of the form

$$y = \mathbf{Xb} + e$$

which is interpreted to mean

$$\text{Prob}(y = 1) = \Phi(\mathbf{Xb})$$

where y is the binary dependent variable, $\mathbf{X}$ is a vector of independent variables, $\mathbf{b}$ is a vector of unknown regression coefficients, e is a normally distributed random error, and Φ is the cumulative normal distribution. The normality assumption is an essential characteristic of the PROBIT model; alternative distributional assumptions give rise to different statistical models, such as LOGIT.

The purpose of PROBIT analysis is to produce an estimate of the probability that the value of the dependent variable is equal to 1 for any set of independent variable values, and to identify those independent variables that are significant predictors of the outcome. The estimated coefficients, **b,** are assumed to generate a predicted z score, **Xb**.

Interpreting the Results

The simplest interpretation of the output is obtained by noting the significant variables and identifying them as useful predictors of the dependent variable. More sophisticated interpretation requires scaling the coefficients into derivatives. While the predicted effect of an independent variable on the z score is linear, the effect on the probability that the dependent variable equals 1 is nonlinear. The derivative of this probability with respect to the i'th independent variable is given by

$$b_i f(\mathbf{Xb})$$

where $f(\mathbf{Xb})$ is the normal density evaluated at the predicted z score.

This derivative will differ for each observation in the data set. The correct way to estimate this derivative for the sample is to evaluate it for each observation and then average all the observations. A good approximation can be obtained by evaluating the s score for the mean set of X's and using the above scaling formula, or using the normal density evaluated at the x score, which would split the sample to match the observed split.

Probit Analysis in SYSTAT

Probit Analysis Main Dialog Box

To open the Probit dialog box, from the menus choose:

Statistics
  Regression
    Probit...

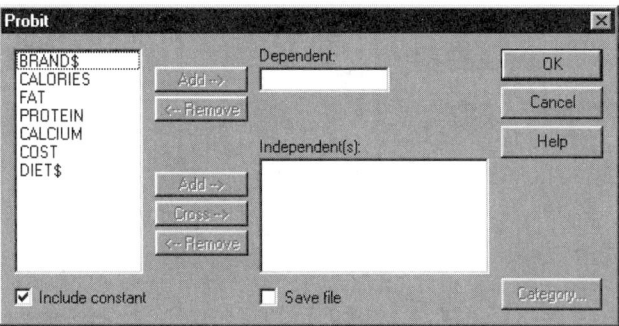

Dependent. The variable you want to examine. The dependent variable should be a binary numeric variable. Normally, the dependent variable is coded so that the larger value denotes the reference group.

Independent(s). Select one or more variables. Categorical variables must be designated using the Category button. To add an interaction to your model use the Cross button. For example, add income to the Independent list and then use the Cross button to add education, which will look like income*education. A variable with a positive correlation with the dependent variable should have a positive coefficient when fitted alone. To reverse the direction of this coding, use ORDER with a descending sort for the dependent variable.

Include constant. Includes the constant in the regression equation. Deselect this option to remove the constant. You rarely want to remove the constant, and you should be familiar with no-constant regression terminology before considering it.

Save file. Saves statistics into *filename.SYD*.

Categories

Independent variables (predictors) in a PROBIT model can be either categorical or continuous. To prevent category codes from being treated as continuous data, specify categorical variables as such using the Categories dialog box.

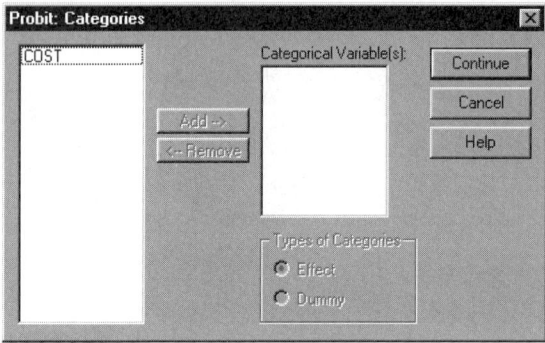

All independent variables selected for the model appear in the variable list.

Categorical Variable(s). You want to categorize an independent variable when it has several categories such as education levels, which could be divided into the following categories: less than high school, some high school, finished high school, some college, finished bachelor's degree, finished master's degree, and finished doctorate. On the other hand, a variable such as age in years would not be categorical unless age were broken up into categories such as under 21, 21–65, and over 65.

You must indicate the coding method to apply to categorical variables. The two available options include:

- **Effect.** Produces parameter estimates that are differences from group means.
- **Dummy.** Produces dummy codes for the design variables instead of effect codes. Coding of dummy variables is the classic analysis of variance parameterization, in which the sum of effects estimated for a classifying variable is 0. If your categorical variable has k categories, $k - 1$ dummy variables are created.

Using Commands

Select a data file using USE filename and continue with:

```
PROBIT
    MODEL yvar = CONSTANT + xvarlist + xvar*xvar + ... / PROBIT
    CATEGORY grpvarlist / MISS  EFFECT or DUMMY
    ESTIMATE
```

PROBIT must be specified in MODEL. Use an * between variables to specify interactions.

Usage Considerations

Types of data. PROBIT uses rectangular data only.

Print options. Coefficient estimates and their covariance matrix are printed in all circumstances.

Quick Graphs. PROBIT produces no Quick Graphs.

Saving files. In the PROBIT model, the predicted value of the dependent variable is a normal z score. If you want to save this variable, you can issue a SAVE command. This will produce a SYSTAT system file with the variable's z score, the predicted z score from the last model estimated, and *MILLS*, the hazard function evaluated at the predicted z score. By using the cumulative normal probability function in the DATA module, you can convert the z score into a predicted probability. The *MILLS* variable is often used as a selectivity bias correction variable in regression models with nonrandom sampling. For further details, see the references at the end of this chapter.

Additional variables saved are *SEZSCORE* (standard errors), *PROB* (corresponding probability), *DENSITY* (associated density value), and confidence intervals for the parameters.

BY groups. PROBIT analyzes data by groups. Your file need not be sorted on the BY variable(s).

Bootstrapping. Bootstrapping is not available in this procedure.

Case frequencies. FREQ = <variable> increases the number of cases by the FREQ variable. This feature does not use extra memory.

Case weights. WEIGHT is not available in PROBIT.

Examples

Example 1
Probit Analysis (Simple Model)

This example shows a simple linear PROBIT model. The data, which have been extracted from the National Longitudinal Survey of Young Men, 1979, includes school enrollment status (*NOTENR* = 1 if not enrolled), age (*AGE*), highest completed grade

(*EDUC*), mother's education (*MED*), an index of reading material available in the home (*CULTURE*), and an IQ score (*IQ*) for 38 individuals. The input is:

```
USE NLS
PROBIT
MODEL NOTENR = CONSTANT + EDUC + AGE / PROBIT
ESTIMATE
```

The resulting output is:

```
Variables in the SYSTAT Rectangular file are:
NOTENR     CONSTONE    BLACK        SOUTH       EDUC         AGE
FED        MED         CULTURE      NSIBS       LW           IQ
FOMY

Categorical values encountered during processing are:
NOTENR (2 levels)
      0,        1
Categorical variables are effects coded with the highest value as reference.

                        Binary Probit Analysis

Dependent variable     : NOTENR
Input records          :         200
Records kept for analysis: 200

Convergence achieved after 4 iterations.
Relative tolerance =         0.000

Number of observations : 200.000

Number with NOTENR = 0          (non-response) :      28.000
Number with NOTENR = 1          (response)     :     172.000


Results of estimation

Log Likelihood:        -75.240
    Parameter             Estimate         S.E.       t-ratio      p-value
 1 CONSTANT                  2.187         1.148        1.905        0.057
 2 EDUC                     -0.161         0.051       -3.185        0.001
 3 AGE                       0.048         0.040        1.184        0.236
-2 * L.L. ratio = 11.505 with 2 degrees of freedom
Chi-Sq. p-value =          0.003


Covariance Matrix
              1              2              3
   1      1.318
   2     -0.027          0.003
   3     -0.035         -0.000          0.002
```

PROBIT always reports the number of cases processed and the means of the dependent variables for each of the two subgroups defined by the value of the dependent variable. If all observations have the same value of the dependent variable, PROBIT will return an error message indicating that the model cannot be estimated.

Before printing the coefficient estimates, PROBIT reports whether it has achieved convergence, the value of the likelihood function, the percentage change in the likelihood achieved in the last iteration, the convergence criterion, the number of iterations required, the size of the two subsamples of the data, and the likelihood ratio chi-square test of the null hypothesis that all coefficients except the constant are equal to 0. If there isn't a constant specified on the model statement, this last statistic will not be computed. Next, the coefficient estimates, standard errors, and t statistics are presented. The coefficients, analogous to regression coefficients, represent the change in a score that is predicted by a unit change in the independent variable. Finally, the variance-covariance matrix of the coefficient estimates is printed. This matrix, analogous to the inverse (X'X) of a linear regression model, can be used to conduct hypothesis tests.

Example 2
Probit Analysis with Interactions

This example adds an interaction term to the simple model from the other example. When doing so, it is useful to standardize variables in product terms so that they do not "soak up variance" from main effects simply because they become highly correlated due to scale effects. You can compare the results with and without standardization. The input is:

```
USE NLS
STANDARDIZE EDUC AGE
PROBIT
MODEL NOTENR= CONSTANT + EDUC + AGE + EDUC*AGE / PROBIT
ESTIMATE
```

The resulting output is:

```
Variables in the SYSTAT Rectangular file are:
 NOTENR       CONSTONE     BLACK        SOUTH        EDUC         AGE
 FED          MED          CULTURE      NSIBS        LW           IQ
 FOMY

  200 cases and 13 variables processed and saved.

Categorical values encountered during processing are:
NOTENR (2 levels)
       0,      1
Categorical variables are effects coded with the highest value as reference.

                        Binary Probit Analysis

 Dependent variable      : NOTENR
 Input records           :              200
 Records kept for analysis: 200
```

```
Convergence achieved after 4 iterations.
Relative tolerance =        0.000

Number of observations : 200.000

Number with NOTENR = 0          (non-response) :      28.000
Number with NOTENR = 1          (response)     :     172.000

Results of estimation

Log Likelihood:      -72.805
    Parameter              Estimate        S.E.      t-ratio    p-value
 1  CONSTANT                 1.176        0.125        9.381      0.000
 2  EDUC                    -0.479        0.137       -3.505      0.000
 3  AGE                      0.067        0.126        0.530      0.596
 4  EDUC*AGE                 0.274        0.128        2.141      0.032


-2 * L.L. ratio = 16.375 with 3 degrees of freedom
Chi-Sq. p-value =        0.001


Covariance Matrix
            1            2            3            4
    1   0.016
    2  -0.006        0.019
    3  -0.000        0.002        0.016
    4   0.002       -0.006       -0.004        0.016
```

Notice that the education main effect remains significant and the interaction is itself moderately significant in this expanded model.

Computation

All of the computations are in double precision.

Algorithms

PROBIT maximizes the likelihood function for the binary PROBIT model by the Newton-Raphson method.

Missing Data

Cases with missing data for any variable in the model are deleted.

References

Amemiya, T. (1981). Qualitative response models: A survey. *Journal of Economic Literature*, December, 1483–1536.

Finney, D. J. (1971). *Probit analysis*, 3rd ed. Cambridge: Cambridge University Press.

Heckman, J. (1979). Sample bias as a specification error. *Econometrica*, 1153–162.

McFadden, D. (1982). Qualitative response models. In W. Hildebrand (ed.), *Advances in Econometrics,* Cambridge: Cambridge University Press.

Chapter 9

Set and Canonical Correlation

Jacob Cohen and Leland Wilkinson

SETCOR computes set correlations (Cohen, 1982) and canonical correlations (Hotelling, 1935, 1936). Although it is based on algorithms developed initially for the mainframe program CORSET (Cohen and Nee, 1983) and subsequently for the PC program SETCORAN (Eber and Cohen, 1987), the SYSTAT program is completely new source code. Recent corrections in statistical tests by Jacob Cohen and Charles Lewis (1988) have been incorporated into the SYSTAT version.

Finally, SETCOR also computes the Stewart and Love (1968) canonical redundancy index and rotates canonical variates.

Statistical Background

Set correlation (SC) is a realization of the multivariate general linear model and therefore is a natural generalization of simple and multiple correlation. In its standard form, it generalizes bivariate and multiple regression to their multivariate analogue. The standard univariate and multivariate methods provided by the SYSTAT MGLH module (for example, multivariate analysis of variance and covariance, discriminant function analysis) may be viewed as special cases of SC. SC thus provides a single general framework for the study of association. In contrast to canonical correlation, it yields a partitioning of variance in terms of the original variables, rather than their canonical transformations.

Sets

The building blocks of SC are sets of variables, which may be categorical or quantitative. They may also comprise interactions or products of measured variables. If they are nonlinearly related to each other, they should be transformed prior to analysis to avoid misleading conclusions. The same assumptions underlying ANOVA, linear regression, and other linear models are appropriate to SC.

Partialing

By partialing a set A from a set B (residualizing B by A), there is produced a new set $B|A$ whose variables have zero correlations with the set A variables. (The notation $B.A$, used in some of the cited papers, is equivalent to the notation $B|A$ here.) This device has several uses in data analysis, including the statistical adjustment for irrelevant or spurious sources of variance or covariance (as in the analysis of covariance), the representation of curvilinear components and of interactions (Cohen, 1978), and the representation of contrasts among means.

In MRC, the use of sets and partialing apply to the right side of the equation, the independent variables, which is where the multiplicity lies. The dependent variable y is a single variable. SC is a generalization of MRC such that a set of dependent variables Y may be related to a set X, either of which may be a partialed set. Given that virtually any information may be expressed as a set of variables, SC offers the possibility of a flexible general data-analysis method.

The basic reference for SC is Cohen (1982), reprinted in Cohen & Cohen (1983, Appendix 4), referred to hereafter as CSC. Cohen & Nee (1984) give estimators for two measures of association (shrunken $R^2_{Y,X}$ and $T^2_{Y,X}$), and Cohen (1988b, Chapter 10) provides a full treatment of power analysis in SC. Van den Burg and Lewis (1988) describe the properties of the association measures and provide formal proofs. The various devices for the representation of information as sets of variables are described and illustrated in detail in Cohen and Cohen (1983, chapters 4–9, 11), referred to hereafter as C&C. This chapter focuses on the "nuts and bolts" of the method and illustrates its chief features as they are represented in the input and output of **SETCOR**.

Notation

In what follows, the symbols Y_B and X_B represent basic sets: set Y_B may be a set of dependent variables Y, or a set of dependent variables Y from which another set Y_P has been partialed, represented as $Y|Y_P$. Similarly, set X_B may be a set of independent variables X, or a set of independent variables X from which another set X_P has been partialed, $X|X_P$. (The term *basic* replaces the term *generic* used in CSC.) All references to sets Y and X in formulas that follow are to be understood to mean Y_B and X_B, the "left-hand" and "right-hand" sets, whether or not either has been partialed. Where Y and Y_B or X and X_B must be distinguished, this will be done so in the notation.

Measures of Association Between Sets

It is desirable that a measure of association between sets be a natural generalization of multiple R^2, bounded by 0 and 1, invariant over full-rank linear transformation (rotation) of either or both sets, and symmetrical (that is, $R^2_{Y,X} = R^2_{X,Y}$). Of the measures of multivariate association that have been proposed (Cramer and Nicewander, 1979), three have been found to be particularly useful: multivariate $R^2_{Y,X}$ and the symmetric ($T^2_{Y,X}$) and asymmetric ($P^2_{Y,X}$) squared trace correlations.

$R^2_{Y,X}$ Proportion of Generalized Variance

Using determinants of correlation matrices,

$$R^2_{Y,X} = \frac{1 - |\mathbf{R}_{YX}|}{|\mathbf{R}_{YY}| \cdot |\mathbf{R}_{XX}|},$$

where

- $\mathbf{R}_{YX}$ is the full correlation matrix of the Y_B and X_B variables,
- $\mathbf{R}_{YY}$ is the matrix of correlations among the variables of set Y_B, and
- $\mathbf{R}_{XX}$ is the matrix of correlations among the variables of set X_B.

This equation also holds when variance-covariance (**S**) or sums of squares and cross-products (**C**) matrices replace the correlation matrices.

$R^2_{Y,X}$ may also be written as a function of the q squared canonical correlations (C^2) where $q = \min(k_Y, k_X)$, the number of variables in the smaller of the two basic sets:

$$R^2_{Y,X} = 1 - (1 - C_1^2)(1 - C_2^2)\ldots(1 - C_q^2)$$

$R^2_{Y,X}$ is a generalization of the simple bivariate $r^2_{y,x}$ and of multiple R^2 and is properly interpreted as the proportion of the generalized variance (multivariance) of set Y_B accounted for by set X_B (or vice versa, because like all product-moment correlation coefficients, it is symmetrical). Generalized variance is the generalization of the univariate concept of variance to a set of variables and is defined here as the determinant of the covariance matrix of the variables in the set. You can interpret proportions of generalized variance much as you interpret proportions of variance of a single variable. $R^2_{Y,X}$ does not vary with changes in location or scale of the variables, with nonsingular transformations of the variables within each set (for example, orthogonal or oblique rotations), or with different single degree-of-freedom codings of nominal scales. $R^2_{Y,X}$ makes possible a multiplicative decomposition in terms of squared (multiple) partial (but not semipartial) correlations. See CSC and Van den Burg and Lewis (1988) for the justification of these statements and a discussion of these and other properties of $R^2_{Y,X}$.

$T^2_{Y,X}$ and $P^2_{Y,X}$ Proportions of Additive Variance

Two other useful measures of multivariate association are based on the trace of the variance-covariance matrix, $\mathbf{M}_{YX} = \mathbf{S}_{YY}^{-1}\mathbf{S}_{YX}\mathbf{S}_{XX}^{-1}\mathbf{S}_{XY}$, where Y and X are again taken as basic. It can be shown that the trace of this matrix,

$$tr(\mathbf{M}_{YX}) = \sum_q C^2$$

is the sum of the q squared canonical correlations. $T^2_{Y,X}$, the symmetric squared trace correlation, is the trace divided by q, or the mean of the q squared canonical correlations,

$$T^2_{Y,X} = \frac{tr(\mathbf{M}_{YX})}{q} = \sum_q \frac{C^2}{q}$$

A space may be defined by a set of variables, and any nonsingular linear transformation (for example, rotation) of these variables defines the same space. Assume that $k_Y < k_X$ and consider any orthogonalizing transformation of the (basic) Y

variables. Find the multiple R^2's of each of the orthogonalized Y variables with set X_B; their sum equals $tr(\mathbf{M}_{YX})$, so the mean of these multiple R^2's is $T^2_{Y,X}$. This symmetric squared trace correlation also has a proportion of variance interpretation, but unlike $R^2_{Y,X}$, the definition of variance is that of additive (or total) variance, the sum of the unit variances of the smaller set; that is, q. $T^2_{Y,X}$ provides an additive decomposition into squared semipartial (but not partial) correlations. It may, however, decrease when a variable is added to the lesser of k_Y and k_X (CSC; van den Burg and Lewis, 1988).

$P^2_{Y,X}$ is the trace divided by k_Y, the number of dependent variables, and is therefore asymmetric. When $k_Y > k_X$, its maximum is k_X/k_Y. It shares with $R^2_{Y,X}$ and multiple R^2 the property that the addition of a variable to either X or Y cannot result in a decrease. When $k_Y \leq k_X$ (the usual case), $P^2_{Y,X} = T^2_{Y,X}$. In a comprehensive analysis of their properties, van den Burg and Lewis (1988) argue that $P^2_{Y,X}$ (rather than $T^2_{Y,X}$) is a direct generalization of multiple R^2.

Interpretations

The varied uses of partialing (residualization), made familiar by MRC, makes possible a functional analysis of data in terms of research factors as defined above. The basic set X_B, made up of $X|X_P$, may be used in the following ways:

- The statistical control of the research factor(s) in X_P when X is to be related to Y_B. If the model to be tested posits an independent effect of X on Y_B, then $X|X_P$ holds X_P constant; without X_P partialed, the effect found for X may be a spurious consequence of the association of X_P with both X and Y_B. In the analysis of covariance (univariate and multivariate), partialing the covariates also has the effect of reducing the error variance, and thus increases power.

- The representation of interactions of any order for research factors of any kind. For example, the $U \times V$ interaction set is constructed as $X|X_P$, where X is UV, the set of $k_U k_V$ product variables that result from multiplying each of the variables in research factor U by each of the variables in research factor V, and X_P is $U + V$, the $k_{YU} + k_{YV}$ variables of the combined U and V research factors (C&C, Chapter 8).

- The representation of curve components in polynomial (curvilinear) regression. For example, for the cubic component of a variable v, set X is v^3 and set X_P is made up of v and v^2 (C&C, Chapter 6).

- The representation of a particular contrast within a set of means of the categories of a nominal scale. Here, X contains a single suitably coded variable and X_P contains the remaining variables carrying other contrasts (C&C, Chapter 5).

- The "purification" of a variable to its "uniqueness," as when X is made up of one subtest of a battery of intercorrelated measures and X_P contains the remaining subtests. Examples of X are the Digit Symbol subtest of the Wechsler Adult Intelligence Scale or the Schizophrenia scale score of the Minnesota Multiphasic Personality Inventory, with X_P in each instance the respective remaining subtest/scale scores.

- The use of missing data as positive information. Here, X represents a research factor for which some subjects, having no data, are assigned an arbitrary constant (usually the mean), and X_P is a single binary variable coded 1 for the cases with missing data and 0 for those with data present (C&C, Chapter 7).

In SC, the partialing devices described above for the set X_P may equally be employed in the Y_B set as $Y|Y_P$. Thus, you may control a dependent variable for age, sex, and socioeconomic status, or represent curve components, interactions, missingness, or uniqueness of a dependent variable or set of dependent variables. (See CSC for examples.)

Types of Association between Sets

Given the option of partialing, there are five types of association possible in SC:

	Set Y		Set XB
Whole	set Y	with	set X
Partial	set $Y|Y_p$	with	set $X|X_p$ (where $X_p=Y_p$)
Y semipartial	set $Y|Y_p$	with	set X
X semipartial	set Y	with	set $X|X_p$
Bipartial	set $Y|Y_p$	with	set $X|X_p$

Formulas for the covariance matrices required for the computation of $R^2_{Y,X}$ and $T^2_{Y,X}$ for the five types of association are given in CSC, Table 1. Following an SC analysis, further analytic detail is provided by output for MRC analyses for each basic y variable on the set of basic x variables, y and x being single variables in their respective sets. Thus, it is for the individual variables, partialed or whole depending on the type of association, that the regression and correlation results are provided. The information provided in the output for these individual basic variables (betas, multiple R^2's) facilitates the interpretation of the SC results of the X_B and Y_B sets that they constitute.

Testing the Null Hypothesis

Throughout this section, X and Y are to be understood as basic. For purposes of testing the hypothesis of no association between sets X and Y, we treat Y as the dependent variable set, X as independent, and employ the fixed model. Wilks' likelihood ratio Λ is the ratio of the determinant of the error covariance matrix E to the determinant of the sum of the error and hypothesis H covariance matrices,

$$\Lambda = \frac{|\mathbf{E}|}{|\mathbf{E+H}|}$$

where H is the variance-covariance accounted for in the Y variables by X, where

$$H = S_{YX} S_{XX}^{-1} S_{XY}$$

The definition of E depends on whether the test is to employ Model 1 or Model 2 error. Model 1 error is defined as

$$E_1 = S_{YY} - S_{Y,XX_p} R_{XX_p}^{-1} S_{XX_p,Y}$$

that is, the residual covariance matrix when covariance associated with sets X and X_P have been removed.

Model 2 error is employed when there exists a set G, made up of variables in neither X nor X_P, that can be used to account for additional variance in S_{YY} and thus reduce E below E_1 in the interest of unbiasedness and increased statistical power. This occurs when, with multiple research factors, the analyst wishes to use "pure" error, for example, the within-cell variance in a factorial design. In this case, the error-reducing set G is made up of the variables comprising the research factors ("main effects") and interactions other than the factor or interaction under test, as is done traditionally in MANOVA and MANCOVA factorial designs.

$$E_2 = S_{YY} - S_{Y,XX_pG} R_{XX_pG}^{-1} S_{XX_pG,Y}$$

In whole and Y semipartial association, where X_P does not exist, it is dropped from E_1 and E_2. Formulas for the H and E matrices for the five types of association are given in CSC, Table 2. (See "Algorithms" on p. 270 for corrections to the CSC formulas.)

When Model 1 error (no set G) is used, for the whole, partial, and Y semipartial types of association, it can be shown that

$$\Lambda = 1 - R_{Y,X}^2$$

Once Λ is determined for a sample, Rao's F test (1973) may be applied to test the null hypothesis. As adapted for SC, the test is quite general, covering all five types of association and both error models. When $k_Y = 1$, where multivariate $R_{Y,X}^2$ specializes to multiple R^2's, the Rao F test specializes to the standard null hypothesis F test for MRC. For this case, and for the case where the smaller set is made up of no more than two variables, the Rao F test is exact; otherwise, it is approximate (Cohen & Nee, 1987).

$$F = \left(\Lambda^{-\frac{1}{s}} - 1\right)\frac{v}{u}, \text{ where}$$

$u = $ numerator $df = k_Y k_X$,
$v = $ denominator $df = ms + 1 - u/2$ where
$m = N - \max(k_{Yp}, k_{Xp} + k_G) - (k_Y + k_X + 3)/2$, and

$$s = \sqrt{\frac{k_Y^2 k_X^2 - 4}{k_Y^2 + k_X^2 - 5}}$$

except that when $k_Y^2 k_X^2 = 4$, $s = 1$. For partial $R_{Y,X}^2$, set $X_P = $ set Y_P, so $k_{Xp} = k_{Yp}$ is the number of variables in the set that is being partialed, and for whole $R_{Y,X}^2$, neither set X_P nor set Y_P exists. Further, k_{Yp}, k_{Xp}, and k_G are 0 when the set does not exist for the type of association or error model in question. The test assumes that the variables in X are fixed and those in Y are multivariate normal, but the test is quite robust against assumption failure (Cohen & Nee, 1989; Olson, 1974).

Estimates of the Population $R^2_{Y,X}$, $T^2_{Y,X}$, and $P^2_{Y,X}$

Like all squared correlations, $R_{Y,X}^2$, $T_{Y,X}^2$, and $P_{Y,X}^2$ are positively biased. Shrunken values (almost unbiased population estimates) are given by

$$\tilde{R}_{Y,X}^2 = 1 - (1 - R_{Y,X}^2)\left(\frac{v + u}{v}\right)^s,$$

$$\tilde{T}_{Y,X}^2 = 1 - (1 - T_{Y,X}^2)\left(\frac{w+u}{v}\right)^s, \text{ and}$$

$$\tilde{P}_{Y,X}^2 = \tilde{T}_{Y,X}^2 \frac{k_Y}{k_X}$$

where w is the denominator df of the Pillai (1960) F test for

$$T_{Y,X}^2: w = q[N - k_Y - k_X - \max(k_{Yp}, k_{Xp} - 1)]$$

(Cohen & Nee, 1984). When $q = 1$, both $\tilde{R}_{Y,X}^2$ and $\tilde{T}_{Y,X}^2$ specialize to Wherry's formula for the shrunken multiple R^2 (1931).

Set and Canonical Correlations in SYSTAT

Set and Canonical Correlations Main Dialog Box

To open the Set and Canonical Correlations dialog box, from the menus choose:

Statistics
  Correlations
    Set and Canonical...

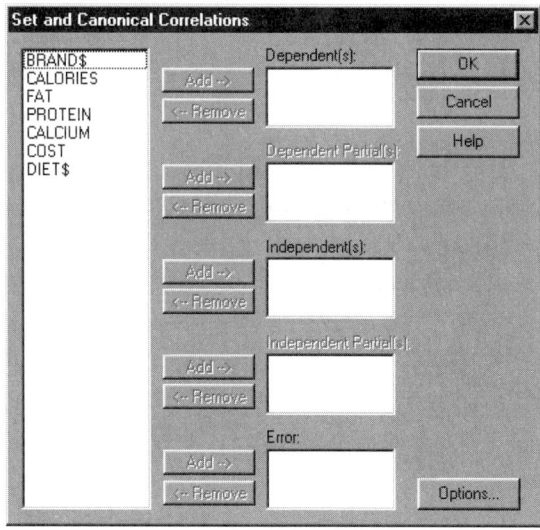

To do a SETCOR analysis, first specify a model.

Dependent(s). Enter the dependent variables you want to examine.

Dependent Partial(s). You can specify the variables to be partialed out of the dependent set, which produces a new set whose variables have zero correlation with the partialed set. The partial variables are optional for dependent variables. The simple canonical correlation model does not have a partial variable list.

Independent(s). Select one or more continuous or categorical variables (grouping variables).

Independent Partial(s). You can specify the variables to be partialed out of the independent set, which produces a new set whose variables have zero correlation with the partialed set. The partial variables are optional for independent variables. The simple canonical correlation model does not have a partial variable list.

Error. Specify a set of variables to be used in computing error terms for statistical tests. Error variables are optional.

Set and Canonical Correlation Options

The Options dialog box controls the rotation and sample size options for estimation.

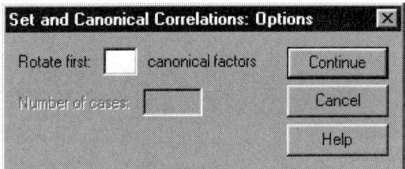

The following options can be specifed:

- **Rotate first.** Enter the number of canonical factors to rotate using the varimax rotation.
- **Number of cases.** If you enter a triangular matrix (correlation), specify the number of cases from which the matrix was computed. This is required if you are using a correlation matrix instead of raw data.

Set and Canonical Correlation

Using Commands

After specifying the data with USE filename, continue with:

```
SETCOR
    MODEL yvarlist | ypartials = xvarlist | xpartials
    ERROR = varlist
    ESTIMATE / N=n  ROTATE=n
```

Usage Considerations

Types of data. SETCOR normally uses rectangular data. SETCOR will also accept a lower triangular Pearson correlation matrix, which is produced by SYSTAT's CORR module, in which case n must be specified in the ESTIMATE command. You may be tempted to solve missing data problems by using a correlation matrix produced by CORR using its pairwise deletion option with an average or minimum n. Although this may produce reasonable results when data are randomly missing, you should consider Wilkinson's (1988) and Cohen and Cohen's (1983) warnings concerning pairwise matrices. A better technique for dealing with missing data is to use the maximum likelihood (EM) estimation of the covariance or correlation matrix in the CORR module. See Chapter 7 of Cohen and Cohen (1983) for a detailed discussion of missing data.

Unlike the MGLH module in SYSTAT, SETCOR cannot handle products of variables when sets are defined. Thus, with *AGE* and *SEX* as variables in a rectangular file, naming *AGE*SEX* or *AGE*AGE* as a variable in a set will result in an error message. To use product (or other) functions of variables, they must be created using SYSTAT BASIC.

SETCOR can use nominal (qualitative or categorical) scales in any of the sets it employs by means of a variety of coding methods. The most useful of these, which are dummy, effects, and contrast coding, are discussed in detail in Chapter 5 of Cohen and Cohen (1983), and their use in set correlation illustrated in Cohen (1982) and in Cohen (1988a). The CATEGORY command codes these variables.

Print options. For PRINT=SHORT, the output gives n, the type of association, the variables in sets *YPARTIAL*, *XPARTIAL*, and *G* (when present), the Rao F (with its df and p value), and their shrunken values, and the following results for the basic y and x variables: the within-set correlation matrices for the y and x variables, the rectangular between-set correlation matrix, the betas for estimating each y variable from the x set (with their standard errors and p values), a matrix of the intercorrelations of the estimated *y* values whose diagonal is the multiple of each *y* variable with the *x* set, and the *F* test and *p* for the latter.

PRINT=LONG gives, in addition to the above results for basic *y* and *x*, the Stewart and Love redundancy index for *y* given *xb*, the canonical correlations and their Bartlett chi-square tests, and the canonical coefficients, loadings, and redundancies for both sets. When PRINT=LONG, the option ROTATE rotates the dependent and independent canonical loadings and the canonical correlations.

Quick Graphs. SETCOR produces no Quick Graphs.

Saving files. SETCOR does not save results.

BY groups. SETCOR analyzes data by groups.

Bootstrapping. Bootstrapping is available in this procedure.

Case frequencies. SETCOR uses the FREQ variable, if present, to duplicate cases. This inflates the total degrees of freedom to be the sum of the number of frequencies. Using a FREQ variable does not require more memory, however.

Case weights. SETCOR weights sums of squares and cross products using the *WEIGHT* variable for rectangular data input. It does not require extra memory.

Examples

Example 1
Canonical Correlations—Simple Model

This example shows a simple canonical correlation model. The data, which have been extracted from the National Longitudinal Survey of Young Men, 1979, includes school enrollment status (*NOTENR*, set to 1 if not enrolled), age (*AGE*), highest completed grade (*EDUC*), mother's education (*MED*), an index of reading material available in the home (*CULTURE*), and an IQ score (*IQ*) for 38 individuals. The input is:

```
USE ANXIETY
SETCOR
MODEL S(1)..S(2) = P(1)..P(3)
ESTIMATE / N=48
```

The resulting output is:

```
Variables in the SYSTAT Correlation file are:
 S(1..2)      P(1..3)

Whole set correlation analysis (Y VS. X)

Number of cases on which analysis is based: 48.
RAO F =      3.675   df =         6.0,       86.0   Prob=      0.003
R-Square =           0.367              Shrunk R-Square =      0.275
T-Square =           0.202              Shrunk T-Square =      0.090
P-Square =           0.202              Shrunk P-Square =      0.090


Within basic set y correlations

                       S(1)        S(2)

            S(1)      1.000
            S(2)      0.303       1.000

Within basic set x correlations

                       P(1)        P(2)        P(3)

            P(1)      1.000
            P(2)      0.304       1.000
            P(3)      0.403       0.589       1.000

Between basic y (col) and basic x (row) correlations

                       S(1)        S(2)

            P(1)      0.391       0.106
            P(2)      0.298      -0.028
            P(3)      0.197       0.321

Estimated (from x-set) y intercorrelations (R-square on diagonal)

                       S(1)        S(2)

            S(1)      0.193
            S(2)      0.002       0.175

Significance tests for prediction of each basic y variable

Variable      F-statistic   Probability
S(1)             3.505         0.023
S(2)             3.115         0.036

Betas predicting basic y (col) from basic x (row) variables

                       S(1)        S(2)

            P(1)      0.353      -0.001
            P(2)      0.243      -0.332
            P(3)     -0.088       0.517

Standard errors of betas

                       S(1)        S(2)

            P(1)      0.149       0.150
            P(2)      0.168       0.170
            P(3)      0.175       0.177
```

```
T-statistics for betas

                    S(1)        S(2)

          P(1)      2.374      -0.010
          P(2)      1.442      -1.953
          P(3)     -0.503       2.921

Probabilities for betas

                    S(1)        S(2)

          P(1)      0.022       0.992
          P(2)      0.156       0.057
          P(3)      0.618       0.005


Stewart-Love canonical redundancy index =        0.184

Canonical correlations

                      1           2

                    0.511       0.377

Bartlett test of residual correlations

    Correlations 1 through 2
        Chi-square statistic =      20.087    df =    6    prob=    0.003

    Correlations 2 through 2
        Chi-square statistic =       6.754    df =    2    prob=    0.034

Canonical coefficients for dependent (y) set

                      1           2

          S(1)     -0.893       0.551
          S(2)      0.796       0.684

Canonical loadings (y variable by factor correlations)

                      1           2

          S(1)     -0.652       0.759
          S(2)      0.525       0.851

Canonical redundancies for dependent set

                      1           2

                    0.092       0.092

Canonical coefficients for independent (x) set

                      1           2

          P(1)     -0.618       0.513
          P(2)     -0.941      -0.247
          P(3)      0.959       0.809
```

```
Canonical loadings (x variable by factor correlations)
                        1           2

           P(1)      -0.518       0.764
           P(2)      -0.564       0.385
           P(3)       0.156       0.870

Canonical redundancies for independent set
                        1           2

                      0.053       0.071
```

Because this is a whole association, the "basics" are the original unpartialed variables. Note that there is considerable shrinkage. The overall association ($R^2 = 0.367$) is nontrivial and significant ($PROB = 0.003$).

The individual regression analyses provide detail: $p(1..3)$ are significantly related to $s(1)$ (multiple $R = 0.193$), with $p(1)$ yielding a significant beta. They are also significantly related to $s(2)$ (multiple $R = 0.175$), with $p(3)$'s beta significant.

Example 2
Partial Set Correlation Model

This example shows a partial set correlation model. In a large-scale longitudinal study of childhood and adolescent mental health (Cohen and Brook, 1987), data were obtained on personal qualities that the subjects admired and what they thought other children admired, as well as the sex and age of the subjects. The admired qualities were organized into scales for antisocial, materialistic, and conventional values for the self and as ascribed to others. In one phase of the investigation, the researchers wanted to study the relationship between the sets of self versus others. However, several of these scales exhibited sex differences, were nonlinearly (specifically quadratically) related to age, and/or were differently related to age for the sexes. For the self-other association to be assessed free of the confounding influence of age, sex, and their interactions, it was desirable to partial those effects from the association. Accordingly, using SYSTAT BASIC, the variables *AGE*, *SEX* times *AGE* and their squares were created, which, together with *AGE* and *SEX*, constituted both the *YPARTIAL* and

Chapter 9

XPARTIAL sets in the partial association. The resulting rectangular data file, *ADMIRE.SYD*, was analyzed as follows:

```
USE ADMIRE
SETCOR
MODEL ANTISO_O,MATER_O,CONVEN_O | ,
      AGE,SEX,AGESQ,SEXAGE,SEXAGESQ = ,
      ANTISO_S,MATER_S,CONVEN_S | ,
      AGE,SEX,AGESQ,SEXAGE,SEXAGESQ
ESTIMATE
```

The resulting output is:

```
Variables in the SYSTAT Rectangular file are:
   ID$          ANTISO_S     MATER_S      CONVEN_S     ANTISO_O     MATER_O
   CONVEN_O     AGE          SEX          AGESQ        SEXAGE       SEXAGESQ

Partial set correlation analysis (Y|YPAR VS. X|XPAR, WHERE YPAR=XPAR)

Number of cases on which analysis is based: 755.

Dependent set y partialled by these variables:
     AGE
     SEX
     AGESQ
     SEXAGE
     SEXAGESQ

Independent set x partialled by these variables:
     AGE
     SEX
     AGESQ
     SEXAGE
     SEXAGESQ
RAO F  =       52.169    df =           9.0,       1810.9   Prob=        0.000
R-Square =         0.429                        Shrunk R-Square =        0.422
T-Square =         0.169                        Shrunk T-Square =        0.159
P-Square =         0.169                        Shrunk P-Square =        0.159

Within basic set y correlations

                          ANTISO_O     MATER_O      CONVEN_O

              ANTISO_O     1.000
              MATER_O      0.200       1.000
              CONVEN_O    -0.417       0.105        1.000

Within basic set x correlations

                          ANTISO_S     MATER_S      CONVEN_S

              ANTISO_S     1.000
              MATER_S      0.206       1.000
              CONVEN_S    -0.258       0.063        1.000

Between basic y (col) and basic x (row) correlations

                          ANTISO_O     MATER_O      CONVEN_O

              ANTISO_S     0.393       0.077       -0.066
              MATER_S      0.133       0.456        0.046
              CONVEN_S    -0.111       0.120        0.351
```

Set and Canonical Correlation

Estimated (from x-set) y intercorrelations (R-square on diagonal)

	ANTISO_O	MATER_O	CONVEN_O
ANTISO_O	0.157		
MATER_O	0.052	0.216	
CONVEN_O	-0.028	0.053	0.124

Significance tests for prediction of each basic y variable

Variable	F-statistic	Probability
ANTISO_O	46.436	0.000
MATER_O	68.673	0.000
CONVEN_O	35.358	0.000

Betas predicting basic y (col) from basic x (row) variables

	ANTISO_O	MATER_O	CONVEN_O
ANTISO_S	0.377	0.009	0.022
MATER_S	0.056	0.448	0.018
CONVEN_S	-0.017	0.094	0.356

Standard errors of betas

	ANTISO_O	MATER_O	CONVEN_O
ANTISO_S	0.036	0.034	0.036
MATER_S	0.035	0.033	0.035
CONVEN_S	0.035	0.034	0.036

T-statistics for betas

	ANTISO_O	MATER_O	CONVEN_O
ANTISO_S	10.543	0.249	0.616
MATER_S	1.611	13.430	0.520
CONVEN_S	-0.486	2.783	9.965

Probabilities for betas

	ANTISO_O	MATER_O	CONVEN_O
ANTISO_S	0.000	0.803	0.538
MATER_S	0.108	0.000	0.603
CONVEN_S	0.627	0.006	0.000

Stewart-Love canonical redundancy index =   0.166

Canonical correlations

	1	2	3
	0.487	0.401	0.329

Bartlett test of residual correlations

Correlations 1 through 3
  Chi-square statistic =   418.286   df =   9   prob=   0.000

Correlations 2 through 3
  Chi-square statistic =   216.191   df =   4   prob=   0.000

Correlations 3 through 3
  Chi-square statistic =   85.145   df =   1   prob=   0.000

```
Canonical coefficients for dependent (y) set

                    1          2          3
      ANTISO_O    0.462      1.039     -0.114
      MATER_O     0.733     -0.671     -0.320
      CONVEN_O    0.471      0.448      0.919

Canonical loadings (y variable by factor correlations)

                    1          2          3
      ANTISO_O    0.412      0.718     -0.561
      MATER_O     0.875     -0.416     -0.246
      CONVEN_O    0.356     -0.056      0.933

Canonical redundancies for dependent set

                    1          2          3
                  0.084      0.037      0.045

Canonical coefficients for independent (x) set

                    1          2          3
      ANTISO_S    0.392      0.986     -0.077
      MATER_S     0.745     -0.585     -0.404
      CONVEN_S    0.470      0.196      0.910

Canonical loadings (x variable by factor correlations)

                    1          2          3
      ANTISO_S    0.425      0.815     -0.395
      MATER_S     0.856     -0.369     -0.362
      CONVEN_S    0.416     -0.095      0.904

Canonical redundancies for independent set

                    1          2          3
                  0.086      0.043      0.040
```

The partial association is substantial (0.429), significant, and because of the large *n* and small *x* and *y* sets, hardly affected by shrinkage. The within and between basic *x* and *y* set correlation coefficients are all partial correlation coefficients because the basic *x* and *y* sets are respectively X|XPARTIAL and Y|YPARTIAL with XPARTIAL=YPARTIAL, and it is for these partialed variables that the multiple-regression output (betas, multiple *R* squares, etc.) is given.

For example, the significant beta = 0.377 for *ANTISO_S* in estimating *ANTISO_O* are for both with the variables *AGE*, *SEX*, *AGESQ*, *SEXAGE*, and *SEXAGSQ* partialed, and *ANTISOC_S* is further partialed by *MATER_S* and *CONVEN_S*. Note that each _O variable has significant betas with its paired _S variable. In addition, *MATER_O*'s beta for *CONVEN_S* is significant. All the partialed *y* variables have significant multiple *R* squares with the partialed *x* set, that for *MATER_O* being the largest.

Example 3
Contingency Table Analysis

From the perspective of set correlations, a two-way contingency table displays the association between two nominal scales, each represented by a suitably coded set of variables. A nominal scale of n levels (categories) is coded as $n-1$ variables, and when each is partialed by the other $n-2$ variables, it carries a specific contrast or comparison, its nature depending on the type of coding employed. The major types of coding—dummy, effects, and contrast—are described in Chapter 5 of Cohen and Cohen (1983); their use in contingency table analysis is illustrated in Cohen (1982).

Zwick and Cramer (1986) compared the application of various multivariate methods in the analysis of contingency tables using a fictitious example from Marascuilo and Levin (1983), and Cohen (1988a) provides a complete set correlation analysis of this example. It is of responses by 500 men to the question "Does a woman have the right to decide whether an unwanted birth can be terminated during the first three months of pregnancy?" The response alternatives were crosstabulated with religion, resulting in the following table of frequencies:

	Protestant	Catholic	Jewish	Other	Total
Yes	76	115	41	77	309
No	64	82	8	12	166
No opinion	11	6	2	6	25
Total	151	203	51	95	500

Religion and response are represented by ordinal numbers in the data file *SURVEY3.SYD*. Religion is effects-coded as E(1), E(2), and E(3). When from each of these the other two are partialed, the resulting variable compares that group with the unweighted combination of all four groups; that is, it estimates that group's "effect." Notice how we use the FREQ command to determine the cell frequencies:

```
USE SURVEY3
CATEGORY RELIGION$ RESPONSE$
FREQ=COUNT
SETCOR
MODEL RESPONSE$=RELIGION$
ESTIMATE
```

The resulting output is:

```
Variables in the SYSTAT Rectangular file are:
  RELIGION$    RESPONSE$    COUNT

    Case frequencies determined by value of variable COUNT.

Categorical values encountered during processing are:
RELIGION$ (4 levels)
    Catholic, Jewish, Other, Protestant
RESPONSE$ (3 levels)
    No, No_opinion, Yes

Whole set correlation analysis (Y VS. X)

Number of cases on which analysis is based: 640.
RAO F =       50.311    df =          6.0,      1270.0   Prob=      0.000
R-Square =             0.347                Shrunk R-Square =        0.341
T-Square =             0.182                Shrunk T-Square =        0.174
P-Square =             0.182                Shrunk P-Square =        0.174

Within basic set y correlations

                      RESPONSE$ 1 RESPONSE$ 2

        RESPONSE$ 1   .     1.000
        RESPONSE$ 2        -0.569        1.000

Within basic set x correlations

                      RELIGION$ 1 RELIGION$ 2 RELIGION$ 3

        RELIGION$ 1        1.000
        RELIGION$ 2       -0.123        1.000
        RELIGION$ 3       -0.269       -0.381        1.000

Between basic y (col) and basic x (row) correlations

                      RESPONSE$ 1 RESPONSE$ 2

        RELIGION$ 1       -0.147        0.189
        RELIGION$ 2       -0.186        0.274
        RELIGION$ 3        0.545       -0.405

Estimated (from x-set) y intercorrelations (R-square on diagonal)

                      RESPONSE$ 1 RESPONSE$ 2

        RESPONSE$ 1        0.298
        RESPONSE$ 2       -0.217        0.195

Significance tests for prediction of each basic y variable

Variable       F-statistic    Probability
RESPONSE$         89.841         0.000

Betas predicting basic y (col) from basic x (row) variables

                      RESPONSE$ 1 RESPONSE$ 2

        RELIGION$ 1        0.006        0.129
        RELIGION$ 2        0.027        0.174
        RELIGION$ 3        0.557       -0.304
```

Set and Canonical Correlation

Standard errors of betas

	RESPONSE$ 1	RESPONSE$ 2
RELIGION$ 1	0.036	0.019
RELIGION$ 2	0.037	0.020
RELIGION$ 3	0.038	0.020

T-statistics for betas

	RESPONSE$ 1	RESPONSE$ 2
RELIGION$ 1	0.168	6.846
RELIGION$ 2	0.735	8.866
RELIGION$ 3	14.551	-15.080

Probabilities for betas

	RESPONSE$ 1	RESPONSE$ 2
RELIGION$ 1	0.867	0.000
RELIGION$ 2	0.463	0.000
RELIGION$ 3	0.000	0.000

Stewart-Love canonical redundancy index =   0.246

Canonical correlations

	1	2
	0.558	0.228

Bartlett test of residual correlations

Correlations 1 through 2
    Chi-square statistic =   271.251   df =   6   prob=   0.000

Correlations 2 through 2
    Chi-square statistic =   34.099   df =   2   prob=   0.000

Canonical coefficients for dependent (y) set

	1	2
RESPONSE$ 1	0.815	0.904
RESPONSE$ 2	-0.279	1.184

Canonical loadings (y variable by factor correlations)

	1	2
RESPONSE$ 1	0.973	0.229
RESPONSE$ 2	-0.743	0.670

Canonical redundancies for dependent set

	1	2
	0.233	0.013

Canonical coefficients for independent (x) set

	1	2
RELIGION$ 1	-0.056	-0.690
RELIGION$ 2	-0.047	-1.008
RELIGION$ 3	0.965	-0.626

```
            Canonical loadings (x variable by factor correlations)
                                 1          2
              RELIGION$ 1      -0.309     -0.398
              RELIGION$ 2      -0.408     -0.684
              RELIGION$ 3       0.998     -0.056

       Canonical redundancies for independent set
                                 1          2
                               0.131      0.011
```

The whole association is modest (0.347) but highly significant, and provides some Fisherian protection for the tests of specific hypotheses that follow. To determine where this overall association is coming from, assess the association of religion with the Yes-No contrast C(l).C(2) using y semipartial association.

To analyze the effects of the religious groups on the Yes-No contrast, we turn to the betas for E(1..3). Since these are partial regression coefficients, each reflects a comparison of its religious group with an equally weighted combination of the four groups on the Yes versus No contrast. For example, the Protestant group (beta = 0.129) shows a greater proclivity to respond "No" (compared to "Yes") with $t = 6.846$, $df = 495$, $p = 0.000$. (For dealing with the implicitly coded "Other" group, see Chapter 5 of Cohen and Cohen, 1983.) Further analyses of these data using contrast functions of religious group membership and bipartial association are given in Cohen (1988a).

Computation

All the computations are in double precision.

Algorithms

Table 2 in Cohen (1982) contains errors in two of the matrix expressions for the Y semipartial. The expression for H should read (in Cohen's notation)

$$H = C_{D.C,B.C} C_{B.C}^{-1} C'_{D.C,B.C}$$

and in E_2, B should be replaced with $B.C$. E_1 is correct as is. We are indebted to Charles Lewis for this correction.

Missing Data

When a rectangular data file is used in SETCOR, the program computes a Pearson correlation matrix on all the numeric variables in the file on a listwise basis. This means that if a value is missing for any variable in the file, the case is dropped and n is reduced accordingly. If the pattern of missing data makes n small, you should impute missing values by maximum likelihood (EM) in the CORR module.

References

Cohen, J. (1982). Set correlation as a general multivariate data-analytic method. *Multivariate Behavioral Research*, 17, 301–341.

Cohen, J. (1988a). Set correlation and contingency tables. *Applied Psychological Measurement*, 12, 425–434.

Cohen, J. (1988b). *Statistical power analysis for the behavioral sciences,* 2nd ed. Hillsdale, N.J.: Lawrence Erlbaum Associates.

Cohen, P. and Brook, J. (1987). Family factors related to the persistence of psychopathology in childhood and adolescence. *Psychiatry*, 50, 332–345.

Cohen, J. and Cohen, P. (1983). *Applied multiple regression/correlation analysis for the behavioral sciences,* 2nd ed. Hillsdale, N.J.: Lawrence Erlbaum Associates.

Cohen, J. and Nee, J. C. M. (1983). CORSET, A Fortran IV program for set correlation. *Educational and Psychological Measurement*, 43, 817–820.

Cohen, J. and Nee, J. C. M. (1984). Estimators for two measures of association for set correlation. *Educational and Psychological Measurement*, 44, 907–917.

Cohen, J. and Nee, J. C. M. (1987). A comparison of two noncentral F approximations, with applications to power analysis in set correlation. *Multivariate Behavioral Research*, 22, 483–490.

Cohen, J., and Nee, J. C. M. (1989). Robustness of Type I error and power in set correlation analysis of contingency tables. *Multivariate Behavioral Research*, 23.

Cramer, E. M. and Nicewander, W. A. (1979). Some symmetric, invariant measures of set association. *Psychometrika*, 44, 43–54.

Eber, H. W. and Cohen, J. (1987). SETCORAN: A PC program to implement set correlation as a general multivariate data-analytic method. Atlanta: Psychological Resources.

Hotelling, H. (1935). The most predictable criterion. *Journal of Educational Psychology*, 26, 139–142.

Hotelling, H. (1936). Relations between two set of variates. *Biometrika*, 28, 321–377.

Marascuilo, L. A., and Levin, J. R. (1983). *Multivariate statistics in the social sciences.* Monterey, Calif.: Brooks/Cole.

Olson, C. L. (1974). Comparative robustness of six tests in multivariate analysis of variance. *Journal of the American Statistical Association*, 69, 894–908.

Pedhazur, E. J. (1982). *Multiple regression in behavioral research*, 2nd ed. New York: Holt, Rinehart & Winston.

Pillai, K. C. S. (1960). *Statistical tables for tests of multivariate hypotheses.* Manila: The Statistical Institute, University of the Philippines.

Rao, C. R. (1973). *Linear statistical inference and its applications,* 2nd ed. New York: John Wiley & Sons, Inc.

Stewart, D., and Love, W. (1968). A general canonical correlation index. *Psychological Bulletin*, 70, 160–163.

van den Burg, W., and Lewis, C. (1988). Some properties of two measures of multivariate association. *Psychometrika*, 53, 109–122.

Wherry, R. J. (1931). The mean and second moment coefficient of the multiple correlation coefficient in samples from a normal population. *Biometrika*, 22, 353–361.

Wilkinson, L. (1988). *SYSTAT. The system for statistics.* Evanston Ill.: Systat, Inc.

Wilks, S. S. (1932). Certain generalizations in the analysis of variance. *Biometrika*, 24, 471–494.

Zwick, R. and Cramer, E. M. (1986). A multivariate perspective on the analysis of categorical data. *Applied Psychological Measurement*, 10, 141–145.

Chapter 10

Signal Detection Analysis

Herb Stenson

The SIGNAL module provides analyses of data that are appropriate for the theory of signal detection as described by Green and Swets (1966), Egan (1975), and many others. For some interesting recent applications, see Swets and Pickett (1982), Swets (1986), and Kraemer (1988).

The response data to be analyzed by SIGNAL can consist of from 2 to 11 response categories. Thus, either binary or rating-scale data can be analyzed. An iterative technique is used in order to produce maximum likelihood estimates of all model parameters, including the locations of the category boundaries. Graphical displays of ROC curves are available in addition to the numerical output.

SIGNAL allows analyses based on a number of statistical models in addition to the more usual normal distribution and nonparametric models. The additional models are the logistic, negative exponential, chi-square, Poisson, and gamma distribution models. These models are useful for various types of detection tasks in which the sets of assumptions concerning the nature of the detector dictate one of these models. For a discussion of these alternative models, see Egan (1975).

The parameter estimates from any model can be saved into a SYSTAT file, as can the coordinates of any ROC curve.

Statistical Background

The theory of signal detectability (TSD) emerged after World War II as a synthesis of existing methods for representing the characteristics of a receiver or sensing device (Peterson, Birdsall, and Fox, 1954). Although its origins were in electrical engineering, the abstraction of the theory made it especially suited to analysis of human perception in general and of any system involving detection of a weak signal against a background of noise: perception of visual and auditory signals, medical diagnosis based on signs or symptoms, robotic perception, and so on. TSD is now widely used in medical research for evaluating the sensitivity and specificity of diagnostic equipment and clinicians. In radiology, for example, TSD can be used to quantify the performance of radiologists reading diagnostic X-rays when the "signal" (true diagnosis) is known from subsequent events or external criteria. See Hanley and McNeil (1982) for an example.

Detection Parameters

The signal detection theory literature abounds with various indices of the detectability of a signal and associated parameters. Because of this proliferation and the confusion that it can cause, the indices and parameters that are estimated by SIGNAL are described here in some detail. You can read more about these indices in books by Swets and Pickett (1982), Egan (1975), and Green and Swets (1966). Coombs, Dawes, and Tversky (1970) provide the best summary.

Except for the NPAR model, the output printed by SIGNAL contains a standard set of parameters and indices of detectability for all of the models. The NPAR model is nonparametric, so there are no parameters to estimate. The only index of detection that is given for it is the area under the ROC curve obtained by joining the points on the ROC graph by straight lines. See Bamber (1975) for ways to test hypotheses about this area measure.

For every model involving a statistical distribution, SIGNAL prints the mean and standard deviation of the noise (N) distribution and the mean and standard deviation of the signal+noise ($S + N$) distribution. For compactness, let us call these *MN, SN, MS,* and *SS*, respectively. For the normal distribution model, *MN* will always be 0 and *SN* will always be unity because these two parameters are chosen as the origin and unit of the scale for the decision axis. They are a part of the standard output because they do not take on these fixed values for all of the models.

Using these means and standard deviations, SIGNAL computes and prints three measures of the separation of the $S + N$ and N distributions for each of the models. These measures are labeled as *D-Prime, D Sub-A,* and *Sakitt D* in the output.

D-Prime (d') is the most common index of detectability used in detection research. It is defined as $(MS - MN)/SN$. As has been pointed out by many authors, it suffers from the lack of information about the standard deviation of the $S + N$ distribution when this information is available. The other two measures computed by SIGNAL take this information into account.

D Sub-A (d_a) uses as a denominator the square root of the mean of the N and $S + N$ variances. Let us call this number x. Thus, you would square both SN and SS, add these squares, divide by two, and take the square root of the result in order to find x. Then the index $D\ Sub\text{-}A$ is defined as $(MS - MN)/x$. This index is related to the area under the ROC curve for normal distributions and has other statistical niceties. See Simpson and Fitter (1973) for further discussion.

Sakitt D is another measure of detectability that takes into account the variances of both the N and $S + N$ distributions. It was proposed by Sakitt (1973). It uses as a denominator the square root of the product of SN and SS. Thus, this index is defined as $(MS - MN)/(\sqrt{SN \times SS})$. Egan (1975) proposes this as the best detection index for chi-square, gamma, and Poisson models.

In addition to these measures of the separation of the $S + N$ and N distributions, SIGNAL also prints in the output for each model the ratio of SS to SN. It is labeled *SD-Ratio*, which stands for *standard deviation ratio*.

The most general measure of detection available is the area under the theoretical ROC curve that is fitted to your data. This measure is computed by SIGNAL and is labeled ROC *Area* in the output for each model. The remainder of the output is discussed in sections that follow, where each model is described.

Signal Detection Analysis in SYSTAT

Signal Detection Analysis Main Dialog Box

To open the Signal Detection dialog box, from the menus choose:

Statistics
  Signal Detection...

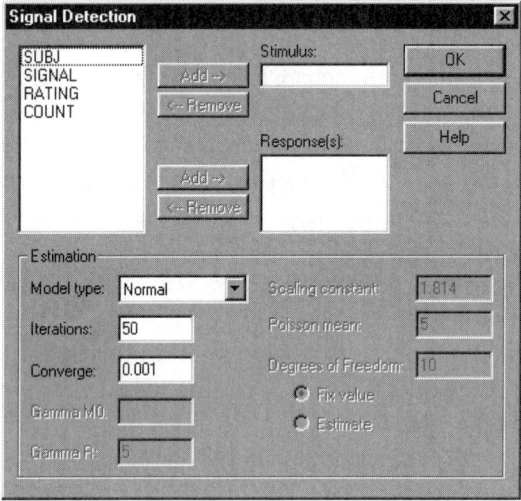

Signal detection models are computed with a model specification and estimation stage.

Stimulus. Select the variable that shows the true state of the signal on each trial for signal-detection data. The stimulus variable can only contain the numbers 0 (for noise occurrences) and 1 (for signal+noise occurrences) to indicate the stimulus state on trial. The stimulus variable remains in effect until you change it or use a different data file.

Response(s). Select the variable(s) that contain the response(s) to the stimulus by one or more detectors. The response variable can contain numbers only between −10 and +10 and there can be only 11 categories of response. (for example, 0 through 10 or −5 through +5). If the input data contain decimals, they will be truncated instead of rounded. The response variable remains in effect until you change it or use a different data file.

Model type. With the exception of the nonparametric model, each model assumes that the trials on which noise alone occurred (N) and the trials on which both signal and noise occurred ($S + N$) are samples from a particular kind of statistical distribution, with possibly different parameters for the N and $S + N$ distributions. Possible models include:

- **Chi Square.** You can think of the chi-square model as a generalization of the exponential model. To enter a fixed value for the degrees of freedom, select **Fix value** and enter a positive number in the Degrees of Freedom box. Alternatively you can specify a starting value for the degrees of freedom and signal analysis will attempt to find the best-fitting value for the degrees of freedom during iteration. To specify a starting value for degrees of freedom, select **Estimate** and enter a positive number in the Degrees of Freedom box.

- **Exponential.** The negative exponential density function is algebraically identical to a chi-square density function with two degrees of freedom. However, its simple properties and usefulness justify treating it as a separate model.
- **Gamma.** Use the gamma model when your experiment can be described as a Poisson process and the detector uses the time required to accumulate a fixed number of rare events as the basis of the response. The length of a trial is determined by the detector as opposed to a Poisson counting observer, who counts events during fixed interval trial. You can specify both the M0 parameter and the number of events (R) that the detector is waiting to accumulate. If you do not enter a fixed value for R, the default starting value (5) will be used and the program will estimate a value of R at every iteration.
- **Logistic.** The logistic model models the noise or signal+noise distributions and is a good approximation for the normal, while being mathematically more tractable.
- **Normal.** Use this model to indicate that the noise *(N)* and signal+noise *(S + N)* distributions are Gaussian.
- **Npar.** A nonparametric model offers a simple way to get a quick look at your data. If you believe that the assumptions of any of the parametric models that you can use are not justifiable for your data, then use the nonparametric model.
- **Poisson.** Select a Poisson model when the detector is basing a response on a small number of countable, rare events that occur on each trial. For a Poisson model, you can specify the mean of the noise distribution. The mean of the Poisson distribution is the average number of occurrences per trial of the event being counted. The mean for the signal+noise distribution will be estimated to give the best fit to your data.

Scaling constant. For both the logistic and exponential models, the default scaling constant is $\pi/\sqrt{3}$, which is approximately 1.814. With the default value in effect, the standard deviation of the noise distribution will be 1.00. You can set the scaling constant to be any positive number.

Iterations. This option controls the maximum number of iterations that you want to allow the program to perform in order to estimate the parameters. The default value is 50, which for most applications is more than enough. However, if you have a lot of response categories, a small value of CONVERGE, and "difficult" data, you may need more than this for some models.

Converge. The CONVERGE option controls the degree of accuracy sought in the estimations. Its default value is 0.001, which means that the estimates are to be accurate

Chapter 10

to 0.001 times their values. You can set CONVERGE to any number from 0.1 to 0.00001.

Using Commands

After selecting the data with USE filename, continue with:

```
SIGNAL
    MODEL responsevarlist = stimulusvar
    ESTIMATE / type  CONVERGE=d  ITERATIONS=n ,
                    M0=d  R=d  C=d  MEAN=d  DF=d
```

Type must be one of the following:

NORMAL	NPAR	LOGISTIC
EXPONENTIAL	CHI_SQUARE	POISSON
GAMMA		

For a single detector, the response variable list contains a single variable. Multiple detectors (for example, judges) of a single signal can be fit in a single model.

When analyzing your data, SIGNAL computes initial estimates (starting values) for each parameter that is to be estimated by the iterative process. Typing ESTIMATE again after an analysis has finished will cause SIGNAL to use the most recent estimates of parameters as starting values for continuing the analysis, rather than computing new ones. You can, if you want, change the options for ESTIMATE when restarting the program in this way. However, this restart procedure will not work if you specify a new MODEL or use FREQ after an analysis terminates. It also will not work if you are using the BY command. You can, however, use any of the other commands (except USE) before restarting the program.

The values of CONVERGE and ITER always revert to their default values for each use of ESTIMATE. Therefore, they must be stated explicitly each time that you use ESTIMATE if you don't want to use the default settings. The value that you use for CONVERGE is irrelevant, and therefore unnecessary, if you specify ITER=0. Because no iterations will occur, there is no accuracy of estimation to worry about. Similarly, since no iterations are used for the NPAR model, both ITER and CONVERGE are inappropriate options for this model.

The capability to restart the program using the most recent values, combined with the options for ESTIMATE, enables you to be flexible in the way that you approach the analysis of your data. You could, for example, set CONVERGE to a large value, such as 0.1, and set ITER to a small value, such as 4. This will cause the iterative process to proceed rather quickly. After a look at the output, you could restart the program by typing ESTIMATE again with a smaller value for CONVERGE, and perhaps with a different number for ITER.

Usage Considerations

Types of data. The format of input data for SIGNAL is quite flexible in order to easily accommodate data from a variety of experimental designs commonly used in signal detection studies. The program requires a SYSTAT data set containing a minimum of two numeric variables: One that shows the true state of the signal on each trial of your experiment, and the other that shows the response of a detector to that signal state. Thus, the cases in your SYSTAT file represent trials (instances of the signal or lack thereof) in a detection experiment.

If you have more than one detector responding to exactly the same sequence of stimuli, responses from the additional detectors can also be coded as variables in the SYSTAT data file. In this case, there should be only one variable that indicates the true state of the signal on each trial. You could also have more than one variable that designates the true state of the signal on each trial. For example, if each detector was exposed to a different sequence of signal states, you could have a separate variable that indicates the true state of the signal for each detector.

The example below shows how to enter data for a hypothetical experiment in which each of three detectors (HS, LB, and LW) responded on each of five trials to exactly the same sequence of signal states. (You would, of course, have many more trials than this for a real experiment.) Imagine that a response was to be one of the numbers -2, -1, 0, 1, or 2, with a -2 indicating that the detector was sure that no signal was present on a trial, a 2 indicating that the detector was sure that a signal was present on a trial, and the other numbers indicating degrees of certainty as to whether a signal was present or not. The true state of the signal (present or not present) is coded as the variable labeled *STATE*.

```
BASIC
SAVE MYFILE
INPUT STATE,HS,LB,LW
RUN
  1   0   1   2
  0  -1  -2  -1
  0   0  -1   0
  1   2   1   1
  0  -1   0  -1
```

Another way to encode these same data would be to create either a string or numeric variable to identify a detector (for example, *UNIT$*), a variable to show the true state of the stimulus, (for example, *STATE*), and a third variable to indicate the response of the detector (for example, *RATING*). Then, on each line of the data set, you would enter the identifier for the detector, the state of the stimulus on the trial in question, and the response of the detector. Such a data set would then contain as many cases as there were trials times the number of detectors. You then could use the SELECT command within the SIGNAL module to identify which of the detectors you want to analyze, or you could use the BY command to analyze each detector sequentially. This would be an easy way to enter data if each detector had been exposed to a different sequence of signal states. However, this would not be an optimal way to enter data when each detector was exposed to exactly the same sequence of signal states because you are repeating the same set of numbers representing the signal states for each detector.

The availability of negative numbers as response options makes it possible to encode responses from a particular kind of signal detection task that is sometimes used. In this task, the detector (usually a human detector) is to specify first whether or not a given trial contained a signal, and then is asked to rate his or her confidence that his or her response is correct on, say, a five-point rating scale. A way to encode such data for SIGNAL would be to treat all confidence ratings on trials when the subject reported the absence of a signal as the numbers –1 through –5, and to treat the ratings on trials when the subject reported that there was a signal present as the numbers +1 through +5. A similar encoding strategy can be used when a detector reports the presence or absence of a signal, and the reaction time for the response is categorized and used as a *confidence rating*, with quick times indicating a high degree of confidence in the response. You would encode the reaction times into categories acceptable to SIGNAL for this experimental paradigm.

SIGNAL treats the response categories as ordinal data. Thus, it makes no difference in the analysis what numbers are used, even if there are gaps in the sequence used. All that is necessary is that the higher numbers indicate a "signal-like" response and the lower ones indicate a "noise-like" response. For example, using the response categories 1, 2, and 3 would result in the same analysis as using the categories –6, 0, and +2 for the same data. Only the category labels would be affected in the program output. Notice that gaps can occur in the response category sequence either because certain numbers were not available to the detector as response options or because the detector never used one of the available options. The program obviously cannot distinguish which of these is the case.

You can specify more than one variable as a response. This allows the pooling of responses of detectors that were exposed to the same stimulus sequence, or the pooling of responses from one detector that was exposed to the same sequence of stimuli on more than one occasion. Each occasion would have to be entered into the data set as a separate variable. For example, to pool the responses from detectors HS and LW from the data set *MYFILE* (above), you would type:

MODEL HS,LW = STATE

The resulting signal detection analysis would treat all responses from these two detectors as being from the same detector. Thus, the resulting detection parameter estimates would apply to this group of detectors instead of to one of them individually.

If you used a different coding scheme, like the one used for the data set *SWETSDTA* in the first example, where each detector has an identifier code, you could pool detectors by simply not using a SELECT or BY command when you analyzed the data. SIGNAL would then treat all response entries as coming from the same detector. You could also use the SELECT command with multiple identifier variables, such as sex and age, to pool data within these subgroups. The resulting analyses would then apply to whatever group(s) you selected to pool.

Print options. The output is standard for all PRINT options.

Quick Graphs. SIGNAL plots the receiver operating characteristic (ROC) curve.

Saving files. If you save before you estimate, SIGNAL will save parameter estimates into a file. If you add SAVE / ROC, SIGNAL will save the ROC curve coordinates.

BY groups. SIGNAL analyzes data by groups. Your file need not be sorted on the BY variable(s).

Bootstrapping. Bootstrapping is not available in this procedure.

Case frequencies. If a file contains frequencies of each type of response to each of two stimulus states, the frequencies of responses then can be used as a FREQ variable in the SIGNAL module. This can be useful if your data are already aggregated in this way or if you want to make up a table of hypothetical data to model some signal detection task.

Case weights. SIGNAL does not allow case weighting.

Examples

Example 1
Normal Distribution Model for Signal Detection

This example shows frequency data for two detectors (subjects) in a study by Swets, Tanner, and Birdsall (1961) as reported by Swets and Pickett (1982, pp. 216–219). Each of the subjects in the experiment used a six-category rating scale to indicate his or her confidence that a signal was present on each of 597 trials when the signal was present, and on 591 randomly-mixed trials on which the signal was not present. The *COUNT* variable shows the number of times a subject gave a particular rating to a given signal state. Notice that the identifier *SUBJ* is a numeric variable in this case (but would not have to be).

By far, the most common model used for signal detection analysis is the normal (Gaussian) model, in which the noise (*N*) distribution and the signal+noise (*S* + *N*) distribution are both assumed to be Gaussian density functions. These functions have the same variance in the case of binary response data, or have possibly unequal variances in the case of more than two response categories.

Here we use the data set named *SWETSDTA* that was described earlier. To perform a signal detection analysis using the normal distribution model for the first subject in the data set, we type:

```
USE SWETSDTA
SELECT SUBJ=1
SIGNAL
MODEL RATING=SIGNAL
FREQ=COUNT
ESTIMATE
```

Notice that the SELECT command is used to specify which detector to analyze. SELECT remains in effect throughout any subsequent analyses until you change the selection by using the SELECT command again (or cancel it completely by typing SELECT with nothing after it).

The FREQ command is used in the same way as it is in the rest of SYSTAT. Here it specifies the variable that shows the frequencies with which response categories were used for the two different signal states. If you were using a data set that was coded in a manner similar to *MYFILE*, you obviously would not use the FREQ command.

Signal Detection Analysis

Following is the output produced:

```
Variables in the SYSTAT Rectangular file are:
    SUBJ         SIGNAL        RATING        COUNT

    Case frequencies determined by value of variable COUNT.

Number of stimulus events (cases) responded to:      1188

Number of detectors (variables) observing an event:     1

Number of response categories used:                     6

Number of responses to noise events:                  591

Number of responses to signal events:                 597

Total number of responses:                           1188

Number of instances of missing data:                    0

Response  Frequency     Joint Probability  Conditional Prob.   Cum.Cond.Prob.
Category  Noise Signal    Noise   Signal     Noise   Signal     Noise   Signal
    1       174    46    0.14646  0.03872   0.29442  0.07705   0.29442  0.07705
    2       172    57    0.14478  0.04798   0.29103  0.09548   0.58545  0.17253
    3       104    66    0.08754  0.05556   0.17597  0.11055   0.76142  0.28308
    4        92   101    0.07744  0.08502   0.15567  0.16918   0.91709  0.45226
    5        41   154    0.03451  0.12963   0.06937  0.25796   0.98646  0.71022
    6         8   173    0.00673  0.14562   0.01354  0.28978   1.00000  1.00000

  Total     591   597    0.4975   0.5025    1.0000   1.0000


Initial estimates of parameters: Gaussian model
     Mean(Noise)     SD(Noise)          Mean(Sig+Noise)  SD(Sig+Noise)
         0.0           1.000                  1.495          1.392
       D-Prime        D Sub-A      Sakitt D      SD-Ratio      ROC Area
        1.495          1.234        1.267         1.392         0.808
Upper Category Boundaries:
        -0.523         0.204        0.706         1.366         2.229


Goodness of Fit:  Log(Likelihood)   ChiSq(3 df)   Prob(ChiSq)
                    -1921.418606       2.364         0.500


Iterative maximum-likelihood estimation of parameters with tolerance = 0.00100
Iter  -Log(Like)    D-Prime     SD-Ratio     Category Boundaries
   0  .1921419D+04  .14949D+01  .13917D+01   -.52284D+00 .20391D+00 .70596D+00
                                              .13661D+01 .22293D+01
   1  .1920995D+04  .15075D+01  .14088D+01   -.53627D+00 .20024D+00 .70545D+00
                                              .13599D+01 .22829D+01
   2  .1920986D+04  .15219D+01  .14174D+01   -.53395D+00 .20431D+00 .71050D+00
                                              .13673D+01 .22951D+01
   3  .1920985D+04  .15182D+01  .14160D+01   -.53279D+00 .20448D+00 .70969D+00
                                              .13656D+01 .22945D+01
   4  .1920985D+04  .15182D+01  .14160D+01   -.53279D+00 .20448D+00 .70969D+00
                                              .13656D+01 .22945D+01
   5  .1920985D+04  .15189D+01  .14166D+01   -.53304D+00 .20410D+00 .70956D+00
                                              .13662D+01 .22937D+01
   6  .1920985D+04  .15189D+01  .14166D+01   -.53304D+00 .20390D+00 .70956D+00
                                              .13662D+01 .22937D+01
```

```
Final parameter estimates using upper category boundaries: Gaussian model
   Mean(Noise)     SD(Noise)           Mean(Sig+Noise)  SD(Sig+Noise)
      0.0           1.000                   1.519           1.417


Ctgry                                        Upper
Label   Far     HR    FINV(FAR)  FINV(HR)  Boundary       Beta    Log(Beta)
  1   0.7056 0.9229    -0.541    -1.425    -0.533        0.285     -1.255
  2   0.4146 0.8275     0.216    -0.944     0.204        0.468     -0.758
  3   0.2386 0.7169     0.711    -0.574     0.710        0.771     -0.260
  4   0.0829 0.5477     1.386    -0.120     1.366        1.785      0.579
  5   0.0135 0.2898     2.210     0.554     2.294        8.437      2.133
      D-Prime        D Sub-A     Sakitt D   SD-Ratio    ROC Area
       1.519          1.239       1.276      1.417       0.809

Goodness of Fit: Log(Likelihood)  ChiSq(3 df)   Prob(ChiSq)
                   -1920.984805      1.497        0.683
EXPORT successfully completed.
```

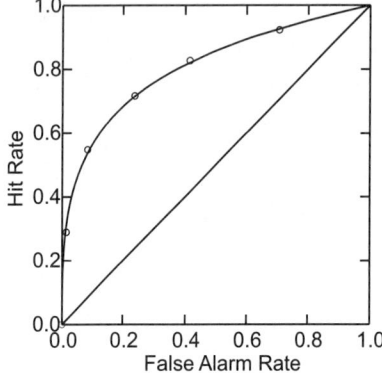

Receiver Operating Characteristic (ROC) Plot

The meanings of the first two sections of output are self-evident. The first is a report on the data read, and the second is a tabulation of frequencies and probabilities (relative frequencies) compiled from the input data. The final column of the frequency table is *Cumulative Conditional Probabilities*. The false-alarm rates (*FAR*) and hit-rates (*HR*) shown later in the output are computed by subtracting these cumulative probabilities from unity. This results in *FAR* and *HR* being associated with the upper category boundary of a labeled category. The report on the data read and the frequency table are a standard part of the output for every model that can be used in SIGNAL.

The next section of output, labeled *Initial estimates of parameters*, contains the detection parameters discussed earlier as well as a line of numbers labeled *Upper Category Boundaries*. The latter are the standard normal deviates (z scores) that correspond to the area of the noise distribution that is above the upper boundary of each successive response category. Notice that there is one fewer of these than there are categories. This section of output is referred to as **initial estimates** because they are the starting estimates that the iterative procedure uses to compute maximum likelihood estimates of these same parameters.

At the end of the output for initial estimates, there is a line labeled *Goodness of Fit*. The data on this line indicate how well the initial parameter estimates account for the empirical data in your data file. The estimated parameters and category boundaries for the two normal distributions (N and $S + N$) allow the estimation of the probability that a given response will occur given either an N trial or an $S + N$ trial. We compute these probabilities for each response that occurred on each trial of the experiment. The product of all these probabilities gives us the probability (likelihood) of obtaining the data that we in fact obtained, given that the model and its parameters are correct. Instead of computing this product, SIGNAL finds the natural logarithm of each probability and adds them together, rather than multiplying the probabilities themselves. The first goodness-of-fit indicator is the sum of these logarithms for the input data, given the estimates of the model that were made from the data. Thus, it is labeled *Log(Likelihood)*.

The log-likelihood is useful for certain analytic purposes, but it is not very intuitively appealing. For this reason, SIGNAL also computes a Pearson chi-square statistic indicating how well the model with its parameter estimates fits the input data. The theoretical probability of each type of response, mentioned in the preceding paragraph, allows the calculation of an expected frequency of each response for both N and $S + N$ trials. Differences between the actual frequencies and the expected frequencies, based on the model, are used to calculate the chi-square statistic in the usual way. For the normal model, it will have degrees of freedom three fewer than the number of response categories used. This chi-square value, its degrees of freedom, and the associated chi-square probability are shown along with the log(likelihood) as goodness-of-fit statistics. The probability of the chi-square value will be unity if the fit is perfect and will approach 0 for very bad fits to the data.

The next section of output is a history of the iterative estimation of the model parameters. The value of –log(likelihood) is shown for each iteration along with the estimated values of the model parameters for the iteration. As you can see from the output, the value of –log(likelihood) decreases at each iteration until it levels off, and the program ceases to iterate. As the value of –log(likelihood) decreases, the likelihood of having gotten the data that were obtained increases, hence the term **maximum likelihood estimation**. When the program can no longer produce significant increases in this likelihood by adjusting the parameters and is not producing parameter values that differ much from iteration to iteration, it ceases. The letter D that appears in this numerical output should be interpreted in the same way an E is when using scientific notation. Using *D* rather than *E* merely signifies that double-precision arithmetic is being used in the calculations.

As you can see in the output for the iterative estimations, SIGNAL estimates *D-Prime*, the *SD-Ratio* and the *Upper Category Boundaries* on each iteration. *D-Prime* could just as easily be labeled *Mean S + N*, and *SD-Ratio* could be labeled *Standard Deviation of S + N* because we have assumed the mean and standard deviation of *N* to be 0 and 1, respectively. As stated earlier, the numbers for the upper category boundaries are standard normal deviates (z scores) relative to the *N* distribution. Following the history of iteration is a table showing the final estimates of the parameters along with some other information.

In this table of final parameter estimates, you will see a column labeled *FINV(FAR)* and another labeled *FINV(HR)*. These are the z scores corresponding to the *FAR* and *HR*, respectively. These z scores are the inverse function of the *FAR* and *HR* values, hence the more general label *FINV*. This is very useful when models other than the normal distribution are used because then we are not necessarily dealing with standard normal deviates. Also shown in this table are the *Upper Category Boundaries*, which have already been described, and two columns labeled *Beta* and *Log(Beta)*. **Beta** is the ratio of the height of the normal distribution for *S + N* to the height of the normal distribution for *N* at a given upper category boundary. **Log(Beta)** is the natural logarithm of Beta.

Following the table of final estimates are the computed values for all of the detection indices described earlier, as well as the values of the same goodness-of-fit measures that were described for the table of initial estimates. The plot shows the usual ROC curve for the input data. *HR* is plotted against *FAR*, and the theoretical ROC curve that results from the final parameter estimates is shown.

When you analyze data that have fewer than four response categories using the NORMAL model, you will notice that no iterations occur. This is because the *HR* and *FAR* data can always be fit perfectly by an algebraic procedure for fewer than four categories. There are not enough degrees of freedom in the data to allow any error of estimation. Thus, for these cases, all that you will get is a table of final estimates, and the goodness-of-fit measures will show a perfect fit.

Example 2
Nonparametric Model for Signal Detection

If you use the NPAR option of the ESTIMATE statement, you will get some very simple output. In addition to the data report and the frequency table, you will get the *HR* and *FAR* for each category and the area under the nonparametric ROC function. This ROC is constructed by connecting the empirical points on the graph with straight lines. The area referred to is the area to the right and below the function defined by these lines. Bamber (1975) showed that this nonparametric ROC was essentially the same thing that mathematicians call an *ordinal dominance graph*. He finds that the area under such a graph is closely related to the Mann-Whitney *U* statistic, thus enabling hypotheses about such an area to be tested.

The nonparametric model is a simple way to get a quick look at your data, and if you believe that the assumptions of any of the parametric models that you can use are not justifiable for your data, then NPAR is the model for you. The input is:

```
USE SWETSDTA
SELECT SUBJ=1
SIGNAL
MODEL RATING=SIGNAL
FREQ=COUNT
ESTIMATE / NPAR
```

Following is the output:

```
Variables in the SYSTAT Rectangular file are:
   SUBJ        SIGNAL       RATING        COUNT

   Case frequencies determined by value of variable COUNT.

Number of stimulus events (cases) responded to:      1188

Number of detectors (variables) observing an event:     1

Number of response categories used:                     6

Number of responses to noise events:                  591

Number of responses to signal events:                 597

Total number of responses:                           1188

Number of instances of missing data:                    0
```

```
Response   Frequency       Joint Probability  Conditional Prob.   Cum.Cond.Prob.
Category   Noise Signal     Noise    Signal    Noise    Signal    Noise    Signal
    1       174    46      0.14646  0.03872   0.29442  0.07705   0.29442  0.07705
    2       172    57      0.14478  0.04798   0.29103  0.09548   0.58545  0.17253
    3       104    66      0.08754  0.05556   0.17597  0.11055   0.76142  0.28308
    4        92   101      0.07744  0.08502   0.15567  0.16918   0.91709  0.45226
    5        41   154      0.03451  0.12963   0.06937  0.25796   0.98646  0.71022
    6         8   173      0.00673  0.14562   0.01354  0.28978   1.00000  1.00000

Total       591   597      0.4975   0.5025    1.0000   1.0000
Nonparametric analysis using upper category boundaries
   False-alarm rates for successive categories:
       0.706        0.415        0.239       0.083       0.014
   Hit rates for successive categories:
       0.923        0.827        0.717       0.548       0.290
   Area under ROC =        0.803
EXPORT successfully completed.
```

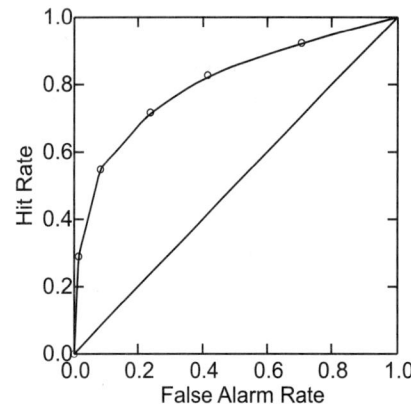

Receiver Operating Characteristic (ROC) Plot

Example 3
Logistic Model for Signal Detection

This model uses the logistic distribution as the model for the N and $S + N$ distributions. The cumulative probability function for the logistic distribution is $1/(1 + exp(-Y))$, where Y is the random variable on which the distribution is defined. In SIGNAL, Y is replaced by $c \times X$, where c is a scaling constant, and X is the decision axis of the detection model. The default value of c is $\pi/(\sqrt{3})$, which is approximately 1.81. This has the effect of making the variance of X equal unity. Thus, with the default in effect, the standard deviation of the N distribution will be 1.00. You can set the value of c to be any positive number because c is an option that can be appended to the ESTIMATE command for this model.

You might very well want to use 1.7 for c because, if you do, the cumulative probabilities for the N distribution will differ from standard normal (Gaussian) probabilities by less than 0.01 for all values of X (with a mean of 0). The standard deviation of X for the N distribution will not be unity, however. It will be equal to $\pi/(1.7\sqrt{3})$, or about 1.07. Thus, the logistic distribution is a good approximation for the normal, and it is mathematically more tractable.

The format of the output from SIGNAL for the logistic model does not differ from that for the normal model, except that the program reports the value of c that was used, and the variance of N is not necessarily unity, depending on this value of c. The values of *FINV* in both the numerical and the Quick Graph output are computed as

$$FINV = \ln((1-p)/p)/c$$

where the probability p is either an *HR* or an *FAR*. As with the normal model, the values shown for upper category boundaries are scaled on the N distribution. You can examine the input and output by changing NPAR to LOGISTIC in the last example.

Treisman and Faulkner (1985) show the relationships between ROC curves derived from a logistic model and aspects of the choice theory proposed by Luce (1959). Thus, the use of this model lends theoretical elegance to signal detection theory.

Example 4
Negative Exponential Model for Signal Detection

The negative exponential density function is algebraically identical to a chi-square density function with two degrees of freedom. However, its simple properties and usefulness justify treating it as a separate model. A simple (somewhat limited) way to think of the distribution is to imagine a detector that on each trial of an experiment receives two random observations from a normal distribution that is either N or $S + N$ in nature. The detector is built to compute the variance, or sum of squared deviations of the two observations, and bases its response on that computation. Thus, it tries to distinguish $S + N$ from N, based on the variance of each. A chi-square distribution with two degrees of freedom is an appropriate model for such a detector.

The cumulative probability function for the negative exponential distribution is $1 - e^{cX}$, where X is a random variable (the decision axis in this case) and c is a constant. The mean and standard deviation of the distribution are both equal to $1/c$. Therefore, if we have an N distribution with the value of $c = c_N$ and an $S + N$ distribution with the value of $c = c_S$, D-Prime is $(c_N/c_S) - 1$ and the ratio of the $S + N$ standard deviation to the N standard deviation is c_N/c_S. A little algebra shows that the ROC is given by a power law: The *HR* is the *FAR* raised to the c{S}/c{N} power. The area under the ROC curve is $1/(1 + (c_S/c_N))$.

The implementation of this model in SIGNAL allows the user to choose a value of *c* for the *N* distribution. The program then finds the best-fitting value of *c* for the *S* + *N* distribution given the input data. Thus, the user-supplied value of *c* is simply a scaling constant for the decision axis, and there is only one parameter left for the program to estimate from the data (in addition to the category boundaries). The default value of *c* for the *N* distribution is unity. This is the only option for the MODEL statement when the model is exponential.

The format of the output for this model differs from the format of the normal model in only two respects. First, the values of *c* are given for the *N* and *S* + *N* distributions in both the table of initial estimates and the table of final estimates. Second, rather than listing *D-Prime* and *SD-Ratio* as parameters being estimated during the iterative process, the value of the mean of *S* + *N* and the value of the mean of *N* are listed instead. The mean of *N* is $1/c$ and, of course, remains constant during the iterations. It is simply filling space in the table. The mean of *S* + *N* is $1/c_S$, where c_S is the constant for the *S* + *N* distribution. Thus, iteratively estimating the mean is the same thing as iteratively estimating c_S.

The values for *FINV* in the numerical as well as the Quick Graph output are computed by finding the logarithm of the probability involved and dividing it by $-c_S$ or $-c_N$, whichever is appropriate. The upper category boundaries shown in the output are scaled using the standard deviation of the *N* distribution as the unit of measure and absolute 0 as the origin. With regard to origin, notice that the linear ROC line always starts at the (0,0) coordinate of the plot, as it must for the exponential model.

As you will notice in the output, the degrees of freedom for the chi-square goodness of fit are equal to the number of response categories minus 2, rather than minus 3 as for the normal and logistic distributions. This is because there is one less parameter to estimate for the exponential model than for the other two. The input is:

```
USE SWETSDTA
SELECT SUBJ=1
SIGNAL
MODEL RATING=SIGNAL
FREQ=COUNT
ESTIMATE / EXPONENTIAL
```

Signal Detection Analysis

The output is as follows:

```
Variables in the SYSTAT Rectangular file are:
  SUBJ         SIGNAL        RATING         COUNT

  Case frequencies determined by value of variable COUNT.

Number of stimulus events (cases) responded to:       1188

Number of detectors (variables) observing an event:      1

Number of response categories used:                      6

Number of responses to noise events:                   591

Number of responses to signal events:                  597

Total number of responses:                            1188

Number of instances of missing data:                     0

Response   Frequency      Joint Probability   Conditional Prob.    Cum.Cond.Prob.
Category  Noise  Signal    Noise    Signal    Noise    Signal     Noise    Signal
   1       174     46     0.14646  0.03872   0.29442  0.07705    0.29442  0.07705
   2       172     57     0.14478  0.04798   0.29103  0.09548    0.58545  0.17253
   3       104     66     0.08754  0.05556   0.17597  0.11055    0.76142  0.28308
   4        92    101     0.07744  0.08502   0.15567  0.16918    0.91709  0.45226
   5        41    154     0.03451  0.12963   0.06937  0.25796    0.98646  0.71022
   6         8    173     0.00673  0.14562   0.01354  0.28978    1.00000  1.00000

Total      591    597     0.4975   0.5025    1.0000   1.0000
Initial estimates of parameters: exponential model
    Multiplicative constant for noise          =      1.000
    Multiplicative constant for signal+noise   =      0.258

  Mean(Noise)    SD(Noise)           Mean(Sig+Noise)  SD(Sig+Noise)
     1.000         1.000                  3.870           3.870
    D-Prime       D Sub-A     Sakitt D    SD-Ratio      ROC Area
     2.870         1.015        1.459       3.870         0.795
Upper Category Boundaries:
     0.346         0.871        1.424       2.480         4.333

Goodness of Fit:  Log(Likelihood)   ChiSq(4 df)   Prob(ChiSq)
                    -1927.548455      15.180         0.004
Iterative maximum-likelihood estimation of parameters with
Tolerance =0.00100
Iter  -Log(Like)    Mean(S+N)    Mean(N)    Category Boundaries
  0   .1927548D+04  .38702D+01  .10000D+01  .34633D+00 .87132D+00 .14240D+01
                                            .24800D+01 .43331D+01
  1   .1922809D+04  .39983D+01  .10000D+01  .34193D+00 .84605D+00 .14066D+01
                                            .24759D+01 .48555D+01
  2   .1922807D+04  .40085D+01  .10000D+01  .34293D+00 .84660D+00 .14073D+01
                                            .24772D+01 .48693D+01
  3   .1922807D+04  .40085D+01  .10000D+01  .34293D+00 .84660D+00 .14073D+01
                                            .24772D+01 .48693D+01
  4   .1922807D+04  .40088D+01  .10000D+01  .34263D+00 .84679D+00 .14077D+01
                                            .24758D+01 .48705D+01
Final parameter estimates using upper category boundaries: Exponential model
    Multiplicative constant for noise          =      1.000
    Multiplicative constant for signal+noise   =      0.249
  Mean(Noise)    SD(Noise)           Mean(Sig+Noise)  SD(Sig+Noise)
     1.000         1.000                  4.009           4.009
```

```
Ctgry                                           Upper
Label   Far     HR    FINV(FAR)  FINV(HR)   Boundary         Beta    Log(Beta)
  1   0.7056 0.9229     0.349     0.080       0.343         0.323     -1.131
  2   0.4146 0.8275     0.881     0.189       0.847         0.471     -0.753
  3   0.2386 0.7169     1.433     0.333       1.408         0.718     -0.332
  4   0.0829 0.5477     2.490     0.602       2.476         1.600      0.470
  5   0.0135 0.2898     4.302     1.239       4.871         9.651      2.267
       D-Prime         D Sub-A   Sakitt D    SD-Ratio     ROC Area
        3.009           1.030     1.503       4.009         0.800

Goodness of Fit:  Log(Likelihood)  ChiSq(4 df)   Prob(ChiSq)
                    -1922.806648      5.579         0.233
EXPORT successfully completed.
```

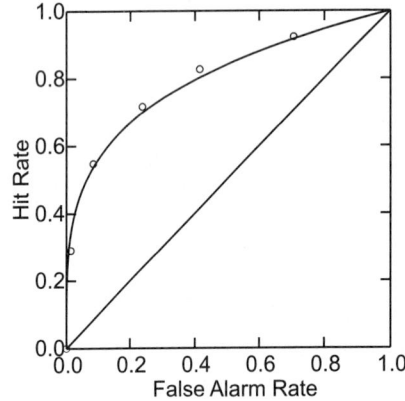

Receiver Operating Characteristic (ROC) Plot

Egan (1975) discusses the negative exponential model at some length. He points out its relationship to the Rayleigh distribution and notes that it represents the probability distribution of a randomly selected sinusoid in the Rice model of Gaussian noise.

Example 5
Chi-Square Model for Signal Detection

We can think of the chi-square model as a generalization of the exponential model that was just discussed. Imagine that the hypothetical detector now receives k random observations of N, or k random observations of $S + N$ on a trial, and that N and $S + N$ are normally distributed. As before, the detector bases its response on the sums of squared deviations for the k observations. The appropriate model for such a detector is the (unstandardized) chi-square distribution with k degrees of freedom (or $k - 1$ degrees of freedom if the detector does not know and must estimate the true means of

N and $S + N$ from the data). For SIGNAL, we assume that k is the same for both $S + N$ and N trials.

Let us designate a χ^2 variable that represents the sum of squared deviations for k observations from the N distribution divided by the population variance of the parent (normal) distribution as CSN. Let CSS be the corresponding χ^2 variable for the $S + N$ trials. The distributions of sums of squared deviations are then $CSN \times VAR(N)$ and $CSS \times Var(S + N)$, the so-called unstandardized χ^2 distributions. Here, $Var(N)$ represents the variance of the parent noise distribution, and $Var(S + N)$ represents the variance of the signal+noise distribution. Some algebra shows that the sum of squared deviations for $S + N$ is the sum of squared deviations for N times $Var(S + N)/Var(N)$, which turns out to be the ratio of the standard deviations (not variances) of the unstandardized χ^2 variables for $S + N$ and N. We must be careful here to distinguish the variances of the parent N and $S + N$ distributions, $Var(N)$ and $Var(S + N)$, from the variance or standard deviations of the unstandardized χ^2 distributions to which they give rise. It is the latter that form the model of what the detector is doing.

In the SIGNAL output for this model, one of the estimated parameters is called *SD-Ratio*. This is the ratio of the standard deviation of the $S + N$ unstandardized χ^2 variable to the standard deviation of the N unstandardized χ^2 variable. As stated above, this is also the ratio of $Var(S + N)$ to $Var(N)$. The unstandardized χ^2 for $S + N$ is a constant times the unstandardized χ^2 for N. The constant is the *SD-Ratio*. The means and standard deviations that SIGNAL prints for the N and $S + N$ distributions are based on the assumption that $Var(N)$ is unity. The mean for the N unstandardized χ^2 is then simply the degrees of freedom, k. The mean for the $S + N$ unstandardized χ^2 is then *SD-Ratio* times k. Of course, the *SD-Ratio* then has unity as its denominator so that it is just equal to the standard deviation of the unstandardized χ^2 distribution for $S + N$.

The other parameter that can be estimated by the program is the correct degrees of freedom *(df)* to use. It is allowed to be a non-integer value. You do not have to allow SIGNAL to try to estimate *df*. If you want to fix *df* at some value, you can use an option of the MODEL command to do this. For example, if you want to fix *df* at 4, you should type:

```
ESTIMATE / CHISQ,DF=4
```

Consequently, the *df* will not change during the iterations. You can fix *df* at any positive value. There is another option available here that will give you some flexibility about the *df*. You may, for example, type:

```
ESTIMATE / CHISQ,START,DF=12.8
```

This will cause SIGNAL to use 12.8 (or any other positive number that you type) as a starting value for the iterations. SIGNAL will (probably) move away from this starting value during the iterations in an attempt to find the best-fitting value for *df*.

There is a potential problem with allowing SIGNAL to do this. The procedure for trying to iteratively determine *df* seems particularly prone to the problem of local minima for some kinds of data. This means that, at some point in the process, the parameter estimates do not change much for a few iterations, and so the program stops iterating as though the minimum value for the –log(likelihood) has been found. However, it is not the global minimum but a local minimum that has been found. It is a good idea to always use the START option to start the program at a different value of *df* once you think that you have found the maximum likelihood solution. There may be a still better value for *df*. Better yet, if you have some idea of what *df* should be, either fix *df* at this value or START at it. The default starting value for *df* is 10.

If you allow the program to find the *df*, a degree of freedom is lost for the Pearson χ^2 goodness-of-fit statistic. This will not occur for the initial estimates because these are based on either the default starting value or a number that you assign to *df*. However, if you let the program iteratively find *df*, then the Pearson χ^2 will show one less degree of freedom for the final estimates.

These degrees of freedom are the number of categories minus 3 if the program estimates *df*, or the number of categories minus 2 if you fix *df* at a value. There is an unresolved theoretical problem here. If you use three categories of response and allow SIGNAL to iteratively find *df*, there will be one degree of freedom for the initial Pearson statistic (the starting value for *df* is given) and zero degrees of freedom for the final Pearson statistic. Zero degrees of freedom would seem to imply that a perfect fit is a necessity, but it is not, as can easily be demonstrated with an example. In this case, the program still computes the empirical value for the Pearson statistic and finds the probability of that value based on one degree of freedom. However, the printout will show that there are zero degrees of freedom. There seems to be no resolution for this problem at present. This model also is a bit slower in execution than some others because of the complexity of finding inverse values for χ^2 probabilities, and because of the necessity to use an iterative technique to measure the area under the ROC.

As with the other models, the values for the upper category boundaries are measured on the *N* distribution. The printout for this model is so similar to the others that have been described that it will not be discussed further here. For further information on this model and ways in which it can be used, see Egan (1975).

Example 6
Poisson Model for Signal Detection

This model is appropriate when the detector is basing a response on a count of rare events of some kind that occur during a trial. On N trials, only a very few of the events are liable to occur; and on $S + N$ trials, more of the events occur, although they are still rare. Think, for example, of a rare form of bacteria that is present to some small degree in every person. Suppose that the presence of a certain disease is indicated by a small increase in the count of this bacteria as seen on a microscope slide. A slide containing a very small number of these organisms is considered to be from a normal person (a noise trial), and a slide with more of the bacteria is considered to have come from a diseased person (the signal+noise condition). It must be decided on the basis of small differences in count whether a person is diseased or not (or a rating scale of the likelihood of disease could be used). When the number of possibilities for bacteria is large, as on the slide, but the probability of finding very many is small, the Poisson model is appropriate.

The Poisson is a discrete distribution with probabilities defined only for the non-negative integers. This would seem to lead to a theoretical ROC function that was composed of discrete points on the graph, one for each integer. However, Egan (1975) and others have argued that a guessing strategy when an ambiguous count is received by the detector allows us to "close" the ROC by connecting the points with straight lines.

If the detector were mechanical or electrical, you would have to assume that when an ambiguous count was received on a trial, the detector would sometimes act as though the next highest integer was appropriate and sometimes act as though the next lowest was appropriate, perhaps with unequal probabilities. This behavior allows us to close the ROC with the aforementioned straight lines. This is the approach taken in SIGNAL.

The decision axis is the scale of non-negative real numbers; and while the probabilities of various counts theoretically can occur only at integer values, the closing of the ROC implies that boundaries between response categories can occur at any real number. Thus, the scale of the decision axis is fixed by the non-arbitrariness of the counting numbers. The question then becomes, "What two Poisson distributions defined on these numbers best fit the response data given?"

Formulas for the Poisson distribution are given in many statistics texts. The mean (λ) of the Poisson distribution is the average number of occurrences per trial of the event being counted. A trial can be a spatial and/or temporal entity. The variance of the Poisson is also λ. Thus, there are two model parameters to deal with here (in addition to category boundaries): the mean of the N distribution and the mean of the $S + N$ distribution.

If you fix one of these means at some value, a priori, then there is only the other mean and the category boundaries for SIGNAL to estimate. That is exactly what one of the ESTIMATE options allows you to do. You can specify that the mean of the N distribution be fixed at some value. For example, if you type

```
ESTIMATE / POISSON,MEAN=4
```

the program will fix the mean of the N distribution at 3 and then estimate the value for the $S + N$ mean that gives the best fit to your data. The two means completely specify the two distributions. The default value for the MEAN option is 5.

The START option used here works in a manner similar to that described for the chi-square model. It makes the initial value of the mean of N equal to the set value. The program would then include values of the mean of N in the iterative process, trying to find a best-fitting value for the mean (that is, trying to find the most appropriate Poisson distribution). The same comments that were made above in the chi-square model regarding the Pearson fit statistic apply here as well.

Like the chi-square model, the iterative routine seems to be susceptible to a local minimum problem for many Poisson data sets. Thus, the best strategy, if you do not know the value of the mean for N, is to try a wide range of fixed values for it in successive runs of the model. Then pick the fixed value that gave you the lowest value of $-\log(\text{likelihood})$ and use it along with the START option to allow the program to iterate near that value.

By the time you have read this far, the nature of the output should be self-evident to you. It is very much the same for all of the models discussed. The program is somewhat slower for the Poisson because of the iterative techniques that needed to be used to find *FINV* for *HR* and *FAR* and to find the area under the ROC.

Example 7
Gamma Model for Signal Detection

Suppose that in an experiment, the N and $S + N$ trials can be described as a Poisson process as described for the Poisson model. That is, a small number of discrete, countable, and rare events occur on each trial. But now suppose that the detector adopts or is programmed for the following strategy: The detector uses the time required to accumulate a fixed number of the rare events as the basis of the response. If that fixed number accumulates very slowly, the detector gives a "noise-like" response. If the fixed number accumulates more rapidly, the detector gives a "signal-like" response. Thus, the detector's response (binary or rating category) is based on time—the time it takes to accumulate a predetermined number of discrete events. Notice that the length of a trial is determined by the detector, as opposed to the Poisson-counting observer described above, who counts events during a fixed-interval trial. In the former case, the gamma distribution is an appropriate detection model.

Formulas for the gamma distribution are found in advanced statistics textbooks. Suffice it to say here that the distribution has two parameters: m and r. Let us call the number of events that the detector is waiting to accumulate r. The mean of the gamma distribution is r/m so that m times the mean is r, and m is then a scaling constant. For a detection problem, there is only one value of r; but there are two values of m: one for the N distribution and one for the $S + N$ distribution. Let us call these m_o and m_1, respectively. The mean of the time that it takes for r (Poisson) events to accumulate if the N process is in effect is then r/m_o, and the mean of the time that it takes for r events to accumulate if the $S + N$ process is in effect is r/m_1. The variance of a gamma distribution is r divided by m^2, so knowing r and m defines both the mean and variance.

Thus, in addition to category boundaries, there are three parameters for our model: R, M0, and Ml. In SIGNAL, we fix M0 at a value predetermined by the program (the default value) or by the user via the option described below. The default value is unity. If you want to change the value of M0, for example, to 3, you would type:

```
ESTIMATE / GAMMA,M0=3
```

The value of Ml is then estimated by the program after M0 is determined. Note that M0 is never estimated. It either keeps its default value or the value that you assign. These values, along with R, determine the means and variances of the N and $S + N$ distributions. The value of R has a default value of 5. You can change it in a manner similar to that for M0. If you want to change both M0 and R, you must list them both in the same MODEL statement.

If you do not exercise the option to fix R, then the default starting value will be used and the program will estimate a value of R at every iteration. You can also choose to let this happen but pick your own starting value for R, just as in the previous two models. For example, you could type

```
ESTIMATE / GAMMA,M0=3,START
```

to accept the default value of R and let M0 change over iterations. All of the discussion of local minima in the previous two models applies here as well. Do not let the program do your thinking for you.

If you think about it, you will realize that the *N* and *S* + *N* distributions have to be reversed from their usual positions on the decision axis for this model. The *N* trials result in longer waiting times, and the *S* + *N* trials result in shorter waiting times. Also, for the same reason, *HR* and *FAR* are in the lower tail instead of the upper tails of the distributions in this case. This has all been taken care of for you with SIGNAL. Everything that needs to be reversed has been reversed so that, for example, you do not get negative values of *D-Prime* when you should not. (That doesn't mean that negative values cannot occur.)

Again, the output is in the same approximate format as for the other models already described. The few differences should be self-evident. It should also be evident that this model was specifically designed to handle waiting-time data. If you use it as a general GAMMA model, you will have to remember all of the design features mentioned here, especially the reversal of the direction of the decision axis and the fact that *HR* and *FAR* are computed from the lower tails of the distributions.

For more in-depth discussion of this model, you should again consult Egan (1975), who also makes some interesting comparisons of Poisson counting detectors versus gamma timing detectors.

Computation

All arithmetic is double precision.

Algorithms

The algorithm used to minimize negative log-likelihood is an adaptation of the Nelder-Mead simplex method as presented by O'Neill (1985). This method does not require derivatives, making it useful for all of the present models simultaneously. It is, however, less time-efficient than methods that use derivatives.

The area under the ROC is not directly computable for certain of the models (CHISQ, POISSON, and GAMMA). An algorithm was written to approximate this area by successively dividing it into smaller and smaller trapezoids and using the trapezoidal rule to accumulate the area. On successive iterations, the area is subdivided into trapezoidal panels, first two, then four, then eight, etc. If the increase in accumulated area is less than the value of CONVERGE from one iteration to the next, the subroutine ceases and returns the most recent value of the area. If, after 512 panels have been constructed, the stopping rule has not been met, the routine prints a warning message, returns the most recent area estimate, and ceases.

The initial estimates for the NORMAL and LOGISTIC models are obtained by finding the eigenvector of the *FINV(HR)* and *FINV(FAR)* vectors. The category boundaries are located by projecting the data points onto this vector and then scaling to the units of the *N* distribution. Similar methods are used for the other models, with the restriction that the least-squares vector on which the boundaries are located must pass through the point 0,0 on the linear ROC.

Missing Data

Missing data are treated as though the trial or trials that are missing the data did not exist only for the particular detector missing the data.

References

Bamber, D. (1975). The area above the ordinal dominance graph and the area below the receiver operating characteristic graph. *Journal of Mathematical Psychology,* 12, 387–415.

Egan, J. P. (1975). *Signal detection theory and ROC analysis.* New York: Academic Press.

Coombs, C. H., Dawes, R. M., and Tversky, A. (1970). *Mathematical psychology: An elementary introduction.* Englewood Cliffs, N.J.: Prentice-Hall, Inc.

Green, D. M. and Swets, J. A. (1966). *Signal detection theory and psychophysics.* New York: John Wiley & Sons, Inc.

Hanley, J. A. and McNeil, B. J. (1982). The meaning and use of the area under a receiver operating characteristic (ROC) curve. *Radiology,* 143, 29–36.

Kraemer, H. C. (1988). Assessment of 2 x 2 associations: Generalization of signal detection methodology. *The American Statistician,* 42, 37–49.

Luce, D. (1959). *Individual choice behavior.* New York: John Wiley & Sons, Inc.

O'Neill, R. (1985). Function minimization using a simplex procedure. In Griffiths, P. and Hill, I. D. (eds.), *Applied statistics algorithms.* Chichester, England: Ellis Horwood Limited. 79–87.

Peterson, W. W., Birdsall, T. G., and Fox, W. C. (1954). The theory of signal detectability. *Institute of Radio Engineers Transactions,* PGIT-4, 171–212.

Sakitt, B. (1973). Indices of discriminability. *Nature,* 241, 133–134.

Simpson, A. J. and Fitter, M. J. (1973). What is the best index of detectability? *Psychological Bulletin,* 80, 481–488.

Swets, J. A. (1986). Indices of discrimination or diagnostic accuracy: Their ROCs and implied models. *Psychological Bulletin,* 99, 110–117.

Swets, J. A. and Pickett, R. M. (1982). *Evaluation of diagnostic systems.* New York: Academic Press.

Swets, J. A, Tanner, W. P., and Birdsall, T. G. (1961). Decision processes in perception. *Psychological Review,* 68, 301–340.

Treisman, M. and Faulkner, A. (1985). On the choice between choice theory and signal detection theory. *Quarterly Journal of Experimental Psychology,* 37A, 387–405.

Chapter

11

Smoothing

Leland Wilkinson

The SMOOTH module applies nonparametric smoothers for data exploration in two or three dimensions. In nonparametric smoothing, a weighted function of a data subset provides a local estimate for a region. Because each region receives a smooth estimate, the agglomeration of these estimates captures local variations well without the need for complicated models or additional parameters found in parametric smoothing.

Constructing a nonparametric smoother involves:

- Specifying the size of the estimation regions. Estimation regions are defined by the number of neighboring points or as a fixed range of data.
- Defining the weighting function. Smoothing offers seven functions for data weighting: Epanechnikov, biweight, triweight, tricube, uniform, Gaussian, and Cauchy.
- Assigning a method of combining the weighted observations. Estimates can be computed as means, trimmed means, medians, polynomial regression estimates, or robust estimates.

The combinations of estimation window, weighting function, and smoothing method result in 126 possible nonparametric smoothers. For each smoother, you can estimate values at either specified gridpoints or at the predictor data values, saving the results to SYSTAT files for subsequent analyses.

Statistical Background

Smoothers fit functions to data. Nonparametric smoothers fit functions to overlapping subsets of data. Each subset receives its own fit so that the overall smoother adapts to local variations in the data. Unlike parametric smoothers (such as linear or polynomial regression) nonparametric smoothers have no global model equation or simple parameters; instead, they have a collection of local estimates. Consequently, they are designed for data exploration and local prediction rather than parametric modeling. There is a large statistical literature in this area (e.g., Härdle, 1990; Hastie and Tibshirani, 1990; Green and Silverman, 1994; Fan and Gijbels, 1996; Simonoff, 1996). It is worth consulting one of these references before using SMOOTH.

Tukey (1977) used the word *smooth* for a procedure that describes given data as follows:

data = smooth PLUS rough

This equation is a species of a more general Tukey paradigm:

data = fit PLUS residual

If we had perfect knowledge of the process that led to our observed data values, then we might construct a complete description of our data. We are usually safer in regarding our fit as an incomplete description, however. As Tukey says:

data = incomplete description PLUS residual

As we shall see, smoothing in practice inevitably produces an incomplete description. It involves a variety of trade-offs and requires careful judgment. This introduction will summarize several of these trade-offs.

The Three Ingredients of Nonparametric Smoothers

Nonparametric smoothers are usually assembled from three ingredients: 1) A **kernel function**, 2) a **bandwidth function**, and 3) a **smoothing function**. The kernel function is a probability function that is used to weight points in the computation of each local smoothing estimate. Points farther from the location of the estimate are usually weighted less than points nearer. The bandwidth function determines the size of the region over which each local estimate is computed. It does this by setting the spread or width of the kernel function. Finally, the smoothing function is the method for computing a smoothed estimate over the subset of points lying within the smoothing window.

These three ingredients are assembled in a single algorithm. They are interdependent (choice of bandwidth depends on choice of kernel, for example), although I will describe them in order. I will restrict the analysis to the case of 2D smoothing, where we compute a smoothed y_s value for a given x_s value on the basis of a collection of points measured in (x, y) pairs. The 3D algorithm, in which we compute a smoothed z_s value for given x_s and y_s values, is a straightforward extension of the same principles.

A Sample Dataset

In order to make systematic comparisons, we will use an artificial dataset that exploits differences among the various smoothers. The following SYSTAT code generates a dataset based on a damped sine wave: $\sin(4x)/x$. I have added Gaussian error to this function as well as higher-variance Gaussian noise 20 percent of the time. Also, I have applied the square-root transformation to the *x* values in order to make them unequally spaced. This will become relevant in comparing fixed-width windows with *k* nearest neighbor windows. The following plot shows 150 cases generated by this program, the function underlying the process, and the marginal distributions of the cases displayed as stripes at the borders.

```
BASIC
SAVE DAMP
RSEED=1357
REPEAT 150
LET X=SQR(CASE/10)
LET Y=SIN(4*X)/X+ZRN/2+1.5*ZRN*(URN>.8)
RUN
EXIT
USE DAMP
BEGIN
PLOT Y*X/XMIN=0,XMAX=4,YMIN=-4,YMAX=4,BORDER=STRIPE
FPLOT Y=SIN(4*X)/X ; XMIN=0,XMAX=4,YMIN=-4,YMAX=4,
                    AX=0,SC=0,COLOR=RED
END
```

Chapter 11

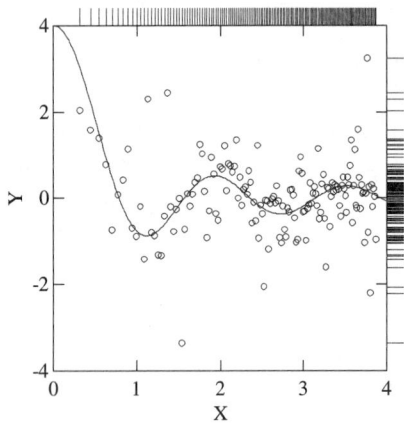

It is tempting to use this plot as a criterion for evaluating the goodness of the smoothing methods we will try, and to some extent this makes sense. Some combinations of the three smoothing parameters we will review do better than others in approximating the known smooth function. We must keep in mind, however, that one example cannot suffice for a global evaluation. First of all, the sinusoidal function we are using has some characteristics (periodic form, for example) more suitable for some methods than for others. Other functions would be more suited to other smoothing methods. Secondly, there are formal analytic results given in the references that should take precedence over eye-balling graphics when deciding on parameter choices. Third, there is room in this chapter to present only a limited subset of possible smoothing parameter combinations. With 7 kernel functions, 2 window types for determining bandwidth, and 9 smoothing methods, there are 126 different smoothers available in this package. This figure does not include the possible choices for bandwidth itself.

Kernels

The first ingredient of a nonparametric smoothing is a kernel function. Although many weighting functions have been proposed for smoothers at one time or another by applied researchers, the statistical literature has focused on a set of related kernel functions that are suited to formal analysis of their properties. They are shaped as follows:

Smoothing

uniform: $f(x) = a : (-h \leq x \leq h)$, else 0

epanechnikov: $f(x) = a(1 - (x/h))^2 : (-h \leq x \leq h)$, else 0

biweight: $f(x) = a(1 - (x/h)^2)^2 : (-h \leq x \leq h)$, else 0

triweight: $f(x) = a(1 - (x/h)^2)^3 : (-h \leq x \leq h)$, else 0

tricube: $f(x) = a(1 - |x/h|^3)^3 : (-h \leq x \leq h)$, else 0

gaussian: $f(x) = ae^{-(x/h)^2}$

cauchy: $f(x) = a/(b + (x/h)^2)$

The constant *a* scales these formulas as probability kernel functions. This constant may be set to 1 for smoothers because it cancels out in the algorithms. The constant *h* is the bandwidth that determines the width of the window or, for kernels like *gaussian* and *cauchy* that have nonzero tails, the spread of the kernel. We can adapt these functions to 3D smoothing (assuming *x* and *y* are independent and identically distributed) by transforming them into polar coordinates. Non-circular 3D window functions are slightly more complex.

You may wish to try plotting these kernel functions in SYSTAT to learn more about the behavior of their parameters. I used the following commands to make the graphics on the left of each equation (from top to bottom):

```
fplot F=.5*(x>-1)*(x<1) ; xmin=-2,xmax=2,ymin=0,ymax=2
fplot F=.75*(1-x^2)*(x>-1)*(x<1); xmin=-2,xmax=2,ymin=0,ymax=2
fplot F=.9375*((1-x^2)^2)*(x>-1)*(x<1) ; xmin=-2,xmax=2,
                                         ymin=0,ymax=2
fplot F=1.094*((1-x^2)^3) *(x>-1)*(x<1); xmin=-2,xmax=2,
                                         ymin=0,ymax=2
fplot F=.864*((1-abs(x)^3)^3)*(x>-1)*(x<1) ; xmin=-2,xmax=2,
                                         ymin=0,ymax=2
fplot F=.399*exp(-x^2) ; xmin=-2,xmax=2,ymin=0,ymax=2
fplot F=.32/(1+x^2) ; xmin=-2,xmax=2,ymin=0,ymax=2
```

The following figure shows the effect of these kernels on a running-mean smoother applied to our data. Some differences are subtle because of the similarity of shapes among some kernels, because of other default parameter settings such as bandwidth, and because of the particular dataset we are using. Nevertheless, there are some differences worth noting. First, the Uniform kernel tends to downplay local variation because it weights all points in the window equally. By contrast, the Triweight weights points near the center of the window (where the estimate is computed) more heavily. Epanechnikov and Biweight are between these two kernels in this regard. The Gaussian and Cauchy functions have infinitely long tails and central peaks, but when they are scaled to the interval used for the other smoothers (as in the function plots shown above), they more closely resemble flatter weighting functions.

```
USE DAMP
SMOOTH
MODEL Y=X
ESTIMATE / SMOOTH=MEAN,KERNEL=UNIFORM
ESTIMATE / SMOOTH=MEAN,KERNEL=EPANECHNIKOV
ESTIMATE / SMOOTH=MEAN,KERNEL=BIWEIGHT
ESTIMATE / SMOOTH=MEAN,KERNEL=TRIWEIGHT
ESTIMATE / SMOOTH=MEAN,KERNEL=TRICUBE
ESTIMATE / SMOOTH=MEAN,KERNEL=GAUSSIAN
ESTIMATE / SMOOTH=MEAN,KERNEL=CAUCHY_
```

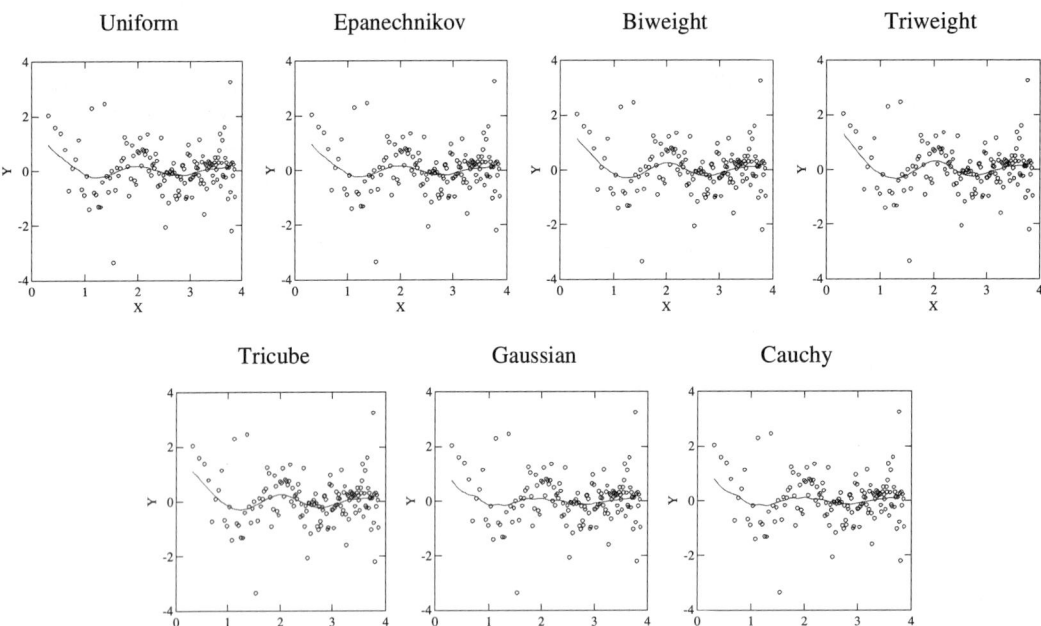

Bandwidth

The second ingredient of a nonparametric smoothing is a bandwidth function. To compute a smoothed y_s value for a given x_s value, we need to compute the bandwidth function h at x_s so that we can scale the width of our kernel. There are several ways to do this.

The simplest way is to set the bandwidth to a constant, fixed value for all x_s values. For every x_s, the *fixed-bandwidth method* weights points the same amount when they are the same distance from x_s. This method works well when the x coordinates of the data values are fairly uniformly distributed. It is the method underlying popular time series smoothers such as moving averages.

Alternatively, we may devise an adaptive or variable method that yields a different bandwidth value for each x_s. One way to achieve this goal is to choose a subset size k less than or equal to the number of points n; this is the number of points on which we want every smoothed value to be based. A popular choice is $k=n/2$. For any x_s, we then choose the k points that are nearest neighbors to x_s and then set the bandwidth to the distance between x_s and the farthest neighbor in this set. This assures that there are at least k data points within the bounds $[x_s-h, x_s+h]$. If there are ties, we may have to modify this approach slightly. This *k nearest-neighbors method* (KNN) offers a useful alternative to fixed bandwidth methods. Other adaptive bandwidth methods (not available in SYSTAT) compute h as a function of the distribution of points around x_s.

The following figure shows the consequences of different bandwidths for the behavior of a local cubic polynomial smoother. I have chosen a degree 3 polynomial to emphasize the behavior different bandwidths produce. In this instance, the PROPORTION parameter determines the proportion of the range of the data that is used to calculate the bandwidth. Notice that smaller bandwidths make the smoother respond to local features and larger bandwidths make the smoother behave more globally. This behavior is similar to what we see when the TENSION parameter is manipulated in the

Dynamic Explorer when we use nonparametric smoothers (such as LOWESS) in SYGRAPH.

```
USE DAMP
SMOOTH
MODEL Y=X
ESTIMATE  /  SMOOTH=POLY,DEGREE=3,PROPORTION=.1
ESTIMATE  /  SMOOTH=POLY,DEGREE=3,PROPORTION=.3
ESTIMATE  /  SMOOTH=POLY,DEGREE=3,PROPORTION=.5
ESTIMATE  /  SMOOTH=POLY,DEGREE=3,PROPORTION=.7
```

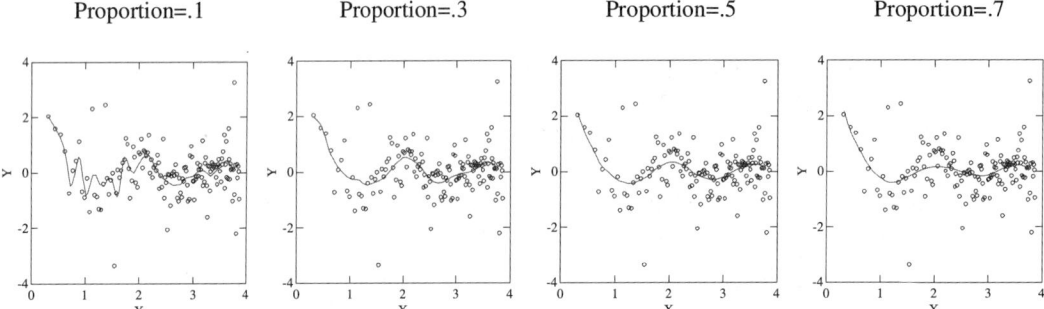

There is an extensive literature for determining "optimal" bandwidths for fixed window-width smoothers. This is summarized in the references. Erring in the direction of too-small a bandwidth introduces extraneous variance and erring in the direction of too-large a bandwidth favors bias in the smoother. It is often best to start with the default settings and to explore other nearby bandwidth values to see if systematic structure becomes apparent. The default settings in SYSTAT generally err on the side of large bias and small variance (over-smoothing). It is a good idea to observe the bandwidth chosen by the program and then to reduce it in subsequent runs to determine if the fit to local features improves without picking up random noise.

As mentioned above, there is a dependency between the choice of bandwidth and the type of kernel used. A bandwidth of .5, say, may be optimal for a uniform kernel, but not for a biweight. Because of its peculiar shape, each kernel has its own "effective bandwidth" where most of the heavy-weighting of points occurs. Marron and Nolan (1988) offer a way to normalize the bandwidth to a "canonical bandwidth" that produces the same relative degree of smoothness across different kernels at the same bandwidth setting. This feature is implemented in SYSTAT with the CANONICAL option. After an "optimal" bandwidth is determined for a particular kernel, we can explore how another smoother appears without having to change the BANDWIDTH setting. We simply add the CANONICAL option and the program automatically adjusts the bandwidth to the optimal setting for the new kernel.

The four bandwidths in the figure above were computed for a fixed-width window. That is, the bandwidth is kept constant across all locations where estimates are computed. This approach is especially suited when the data are fairly uniformly distributed on the *x* variable. When the data are substantially non-uniform on *x*, we may wish to reduce the size of the bandwidth in regions where the data are relatively dense on *x* and enlarge it where the data are sparse. A simple way to produce such an adaptive window width is to determine the bandwidth directly from the number of nearest neighbors. For example, we might decide that we want every estimate (point on the smoother) to be based on 30 points from our dataset. In that case, the bandwidth will be wider for lower values of *x* (say, below 2) in our dataset than for larger, because the points are concentrated at the higher values of *x*. The following figure shows the difference between the KNN (*k* nearest-neighbors) adaptive bandwidth and the fixed bandwidth.

The result is that the KNN window picks up more detail at the right-end of the smoother than the fixed window. Our choice of *k* (the number of neighbors) still determines whether we over- or under-smooth; the KNN window does not save us from having to make that decision. But it does provide more detail in areas of high data density. Combined with a robust smoothing method (such as Cleveland's LOESS), the KNN window can form the basis of an effective general-purpose smoother.

```
ESTIMATE / SMOOTH=POLY,WINDOW=FIXED,BANDWIDTH=.5
ESTIMATE / SMOOTH=POLY,WINDOW=KNN,NEIGH=30
```

Fixed Width Window   KNN Window

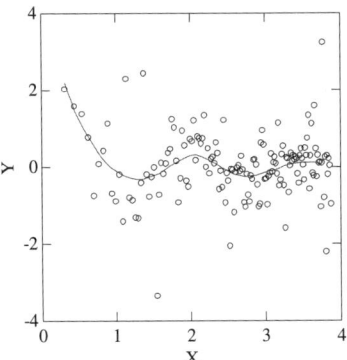
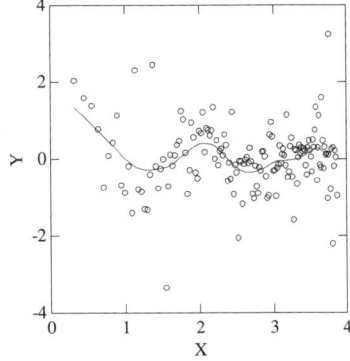

Smoothing Functions

The third ingredient in the smoothing algorithm is the smoothing function applied to data points using the kernel function to weight or select points. The smoothing function has only one requirement: it must yield a unique value y_s for any value x_s. In practice, the most popular functions are the same ones we use for statistical estimators: the mean, median, linear or polynomial regression estimate at x_s, and so on. In using these functions for smoothing, we must weight each point (x_i, y_i) by the kernel function value at $(x_s - x_i)$, but otherwise the computations are the same.

The literature suggests that polynomial smoothers tend to perform better, particularly at the endpoints of the smooth, than do mean smoothers. As the figure below shows, the MEAN smoothing function produces a smooth that tends to regress toward the mean of y at both ends. The TRIM and MEDIAN smoother are more resistant to outliers than the MEAN, but they have the same endpoint deficiency. The ROBUST polynomial smoothers have both good resistance to outliers and endpoint performance. The only drawback to using them is computation time. LOESS and other ROBUST smoothers require several additional passes through the data to achieve stable estimates.

The degree of the polynomial contributes to the local adaptiveness of the smoother. For curves that wiggle, degree 2 and 3 polynomials capture the bends better. It is best not to use higher polynomials if the data follow a monotonic path (increasing or decreasing), however. Higher degrees require more parameters and increase the risk of over-fitting. The following graphics show the different smoothers applied to our sample data.

```
SMOOTH
MODEL Y=X
ESTIMATE  /  SMOOTH=MEAN
ESTIMATE  /  SMOOTH=TRIM
ESTIMATE  /  SMOOTH=MEDIAN
ESTIMATE  /  SMOOTH=POLY,DEGREE=1
ESTIMATE  /  SMOOTH=POLY,DEGREE=2
ESTIMATE  /  SMOOTH=POLY,DEGREE=3
ESTIMATE  /  SMOOTH=ROBUST,DEGREE=1
ESTIMATE  /  SMOOTH=ROBUST,DEGREE=2
```

Smoothness

A remarkable aspect of the outcome of the nonparametric smoothing process is that we can produce a globally smooth curve from separate, local smooths. This happens most surely when we employ a bandwidth that weights a substantial subset of the data, and when we use a smoothing method that produces a continuous function (such as polynomial regression). Other combinations of kernels and smoothers produce a smooth global smooth for all practical purposes. This happens when kernel bandwidths are large enough to include sufficient data points for stable estimates and when smoothing functions are relatively continuous over the data.

Not all smoothing and kernel functions produce smooth smooths, however. If we use a smoothing function like the median or a relatively small bandwidth, we may find discontinuities in the global smooth. Discontinuities may not be undesirable. The point of smoothing is not to produce a smooth curve, but to produce an accurate summary y_s of the y_i data values whose paired x_i values lie near x_s, and to do so for every x_s value in the region of interest.

Interpolation and Extrapolation

Generally, we compute the smooth within the region bounded by the actual (x, y) pairs. Because smoothing is usually a symmetrically-weighted function of the data, extrapolation can be problematic. Even with careful attention to endpoint problems, nonparametric smoothers are least trustworthy at the extremes of the data. On the other hand, smoothing can be especially useful for interpolation or predicting in sparse x regions between the endpoints where there is less information about y. If you are interested in forecasting, it is better to employ models designed for that purpose, such as ARIMA and exponential smoothing (see the SERIES module).

Close Relatives (Roses by Other Names)

As a consequence of their evolution, nonparametric smoothers have acquired many different names. For example, a ***running-means*** or ***moving-averages*** smoother (Makridakis and Wheelwright, 1989) is a UNIFORM kernel smoother with MEAN smoothing function. The Nadaraya-Watson kernel smoother (Nadaraya, 1964; Watson, 1964) is an EPANECHNIKOV kernel with a MEAN smoothing function. Shepard's smoother (Shepard, 1965), sometimes called an ***inverse-distance*** smoother (McLain, 1974), is closely related to a CAUCHY kernel with MEAN smoothing function. The ***distance-weighted least squares*** (DWLS) smoother (McLain, 1974) is closely related to a quadratic polynomial smoother (SMOOTH=POLYNOMIAL, DEGREE=2) with a GAUSSIAN kernel. The ***step*** smoother (Cleveland, 1995) is a k nearest-neighbor smoother (WINDOW=KNN) with the number of nearest neighbors set to 1 (NEIGHBOR=1). The image-processing digital filter called a ***discrete gaussian convolution*** that is used to smooth black-and-white images (Gonzalez and Wintz, 1977) is a MEAN smoother with a GAUSSIAN kernel and KNN bandwidth function. It is a KNN method because the pixels on which it operates are evenly spaced, so it does weighted averages over a fixed number of pixels. Finally, Cleveland's ***LOESS*** smoother (Cleveland and Devlin, 1988) is a ROBUST smoother with DEGREE=1 or 2 and a

TRICUBE kernel. The LOWESS smoother in SYGRAPH is based on an older, scatterplot smoothing version of this smoother. The LOESS option in SMOOTH is a shortcut to setting KERNEL=TRICUBE, SMOOTH=ROBUST, WINDOW=KNN. Finally, the running median smoother in Tukey (1977) is produced with WINDOW=KNN, SMOOTHER=MEDIAN, and KERNEL=UNIFORM. For all of these smoothers, results will often differ slightly due to parameter settings and peculiarities of the algorithms in older versions.

Ties

SYSTAT handles tied data in SMOOTH by randomly perturbing x values by a negligible amount before performing the smooth. This works well when there are not numerous observations at a given value of x. If your data contain many ties on x, it is best to preprocess them in the STATS module to aggregate y values at each x value. When estimating the smooth, use the mean of the y values at each x plus a WEIGHT set to the number of cases used to compute each mean. Hastie and Tibshirani (1990) discuss this procedure.

Gridpoints vs. Datapoints

We usually compute smoothed values on y at equally spaced values x_s that are not necessarily located at the data points. This yields a smoothed curve. The Quick Graph in SYSTAT plots the data and a curve through the smoothed points using a spline interpolator. It is often useful to SAVE the smoothed values so that they can be examined more closely and plotted directly in SYGRAPH. One of the examples below shows how to do this. Because they employ the additional step of spline-smoothing the smoothed values (in order to save computation time), the 2D and 3D Quick Graphs are intended only for an initial glimpse at the smoothed results. You should always SAVE your results and plot them yourself after you are satisfied that a smooth is reasonable.

Often, we wish to plot residuals before settling on a particular smooth. This is done by setting GRID=0. In that case, the smoothed values are computed only at the values of the x_i data points. Examining residuals for specific smooths is as important in nonparametric as in parametric smoothing. You should look for the same features in the residuals in both cases: systematic departures from a rough horizontal band of residuals. A robust method such as LOESS will highlight outliers, however, while less resistant methods will mask them in the residuals. Of more concern than outliers is systematic trend or local variation that is not picked up by the smoother.

Smoothing in SYSTAT

Smooth Main Dialog

To fit a smoother, from the menus choose:

Statistics
  Smoothing…

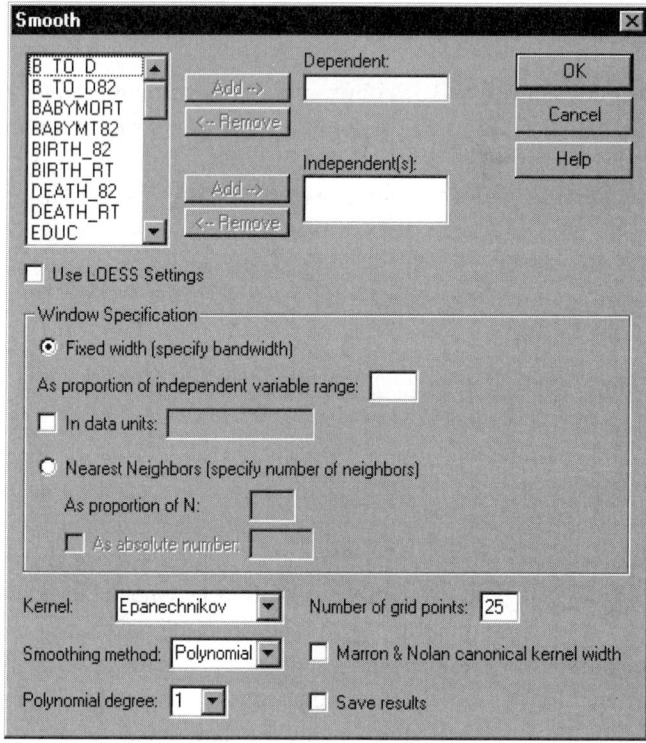

Select the dependent and independent variables. Define the smoother by selecting from the following options:

Use LOESS settings. Uses the nearest 50% of the data for each estimate, employing a tricube kernel with robust smoothing. Unchecking this option allows you to specify a custom smoothing technique by selecting an estimation window, a kernel function, and a smoothing method.

Smoothing

Window Specification. Define the region, or "window", containing the data to be used in calculating the smooth estimate for each point. Select either:

- Fixed Width. For all data values, the estimation window has a constant width. Specify this width as a proportion of the largest independent variable range or in data units.
- Nearest neighbors. For all data values, the number of points used to generate the estimate is constant. Specify this number as a proportion of the sample size or as an absolute number.

Kernel. Select the function used to weight each point. Kernel functions include: Epanechnikov, Uniform, Biweight, Triweight, Tricube, Gaussian, and Cauchy.

Smoothing method. Select the method for combining the kernel-weighted observations into a single estimate. Smoothing methods include: Mean, Trim, Median, Polynomial, and Robust.

Polynomial degree. For polynomial, robust, and LOESS smoothing, specify the degree of the polynomial. The curve can be linear (1), quadratic (2), or cubic (3).

Number of grid points. Specify the number of smooth estimates to compute. SYSTAT divides the independent variable range into intervals of equal length yielding the desired number of grid points.

Marron & Nolan canonical kernel width. Normalizes the window width. Use this option when comparing results across different kernel functions.

Save results. Saves either the grid values with corresponding predicted values or the predicted values with residuals. The statistics saved depend on the number of grid points.

Kernel Functions

The kernel function determines the weights assigned to points used in calculating a particular smoothing estimate. Select one of the following functions:

Uniform. All data receive equal weights.

Epanechnikov. Data near the current point receive higher weights than extreme data receive. This function weights extreme points more than the triweight, biweight, and tricube kernels, but less than the Gaussian and Cauchy.

Biweight. Data far from the current point receive more weight than the triweight kernel allows, but less weight than the Epanechnikov kernel permits.

Tricube. Data close to the current point receive higher weights than both the Epanechnikov and biweight kernels allot.

Triweight. Data close to the current point receive higher weights than any other kernel allows. Extreme cases get very little weight.

Gaussian. Weights follow a normal distribution, resulting in higher weighting of extreme cases than the Epanechnikov, biweight, tricube, and triweight kernels.

Cauchy. Extreme values receive more weight more than the other kernels, with the exception of the uniform, allow.

Smoothing Methods

The smoothing method determines how the kernel-weighted points are combined into an estimate. Select one of the following methods:

Mean. The arithmetic average of the weighted points.

Trim. The mean of the weighted points after discarding the most extreme 50% in the current region.

Median. The median of the weighted points.

Polynomial. The polynomial regression estimate at the current point. Select either a linear, quadratic, or cubic polynomial by specifying a degree of 1, 2, or 3.

Robust. A polynomial regression estimate resistant to outliers. Select either a linear, quadratic, or cubic polynomial by specifying a degree of 1, 2, or 3.

Using Commands

After selecting a data file with USE, continue with:

```
SMOOTH
USE datafile
MODEL dep = pred1 pred2
SAVE outfile
```

```
ESTIMATE / WINDOW = FIXED
                    KNN,
          KERNEL  = UNIFORM
                    EPANECHNIKOV
                    BIWEIGHT
                    TRIWEIGHT
                    TRICUBE
                    GAUSSIAN
                     CAUCHY
          SMOOTHER = MEAN
                     TRIM
                     MEDIAN
                     POLY
                      ROBUST
          BANDWIDTH = b
          NEIGHBORS = n
          PROPORTION = p
          GRID = n
          CANONICAL
          LOESS
```

Usage Considerations

Types of data. Smoothing requires a rectangular data file.

Print options. The output is standard for all PRINT options.

Quick Graphs. If a grid has been defined, the plot displays the data with the smoothing line for two-dimensional smoothing and creates a contour plot for three-dimensional smoothing. If no grid points are defined, the plot contains the residuals versus the smoothed values.

Saving files. SMOOTH saves predicted values and residuals if the number of grid points equals 0. Otherwise, the saved file contains grid points and smooth estimates.

BY groups. SMOOTH performs separate analyses for each level of any BY variables.

Bootstrapping. Bootstrapping is available in this procedure.

Case frequencies. You can use a FREQUENCY variable to duplicate cases.

Case weights. Smoothing uses a WEIGHT variable, if present, to weight cases.

Examples

Example 1
Smoothing: Saving and Plotting Results

This example shows how to save and replot a smooth. We use the artificial dataset from the introduction to this chapter. I have added the known function so that direct comparison is possible. In real data applications, you may still want to superimpose parametric models on nonparametric smooths as one type of validation method to supplement more formal tests of goodness of fit.

```
BASIC
  SAVE DAMP
  RSEED=1357
  REPEAT 150
  LET X=SQR(CASE/10)
  LET Y=SIN(4*X)/X+ZRN/2+1.5*ZRN*(URN>.8)
  RUN
EXIT
USE DAMP
SMOOTH
MODEL Y=X
SAVE TEMP
ESTIMATE / LOESS,DEGREE=2
USE TEMP
BEGIN
PLOT SMOOTH*XGRID / LINE,XMIN=0,XMAX=4,
                    YMIN=-4,YMAX=4,FILL
FPLOT Y=SIN(4*X)/X ; XMIN=0,XMAX=4,YMIN=-4,YMAX=4,
                    AXES=0,SCALE=0,COLOR=RED
END
```

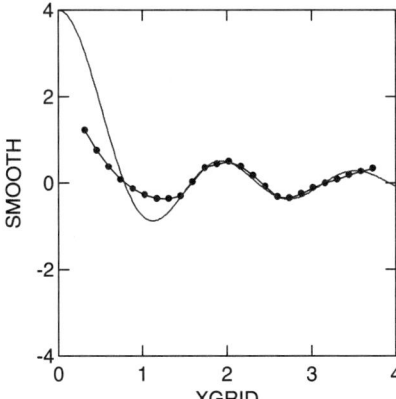

Example 2
Confidence Intervals for Smoothers

Confidence intervals on nonparametric smoothers can often be difficult to construct. One way around this problem is to bootstrap a smoother and examine the estimated values to get an idea of the shape of the envelope for a particular number of samples. The following example computes 100 bootstrap replications of the fit in the "Smoothing: Saving and Plotting Results" example. I have superimposed the theoretical curve on the sample results.

```
GRAPH NONE
USE DAMP
SMOOTH
MODEL Y=X
SAVE TEMP
RSEED=1357
ESTIMATE / LOESS,GRID=25,DEGREE=2,SAMPLE=BOOT(100)
USE TEMP
BEGIN
```

```
            PLOT SMOOTH*XGRID / SIZE=.5,XMIN=0,XMAX=4,
                               YMIN=-4,YMAX=4,FILL
            FPLOT Y=SIN(4*X)/X ; XMIN=0,XMAX=4,YMIN=-4,YMAX=4,
                                 AXES=0,SCALE=0,COLOR=RED
            END
            GRAPH
```

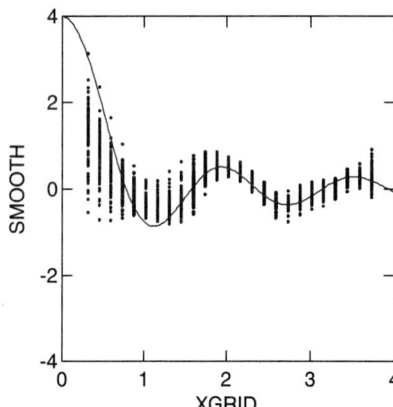

Notice that the estimates fail to envelop the leftmost segment of the curve. There are not enough points in the original sample to capture the variation in this area. This is, in part, a consequence of the original sampling scheme I chose, which produced fewer points at small x values than at larger.

How good are these bootstrap intervals? One way to find out in this case is to take 100 samples from the population and fit a LOESS to each sample. The following program generates 100 DAMP datasets. All 100 datasets are grouped together in a single file of 15000 cases, with an additional grouping variable G to denote the sample number. Because we reset the random number seed to the value used in the "Smoothing: Saving and Plotting Results" example, the first sample is identical to the data used in that example.

```
            BASIC
            NEW
            SAVE DAMP2
            RSEED=1357
```

Smoothing

```
REPEAT 15000
LET X=SQR((1+MOD((CASE-1),150))/10)
LET Y=SIN(4*X)/X+ZRN/2+1.5*ZRN*(URN>.8)
LET G=1+INT((CASE-1)/150)
```

The following program runs 100 different LOESS smoothings and saves the results into a single file. Then we plot the results as before.

```
GRAPH NONE
USE DAMP2
BY G
SMOOTH
MODEL Y=X
SAVE TEMP
ESTIMATE / LOESS,GRID=25,DEGREE=2
USE TEMP
BEGIN
PLOT SMOOTH*XGRID / SIZE=.5,XMIN=0,XMAX=4,
                    YMIN=-4,YMAX=4,FILL
FPLOT Y=SIN(4*X)/X ; XMIN=0,XMAX=4,YMIN=-4,YMAX=4,
                    AXES=0,SCALE=0,COLOR=RED
END
RUN
GRAPH
```

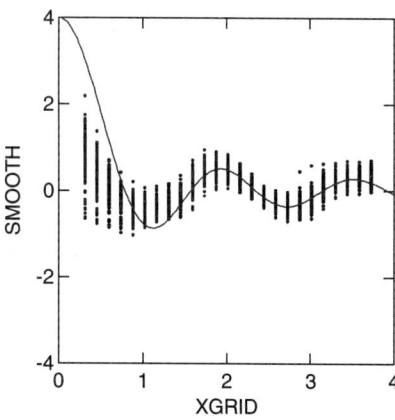

Chapter 11

Example 3
Polynomial Regression and Smoothing

In this example, we illustrate the correspondence between polynomial smoothing in scatterplots and in the SMOOTH procedure. We also compare nonparametric smooths with their parametric counterparts. Throughout this example, we focus on the relationship between military and health spending.

```
USE ourworld
PLOT HEALTH*MIL / BORDER=NORMAL SMOOTH=LINEAR
```

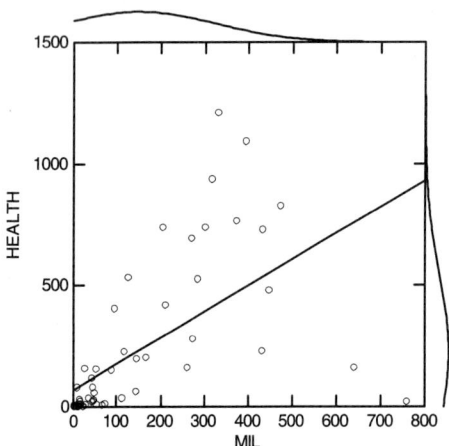

Notice the large number of observations in the lower left corner of the plot. The border plots reveal a heavy concentration of cases at the low end of each axis and a few cases at the high end. Data of this type are not well suited for linear regression. However, transforming the data may improve the situation. Use the Dynamic Explorer to investigate the effects of transforming both variables.

The plot resulting from applying the log transformation to both axes follows:

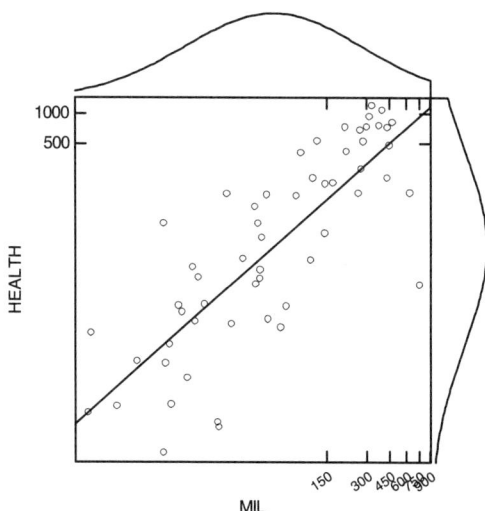

The border plots for the log transformed data (setting X-Power to 0 and Y-Power to 0 in the Dynamic Explorer) reveal the improvement in the distributions for both variables; the transformations eliminate the long tail corresponding to large values of spending for each distribution.

Let's look at the residuals before and after log transforming the data.

```
USE ourworld
BEGIN
PLOT HEALTH*MIL / RESID=LINEAR YLIM=0 LOC=-3IN,0IN,
                  TITLE='Raw Data'
PLOT HEALTH*MIL / RESID=LINEAR YLOG YLIM=0 LOC=3IN,0IN,
                  TITLE='Log Y-Axis'
PLOT HEALTH*MIL / RESID=LINEAR XLOG YLOG YLIM=0,
                  LOC=0IN,-6IN,
                  TITLE='Log Y-Axis and Log X-Axis'
END
```

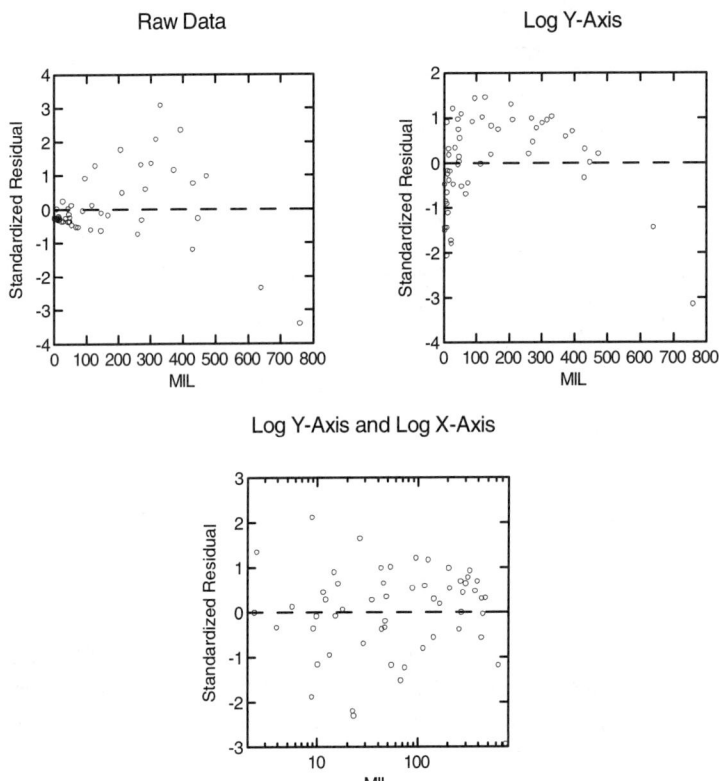

The residual plot for the raw data displays a pattern commonly referred to as a *right-opening megaphone*. As military spending increases, the residuals tend to get larger. This pattern often occurs when the dependent variable varies over a large range (from .385 to 1209.077, in this example). One common procedure used to alleviate the resulting nonconstant variance involves applying the log transformation to the dependent variable.

In the second plot, only the dependent variable (*HEALTH*) is log transformed. The plot displays a distinct nonlinear relationship; the extreme *MIL* values correspond to negative residuals and values between 100 and 400 yield positive residuals. To control for this pattern, transform the independent variable or use a nonlinear model.

Applying the log transformation to both variables results in the final plot. The residuals appear randomly scattered with a few possible outliers. The lack of an apparent relationship between the independent variable and the residuals suggests transforming the raw data to logs before fitting linear regression models.

Similar residual plots occur for a quadratic smooth. The commands follow:

```
USE ourworld
BEGIN
PLOT HEALTH*MIL / RESID=QUADRATIC YLIM=0 LOC=-3IN,0IN,
                  TITLE='Raw Data'
PLOT HEALTH*MIL / RESID=QUADRATIC YLOG YLIM=0 LOC=3IN,0IN,
                  TITLE='Log Y-Axis'
PLOT HEALTH*MIL / RESID=QUADRATIC XLOG YLOG YLIM=0,
                  LOC=0IN,-6IN,
                  TITLE='Log Y-Axis and Log X-Axis'
END
```

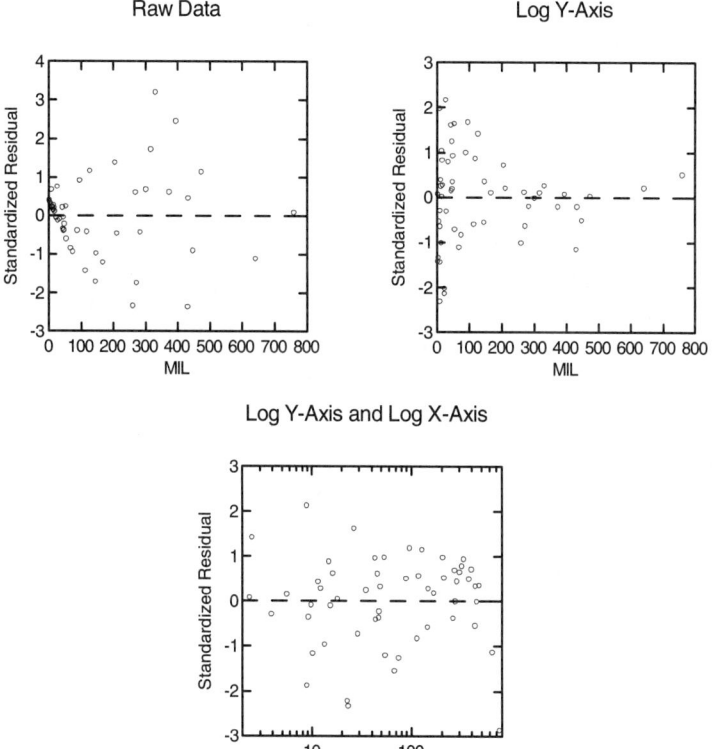

The first plot displays a right-opening megaphone. In contrast to the linear smooth, however, transforming the dependent variable yields decreasing residual variance as *MIL* increases (a left-opening megaphone). Transforming both variables results in a random scatter of residuals.

Polynomial Smoothing

The SMOOTH option for PLOT offers linear and quadratic polynomial smoothing. The SMOOTH procedure also fits polynomial models, but allows more control by allowing local fitting to data regions instead of global fitting of all observed data. In addition, cubic smoothing is available. Here we fit three polynomial models, as well as a LOESS smooth, to the health and military spending data:

```
USE ourworld
LET log_mil=L10(mil)
LET log_heal=L10(health)
GRAPH NONE
SMOOTH
MODEL LOG_HEAL = LOG_MIL
SAVE LINGRID
ESTIMATE / KERNEL=Uniform SMOOTHER=Polynomial,
          WINDOW=KNN PROPORTION=1 DEGREE=1
SAVE QUADGRID
ESTIMATE / KERNEL=Uniform SMOOTHER=Polynomial,
          WINDOW=KNN PROPORTION=1 DEGREE=2
SAVE CUBGRID
ESTIMATE / KERNEL=Uniform SMOOTHER=Polynomial,
          WINDOW=KNN PROPORTION=1 DEGREE=3
SAVE LOEGRID
ESTIMATE / LOESS DEGREE=1 GRID=25
GRAPH
BEGIN
USE LINGRID
PLOT smooth*xgrid / LINE SIZE=0 COLOR=RED LOC=-3IN,0IN,
                    TITLE='Linear Polynomial',
                    YMIN=-1 YMAX=4 YLAB='' XLAB=''
PLOT log_heal*log_mil / LOC=-3IN,0IN
```

```
USE QUADGRID
PLOT smooth*xgrid / LINE SIZE=0 COLOR=RED LOC=3IN,0IN,
                    TITLE='Quadratic Polynomial',
                    YMIN=-1 YMAX=4 YLAB='' XLAB=''
PLOT log_heal*log_mil / LOC=3IN,0IN
USE CUBGRID
PLOT smooth*xgrid / LINE SIZE=0 COLOR=RED LOC=-3IN,-6IN,
                    TITLE='Cubic Polynomial',
                    YMIN=-1 YMAX=4 YLAB='' XLAB=''
PLOT log_heal*log_mil / LOC=-3IN,-6IN
USE LOEGRID
PLOT smooth*xgrid / LINE SIZE=0 COLOR=RED LOC=3IN,-6IN,
                    TITLE='LOESS (degree=1)',
                    YMIN=-1 YMAX=4 YLAB='' XLAB=''
PLOT log_heal*log_mil / LOC=3IN,-6IN
END
```

By default, SMOOTH generates estimates at 25 grid points. For the linear, quadratic, and cubic models, we set the proportion of neighbors included when generating each estimate to 1 resulting in a global smooth of all data. By using a uniform kernel, all data points receive equal weighting. These specifications result in smooths that correspond to their parametric counterparts. For example, the polynomial of degree one is equivalent to fitting a linear least-squares regression to the data. However, by adjusting the proportion, kernel function, or smoothing method, you can modify the model to better describe the relationships in your data.

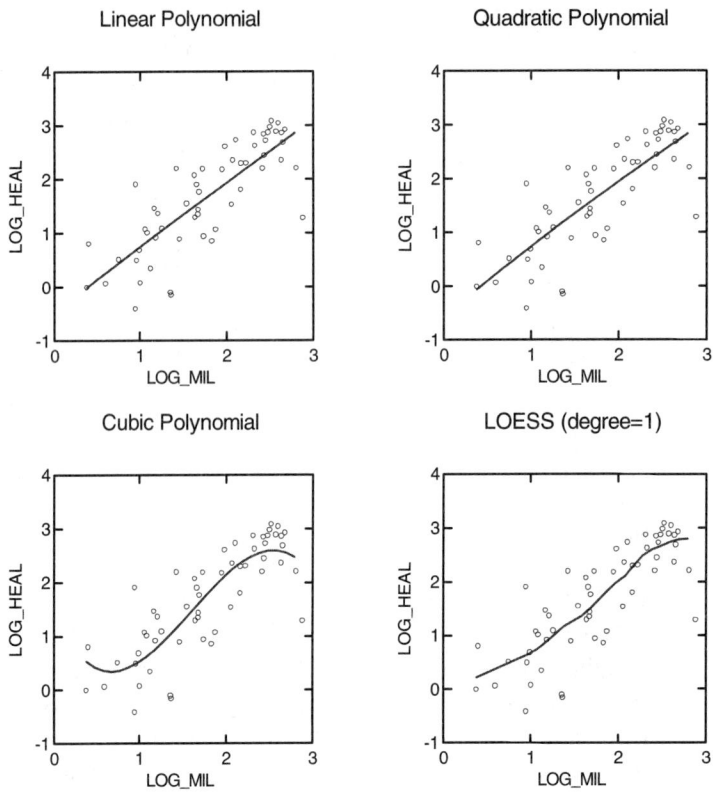

The linear and quadratic smooths are practically indistinguishable. The cubic smooth begins turning up at the left end and turning down at the right end. Cubic models often respond dramatically to data at the extremes of the observed range. In contrast, the LOESS smooth merely levels off slightly at the upper end in response to the two values at the right extreme. It appears that a first degree polynomial describes the relationship between the two transformed variables adequately; polynomials of higher degree overfit this data.

Mean Squared Error in Smoothing

When the number of grid points equals 0, SMOOTH generates a smooth estimate for each case and reports an MSE value. However, this mean squared error differs from the

Smoothing

MSE typically reported in regression programs. To illustrate this difference, we fit a linear model using both GLM and SMOOTH:

```
USE ourworld
LET log_mil=L10(mil)
LET log_heal=L10(health)
GRAPH NONE
SMOOTH
MODEL LOG_HEAL = LOG_MIL
SAVE LINRES
ESTIMATE / KERNEL=Uniform SMOOTHER=Polynomial,
          WINDOW=KNN PROPORTION=1 DEGREE=1 GRID=0
GLM
MODEL log_heal = CONSTANT + log_mil
ESTIMATE
GRAPH
```

The output follows:

```
Model: LOG_HEAL = LOG_MIL

K-nearest neighbor smoothing
Uniform kernel
Smoothing method is kernel weighted polynomial regression
Degree of polynomial is: 1
Number of cases input:   57
Number of nonmissing cases smoothed: 56
Number of cases in window: 56
MSE (square root of average squared residual) : 0.573
Predicted values and residuals have been saved.


1 case(s) deleted due to missing data.

Dep Var: LOG_HEAL    N: 56    Multiple R: 0.808    Squared multiple R: 0.653

Adjusted squared multiple R: 0.646    Standard error of estimate: 0.583
```

Effect	Coefficient	Std Error	Std Coef	Tolerance	t	P(2 Tail)
CONSTANT	-0.451	0.224	0.000	.	-2.016	0.049
LOG_MIL	1.191	0.118	0.808	1.000	10.073	0.000

```
                    Analysis of Variance

Source            Sum-of-Squares    df   Mean-Square    F-ratio        P

Regression            34.516         1      34.516      101.467      0.000
Residual              18.369        54       0.340
-------------------------------------------------------------------------


*** WARNING ***
Case           22 is an outlier        (Studentized Residual =     -3.281)

Durbin-Watson D Statistic       1.472
First Order Autocorrelation     0.248
```

The mean-square error (residual) from the ANOVA table for the linear model is 0.340. But the smoothing output reports a MSE value of 0.573 for this model. How is this possible?

To calculate the MSE for smoothing, SYSTAT squares the residuals, determines the average of these squared terms, and reports the square root of this average. The following commands compute the squared MSE value for the linear model.

```
USE linres
LET sqres=residual*residual
STATS
STATISTICS sqres / N SUM MEAN
```

The output from **STATS** follows:

```
                     SQRES
N of cases             56
Sum                 18.354
Mean                 0.328
```

The reported mean equals 18.354 / 56. Taking the square root of the mean:

CALC SQR(.328)

results in the reported MSE value of .573.

Notice that the sum of the squared residuals from SMOOTH equals the sum-of-squares (SS) for Residual in GLM. In GLM, the MS for error equals the SS for error divided by the degrees of freedom for error. In this case, 18.369 / 54 = 0.340. Thus, the two procedures differ in divisors for the sum of squared residuals (56 vs 54). In the regression approach, we divide by (the number of cases - the number of estimated parameters). In the nonparametric smoothing approach, no parameters are being estimated, so we simply divide by the number of cases. Furthermore, the MSE in GLM is a sum of squares divided by a divisor. In SMOOTH, the MSE equals the *square root* of a sum of squares divided by a divisor.

Example 4
Smoothing Binary Data in Three Dimensions

This example shows a smooth of binary data using two predictors: Graduate Record Examination Verbal and Quantitative scores. The dependent variable is a binary indicator of whether or not a student was awarded a Ph.D. in a graduate psychology department. We employ the LOESS smoother.

```
USE ADMIT
SMOOTH
MODEL PHD=GREV GREQ
SAVE TEMP
ESTIMATE / LOESS
```

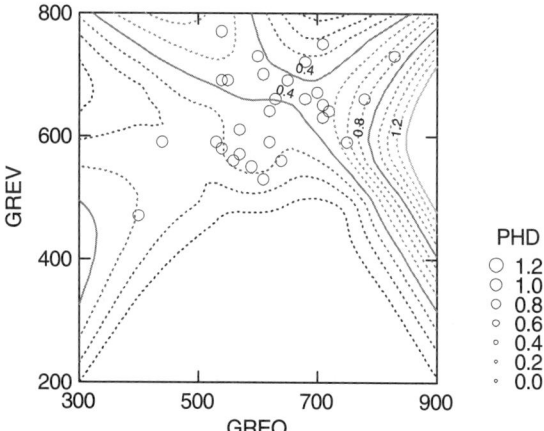

The Quick Graph uses a contour plot to represent the smoothed surface when there are two predictors. The size of the data points is proportional to the values on the dependent variable. The fitted surface is highest for Verbal GRE scores around 600 and Quantitative GRE scores around 700-800.

3D Scatter Plots

We plot the saved values as follows:

```
USE TEMP
PLOT SMOOTH*YGRID*XGRID  /  XLAB='Quantitative GRE',
                            YLAB='Verbal GRE'
```

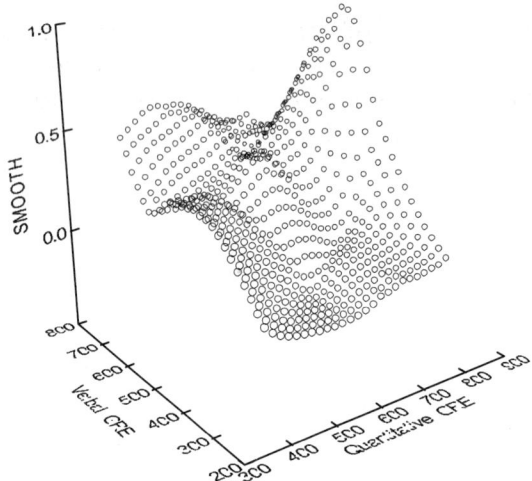

It is often preferable to use a large GRID setting (e.g., GRID=40) rather than to attempt to fit a surface to these points. This will also reveal where estimates cannot be made because there are computational problems or missing values in a larger region. Especially with 3D smooths, it is better to trust the plot of the estimates on the grid than the smoothed estimates in the Quick Graph.

You can set the SIZE of the points smaller (e.g., SIZE=.5) with a finer grid to make the surface less coarse. Plotting the smooth in one color and the data in another allows us to see both objects without either hiding the other.

References

Cleveland, W.S. (1995). *Visualizing Data*. Summit, NJ: Hobart Press.

Cleveland, W.S., and Devlin, S. (1988). Locally weighted regression analysis by local fitting. *Journal of the American Statistical Association, 83*, 596-640.

Fan, J., and Gijbels, I. (1996). *Local Polynomial Modelling and Its Applications*. London: Chapman & Hall.

Gonzalez, R.C., and Wintz, P. (1977). *Digital Image Processing*. Reading, MA: Addison-Wesley.

Green, P.J. and Silverman, B.W. (1994). *Nonparametric Rression and Generalized Linear Models: A Roughness Penalty Approach*. London: Chapman and Hall.

Härdle, W. (1990). *Applied Nonparametric Regression*. Cambridge, UK: Cambridge University Press.

Hastie, T. and Tibshirani, R. (1990). *Generalized Additive Models*. London: Chapman and Hall.

McLain, D.H. (1974). Drawing contours from arbitrary data points. *The Computer Journal, 17*, 318-324.

Makridakis, S., and Wheelwright, S.C. (1989). *Forecasting Methods for Management* (5th ed.). New York: John Wiley & Sons.

Marron, J.S., and Nolan, D. (1988). Canonical kernels for density estimation. *Statistics & Probability Letters, 7*, 195-199.

Nadaraya, E.A. (1964). On estimating regression. *Theory of Probability and its Applications, 10*, 186-190.

Shepard, D. (1965). A two-dimensional interpolation function for irregularly spaced data. *Proceedings of the 23rd National Conference of the ACM,* 517.

Simonoff, J.S. (1996). *Smoothing Methods in Statistics*. New York: Springer-Verlag.

Tukey, J.W. (1977). *Exploratory Data Analysis*. Reading, MA: Addison-Wesley.

Watson, G.S. (1964). Smooth regression analysis. *Sankhya, Series A, 26*, 359-372.

Chapter

12

Spatial Statistics

Leland Wilkinson

Spatial statistics compute a variety of statistics on a 2-D or 3-D spatially oriented data set. Variograms assist in the identification of spatial models. Kriging offers 2-D or 3-D kriging methods for spatial prediction. Simulation realizes a spatial model using Monte Carlo methods. Finally, a variety of point-based statistics are produced, including areas (volumes) of Voronoi polygons, nearest-neighbor distances, counts of polygon facets, and quadrat counts. Graphs are automatically plotted and summary statistics are printed for many of these statistics.

The geostatistical routines in SYSTAT Spatial are based on GSLIB (Deutsch and Journel, 1998). Point statistics are computed from a Voronoi/Delaunay partition of 2-D or 3-D configurations.

Statistical Background

Spatial statistics involve a variety of methods for analyzing spatially distributed data. SYSTAT Spatial covers two principal areas: fixed-point methods (kriging and Gaussian simulation) and random-point methods (nearest-neighbor distances, polygon area/volumes, quadrat procedures). All of these procedures can be defined through a basic spatial model.

The Basic Spatial Model

The basic spatial model can be defined as follows. Assume $\mathbf{s}_0 \in \Re^d$ is a "site" or point in d-dimensional Euclidean space. The random variable $Z(\mathbf{s}_0)$ represents a possible observation of some quantity or quality at the site $\mathbf{s}_0$. Instead of fixing $\mathbf{s}_0$ at a single site, however, we can let **s** vary over the index set $D \subset \Re^d$, so as to make $Z(\mathbf{s})$ a *stochastic process* or a *random field*:

$$\{Z(\mathbf{s}): \mathbf{s} \in D\}$$

There are two principal variants of this random process. If D is a *fixed* subset of $\Re^d$, then we have a *geostatistical* model in which points are at predetermined locations and $Z(\mathbf{s})$ is sampled at these points. Although points are taken at fixed locations, the geostatistical model assumes **s** can vary continuously over $\Re^d$. On the other hand, if D is a *random* subset, then we have a *point process* in which $Z(\mathbf{s})$, or **s** itself, is sampled at random locations.

Conventional statistical procedures are unsuited for either of these models for several reasons. The major reason involves independence of observations. As with time series (see the SERIES module in SYSTAT), spatial models normally involve dependence among observations. We cannot assume that errors for a conventional statistical model applied to spatial data will be independent.

In the geostatistical model, the value of $Z(\mathbf{s}_i)$ is usually correlated with the value of $Z(\mathbf{s}_j)$. For example, if we sample groundwater level at a site, the value we find there can be predicted, in part, by the value at a nearby site. Furthermore, the nature of this relationship may be more complex than the one-dimensional dependencies found in a time series. The dependency structure may vary with direction, distance, and time. We expect nearby sites to be related. We might even find that groundwater level is related (perhaps negatively) to the level at a distant site and this relationship might vary over time.

In the point process model, we face a similar dependency issue even though sites are randomly distributed. We also encounter another problem: the statistics we construct in order to examine patterns and test hypotheses are not usually normal. The distribution of distances between pairs of points, the counts of points in fixed areas, the areas of clear space around points, and other spatial statistics are not normally distributed. So even if our interest is focused only on the distribution of sites (that is, we have no $Z(\mathbf{s})$ or $Z(\mathbf{s}) = \mathbf{s}$), we cannot resort to conventional statistical procedures.

I will first introduce the approaches designed to handle these problems in geostatistics and then summarize the basic approaches in point processes. The examples in the following sections should further highlight these issues.

The Geostatistical Model

The classic geostatistical model involves the random variate $Z(\mathbf{s})$ over a fixed field for $\mathbf{s}$ defined on the real numbers. The set

$$\{Z(\mathbf{s}) : \mathbf{s} \in D\}$$

where D is the collection of sites being studied, is a *random function* of the sites. The cumulative distribution function of $Z(\mathbf{s})$ is

$$F(\mathbf{s};z) = \text{Prob}\{Z(\mathbf{s}) \leq z\}$$

Fitting models and making inferences about $Z(\mathbf{s})$ requires us to make a global assumption about its behavior over all members of the set D. That is, summarizing $Z(\mathbf{s})$ usually requires using information from neighboring sites, and how that information is used depends on our global assumptions. These assumptions usually involve some form of *stationarity*. In its strong form, stationarity requires that

$$F(\mathbf{s}_1;z_1, \mathbf{s}_2;z_2, \ldots, \mathbf{s}_n;z_n) = F(\mathbf{s}_1 + \mathbf{h};z_1, \mathbf{s}_2 + \mathbf{h};z_2, \ldots, \mathbf{s}_n + \mathbf{h};z_n)$$

for all $\mathbf{s}_i \in D$, $\mathbf{s}_i + \mathbf{h} \in D$, $\mathbf{h} \in \Re^d$, and any finite n.

Because $\mathbf{h}$ acts as a translation vector, this condition is also called *stationarity under translation*. In geostatistical modeling, we often use a weaker form of the stationarity assumption:

$$E(Z(\mathbf{s})) = \mu \text{ for all } \mathbf{s} \in D, \text{ and}$$

$$\text{cov}(Z(\mathbf{s}_1), Z(\mathbf{s}_2)) = C(\mathbf{s}_1 - \mathbf{s}_2) \text{ for all } \mathbf{s}_1, \mathbf{s}_2 \in D$$

The parameter μ is called the stationary mean. The function $C(.)$ is called a *covariogram*. These two conditions define weak, or *second-order stationarity* for $Z(\mathbf{s})$. The first implies that the mean is invariant over sites. The second implies that the covariance of random functions $Z(.)$ between all pairs of sites is a function of the difference between sites. Furthermore, if $C(.)$ is independent of direction (that is, it depends only on the Euclidean distance between $\mathbf{s}_1$ and $\mathbf{s}_2$), then we call it *isotropic*.

Variogram

Instead of $C(.)$, geostatisticians usually work with a different but related function. This function is constructed from the variance of the first differences of the process:

$$2\gamma(\mathbf{s}_1 - \mathbf{s}_2) = var(Z(\mathbf{s}_1) - Z(\mathbf{s}_2))$$

The function $2\gamma(\mathbf{h})$, where $\mathbf{h}$ is the difference over all sites, is called the *variogram* and the function $\gamma(\mathbf{h})$ is called the *semi-variogram*. The classical estimator of the variogram function is:

$$2\hat{\gamma}(\mathbf{h}) = \frac{1}{N_{ij}} \sum_{i=1}^{n} \sum_{j<i} (Z(\mathbf{s}_i) - Z(\mathbf{s}_j))^2, \text{ where } \mathbf{h} = \mathbf{s}_i - \mathbf{s}_j$$

When the data are irregularly spaced, the classical variogram estimator is computed with a "tolerance" region. The following figure shows the parameters for defining this region. The *angle* parameter determines the direction along which we want to compute the variogram. The *number of lags,* the *lag distance*, and the *lag tolerance* determine the maximum distance in this direction. The *bandwidth* determines the width of the band covering sites to be included in the calculations. And the *angle tolerance* determines the amount of tapering at the origin-end of the covering region. If this value is greater than 90 degrees, SYSTAT creates an omni-directional variogram, in which the full 360 degree sweep is used for computing lags. For three-dimensional spatial fields, these parameters are extended to the depth dimension from the usual horizontal (East) and vertical (North) dimensions.

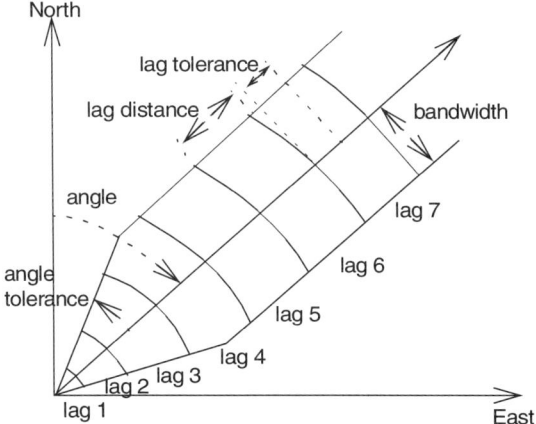

Variogram Models

We often want to construct a *variogram model* that fits well our empirical variogram. The smooth functions we use for variogram models not only help summarize the behavior of our process but they also give us a numerical method for fitting $Z(\mathbf{s})$ by least squares. There are several popular functions for modeling the semi-variogram. The ones provided in SYSTAT (with scalar $h = \|\mathbf{h}\|$) are:

- **Spherical**

$$\gamma(h) = \begin{cases} 0, & h = 0 \\ c_0 + c\left[1.5\left(\frac{h}{a}\right) - 0.5\left(\frac{h}{a}\right)^3\right], & 0 < h \leq a \\ c_0 + c, & h > a \end{cases}$$

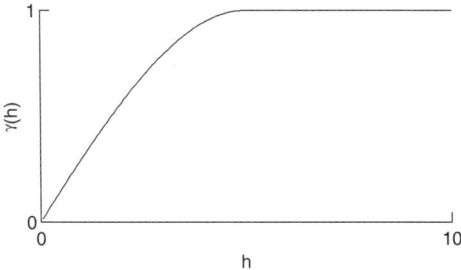

Chapter 12

- **Exponential**

$$\gamma(h) = \begin{cases} 0, & h = 0 \\ c_0 + c\left[1 - \exp\left(-\dfrac{3h}{a}\right)\right], & h > 0 \end{cases}$$

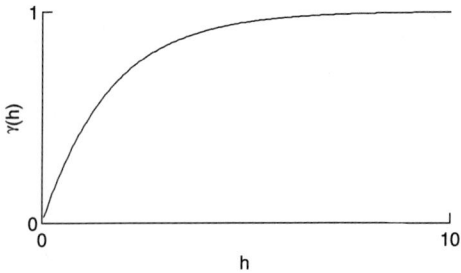

- **Gaussian**

$$\gamma(h) = \begin{cases} 0, & h = 0 \\ c_0 + c\left[1 - \exp\left(-\dfrac{3h}{a}\right)^2\right], & h > 0 \end{cases}$$

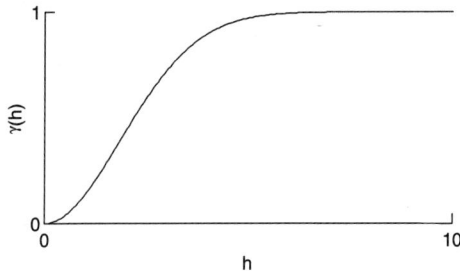

- **Power**

$$\gamma(h) = \begin{cases} 0, & h = 0 \\ c_0 + ch^a, & h > 0, \ 0 < a < 2 \end{cases}$$

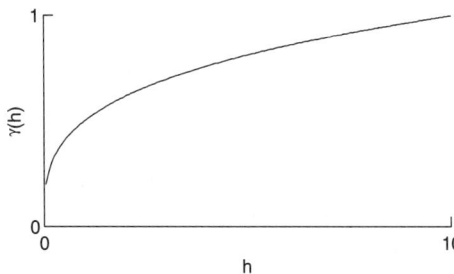

◼ Hole, or wave

$$\gamma(h) = \begin{cases} 0, & h = 0 \\ c_0 + c\left[1 - \cos\left(\dfrac{\pi h}{a}\right)\right], & h > 0 \end{cases}$$

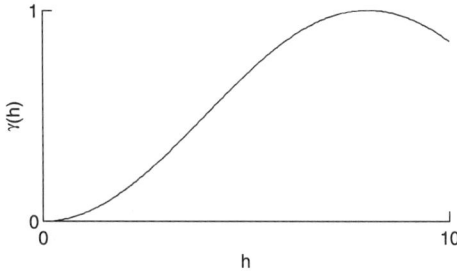

The hole model is sometimes parameterized equivalently with *sin* instead of *cos*. There is a variant of the hole effect model that includes a damping factor (usually exponential) for larger values of h. This model is not included in SYSTAT.

For most of these models, the parameter c is called the *sill*, and the parameter a is called the *range*. When appropriate, the sill is the maximum value of the function on the ordinate axis; in other cases, it is an asymptote. The range is the value of h for which $\gamma(h) = c_0 + c$. For other models, it is the value of h for which $\gamma(h)$ approaches $c_0 + c$. Another parameter is called the *nugget effect* (c_0). The nugget is an offset parameter measured at $\gamma(h)$ near zero. It raises the height of the entire curve (except for $\gamma(h) = 0$). Estimating these parameters for typical geophysical data presents some difficulties, as Cressie (1991) discusses, but most smoothing methods that use a variogram model are fairly robust against minor deviations in their values.

Variogram models can be combined in what Deutsch and Journel (1998) call the "nested model." This is a linear combination of submodels with separate parameter specifications for each. SYSTAT allows up to three submodels in a specification.

Pannatier (1996) offers an interactive program for variogram modeling (VARIOWIN) that is based on the same parameterizations as GSLIB and SYSTAT. Both VARIOWIN and SYSTAT offer variants of semi-variograms derived from GSLIB, such as the covariogram, correlogram, and semi-madogram. See Deutsch and Journel (1998) for details on these methods.

Anisotropy

If the variogram for a process is not identical for all directions, then it lacks isotropy. This *anisotropy* condition requires a more complex variogram model. The more basic type of anisotropy is *geometric*. This condition can be modeled by weighting distance according to direction, in a manner similar to the computation of Mahalanobis distance in discriminant analysis (see the Discriminant procedure). That is, we compute $\gamma(h_w)$ instead of $\gamma(h)$, where

$$h = \|\mathbf{h}\| = [(\mathbf{s}_1 - \mathbf{s}_2)^T(\mathbf{s}_1 - \mathbf{s}_2)]^{1/2} \text{ and}$$

$$h_w = \|\mathbf{h}_w\| = [(\mathbf{s}_1 - \mathbf{s}_2)^T \mathbf{W}(\mathbf{s}_1 - \mathbf{s}_2)]^{1/2}$$

The weight matrix **W** is usually a positive definite composition of linear transformations involving rotation and dilatation. This turns the circular isometric locus for the isotropic model into an ellipse. SYSTAT specifies this matrix through several parameters. The first group specifies the angles for rotation: ANG1 is a deviation from north in a clockwise direction, ANG2 is a deviation from horizontal (for 3-D models), and ANG3 is a tilt angle. The second group specifies the shape of the ellipse that comprises a level curve for a given distance calculation: AHMAX is the maximum extent, AHMIN is the minimum extent, and AVERT is the 3-D (vertical) extent. An anisotropy index is calculated from these measures:

ANIS1=AHMIN/AHMAX and, for 3-D, ANIS2=AVERT/AHMAX.

A second type of anisotropy is called *zonal*. This condition exists when different models apply to different directions. SYSTAT allows this type of modeling through nested variogram models. When the anisotropy parameter settings are different for each type of model in a nested structure, then we have a zonal isotropic model. See Journel and Huijbregts (1978) or Deutsch and Journel (1969) for further details.

Simple Kriging

The most popular geostatistical prediction method is called kriging, named after a South African mining engineer (Krige, 1962). Cressie (1990) provides a history of its origins in a variety of fields, including meteorology and physics. The simple kriging prediction model for $Z(\mathbf{s})$ is:

$$Z(\mathbf{s}) = \sum_{i=1}^{n} \lambda_i Z(\mathbf{s}_i) + \left(1 - \sum_{i=1}^{n} \lambda_i\right)\mu$$

where λ_i are weights and μ is the stationary mean. Kriging estimates weights λ_i that minimize the error variance over all estimated points $Z(\mathbf{s})$, not necessarily measured at the given sites. The numerical estimation procedure requires a variogram model to be specified through the MODEL statement in SYSTAT.

Ordinary Kriging

By setting $\Sigma \lambda_i = 1$, we restrict the model and exclude the stationary mean. This constrained model is called *ordinary kriging*, the default method used in SYSTAT. The model is of the same form as that for simple kriging. Notice that, because the sum of the kriging weights is 1, the last summation term drops out of the model.

Universal Kriging

We may not be able to assume that $E(Z(\mathbf{s})) = \mu$ for all $\mathbf{s} \in D$, as we do in simple and ordinary kriging. Instead, we may want to assume that $E(Z(\mathbf{s}))$ is a linear combination of known functions $\{f_0(\mathbf{s}), ..., f_p(\mathbf{s})\}$. This allows us to model Z(s) with trend components across the field. While these functions may be more general, it is customary to fit polynomial components to model this global trend in the following form:

$$Z(\mathbf{s}) = \sum_{j=0}^{p} \beta_j f_j(\mathbf{s}) + \delta(\mathbf{s})$$

The $\delta(\mathbf{s})$ term represents a stationary random process. SYSTAT offers linear and quadratic function terms for this type of modeling, including interactions. The terms are specified in the TREND command. Deutsch and Journel (1998) eschew the term "universal kriging" and instead call this method "kriging with a trend model." The SMOOTH=KRIG option of the PLOT command in SYSTAT is an independent implementation of universal kriging. This exploratory smoother does not offer the full modeling and output capabilities of the KRIG command in SPATIAL, however.

Simulation

Stochastic simulation offers the opportunity to create a realization of a spatial process to view the implications of a particular model or to estimate standard errors through Monte Carlo methods. Gaussian simulation generates the realization $\{z(\mathbf{s}): \mathbf{s} \in D\}$ from the multivariate Gaussian $N(\mu, \Sigma)$, where the parameters for the centroid vector and covariance matrix are taken from the stationary means and covariances over the field.

SYSTAT implements the LUSIM algorithm from GSLIB (Deutsch and Journel, 1998). This algorithm requires the number of grid points and number of data points to be relatively small. It is designed to be most suited for a large number of realizations at a small number of nodes. SYSTAT executes one realization per use of the command, however, so the simulation is less useful for this purpose. To compensate, the memory requirements have been increased so that somewhat larger problems can be handled. See Deutsch and Journel (1998) and Haining (1990) for further details.

Point Processes

Cressie (1991) and Upton and Fingleton (1985) cover various models and applications that can be loosely grouped under the heading of point processes. Unlike traditional geostatistical methods, our focus of interest in these areas is on the distribution of sites themselves or functions of that distribution. We usually consider the location of sites in these cases to be a random variable.

The statistical indexes of the distribution of sites in a field are numerous. Most are based on some fundamental geometric measures. A biological example helps to illustrate these measures. The following plot shows the location of fiddler-crab holes in an 80 by 80 centimeter plot of the Pamet river marsh in Truro, Massachusetts (Wilkinson, 1998).

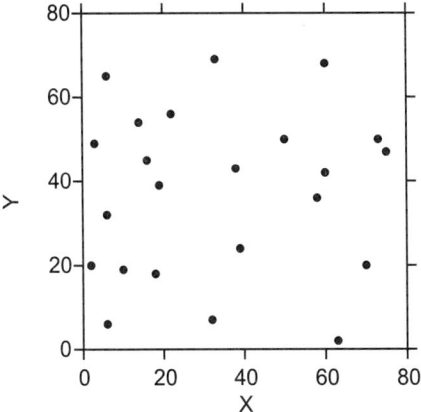

We might ask a number of questions about these data. First of all, are the holes randomly distributed in the plane? SYSTAT does not offer test statistics for answering this question directly but does provide the fundamental measures needed for a variety of such tests. The most widely used measure for spatial hypotheses of this sort is the nearest-neighbor distance, represented by the minimum spanning tree in the following figure (drawn with the SPAN option of the PLOT command in SYSTAT):

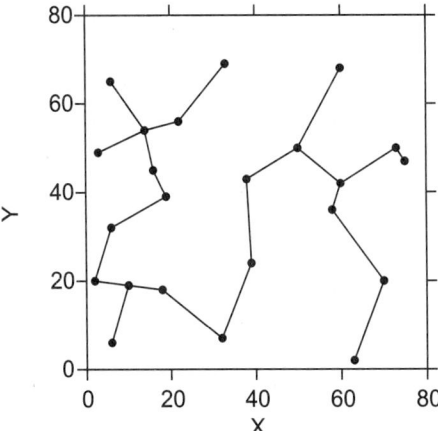

Upton and Fingleton (1985, Table 1.10) and Cressie (1993, Table 8.6) discuss a large number of statistical tests that are simple functions of these distances. The density of the nearest-neighbor distance under complete spatial randomness in two dimensions is:

$$g(d) = 2\pi\lambda d \, \exp(-\pi\lambda d^2), \quad d > 0$$

where λ is an intensity parameter, like the Poisson λ. Here is a graph of this density:

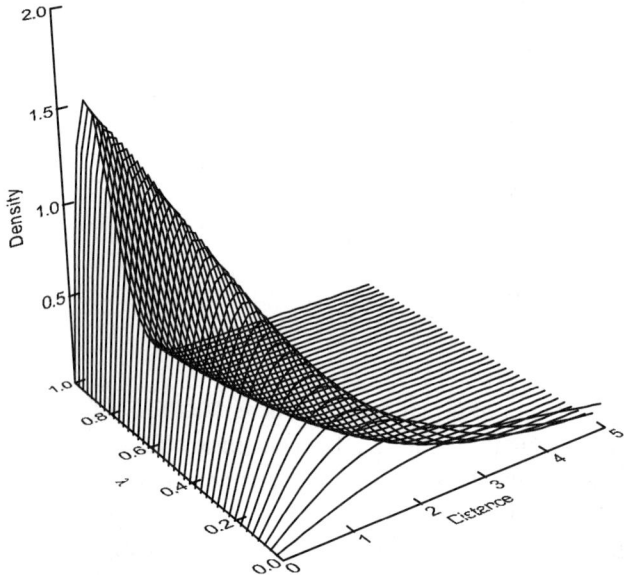

The density resembles the chi-square, with the shape evolving from normal to skewed as a function of the intensity parameter.

SYSTAT plots a histogram of these nearest-neighbor distances after the POINT command is issued. For our crabs, this distance has substantive meaning that can be useful for further modeling with other variables. The nearest-neighbor distance is the shortest distance from any crab hole to another in the sampled area. A crab is, all other things being equal, most likely to compete with the nearest-neighbor crab for local resources (absent remote foraging).

Another statistic used for tests of randomness is the Voronoi area, or volume if we have a 3-D configuration (flying crabs?). The following plot shows the Voronoi polygons (Dirichlet tiles) for the crab data. I used the VORONOI option of the PLOT command to draw these:

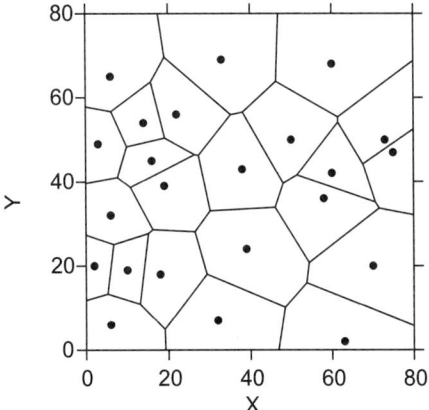

The Voronoi polygons delimit the area around each hole (point) within which every possible point is closer to the crab's hole than to any other. For our crabs, they might represent the area around each hole in which a crab might wander before hitting a neighbor who wanders with equal vigor. Upton and Fingleton (1985) discuss statistical tests based on these areas and the wide applications based on this measure. Okabe et al. (1992) cover Voronoi tessellations in depth.

A third statistic, also based on the Voronoi tessellation, is the count of the number of facets in each Voronoi polygon. For our crabs, this is a measure of the number of near neighbors each crab must contend with. It is positively correlated with the area measure, but is nevertheless distributed differently. Upton and Fingleton (1985) discuss applications.

A fourth measure of point intensity is the quadrat count. We simply count the number of points found in a set of rectangles defined by a grid (the SYSTAT GRID command). Upton and Fingleton (1985) discuss statistical tests based on this measure. Not surprisingly, several are chi-square based, following the rationale for using chi-square tests on binned one-dimensional variates.

Finally, Cressie (1991) and Upton and Fingleton (1985) discuss edge effects that can influence the distribution of many of these statistics. For example, the Voronoi areas (volumes) for points at the periphery of the configuration may be infinite or, because of the distribution of a few neighboring points, substantial outliers. These edge points also tend to have fewer neighbors as candidates for distance calculations. Consequently, it is often useful to be able to identify the points that lie on the convex hull in two or three dimensions. The following figure shows the hull for the 2-D crab data.

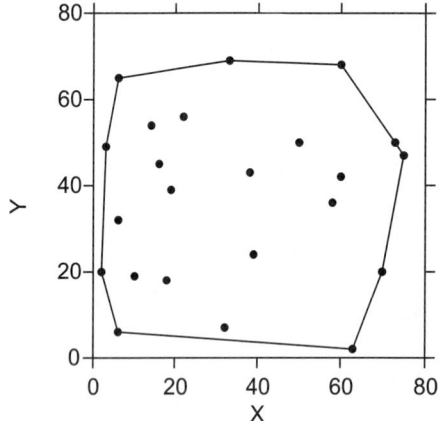

You may want to exclude points on the hull from analyses based on some of the above measures. Cressie (1991) discusses other methods for eliminating edge effects, including bordering the configuration and excluding points in the border.

Spatial Statistics in SYSTAT

Deutsch and Journel (1998) discuss various kriging models and provide the algorithms in a package called GSLIB, on which the kriging program in SYSTAT is based. If you do not already own this book, you should buy it before using the kriging and simulation methods in SYSTAT. The theoretical and applied material in this book provides essential background that necessarily exceeds the scope of a computer manual. For other procedures in SYSTAT Spatial, you can consult other references given in this chapter.

Spatial Statistics Main Dialog Box

To open the Spatial Statistics main dialog box, from the menus choose:

Statistics
  Spatial Statistics...

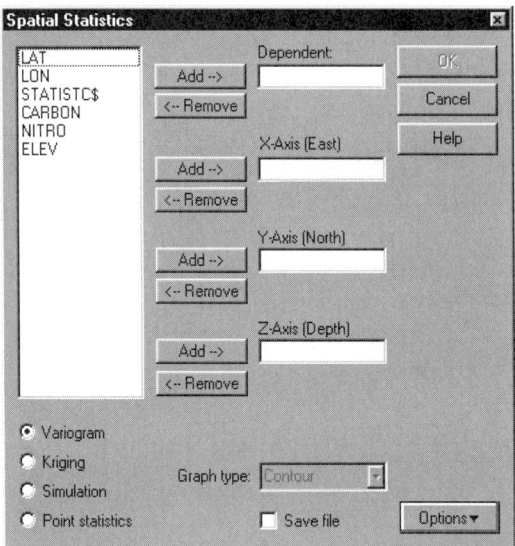

Specify the variables and select one of the following analyses:

- **Variogram.** Computes spatial dissimilarity measures over varying distances.
- **Kriging.** Generates predictions by minimizing the error variance over all estimated points.
- **Simulation.** Uses the multivariate normal distribution to generate a realization for a defined model. Simulation is often used to study a particular model or to estimate standard errors.
- **Point statistics.** Yields areas (volumes) of Voronoi polygons, nearest-neighbor distances, counts of polygon facets, and quadrat counts for sites by treating site locations as a random variable.

Define options specific to each analysis using the Options button.

For Kriging and Simulation, select the graph type to display:

- **Tile.** Produces a plot contoured with shading fill patterns in color gradations.
- **Contour.** Produces a plot contoured with gradation lines.
- **Surface.** Produces a three-dimensional surface plot.

If the analysis involves East, North, *and* Depth variables, no graphs are produced.

Model Options

The Model Options dialog box offers settings for defining the variogram model. Up to three nesting structures are allowed.

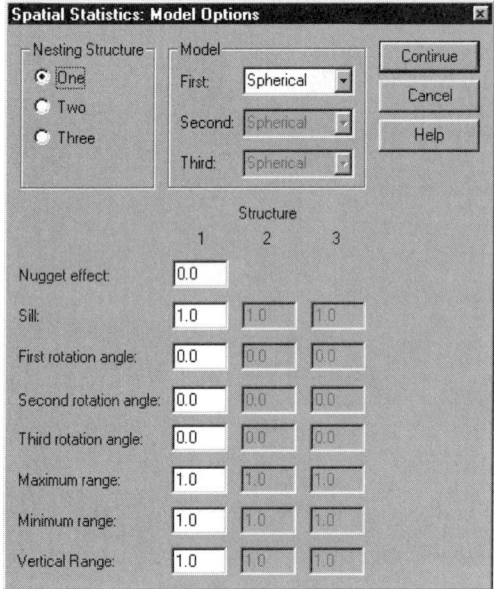

Nesting Structure. Specify the number of nested structures.

For each structure, specify the form of the model. Alternatives include:

- **Spherical.** Near the origin, the spherical model is linear. The tangent to the curve at the origin reaches the sill at a distance of two-thirds of the distance at which the curve reaches the sill.
- **Exponential.** Near the origin, the exponential model is also linear. The tangent to the curve at the origin reaches the sill at a distance of one-third of the distance at which the value of the curve reaches 95% of the sill.
- **Gaussian.** Near the origin, this model is parabolic.
- **Power.** This model does not reach a sill. For exponents between 0 and 1, the model is concave; for values between 1 and 2, the model is convex. An exponent of 1 yields a linear variogram.
- **Hole.** The hole model oscillates around the sill.

Spatial Statistics

In addition, specify the following:

Nugget effect. Enter the value at which the variogram intersects the vertical axis. Specifying a nugget raises the height of the variogram.

Sill. Enter the maximum value attained by the function. For some models, the sill is the asymptote of the function.

Rotating and dilating the orientation helps control for geometric anisotropy by transforming the ellipse (or ellipsoid) into a circle (or sphere). All angles must be specified in degrees.

- **First rotation angle.** The clockwise deviation from north.
- **Second rotation angle.** The deviation from horizontal.
- **Third rotation angle.** The tilt angle.
- **Maximum range.** The maximum extent. For power models, the maximum range defines the exponent.
- **Minimum range.** The minimum extent.
- **Vertical range.** The vertical extent.

In two dimensions, the anisotropy index is the minimum extent divided by the maximum extent. In three dimensions, a second index is the vertical extent divided by the maximum extent.

Variogram

The Variogram dialog box provides the settings for specifying how the variogram is to be computed. For irregularly spaced data, SYSTAT computes variogram estimates using a tolerance region defined by lag and azimuth parameters.

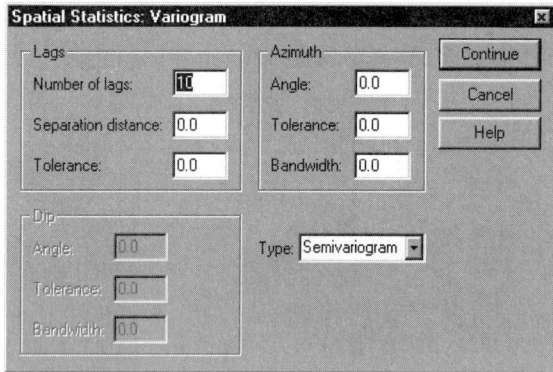

The lag parameters determine the maximum distance in the direction defined by the azimuth angle.

- **Number of lags.** Enter the number of lags used for calculating the spatial similarity measure.
- **Separation distance.** Specify the length of each lag.
- **Tolerance.** Specify a length to add to the separation distance to account for data on an irregular grid. This value is usually one-half of the separation distance (or smaller).

The azimuth parameters define the direction and width of the region used for the variogram.

- **Angle.** Defines the direction (in degrees clockwise from the North axis) along which the variogram is computed.
- **Tolerance.** Specify the amount of tapering (in degrees) near the origin for the covering region. For values exceeding 90 degrees, an omni-directional variogram results.
- **Bandwidth.** Specify the width of the band covering sites. Variogram calculations include points lying within the specified value in either direction from the vector defined by the azimuth angle.

For three-dimensional models, three additional dip parameters extend the variogram to include the depth dimension. (The dip angle is measured in degrees clockwise from the East axis.)

Variograms in SYSTAT differ with respect to the spatial dissimilarity measure [γ(h)] used. Select one of the following measures:

- **Semivariogram.** Half of the average squared difference.
- **Covariance.** The covariance between points.
- **Correlogram.** Standardized covariances.
- **General.** The semi-variogram divided by the squared mean for each lag.
- **Pairwise.** Half of the average squared normalized difference, where each pair is normalized by their mean before squaring.
- **Log.** Semi-variogram of the logged values.
- **Madogram.** Mean absolute deviation.

Grid

The Grid dialog box offers settings for determining the size and shape of the grid used for the kriging estimates and for quadrat counting in the point methods.

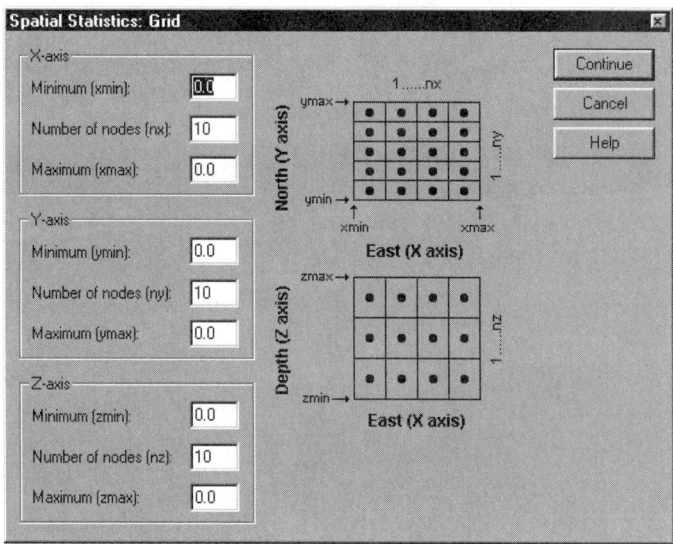

For each axis, specify:

- **Minimum.** The minimum value for the grid along the axis.
- **Number of nodes.** The number of points along the axis.
- **Maximum.** The maximum value along the axis.

SYSTAT uses equal spacing between consecutive nodes for each axis.

Kriging

Kriging yields estimates of the dependent variable based on nearby points, taking into account spatial relationships.

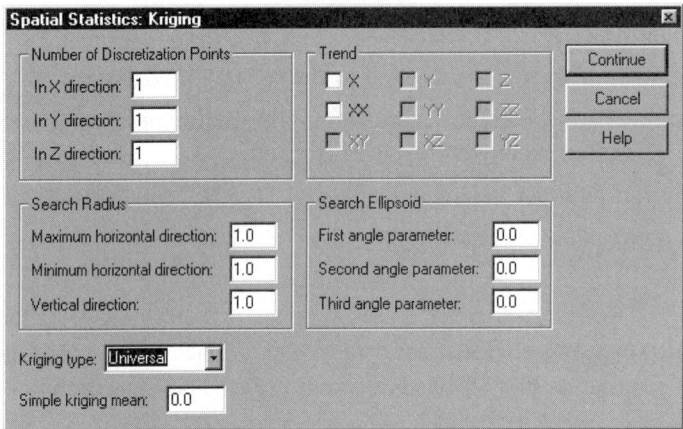

Number of Discretization Points. Specify the number of points for each block in the kriging analysis.

Trend. Defines polynomial trend components to add to the universal kriging analysis. X, Y, and Z correspond to the East, North, and Depth variables, respectively. For example, suppose the x axis (East) variable is *LONG*. Selecting XX adds the term *LONG*LONG* to the kriging model.

Search Radius. Defines the size of the region used to compute the kriging estimates.

Search Ellipsoid. Defines the orientation of the region used to compute the kriging estimates.

Three types of kriging are available:

- **Ordinary.** Constrains the sum of the kriging weights to be 1.
- **Simple.** Uses unconstrained weights. For simple kriging, specify the stationary mean.
- **Universal.** Kriging with polynomial trend components.

Using Commands

First, specify your data with USE filename. Continue with:

```
SPATIAL
MODEL var = varlist / NUGGET = d,
                      SILL = d,
                      ANG1 = d,
                      ANG2 = d,
                      ANG3 = d,
                      AHMIN = d,
                      AHMAX = d,
                      AVERT = d,
                      TYPE = SPHERICAL
                             EXPONENTIAL
                             GAUSSIAN
                             POWER
                             HOLE,
                    / repeat options,
                    / repeat options
```

There are two arguments in varlist for 2-D distributions and three for 3-D. Submodels are expressed by using slashes up to three times and specifying the optional arguments separately for each submodel, all in one statement.

For variograms:

```
VARIOGRAM /NLAG = n,
           XLAG = d,
           XLTOL = d,
           AZM = d,
           ATOL = d,
           BANDH = d,
           DIP = d,
           DTOL = d,
           BANDV = d,
           TYPE = SEMI
                  COVARIANCE
                  CORRELOGRAM
                  GENERAL
                  PAIRWISE
                  LOG
                  MADOGRAM
```

For kriging:

```
KRIG / NXDIS = n,
       NYDIS n,
       NZDIS = n,
       NDMIN = d,
       NDMAX = d,
       RADMIN = d,
       RADMAX = d,
       RADVER = d,
       SANG1 = d,
       SANG2 = d,
       SANG3 = d,
       SKMEAN = d,
       TREND,
       TYPE = SIMPLE
              ORDINARY,
       GRAPH = CONTOUR
               TILE
               SURFACE
```

For universal kriging, use **TYPE=ORDINARY** and the **TREND** option. In addition, specify the form of the trend using the **TREND** command:

```
TREND xvar + yvar + zvar + ,
      xvar*xvar + yvar*yvar + zvar*zvar +
      xvar*yvar + xvar*zvar + yvar*zvar
```

The syntax of the **GRID** statement is:

```
GRID/XMIN = d,
     YMIN = d,
     ZMIN = d,
     XMAX = d,
     YMAX = d,
     ZMAX = d,
     NX = n,
     NY = n,
     NZ = n
```

The syntax of the **SIMULATE** and **POINT** statements follows:

```
SIMULATE/GRAPH = CONTOUR
                 TILE
                 SURFACE,
POINT varlist
```

Usage Considerations

Types of data. SPATIAL uses rectangular data only. The basis (spatial) variables are expected to be measures of latitude, longitude, depth, or other spatial dimensions. The dependent variable is expected to be symmetrically distributed or transformed to a symmetrical distribution.

Print options. There are no print options. Output reports parameter settings. Data are saved into files. Graphs show the distributions and fitted models.

Quick Graphs. SPATIAL produces variograms, kriging surfaces, simulations, and nearest-neighbor histograms. You can choose the type of graph used to display the results of the KRIG and SIMULATE commands by using the GRAPH option.

Saving files. SPATIAL saves variograms, kriging estimates, simulated values, and point statistics.

BY groups. SPATIAL analyzes data BY groups. Your file need not be sorted on the BY variable(s).

Bootstrapping. SPATIAL allows bootstrapping.

Case frequencies. FREQ=<variable> increases the number of cases by the FREQ variable.

Case weights. WEIGHT is not available in SPATIAL.

Examples

The examples begin with a kriging analysis of a spatial data set and proceed to simulation and point processes. Data in the "Point Statistics" example are used with the permission of Kooijman.

Example 1
Kriging (Ordinary)

The data in this example were taken from a compilation of worldwide carbon and nitrogen soil levels for more than 3500 scattered sites. These data were compiled by P. J. Zinke and A. G. Stangenberger of the Department of Forestry and Resource Management at the University of California, Berkeley. The full data set is available at the U.S. Carbon

Dioxide Information Analysis Center (CDIAC) site on the World Wide Web. For our purposes, I have restricted the data to the continental U.S. and have averaged duplicate measurements at single sites by analyzing BY the *LAT* and *LON* variables using the STATS module and saving the averages.

The first step in the analysis is to examine the dependent variable (*CARBON*). The sample histogram for this variable is positively skewed.

```
USE SOIL
HIST CARBON
```

Here is the resulting histogram of the carbon levels:

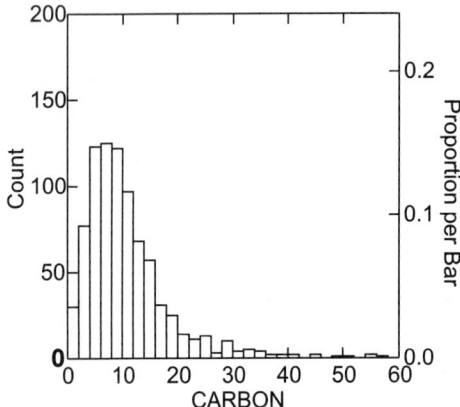

We can use the Dynamic Explorer in the graphics window to transform the *CARBON* variable so that it looks more normally distributed. A value near 0 in the X-Power spin-box produces a normal-appearing histogram, suggesting that a log transformation can approximately symmetrize these data.

```
LET CARBON = L10(CARBON)
HIST CARBON
```

Here is the histogram for the log10 transformed data:

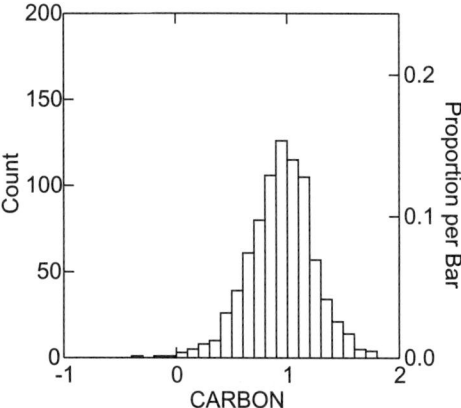

We will proceed using these log-transformed data.

The first step on the way to fitting a kriging surface is to identify a model through the variogram. We can get preliminary guidance for choosing a variogram model by using the default values of the VARIOGRAM command:

```
SPATIAL
    MODEL CARBON = LON LAT
    VARIOGRAM
```

The MODEL statement specifies that *CARBON* is to be a function of *LON* (longitude of the sampling site) and *LAT* (latitude). The VARIOGRAM statement produces an omni-directional semi-variogram by default. The output follows:

```
Structural Model
  Nugget (c0): 0.000000
    First rotation angle (azimuth, or degrees clockwise from North): 0.000000
    Second rotation angle (dip, or degrees down from azimuthal): 0.000000
    First anisotropy index (anis1=ahmin/ahmax): 1.000000
    Sill (c): 1.000000
    Range (a): 1.000000

Semivariogram
  Direction: 0.000000
  Number of lags: 10
  Lag distance: 5.630000
  Lag tolerance: 2.815000
  Angular tolerance: 90.000000
  Maximum horizontal bandwidth: 5.630000
```

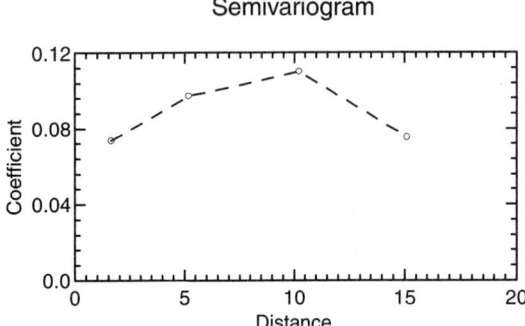

The semi-variogram suggests several things. First, we need a nugget and sill value to offset our model semi-variogram high enough to reach a maximum value somewhere around 0.10. Second, we need to specify a range value so that the model variogram asymptotes near a distance of 10.

By adding options to the MODEL statement, we manage to fit a theoretical variogram to the observed results. The AHMAX and AHMIN parameters specify that the range for both the major and the minor axes is 10 degrees. We choose a lag distance (XLAG) of 1 degree (latitude and longitude) to base our variogram model on relatively local detail. Finally, we again use the default angular tolerance to produce an omni-directional semi-variogram.

```
MODEL CARBON = LON LAT /
  SILL=.05,NUGGET=.05,AHMAX=10,AHMIN=10
VARIOGRAM / XLAG=1
```

The output follows:

```
Structural Model
   Nugget (c0): 0.050000
     First rotation angle (azimuth, or degrees clockwise from North): 0.000000
     Second rotation angle (dip, or degrees down from azimuthal): 0.000000
     First anisotropy index (anis1=ahmin/ahmax): 1.000000
     Sill (c): 0.050000
     Range (a): 10.000000

  Semivariogram
     Direction: 0.000000
     Number of lags: 10
     Lag distance: 1.000000
     Lag tolerance: 0.500000
     Angular tolerance: 90.000000
     Maximum horizontal bandwidth: 1.000000
```

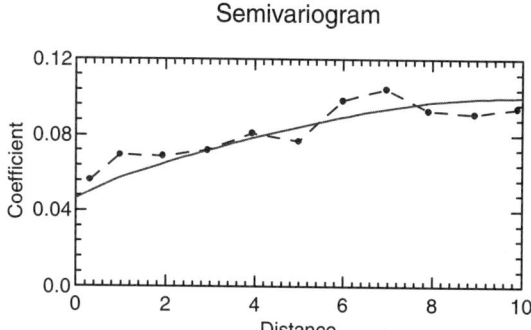

We can check whether we need to worry about anisotropy by checking semi-variograms for different angles. Here are two excursions, 90 degrees separated. By setting angular tolerance (ATOL) to 20 degrees, we keep the lagging window narrow at its origin-end.

```
VARIOGRAM / XLAG=1,AZM=45,ATOL=20
VARIOGRAM / XLAG=1,AZM=135,ATOL=20
```

The output is:

```
Semivariogram
    Direction: 45.000000
    Number of lags: 10
    Lag distance: 1.000000
    Lag tolerance: 0.500000
    Angular tolerance: 20.000000
    Maximum horizontal bandwidth: 1.000000
```

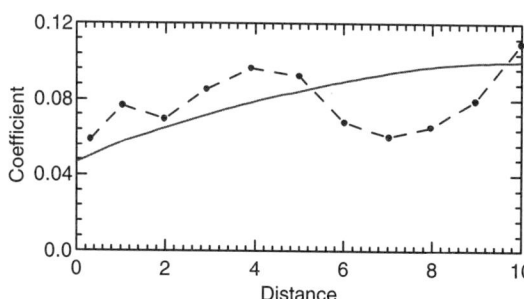

```
Semivariogram
   Direction: 135.000000
   Number of lags: 10
   Lag distance: 1.000000
   Lag tolerance: 0.500000
   Angular tolerance: 20.000000
   Maximum horizontal bandwidth: 1.000000
```

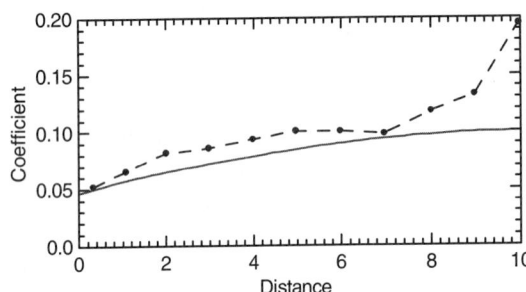

There is enough difference to suggest the possibility of anisotropy, but not enough to radically alter the results. Some of this variety is likely due to the uneven scattering of the sites. This can induce negative or fluctuating spatial correlations, as evidenced by a wavy semi-variogram. If these are pronounced, one might consider a wave or hole-effect semi-variogram model.

We will keep our metric spherical nevertheless. This uneven scattering is not comforting, however; kriging normally should rest on fairly evenly distributed sampling sites or on a regular grid. Our data are received, however, so the sites are given.

Now we can use the spherical model to fit a surface to the carbon data. We add a GRID statement to specify the grid points where estimates are to be made. We also SAVE the estimates into a file called *KRIG*. The options to the KRIG statement specify the minimum number of data points to be included in an estimate (NDMIN), the maximum (NDMAX), the minimum and maximum radii for searching for neighboring sites to include in an estimate (RADMIN and RADMAX), and finally the type of graph (a CONTOUR plot).

```
GRID /  NX=10, XMIN=-125, XMAX=-65,
        NY=10, YMIN=30, YMAX=50
SAVE KRIG
KRIG / NDMIN=2, NDMAX=20,
       RADMAX=5, RADMIN=5,
       GRAPH=CONTOUR
```

Here is the output:

```
Ordinary Kriging
  Search radius1: 5.000000
  Search radius2: 5.000000
  Search angle 1: 0.000000
  Search angle 2: 0.000000

Number of blocks used in estimation: 92

Average estimated value: 0.882166
Variance of estimated values: 0.023829
```

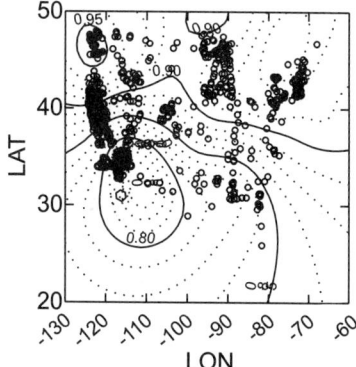

Our model shows the lowest soil carbon concentrations in the southwest and the highest in the north, particularly the northwest.

We can use our saved data to overlay these estimates on a map of the U.S. I have used a stereographic projection and set the axis limits to make the two graphs correspond.

```
BEGIN
USE USSTATES
MAP / PROJ=STEREO,AX=4,SC=2,YMIN=20,YMAX=50
USE KRIG
PLOT ESTIMATE*GRID(2)*GRID(1)/PROJ=STEREO,CONTOUR,
                    YMIN=20,YMAX=50,SMOO=INVS,
                    AX=0,SC=0,SIZE=0,ZTICK=20
END
```

Chapter 12

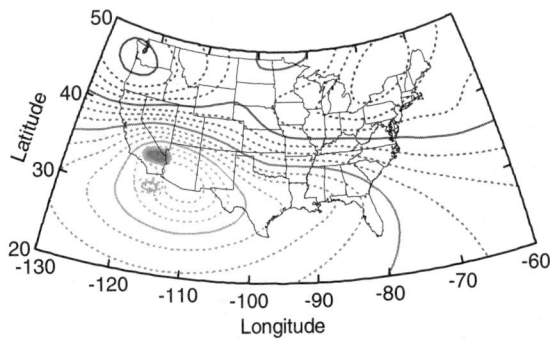

A final note: We have fit a surface to data distributed on the continental U.S. This represents a relatively small portion of the global sphere, so I have assumed the data to lie on a plane. The map projection makes clear that there is some distortion to be expected when we ignore the spherical nature of the coordinates, however. Cressie (1991) discusses spherical kriging methods, but they are not available in SYSTAT. Smaller areas, such as state, province, or county data, should be little cause for concern.

Example 2
Simulation

We now compute a single realization based on the model we fit in the kriging example.

```
USE soil
LET CARBON = L10(CARBON)
SPATIAL
    MODEL CARBON = LON LAT / SILL=.05,NUGGET=.05,AHMAX=10,
                             AHMIN=10
    SIMULATE / GRAPH=CONTOUR
```

The resulting output is:

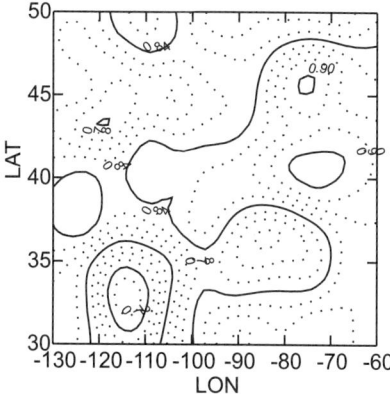

The results follow the same pattern found in the kriging. Higher carbon levels occur in the northeast and northwest. The time to compute a single simulation is greatly affected by the number of grid nodes specified in the GRID command. Grids larger that 10 cuts per variate, particularly for larger data sets, can increase the memory and time requirements substantially.

Example 3
Point Statistics

The data for this example are from Kooijman (1979), reprinted in Upton and Fingleton (1990). They consist of the locations of beadlet anemones (Actinia equina) on the surface of a boulder at Quiberon Island, off the Brittany coast, in May, 1976. I have added bordering histograms to the scatterplot shown in Figure 1.26 of Upton and Fingleton. The size of the points is proportional to the measured diameter of the anemones (D).

```
USE KOOIJMAN
PLOT Y*X / HEIGHT=2IN, WIDTH=3IN, SIZE=D, BORDER=HIST
```

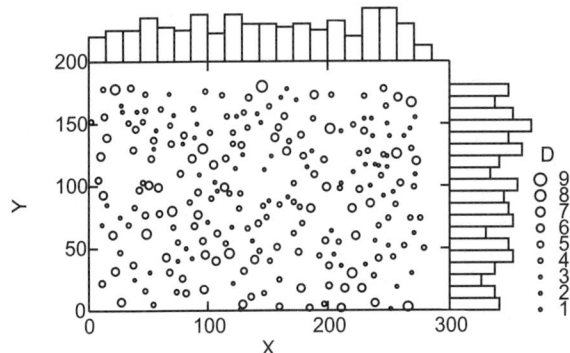

The bordered histograms reveal that the distribution of the anemones is fairly uniform in both marginal directions.

We can get an elevated view of the distribution by computing a 3-D histogram of the anemone locations. A 3-D density kernel provides a smooth estimate of the density. It is available in the SYSTAT graphing module:

```
DEN .*Y*X / HEIGHT=2IN, WIDTH=3IN, ALT=2IN, AXES=CORNER,
            ZGRID
DEN .*Y*X / KERNEL, HEIGHT=2IN, WIDTH=3IN, AXES=0,
            SCALES=0
```

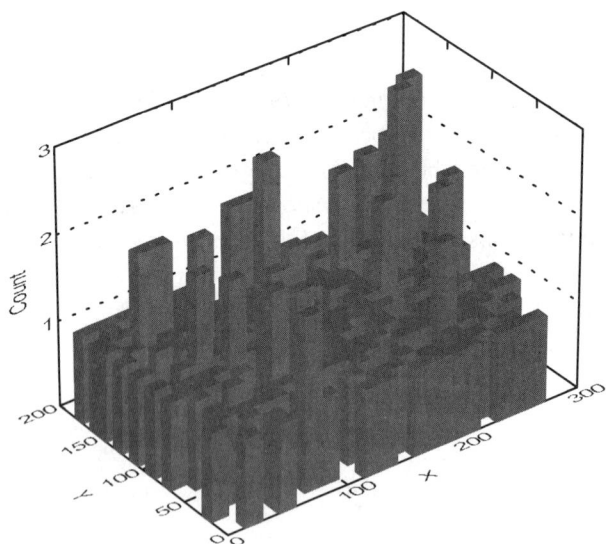

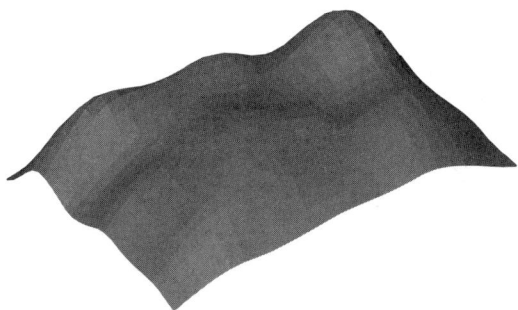

With a few exceptions, the intensity of the distribution appears to be fairly uniformly distributed over the sampled area

Now we proceed to examine the measures of spatial variation. The first graph shows the Voronoi tessellation of this configuration. The second, the minimum spanning tree, highlights the nearest-neighbor distances. The final graph, the convex hull, highlights the outermost bordering points:

```
PLOT Y*X / VORONOI, HEIGHT=2IN, WIDTH=3IN
PLOT Y*X / SPAN, HEIGHT=2IN, WIDTH=3IN
PLOT Y*X / HULL, HEIGHT=2IN, WIDTH=3IN
```

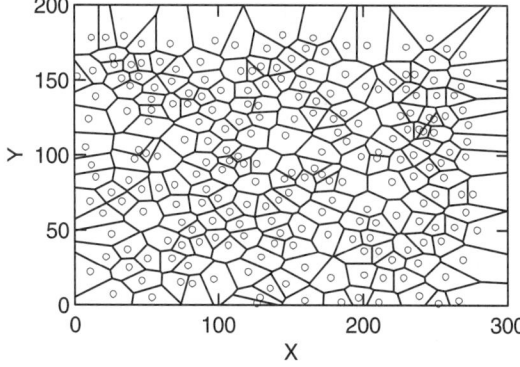

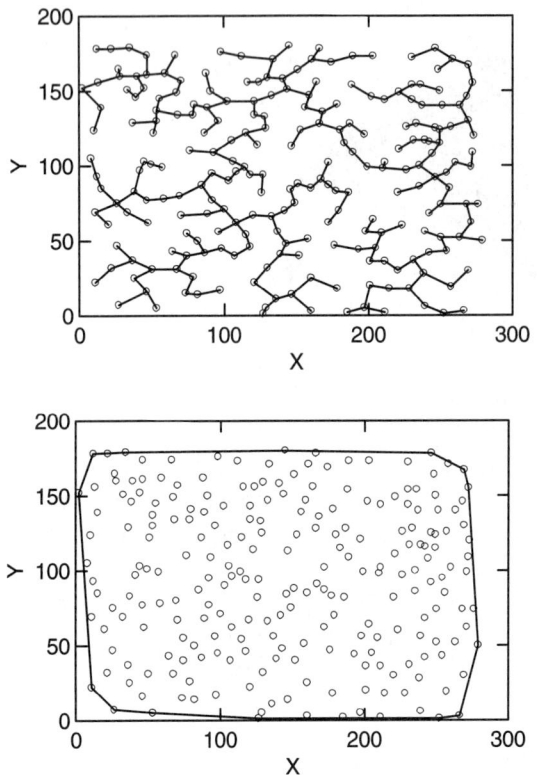

Now we proceed to compute the various point statistics:

```
SPATIAL
   SAVE POINTS
   POINT X Y
```

Here is the histogram of the nearest-neighbor distances:

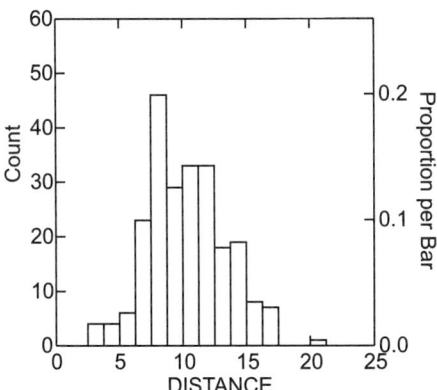

We can do a probability plot of these distances by merging the point measures with the original data:

```
MERGE KOOIJMAN POINTS
PPLOT DISTANCE
```

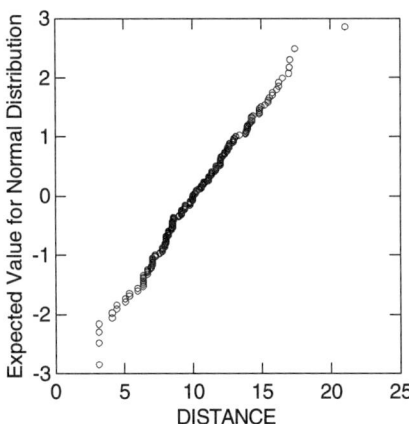

They appear to be quite normally distributed. Now we examine the relation of Kooijman's measurement of the diameter of the anemones to the other spatial measures. We also construct a new variable called *CROWDING* by taking the inverse of *VOLUME*. The D variable is Kooijman's anemone diameter. It is correlated with distance, as Upton and Fingleton point out, but even more strongly related to the inverse Voronoi area of the anemones. This relationship holds even after deleting the four outlying values of *CROWDING*.

```
CORR
LET CROWDING = 1/VOLUME
PEARSON D..CROWDING
```

The output follows:

```
Means
                  D        DISTANCE        VOLUME         FACETS        CROWDING
              4.263           7.176       954.669          5.829           0.005

Pearson correlation matrix
                  D        DISTANCE        VOLUME         FACETS        CROWDING
D             1.000
DISTANCE      0.249           1.000
VOLUME        0.092           0.144         1.000
FACETS        0.085           0.285         0.082          1.000
CROWDING     -0.291          -0.680        -0.342         -0.237           1.000

Number of observations: 217
```

Here is the SPLOM of these measures output by the CORR procedure:

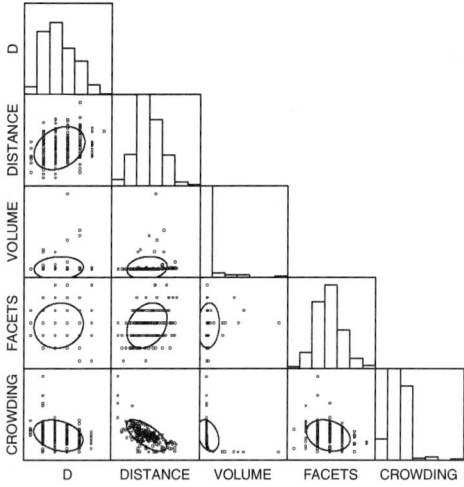

Example 4
Unusual Distances

The transformation and programming capabilities of SYSTAT can be used to compute statistics needed for other spatial analyses. The following example computes Euclidean and city-block distances for the crab data and plots them against each other. The distances are computed from a central point (*px*, *py*) in the field. The city-block distances have particular significance for fiddler crabs in Truro because the encroachment of recent residential and commercial development may force the crabs to follow a rectangular traffic grid to go about their business. The input is:

```
USE CRABS
LET PY=40
LET PX=40
LET EUCL=SQR((Y-PY)^2+(X-PX)^2)
LET CITY=ABS(Y-PY)+ABS(X-PX)
PLOT EUCL*CITY / BORDER=HIST,XMIN=0,XMAX=70,YMIN=0,YMAX=70
```

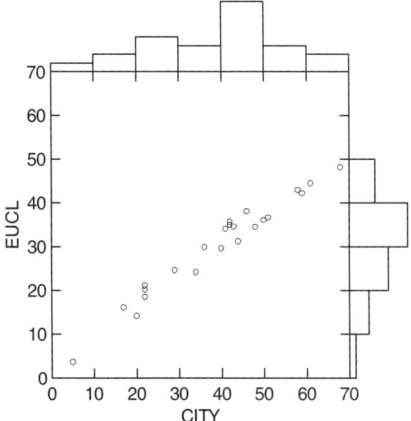

Several other useful distance statistics can be calculated directly from coordinate information. Distance between two points on the circumference of a circle given angle coordinates in degrees is:

```
LET CDIST = 2*3.14159*RADIUS*ABS(ANG1-ANG2)/360.
```

The great-circle global distance in statute miles between two points is:

```
REM DEGRAD = RADIANS PER DEGREE
REM AY = NORTH LATITUDE OF POINT A
REM AX = WEST LONGITUDE OF POINT A
REM BY = NORTH LATITUDE OF POINT B
REM BX = WEST LONGITUDE OF POINT B
REM MR = STATUTE MILES PER RADIAN
REM THIS EXAMPLE SETS THE REFERENCE POINT (AX,AY) NEAR CHICAGO

LET DEGRAD=2*3.1415926/360
LET MR=69.09332414/DEGRAD
LET AY=45*DEGRAD
LET AX=-90*DEGRAD
LET BY=LABLAT*DEGRAD
LET BX=LABLON*DEGRAD
LET GCDIST = MR * ACS(SIN(AY)*SIN(BY) ,
            + COS(AY)*COS(BY)*COS(AX-BX))
```

Computation

All computations are in double precision.

Missing Data

Cases with missing data are deleted from all analyses.

Algorithms

SPATIAL uses kriging, simulation, and variogram algorithms documented in Deutsch and Journel (1998). Point statistics are computed by a Voronoi tessellation algorithm. SYSTAT applies the inverse distance smoother to the estimated grid values for kriging and simulation when producing Quick Graphs (see the description of this algorithm in *SYSTAT Graphics*). For sparser grids, this can lead to a high degree of interpolation of the estimated values. To view the actual estimates, save the results into a file and plot them separately without a smoother. You can also specify a large number of grid points (more than 40) to minimize the effects of the inverse smoother.

References

Cressie, N. A. C. (1990). The origins of kriging. *Mathematical Geology*, 22, 239–252.

Cressie, N. A. C. (1991). *Statistics for spatial data*. New York: John Wiley & Sons, Inc.

Deutsch, C. V. and Journel, A. G. (1998). *GSLIB: Geostatistical software library and user's guide* (2nd ed.). New York: Oxford University Press.

Haining, R. (1990). *Spatial data analysis in the social and environmental sciences*. Cambridge: Cambridge University Press.

Journel, A. G. and Huijbregts, C. J. (1978). *Mining geostatistics*. New York: Academic Press.

Kooijman, S. A. L. M. (1979). The description of point patterns. In R. M. Cormack and J. K. Ord (eds.), *Spatial and Temporal Analysis in Ecology*. Fairland, Md.: International Co-operative Publishing House, pp. 305–332.

Krige, D. G. (1966). Two-dimensional weighted average trend surfaces for ore evaluation. In *Proceedings of the Symposium on Mathematical Statistics and Computer Applications in Ore Valuation*. Johannesburg, 13–38.

Okabe, A., Boots, B., and Sugihara, K. (1992). *Spatial tessellations: Concepts and applications of voronoi diagrams*. New York: John Wiley & Sons, Inc.

Pannatier, Y. (1996). *VARIOWIN: Software for spatial data analysis in 2D*. New York: Springer-Verlag.

Ripley, B. D. (1981). *Spatial statistics*. New York: John Wiley & Sons, Inc.

Upton, G. J. G. and Fingleton, B. (1990). *Spatial data analysis by example* (2 vols.). New York: John Wiley & Sons, Inc.

Wilkinson, L. (1998). *The grammar of graphics*. Unpublished manuscript.

Chapter 13

Survival Analysis

Dan Steinberg, Dale Preston, Doug Clarkson, and Phillip Colla

SURVIVAL can be used to explore grouped, right-censored, and interval-censored survival data and to estimate nonparametric, partially parametric, and fully parametric models by maximum likelihood. The SURVIVAL module's ability to handle disjoint and overlapping interval-censored data and combinations of interval censoring, right censoring, and exact failure times is a major enhancement over other programs.

The facilities provided in SURVIVAL include the Kaplan-Meier estimator, Turnbull's generalization of the Kaplan-Meier estimator for interval-censored data, plots of failure and censoring times, quantile plots for standardized reference distributions, log-rank tests, the proportional hazards (Cox) regression, and the Weibull, log-normal, logistic, and exponential regression models. All models can be estimated with or without covariates, either directly or by stepwise regression procedures. The Kaplan-Meier estimator, quantile plots, and Cox regression all permit stratification. The survivor function, hazard function, reliabilities, and quantiles can be generated from parametric models for specific covariate values, and the baseline hazards can be derived from the Cox and stratified Cox models.

The results of most analytic techniques can be saved into SYSTAT files for further manipulation and analysis with other SYSTAT modules.

Statistical Background

SURVIVAL contains a collection of tools for the analysis of survival or reliability data. Typically, the dependent variable is a duration, such as the length of time it takes a woman to conceive after cessation of birth control pills, the survival times of cancer patients on experimental drugs, or the time a motor runs before it fails. The methods have been used to analyze a broad range of topics including unemployment durations, stability of marriages, people's willingness to pay for public goods, and the lengths of pieces of yarn. It could conceivably be used for the modeling of any strictly positive quantity. These topics are also studied under other names—reliability, duration, waiting time, failure time, event history, and transition data analysis are each titles under which survival topics have been discussed. (References are provided below.)

The distinguishing mark of survival analysis, besides the special parametric models typically used, is that the dependent variable can be censored. SURVIVAL allows for two types of such incomplete data: right-censored and interval-censored data. When a case is right-censored, the dependent variable is known to be greater than a specified number, but its true value is not known. When data are subject to interval censoring, failure times may be known only to have occurred within some specified time interval. Left censoring can be handled by SURVIVAL when it coincides with interval censoring with a zero lower bound.

Interval censoring naturally arises in data collected by periodic inspection (Nelson, 1978). For example, a utility company might check gas meters at three-month intervals. A study of the time between meter failures would be conducted on interval-censored data because the exact failure times would never be known. Meters that had failed would only be known to have failed within some three-month interval, and meters that had not failed would be censored.

In general, censoring can occur because a study is ended after a predetermined time period, after a fixed number of failures has occurred, because of periodic inspection, because cases are subject to competing risks (Cox and Oakes, 1984), or for other reasons. A fairly extensive discussion can be found in Lawless (1982). For the methods of this program to be applicable, the censoring scheme should have nothing to do with the future survival of the case. That is, the censoring process cannot be informative. Conditional on having survived to some time t, cases that are censored at that time should be representative of all cases with the same explanatory variables surviving to time t. If the fact that a case is censored provides information about its expected lifetime that distinguishes it from other cases that have not been censored, the assumptions underlying the models estimable with SURVIVAL are violated. For example, censoring will not be independent of future survival if an investigator removes all persons with good or bad prognoses; results will also be subject to severe bias if patients remove themselves from a study when they feel they are making little progress. (See Cox and Oakes, 1984, or Lagakos, 1979, for further discussion.) For the remainder of this chapter, we assume that the censoring scheme, whatever it may be, is not informative; you should check the conditions under which your data were gathered to ensure that this condition is met prior to analysis.

Graphics

We're going to reproduce (approximately) Figures 2.1 and 2.2 in Parmar and Machin (1995) to give you an idea of how survival measurements differ from other types of data. This should also give you some ideas about using SYSTAT's graphics to produce survival graphs for publication. The first figure shows patients entering a prospective clinical study at different dates, with known survival times indicated by a solid black symbol and censored times by a pale symbol. The input file looks like this:

```
BASIC
INPUT ENTRY$,DAYS_IN,DAYS_OUT,CENSOR,SURVIVAL
RUN
  01/01/91        0      910    0      910
  01/01/91        0      752    1      752
  03/26/91       86     1092    0     1006
  04/26/91      116      452    1      336
  06/23/91      175     1098    1      923
  07/09/91      190      308    1      118
  07/22/91      203      817    0      614
  08/02/91      214      763    1      549
  09/01/91      244     1098    1      854
  10/07/91      280      432    0      152
  12/14/91      348      645    1      297
  12/26/91      360     1001    0      641
~
SAVE PMA
LET PATIENT=CASE
LET ENTER=DOC(ENTRY$,'MM/DD/YY')
LET EXIT=ENTER + DAYS_OUT - DAYS_IN - 2
RUN
EXIT
USE PMA
CATEGORY PATIENT,CENSOR
BEGIN
PLOT PATIENT*EXIT / XFORM='MMM. YYYY',
            XTICK=2,XPIP=12,
            XMIN=33238,XMAX=34333,
            INDENT,SIZE=1.5,
            YREVERSE,VECTOR=ENTER,PATIENT,
            HEIGHT=3IN,WIDTH=4IN,SC=2,AX=C,
            XLAB=' ',YLAB='PATIENT',
            FILL=CENSOR,LEGEND=NONE
DRAW LINE / FROM=1.4IN,0IN,TO=1.4IN,3IN
DRAW LINE / FROM=3.81IN,0IN,TO=3.8IN,3IN
WRITE 'Patient accrual period' /LOC=.7IN,3.3IN
                      HEI=5PT,WID=5PT,
                      CENTER
WRITE 'Observation only period'/LOC=2.6IN,3.3IN,
                      HEI=5PT,WID=5PT,
                      CENTER
END
```

We've included the raw data so that you can see something about entering and coding time. First of all, if your data source does not have day-of-the-century values (which most spreadsheets use for their time variable), it is easier to import the data as ASCII dates. Don't worry about the year 2000. SYSTAT's dates are good for several more centuries.

Parmar and Machin use British notation in their Table 2.1 for the dates (for example, 26.12.91 instead of 12/26/91). If you want to enter data that way, change the day-of-century conversion in the program from

```
LET ENTER=DOC(ENTRY$,'MM/DD/YY')
```

to

```
LET ENTER=DOC(ENTRY$,'DD.MM.YY')
```

Notice how the separator symbol is understood by SYSTAT because you put it in the format string. Any character other than Y, M, D, H, M, or S will do as well. By converting dates to day-of-the-century form, we can now do date arithmetic, calculating the exit times for our graph. We then exit BASIC and plot our first graph. Notice, also, how powerful the formatting facility for dates is once we code time as day-of-the-century. We can request the output format for any axis with a simple format string. SYSTAT takes care of choosing round tick-mark values (allowing for leap years and different-length months). Again, if you want another date format, simply change it. For example,

```
XFORM='DD MMM, YYYY'
```

Most of the commands and options are needed to duplicate Parmar and Machin's format. The main idea, however, is that we are seeking a graph that shows how entry and exit times from a study fit on a common time line. Notice, incidentally, that we treat *PATIENT* as a categorical variable, so that each patient is given a tick mark, instead of treating the patient ID's as numbers on a continuous scale. Following is the result:

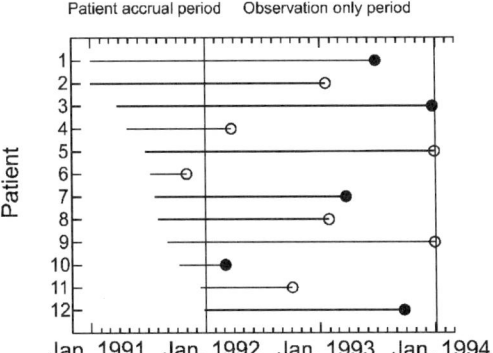

The second graph changes the time line from calendar time to survival time. Following is the input:

```
USE PMA
CATEGORY PATIENT
ORDER PATIENT/SORT=6,10,11,4,8,7,12,2,9,1,5,3
LET ZERO=0
LET SURVIVAL=SURVIVAL/30
PLOT PATIENT*SURVIVAL / ,
              INDENT,SIZE=1.5,YREVERSE,
              HEIGHT=3IN,WIDTH=4IN,SC=2,AX=2,
              XMIN=0,XMAX=36,XTICK=6,XPIP=6,
              VECTOR=ZERO,PATIENT,FILL=CENSOR,
              LEGEND=NONE,
              XLAB='Survival time (months)',
              YLAB='Patient'
```

This time, Parmar and Machin order the patients according to survival time, so we use the ORDER command to sort the indices. Since *PATIENT* is categorical, the tick marks will be labeled in that order. We create a *ZERO* value so that we can draw the lines for the dot plot starting at zero survival time.

We used a simple recoding of SURVIVAL to get months:

```
LET SURVIVAL=SURVIVAL/30
```

If we were concerned about accuracy, we could do the time arithmetic exactly with SYSTAT's date functions. (See *SYSTAT: Data* for more information.) The difference between 30 and 31 days could not be detected in the range of this graph, however.

Following is the result:

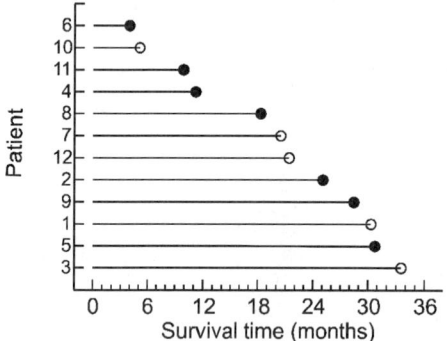

Parametric Modeling

Parametric modeling in SURVIVAL involves the fitting of a fully specified probability model (up to a finite number of unknown parameters) by the method of maximum likelihood. Because the *a priori* commitment to a specific functional form can result in rather poor fits, it is important to explore the fitted model, to examine generalized residuals, and to compare the fitted survivor function to nonparametric and partially parametric models.

The parametric models available in SURVIVAL are based on the exponential, Weibull, log-normal, and log-logistic distributions. Each model can be fit with or without covariates. The exponential and Weibull distributions have two options to allow for the alternative parameterizations discussed below. The Weibull, log-normal, and log-logistic distributions are each specified as two-parameter distributions generalized to include the effects of covariates on survival times. Each is an accelerated life model in which the logarithm of survival time is a linear function of the covariates.

Accelerated Failure Time Distributions

A random variable has an accelerated failure time distribution if the natural logarithm of time can be modeled as

$$\ln(t) = \mu + \beta'z + \sigma w$$

where μ, β, and σ are parameters to be estimated, $\mathbf{z}$ is a vector of covariates, and w is a random variable with the known distribution function $F(w)$. Writing

$$w(t) = \ln(t) - \mu - \beta'\mathbf{z}/\sigma$$

the survivor function of t is given by

$$s(t) = 1 - F(w(t))$$

The distributions available for accelerated life models in SURVIVAL use the following definitions of $F(w)$:

Distribution Function $F(w)$	Model
extreme value: 1-exp[-exp(w)]	EWB, EEXP
logistic: $1/[1 + \exp(-w)]$	LGST
standard normal: $\Phi(w)$	LNOR

The Weibull and exponential models can also be estimated in the more familiar proportional hazards parameterization with the WB and EXP commands. The survivor function is now written as

$$s(t) = \exp - (\pi t)^\delta$$

where $\pi = \alpha \exp(\mathbf{z}'\beta)$ is proportional to the mean of the distribution and δ is the shape parameter. The exponential distribution is a special case of the Weibull distribution with the shape parameter constrained to 1. In terms of the accelerated life formulation, μ equals $\ln(\alpha)$ and σ equals $1/\delta$. The Weibull distribution is the only distribution that can be equivalently parameterized as either a proportional hazards or an accelerated life model.

Some authors prefer to parameterize the Weibull model in terms of $1/\alpha$ rather than α (for example, Cox and Oakes, 1984). To facilitate comparisons with different texts, the SURVIVAL output includes several transformations of this parameter. Regardless of the parameterization, the log-likelihood, coefficient estimates, and standard errors for the covariates will be the same. Parameter estimates and standard errors for the location and shape parameters will differ, however. Choose whatever parameterization is most convenient.

In the output, the fundamental scale (shape) and location parameters are labeled _B(1)_ and _B(2)_, respectively. The table below lists their meaning for each of the possible models:

Model	Hazard Shape	_B(1)_	_B(2)_
WB	increasing for $\delta > 1$ decreasing for $\delta < 1$	shape δ	location α proportional to mean time
EWB	increasing for $\sigma > 1$ decreasing for $\sigma < 1$	shape σ	location μ proportional to log mean time
EXP	constant	shape $\delta = 1$	location α equal to mean time if no covariates
EEXP	constant	shape $\sigma = 1$	location μ equal to log mean time if no covariates
LNOR	non-monotonic	scale σ	location μ
LGST	decreasing for $\sigma > 1$ single-peaked for $\sigma < 1$	scale σ	location μ

Choosing a Parametric Form

Quantile plots of the unadjusted data can be useful in assessing the suitability of a functional form when we are interested in the unconditional distribution of the failure times. When the unconditional distribution may differ substantially from the conditional distribution (conditioning on covariates), the PPLOT output may not be helpful in deciding on a model with covariates. You can also examine the quantile Quick Graph plot produced automatically after fitting parametric models.

Selection of a parametric form can also be guided by thinking about the shape of the hazard. This is the approach taken by Barlow and Proschan (1965) and Allison (1984), among others. Since the probability models available in SURVIVAL have sharply different implications for the hazard, any strong prior notions about the hazard time profile can rule out certain models.

The table above lists hazard shapes that are possible for each of the failure models. For example, the exponential model implies a hazard that is constant over time. This means that given a set of covariates, the conditional probability of failure does not depend on the length of the survival time and exhibits duration independence. In contrast, the Weibull model will imply either an increasing or a decreasing hazard, depending on the value of the shape parameter. For example, for much mechanical equipment, the conditional probability of failure is an increasing function of its age (survival time), and a Weibull model is often appropriate.

The remaining two models are a little more complex. The log-normal model yields a nonmonotonic hazard rising to a peak and then declining. If the scale parameter is large, however, the hazard will look like an increasing function over any range of outcomes with appreciable probability. Finally, the log-logistic hazard will be decreasing if the scale parameter is greater than 1; otherwise, it will be nonmonotonic with a single maximum (Cox and Oakes, 1984).

It is important to be aware of the potential effect of unobserved heterogeneity on the estimated hazard function. In general, when cases differ along unmeasured dimensions that are relevant to the hazard, the estimated hazard will tend to exhibit a more negative duration dependence than would be obtained with a correctly specified model. For example, Cox and Oakes (1984) point out that if every case has an exponential hazard with a mean parameter distributed as a gamma random variable, the population hazard (a compound exponential) will follow a Pareto distribution with negative duration dependence. This topic has been discussed briefly in the biostatistical literature (Vaupel et al., 1979; Hougaard, 1984; Manton et al., 1986) and has received considerable attention in the econometric literature. See, for example, the *Journal of Econometrics*, Vol. 28 (1985), which is devoted to duration analysis.

Survival Analysis in SYSTAT

Survival Analysis Main Dialog Box

Survival analyses are computed by specifying a model and estimating it. This is true for both parametric models, such as the Weibull, and for nonparametric models, such as Cox regression and Kaplan-Meier curves. For all models, including the Kaplan-Meier and others without covariates, specifying a model may simply be a way of naming the survival, censoring, or strata variables. Post hoc analyses, such as plotting survivor functions, computing life tables from a model, and requesting quantiles, are also available.

To open the Survival dialog box, from the menus choose:
Statistics
  Survival...

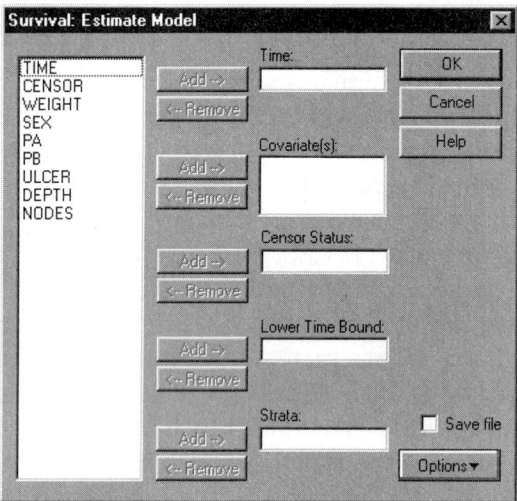

Time. Specify the survival variable. The survival variable is usually a measurement of time, such as the survival duration of a cancer patient or the length of a spell of unemployment, but it could be a weight, a trip length, or any other variable for which negative or zero values would be meaningless.

Covariate(s). Specify covariate variables. Covariates are quantitative predictor variables.

Censor Status. Specify a censoring indicator variable. The censoring variable is usually an indicator variable coded as 1 for durations that are complete (uncensored) and 0 for durations that are incomplete (censored). The censoring variable is sometimes called an event variable because it indicates whether or not an event, such as a birth or death, was observed. Survival analysis allows for but does not require censored data; if your observations are all current, each case would have the censoring variable equal to 1.

Lower Time Bound. Specify a lower-bound variable, which is used for interval censoring. This variable need not appear in the data set if the data are subject to right censoring and exact failures alone.

The coding of the survival variable, the censoring variable, and the lower-bound variable depends on whether the data are interval-censored or not. Use the following coding scheme:

Survival Analysis

Case status	Survival variable	Censoring variable	Lower-bound variable
Exact failure	failure time	1	
Right censored	censoring time	0	
Interval censored	upper bound	−1	lower bound

If the lower-bound variable is specified, it should be coded according to the above scheme. Certain internal data changes are made to the lower bound and censoring variables as the data are entered. For exact failures, the lower bound, if it is included, is set equal to the survival variable. For right-censored cases, the lower bound, if it is being input, is set to −1. For interval-censored cases, the lower-bound value should be non-negative and less than or equal to the survival variable value. If SURVIVAL finds an interval-censored observation with the lower bound equal to the survival time, the censoring is changed to an exact failure (the censoring variable is set to 1). These changes are made solely for the convenience of SURVIVAL, and you will see them only if you save the data during the input process.

In addition, you can specify a stratification (blocking) variable.

Estimation Options

Survival estimation options are available when you click Options.

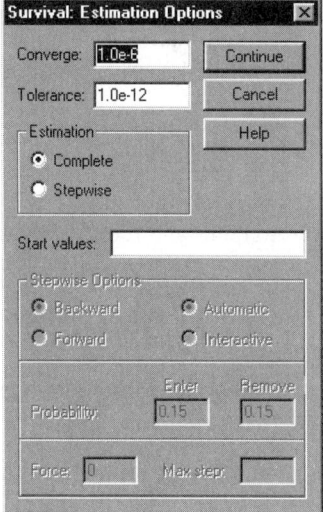

Estimation options allows you to specify convergence, a tolerance level, select complete or stepwise estimation, and specify entry and removal criteria.

Converge. Sets the convergence criterion. This is the largest relative change in any coordinate before iterations terminate.

Tolerance. Prevents the entry of a variable that is highly correlated with the independent variables already included in the model. Enter a value between 0 and 1. Typical values are 0.01 or 0.001. The higher the value (closer to 1), the lower the correlation required to exclude a variable.

Estimation. Controls the method used to enter and remove variables from the equation. For complete estimation, in which all independent variables are entered in a single step, you can enter start values. Start values for the computation routines are calculated automatically whenever a model is specified. We suggest that you use these start values unless you have compelling reasons to provide your own or wish to conduct score tests with the Cox model.

For stepwise estimation, in which variables are entered or removed from the model one at a time, the following alternatives are available for stepwise entry and removal:

- **Backward.** Begins with all candidate variables in the model. At each step, SYSTAT removes the variable with the largest Remove value.
- **Forward.** Begins with no variables in the model, and at each step SYSTAT adds the variable with the smallest Enter value.
- **Automatic.** For Backward, at each step SYSTAT automatically removes a variable from your model. For Forward, SYSTAT automatically adds a variable to the model at each step.
- **Interactive.** At each step in the model building process, you select the variable to enter or remove from the model.

Probability. You can also control the criteria used to enter and remove variables from the model:

- **Enter.** Enters a variable into the model if its alpha value is less than the specified value. Enter a value between 0 and 1 (for example, 0.025).
- **Remove.** Removes a variable from the model if its alpha value is greater than the specified value. Enter a value between 0 and 1 (for example, 0.025).

Force. Forces the first *n* variables listed in your model to remain in the equation.

Max Step. You can define the maximum number of steps that the stepwise estimation should perform.

Tables and Graphs

You can also select from a variety of output tables and regression models when you click Options.

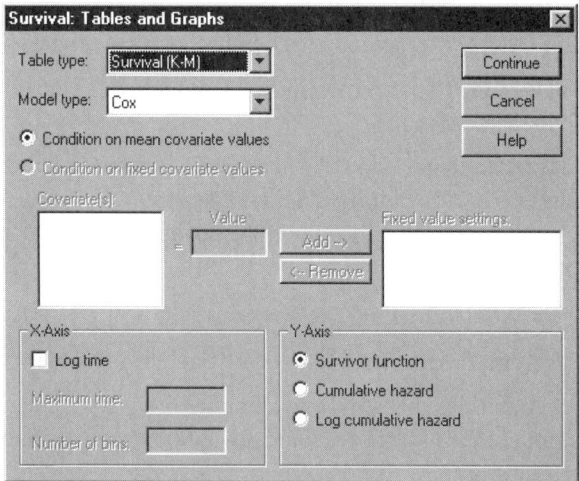

Table Type. From the drop-down list, select the type of table you would like displayed.

- **Survival K-M.** Survival K-M is a simple nonparametric estimator that produces a life table and a plot of the estimated survivor curve.
- **Actuarial Life.** Divides the time period of observations into time intervals. Within each interval, the number of failing observations is recorded.
- **Actuarial Hazard.** Requests that the hazard function be tabled instead of the standard actuarial survival curve.
- **Conditional Life.** Requests that the conditional survival be tabled instead of the standard actuarial survival curve. This table displays the probability of survival given an interval.
- **Parametric Quantiles.** Requests approximate confidence intervals for quantiles and quick graphs based on the last parametric model estimated.
- **Parametric Reliability.** Requests reliability confidence intervals and quick graphs based on the last parametric model estimated.
- **Parametric Hazard.** Requests Quick Graphs and approximate confidence intervals for values of the hazard function at specified times, based on the last parametric model estimated.

Model Type. Select the type of regression model you want to use from the drop-down list. You can choose from Cox regression, logistic model, exponential model, extreme value exponential model, Weibull model, extreme value Weibull model, and log-normal model.

Tables, quantiles, hazards, and reliabilities vary as a function of the covariates in the model (if any). SYSTAT offers two methods for dealing with covariates:

- **Condition on mean covariate.** The survivor curve by default will be evaluated with all covariates set to their means.
- **Condition on fixed covariate values.** You can specify fixed values on the covariates over which tables are produced. Highlight a covariate, enter the fixed value in the Value field, and click Add. The fixed value on the covariate will be displayed in the Fixed value settings list.

In addition, you can specify the following plot options:

- **Log time.** Expresses the x axis in units of the log of time, or log(time).
- **Maximum time.** For reliabilities, hazards, and actuarial life tables, you can specify the maximum time limit of the plot. This should always be expressed as a time even if you select a Log time axis.
- **Number of bins.** For reliabilities, hazards, and actuarial life tables, enter the desired length of the plot along the time or log time axis. If not specified, 10 bins are used.
- **Survivor function.** Plots the survivor function on the y axis.
- **Cumulative hazard.** The negative of the log of the survivor function is plotted on the y axis.
- **Log cumulative hazard.** Plots the log of the negative of the log of the survivor function (log(-log(survivor))) on the y axis.

Time Varying Covariates

To specify time varying covariates, click the Options button in the Survival dialog box.

Survival Analysis

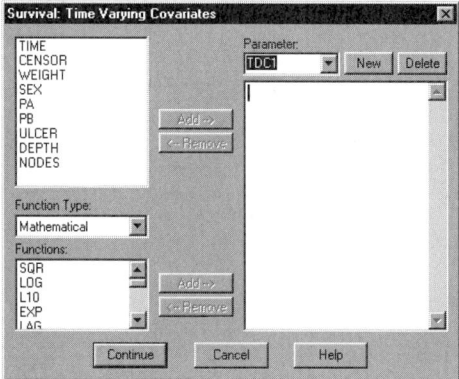

You can define set names for time-dependent covariates and create, edit, or delete time-dependent covariates.

Parameter. To modify an existing time-dependent variable, select it from the Parameter drop-down list. To set up a new time-dependent covariate, click New. Define the covariate in the large text field on the right. You can use existing variables and choose functions of different types. You may state as many functions of parameters as you want.

You must define a function for each covariate selected in this dialog box. When you click Continue, SYSTAT will check that each time-dependent covariate has a definition. If a name exists but no variables were assigned to it, the time-dependent covariate is discarded and the name will not be in the drop down list when you return to this dialog box. To delete a covariate, select it in the Parameter drop-down list and click Delete.

Using Commands

After selecting the data file with USE filename, continue with:

```
SURVIVAL
    MODEL timevar = covarlist | tdcovarlist /,
                    CENSOR=var  LOWER=var  STRATA=var
    FUNPAR tdcovar=expression
(There is one FUNPAR statement for each time-dependent covariate)
    ESTIMATE / method , START=d,d,d ... , TOLERANCE=d ,
               CONVERGE=d
```

Stepwise model fitting is accomplished with the START, STEP, and STOP commands in place of ESTIMATE:

```
START / method , BACKWARD  FORWARD  ENTER=p  REMOVE=p,
                FORCE=n , MAXSTEP=n  TOLERANCE=d  CONVERGE=d
STEP var or  +   or - or / AUTO
STOP
```

METHOD is one of:

```
COX    LGST   EXP    EEXP
WB     EWB    LNOR
```

Finally, there are several commands for producing tables and graphs following a model estimation.

```
LTAB / TLOG covar=d,covar=d   CHAZ   LCHAZ
ACT d,n / TLOG   LIFE   CONDITIONAL   HAZARD
QNTL / TLOG
RELIABILITY d,n / TLOG
HAZARD d,n / TLOG
```

Usage Considerations

Types of data. SURVIVAL uses rectangular data and distinguishes three types of data organization, depending on the type of censoring:

- Data are either exact failures or right-censored.

- Interval-censored and right-censored data intervals do not overlap, and right censoring occurs at the upper boundary of an interval--no exact failures.

- Any other data type, typically, interval-censored data with overlapping intervals, or a mixture of interval-censored and exact failure data.

SURVIVAL automatically classifies the data; the type of data will determine the kinds of analysis you can perform. The fully parametric models can be estimated for any type of data, but the Cox proportional hazards model can be fit only to the first data type, and the K-M estimator is replaced with Turnbull's (1976) generalized K-M estimator for the third data type. When checking for overlapping intervals, SURVIVAL does not consider a shared endpoint to be an overlap.

The CATEGORY command for categorizing variables works only for stratification. If you have categorical covariates, recode them with the CODE command in SYSTAT BASIC before using SURVIVAL.

Print options. PRINT=LONG adds covariance matrices of parameters to the output.

Quick Graphs. Quick Graphs produced by SURVIVAL include Kaplan-Meier curves and survival functions for parametric models.

Saving files. Almost every command in SURVIVAL allows you to save selected output to a SYSTAT data file. Any command that produces a table or a plot permits a prior SAVE command; this is especially useful if you wish to pursue another type of analysis not presently supported within SURVIVAL.

BY groups. BY group analysis is not allowed in SURVIVAL.

Bootstrapping. Bootstrapping is not available in this procedure.

Case frequencies. FREQ=<variable> increases the number of cases by the FREQ variable. It does not use extra memory.

Case weights. WEIGHT is not available in SURVIVAL.

Examples

Example 1
Life Tables: The Kaplan-Meier Estimator

The nonparametric estimator available in SURVIVAL is the Kaplan-Meier or product limit estimator (for example, Kaplan and Meier, 1958, or Lee, 1980). The input for this follows. Notice that we estimate a model based solely on time and the censoring structure and then ask for the survival table with the LTAB command. The default survival table produced by LTAB is Kaplan-Meier. The input is:

```
USE MELANOMA
SURVIVAL
MODEL TIME/CENSOR=CENSOR
ESTIMATE
LTAB
```

Chapter 13

Following is the output:

```
Variables in the SYSTAT Rectangular file are:
   TIME         CENSOR       WEIGHT       SEX          PA           PB
   ULCER        DEPTH        NODES        SEX$


  Time variable: TIME
Censor variable: CENSOR
Weight variable: 1.0
Input records:             69
Records kept for analysis:             69

                                      Weighted
  Censoring         Observations     Observations

Exact Failures                   36
Right Censored                   33


Type 1, exact failures and right censoring only.
Analyses/estimates: Kaplan-Meier, Cox and parametric models
Overall time range: [     72.000 ,     7307.000]
Failure time range: [     72.000 ,     1606.000]

Kaplan-Meier estimation
All the data will be used

          Number       Number                  K-M         Standard
          At Risk      Failing       Time    Probability    Error

          69.000       1.000       72.000      0.986        0.014
          68.000       1.000      125.000      0.971        0.020
          67.000       1.000      127.000      0.957        0.025
          66.000       1.000      133.000      0.942        0.028
          65.000       1.000      142.000      0.928        0.031
          64.000       1.000      151.000      0.913        0.034
          63.000       1.000      154.000      0.899        0.036
          62.000       1.000      176.000      0.884        0.039
          61.000       1.000      184.000      0.870        0.041
          60.000       1.000      229.000      0.855        0.042
          59.000       1.000      251.000      0.841        0.044
          58.000       1.000      256.000      0.826        0.046
          57.000       1.000      320.000      0.812        0.047
          56.000       1.000      362.000      0.797        0.048
          55.000       1.000      391.000      0.783        0.050
          54.000       1.000      414.000      0.768        0.051
          53.000       1.000      422.000      0.754        0.052
          52.000       1.000      434.000      0.739        0.053
          51.000       1.000      441.000      0.725        0.054
          49.000       1.000      465.000      0.710        0.055
          48.000       1.000      471.000      0.695        0.055
          47.000       1.000      495.000      0.680        0.056
          45.000       1.000      544.000      0.665        0.057
          44.000       1.000      584.000      0.650        0.058
          43.000       1.000      645.000      0.635        0.058
          42.000       1.000      659.000      0.620        0.059
          41.000       1.000      749.000      0.605        0.059
          39.000       1.000      788.000      0.589        0.060
          37.000       1.000      803.000      0.573        0.060
          36.000       1.000      812.000      0.557        0.061
          32.000       1.000     1020.000      0.540        0.061
          31.000       1.000     1042.000      0.523        0.062
          28.000       1.000     1151.000      0.504        0.062
          26.000       1.000     1239.000      0.484        0.063
          13.000       1.000     1579.000      0.447        0.068
          12.000       1.000     1606.000      0.410        0.072
```

```
Group size                    =      69.000
Number failing                =      36.000
Product limit likelihood      =    -173.084

Mean survival time =    1034.958

Survival Quantiles

        75.000%          422.000
        50.000%         1151.000
        41.000%         1606.000

Kaplan-Meier estimation
EXPORT successfully completed.
```

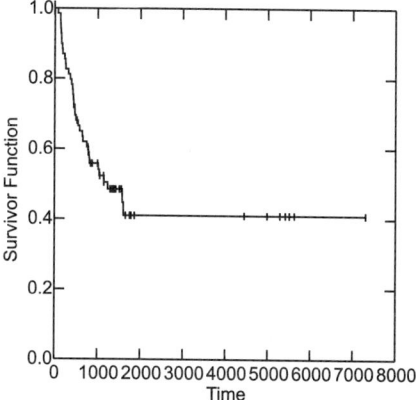

The standard error reported for the survivor function is computed using Greenwood's formula (Kalbfleisch and Prentice, 1980). The K-M estimate is a step function with jumps at each exact failure time.

By default, the plots produced by the K-M option are of the survivor function plotted against time. You can also obtain the cumulative hazard plot (time against the negative of the log of the survivor function) or log-cumulative hazard plots (log(−log(survivor))) with the CHAZ and LCHAZ options of the LTAB command.

Example 2
Actuarial Life Tables

Actuarial life tables divide the time period of observations into time intervals. Within each interval, the number of failing observations is recorded. To see an actuarial table, you must first specify and estimate a model. We already did so in the Life Tables example.

```
USE MELANOMA
SURVIVAL
MODEL TIME/CENSOR=CENSOR
ESTIMATE
ACT 2000,4
```

We use the required TIME parameter to specify the maximum time (2000) and the optional number of intervals (4) to keep the table brief. The default number of intervals is 10. Following is the output:

Lower Interval Bound	Interval Midpoint	Interval Width	Number Entering Interval	Number Failed	Number Censored
0.0	250.000	500.000	62.000	22.000	1.000
500.000	750.000	500.000	39.000	8.000	5.000
1000.000	1250.000	500.000	26.000	4.000	14.000
1500.000	1750.000	500.000	8.000	2.000	6.000

Hazard Function

You can request that the hazard function be tabled instead of the standard actuarial survival curve. Following is the input:

```
ACT 2000,4 / HAZARD
```

Following is the output:

Lower Interval Bound	Interval Midpoint	Probability Density Function	S.E. PDF	Hazard Rate	S.E. Hazard Rate
0.0	250.000	0.001	0.003	0.001	0.000
500.000	750.000	0.000	0.002	0.000	0.000
1000.000	1250.000	0.000	0.002	0.000	0.000
1500.000	1750.000	0.000	0.004	0.001	0.001

Survival Analysis

Conditional Survival

You can also request that the conditional survival be tabled instead of the standard actuarial survival curve. This table displays the probability of survival given an interval. Following is the input:

```
USE MELANOMA
SURVIVAL
MODEL TIME/CENSOR=CENSOR
ESTIMATE
ACT 2000,4 / CONDITIONAL
```

Following is the output:

Number Interval Midpoint	Conditional Exposed To Risk	Conditional Probability Of Failure	Cumulative Probability Of Survival	S.E. Probability Of Survival	Cum. Prob. Of Survival
250.000	61.500	0.358	0.642	1.000	
750.000	36.500	0.219	0.781	0.642	0.061
1250.000	19.000	0.211	0.789	0.502	0.065
1750.000	5.000	0.400	0.600	0.396	0.069

Example 3
Stratified Kaplan-Meier Estimation

Nonparametric analysis can be refined further by the use of a stratification variable. There is no fixed upper limit on the number of strata that can be used, and with moderate-sized data sets, a large number of strata are possible. In the *MELANOMA* data set, the variable *SEX* is coded as 1 for males and 0 for females, respectively. By adding the STRATA option, we will get a single plot with the two estimated survivor curves:

```
USE MELANOMA
SURVIVAL
MODEL TIME / CENSOR=CENSOR, STRATA=SEX
LABEL SEX / 1="Male",0="Female"
PRINT=LONG
ESTIMATE
LTAB
```

Following is the output:

```
Variables in the SYSTAT Rectangular file are:
  TIME       CENSOR       WEIGHT        SEX           PA           PB
  ULCER      DEPTH        NODES         SEX$


 Time variable: TIME
Censor variable: CENSOR
Weight variable: 1.0
Input records:              69
Records kept for analysis:              69
                                         Weighted
  Censoring          Observations      Observations

Exact Failures              36
Right Censored              33


Type 1, exact failures and right censoring only.
Analyses/estimates: Kaplan-Meier, Cox and parametric models
Overall time range: [     72.000 ,    7307.000]
Failure time range: [     72.000 ,    1606.000]

Stratification on SEX specified, 2 levels

Kaplan-Meier estimation
With stratification on SEX
All the data will be used


The following results are for SEX = Female.

     Number       Number                    K-M        Standard
    At Risk      Failing       Time      Probability     Error

     31.000       1.000      133.000       0.968        0.032
     30.000       1.000      184.000       0.935        0.044
     29.000       1.000      251.000       0.903        0.053
     28.000       1.000      320.000       0.871        0.060
     27.000       1.000      391.000       0.839        0.066
     26.000       1.000      414.000       0.806        0.071
     25.000       1.000      434.000       0.774        0.075
     23.000       1.000      471.000       0.741        0.079
     22.000       1.000      544.000       0.707        0.082
     20.000       1.000      788.000       0.672        0.085
     19.000       1.000      812.000       0.636        0.088
     15.000       1.000     1151.000       0.594        0.092
     13.000       1.000     1239.000       0.548        0.095
      5.000       1.000     1579.000       0.438        0.124
      4.000       1.000     1606.000       0.329        0.133

Group size                   =       31.000
Number failing               =       15.000
Product limit likelihood     =      -58.200

Mean survival time =     1142.022

Survival Quantiles

    74.000%          471.000
    55.000%         1239.000
    33.000%         1606.000
```

Survival Analysis

The following results are for SEX = Male.

Number At Risk	Number Failing	Time	K-M Probability	Standard Error
38.000	1.000	72.000	0.974	0.026
37.000	1.000	125.000	0.947	0.036
36.000	1.000	127.000	0.921	0.044
35.000	1.000	142.000	0.895	0.050
34.000	1.000	151.000	0.868	0.055
33.000	1.000	154.000	0.842	0.059
32.000	1.000	176.000	0.816	0.063
31.000	1.000	229.000	0.789	0.066
30.000	1.000	256.000	0.763	0.069
29.000	1.000	362.000	0.737	0.071
28.000	1.000	422.000	0.711	0.074
27.000	1.000	441.000	0.684	0.075
26.000	1.000	465.000	0.658	0.077
25.000	1.000	495.000	0.632	0.078
23.000	1.000	584.000	0.604	0.080
22.000	1.000	645.000	0.577	0.081
21.000	1.000	659.000	0.549	0.081
20.000	1.000	749.000	0.522	0.082
18.000	1.000	803.000	0.493	0.082
16.000	1.000	1020.000	0.462	0.083
15.000	1.000	1042.000	0.431	0.083

```
Group size                 =      38.000
Number failing             =      21.000
Product limit likelihood   =     -89.404
```

Mean survival time =   703.643

Survival Quantiles

```
    74.000%         362.000
    49.000%         803.000
    43.000%        1042.000
```

Kaplan-Meier estimation

Log-rank test, stratification on SEX strata range 1 to 2

```
                   Method: MANTEL
         Chi-Sq statistic:         0.568 with 1 df
Significance level (p value):      0.451

                   Method: BRESLOW-GEHAN
         Chi-Sq statistic:         1.589 with 1 df
Significance level (p value):      0.207

                   Method: TARONE-WARE
         Chi-Sq statistic:         1.167 with 1 df
Significance level (p value):      0.280
```
EXPORT successfully completed.

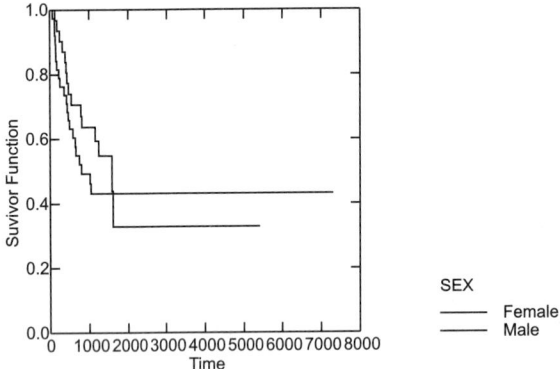

The plot can be used to see if the survivor curves are similar in shape and how far apart they lie. By computing the survivor curves in their log(-log(survivor)) transforms (with the LCHAZ option), you can check for parallelism. Parallel curves, even if the curves themselves are not linear, suggest that the stratification variable acts as a covariate in a proportional hazards model. (See Kalbfleisch and Prentice, 1980, and the Cox regression examples for further discussion of this point.)

If the SAVE command is issued just prior to the LTAB command, a log-cumulative hazard function for each stratum will be saved.

Rank Tests

This output includes three variations of the log-rank test. The first, the Mantel-Haenszel test, is what is conventionally called the log-rank test. The remaining tests are versions of Wilcoxon tests, and they offer different weighting schemes in calculating the difference between observed and expected failures at each failure time in a contingency table analysis. The simple log-rank test uses unit weights so that each failure time has equal weighting. The Breslow-Gehan version weights each failure time by the total number at risk at that time so that earlier times receive greater weight than later times. The Tarone-Ware version weights by the square root of the total number at risk, placing less emphasis on later failure times.

Discussions of log-rank tests can be found in Kalbfleisch and Prentice (1980), Lawless (1982), Miller (1981), and Cox and Oakes (1984). The tests themselves were introduced by Mantel and Haenszel (1959), Gehan (1965), Breslow (1970), and Tarone and Ware (1977). If there are no tied failures, the simple LRANK test is equivalent to a score test of the proportional hazards model containing a dummy variable for each stratum.

Example 4
Turnbull Estimation: K-M for Interval-Censored Data

The Kaplan-Meier estimator, as originally introduced in 1958, is restricted to exact failure and right-censored data. It is simply defined as:

$$S_{KM}(t\{i\}) = \prod_{j^*}\left(1 - \frac{d\{j\}}{r\{j\}}\right)$$

where j^* is the set j such that $t\{j\} < t\{i\}$, $d\{j\}$ is the number of deaths at time $t\{j\}$, and $r\{j\}$ is the number at risk (those that have not yet failed or been censored immediately before time $t\{j\}$).

For data of type 2, in which there are disjoint intervals and possibly right censoring, the K-M estimator is extended so that the above definition still applies. Now $d\{j\}$ denotes the number of failures in the jth interval and right censoring is assumed to have occurred immediately after the upper boundary of the appropriate interval.

For data of type 3, the generalization of the Kaplan-Meier estimator requires a major departure from this equation. A version of this generalized K-M estimator was first suggested by Peto (1973) and was further developed by Turnbull (1976). As type 3 data have overlapping interval-censored data and may have exact failures and right censoring as well, the first task is to determine the intervals over which the survivor function is estimated to decrease. Because this estimator is not discussed in the standard texts, we provide a brief exposition of the method here.

When data are of type 3, every case is considered to have left and right time boundaries ($L\{i\}$, $R\{i\}$) defining its interval of censoring or failure. Cases with exact failures have $L\{i\} = R\{i\}$; a right-censored observation will have $R\{i\}$ equal to infinity; and an interval-censored failure will have $L\{i\} < R\{i\}$. The Peto-Turnbull generalization begins by identifying a unique set of disjoint time intervals for which failure probabilities will be estimated. These intervals are constructed by selecting lower boundaries from the left boundaries and upper boundaries from the right boundaries, such that these new intervals do not contain any observed $L\{i\}$ or $R\{i\}$ except at the boundaries.

For example, consider the type 3 data set *TYPE3A*:

LTIME	TIME	WEIGHT	CENSOR
1.0	2.0	4	−1
1.0	2.0	5	−1
1.9	3.0	5	−1
4.0	5.1	3	−1
4.0	4.2	8	−1
5.0	6.0	10	−1
7.0	8.0	6	−1
7.0	9.0	4	−1

There are seven different observed intervals in the data, and the following four intervals are generated by the Turnbull estimator:

lower (q)	upper (p)
1.9	2.0
4.0	4.2
5.0	5.1
7.0	8.0

The lower and upper boundaries are referred to as q's and p's, respectively, by both Peto (1973) and Turnbull (1976). We will explain the determination of the first interval. Cases 1 through 3 overlap each other somewhere on the interval (1.0, 3.0) with distinct left boundaries being 1.0 and 1.9 and distinct right boundaries being 2.0 and 3.0. The interval (1.9, 2.0) is the only interval constructible out of these boundaries that does not itself contain another endpoint. For example, (1.0, 2.0) contains the left endpoint 1.9. The constructed intervals are of minimal size and involve a maximal overlap of cases spanning the interval.

A similar method is used to generate the remaining intervals. Intuitively, the goal is to determine where in the interval the probability of failure lies. Given that a failure occurs between 1.9 and 3.0, and also that a failure occurs between 1.0 and 2.0, our attempt to assign all the probability to the smallest possible interval leads to the choice of the subinterval (1.9, 2.0).

Turnbull shows that a maximum likelihood nonparametric cumulative distribution function (CDF) can assign probability only to these intervals. Further, for a given set of probability assignments, the likelihood is independent of the behavior of the CDF within the interval, meaning that the CDF may be entirely arbitrary within the interval (Wang, 1987).

The second stage of the generalized Kaplan-Meier estimator computation is to assign probability to each ($q\{i\}$, $p\{i\}$) interval, which will define the CDF that maximizes the likelihood of the data. The solution vector of probabilities s is obtained by the EM algorithm of Dempster, Laird, and Rubin (1977). Specifically, the observed frequency distribution of the data should be equal to the expected frequency, given s.

Following is the input for the analysis:

```
USE TYPE3A
SURVIVAL
MODEL TIME / CENSOR=CENSOR, LOWER=LTIME
FREQ=WEIGHT
ESTIMATE
LTAB
```

The *TYPE3A* data set yields the following output:

```
Variables in the SYSTAT Rectangular file are:
  LTIME        TIME         WEIGHT         CENSOR

   Case frequencies determined by value of variable WEIGHT.


  Time variable: TIME
Censor variable: CENSOR
Weight variable: WEIGHT
Weight variable: LTIME
Sorting was found to be required on the following special variables:
TIME
Sorting activated, input continues.

   Case frequencies determined by value of variable WEIGHT.
Input records:                  8
Records kept for analysis:               8

                                     Weighted
   Censoring         Observations   Observations

Exact Failures                 0
Right Censored                 0
Interval Censored              8

Type 3, general censoring (left censoring and/or nondistinct intervals).
Analyses/estimates: Kaplan-Meier (generalized) and parametric models
Overall time range: [      1.000 ,      9.000]
Failure time range: [      1.000 ,      9.000]

Turnbull K-M estimation
All the data will be used

Iter         L-L
   0      -60.304
   1      -59.757
   2      -59.757
```

```
        Convergence achieved in 2 iterations
     Final convergence criterion:     0.0      -59.757

                         Turnbull K-M      Density
  Lower Time   Upper Time Probability      Change

        1.900      2.000       0.689        0.311
        4.000      4.200       0.481        0.207
        5.000      5.100       0.222        0.259
        7.000      8.000       0.0          0.222
  Turnbull K-M estimation
```

The EM algorithm is frequently slow to converge, but it has the advantage of increasing the likelihood on each iteration. For a theoretical discussion of EM convergence, see Wu (1983).

Example 5
Cox Regression

Proportional hazards regression (Cox, 1972) is a hybrid model--partly nonparametric, in that it allows for an arbitrary survivor function like the Kaplan-Meier estimator, and partly parametric, in that covariates are assumed to induce proportional shifts of the arbitrary hazard function. The Kaplan-Meier (product limit) estimator is equivalent to the Cox model without covariates. In SURVIVAL, Cox models are allowed only for type 1 data. The proportional hazards model is assumed to take the form

$$h(t, z) = b(t)f(z.\beta)$$

where $b(t)$ is the nonparametric baseline hazard, and $f(z.\beta)$ is a parametric shift function of the covariate vector z and the parameter vector β. Typically, $f(z.\beta)$ is specified as $exp(z'\beta)$, where $z'\beta$ is an inner vector product, and this is the form used in SURVIVAL.

SURVIVAL reports maximum likelihood estimates for β and allows access to $h(t,z)$ and $b(t)$ via the LTAB command. Models are specified with the MODEL command and a list of covariates.

Following is an example:

```
USE MELANOMA
SURVIVAL
MODEL TIME = ULCER,DEPTH,NODES / CENSOR=CENSOR
ESTIMATE / COX
```

The input above will fit the proportional hazards model with three covariates and display:

```
Variables in the SYSTAT Rectangular file are:
   TIME        CENSOR      WEIGHT      SEX         PA          PB
   ULCER       DEPTH       NODES       SEX$

  Time variable: TIME
Censor variable: CENSOR
Weight variable: 1.0
Input records:              69
Records kept for analysis:              69
                                       Weighted
   Censoring          Observations    Observations

 Exact Failures              36
 Right Censored              33

Covariate means

ULCER     =      1.507
DEPTH     =      2.562
NODES     =      3.246

Type 1, exact failures and right censoring only.
Analyses/estimates: Kaplan-Meier, Cox and parametric models
Overall time range: [     72.000 ,      7307.000]
Failure time range: [     72.000 ,      1606.000]

Cox Proportional Hazards Estimation
Time variable: TIME
Censoring: CENSOR

Weight variable: 1.0
Lower time: Not specified

Iter  Step           L-L
  0     0         -137.527
  1     0         -136.100
  2     0         -127.887
  3     0         -127.813
  4     0         -127.813


              Results after 4 iterations
                Final convergence criterion:         0.000
                 Maximum gradient element:           0.000
             Initial score test of regression:     37.083 with 3 df
                  Significance level (p value):     0.000
                       Final log-likelihood:      -127.813
                   -2*[LL(0)-LL(4')] TEST:         19.429 with 3 df
                  Significance level (p value):     0.000


            Parameter       Estimate        S.E.      t-ratio     p-value
            ULCER            -0.776        0.376      -2.063       0.039
            DEPTH             0.094        0.050       1.885       0.059
            NODES             0.131        0.053       2.490       0.013

                                     95.0 % Confidence Intervals
            Parameter       Estimate       Lower        Upper
            ULCER            -0.776       -1.514       -0.039
            DEPTH             0.094       -0.004        0.192
            NODES             0.131        0.028        0.235
```

```
Covariance matrix

               ULCER          DEPTH          NODES
    ULCER      0.142
    DEPTH      0.006          0.002
    NODES     -0.005         -0.000          0.003


Correlation matrix

               ULCER          DEPTH          NODES
    ULCER      1.000
    DEPTH      0.293          1.000
    NODES     -0.255         -0.052          1.000
```

We are provided with a summary of the iteration log. The partial likelihood began at -137.527 when the parameter vector was all 0's and ended at -127.813.

The output also reports the score test of the hypothesis that all three coefficients are equal to their start values (in this case 0); the chi-square statistic is 37.083 with three degrees of freedom and has a p value less than 0.001. This test is analogous to the F-test reported by the SYSTAT module MGLH for a linear regression, and is simply a test of the hypothesis that the gradient of the log-likelihood function is 0 when evaluated at the start values of the coefficients.

Since the start values are 0 for the Cox model (unless specifically set otherwise by the user), the statistic yields a test of a standard null hypothesis. (Other null hypotheses could be conveniently tested by using the START and MAXIT = 1 options of the ESTIMATE command.) Asymptotically, the score test above is equal to the likelihood-ratio test defined as twice the difference between the final and initial likelihood values. In larger samples, there is typically good agreement between the two tests. In small samples, as in this case, the statistics may be quite different.

When comparing the parameter estimates of a Cox model with those of a fully parametric model such as the Weibull, it is important to note that the coefficients are expected to have opposite signs and will differ by a scale factor. If the data actually follow a Weibull model with coefficients β and shape parameter σ, then the proportional hazards parameters will be $(-\beta/\sigma)$ (Kalbfleisch and Prentice, 1980).

Example 6
Stratified Cox Regression

The proportional hazards assumption implies that groups with different values of the covariates have unchanging relative hazard functions over time. Thus, in a study of male and female survival, the ratio of male to female hazard functions would be assumed constant if sex were a covariate. If we thought the hazard function for males was increasing relative to the hazard function for females over time, we would have a violation of the proportional hazards assumption for the *SEX* variable.

To accommodate such potential assumption violations, an important generalization of the Cox model is allowed in SURVIVAL. This is the use of stratification (sometimes also referred to as *blocking*). Stratification relaxes the assumption of a single underlying baseline hazard for the entire population. Instead, it permits each stratum to have its own baseline hazard, with considerably different stratum-specific time profiles possible. Stratification stops short of estimating a separate model for each group because the coefficients for the covariates are common across all the strata. To estimate a stratified Cox model, we proceed with the following input. We have added an LTAB command to plot a cumulative hazard life table for the model.

```
USE MELANOMA
SURVIVAL
MODEL TIME = ULCER,DEPTH,NODES / ,
            CENSOR=CENSOR,STRATA=SEX
ESTIMATE / COX
LTAB / ULCER=0,DEPTH=0,NODES=0,LCHAZ
```

Following is the output:

```
Variables in the SYSTAT Rectangular file are:
 TIME         CENSOR       WEIGHT       SEX          PA           PB
 ULCER        DEPTH        NODES        SEX$

  Time variable: TIME
Censor variable: CENSOR
Weight variable: 1.0
Input records:               69
Records kept for analysis:           69

                                    Weighted
  Censoring           Observations  Observations

Exact Failures              36
Right Censored              33

Covariate means

ULCER       =     1.507
DEPTH       =     2.562
NODES       =     3.246

Type 1, exact failures and right censoring only.
Analyses/estimates: Kaplan-Meier, Cox and parametric models
Overall time range: [      72.000 ,       7307.000]
Failure time range: [      72.000 ,       1606.000]

Stratification on SEX specified, 2 levels

Cox Proportional Hazards Estimation
with stratification on SEX
Time variable: TIME
Censoring: CENSOR
```

```
Weight variable: 1.0
Lower time: Not specified

Iter  Step          L-L
  0    0        -112.564
  1    0        -108.343
  2    0        -103.570
  3    0        -103.533
  4    0        -103.533

            Results after 4 iterations
              Final convergence criterion:    0.000
              Maximum gradient element:       0.000
            Initial score test of regression: 32.533 with 3 df
              Significance level (p value):   0.000
              Final log-likelihood:          -103.533
              -2*[LL(0)-LL(4')] TEST:        18.063 with 3 df
              Significance level (p value):   0.000
 Parameter       Estimate         S.E.       t-ratio      p-value
 ULCER            -0.817         0.385       -2.123        0.034
 DEPTH             0.083         0.053        1.587        0.112
 NODES             0.131         0.057        2.289        0.022

                            95.0 % Confidence Intervals
 Parameter       Estimate       Lower         Upper
 ULCER            -0.817        -1.570        -0.063
 DEPTH             0.083        -0.020         0.186
 NODES             0.131         0.019         0.243

Covariance matrix

              ULCER          DEPTH         NODES
 ULCER        0.148
 DEPTH        0.006          0.003
 NODES       -0.006         -0.000          0.003


Correlation matrix

              ULCER          DEPTH         NODES
 ULCER        1.000
 DEPTH        0.301          1.000
 NODES       -0.287         -0.096          1.000



Life table for last Cox model
1 evaluation covariate vector
All the data will be used
```

Survival Analysis

The following results are for SEX = 0.
No tied failure times

Number At Risk	Number Failing	Time	Model Survival Probability	Model Hazard Rate
31.000	1.000	133.000	0.941	0.059
30.000	1.000	184.000	0.883	0.062
29.000	1.000	251.000	0.826	0.065
28.000	1.000	320.000	0.769	0.069
27.000	1.000	391.000	0.712	0.074
26.000	1.000	414.000	0.658	0.076
25.000	1.000	434.000	0.606	0.078
23.000	1.000	471.000	0.554	0.086
22.000	1.000	544.000	0.501	0.096
20.000	1.000	788.000	0.445	0.112
19.000	1.000	812.000	0.392	0.117
15.000	1.000	1151.000	0.337	0.142
13.000	1.000	1239.000	0.277	0.177
5.000	1.000	1579.000	0.159	0.427
4.000	1.000	1606.000	0.070	0.556

Group size   =   31.000
Number failing   =   15.000

The following results are for SEX = 1.
No tied failure times

Number At Risk	Number Failing	Time	Model Survival Probability	Model Hazard Rate
38.000	1.000	72.000	0.996	0.004
37.000	1.000	125.000	0.953	0.044
36.000	1.000	127.000	0.909	0.046
35.000	1.000	142.000	0.866	0.048
34.000	1.000	151.000	0.823	0.049
33.000	1.000	154.000	0.782	0.050
32.000	1.000	176.000	0.742	0.051
31.000	1.000	229.000	0.703	0.052
30.000	1.000	256.000	0.665	0.055
29.000	1.000	362.000	0.627	0.057
28.000	1.000	422.000	0.590	0.059
27.000	1.000	441.000	0.552	0.063
26.000	1.000	465.000	0.514	0.069
25.000	1.000	495.000	0.476	0.074
23.000	1.000	584.000	0.439	0.077
22.000	1.000	645.000	0.401	0.086
21.000	1.000	659.000	0.361	0.099
20.000	1.000	749.000	0.324	0.105
18.000	1.000	803.000	0.287	0.113
16.000	1.000	1020.000	0.250	0.129
15.000	1.000	1042.000	0.215	0.139

Group size   =   38.000
Number failing   =   21.000
  Cox estimation

```
Log-rank test, stratification on SEX strata range 1 to 2
                    Method: MANTEL
          Chi-Sq statistic:        0.568 with 1 df
Significance level (p value):      0.451
                    Method: BRESLOW-GEHAN
          Chi-Sq statistic:        1.589 with 1 df
Significance level (p value):      0.207
                    Method: TARONE-WARE
          Chi-Sq statistic:        1.167 with 1 df
Significance level (p value):      0.280
EXPORT successfully completed.
```

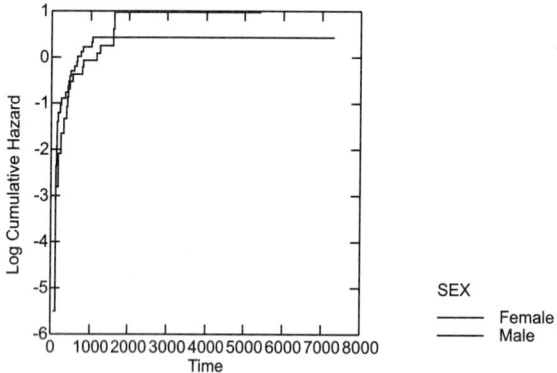

Stratification allows the survival pattern to vary markedly for cases with different values of the stratification variable while keeping the coefficients governing hazard shifts common across strata. In the above models, allowing *SEX* to be a stratification variable does not alter the coefficients by much.

Comparison of the baseline hazards across the strata allows you to decide whether the stratification variable can be modeled as a covariate. If the log(-log(survivor)) plots are roughly parallel, the stratification variable is acting to shift the baseline hazard and is correctly considered to be a covariate. If, on the other hand, the curves are quite different in shape, the variable is best left as a stratification variable and should not be included as a covariate. Only one stratification variable can be specified at any given time.

The baseline survivor function derived from the Cox model is produced with the LTAB command followed by zero settings for the covariates, as in our example. By adding the LCHAZ option, we get a baseline hazard for each of the two sexes and a log(-log) plot of the survivor functions against time. As Kalbfleisch and Prentice (1980) point out, this technique can be applied repeatedly, swapping the roles of covariates and stratification variables until you are satisfied with a particular model. With so few data points, it is difficult to draw firm conclusions, but the log(-log(survivor)) curves do look largely parallel. This suggests that *SEX* can appear as a covariate in this model, albeit not a significant one.

A more conservative analytic procedure than stratification would first split the sample into the subgroups that are suspected of having different survival behavior and then estimate separate models for each group. A likelihood-ratio test based on the summed log-likelihoods of the separate subgroup models and the likelihood for the stratified Cox model could form the basis of a test of whether stratification is sufficient to capture the group differences. If stratification is accepted, you could then proceed to investigate whether the stratification variable could enter as a covariate.

Example 7
Stepwise Regression

When there is little theoretical reason to prefer one model specification over another, stepwise methods of covariate selection can be useful, particularly if there is a large number of potential covariates. SURVIVAL allows both forward and backward stepwise covariate selection, with optional forcing of certain covariates into the model and control over the addition and deletion criteria. The stepping can be used with any model (except stratified ones) in SURVIVAL, although the forward selection (STEP/FORWARD) cannot be used with the Cox model unless at least one covariate is forced into the model. In general, we advise you to use backward elimination (STEP/BACKWARD) with all stepwise procedures because it is less likely to miss potentially valuable predictors.

The criterion for adding a variable is based on a Lagrange multiplier test (or Rao's score test) of the hypothesis that the variable has a zero coefficient when added to the current list of covariates (Peduzzi, Holford, and Hardy, 1980; Engel, 1984). The signed square root of this chi-square statistic on one degree of freedom is then treated as a normal random variable for significance computation.

For variable deletion, the *t* statistic (actually the asymptotic normal statistic) based on the ratio of the coefficient to its standard error, as derived from the inverse of the information matrix, is used. If the default ENTER and REMOVE levels are overridden, care should be taken to prevent cycling of variables into and out of the model.

Stepwise model selection in nonlinear contexts is subject to the same criticisms as stepwise linear regression. In particular, conventional hypothesis testing can be misleading, and models will look much better than they really are. For a general

Chapter 13

discussion of stepwise modeling problems, see Hocking (1983) and additional references cited for General Linear Models.

Following is an example. The input is:

```
USE MELANOMA
SURVIVAL
MODEL TIME = ULCER,DEPTH,NODES / CENSOR=CENSOR
START / COX,BACK,REMOVE=.05
STEP / AUTO
```

We have changed the "remove p" value to 0.05 from the default of 0.15 in order to force out of the model any nonsignificant effects.

The output follows:

```
Variables in the SYSTAT Rectangular file are:
  TIME          CENSOR        WEIGHT        SEX           PA            PB
  ULCER         DEPTH         NODES         SEX$

   Time variable: TIME
Censor variable: CENSOR
Weight variable: 1.0
Input records:              69
Records kept for analysis:              69

                                        Weighted
   Censoring             Observations   Observations

Exact Failures                    36
Right Censored                    33

Covariate means

ULCER       =       1.507
DEPTH       =       2.562
NODES       =       3.246

Type 1, exact failures and right censoring only.
Analyses/estimates: Kaplan-Meier, Cox and parametric models
Overall time range: [       72.000 ,      7307.000]
Failure time range: [       72.000 ,      1606.000]


Step number 0
Log-likelihood = -127.813
                     t-ratio              "p"
Further stepping impossible.
Variables included:
  ULCER             -2.063             0.039
  DEPTH              1.885             0.059
  NODES              2.490             0.013
```

```
Step number 1
Log-likelihood = -129.259
                       t-ratio              "p"
Further stepping impossible.
Variables included:
  ULCER               -2.577             0.010
  NODES                2.524             0.012
Variables excluded:
  DEPTH                1.941             0.052


Final Model Summary
       Parameter           Estimate        S.E.      t-ratio     p-value
       ULCER                 -0.926       0.359       -2.577       0.010
       NODES                  0.136       0.054        2.524       0.012

                                    95.0 % Confidence Intervals
       Parameter           Estimate        Lower        Upper
       ULCER                 -0.926       -1.631       -0.222
       NODES                  0.136        0.030        0.241

Covariance matrix
                ULCER          NODES
       ULCER    0.129
       NODES   -0.005          0.003


Correlation matrix
                ULCER          NODES
       ULCER    1.000
       NODES   -0.280          1.000
```

Example 8
The Weibull Model for Fully Parametric Analysis

This example fits an accelerated life model using the Weibull distribution. When we fit parametric models, we automatically get a plot of the log failure times against the quantiles of the chosen distribution. Following is the input:

```
USE MELANOMA
SURVIVAL
MODEL TIME = ULCER,DEPTH,NODES / CENSOR=CENSOR
ESTIMATE / EWB
QNTL
```

Following is the output:

```
Variables in the SYSTAT Rectangular file are:
   TIME         CENSOR        WEIGHT        SEX          PA           PB
   ULCER        DEPTH         NODES         SEX$


 Time variable: TIME
Censor variable: CENSOR
Weight variable: 1.0
Input records:              69
Records kept for analysis:              69

                                             Weighted
  Censoring           Observations          Observations

Exact Failures                 36
Right Censored                 33

Covariate means

ULCER        =        1.507
DEPTH        =        2.562
NODES        =        3.246

Type 1, exact failures and right censoring only.
Analyses/estimates: Kaplan-Meier, Cox and parametric models
Overall time range: [     72.000 ,    7307.000]
Failure time range: [     72.000 ,    1606.000]

Weibull distribution B(1)--shape, B(2)--location
Extreme value parameterization
Time variable: TIME
Censoring: CENSOR

Weight variable: 1.0
Lower time: Not specified

Iter   Step          L-L      Method
  0      0       -346.029     BHHH
  1      0       -333.961     BHHH
  2      0       -325.721     BHHH
  3      0       -318.696     BHHH
  4      0       -316.158     BHHH
  5      0       -312.058     N-R
  6      0       -307.552     BHHH
  7      0       -306.814     BHHH
  8      1       -306.615     N-R
  9      0       -306.510     N-R
 10      0       -306.508     N-R
 11      0       -306.508     N-R

           Results after 11 iterations
             Final convergence criterion:           0.000
              Maximum gradient element:             0.000
         Initial score test of regression:        14.738 with 5 df
             Significance level (p value):          0.012
                     Final log-likelihood:       -306.508

  Parameter              Estimate      S.E.      t-ratio     p-value
    _B(1)_  (SHAPE)         1.202     0.161        7.470       0.000
    _B(2)_  (LOCATION)      7.277     0.728        9.990       0.000
     ULCER                  0.776     0.431        1.800       0.072
     DEPTH                 -0.154     0.057       -2.675       0.007
     NODES                 -0.063     0.020       -3.162       0.002

  1.0/_B(1)_  =      0.832, EXP(_B(2)_) =     1446.887
```

Survival Analysis

```
                    Mean
Vector       Failure Time      Variance

ZERO            1595.592      3716876.399
MEAN             900.377      1183539.543

Coefficient of variation:            1.208
                                           95.0 % Confidence Intervals
      Parameter               Estimate       Lower         Upper
      _B(1)_ (SHAPE)             1.202       0.886         1.517
      _B(2)_ (LOCATION)          7.277       5.849         8.705
      ULCER                      0.776      -0.069         1.622
      DEPTH                     -0.154      -0.266        -0.041
      NODES                     -0.063      -0.102        -0.024

Covariance matrix
                     _B(1)_        _B(2)_    ULCER       DEPTH       NODES
       _B(1)_        0.026
       _B(2)_        0.003         0.531
       ULCER         0.007        -0.288     0.186
       DEPTH        -0.001        -0.021     0.007       0.003
       NODES        -0.000        -0.003     0.001       0.000       0.000


Correlation matrix
                     _B(1)_        _B(2)_    ULCER       DEPTH       NODES
       _B(1)_        1.000
       _B(2)_        0.024         1.000
       ULCER         0.108        -0.915     1.000
       DEPTH        -0.132        -0.511     0.291       1.000
       NODES        -0.077        -0.199     0.079       0.020       1.000

Group size           =    69.0000
Number failing       =    36.0000

Quantile 95.0 confidence intervals
   for last model estimated: EWB (Weibull distribution)

Covariate vector:
ULCER=1.5072, DEPTH=2.5620, NODES=3.2464

                                  Lower         Upper        Log Of        S.E. Of
                   Estimated       Time          Time       Estimated        Log
       Quantile      Time         Bound         Bound         Time          Time

        0.9990       0.6373       0.0786        5.1662       -0.4506       1.0677
        0.9950       4.4185       0.8945       21.8251        1.4858       0.8149
        0.9900      10.1932       2.5485       40.7694        2.3217       0.7073
        0.9750      30.9354      10.1861       93.9516        3.4319       0.5668
        0.9500      72.2627      29.1689      179.0230        4.2803       0.4629
        0.9000     171.6176      84.2625      349.5338        5.1453       0.3629
        0.7500     573.7870     353.0871      932.4371        6.3523       0.2477
        0.6667     866.6446     560.8401     1339.1924        6.7646       0.2220
        0.5000    1650.6876    1101.2413     2474.2710        7.4089       0.2065
        0.3333    2870.8589    1861.9127     4426.5399        7.9624       0.2209
        0.2500    3796.5470    2386.6769     6039.2630        8.2418       0.2368
        0.1000    6985.1899    3989.1996    12231.2453        8.8515       0.2858
        0.0500    9583.1488    5152.7473    17822.8689        9.1678       0.3166
        0.0250   12306.2149    6287.2253    24087.4026        9.4179       0.3427
        0.0100   16065.7917    7752.8895    33292.0604        9.6844       0.3718
        0.0050   19013.9159    8840.9176    40892.7006        9.8529       0.3907
        0.0010   26151.5267   11313.1214    60452.1357       10.1717       0.4275
```

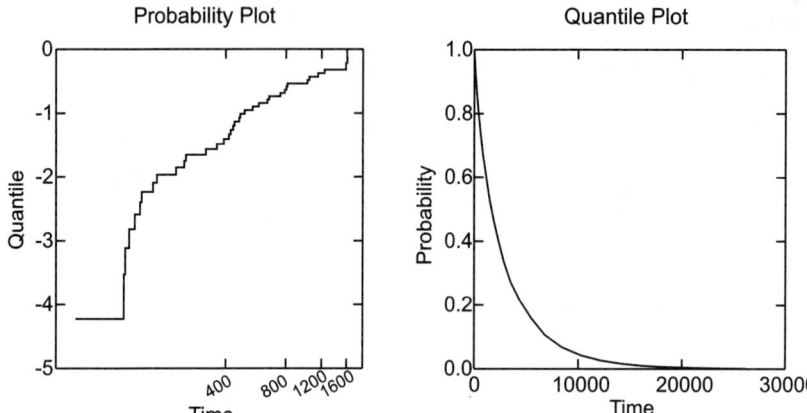

In the output, the fundamental scale (shape) and location parameters are labeled _B(1)_ and _B(2)_, respectively. Also, notice that SURVIVAL selected the BHHH method in early iterations to ensure a positive definite information matrix. It then switched to conventional Newton-Raphson.

The probability plot should follow a relatively straight line if the distribution used is appropriate. You should compute several distributions and examine this graph as a diagnostic aid. We also present the fitted distribution's quantiles in a table and Quick Graph.

Computation

All computations are in double precision.

Algorithms

Start values for the computation routines are calculated automatically whenever a model is specified. In SURVIVAL, start values are obtained from a linear regression based on an accelerated life model without covariates. The model is:

$$\ln(t) = \mu + \sigma w$$

which specifies the log failure time to be the sum of a constant and a parametric error. We rewrite this in terms of the probability of failure before time t, denoted by p, as

$$\ln(t) = \mu + \sigma F(p)^{-1}$$

where F is the CDF of the Weibull, log-normal, or log-logistic distribution. A linear regression of the observed failure times on a constant and the appropriate transform of the Kaplan-Meier estimate of p for each time yields start values for μ and σ. For the WB form of the Weibull model, we use $a = e^{\mu}$ and $\delta = 1/\sigma$.

Missing Data

SURVIVAL will analyze only cases that have valid data for every special variable and all covariates listed in the MODEL command. If any one of these variables is missing for a case, that record will not be input. Consequently, if you want to analyze data containing missing values for some of the covariates and retain the maximum possible number of cases for each analysis, use the CORR procedure to estimate the missing values via the EM algorithm and save your data with the imputed values.

Parameters

In SURVIVAL, we use the accelerated life parameterization for convenience in computing and interpreting the results. The models behave well and converge quickly, and the notion of a covariate accelerating life is intuitive. Some other texts and programs prefer a different parameterization, most typically for the Weibull and exponential models. To facilitate comparisons, SURVIVAL output prints transformations of the shape and location parameters that will match other parameterizations, and the optional WB and EXP commands use a proportional hazards parameterization. If you observe a difference in the shape and location parameters but identical covariate coefficients (or identical except for sign), you have come across a difference in parameterization. This is no cause for concern; from a mathematical point of view, the sets of results are identical except for a transformation of some parameters.

Centering

In SURVIVAL, the default is to input data without centering. If you do opt to center, and this is advisable particularly for estimation of the WB model, you will discover that your location parameter (_B(2)_) may change. This is analogous to the change in the intercept you would see in a multiple regression if you centered some of your data. Again, the change is of no consequence.

Log-Likelihood

The most common discrepancy between SURVIVAL and textbook results is in the reported log-likelihood at convergence. Some authors such as Kalbfleisch and Prentice (1980) prefer to eliminate any terms in the log-likelihood that are constants or exclusively functions of the data (that is, not functions of the unknown parameters). Thus, in the Weibull model, they drop an $\ln(t)$ term from the likelihood contribution of each uncensored case. While this does not in any way affect the maximum likelihood solutions for the parameter vector, it does result in a log-likelihood much smaller than that reported by SURVIVAL. For example, Kalbfleisch and Prentice (1980) report a Weibull model estimated on the data in their Table 1.2 as having a log-likelihood of –22.952; SURVIVAL reports –144.345. The coefficients and standard errors are identical for both normalizations, however. A similar divergence will be noted on the log-logistic and log-normal models. All of the differences are innocuous and are the result of different normalizations; they do not represent any real differences in results.

Iterations

The maximum likelihood procedures in SURVIVAL are iterative. The basic iteration consists of determination of the gradient of the log-likelihood with respect to the parameter vector, calculation of a parameter change vector, and evaluation of the log-likelihood based on the updated parameter vector. If the new log-likelihood is larger than that of the previous iteration, the iteration is considered complete and a new iteration is begun; if not, a step halving is initiated. SURVIVAL will continue to iterate until convergence has been attained.

A step halving is required if some metric of the parameter change vector is too large, resulting in a more negative log-likelihood. This change vector is simply cut in half, and the log-likelihood is reevaluated. If this log-likelihood is an improvement, the iteration is considered complete and a new iteration is begun; otherwise, another step halving is done.

During this process, if either the total number of complete iterations or the total number of step halvings for a single iteration becomes greater than or equal to the limit specified in the MAXIT option, estimation will stop, and a message stating that the

Survival Analysis

iteration limit was encountered will be given followed by the parameter values, log-likelihood, etc., at this point.

The iteration limit will usually be a problem only for models that typically converge slowly, such as WB and EXP. On the other hand, as the parameter estimates approach their final values and the convergence criterion is almost satisfied, SURVIVAL may have difficulty in improving the log-likelihood. Successively smaller steps will be required to get an improved log-likelihood for the iteration, since there is only a little room left for improvement this far along anyway. If iteration i results in a log-likelihood very close to the optimal value, but the overall convergence criterion is not yet satisfied, then many step halvings are required on iteration $i + 1$ to get an improvement, and the step halving limit may be encountered. This may not be a problem. If the parameters that are printed out appear not to have met the convergence criterion, they probably are near their optimal values anyway. Intelligent control of the convergence criterion and iteration and step halving limits is important here.

Singular Hessian

SURVIVAL will not estimate models that include an exact linear dependency among covariates or that include a constant covariate. For either situation, the Hessian (matrix of second derivatives) is singular, and a message to that effect will be printed in the output. The problem of covariate interdependency is common to all models (parametric and proportional hazards). Stratified proportional hazards models add another level of complexity. If one of the covariates is constant within a stratum, a singular Hessian can result.

Survival Models

We use the symbol $F(t)$ to represent the CDF for the continuous non-negative random variable T. Within SURVIVAL, we require that all failure times be strictly positive (that is, zero failure times are not permitted). The survivor function is defined as

$$S(t) = 1 - F(t) = Prob(T > t)$$

The density function is

$$f(t) = dF(t)/(dt)$$

and the hazard function is

$$h(t) = -d[\ln S(t)]/dt = f(t)/S(t)$$

Censoring occurs when the value of t is not observed completely but is restricted to an interval on the real line. In general, an observation is interval-censored if all we know is that the failure time falls between times t_u and t_j, or

$$t_j < t < t_u$$

The censoring is called *right censoring* when

$$t_j < t < \infty$$

In some contexts, if $t_i = 0$ and t_u is finite, the censoring is called *left censoring,* but we do not distinguish this from general interval censoring in SURVIVAL.

Proportional Hazards Models

Cox's proportional hazards model can be written as

$$h(t, \mathbf{z}, \beta) = h_0(t)\exp(\mathbf{z}'\beta)$$

where $h_0(t)$ is the nonparametric baseline hazard. The survivor function is then

$$S(t, \mathbf{z}, \beta) = S_0(t)^q$$

where $q = \exp(\mathbf{z}'\beta)$. SURVIVAL allows each stratum i to have its own baseline hazard $h_{0i}(t)$.

The Cox model is estimated by maximizing the partial likelihood that does not include the baseline hazard $h_0(t)$. For tied failure times, we use Breslow's generalization of the Cox likelihood. Denoting the ordered failure times for the ith stratum by $t_{(1i)}, \ldots t_{mi}$

$$L = \prod_{i=1}^{I} \prod_{j=1}^{m_i} \exp(s_{(ji)} \cdot \beta) / \left[\sum_{R_{t(ji)}} \exp(z \cdot \beta)^{d(ji)} \right]$$

where m_i is the number of failures in the ith stratum, $d(ji)$ is the number of failures in stratum i at time $t_{(ji)}$, $s_{(ji)}$ is the vector sum of covariate vectors for each of these

$d(ji)$ observations, and R_{tji} is the risk set at failure time $t_{(ji)}$. When there are no tied failures, this formula reduces to Cox's original likelihood.

The recovery of the baseline hazard for a stratum follows Prentice and Kalbfleisch (1979). Defining

$$\alpha_j = 1 - \exp(\mathbf{z}'\boldsymbol{\beta}) / [\sum_{R_{tji}} \exp(\mathbf{z}'\boldsymbol{\beta})]$$

the baseline hazard for covariate vector $\mathbf{z} = \mathbf{0}$ is

$$S(t;0) = \prod_{t_j < t} \alpha_j$$

and for tied failure times,

$$\alpha_j = \exp(-d(ji)) / [\sum_{R_{tji}} \exp(\mathbf{z}'\boldsymbol{\beta})]$$

ln(−ln(survivor)) Plots and Quantile Plots

We can write the log(−log(survivor)) equation as

$$\ln(-\ln(S(t, \mathbf{z}, \boldsymbol{\beta}))) = \ln(-\ln(S_0(t))) + \mathbf{z}'\boldsymbol{\beta}$$

which shows that for different values of the covariate vector $\mathbf{z}$, the curve is simply shifted by an additive constant $\mathbf{z}'\boldsymbol{\beta}$. Although the baseline curve $\ln(-\ln(S_0(t)))$ need not be linear, the curves for different strata satisfying the proportional hazards assumption will be parallel.

For the Weibull model, the baseline hazard can be written as

$$S(t) = e^{-t^\delta}$$

so that

$$\ln(-\ln(S(t))) = \delta \ln(t)$$

which will plot as a straight line against $\log(t)$.

Convergence and Score Tests

The convergence criterion is based on the relative increase in the likelihood between iterations. If

$$[L^{(i)} - L^{(i-1)}]/L^{(i)} < converge$$

convergence is achieved, where $L^{(i)}$ is the value of the log-likelihood at the *i*th iteration.

The relative change in the log-likelihood is also used to decide whether first derivatives or the Newton-Raphson method is used in the search algorithm. By default, if the relative increase exceeds the user-defined threshold, only first derivatives are calculated, and the sum of the outer products of the gradient vector are used as an approximation to the matrix of second derivatives (Berndt, Hall, Hall, and Hausman, 1974); below the threshold, the Newton-Raphson method is used.

The score test (Rao, 1977; Engel, 1984) is a Lagrange multiplier (LM) test of the hypothesis that the entire parameter vector of the Cox model is 0. The statistic is computed as

$$S = \mathbf{U}(\delta)' \mathbf{I}(\delta)^{-1} \mathbf{U}(\delta)$$

where $\mathbf{U}(\delta)$ is the score (gradient) vector evaluated at parameter vector δ, and $\mathbf{I}(\delta)$ is an estimate of the information matrix also evaluated at δ. Under the null hypothesis that $\beta = \delta$, S is asymptotically distributed as a chi-square variate with degrees of freedom equal to the number of elements in β. In SURVIVAL, the score test is computed for δ equal to the start values for β. Ordinarily, these are 0 for the Cox model, but they may be overridden with the START option.

Stepwise Regression

The stepwise algorithm follows the suggestion of Peduzzi, Hofford, and Hardy (1980) and, if unrestricted, begins with a test for downward stepping. The criterion for deletion of a variable is based on the *t* statistic or, more correctly, the asymptotic normal statistic, computed as the ratio of the coefficient to its estimated standard error.

A step up is based on a score test of the hypothesis that a potential covariate not currently in the model has a coefficient of 0. If the model currently has *p* covariates, to test for the addition of the $(p + 1)$th covariate, we need to evaluate the information matrix **I** and the score vector **U** under the null hypothesis. Writing β_0 for the current parameter vector obtained from maximizing the log-likelihood for p parameters, and partitioning the score vector $\mathbf{U} = (\mathbf{U}_1, \mathbf{U}_2)$, the score statistic is

$$\mathbf{U}(\beta_0, \mathbf{0})' \mathbf{I}(\beta_0, \mathbf{0})^{-1} \mathbf{U}(\beta_0, \mathbf{0}) = \mathbf{U}_2' \mathbf{I}^{22} \mathbf{U}_2$$

where $\mathbf{I}^{22}$ is the partitioned inverse of $\mathbf{I}$. The statistic could be expanded to test for a set of potential covariates jointly but is implemented for a single covariate only in the current version of SURVIVAL. The resulting scalar is asymptotically a chi-square variate on one degree of freedom, whose square root is treated as a standard normal.

Variances of Quantiles, Hazards, and Reliabilities

The pth quantile of a distribution for the random variable is that value of t for which $F(t) = p$. For the accelerated life model we have

$$\ln(t) = \mu + \beta'\mathbf{z} + \sigma w$$

and for a given p, a point estimate for $\ln(t)$ is obtained from

$$\ln(t) = \mu + \beta'\mathbf{z} + \sigma F^{-1}(w)$$

where F^{-1} is the inverse of the extreme value, normal, or logistic distribution, depending on the model in use. The variance of $\ln(t)$ is derived under the assumption that the estimated parameters are multivariate normal with mean and covariance matrix given by the maximum likelihood solutions. The confidence intervals are computed in terms of $\ln(t)$ and then transformed to the time scale.

Confidence intervals for reliabilities are computed from asymptotic approximations based on a first-order Taylor series expansion in terms of the estimated parameters of the model. This is sometimes called the **delta method** (Rao, 1977). In SURVIVAL, we compute confidence intervals in terms of the log-odds ratio $\ln(p/(1-p))$ because this quantity does not have any range restrictions and is more nearly a linear function of the parameters. The confidence intervals for the log odds are then transformed to the probability scale.

References

Allison, P. (1984). *Event history analysis.* Beverly Hills, Calif.: Sage Publications.

Anderson, J. A. and Senthilselvan, A. (1980). Smooth estimates for the hazard function. *Journal of the Royal Statistical Society*, Series B, 42, 322–327.

Barlow, R. E. and Proschan, F. (1965). *Mathematical theory of reliability.* New York: John Wiley & Sons, Inc.

Berndt, E. K., Hall, B., Hall, R. E., and Hausman, J. A. (1974). Estimation and inference in non-linear structural models. *Annals of Economic and Social Measurement*, 3, 653–665.

Breslow, N. (1970). A generalized Kruskal-Wallis test for comparing K samples subject to unequal patterns of censorship. *Biometrika*, 57, 579–594.

Breslow, N. (1974). Covariance analysis of censored survival data. *Biometrics*, 30, 89–99.

Cox, D. R. (1972). Regression models and life tables. *Journal of the Royal Statistical Society*, Series B, 34, 187–220.

Cox, D. R. (1975). Partial likelihood. *Biometrika*, 62, 269–276.

Cox, D. R. and Oakes, D. (1984). *Analysis of survival data.* New York: Chapman and Hall.

Cox, D. R. and Snell, E. J. (1968). A general definition of residuals. *Journal of the Royal Statistical Society*, Series B, 30, 248–275.

Dempster, A. P., Laird, N. M., and Rubin, D. B. (1977). Maximum likelihood from incomplete data via the EM algorithm. *Journal of the Royal Statistical Society*, Series B, 39, 1–38.

Elandt-Johnson, R. C. and Johnson, N. L. (1980). *Survival models and data analysis.* New York: John Wiley & Sons, Inc.

Elber, C. and Ridder, G. (1982). True and spurious duration dependence: The identifiability of the proportional hazards model. *Review of Economic Studies*, 49, 402–411.

Engel, R. F. (1984). Wald, likelihood ratio and Lagrange multiplier tests in econometrics. In Z. Griliches and M. Intrilligator (eds.), *Handbook of Econometrics.* New York: North-Holland.

Gehan, E. A. (1965). A generalized Wilcoxon test for comparing arbitrarily singly censored samples. *Biometrika*, 52, 203–223.

Gross A. J. and Clark, V. A. (1975). *Survival distributions: Reliability applications in the biomedical sciences.* New York: John Wiley & Sons, Inc.

Han, A. and Hausman, J. (1986). *Semiparametric estimation of duration and competing risks models.* Department of Economics, Massachusetts Institute of Technology, Cambridge, Mass.

Heckman, J. and Singer, B. (1984). The identifiability of the proportional hazards model. *Review of Economic Studies*, 51, 321–341.

Heckman, J. and Singer, B. (1984). A method for minimizing the impact of distributional assumptions in econometric models for duration data. *Econometrica*, 52, 271–320.

Hougaard, P. (1984). Life table methods for heterogeneous populations: Distributions describing the heterogeneity. *Biometrika*, 71.

Kalbfleisch, J. and Prentice, R. (1980). *The statistical analysis of failure time data*. New York: John Wiley & Sons, Inc.

Kaplan, E. L. and Meier, P. (1958). Nonparametric estimation from incomplete observations. *Journal of the American Statistical Association*, 53, 457–481.

Lagakos, S. (1979). General right censoring and its impact on the analysis of survival data. *Biometrics*, 35, 139–56.

Lancaster, T. (1985). Generalized residuals and heterogeneous duration models: With applications to the Weibull model. *Journal of Econometrics*, 28, 155–169.

Lancaster, T. (1988). *Econometric analysis of transition data*. Cambridge: Cambridge University Press.

Lawless, J. F. (1982). *Statistical models and methods for lifetime data*. New York: John Wiley & Sons, Inc.

Lee, E. T. (1980). *Statistical methods for survival data analysis*. Belmont, Calif.: Wadsworth.

Mantel, N. and Haenszel, W. (1959). Statistical aspects of the analysis of data from retrospective studies of disease. *Journal of the National Cancer Institute*, 22, 719–748.

Manton, K. G., Stallard, E., and Vaupel, J. (1986). Alternative models for the heterogeneity of mortality risks among the aged. *Journal of the American Statistical Association*, 81, 635–644.

Miller, R. (1981). *Survival analysis*. New York: John Wiley & Sons, Inc.

Nelson, W. (1978). Life data analysis for units inspected once for failure. *IEEE Transactions on Reliability*, R-27, 4, 274–279.

Nelson, W. *Applied life data analysis*. New York: John Wiley & Sons, Inc.

Parmar, M. K. B. and Machin, D. (1995). *Survival analysis: A practical approach*. New York: John Wiley & Sons, Inc.

Peduzzi, P. N., Hofford, T. R., and Hardy, R. J. (1980). A stepwise variable selection procedure for nonlinear regression models. *Biometrics*, 36, 511–516.

Prentice, R. L. and Kalbfleisch, J. D. (1979) Hazard rate models with covariates. *Biometrics*, 35, 25–39.

Preston, D. and Clarkson, D. B. (1983). SURVREG: A program for the interactive analysis of survival regression models. *The American Statistician*, 37, 174.

Rao, C. R. (1977). *Linear statistical inference and its applications*, 2nd ed. New York: John Wiley & Sons, Inc.

Steinberg, D. and Monforte, F. (1987). Estimating the effects of job search assistance and training programs on the unemployment durations of displaced workers. In K. Lang and J. Leonard (eds.), *Unemployment and the Structure of Labor Markets*. London: Basil Blackwell.

Tarone, R. E. and Ware, J. (1977). On distribution-free tests for equality of survival distributions. *Biometrika*, 64, 156–160.

Turnbull, B. W. (1976). The empirical distribution function with arbitrarily grouped, censored and truncated data. *Journal of the Royal Statistical Society*, Series B, 38, 290–295.

Vaupel, J. W., Manton, K. G., and Stallard, E. (1979). The impact of heterogeneity in individual frailty on the dynamics of mortality. *Demography*, 16, 439–454.

Wang, M. (1987). *Nonparametric estimation of survival distributions with interval censored data*. John Hopkins University, Baltimore, Md.

White, H. (1982). Maximum likelihood estimation of misspecified models. *Econometrica*, 50, 1–25.

Wu, C. F. J. (1983). On the convergence properties of the EM algorithm. *The Annals of Statistics*, 11, 95–103.

Chapter 14

T Tests

Laszlo Engelman

The following *t* tests are available on the Statistics menu:

Two Groups Two-sample (independent) *t* test. The values of the variable of interest (for example, *INCOME*) are stored in a single column and SYSTAT uses codes of a grouping variable (for example, *GENDER*) to separate the cases into two groups (the codes can be numbers or characters). SYSTAT tests whether the difference between the two means differs from 0.

Paired Paired comparison (dependent) *t* test. For each case used in a paired *t* test, SYSTAT computes the differences between values of two variables (columns) and tests whether the average differs from 0.

One-Sample One-sample *t* test. For the one-sample *t* test, values of a single variable are compared against a constant that you specify.

Statistical Background

The following figure shows four different curves—all probability densities. These were drawn with

$$\text{FPLOT } F = \text{TDF}(T, df)$$

using SYSTAT's *t* density function, where *df* is the degrees-of-freedom parameter. Plotting probability and cumulative density functions is often a good way to see what the distributions we use for confidence intervals and hypothesis tests look like. The dashed curve is the normal density. The other three are *t* densities with 1, 2, and 5 degrees of freedom. Notice that as degrees of freedom increase, the shape of the curve approaches the normal density.

The *t* distribution was found by William S. Gosset (1908) while working at the Guinness brewery in Dublin. His discovery came out of the practical need to analyze the results of small-sample experiments in the brewing process. Prior to Gosset's work, the normal curve, or its parametric variant called the error function, was used to approximate the uncertainty of the mean of a set of measurements. As Gosset and others had noted, this approximation was satisfactory only for large samples. Incidentally, the authorship of his 1908 *Biometrika* paper under the pseudonym "Student" arose from the Guinness corporate desire to conceal this new technology from competitors. It also reflected Gosset's gratitude for help from the statistician Karl Pearson, his "Professor."

Gosset provided a method that enabled reasonable inferences to be drawn from the mean of small random samples. He identified this distribution (later named *t* by Sir Ronald Fisher) by taking repeated random samples of size 4 from a data set and examining the behavior of a statistic based on the ratio of the sample mean to the sample standard deviation.

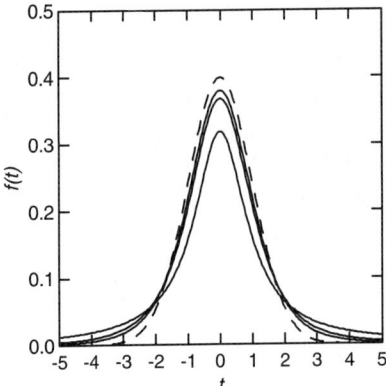

Although Gosset used real data and a somewhat different parameterization of the problem, you can get an idea of what he discovered by running the following Monte Carlo experiment:

```
BASIC
RSEED=3333
REPEAT 750
DIM X(4)
REM Generate 750 samples (n=4) of normal random
numbers
FOR I=1 TO 4
    LET X(I)=ZRN
NEXT
REM Compute a t statistic for each sample
LET T=AVG(X(1)..X(4))/(STD(X(1)..X(4))/SQR(4))
RUN
REM Plot the ordered t values against their
expected values
REM Use a theoretical t distribution with 3 df
PPLOT T / T=3
```

Here is the probability plot output:

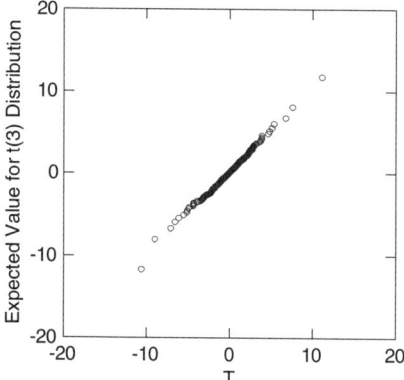

Gosset examined batches of 750 means and noted the extremely long tails of the distribution as compared to the normal. Notice in the probability plot that we see the two most extreme cases having absolute *t* values greater than 10. This would be incredible if we had a sample of 750 from a standard normal distribution. The theoretical chance of seeing values this large or larger from a random sample of a *t* distribution with 3 degrees of freedom, on the other hand, is:

CALC 2 * (1 − TCF(10,3))

which yields 0.0021, or about two cases, which is what we found in this sample.

Degrees of Freedom

The parameter called *degrees of freedom* enters into the definition of the *t* distribution because the estimate of the standard deviation in the denominator depends on it. If we compute *n* deviations from the mean of *n* observations, we can predict perfectly the last (or any) deviation by knowing the mean, *n*, and the other $n - 1$ observations. Stigler (1986) notes that this concept originated in the development of the chi-square distribution in the 19th century. The chi-square is involved in the computation of *t* because it is the distribution of the sample variance (the square of the standard deviation).

When degrees-of-freedom are large enough (say, greater than 30), the *t* and standard normal (*z*) distributions are practically indistinguishable. You can see this by comparing TDF(T,30) to ZDF(Z). On the other hand, you can see from the figure on p. 426 that for small degrees of freedom, the difference between the two curves is substantial, particularly in the tails. This is the gist of Gosset's accomplishment. Gosset quantified the amount of bias scientists are likely to encounter by ignoring degrees of freedom and using *z* instead of *t*.

The T Test

We call a test based on the distribution

$$t = \frac{\bar{x} - \mu}{s/\sqrt{n}}$$

a ***t* test**. Fisher (1925) extended this form to a variety of applications, including tests on regression coefficients and differences of means. Many procedures in SYSTAT use this distribution for various purposes. TTEST focuses on the classic tests of means.

The simplest test is called a **one-sample *t* test**. This is a test of the form:

Null hypothesis: $\mu = \mu_0$
Alternative hypothesis: $\mu \neq \mu_0$

It is occasionally overlooked in practice that μ_0 may be any real value; "null" does not mean "zero." Indeed, this is the point of the one-sample test: to assess the credibility of an observed mean value given an expected value and an estimate of error.

Mathematical constants such as π and certain physical constants are obvious candidates for μ_0 in an hypothesis testing framework.

The prevalence of t tests on *differences* is perhaps what has led to linking of "null" and "zero" in the minds of some applied researchers. There are two species of this test. The first is called the **paired t test (dependent t test)**. In this context, we seek to assess the credibility of an observed difference between the means of two repeated observations x_1 and x_2 being due to a process where no difference exists in the population. Since the difference between two normally distributed variables is itself a normally distributed variable with mean $\mu_1 - \mu_2$ and variance $\sigma_1^2 + \sigma_2^2 - 2\sigma_{12}$, we construct a test on:

Null hypothesis: $\mu_{1-2} = 0$
Alternative hypothesis: $\mu_{1-2} \neq 0$

Computing this test is a matter of taking differences of our data and treating the new variable comprising these differences as we do in a single-sample t test. This differencing improves the power of an experiment when the covariance σ_{12} is large (and positive) relative to the variances because we are implicitly subtracting twice its value from the sum of the variances when we compute our estimate of the variance of the difference. This generally occurs when the pairs of measurements are on the same individual or siblings, for example. Woe to the researcher who encounters negative covariances, however. This may happen when negative feedback biases the measurement process or other lurking variables cause one measurement to covary negatively with the other in each pair.

The second species of t test on differences is slightly different. We have two sets of independent measurements rather than one set of pairs of measurements. We cannot difference pairs of measurements because there are no pairs; the samples may not even be the same size. Our hypotheses are:

Null hypothesis: $\mu_1 - \mu_2 = 0$
Alternative hypothesis: $\mu_1 - \mu_2 \neq 0$

Computing this test requires us to get an estimate of the variance of the difference by using the estimates of the separate variances. If the samples are indeed independent, then this variance is simply the sum of the separate variances and its estimate is a weighted sum of the separate variance estimates. We lose a degree of freedom for *each* sample in the process, however, since the sums of the separate samples are each constrained.

Pooling

Estimating the variance of a difference between means of measurements on two independent samples involves *pooling* sources of variance from each separate sample. This pooling requires us to assume we are combining homogeneous sources of variation. If this is not true, then the computed t statistic does not follow the t distribution. This problem, summarized in Snedecor and Cochran (1989), has been attacked by a number of statisticians. SYSTAT provides a **separate variances t test** for this condition; the test approximates the true distribution of the statistic when the assumption of equal variance (but not distributional shape) is violated.

Assumptions

Throughout this discussion, we have been assuming that the distribution of measurements that determine the means we are testing is normal. For large independent random samples, normality is not as much of a concern because the central limit theorem tells us that the distribution of sample means is normal in these cases, even when the sampled variable is substantially non-normal. The t test, on the other hand, is designed for small samples.

This situation has led Freedman, Pisani, and Purves (1980) to note a predicament: we need to assume normality for the t test, but our sample is too small to be of use in assessing the validity of this assumption. This predicament would be more worrisome were it not for the robustness of the t test against violations of this assumption. There is a considerable Monte Carlo literature in this area, whose general finding is that the primary condition that should concern us is substantial skewness rather than symmetrical departures from normality. SYSTAT provides a graphic with each t test that includes box and dot plots superimposed on normal curves to assess this condition informally. Because of the issue noted by Freedman et al., generally it is not helpful to compute statistical tests of normality on samples sized appropriately for t tests prior to doing the tests. Graphical inspection is to be preferred.

T Tests in SYSTAT

Two-Sample T Test Main Dialog Box

To open the Two-Sample T Test dialog box, from the menus choose:

Statistics
  t-test
    Two Groups...

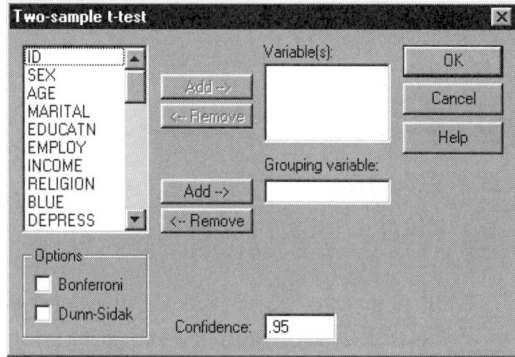

The following must be specified to perform a two-sample *t* test:

Variable(s). Select the variables for which *t* tests are desired. Each variable corresponds to a separate *t* test. When testing several variables, use the optional *p* value adjustments to control for multiple tests.

Grouping variable. The *t* test compares the means for the two groups defined by this variable.

You can also request optional confidence intervals for the mean differences.

Paired T Test Main Dialog Box

To open the Paired T Test dialog box, from the menus choose:

Statistics
 t-test
  Paired...

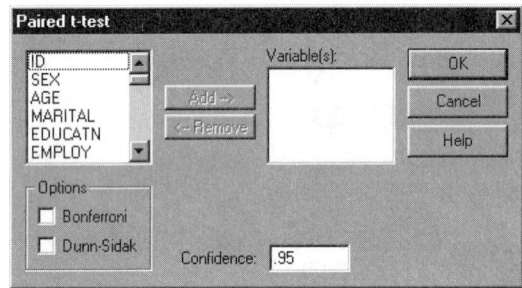

The following must be specified to perform a paired *t* test:

Variable(s). Select the variables for which *t* tests are desired. If more than two variables are selected, each variable pair results in a separate *t* test. When testing several variable pairs, use the optional *p* value adjustments to control for multiple tests.

You can also request optional confidence intervals for the paired mean differences.

One-Sample T Test Main Dialog Box

To open the One-Sample T Test dialog box, from the menus choose:

Statistics
 t-test
  One-Sample...

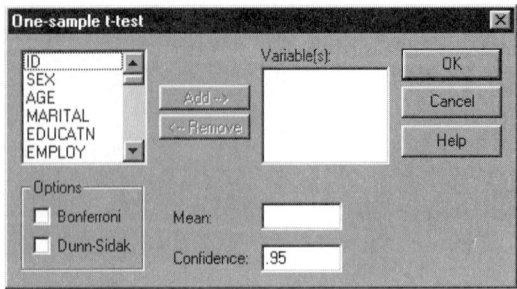

The following must be designated to perform the test:

Variable(s). Select the variables for which *t* tests are desired. Each variable corresponds to a separate *t* test. When testing several variables, use the optional *p* value adjustments to control for multiple tests.

Mean. The constant value to which you want to compare the sample mean for each selected variable.

You can also request optional confidence intervals for the mean differences.

T Test Options

SYSTAT allows you to request tests for several variables with one specification. The *p* value associated with the *t* test assumes that you are making one and only one test. The probability of finding a significant difference by chance alone rapidly increases with the number of tests. So, you should avoid requesting tests for many variables and reporting only those that appear to be significant.

What do you do when you want to study test results for several variables? As protection for multiple testing, SYSTAT offers two adjustments to the probabilities:

- **Dunn-Sidak**. The Dunn-Sidak adjustment is appropriate when more than one test is performed simultaneously. For *n* tests, the Dunn-Sidak adjusted probability is $1 - (1 - p) * n$.
- **Bonferonni**. The Bonferonni adjustment is appropriate when more than one test is performed simultaneously. It drops the second- and higher-order terms from the expression $1 - (1 - p) * n$. The Bonferonni adjusted probability is $n * p$.

Another option available for all three *t* tests is confidence intervals. You can specify the confidence using the following option:

- **Confidence**. Confidence level for the confidence interval. Enter a value between 0 and 1 to specify the likelihood that the confidence interval, a range of values based on the difference between the sample means (or between the sample mean and a specified constant for a one-sample test), includes the difference between the population means. Typical values for the confidence level are 0.95 and 0.99. Higher values (closer to 1) produce wider confidence intervals; lower values produce narrower confidence intervals.

Using Commands

To request a two-sample *t* test, specify your data with USE filename and continue with:

```
TTEST
   TEST varlist * grpvar / BONF  DUNN  CONFI=n
```

Alternatively, to request a paired *t* test, continue with:

```
TTEST
   TEST varlist / BONF  DUNN  CONFI=n
```

Finally, to request a one-sample *t* test, continue with:

```
TTEST
   TEST varlist = constant / BONF  DUNN  CONFI=n
```

Usage Considerations

Types of data. Test variables must be numeric. The grouping variable for the two-sample *t* test can contain either numbers or characters.

Print options. The output is standard for all PRINT options.

Quick Graphs. TTEST produces Quick Graphs. The graph produced depends on the test.

- The two-sample *t* test produces a Quick Graph combining three graphical displays for each group: a box plot displaying the sample median, quartiles, and outliers (if any), a normal curve calculated using the sample mean and standard deviation, and a dit plot displaying each observation.
- The paired *t* test produces a Quick Graph in which, for each case pair, a line connects the values on the two variables.
- The one-sample *t* test produces a Quick Graph combining three graphical displays: a box plot displaying the sample median, quartiles, and outliers (if any), a normal curve calculated using the sample mean and standard deviation, and a dit plot displaying each observation.

Saving files. TTEST does not save the results of the analysis.

BY groups. TTEST analyzes data by groups.

Bootstrapping. Bootstrapping is available in this procedure.

Case frequencies. TTEST uses the FREQ variable, if present, to duplicate cases.

Case weights. TTEST uses the WEIGHT variable, if present, to weight cases.

Examples

Example 1
Two-Sample T Test

Do males tend to earn more than females? We use the *SURVEY2* data to test whether the average income for males differs from that for females. The *SURVEY2* data file has one case for each subject, with the annual income *(INCOME)* and a numeric or character code to identify the sex (the values female and male are stored in the grouping variable *SEX$*). Note that the cases do not need to be ordered by the values of the grouping variable.

In addition to the Quick Graph, which SYSTAT automatically provides with each test, we show alternative ways of viewing these data—a box-and-whiskers plot, a dual histogram, and a kernel density estimator for each group. The input follows:

```
TTEST
   USE survey2
   TEST income * sex$
   DENSITY income * sex$ / BOX   TRANS
   DENSITY income / DUAL=sex$   FILL=0,1
   DENSITY income / GROUP=sex$  OVERLAY KERNEL DASH=1,6
```

The output is:

```
Two-sample t test on INCOME grouped by SEX$

   Group                 N           Mean         SD
    Female              152         20.257      14.828
    Male                104         24.971      16.418


   Separate Variance t =      -2.346 df =  206.2    Prob =       0.020
   Difference in Means =      -4.715    95.00% CI =     -8.676 to    -0.753


     Pooled Variance t =      -2.391 df =  254      Prob =       0.018
   Difference in Means =      -4.715    95.00% CI =     -8.597 to    -0.832
```

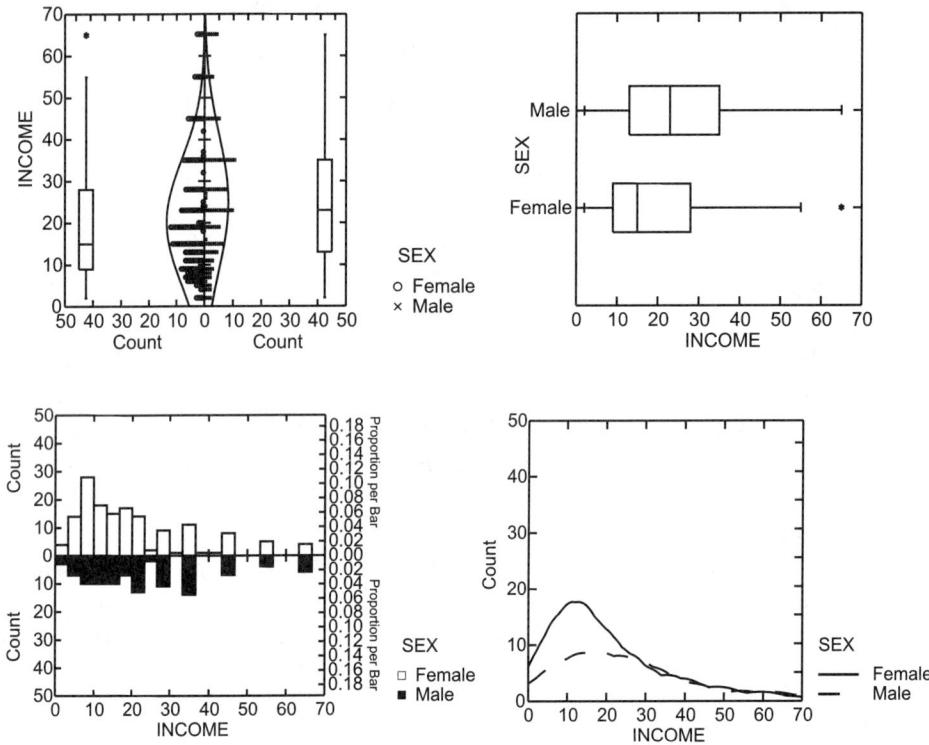

The average yearly income for males in this sample is almost $5,000 more than that for females ($24,971 versus $20,257). The standard deviation (*SD*) for males (16.4) is also larger than that for females (14.8).

The *p* values (*Prob*) for both tests indicate a significant difference in the average incomes of males and females. That is, for the separate variance test, $t = 2.346$ with 206.2 degrees of freedom and an associated probability of 0.02. The values for the pooled test are $t = 2.391$, $df = 254$, and *p* value = 0.018. Which result should you use? Use the pooled test when you are comfortable that the population variances in the two groups are equal. Scan graphical displays for similar shapes and note that the more the sample variances differ, the more the degrees of freedom for the separate variance test drop. You pay a penalty for unequal variances—diminished degrees of freedom mean that your effective sample size decreases. Here, we would use the separate variance *t* test.

The difference in means is –$4,715. The separate variances estimate of the 95% confidence interval for this mean difference extends from –$753 to –$8,676. Note that the interval using the pooled variance estimate is shorter.

T Tests

For each group, three graphical displays are combined in the Quick Graph: a box plot displaying the sample median, quartiles, and outliers (if any), a normal curve calculated using the sample mean and standard deviation, and a dit plot displaying each observation. The median incomes differ more than the mean incomes displayed in the *t* test output. The distribution of female incomes is more right-skewed than the distribution of male incomes. The box plot and normal curve indicate that the distribution of male incomes is fairly symmetric.

Example 2
Bonferroni and Dunn-Sidak Adjustments

How do developed and emerging nations differ? We use the *OURWORLD* file with data for 57 countries. Variables recorded for each case (country) include *URBAN* (percentage of the population living in urban areas), *LIFEEXPF* (years of life expectancy for females), *LIFEEXPM* (years of life expectancy for males), and *GDP$* (grouping variable with codes *Developed* and *Emerging*). The input is:

```
TTEST
   USE ourworld
   FORMAT=8
   TEST urban lifeexpf lifeexpm * gdp$ / BONF DUNN
   FORMAT
```

Following are the results (we used an editor to delete the difference in means and confidence intervals):

```
Two-sample t test on URBAN grouped by GDP$

   Group              N      Mean            SD
   Developed         29   66.10344828    16.84243117
   Emerging          27   38.55555556    19.69446102

   Separate Variance t =   5.60601761 df =    51.4    Prob =   0.00000083
                                    Dunn-Sidak Adjusted Prob =   0.00000248
                                    Bonferroni Adjusted Prob =   0.00000248

     Pooled Variance t =   5.63775383 df =      54    Prob =   0.00000065
                                    Dunn-Sidak Adjusted Prob =   0.00000194
                                    Bonferroni Adjusted Prob =   0.00000194
```

```
Two-sample t test on LIFEEXPF grouped by GDP$

   Group                    N        Mean              SD
     Developed             30    77.43333333       4.47740175
     Emerging              27    62.00000000      11.03490964

     Separate Variance t =    6.78218991  df =    33.6     Prob =    0.00000009
                                    Dunn-Sidak Adjusted Prob =    0.00000027
                                    Bonferroni Adjusted Prob =    0.00000027

       Pooled Variance t =    7.04827869  df =      55     Prob =    0.00000000
                                    Dunn-Sidak Adjusted Prob =    0.00000001
                                    Bonferroni Adjusted Prob =    0.00000001


Two-sample t test on LIFEEXPM grouped by GDP$

   Group                    N        Mean              SD
     Developed             30    70.83333333       3.83345827
     Emerging              27    58.70370370       9.96846881

     Separate Variance t =    5.93974079  df =    32.9     Prob =    0.00000117
                                    Dunn-Sidak Adjusted Prob =    0.00000351
                                    Bonferroni Adjusted Prob =    0.00000351

       Pooled Variance t =    6.18109495  df =      55     Prob =    0.00000008
                                    Dunn-Sidak Adjusted Prob =    0.00000025
                                    Bonferroni Adjusted Prob =    0.00000025
```

On the average, 66.1% of the inhabitants of developed nations live in urban areas, while 38.6% of those in emerging nations live in urban areas. Note that the sample size, N, is 29 + 27 = 56, but there are 57 cases in the *OURWORLD* file (the value of *URBAN* for Belgium is missing). Compare the *df* for the two tests—51.4 versus 54. Thus, considering graphical displays (not shown), the standard deviations, and the small difference between the *df*'s for the two tests, we are not uncomfortable reporting results for the pooled variance test. Significantly more people in developed nations live in urban areas than do people in emerging nations ($t = 5.638$, $df = 54$, p value < 0.0005).

Simply view this output as an illustration of the mechanics of the adjustment features. A difference between a probability of 0.00000083 and 0.00000248 is negligible, considering possible problems in sampling, errors in the data, or a failure to meet necessary assumptions. However, if you scan the results for 100 variables, a probability of 0.0006 for a separate variance *t* test is not significant when multiple testing is considered, since the Bonferroni adjusted probability would be 0.06.

Focusing on female life expectancy, the standard deviation (*SD*) for the emerging nations is more than two times larger than that for the developed nations, and the *df* for the separate variance test drops to 33.6. Using the separate variance test, we conclude that an average life expectancy of 77.4 years differs significantly from 62 years ($t = 6.782$, $df = 33.6$, p value < 0.0005).

Conclusions regarding male life expectancy are similar to those for females, except that for males, life expectancy is, on the average, shorter than that for females—70.8 years in developed nations and 58.7 in emerging nations. You could use a paired *t* test to check if the sex difference is significant.

Example 3
T Test Assumptions

In this example, we examine the dollar amounts that Islamic and New World countries spend per person on health. We request tests of health dollars as measured, in square root units, and for log-transformed values. Since SYSTAT requires that the grouping variable has two values, we remove the European countries from the sample (that is, group$ <> "Europe"). The input is:

```
USE ourworld
TTEST
    SELECT group$ <> "Europe"
    TEST health * group$
    LET sqhealth=SQR(health)
    TEST sqhealth * group$
    LET lghealth=L10(health)
    TEST lghealth * group$
    SELECT
```

Following are the results (we omit the differences in means and confidence intervals):

```
Two-sample t test on HEALTH grouped by GROUP$
    Group              N         Mean          SD
    Islamic           15       20.336      41.736
    NewWorld          21       85.955     200.531

    Separate Variance t =    -1.456 df =    22.4   Prob =      0.159
      Pooled Variance t =    -1.243 df =      34   Prob =      0.222


Two-sample t test on SQHEALTH grouped by GROUP$
    Group              N         Mean          SD
    Islamic           15        3.194       3.295
    NewWorld          21        6.890       6.357

    Separate Variance t =    -2.271 df =    31.5   Prob =      0.030
      Pooled Variance t =    -2.057 df =      34   Prob =      0.047

Two-sample t test on LGHEALTH grouped by GROUP$
    Group              N         Mean          SD
    Islamic           15        0.664       0.777
    NewWorld          21        1.442       0.622

    Separate Variance t =    -3.214 df =    25.9   Prob =      0.003
      Pooled Variance t =    -3.338 df =      34   Prob =      0.002
```

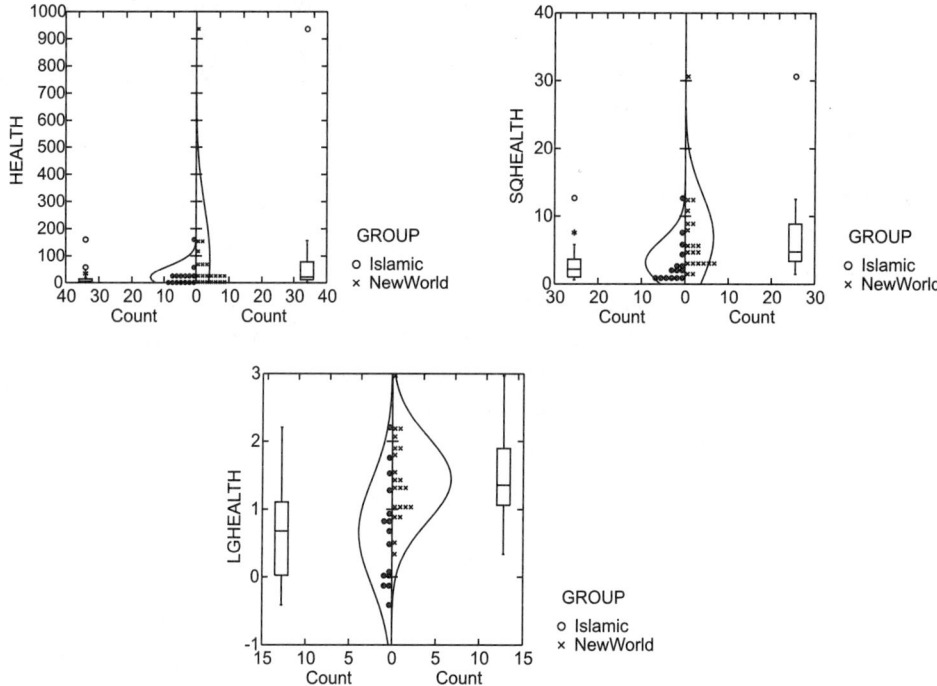

The output includes the results for dollars spent per person for health as recorded (*HEALTH*), in square root units (*SQHEALTH*), and in log units (*LGHEALTH*). In the first panel, it appears that New World countries spend considerably more than Islamic nations ($85.96 versus $20.34, on the average). For these untransformed samples, however, this difference is not significant ($t = -1.456$, $df = 22.4$, p value $= 0.159$).

For the untransformed data, the standard deviation for the New World countries (200.531) is almost five times larger than that for the Islamic nations (41.736). For *SQHEALTH*, the former is approximately two times larger than the latter. For *LGHEALTH*, the difference has reversed. The Islamic group exhibits more spread. Some analysts might want to try a transform between a square root and a log. For example,

```
LET cuberoot = HEALTH^.333
```

But remember, we are selecting a transform using samples of 15 and 21 per group—and the results will have to be explained to others. The graphical displays and test results for the logged data appear to be okay. We conclude that, on the average, New World countries spend significantly more for health than do Islamic nations ($t = -3.338$, $df = 34$, p value = 0.002 for data analyzed in log units).

Each Quick Graph combines three graphical displays: a box plot displays the sample median, quartiles, and outliers (if any), a normal curve calculated using the sample mean and standard deviation, and a dit plot that displays each observation. In the box plots and normal curves, notice that the shapes of the Islamic and New World distributions are most similar for the data in log units. Canada and Libya are far outside values in the box plots for the raw data and the data in square root units. The log transformation tames these outliers.

Example 4
Paired T Test

Do females live longer than males? For each of the 57 countries in the *OURWORLD* data file, life expectancy is recorded for females and males. Each case (country) has two measures in the same units (years of life expectancy), so we use the paired comparison *t* test to test if the means are equal. We include box-and-whiskers plots to illustrate any differences. The input is:

```
TTEST
BEGIN
DENSITY lifeexpf / BOX   TRANS    SCALE=2   AXES=2 ,
                   xmin=35 xmax=85 XLAB="Female Life Expectancy",
                   LOC=-2.5IN,0IN
DENSITY lifeexpm / BOX   TRANS    SCALE=2   AXES=2 ,
                   xmin=35  YMAX=85   XLAB="Male Life Expectancy"
LET dif = lifeexpf - lifeexpm
DENSITY dif / BOX   TRANS   XLAB="Difference" LOC=2.5IN,0IN
END
GRAPH NONE
TEST lifeexpf lifeexpm
```

The output follows:

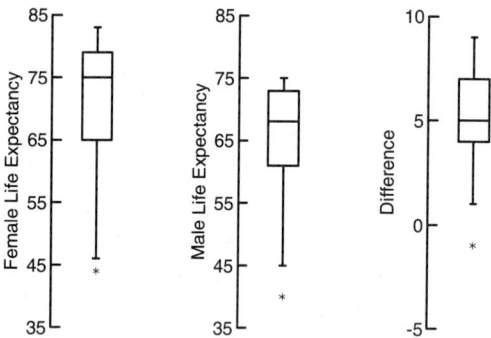

```
Paired samples t test on LIFEEXPF vs LIFEEXPM with 57 cases

    Mean LIFEEXPF    =    70.123
    Mean LIFEEXPM    =    65.088
    Mean Difference  =     5.035    95.00% CI  =    4.415    to       5.655
      SD Difference  =     2.337                                t =  16.264
                                               df =   56    Prob =    0.000
```

The graphs confirm that females tend to live longer, and that only two countries have negative differences (males live longer than females).

In the sample, females, on the average, tend to live 70.123 years and males tend to live 65.088 years. The mean difference between female and male life expectancy is 5.035 years. A 95% confidence interval for this difference in means extends from 4.415 years to 5.655 years.

The interval is computed as follows:

Mean Difference ± $t\{0.975; df\}$ * (*SD Difference*)

A difference of 5.035 years departs significantly from 0 ($t = 16.264$, $df = 56$, p value < 0.005). Females do tend to live longer. To calculate the t statistic manually, first, for each country, compute the difference between female and male life expectancy. Then, compute the average and the standard deviation (*SD*) of the differences. Finally, calculate t where n is the number of countries (or pairs):

$t = (average\ difference) * SQR(n) / SD$

The Bonferroni and Dunn-Sidak adjustments to probability levels are available for protection for multiple testing.

Example 5
One-Sample T Test

Will Europe's population remain stable? You read that for the population to remain stable, the ratio of the birth rate to the death rate should not exceed 1.25—that is, five births for every four deaths. Should you reject the null hypothesis that the average European birth-to-death ratio is 1.25? The input follows:

```
USE ourworld
TTEST
    SELECT group$ = "Europe"
    TEST b_to_d = 1.25
```

The output is:

```
One-sample t test of B_TO_D with 20 cases;   Ho: Mean =        1.250
        Mean =      1.257        95.00% CI  =   1.157 to     1.357
        SD   =      0.213                           t  =      0.147
                                 df  =   19      Prob =       0.884
```

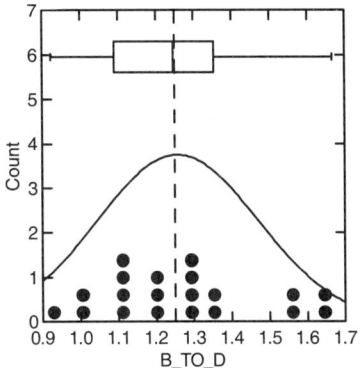

The average birth-to-death ratio for the European countries in the sample is 1.257. We are unable to reject the null hypothesis that the population value is 1.25 ($t = 0.147$, $df = 19$, p value = 0.884). We have no evidence that Europe's population will increase in size.

Do we reach the same conclusion for Islamic nations? Repeat the previous steps, except specify Islamic as *GROUP$*. The output is:

```
One-sample t test of B_TO_D with 16 cases;   Ho: Mean =        1.250

         Mean =       3.478              95.00% CI  =     2.850 to       4.107
         SD   =       1.179                                     t =      7.557
                                         df   =     15       Prob =      0.000
```

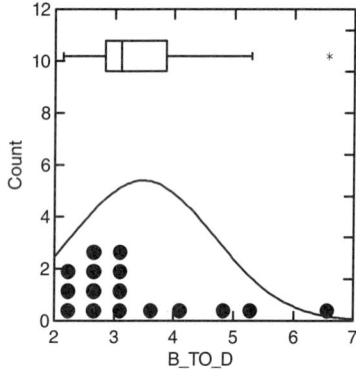

The average birth-to-death ratio for the Islamic countries is 3.478 (more than 2.5 times greater than that of the Europeans). The Islamic birth-to-death ratio differs significantly from 1.25 ($t = 7.557$, $df = 15$, p value < 0.0005). We anticipate a population explosion among these nations.

(As in the other *t* tests, the Bonferroni and Dunn-Sidak adjustments to probability levels are available for protection for multiple testing.)

References

Fisher, R. A. (1925). *Statistical methods for research workers*. London: Oliver and Boyd.
Freedman, D., Pisani, R., and Purves, R. (1980). *Statistics*. New York: W. W. Norton & Co.
Snedecor, G. W. and Cochran, W. G. (1989). *Statistical methods* (8th ed.). Ames: Iowa State University Press.
Stigler, S. M. (1986). *The history of statistics: The measurement of uncertainty before 1900*. Cambridge: Harvard University Press.
"Student." (1908). The probable error of a mean. *Biometrika*, 54, 1–25.

Chapter 15

Test Item Analysis

Herb Stenson

TESTAT provides classical analysis and logistic item-response analysis of tests that are composed of responses to each of a set of test items (variables) by each of a set of respondents (cases). Classical analysis provides test summary statistics, reliability coefficients, standard errors of measurement for selected score intervals, item analysis statistics, and summary statistics for individual cases. Graphical as well as numerical displays are provided.

You also can score individual items for each respondent provided that test items are of the "right versus wrong" variety. However, TESTAT is not limited to these kinds of data; it will accept and analyze any sort of numerical variables that can be used in SYSTAT. Thus, data from true-false tests, multiple-choice tests, rating scales, physiological measures, etc., can all be analyzed with TESTAT using the classical test theory model.

Analysis using logistic, item-response theory is implemented in TESTAT using an iterative, maximum likelihood procedure to estimate item difficulties, item discrimination indices, and subjects' abilities.

Either a one- or two-parameter logistic model can be selected. Item histograms can be printed to examine the fit of each item to the model. TESTAT can save subject scores into a SYSTAT file.

If you use BY, a test can be analyzed for any subgroups of respondents (cases) that you specify. You also have the option of specifying subsets of items (variables) as a subtest to be analyzed. TESTAT also can save item difficulties and discrimination indices into a file for item banking.

Statistical Background

The two statistical approaches to analyzing data from psychological and educational tests have been termed **classical** and **latent trait**. The classical model assumes that items are imperfect measurements of an underlying factor. Like common factor analysis, a single theoretical (unobserved) factor is assumed to comprise a "true" source of variation and random error accounts for the remaining variation in observed scores. Since we cannot observe this true factor, we can estimate it by making assumptions that the random errors are independent and, usually, normally distributed. Thus, the sum of the item scores can yield an estimate of the true score.

The classical model has no role for items of different difficulty. Indeed, it is assumed that any differences in responding to items is due to the ability of the subjects and not to the difficulty of the items. Consequently, tests developed under the classical model tend to have banks of items all of a similar average difficulty or response pattern.

The latent trait model, on the other hand, postulates an underlying distribution that relates item responses to a theoretical trait. This distribution is usually (as in TESTAT) assumed to be logistic, but it can take other forms. In its parameterization, the latent trait model specifically separates subject abilities (individual differences) and item difficulties (scale differences). Tests developed under the latent trait model tend to have a pool of items that vary in difficulty. Some items are failed (or not endorsed) by most subjects and some are passed (or endorsed) by most subjects. Because of this, a latent trait test is especially well suited for measuring larger ranges of abilities or opinions. In addition, the latent trait model allows a more precise description of the performance of an item than simply the item-test correlation. This helps in screening for poor items in a test.

Because of its more elegant parameterization, the latent trait model is generally regarded by test experts to be superior to the classical model for developing surveys and tests of attributes. Indeed, despite the popularity of the classical model (and its associated statistics such as Cronbach's alpha, item-test correlations, and factor loadings) among nonprofessionals and applied researchers, the latent trait model is the one used by the well-known psychological and educational testing organizations. The continuing popularity of the older classical model may be due to its relative simplicity and the lack of availability of latent trait software in the major statistical packages. Until SYSTAT introduced latent trait modeling in a general statistical package, it was confined to specialized software available at selected academic and commercial sites. SYSTAT offers both methods, but we strongly recommend that you learn and apply the latent trait model to develop tests that you intend to reuse.

Classical Model

The principal statistics in the classical model are reliability measures that represent how well a set of items relate to each other (assuming that they all measure a common factor). The reliability, or internal-consistency, coefficients that are produced by TESTAT are the coefficient of correlation between the odd and even test scores, the Spearman-Brown coefficient based on the odd-even correlation, the Guttman-Rulon coefficient, coefficient alpha for all items, coefficient alpha for odd-numbered items, and coefficient alpha for even-numbered items.

The Spearman-Brown coefficient is based on the assumption that the two halves of the test are strictly parallel. The Guttman-Rulon coefficient is based on the assumption that the two halves are parallel in every sense except for having different variances. We call it the Guttman-Rulon coefficient here because the two different formulas for computing it proposed by Guttman (1945) and Rulon (1939) are algebraically equivalent. Coefficient alpha is the internal consistency measure proposed by Cronbach (1951). It is algebraically equivalent to Formula 20 by Kuder and Richardson (KR20) when the test data are dichotomously scored items.

Coefficient alpha deserves a little more discussion here. First, it should be noted that while this coefficient cannot take on values greater than 1.0, it has no lower limit. Therefore, it not only can take on negative values but it can take on negative values less than -1.0, unlike the Pearson correlation coefficient. If you get a value of alpha less than 0, it is because a substantial number of test items have negative correlations with the total test score (or with other items, which is the same thing). You can check the effect of reverse scoring the offending items by using the KEY command with the + and – option (as described later).

Second, a version of alpha called **standardized alpha** is often computed. This coefficient reflects the average size of item-total correlations as opposed to item-total covariances. TESTAT does not produce it for the following reasons. Alpha can be interpreted as the lower limit of reliability for a test that is scored by summing the item scores. If standardized alpha is computed, this coefficient is the lower limit of reliability for a test that is scored by first converting the scores for each item so that all items have equal variances, and then summing these converted scores. Thus, this latter version of alpha does not accurately describe your test unless the items have equal variances. If you need this coefficient, you could first use the DATA module to convert each of your items to z scores and then run these data with TESTAT. The total scores on the test will then be appropriate for the alpha that is computed, which will be the so-called standardized alpha.

More information about all of these test statistics can be found in standard textbooks such as those by Allen and Yen (1979) and Crocker and Aegina (1986).

Latent Trait Model

The latent trait model assigns a probability distribution to responses to each item. Usually, this is a logistic distribution, but it also can be normal. The following figure shows distributions for five hypothetical items. Each curve displays the probability of a correct response on each item by students of different levels of ability. Each item has a common shaped curve based on the cumulative logistic (or normal) distribution function. The only parameter distinguishing the curves is their location. Easier items appear to the left and more difficult items appear to the right. The model generating this graph is called the one-parameter, or Rasch, model.

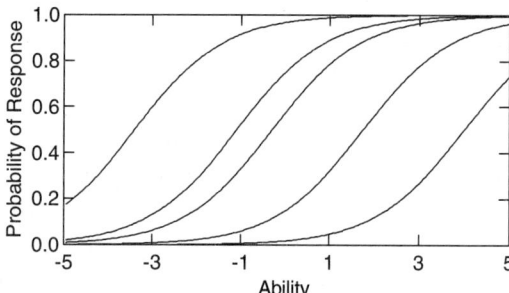

Often, it is more plausible to assume that items vary in discrimination as well as in difficulty. Items with steeper curves discriminate between subjects of different ability more effectively than items with shallower curves. Not surprisingly, this is called a two-parameter model. The following figure shows an example for five hypothetical items. Notice that the second and third items from the left differ noticeably in discrimination as well as in difficulty.

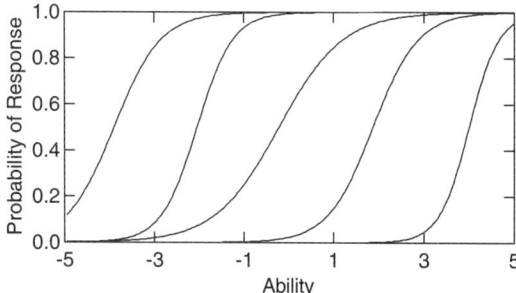

TESTAT fits a one- or two-parameter model to binary responses on a test. The observed data fall into only two categories. The model assumes that these observations were generated by a continuous probability distribution. The computational machinery is similar to that used in logistic regression, but a separate logistic curve must be fit for every item on a test. Correspondingly, a separate curve must be fit for every subject. The graph predicting subjects' response probabilities looks like the figures above, except the *x* axis is *Difficulty* instead of *Ability*.

Test Item Analysis in SYSTAT

Classical Test Item Analysis Main Dialog Box

To open the Classical Test Item Analysis dialog box, from the menus choose:

Statistics
  Test Item Analysis
    Classical…

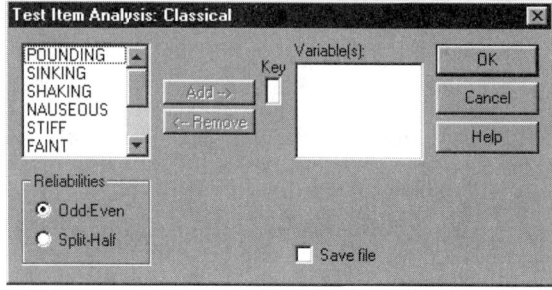

Variable(s). Select a set of test items and move these into the Variable(s) list.

Key. You can alter the nature of the data by scoring each item response as correct or incorrect or by reversing the scoring scale. For each variable enter a scoring key value.

Reliabilities. By default, split-half reliabilities and summary statistics are based on an odd-even split. Instead of using the odd-even split, you can select Split-Half to use the first half of the items versus the last half of items.

Save file. Saves subject scores into *filename.SYD*. The file will include on each record the name of an item and its average score.

Logistic Test Item Analysis Main Dialog Box

To open the Logistic Test Item Analysis dialog box, from the menus choose:

Statistics
  Test Item Analysis
    Logistic…

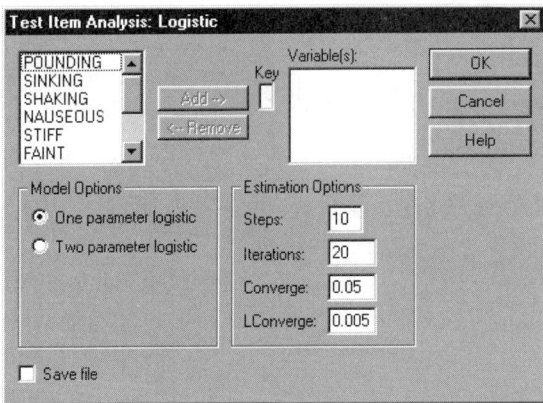

If your data are binary and are coded as zeros and ones, you can analyze your data using item-response theory with the logistic function as the item characteristic curve.

Variable(s). Select a set of test items and move these into the Variable(s) list.

Key. You can alter the nature of the data by scoring each item response as correct or incorrect or by reversing the scoring scale. For each variable enter a scoring key value.

Model Options. Choose between a one-parameter or a two-parameter model. If you select One parameter logistic, the item discrimination index will be the same for every item, but may change values during the iterative process due to rescaling of the abilities. If you select Two parameter logistic, each item can have a different discrimination index.

Estimation Options. The following can be specified:

- **Steps.** Indicate the maximum number of steps that are to be allowed.
- **Iterations.** Enter the maximum number of iterations allowed when estimating a single subject's ability or a single item's parameters within a stage.
- **Converge.** Specify the stopping convergence criterion. Setting a small convergence will decrease the number of steps required to reach a final set of estimates.
- **LConverge.** Specify a value for the likelihood of convergence. The default value is 0.005. This means that if the likelihood of the data increase by less than 0.5 percent, the program will stop at the end of that step. That is, if the likelihood ratio is less than 1.005 at the end of a step, the program will stop and print out the most recent parameter estimates.

Save file. Saves subject scores into *filename.SYD*.

Using Commands

Select a data file using USE filename and continue with:

```
TESTAT
    MODEL varlist
    KEY (values)
    ESTIMATE / CLASSICAL or  LOG1 or  LOG2,
              HALF  STEPS=n  ITER=n  CONVERGE=d  LCONVERGE=d
```

Usage Considerations

Types of data. By default, TESTAT will use whatever data are in the data set to perform the analyses. However, if you want to alter the nature of these data by scoring each item response as correct or incorrect, or by reversing the scoring scale, you can use KEY. It has two forms.

The first form is used as a scoring key to score each item response as a 0 or a 1, which can mean "incorrect" and "correct," or any other meaningful binary designation. To use this form, you must provide the scoring key as a sequence of non-negative numbers corresponding in a one-to-one fashion to the sequence of items on the test (or subtest). The numbers in your data set must not be negative.

Suppose, for example, that your data set consists of five questions that must be answered "true" or "false" and that you have coded the respondents' answers as 0's and 1's. If the correct answer to questions 1, 2, and 4 is "true," and the correct answer to the remainder of the questions is "false," then you would type the KEY command prior to the ESTIMATE command as follows:

```
KEY = 1,1,0,1,0
```

This would cause the item responses to be scored according to your scoring key prior to the analysis by the ESTIMATE command. If you want to create a SYSTAT data set containing the scored items, you must also precede the ESTIMATE command with a SAVE command, naming the data set into which the scored data are to be saved. This data set will contain 1's and 0's indicating correct or incorrect responses for each item and case.

In a similar fashion, the responses to multiple-choice items can also be scored as 0's or 1's using the scoring key. If, for example, your five-question test was made up of four-alternative multiple-choice items, then you can use the numbers 1 through 4 to indicate the correct answers in the scoring key. Of course, the respondents' answers must also be entered into the input data set as the numbers 1, 2, 3, or 4. Suppose that your input data set containing responses to the five questions was named *MYFILE*. Then the following commands would score these data as 0's and 1's, save them into a SYSTAT data set named *SCORED*, and produce test and item histograms:

```
USE MYFILE
TESTAT
MODEL var1,var2,var3,var4,var5
SAVE SCORED
KEY = 3,1,4,2,1
ESTIMATE
```

The data set that is saved (*SCORED* in this case) will contain as an extra variable the total score for each subject (case).

The second form of the KEY command is used to reverse the scoring of selected items. It can be used when the largest data values for one item indicate the same thing as the smallest data values for another item. This scoring key consists of a sequence of "+" and "−" signs to indicate that the item scores are to be multiplied by a +1 or −1, thus reversing the direction of scoring in the case of −1. Reversing the scoring scale in this way will not affect item variances, but it will alter the possible ranges of item means and total scores. Thus, you might use this method to check the effect on alpha of reversing one or more items. If this increases alpha and it makes sense in the context of the test, you may want to use the DATA module to change the scoring of such items so that the highest response score possible would be replaced by the lowest response score possible and so on for the lowest and any intermediate responses.

For example, the following commands will save the input from five items, multiplied by their corresponding weights of +1 and –1, into the data set *WEIGHT*, and produce the default output of ESTIMATE using first-half, last-half as the split-half option:

```
SAVE WEIGHT
KEY +,-,-,+,+
ESTIMATE / HALF
```

Print options. The default output statistics consist of summary statistics for the test and a set of reliability (internal consistency) coefficients. The output statistics are the mean, standard deviation, standard error of the mean, maximum and minimum values, and the number of cases on which these were computed for the following summary variables: total score (summed across the variables), total score/number of items, total score on odd-numbered items, and total score on even-numbered items.

If the total number of items (variables) in the data set is odd, then the total score for odd-numbered items will be based on one more item than the total score for even-numbered items.

Note that the standard deviations, in keeping with tradition in test theory, are based on sums of squared deviations divided by N, rather than $N-1$. To give unbiased estimates, the standard errors of means are computed by dividing the standard deviations by the square root of $N-1$.

If you want to see item analysis statistics in addition to the test statistics, use PRINT LONG.

The first set of additional data that will be provided when you use PRINT LONG is the approximate standard error of measurement for total test scores in each of 15 score intervals. These intervals are each 1/2 standard deviation wide and are centered at the mean. Thus, they are the so-called Stanine intervals. The intervals are shown in both z score and total score metrics, so that, even if you have no need for these standard errors of measurement, the table will be useful for seeing how various total scores translate into z scores.

The standard error of estimate shown for an interval is the square root of the average squared difference between odd and even scores (or first minus last half for cases whose total score is in the interval). This is a method recommended by Livingston (1982) and studied empirically by Lord (1984). Lord showed that standard errors of estimate computed by Livingston's method approximate the standard errors of estimate that he got using a three-parameter logistic model to analyze a large set of achievement test data. However, Lord cautions against the use of these estimates if the number of cases in an interval is small or if the interval is near the minimum or maximum total score that is possible.

The second set of additional data that is provided when you use PRINT LONG is a set of item statistics that are useful in performing an item analysis of a test. Shown for each item are the item mean and standard deviation, the correlation of the item with the total score, the item reliability index (item-total correlation times standard deviation), the item-total correlation if the item is excluded from the total, and the value of coefficient alpha if the item is excluded from the test.

Quick Graphs. If your input data are binary "right versus wrong" data, each item plot shows the percentage of the cases in a z-score interval that got the item correct. That is, the axis labeled *Scaled Mean-Item Score* shows the percentage correct for each interval. However, if your data are not of the "right versus wrong" variety, then the *Scaled Mean-Item Score* is the mean-item score for cases in an interval, scaled so that its minimum possible value is 0 and its maximum possible value is 100. (The minimum and maximum values are found by locating the largest and smallest data values that exist in the input data). Note that the N and percentage listed next to the histograms are the number of cases and percentage of cases with scores in an interval, not the percentage correct. The column labeled *SCORE* gives the actual score.

For the latent trait models, Quick Graphs of the fitted logistic curves are plotted for each item in a grouped array.

Saving files. You can save average item scores ("difficulties" or, in the case of binary items, "p" values) into a SYSTAT file. The file will include, on each record, the name of an item and its average score.

BY groups. TESTAT analyzes data by groups.

Bootstrapping. Bootstrapping is available in this procedure.

Case frequencies. TESTAT uses the FREQ variable, if present, to duplicate cases. This inflates the total degrees of freedom to be the sum of the number of frequencies. Using a FREQ variable does not require more memory, however.

Case weights. TESTAT weights sums of squares and cross products using the WEIGHT variable for rectangular data input. It does not require extra memory.

Examples

Example 1
Classical Test Analysis

The following data are reports of fear symptoms by selected United States soldiers after being withdrawn from World War II combat. The data were originally reported by Suchman in Stouffer et al. (1950). The variable *COUNT* contains the number of soldiers in each profile of symptom reports.

Notice that we use the FREQ command to implement the case weighting variable *COUNT*. TESTAT weights the cases according to this count before computing statistics. We also save the estimates. The input is:

```
USE COMBAT
TESTAT
MODEL POUNDING..URINE
FREQ=COUNT
IDVAR=COUNT
SAVE TEMP/ITEM
ESTIMATE/CLASSICAL
```

Following is the output:

```
Variables in the SYSTAT Rectangular file are:
  POUNDING    SINKING     SHAKING     NAUSEOUS    STIFF       FAINT
  VOMIT       BOWELS      URINE       COUNT

   Case frequencies determined by value of variable COUNT.

Data below are based on 93 complete cases for 9 data items.

Test score statistics

                       Total      Average      Odd         Even
Mean                   4.538      0.504        2.473       2.065
Std Dev                2.399      0.267        1.333       1.277
Std Err                0.250      0.028        0.139       0.133
Maximum                9.000      1.000        5.000       4.000
Minimum                1.000      0.111        0.0         0.0
N cases               93.000     93.000       93.000      93.000

Internal consistency data

Split-half correlation              0.690
Spearman-Brown Coefficient          0.816
Guttman (Rulon) Coefficient         0.816
Coefficient Alpha - all items       0.787
Coefficient Alpha - odd items       0.613
Coefficient Alpha - even items      0.661
```

```
Approximate standard error of measurement of total score
for 15 z score intervals

 z score  Total score     N    Std Error
 -3.750     -4.458        0      .
 -3.250     -3.258        0      .
 -2.750     -2.059        0      .
 -2.250     -0.860        0      .
 -1.750      0.340       10     1.000
 -1.250      1.539       16     1.000
 -0.750      2.739        6     1.000
 -0.250      3.938       29     1.390
  0.250      5.137       10     1.095
  0.750      6.337        8     1.000
  1.250      7.536        8     0.0
  1.750      8.735        6     1.000
  2.250      9.935        0      .
  2.750     11.134        0      .
  3.250     12.334        0      .

Item reliability statistics

                                      Item-    Item    Excl    Excl
                                      Total   Reliab   Item    Item
Item    Label      Mean    Std Dev      R     Index     R      Alpha
  1   POUNDING    0.903     0.296     0.331   0.098   0.215    0.794
  2   SINKING     0.785     0.411     0.499   0.205   0.354    0.782
  3   SHAKING     0.559     0.496     0.678   0.336   0.539    0.757
  4   NAUSEOUS    0.613     0.487     0.721   0.351   0.599    0.747
  5   STIFF       0.538     0.499     0.693   0.346   0.559    0.754
  6   FAINT       0.452     0.498     0.715   0.356   0.588    0.749
  7   VOMIT       0.376     0.484     0.622   0.301   0.472    0.767
  8   BOWELS      0.215     0.411     0.625   0.257   0.502    0.763
  9   URINE       0.097     0.296     0.503   0.149   0.402    0.777
```

Use PRINT=LONG to see item histograms for this test.

Example 2
Logistic Model (One Parameter)

If your data are binary and are coded as 0's and 1's or recoded with the KEY command, you can analyze your data using item-response theory with the LOGISTIC function as the item characteristic curve. Either a one-parameter (Rasch) model or a two-parameter logistic model can be implemented by using the MODEL command. The one-parameter model is the default. The input is:

```
USE COMBAT
TESTAT
MODEL POUNDING..URINE
FREQ=COUNT
IDVAR=COUNT
SAVE TEMP/ITEM
ESTIMATE/LOG1
```

Test Item Analysis

Under the single-parameter logistic model, the item discrimination index will be the same for every item but may change values during the iterative process due to rescaling of the abilities. The initial values of all parameters are computed by a technique given by Cohen (1979) to approximate the abilities and item difficulties of a one-parameter logistic model. They are scaled to have a mean of 0 and a standard deviation of 1 for the ability estimates.

Following is the output:

```
   Case frequencies determined by value of variable COUNT.

93 cases were processed, each containing 9 items
6 cases were deleted by editing for missing data or for zero or
Perfect total scores after item editing.
0 items were deleted by editing for missing data or for zero or
Perfect total scores after item editing.

Data below are based on 87 cases and 9 items

Total score mean =        4.230     2.164, standard deviation = .

-Log(Likelihood) using initial parameter estimates =   270.981602


STEP 1 convergence criterion = 0.050000

Stage 1: estimate ability with item parameter(s) constant.

   -Log(Likelihood)        Change        Likelihood Ratio
      270.070977         -0.910626             2.485877

Greatest change in ability estimate was for case 87

Change from old estimate =      0.134095 , current estimate =     2.005331


Stage 2: estimate item parameter(s) with ability constant.

   -Log(Likelihood)        Change        Likelihood Ratio
      269.662219         -0.408757             1.504946

Greatest change in difficulty estimate was for item BOWELS
Change from old estimate =       0.084109, current estimate =     1.301014
Current value of discrimination index =       1.205582

STEP 2 convergence criterion = 0.050000

Stage 1: estimate ability with item parameter(s) constant.

   -Log(Likelihood)        Change        Likelihood Ratio
      269.590283         -0.071937             1.074588

Greatest change in ability estimate was for case 80

Change from old estimate =      0.006024 , current estimate =     2.011354

Stage 2: estimate item parameter(s) with ability constant.

   -Log(Likelihood)        Change        Likelihood Ratio
      269.548875         -0.041408             1.042277

Greatest change in difficulty estimate was for item BOWELS
Change from old estimate =       0.031751, current estimate =     1.315291
Current value of discrimination index =       1.225624
```

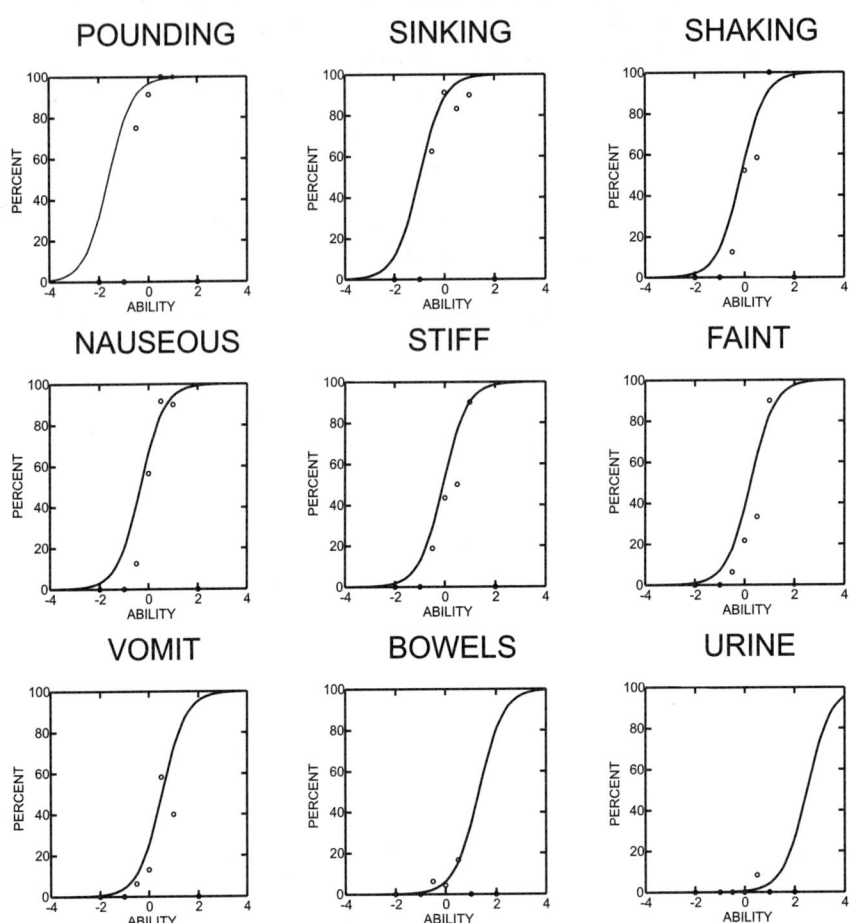

Three levels of the iterative process must be distinguished here. The program operates in what are labeled *STEPS* in the output. Each step consists of two stages. In stage 1, the subjects' abilities are estimated, one at a time, holding the item parameters constant at their most recent values. At the end of stage 1, the resulting abilities are rescaled so as to have a mean of 0 and a standard deviation of 1. The item parameters are also rescaled to conform to the new ability scale. In stage 2, the item parameter(s) are estimated, one item at a time, holding the abilities constant at their most recent values. A new step is then begun, if necessary, in which this two-stage process is repeated.

Within each stage is the third level of the iterative process, called *ITER*. Here, as a single ability (in stage 1) or a single item's parameters (in stage 2) are being estimated, successive iterations are performed until the parameter being estimated does not change by more than a tolerance value called *TOL*. When this criterion is met, the program moves on to estimate the ability for the next case (in stage 1) or the next item's parameters (in stage 2). This iterative process is repeated within a stage until the data are exhausted. Then the next stage is begun.

There are two criteria for stopping the stepwise process. At the end of each stage, the likelihood of obtaining the test data that are in the input data set is computed, given the current values of all parameters. The negative logarithm of this likelihood and the change in this value from the previous stage are printed. The ratio of the current likelihood to the previous likelihood is also computed and printed. If, at the end of a step (after stage 2), this likelihood ratio is less than a value specified by a stopping criterion called **LCONVERGE**, no further steps are run, and the final item parameters are printed. This is the first stopping criterion.

The second stopping criterion relies on the maximum change in parameter estimates between stages. At the end of a stage, the maximum change in the parameters being estimated in that stage is printed. If, at the end of a step, no parameter estimated in either stage of that step changed more than the value of **CONVERGE**, the stagewise process is terminated, and the final item parameters are printed. Thus, the program will stop entering new steps whenever either of the two stopping criteria is met, whichever occurs first.

The final parameter estimates are, thus, a type of maximum likelihood estimate. However, you should realize that because the process alternates between estimating item parameters and abilities, the final parameter estimates are not a true maximum likelihood estimate of all parameters simultaneously. As with other programs that use this same type of alternating estimation technique, the process does converge for all but very unusual data sets.

Example 3
Logistic Model (Two Parameter)

The 20-item version of the Social Desirability Scale described by Strahan and Gerbasi (1972) was administered as embedded items in another test to 359 undergraduate students in psychology. The social desirability items were scored for the "social desirability" of the response and coded as 0's and 1's in a SYSTAT data set named

Chapter 15

SOCDES.SYD. The following commands were used to produce the output for this example:

```
USE SOCDES
TESTAT
MODEL X(1..20)
SAVE TEMP / ITEMS
ESTIMATE / LOG2,STEP=2,CONVERGE=.1
```

Following is the output:

```
359 cases were processed, each containing 20 items
4 cases were deleted by editing for missing data or for zero or
Perfect total scores after item editing.
0 items were deleted by editing for missing data or for zero or
Perfect total scores after item editing.

Data below are based on 355 cases and 20 items

Total score mean =         9.386       3.992, standard deviation = .

-Log(Likelihood) using initial parameter estimates =   3634.928345

STEP 1 convergence criterion = 0.100000

Stage 1: estimate ability with item parameter(s) constant.

    -Log(Likelihood)        Change          Likelihood Ratio
        3634.122209       -0.806136               2.239239

Greatest change in ability estimate was for case 22

Change from old estimate =    -0.105724 , current estimate =       2.956047

Stage 2: estimate item parameter(s) with ability constant.

    -Log(Likelihood)        Change          Likelihood Ratio
        3622.569856      -11.552353             104021.506702

Greatest change in difficulty estimate was for item X(19)
Change from old estimate =     0.021791, current estimate =       0.946823
Greatest change in discrimination estimate was for item X(8)
Change from old estimate =    -0.163600, current estimate =       0.530705

STEP 2 convergence criterion = 0.100000

Stage 1: estimate ability with item parameter(s) constant.

    -Log(Likelihood)        Change          Likelihood Ratio
        3619.922513       -2.647343              14.116484

Greatest change in ability estimate was for case 66

Change from old estimate =    -0.180754 , current estimate =      -2.265529

Stage 2: estimate item parameter(s) with ability constant.

    -Log(Likelihood)        Change          Likelihood Ratio
        3612.343024       -7.579488            1957.627103

Greatest change in difficulty estimate was for item X(4)
Change from old estimate =    -0.580964, current estimate =      -1.770080
Greatest change in discrimination estimate was for item X(4)
Change from old estimate =    -0.153424, current estimate =       0.407619
```

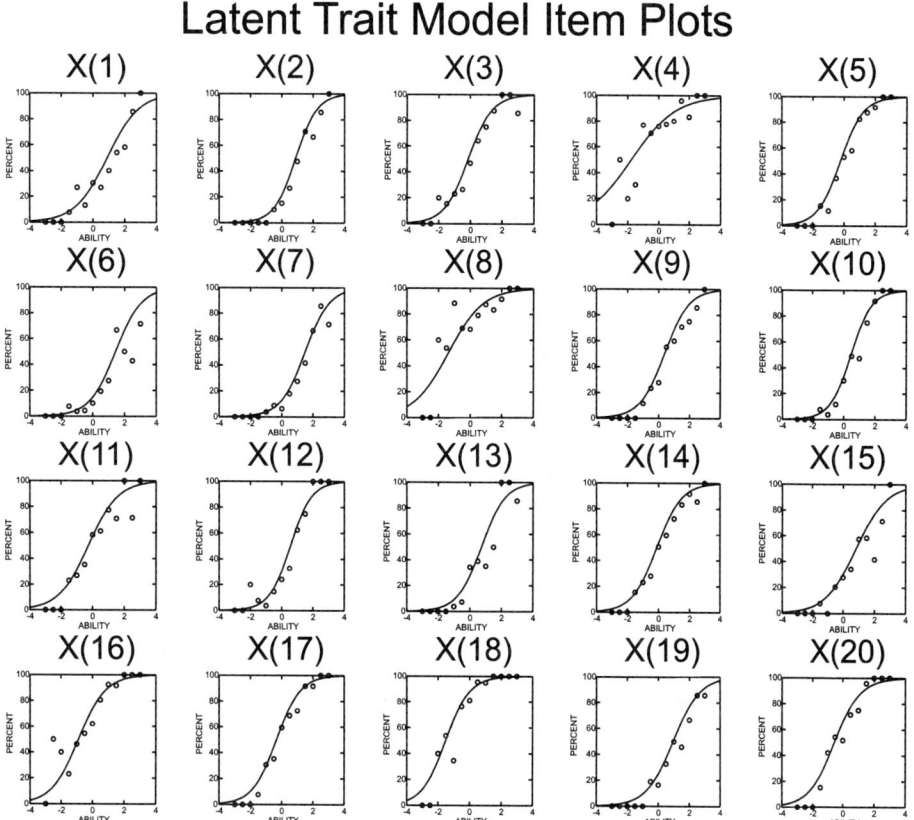

You can see that the second item discriminates better than the first and that both items seem to fit the model moderately well.

Computation

All calculations are in double precision arithmetic, with provisional algorithms used for calculating all means and sums of squares that are needed. The formulas for all of the statistics that are shown in the output can be found in the references given below.

Algorithms

Provisional algorithms are used for means and sums of squares. The calculations for the classical and logistic models are as follows:

Classical Model

Your data must have at least four variables (test items). The number of cases (respondents) must be at least two. Cases with missing data are not used in any of the statistical analyses. Such cases are identified in the case by case listing, if this listing is requested. If you want to substitute a value, such as 0, for missing data, you should do this when you create the SYSTAT data set in the DATA module.

During the calculations, TESTAT creates two temporary data sets on your data disk. Together, they are about as large as your input data set, so you should make sure that there is enough room for them on your disk.

Logistic Model

While the number of variables (items) may be as small as 4, unreliable results will be obtained if the number is less than about 20. The minimum number of cases (respondents) is two, but this is obviously far too small a number for reliable results.

As with the classical model, cases with missing data are not used in any of the calculations. In addition, the item-response routines require that no case have either a 0 or perfect total score on the test or subtest being analyzed. Thus, an editing routine finds and marks such cases for exclusion from the analysis. Likewise, any item (variable) that is responded to in exactly the same way by all respondents must be excluded from the analysis. The editing routine looks for such items after first excluding offending cases. Once any such items are marked for exclusion, the routine again looks for inappropriate cases, using only the remaining items. It iterates in this fashion until no inappropriate cases or items remain. Any items or cases that have been excluded from the analysis are reported by the output routines. The same temporary data sets that are mentioned above for the classical model are also created for the logistic model. Make sure that your disk has room for them.

The algorithm for finding the maximum likelihood (actually, the minimum of the negative logarithm of the likelihood) for each ability in stage 1 and for each item's parameter(s) in stage 2 is based on Fletcher-Powell minimization (Press et al., 1986).

The logistic model that is used in this program is the now-familiar two-parameter formula found in Lord (1980), Hulin, Drasgow, and Parsons (1983), and many other references.

The discrimination parameter for an item is a and the difficulty is b, while the subject's ability is 0. In TESTAT, the function to be minimized is designed to place limits on the values of 0 and a by "driving the iterative routine away" from estimates greater than these limits. The limits are 6.00 for the absolute value of 0 and 3.00 for the absolute value of a, the discrimination index. If your data imply a lot of items with extreme values of a, or a lot of extreme values of 0, you may find that the program will start to oscillate around some value of the likelihood ratio that is not less than the stopping value. You cannot change these limits because to make them very much larger could result in illegally large values for the exponent (x) in the model.

As with any iterative estimation procedure, you should beware of local minima. If you suspect that such a problem exists after inspecting your output, try running the first few steps with a very large value of CONVERGE and then switching to a smaller value.

Missing Data

Any case with missing values on any item is deleted.

References

Allen, M. J. and Y, W. M. (1979). *Introduction to measurement theory*. Belmont, Calif.: Wadsworth.

Cohen, L. (1979). Approximate expressions for parameter estimates in the Rash model. *British Journal of Mathematical and Statistical Psychology*, 32, 113–120.

Coombs, C. H., Dawes, R. M., and Tversky, A. (1970). *Mathematical psychology: An elementary introduction*. Englewood Cliffs, N.J.: Prentice-Hall, Inc.

Crocker, L. and Algina, J. (1986). *Introduction to classical and modern test theory*. New York: Holt Rinehart Winston.

Cronbach, L. J. (1956). Coefficient alpha and the internal structure of tests. *Psychometrika*, 16, 297–334.

Guttman, L. (1945). A basis for analyzing test-retest reliability. *Psychometrika*, 10, 255–282.

Hulin, C. L., Drasgow, F., and Parsons, C. K. (1983). *Item response theory: Application to psychological measurement*. Homewood, Ill.: Dow Jones-Irwin.

Livingston, S. (1982). Estimation of conditional standard error of measurement for stratified tests. *Journal of Educational Measurement*, 19, 135–138.

Lord, F. M. (1980). *Applications of item response theory to practical testing problems.* Hillsdale, N.J.: Erlbaum.

Lord, F. M. (1984). Standard error of measurement at different ability levels. Technical Report Number RR-84-8. Princeton, N.J.: Educational Testing Service.

Press, W. H., Flannery, B. P., Teukolsky, S. A., and Vetterling, W. T. (1986). *Numerical recipes: The art of scientific computing.* Cambridge: Cambridge University Press.

Rulon, P. J. (1939). A simplified procedure for determining the reliability of a test by split-halves. *Harvard Educational Review*, 9, 99–103.

Stouffer, S. A., Guttman, L., Suchman, E. A., Lazarsfeld, P. F., Staf, S. A., and Clausen, J. A. (1950). *Measurement and prediction.* Princeton, N.J.: Princeton University Press.

Strahan, R. and Gerbasi, K. C. (1972). Short, homogeneous versions of the Crowne-Marlowe social desirability scale. *Journal of Clinical Psychology*, 28, 191–193.

Chapter

16

Time Series

Leland Wilkinson and Yuri Balasanov

Time Series implements a wide variety of time series models, including linear and nonlinear filtering, Fourier analysis, seasonal decomposition, nonseasonal and seasonal exponential smoothing, and the Box-Jenkins (1976) approach to nonseasonal and seasonal ARIMA. You can save results from transformations, smoothing, the deseasonalized series, and forecasts for use in other SYSTAT procedures.

The general strategy for time series analysis is to:

- Plot the series using T-plot, ACF, PACF, or CCF.
- Transform the data to stabilize the variance across time or to make the series stationary using Transform.
- Smooth the series using moving averages, running medians, or general linear filters using LOWESS or Exponential smoothing.
- Fit your model using ARIMA.
- Examine the results by plotting the smoothed or forecasted results.

Before performing a particular time series analysis, you can specify how missing values should be handled.

- **Interpolate.** Interpolates missing values by using DWLS (Distance Weighted Least Squares). DWLS interpolates by locally quadratic approximating curves that are weighted by the distance to each nonmissing point in the series. With this algorithm, all nonmissing values in the series contribute to the missing data estimates, and thus complex local features can be modeled by the interpolant.

- **Delete.** Prevents interpolation and only the leading nonmissing values are retained for analysis. In series that begin with one or more missing values, the series is deleted from the first missing value following one or more nonmissing values. This option enables you to forecast missing values from a nonmissing subsection of the series, for example. You can then insert these forecasts into the series and repeat the procedure later in the series if necessary.

Statistical Background

Time series analysis can range from the purely exploratory to the confirmatory testing of formal models. Series encompasses both exploratory and confirmatory methods. Among the exploratory methods are smoothing and plotting. Among confirmatory models are two general approaches: time domain and frequency domain. In time-domain models, we examine the behavior of variables over time directly. In frequency-domain models, we examine frequency (periodic) components contributing to a time series.

Time-domain (autoregressive, moving average, and trend) models represent a series as a function of previous points in the same series or as a systematic trend over time. Time-domain models can fit complex patterns of time series with just a few parameters. Makridakis, Wheelwright, and McGee (1983), McCleary and Hay (1980), and Nelson (1973) introduce these models, while Box and Jenkins (1976) provide the primary reference for ARIMA models.

Frequency-domain (spectral) models decompose a series into a sum of sinusoidal (waveform) elements. These models are particularly useful when a series arises from a relatively small set of cyclical functions. Bloomfield (1976) introduces these models.

In this introduction, we will discuss exploratory methods (smoothing), time-domain models (ARIMA, seasonal decomposition, exponential smoothing), and frequency-domain (Fourier) models.

Smoothing

Smoothing is a complex topic whose applications exceed space here; consult Velleman and Hoaglin (1981) or Bloomfield (1976) for more complete discussions.

Moving Averages

One of the simplest smoothers is a moving average. If a data point consists of a smooth component plus random error, then if we average several points surrounding a point, the errors should tend to cancel each other out.

Here are two possible moving averages three and four points wide. The window shows which points are being averaged. The boldface shows which point in the series is replaced with the average.

Three-point window

Series	$y1$	$y2$	$y3$	$y4$	$y5$	$y6$	$y7$	$y8$	$y9$
Window	$y1$	**$y2$**	$y3$						
		$y2$	**$y3$**	$y4$					
			$y3$	**$y4$**	$y5$				
				$y4$	**$y5$**	$y6$			
					$y5$	**$y6$**	$y7$		
						$y6$	**$y7$**	$y8$	
							$y7$	**$y8$**	$y9$
New series	$y1$	$x2$	$x3$	$x4$	$x5$	$x6$	$x7$	$x8$	$y9$

Four-point window

Series	$y1$	$y2$	$y3$	$y4$	$y5$	$y6$	$y7$	$y8$	$y9$	$y10$
Window	$y1$	$y2$	**$y3$**	$y4$						
		$y2$	$y3$	**$y4$**	$y5$					
			$y3$	$y4$	**$y5$**	$y6$				
				$y4$	$y5$	**$y6$**	$y7$			
					$y5$	$y6$	**$y7$**	$y8$		
						$y6$	$y7$	**$y8$**	$y9$	
							$y7$	$y8$	**$y9$**	$y10$
New series	$y1$	$y2$	$x3$	$x4$	$x5$	$x6$	$x7$	$x8$	$x9$	$y10$

Notice that the four-point window does not have a point in the series at its center. Consequently, we replace the right point of the two in the middle with the average of the four points. This rule is followed for all even windows except two-point windows. Two-point windows can thus be used to shift asymmetrical smoothings back to the left.

If you prefer algebra, then the following description shows how the three-point window smooths y into x.

$x_1 = y_1$
$x_2 = (y_1 + y_2 + y_3)/3$
$x_3 = (y_2 + y_3 + y_4)/3$

Notice also that the first and last points in the series are unchanged by the three-point window of moving averages. The four-point window leaves the first two and last two points unchanged.

Weighted Running Smoothing

If you know something about filter design (see Bloomfield, 1976), you can construct a more general linear filter by using weights. In the examples, we illustrate seven- and four-point moving averages with equal weights.

The smoothings in the examples used even weights of 1 for each member in the window since we did not specify otherwise. We could, however, set these weights to any real number; for example, 1,2,1. Some of you may recognize these as Hanning weights (Chambers, 1977; Velleman and Hoaglin, 1981). It is possible to show algebraically that weighting by (1,2,1) in a three-observation window is the same as smoothing twice with equal weights in a two-observation window. The DWLS smoothing method for graphics is a form of weighting in which weights are determined by distance weighted least squares.

Running Median Smoothers

Now, let's look at another smoother—running medians. Sometimes it's handy to have a more robust filter when you suspect the data do not contain Gaussian noise. You can choose this filter with the Median option. It works like the Mean option, except the values in the series are replaced by the median of the window instead of the mean.

Can you see why running mean and running median smoothers with a window of two are the same?

We can use combinations of these smoothers to construct more complex nonlinear filters. The following sequence of smoothings comprises a nonlinear filter because it doesn't involve a simple weighted average of the values in a window (except for the final Hanning step). It uses a combination of running medians instead:

Running median smoother, window 4
Running median smoother, window 2
Running median smoother, window 5
Running median smoother, window 3
Running means smoother, window 3, weights 1, 2, 1

You can read about this filter (called **4253H**) in Velleman and Hoaglin (1981). It is due to the work of Tukey (1977). It happens to be a generally effective compound smoother because it clears outliers out of the sequence in the early stages and polishes up the smooth later. Velleman and Hoaglin use this smoother twice on the same data by smoothing the data, smoothing the residuals from this smooth, and adding the two together. You can do this by using Save with the last smoothing to save the smoothed values into a SYSTAT file. You can then merge the files and compute residuals. In the final step, you can smooth the residuals.

LOWESS Smoothing

Cleveland (1979) presented a method for smoothing values of *Y* paired with a set of ordered *X* values. Chambers et al. (1983) introduce this technique and present some clear examples. If you are not a statistician, by the way, and want some background information on recent advances in statistics, read the Chambers book (and Velleman and Hoaglin if you don't know about Tukey's work).

Scatterplot smoothing allows you to look for a functional relation between *Y* and *X* without prejudging its shape (or its monotonicity). The method for finding smoothed values involves a locally weighted robust regression. SYSTAT implements Cleveland's LOWESS algorithm on equally spaced data values. You can also use LOWESS on scatterplots of unequally spaced data values.

ARIMA Modeling and Forecasting

The following data show the U.S. birth rate (per 1000) for several decades during and following World War II. They were compiled from federal statistics, principally the U.S. census.

YEAR	RATE	YEAR	RATE
1943	22.7	1965	19.4
1944	21.2	1966	18.4
1945	20.4	1967	17.8
1946	24.1	1968	17.5
1947	26.6	1969	17.8
1948	24.9	1970	18.4
1949	24.5	1971	17.2
1950	24.1	1972	15.6
1951	24.9	1973	14.9
1952	25.1	1974	14.9
1953	25.1	1975	14.8
1954	25.3	1976	14.8
1955	25.0	1977	15.4
1956	25.2	1978	15.3
1957	25.3	1979	15.9
1958	24.5	1980	15.9
1959	24.3	1981	15.9
1960	23.7	1982	15.9
1961	23.3	1983	15.5
1962	22.4	1984	15.7
1963	21.7	1985	15.7
1964	21.0		

These data are a **time series** because they comprise values on a variable distributed across time. How can you use these data to forecast birth rates up to the year 2000? A popular statistical method for such a forecast is linear regression. Let's try it. Here is a plot of birth rates against year with the least squares line. The data points are connected so that you can see the series more clearly.

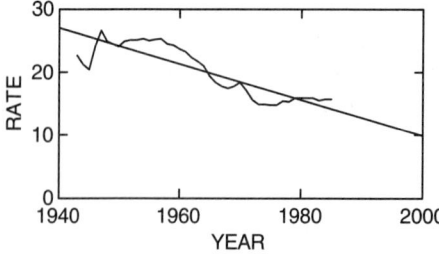

What's wrong with this forecasting method? You may want to read Chapter 14 (if you haven't already). There, we discussed assumptions needed for estimating a model using least squares. We can legitimately fit a line to these data by least squares for the explicit purpose of getting predicted values on the line as close as possible, on average, to observed values in the data. In forecasting, however, we want to use a fitted model to extrapolate beyond the series. The fitted linear model is:

RATE = 579.342 − 0.285 * YEAR

If we want our estimates of the slope and intercept in this model to be unbiased, we need to assume that the errors (ε) in the population model are independent of each other and of *YEAR*. Does our data plot give us any indication of this?

On the contrary, it appears from the data that the randomness in this model is related to *YEAR*. Take any two adjacent years' data. On average, if there is an underprediction one year, there will be an underprediction the next. If there is overprediction one year, there is likely to be overprediction the next. These data clearly violate the assumption of independence in the errors.

Autocorrelation

There is a statistical index that reveals how correlated the residuals are. It is called the **autocorrelation**. The first-order autocorrelation is the ordinary Pearson correlation of a series of numbers with the same series shifted by one observation ($y_2, y_1; y_3, y_2; ...; y_n, y_{n-1}$). In our residuals from the linear model, this statistic is 0.953. If you remember about squaring correlation coefficients to reveal proportion of variance, this means that over 89 percent of the variation in error from predicting one year's birth rate can be accounted for by the error in predicting the previous year's.

The second-order autocorrelation is produced by correlating the series ($y_3, y_1; y_4, y_2; ...; y_n, y_{n-2}$). Computing this statistic involves shifting the series down *two* years. As you may now infer, we can keep shifting and computing autocorrelations for as many years as there are in the series. There is a simple graphical way to display all these autocorrelations. It looks like a bar graph of the autocorrelations sequenced by year, or index in the series. The first bar is the first autocorrelation (0.953). The next highest bar is the second, and so on. Here it is:

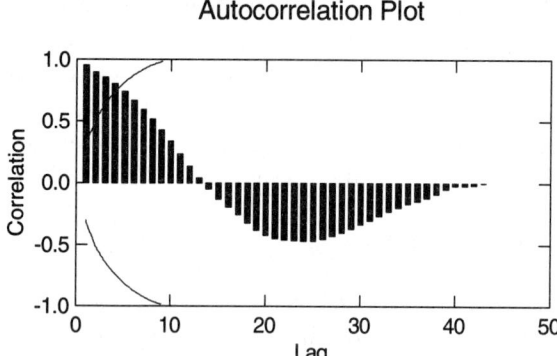

Autocorrelation Plot

This autocorrelation plot tells us about all the autocorrelations in the residuals from the linear model. As you can see, there is a strong dependence in the residuals. As we shift the series far enough back, the autocorrelations become negative, because the series crosses the prediction line and the residuals become negative. Over the entire series, there are three crossings and three corresponding shifts in sign among the autocorrelations.

Autoregressive Models

We would have the same serial correlation problem if we refined our model to include a quadratic term:

$$\text{RATE} = \beta_0 + \beta_1 \text{YEAR} + \beta_2 \text{YEAR}^2 + \varepsilon$$

You can try this model with MGLH, but you will find a large autocorrelation in the residuals even though the curve fits the data more closely. How can we construct a model that includes the autocorrelation structure itself?

The autoregressive model does this:

$$\text{RATE} = \beta_0 + \beta_1 \text{RATE}_{i-1} + \varepsilon_i$$

Notice that this model expresses a year's birth rate as a function of the previous year's birth rate—not as a function of *YEAR*. Time becomes a sequencing variable, not a predictor.

To fit this, we fit an AR(1) model with the ARIMA procedure. Here is the result, with forecasts extending to the year 2000:

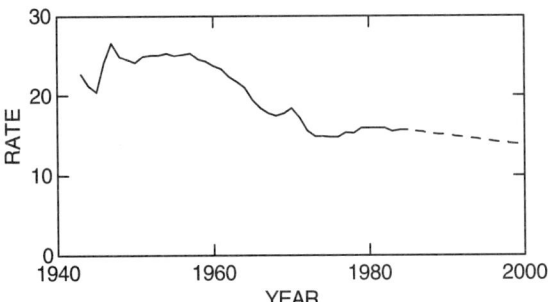

The forecasted values are represented by the dotted line. Unlike the regression model forecast, the autoregressive forecast begins at the last birth rate value and drifts back toward the mean of the series. This forecast behavior is typical of this particular model, which is often called a **random walk**.

Moving Average Models

There is another series model that can account for fluctuations across time. The **moving average model** looks like this:

$$y_i = \varepsilon_i - \beta_1 \varepsilon_{i-1}$$

This models a series as a cumulation of random shocks or disturbances. If this model represented someone's spending habits, for example, then whether the person went on a spending spree one day would depend on whether he or she went on one the day before. Unlike the autoregressive model, which represents an observation as a function of previous observations' *values*, the moving average model represents an observation as a function of the previous observations' *errors*. So you can see the difference between the two, here are examples of first-order autoregressive, or AR(1), and moving average, or MA(1), series:

Chapter 16

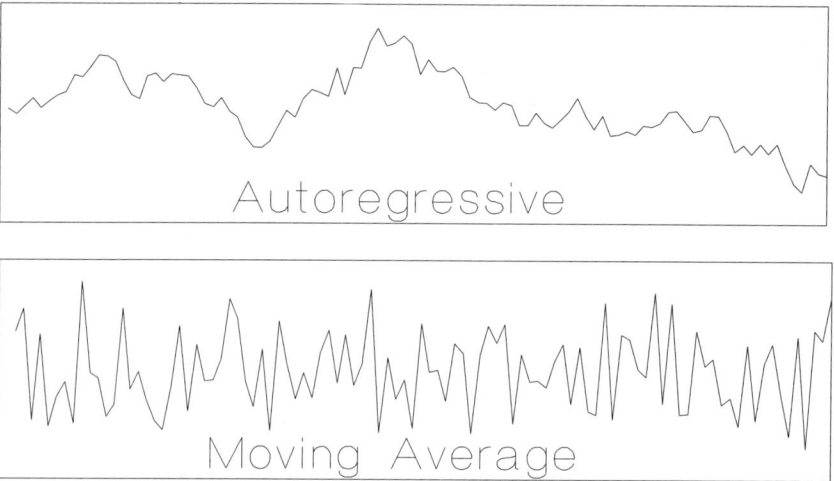

ARMA Models

Autoregressive and moving average models can be mixed to make autoregressive-moving average models. They can be mixed with different orders, for example, AR(2) plus MA(1), which is often expressed as ARMA(2,1). A text on forecasting will offer instances of these more complicated models. You could visually add the two sample series above, however, to see how an ARMA(1,1) model would look.

Identifying Models

Before you can fit an AR, MA, or ARMA model, you need to identify which model is appropriate for your series. You can look at the series plot to find distinctive patterns, as in the figure contrasting AR(1) and MA(1) directly above. Real data seldom fit these ideal types as clearly, however. There are several powerful tools that distinguish these families of models. We have already seen one: the autocorrelation function plot (ACF). The **partial autocorrelation function plot** (PACF) provides additional information about serial correlation. To identify models, we use both of these plots.

Stationarity

Before doing these plots, however, you should be sure the series is **stationary**. This means:

- **The mean of the series is constant across time.** You can use the Trend transformation to remove linear trend from the series. This will not reduce quadratic or other curvilinear trend, however. A better method is to Difference the data. This transformation replaces values by the differences between each value and the previous value, thereby removing trend. For cyclical series, like monthly sales, seasonal differencing may be required before fitting a model (see below). Data that are drifting up or down across the series generally should be differenced.

- **The variance of the series is constant across time.** If the series variation is increasing around its mean level across time, try a Log transformation. If it is decreasing around its mean level across time (a rare occurrence), try a Square transformation. You should generally do this before differencing.

- **The autocorrelations of the series depend only on the difference in time points and not on the time period itself.** If the first half of the ACF looks different from the second, try seasonal differencing after identifying a period on which the data are fluctuating. Monthly, quarterly, seasonal, annual data often cycle this way.

ACF Plots

The autocorrelation function plot displays the pattern of autocorrelations. We have seen in this introduction an ACF plot of the residuals from a linear fit to birth rate. The slow decay of the autocorrelations after the first indicates autoregressive behavior in the residuals.

PACF Plots

The partial autocorrelation function plot displays autocorrelations, but each one below the first is conditioned on the previous autocorrelation. The PACF shows the relationship of points in a series to preceding points after partialing out the influence of intervening points. We examine them for effects that do not depend linearly on previous (smaller lag) autocorrelations.

Identification Using ACF and PACF Plots Together

Let's summarize our identification strategy. First, make sure the series is stationary. If variance is nonconstant, transform it with Log or Square. If trend is present, remove it with differencing. Finally, if seasonality is present, remove it with seasonal differencing. Then examine ACF and PACF plots together. On the facing page is a chart of possible types of patterns. To the right of each series is the ACF plot (in the middle) and the PACF plot (on the right). However, because coefficients in the model can be negative or positive, other representations are possible. The plots shown here are based on one particular combination of signs.

Finally, remember that differencing can remove both trend and autoregressive effects. If an AR(1) model fits your data, as with our birth rate example, then differencing will produce only white noise and your ACF will look uniformly random. As a result, differencing is like constraining an autoregressive parameter to be exactly one.

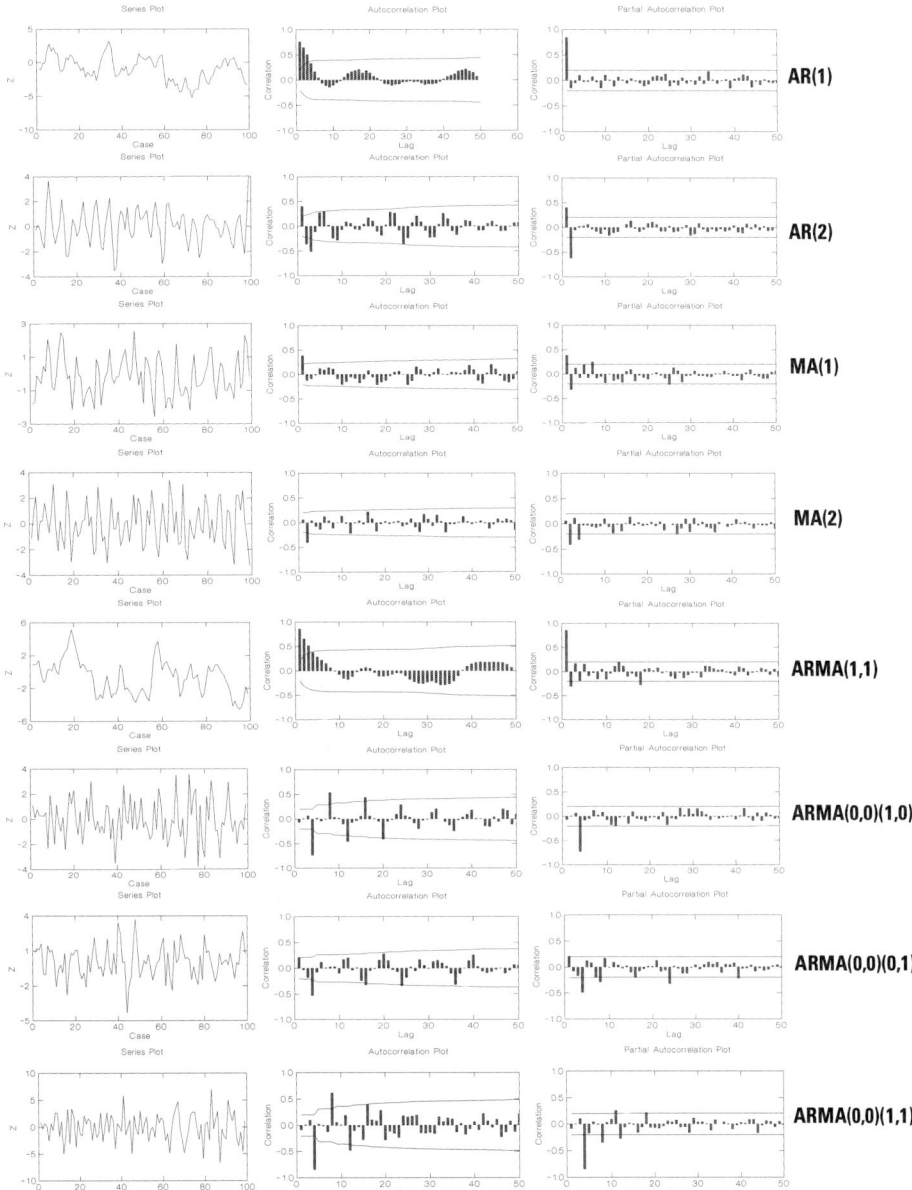

Estimating the ARIMA Model

When you have identified the model as AR, MA, or a mixture, then you can fit it by specifying the AR order (P=n) and the MA order (Q=n). The "I" in ARIMA stands for "Integrated" and is a parameter that has to do with differencing. Any differencing you do while identifying the model will be included automatically in calculating your forecasts.

When you have estimated the model, pay attention to the standard errors of the parameters. If a parameter estimate is much smaller in absolute value than two standard errors away from zero, then it is probably unnecessary in the model. Refit the model without it. If you are uncertain about model identification, you can sometimes use this rule of thumb to compare two different models. The mean square error (MSE) of the model fit can also guide you. Generally, you are looking for a parsimonious model with small MSE.

Problems with Forecast Models

Forecasting is a vast field, and we cannot begin to explain even the basics in such a brief discussion. Makridakis, Wheelwright, and McGee (1983) cover the topic fairly extensively. SYSTAT contains several methods for forecasting, with which you can experiment on these data. Exponential smoothing, for example, should provide similar forecasts to the ARIMA model. Keep in mind several things as you go:

- There is nothing like extrinsic knowledge. We use forecasting methods for SYSTAT budget planning. We always compare them to staff predictions of sales, however. In general, averaging staff predictions does better than the data-driven forecasting models. The reason is simple—staff know about external factors that are likely to affect sales. These are one-time events that are not easily included in models. Although we are not experts on the stock market, we would bet the same is true for investing. "Chartist" models that are based solely on the trends in stocks will not do as well, on average, as strategies based on knowledge of companies' economic performance and, in the illegal extreme, inside trading information.

- Always examine your residuals. The same reasons for using residual diagnostics in ordinary linear regression apply to nonlinear forecasting models. In both cases, you want to see independence, or white noise.

- Don't extrapolate too far. As in regression, predictions beyond the data are shaky. The farther you stray from the ends of the data, the less reliable are the predictions. The confidence limits on the forecasts will give you some flavor of this.

Box and Jenkins (1976) provide the primary reference for these procedures. Financial forecasters should consult Nelson (1973) and Vandaele (1983) for applied introductions. Social scientists should look at McCleary and Hay (1980) for applications to behavioral data.

Many treatments (including Box and Jenkins) outline the ARIMA modeling process in three stages: Identification, Estimation, and Diagnosis. This is the outline we have followed in this introduction. With SYSTAT you identify models with Transform, Case plot, ACF plot, and PACF plot, estimate them with ARIMA, and diagnose their adequacy with more plots. For more complex problems, you may have to use other procedures, also.

ARIMA—Auto Regressive Integrated Moving Average—models can fit many time series with remarkably few parameters. Sometimes, ARIMA and Fourier models can be used effectively on the same data. As with other modeling procedures, decisions about appropriateness of competing models must rest on theoretical grounds. Nevertheless, a researcher should lean toward ARIMA models when it is reasonable to assume that points in a process are primarily functions of previous points and their errors, rather than periodic signal plus noise.

Seasonal Decomposition and Adjustment

A time series can be viewed as a sum of individual components that may include a term for location (level or mean value), a trend component (long-term movements in the level of a series over time), a seasonal component, and an irregular component (the part unique to each time point). We can use the Mean transformation to remove the mean (location) from a series, Trend to remove a linear trend from a series, and Difference to eliminate either a trend or a seasonal effect from a series. Each of these transformations changes the scale of the series but does not directly provide information about the form of the trend or the seasonal component.

Alternatively, you may want to adjust the values in a series for the seasonal component but leave the series in the same scale or unit. This enables you to interpret the value units in the same way as the original series and to compare values in the series after removing differences due to seasonality.

For example, sales data for many products are strongly seasonal. More suntan lotion is sold in the summer than in the winter. It is therefore difficult to compare suntan lotion sales from month to month (going up? going down?) without first taking seasonal differences into account.

Seasonal differences can be accounted for by determining a factor for each period of the cycle. Quarterly data may have a seasonal factor for each of the four quarters. Monthly data may have a seasonal factor for each of the twelve months.

Seasonal factors can take either of two forms: additive (fixed) or multiplicative (proportional). An additive seasonal factor is a fixed number of units above or below the general level of the series; for example, 10,000 more bottles of suntan lotion were sold in July than the average month. In a multiplicative or proportional model, the seasonal factor is a percentage of the level of the series; for example, 200% more bottles of suntan lotion were sold in July than in the average month.

Additive seasonal effects are removed from a series by subtracting estimates of the appropriate seasonal factor from each point in the series. Multiplicative seasonal effects are removed by dividing each point by the appropriate seasonal factor. Seasonal computes either additive or multiplicative seasonal factors for a series and uses them to adjust the original series.

Exponential Smoothing

Exponential smoothing forecasts future observations as weighted averages (a running smoother) of previous observations. For simple exponential smoothing, each forecast is the new estimate of location for the series. For models with trend and/or seasonal components, exponential smoothing smooths the location, trend, and seasonal components separately. For each component, you must specify a smoothing weight between 0 and 1. In practice, weights between 0.10 and 0.30 are most frequently used.

The Exponential Smoothing option allows you to specify a linear or percentage growth (also called exponential or multiplicative) trend or neither, and an additive or multiplicative seasonal component or neither. There is always a location component. Thus, there are nine possible smoothing models from which you can choose.

Smoothing with a linear trend component and no seasonal component is **Holt's method**. Smoothing with both a linear trend and a multiplicative seasonal term is **Winter's three-parameter model**.

The exponential smoothing procedure obtains initial estimates of seasonal components in the same manner as Seasonal. If there is a trend component, SYSTAT uses regression (after adjusting values for any seasonal effects) to estimate the initial values of the location and trend parameters. If there is neither a trend nor a seasonal component, the first value in the series is used as the initial estimate of location.

Fourier Analysis

If you believe your series is cyclical—such as astronomical or behavioral data—then you should consider **Fourier analysis**. The Fourier model decomposes a series into a finite sum of trigonometric components—sine and cosine waves of different frequencies. If your data are cyclical at a particular frequency, such as monthly, then a few Fourier components might be sufficient to capture most of the nonrandom variation.

Fourier analysis decomposes a time series just as a musical waveform can be decomposed into a fundamental wave plus harmonics. The French mathematician Fourier devised this decomposition around the beginning of the nineteenth century and applied it to heat transfer and other physical and mathematical problems. This transformation is of the general form:

$$f(t) = x + x\sin(t) + x\cos(t) + x\sin(2t) + x\cos(2t) + \ldots$$

The Fourier decomposition can be useful for designing a filter to smooth noise and for analyzing the spectral composition of a time series. The most frequent application involves constructing a periodogram which displays the squared amplitude (magnitude) of the trigonometric components versus their frequencies. Fourier can be used to construct these displays. For further details on Fourier analysis, consult Brigham (1974) or Bloomfield (1976).

Fourier transforms are time consuming to compute because they involve numerous trigonometric functions. Cooley and Tukey (1965) developed a fast algorithm for computing the transform on a discrete series that makes the spectral analysis of lengthy series practical. A variant of this Fast Fourier Transform algorithm is implemented in SYSTAT.

The discrete Fourier transform should be done on series with lengths (number of cases) that are powers of 2. If you do not have samples of 32, 64, 128, 256, etc., you should pad your series with zeros up to the next power of 2. If you have a series called Series with only 102 cases, for example, you can recode to add zeros to cases 103 through 128. If you do not pad the file in this way, the Fourier procedure finds the highest power of 2 less than the number of cases in the file and transforms only that number of cases. (In this example, it would have transformed only the first 64 cases.)

A useful graph to accompany Fourier analysis is the **periodogram**. This graph plots magnitude (or squared magnitude) against frequency. It reveals the relative contribution of different frequency waveforms to the overall shape of the series. If the periodogram contains one large spike, then it means that the series can be fit well by a single sinusoidal waveform. The periodogram is itself like a series, so sometimes you may want to smooth it with one of the Series smoothers

Fourier analysis is often used to construct a filter, which works like running smoothers. A filter allows variation of only a limited band of frequencies to pass through. A low-pass filter, for example, removes high-frequency information. It is often used to remove noise in radio transmissions, recordings, and photographs. A high-pass filter, on the other hand, removes low-frequency variation. It is used as one method for detecting edges in photographs. You can construct filters in SYSTAT by computing the Fourier transform, deleting real and imaginary components for low or high frequencies, and then using the inverse transform to produce a smoothed waveform.

If you reproduce a series from a few low-frequency Fourier components, the resulting smooth will be similar to that achieved by a running window of an appropriate width. The Fourier method will constrain the smooth to be more regularly periodic, however, since the selected trigonometric components will completely determine the periodicity of the smooth.

Graphical Displays for Time Series in SYSTAT

Plotting data, autocorrelations, and partial autocorrelations is often one of the first steps in understanding time series data. SYSTAT provides several graphical displays, each of which is discussed in turn.

T-Plot Main Dialog Box

T-plot provides time series plots. This can give you a general idea of a series, enabling you to detect a long-term trend, seasonal fluctuations, and gross outliers.

To open the T-plot dialog box, from the menus choose:

Statistics
  Time Series
    T-plot...

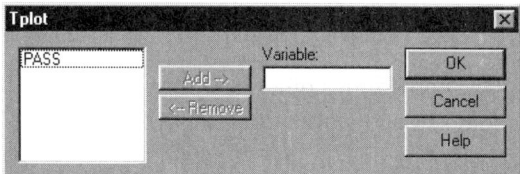

The variable you select is the dependent (vertical axis) variable, and the case number (time series observation) is the independent variable (horizontal axis). The points are connected with a line.

Time Main Dialog Box

Time labels the sequence(s) of values in a file with identifiers that represent the cycle and the periodicity. The identifiers label the T-plot *x* axis for each time point.

To open the Time dialog box, from the menus choose:
Statistics
 Time Series
  Time...

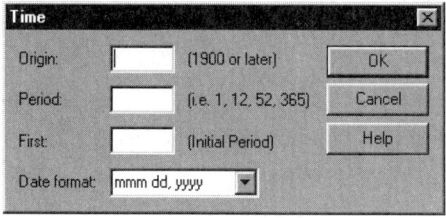

The following options can be specified:

Origin. Starting point of the time series, expressed as a year.

Period. Periods within each year. The value defines the number of observations within each year. For example, specify 12 for months, 52 for weeks, 365 for days, etc. If there is only one observation per year, specify 1.

First. Starting point of the period of observation. For example, if the period is months within each year and the first observation is for June, the First value would be 6.

Date format. The date display format for values on the *x* axis (time axis). Select a format from the drop-down list.

ACF Plot Main Dialog Box

Autocorrelation plots show the correlations of a time series with itself shifted down a specified number of cases. Plots of autocorrelations help you to investigate the relation of each time point to previous time points. If the autocorrelation at lag 1 is high, then each value is highly correlated with the value at the previous time point. If the autocorrelation at lag 12 is high for data collected monthly, then each month is highly correlated with the same month a year before (for example, for monthly sales data, sales in December may be more related to those in previous Decembers than to those in November or January).

To open the ACF Plot dialog box, from the menus choose:

Statistics
  Time Series
    ACF...

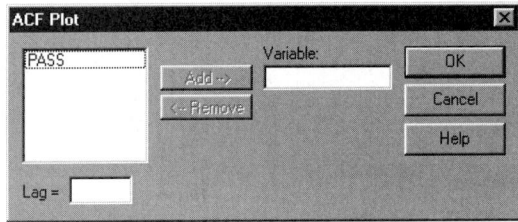

You can specify the maximum number of lags to plot. The plot contains the autocorrelations for all lags between 1 and the number specified.

PACF Plot Main Dialog Box

Partial autocorrelation plots show the relationship of points in a series to preceding points after partialing out the influence of intervening points.

To open the PACF Plot dialog box, from the menus choose:

Statistics
  Time Series
    PACF...

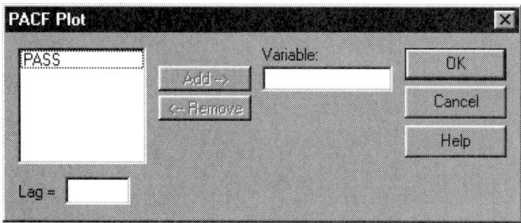

You can specify the maximum number of lags to plot. The plot contains the partial autocorrelations for all lags between 1 and the number specified.

CCF Plot Main Dialog Box

Cross-correlation plots help to identify relations between two different series and any time delays to the relations. A correlation for a negative lag indicates the relation of the values in the first series to values in the second series that number of periods earlier. The correlation at lag 0 is the usual Pearson correlation. Similarly, correlations at positive lags relate values in the first series to subsequent values in the second series.

To open the CCF Plot dialog box, from the menus choose:

Statistics
  Time Series
    CCF...

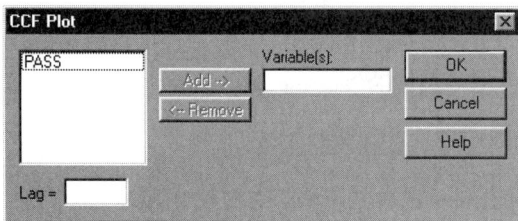

You can specify the number of lags to plot. Approximately half of the lags will be positive and half will be negative.

Using Commands

To graph a time series, first specify your data with USE filename. Continue with:

```
SERIES
     TIME origin period first
     TPLOT var / LAG=n
     ACF var / LAG=n
     PACF var / LAG=n
     CCF var1, var2 / LAG=n
```

Transformations of Time Series in SYSTAT

Transformations Main Dialog Box

To open the Transformations dialog box, from the menus choose:

Statistics
  Time Series
    Transform...

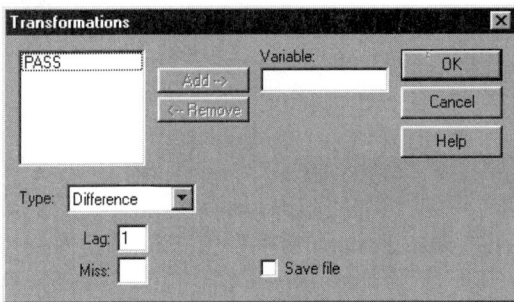

Available transformations include:

- **Mean.** Subtracts the mean from each value in the series.
- **Log.** Replaces the values in a series with their natural logarithms, and thus removes nonstationary variability, such as increasing variability over time.
- **Square.** Squares the values in a series. This is useful for producing periodograms and for normalizing variance across the series.
- **Trend.** Removes linear trend from a series.

- **Difference**. Replaces each value by the difference between it and the previous value, thereby removing trend (nonstationarity in level over time). Using differences between each successive value is called lag 1. A Lag option allows seasonal differences (for example, for data collected monthly, request a lag of 12).
- **Percent Change**. Replaces each value by the difference from the previous value expressed as a percentage change—the difference in values divided by the previous value.
- **Index**. Replaces each value by the ratio of the value to the value of a base observation, which you can specify for Base. By default, SYSTAT uses the first observation in the series.
- **Taper**. Smooths the series with the split-cosine-bell taper. Tapering weights the middle of a series more than the endpoints. Use it prior to a Fourier decomposition to reduce "leakage" between components. For Proportion, enter the proportion (P) of the series to be tapered. Choose a weight function that varies between a "boxcar" (P=0) and a full cycle of a cosine wave from trough to trough (P=1). For intermediate values of P, the weight function is flat in the center section and cosine tapered at either end. Default=0.5.

You can pile up transformation commands in any order, as long as you do not encounter a mathematically undefined result. In that case, SYSTAT displays an error message and the variable is restored to its original value in the file.

All transformations are "in place." That is, the series is stored in the active work area and the transformed values are written over the old ones. The original file is not altered, however, because all the work is done in the memory of the computer. To save the results of a transformation to a SYSTAT file, select Save file.

Clear Series

You can clear any past series transformations from memory and restore the original values of the series. It is not possible to clear only the latest transformation (unless you are saving to files after each step)—Clear Series undoes all the transformations.

To clear series transformations, from the menus choose:

Statistics
 Time Series
  Clear Series...

Using Commands

To transform a time series, first specify your data with USE filename. Continue with:

```
SERIES
    DIFFERENCE var / LAG=n  MISS=n
     LOG var
     PCNTCHANGE var
     MEAN var
     SQUARE var
     TREND var
     INDEX var / BASE=n
     TAPER var / P=n
```

CLEAR var clears transformations from memory.

Smoothing a Time Series in SYSTAT

Sometimes, with a "noisy" time series, you simply want to view some sort of smoothed version of the series even though you have no idea what type of function generated the series. A variety of techniques can smooth, or filter, the noise from such a series.

Smooth Main Dialog Box

To open the Smooth dialog box, from the menus choose:

Statistics
  Time Series
    Smooth...

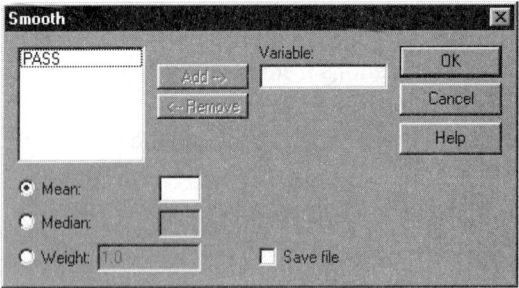

Smooth provides the following methods for smoothing time series:

- **Mean**. Running means (moving averages). Mean of a span of series values surrounding and including the current value. Specify the number of values (observations) to use in the calculation.
- **Median**. Running medians. Median of a span of series values surrounding and including the current value. Specify the number of values (observations) to use in the calculation.
- **Weight**. General linear filters in which you can specify your own weights. Smooth transforms the weights before using them so that they sum to 1.0. Weight=1, 2, 1 is the same as Weight=0.25, 0.5, 0.25 or Weight=3, 6, 3.

To save the results of a smoothing operation to a SYSTAT file, select **Save file**.

LOWESS Main Dialog Box

Cleveland (1979) presented a method for smoothing values of Y paired with a set of ordered X values. Chambers et al. (1983) introduce this technique and present some clear examples. If you are not a statistician, and want a glimpse of some of the details, read the Chambers book and Velleman and Hoaglin (if you are unfamiliar with Tukey's work).

Scatterplot smoothing enables you to look for a functional relation between Y and X without prejudging its shape (or its monotonicity). **LOWESS** is a smoothing method that uses an iterative locally weighted least-squares method to fit a curve to a set of points.

To open the LOWESS dialog box, from the menus choose:

Statistics
  Time Series
    Lowess...

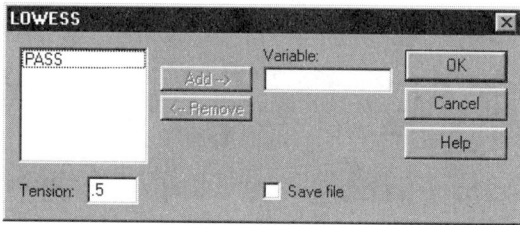

Tension. Tension determines the stiffness of the smooth. It varies between 0 and 1, with a default of 0.5.

To save the results of a LOWESS smooth to a SYSTAT file, select **Save file**.

Exponential Smoothing Main Dialog Box

To open the Exponential Smoothing dialog box, from the menus choose:

Statistics
  Time Series
    Exponential...

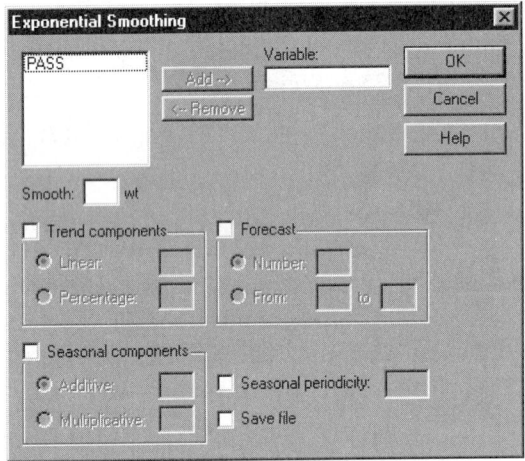

The following options can be specified:

Smooth. Specify a smoothing weight between 0 and 1. In practice, weights between 0.1 and 0.3 are most frequently used.

Trend components. You can supply a weight for either a Linear or Percentage trend component. Values usually range between 0.1 and 0.3. The default is 0.2.

Forecast. Number or the range of new cases to predict. For example, a value of 10 produces forecasts for 10 time points; a range from 144 to 154 produces forecasts for time points 144 through 154.

Seasonal components. You can supply a weight for either Additive or Multiplicative. Values usually range between 0.1 and 0.3. The default is 0.2.

Seasonal periodicity. Indicates the repetitive cyclical variation, such as the number of months in a year or the number of days in a week. The default is 12 (as in months in a year).

To save the forecasts and residuals to a SYSTAT file, select Save file.

Using Commands

To smooth a time series, first specify your data with USE filename. Continue with:

```
SERIES
     SMOOTH var / LOWESS=n  MEAN=n  MEDIAN=n  WT=n1,n2,…
     EXPONENTIAL var / ADDITIVE=n  FORECAST=n (or a,b for a range)
                      LINEAR=n  MULTIPLICATIVE=n  PERCENTAGE=n,
                      SEASON=n  SMOOTH=n
```

Seasonal Adjustments in SYSTAT

Transformations can remove the mean, trends, and seasonal effects from a time series. However, transformations alter the scale of a time series and also yield no information regarding the form of the removed trend or seasonal effect. As an alternative, you can use seasonal adjustments to account for seasonal factors while maintaining the original scale of the time series.

Seasonal Adjustment Main Dialog Box

To open the Seasonal Adjustment dialog box, from the menus choose:

Statistics
  Time Series
    Seasonal Adjustment...

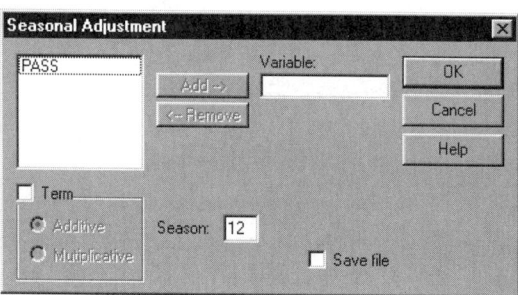

The following options can be specified:

- **Term**. An Additive seasonal factor is a fixed number of units above or below the general level of the series. In a Multiplicative model, the seasonal factor is a percentage of the level of the series.

- **Season**. Indicates the **periodicity**—the repetitive cyclical variation—such as the number of months in a year or the number of days in a week. The default is 12.

To save the deseasonalized series to a SYSTAT file, select **Save file**.

Using Commands

To seasonally adjust a time series, first specify your data with USE filename. Continue with:

```
SERIES
    ADJSEASON var / ADDITIVE  MULTIPLICATIVE  SEASON=n
```

ARIMA Models in SYSTAT

ARIMA (AutoRegressive Integrated Moving Average) models combine autoregressive techniques with the moving average approach. Consequently, each case is a function of previous cases and previous errors.

ARIMA Main Dialog Box

To open the ARIMA dialog box, from the menus choose:

Statistics
  Time Series
    ARIMA...

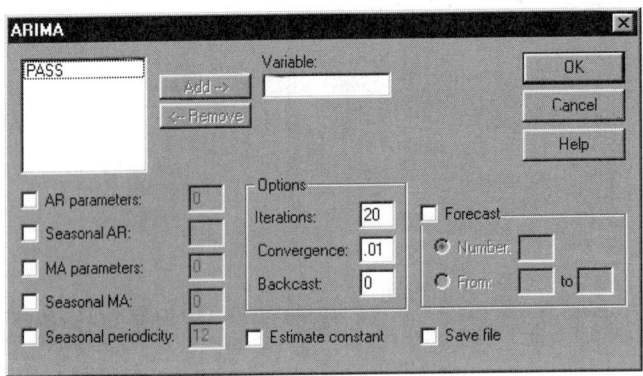

ARIMA provides ARIMA models for time series. The following options can be specified:

AR parameters. Number of autoregressive parameters.

Seasonal AR. Number of seasonal autoregressive parameters.

MA parameter. Number of moving average parameters.

Seasonal MA. Number of seasonal moving average parameters.

Seasonal periodicity. Defines the seasonal periodicity.

Estimate constant. Includes a constant in the model.

Options. You can specify the number of iterations for the ARIMA model, the convergence criterion, and a backcast value to extend the series backwards (forecasting in reverse). Although it slows down computation, you should use backcasting for seasonal models especially and choose a length greater than the seasonal period.

Don't play around with convergence unless you are failing to get convergence of the estimates after many iterations. It is better to increase the number of iterations than to decrease the convergence criterion, since your estimates will be more precise. In any case, it cannot be set greater than one tenth. Sometimes models fail to converge after many iterations because you have misspecified them.

Forecast. Number or the range of new cases to predict. For example, a value of 10 produces forecasts for 10 time points; a range from 144 to 154 produces forecasts for time points 144 through 154.

To save the residuals to a SYSTAT file, select **Save file**.

Using Commands

To fit an ARIMA model, first specify your data with **USE filename**. Continue with:

```
SERIES
    ARIMA var / P=n  PS=n  Q=n  QS=n  SEASON=n  CONSTANT,
          BACKCAST=n  ITER=n  CONV=n,
          FORECAST=n (or time1,time2)
```

Fourier Models in SYSTAT

Fourier models are particularly well-suited to cyclical time series. These models decompose a time series into a sum of trigonometric components.

Fourier Main Dialog Box

The Fourier model decomposes a time series into a finite sum of sine and cosine waves of different frequencies. If your data are cyclical at a particular frequency, such as monthly, then a few Fourier components might capture most of the nonrandom variation.

To open the Fourier dialog box, from the menus choose:

Statistics
  Time Series
    Fourier...

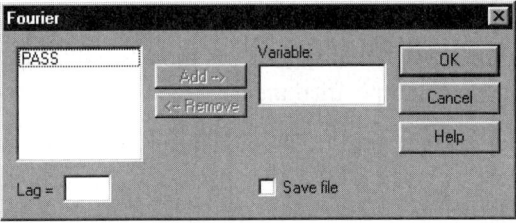

The Lag specification indicates the number of cases to use in the analysis.

If you select two variables, the inverse transformation is computed. The first variable selected is used as the real component, and the second variable is used as the imaginary component. To save the real and imaginary components in a SYSTAT file, select **Save file**. Real and imaginary components are saved instead of magnitude and phase because that allows you to do an inverse Fourier transform.

For example, assume that you have saved the results of a direct transformation into a file *MYFOUR*. That file should contain two variables—*REAL* and *IMAG*—which are the two components of the transformation. To obtain the inverse Fourier transformation:

```
USE myfour
FOURIER real imag
```

Since you specify two variables, SYSTAT assumes that you want the inverse transformation, and that the first variable is the real component, and the second, the imaginary component. The work is done in the active work area, so the resulting real series is stored in the active work area occupied by *REAL* (or whatever you called the first variable corresponding to the real component).

If you absolutely must have magnitude and phase in a SYSTAT file instead of the real and imaginary components, do the following transformations:

```
USE myfour
LET magnitude = SQR(real*real + imag*imag)
LET phase = ATN (imag/real)
```

Using Commands

To fit a Fourier model, first specify your data with USE filename. Continue with:

```
SERIES
    FOURIER varlist / LAG=n
```

Usage Considerations

Types of data. For time series analysis, each case (row) in the data represents an observation at a different time. The observations are assumed to be taken at equally spaced time intervals.

Print options. Output is standard for all PRINT lengths.

Quick Graphs. Smoothing and seasonal adjustments yield a time series plot. Forecasting in ARIMA results in a time series plot of the original series with the forecasts. Fourier analysis produces periodograms (the squared magnitude against frequencies).

Saving files. You can save transformed, smoothed, deseasonalized, and forecasted values, as well as both the real and imaginary parts of the Fourier transform.

BY groups. BY variables are not available in SERIES.

Bootstrapping. Bootstrapping is not available in this procedure.

Case frequencies. FREQ variables have no effect in SERIES.

Case weights. SERIES does not allow case weighting.

Chapter 16

Examples

Example 1
Time Series Plot

To illustrate these displays, we use monthly counts of international airline passengers during 1949–60. Box and Jenkins call the series G. Each of the 144 monthly counts is stored as a case in the SYSTAT file named *AIRLINE*.

TPLOT provides a graphical view of the raw data. Here we plot the *AIRLINE* passenger data. The input follows:

```
USE airline
SERIES
    TIME 1949 12
    TPLOT pass
```

The resulting plot is:

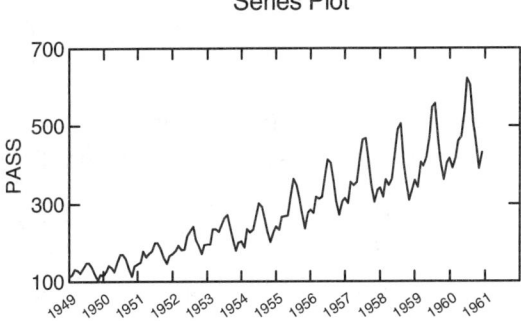

Notice that the counts tend to peak during the summer months each year and that the number of passengers tends to increase over time (a positive trend). Notice also that the spread or variance tends to increase over time. One way to deal with this problem is to log-transform the data.

Applying the log transformation requires the following commands:

```
LOG pass
TPLOT pass
```

The resulting plot follows:

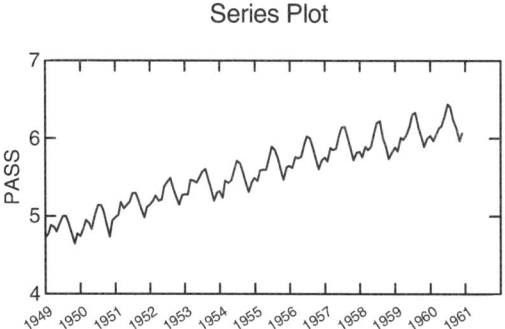

Series Plot

Compare this plot with the previous one—the variance across time now appears more stable, but there is still a positive upward trend over time.

Example 2
Autocorrelation Plot

To display an autocorrelation plot, the input is:

```
USE airline
SERIES
   LOG pass
   ACF pass
```

The plot is:

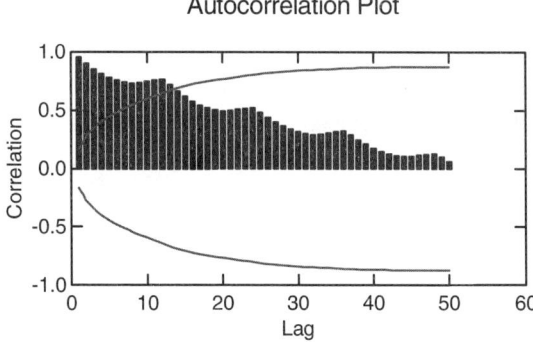

Autocorrelation Plot

Note that we use the logged values of *PASS*. The shading in the display indicates the size of the correlation at each lag (that is, like a bar chart). The correlation of each value with the previous value in time (lag 1) is close to 1.0; with values 12 months before (lag 12), it is around 0.75. The curved line marks approximate 95% confidence levels for the significance of each correlation. Notice the slow decay of these values. To most investigators, this indicates that the series should be differenced.

Example 3
Partial Autocorrelation Plot

To display a partial autocorrelation plot, the input is:

```
USE airline
SERIES
   LOG pass
   PACF pass
```

The plot is:

Partial Autocorrelation Plot

The first autocorrelation is the same as in the ACF plot. There are no previous autocorrelations, so it is not adjusted. The second-order autocorrelation was close to 0.90 in the ACF plot, but after adjusting for the first autocorrelation, it is reduced to −0.118.

Example 4
Cross-Correlation Plot

This example uses the *SPNDMONY* file, which contains two quarterly series, *SPENDING* (consumer expenditures) and *MONEY* (money stock) in billions of current dollars for the United States during the years 1952–1956. The first record (case) in the file contains the *SPENDING* and *MONEY* dollars for the first quarter of 1952; the second record, dollars for the second quarter of 1952, and so on (that is, if each case contains *SPENDING* and *MONEY* values for a quarter). These series are analyzed by Chatterjee and Price (1977).

The input follows:

```
USE spndmony
SERIES
    CCF spending money / LAG=15
```

The resulting plot is:

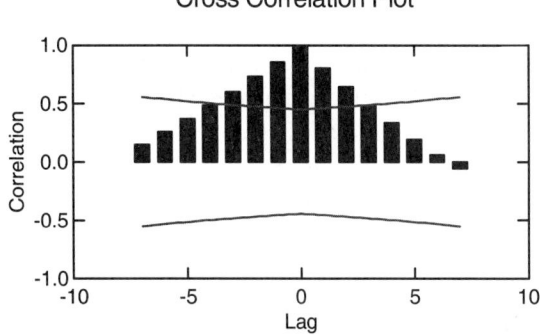

There is strong correlation between the two series at lag 0, tapering off the further one goes in either direction. This is true of all cross-correlation functions between two trended series. Since both series are increasing, early values in both series tend to be small, and final values tend to be large. This produces a large positive correlation.

Differencing

To better understand the relationship, if any, between the series, difference them to remove the common trend and then display a new CCF plot.

To difference both series:

```
USE spndmony
SERIES
   DIFFERENCE spending
   DIFFERENCE money
   CCF spending money / LAG=15
```

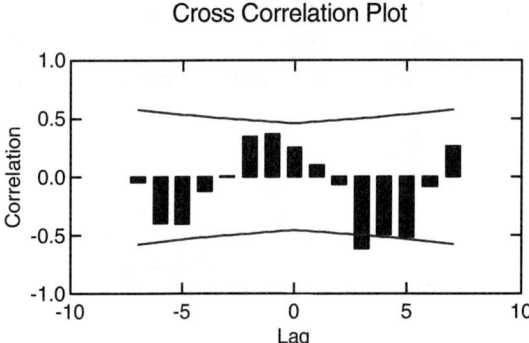

This shows a significant negative correlation at only one time interval: +3 lags of the series. Since we selected *SPENDING* first, we see that consumer expenditures are negatively correlated with the money stock three quarters later. Thus, consumer spending may be a "leading indicator" of money stock.

Example 5
Differencing

Let's replace the values of the series in the *AIRLINE* data with the difference between each value and the previous value—first order (lag) differencing. The input is:

```
USE airline
SERIES
   TIME 1949 12
   LOG pass
   DIFFERENCE pass
   TPLOT pass
   ACF pass / LAG=15
   PACF pass / LAG=15
```

The output follows:

Series Plot

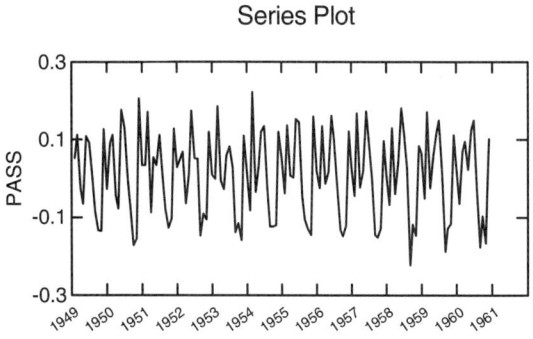

Autocorrelation Plot

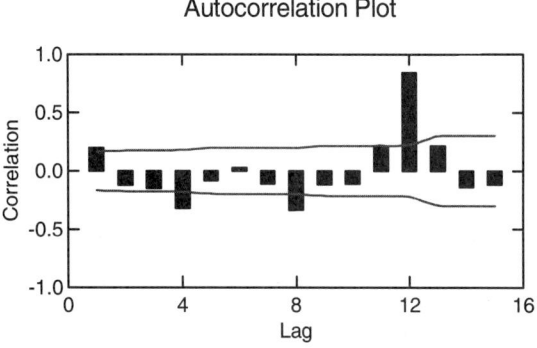

Partial Autocorrelation Plot

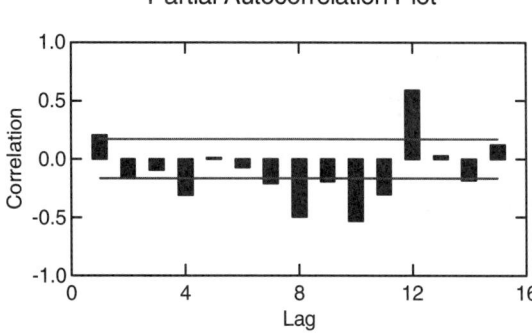

The strong upward trend seen in the undifferenced time series plots is not evident here. Notice also that the scale on this plot ranges from approximately −0.2 to +0.2, while on the plot in the time series plot example, it ranges from 4.6 to 6.4.

The very strong lag 12 ACF and PACF correlations with a decay of strong correlations for shorter lags suggest that the series is seasonal. (We suspected this after seeing the first plot of the data.) Differencing this monthly series by lag 12 can remove cycles from the series.

Order 12 Differencing

Here, we will difference by order 12 and look at the plots. Let's summarize what has happened to the original data. First, the data were replaced by their log values. Next, the data were replaced by their first-order differences. Now we replace these differences with order 12 differences with the following commands:

```
USE airline
SERIES
    LOG pass
    DIFFERENCE pass
    DIFFERENCE pass / LAG=12
    ACF pass / LAG=15
    PACF pass / LAG=15
```

The autocorrelations and partial autocorrelations after differencing by order 12 are shown below:

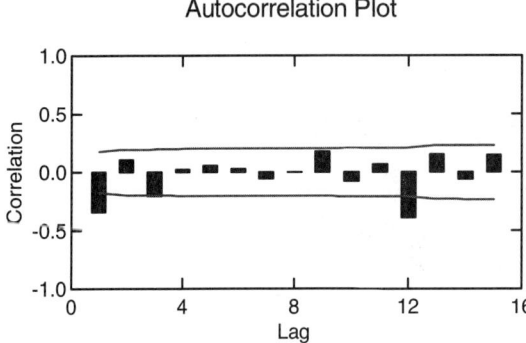

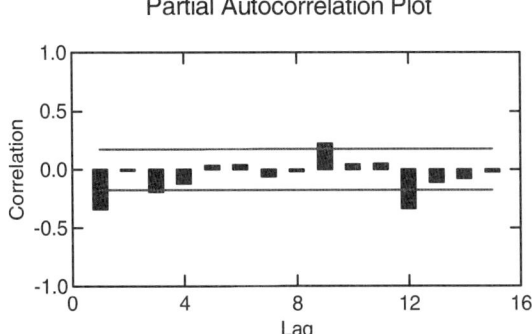

Partial Autocorrelation Plot

The ACF display has spikes at lag 1 and lag 12. We conclude that the number of airline passengers this month depends on the number last month and on the number one year ago during the same month.

Example 6
Moving Averages

The SYSTAT file *AIRCRAFT* contains the results of a "flutter test" (amplitude of vibration) of an aircraft wing (Bennett and Desmarais, 1975). Although the model for these data is known, we are going to try to recover a smooth series without using this information.

Let's try a seven-point moving average on the *AIRCRAFT* data and smooth the resulting smoothed series with a four-point moving average. This should remove some of the jitters. The input is:

```
USE aircraft
SERIES
   SMOOTH flutter / MEAN=7
   SMOOTH flutter / MEAN=4
```

The output follows:

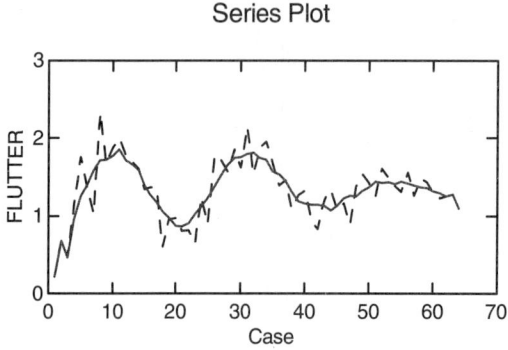

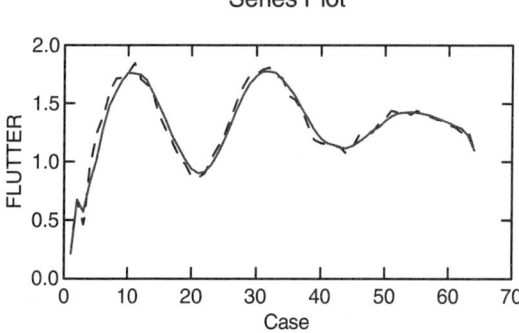

The second plot is even smoother than the first. We chose the lengths of the window by trial and error after looking at the data to see how much they "jitter" to the left and right of each point relative to the overall pattern of the series. You will do better if you know something about the function generating the data.

Example 7
Smoothing (A 4253H Filter)

To fit a 4253H filter to the *AIRCRAFT* data, the input is:

```
USE aircraft
SERIES
   SMOOTH flutter / MEDIAN=4
   SMOOTH flutter / MEDIAN=2
   SMOOTH flutter / MEDIAN=5
   SMOOTH flutter / MEDIAN=3
   SMOOTH flutter / WT=1,2,1
```

A Quick Graph follows each Smooth request. (To omit the display, type GRAPH=NONE.) The displays shown below correspond to the first request (MEDIAN=4) and the final smooth (a running means smoother with weights).

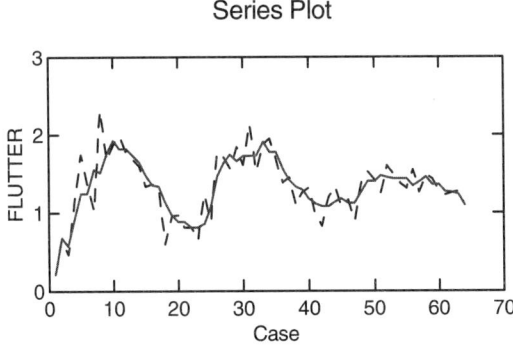

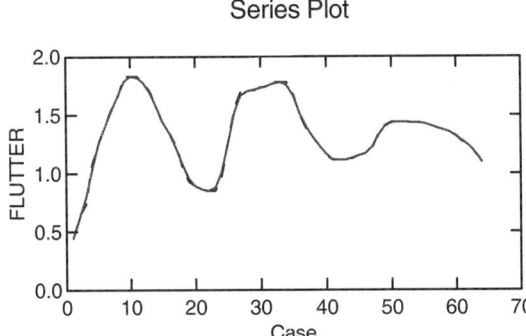

The previous smooth (MEDIAN=3) is marked by dashed lines.

Example 8
LOWESS Smoothing

Here is the flutter variable (in the *AIRCRAFT* data) smoothed with LOWESS smoothing. Use a Tension value of 0.18 to get more of the local detail. The input is:

```
USE aircraft
SERIES
    SMOOTH flutter / LOWESS=.18
```

The resulting plot is:

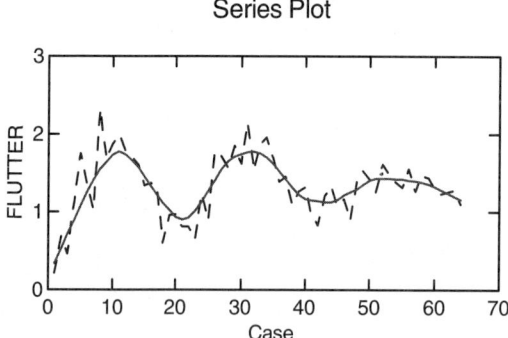

And the Winner Is...

The actual function used to generate the data in the moving average and 4253H filter examples is shown below:

$$Y(t) = 1 - e^{-0.03t} \cos(0.3t)$$

where $t = 1, 2, \ldots, 64$ (the index number of the series). We added normal (Gaussian) noise to this function in inverse proportion to the square root of t. We leave it to the reader to design an optimal filter for the Weight option after looking at the noise distribution in the plot. The generating function on the data is shown below:

```
USE aircraft
BEGIN
PLOT flutter * time / HEI=1.5IN  WID=3.5IN,
            XMIN=0   XMAX=70   YMIN=0   YMAX=3,
            XLABEL='Time'  YLABEL='Flutter',
            SYMB=1   SIZE=.75   FILL=1   COLOR=BLACK
FPLOT y=1-EXP(-0.03*t)*COS(.3*t) + (0.35) ; ,
            HEI=1.5IN   WID=3.5IN,
            XMIN=0   XMAX=70   YMIN=0   YMAX=3,
            XLAB=''   YLAB=''   AXES=NONE   SCALE=NONE
END
```

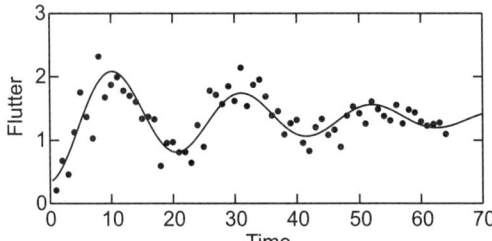

Is there a winner? The LOWESS smooth looks pretty good. Usually, for Gaussian data like these, it is hard to beat running means. Running medians and LOWESS do extremely well on non-Gaussian data, however, because they are less susceptible to outliers in the series. You will also find that exploratory smoothing requires a lot of fine tuning with window widths (tension) and weights.

Example 9
Multiplicative Seasonal Factor

We use the same *AIRLINE* data—from Box and Jenkins (1976)—used in the time series plot example. If you examine the plot there, you can see the strong periodicities. The size of the periodicities depends on the level of the series, so we know that the form of seasonality is multiplicative. Each year, the number of passengers peaks during July and August, but there are also jagged spikes in the data that correspond, apparently, to holidays like Christmas and Easter.

Here we adjust the airline series for the multiplicative seasonal effect implied by the series plot. The input follows:

```
USE airline
SERIES
   TIME 1949 12
   ADJSEASON pass / MULTIPLICATIVE
```

The output is:

```
Series originates at: 1949. Periodicity: 12. First Period: 1.
Adjust series for a seasonal periodicity of 12.
PASS copied from SYSTAT file into active work area
```

Chapter 16

```
Seasonal indices for the series are:
    1:        91.077
    2:        88.133
    3:       100.825
    4:        97.321
    5:        98.305
    6:       111.296
    7:       122.636
    8:       121.652
    9:       105.997
   10:        92.200
   11:        80.397
   12:        90.164

Series is transformed.
```

Airline travel appears heaviest during the summer months, June (6) through September (9).

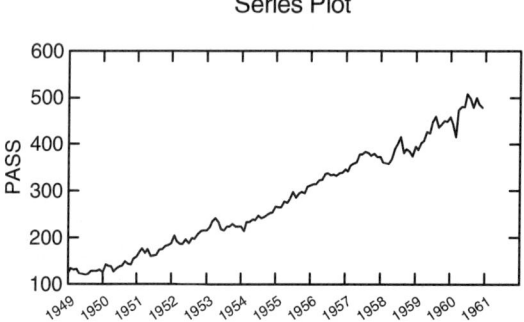

The plot shows that the trend and the irregular components remain, but the seasonal component has been removed from the series.

Example 10
Multiplicative Seasonality with a Linear Trend

In the time series plot example, we looked at the *AIRLINE* data from Box and Jenkins. The plot of the series shows a strong increasing trend and what looks like multiplicative seasonality. We could try to forecast this series with a model having a linear trend and multiplicative seasonality. The input is:

```
USE airline
SERIES
    EXPONENTIAL pass / SMOOTH=.3  LINEAR=.4  MULT=.4 FORECAST=10
```

The output follows:

```
Smooth location parameter with coefficient = 0.300
Linear trend with smoothing coefficient = 0.400
Multiplicative seasonality with smoothing coefficient = 0.400

Initial values

Seasonal indices for the series are:

     1:       91.077
     2:       88.133
     3:      100.825
     4:       97.321
     5:       98.305
     6:      111.296
     7:      122.636
     8:      121.652
     9:      105.997
    10:       92.200
    11:       80.397
    12:       90.164

Initial smoothed value =        88.263
Initial trend parameter =        2.645

Final values

Seasonal indices for the series are:

     1:       87.628
     2:       82.996
     3:       95.362
     4:       98.155
     5:      101.936
     6:      117.471
     7:      133.389
     8:      130.644
     9:      107.631
    10:       93.352
    11:       78.956
    12:       86.086

Final smoothed value =        497.921
Final trend parameter =          8.374

Within series MSE =     325.915, SE =      18.053

     Obs      Forecast

     145.     443.655
     146.     427.158
     147.     498.784
     148.     521.612
     149.     550.243
     150.     643.937
     151.     742.367
     152.     738.027
     153.     617.035
     154.     542.995
```

The output begins with the model and initial parameter estimates. The initial smoothed value is a regression estimate of the level of the seasonally adjusted series immediately before the first observation in the sample. The initial trend parameter is the slope of the regression of observations on observation number—the increase or decrease from one observation to the next due to the overall trend. For a percentage growth model, the trend parameter is the expected percentage change from the previous to the current observation due to trend.

After the values are smoothed, SYSTAT prints the final estimates of the seasonal, location, and trend parameters, plus the within-series forecast error. You can vary the smoothing coefficients and see if they reduce the standard error.

Alternative Smoothing Coefficients

In an attempt to reduce the standard error, we alter the smoothing coefficients:

```
CLEAR
USE airline
SERIES
    TIME 1949 12
    EXPONENTIAL pass / SMOOTH=.2  LINEAR=.2  MULT=.2 FORECAST=10
```

The output is:

```
Smooth location parameter with coefficient = 0.200
Linear trend with smoothing coefficient = 0.200
Multiplicative seasonality with smoothing coefficient = 0.200

Final values

Seasonal indices for the series are:

        1:       90.960
        2:       87.249
        3:       99.846
        4:       98.817
        5:      100.173
        6:      113.664
        7:      126.653
        8:      124.419
        9:      105.075
       10:       91.727
       11:       79.163
       12:       88.002

Final smoothed value =      499.423
Final trend parameter =       4.106

Within series MSE =      220.026,  SE =       14.833
```

```
Obs      Forecast

Jan, 1961   458.008
Feb, 1961   442.905
Mar, 1961   510.954
Apr, 1961   509.745
May, 1961   520.853
Jun, 1961   595.666
Jul, 1961   668.936
Aug, 1961   662.247
Sep, 1961   563.597
Oct, 1961   495.771
```

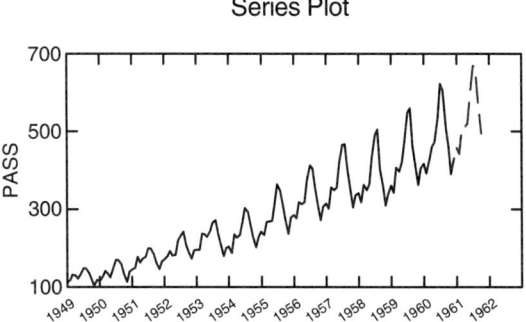

Series Plot

We get a smaller within-series forecast error (220.026 versus 325.915).

In-Series Forecasts

Sometimes it's best to develop a model on a portion of a series and see how well it predicts the remainder. There are 12 years of airline data for a total of 144 monthly observations. The following commands develop the smoothing model with the first 10 years of data (120 observations) and predict the final 2 years (observations 121–144):

```
CLEAR
USE airline
SERIES
    EXPONENTIAL / SMOOTH=.3 LINEAR=.4  MULT=.4 FORECAST=121 .. 144
```

Output from this procedure includes the following forecasts:

```
Within series MSE =      292.090, SE =        17.091
    Obs      Forecast

    Feb, 1959   354.228
    Mar, 1959   423.781
    Apr, 1959   426.328
    May, 1959   447.235
    Jun, 1959   530.144
    Jul, 1959   588.677
```

```
           Aug, 1959         580.174
           Sep, 1959         484.919
           Oct, 1959         420.917
           Nov, 1959         365.250
           Dec, 1959         407.409
           Jan, 1960         427.066
           Feb, 1960         418.752
           Mar, 1960         499.821
           Apr, 1960         501.697
           May, 1960         525.153
           Jun, 1960         621.184
           Jul, 1960         688.343
           Aug, 1960         677.034
           Sep, 1960         564.765
           Oct, 1960         489.287
           Nov, 1960         423.786
           Dec, 1960         471.840
Forecast MSE =           1904.887 SE =           43.645
```

Note that the within-series standard error is not the same as in the previous run because it's now based on only the first 120 observations. The error for the actual forecasts (65.891) is much larger than that for the in-series forecasts (17.091).

For a thorough review of issues and developments in exponential smoothing models, see Gardner (1985). For an introduction to these models, see any introductory forecasting book, such as Makridakis, Wheelwright, and McGee (1983).

Example 11
ARIMA Models

The first thing to consider in modeling the *AIRLINE* passenger data is the increasing variance in the series over time. We logged the data (in the time series plot example) and found that the variance stabilized. An upward trend remained, however, so we differenced the series (in the differencing example). We now identify which ARIMA parameters we want to estimate by plotting the data in several ways. The parameters of the ARIMA model are:

	Name	Description
AR	autoregressive	Each point is a weighted function of a previous point plus random error.
I	difference	Each point's value is a constant difference from a previous point's value.
MA	moving average	Each point is a weighted function of a previous point's random error plus its own random error.

For seasonal ARIMA models, we need three additional parameters: Seasonal AR, Seasonal I, and Seasonal MA. Their definitions are the same as above, except that they apply to points that are not adjacent in a series. The *AIRLINE* data involve seasonal parameters, for example, because dependencies extend across years as well as months.

Checking ACF and PACF Displays

There appears to be at least some differencing needed for the *AIRLINE* data because the series drifts across time (overall level of passengers increases). ACF and PACF plots give us more detailed information on this. The ACF and PACF plots are shown below (here we limit the lags to 15).

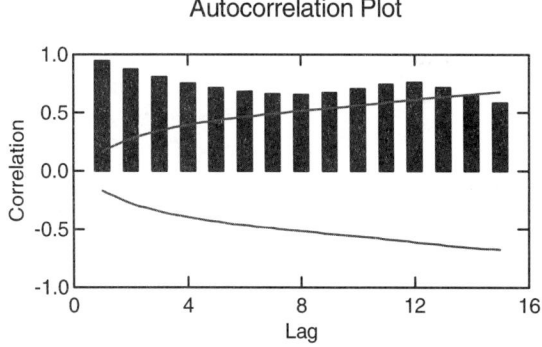

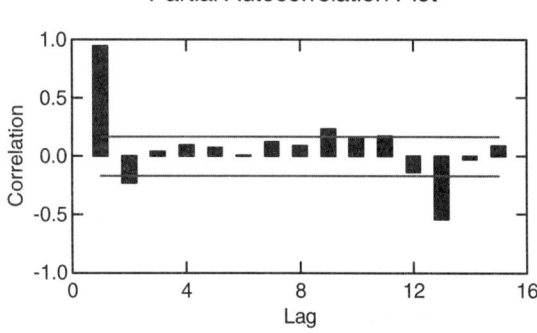

Notice that the autocorrelations are substantial and well outside two standard errors on the plot. There are two bulges in the ACF plot at lag=1 and lag=12, suggesting the nonseasonal (monthly) and seasonal (yearly) dependencies that we supposed. The PACF plot shows the same dependencies more distinctly. Here are the autocorrelations and partial autocorrelations of the differenced series:

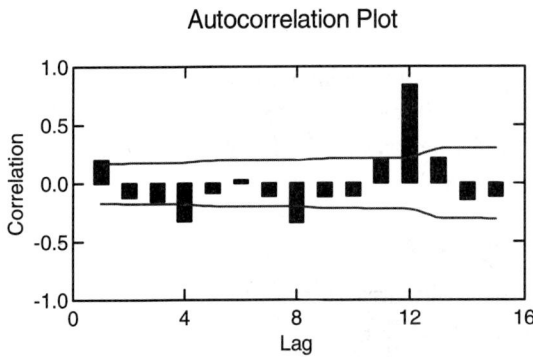

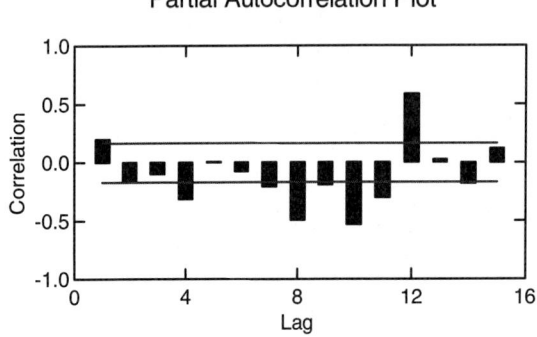

Now we have only 143 points in the series because the first point had no prior value to remove. It was therefore set to missing. The two plots show that the differencing has substantially removed the monthly changes in trend. We still have the seasonal (yearly) trend, however. Therefore, difference again and then replot. The autocorrelations and partial autocorrelations after differencing by order 12 are shown below. With commands:

```
DIFFERENCE / LAG=12
ACF / LAG=15
PACF / LAG=15
```

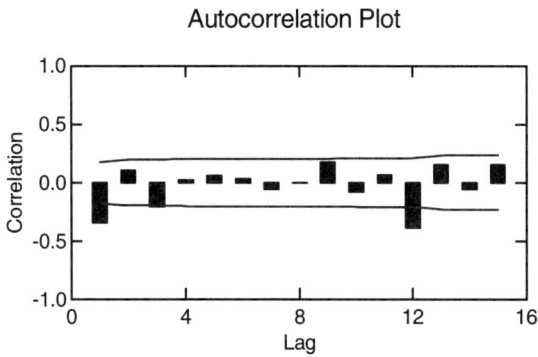

Autocorrelation Plot

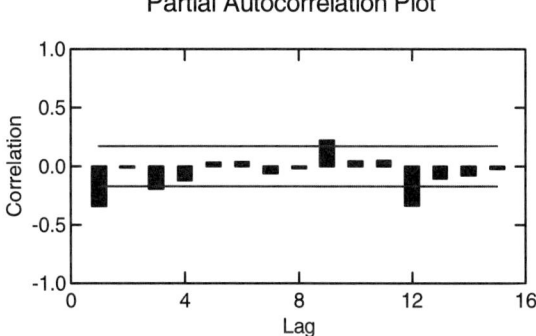

Partial Autocorrelation Plot

Most of the dependency seems to have been removed. Although there are some autocorrelations and partial autocorrelations outside two standard errors, we will not difference again. We will fit a model first because over-differencing can mask the effects of MA parameters. In fact, the pattern in this last plot suggests one regular and one seasonal MA parameter because there are ACF spikes (instead of bulges) at lags 1 and 13, and the PACF shows decay at lags 1 and 13.

Consult the references previously cited for more information on how to read these plots for identification.

Fitting an ARIMA Model

Here we fit a seasonal multiplicative ARIMA model with no autoregressive parameter, one difference parameter, one moving average parameter, no seasonal autoregressive parameter, one seasonal difference parameter, and one seasonal moving average parameter. The input is:

```
USE airline
SERIES
   LOG pass
   DIFFERENCE
   DIFFERENCE / LAG=12
   SAVE resid
   ARIMA /Q=1 QS=1 SEASON=12 BACKCAST=13
USE resid
   ACF / LAG=15
```

We save the residuals into a file to check the adequacy of the model by using the various facilities available in SYSTAT. You can also do normal probability plots, stem-and-leaf plots, Kolmogorov-Smirnov tests, and other statistical tests on residuals. We focus on the serial dependence among the residuals by creating an autocorrelation plot.

The output is:

```
Iteration  Sum of Squares   Parameter values
    0         .2392764D+00    .100   .100
    1         .1835532D+00    .345   .433
    2         .1764962D+00    .449   .633
    3         .1759952D+00    .416   .592
    4         .1758742D+00    .409   .613
    5         .1758463D+00    .392   .614
    6         .1758443D+00    .396   .613
    7         .1758443D+00    .396   .613
    8         .1758443D+00    .396   .613
    9         .1758443D+00    .396   .613
Final value of MSE is         0.001
Index   Type    Estimate       A.S.E.      Lower  <95%> Upper
   1     MA      0.396         0.093       0.212        0.579
   2     SMA     0.613         0.074       0.467        0.760
Asymptotic correlation matrix of parameters

                          1          2

              1        1.000
              2        0.171      1.000
```

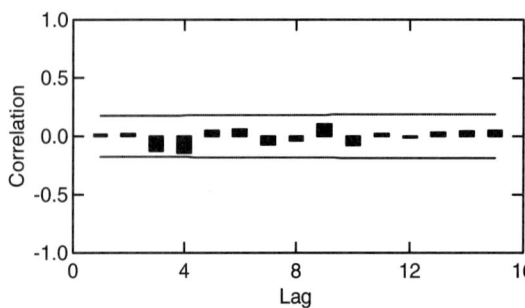

Autocorrelation Plot

None of the autocorrelations are significant.

ARIMA Forecasting

We could have added forecasting by specifying 10 cases to be forecast. The input is:

```
USE airline
SERIES
   LOG pass
   DIFFERENCE
   DIFFERENCE / LAG=12
   SAVE resid
   ARIMA /Q=1 QS=1 SEASON=12 BACKCAST=13 FORECAST=10
```

SYSTAT forecasts the future values of the series:

```
              Forecast Values
Period        Lower95      Forecast     Upper95
      145.    418.862      450.296      484.090
      146.    391.976      426.557      464.189
      147.    438.329      482.099      530.240
      148.    443.296      492.246      546.602
      149.    453.832      508.378      569.480
      150.    516.623      583.439      658.898
      151.    587.307      668.338      760.549
      152.    581.136      666.091      763.464
      153.    484.248      558.844      644.931
      154.    427.648      496.754      577.028
```

Series Plot

The "forecast origin" in this case is taken as the last point in the series. From there, the model computes and prints 10 new points with their upper and lower 95% asymptotic confidence intervals. SYSTAT automatically plots the forecasts.

Example 12
Fourier Modeling of Temperature

Let's look at a typical Fourier application. The data in the *NEWARK* file are 64 average monthly temperatures in Newark, New Jersey, beginning in January, 1964. The data are from the U.S. government, cited in Chambers et al. (1983). Notice that their fluctuations look something like a sine wave, so we might expect that they could be modeled adequately by the sum of a relatively small number of trigonometric components. We have taken exactly 64 measurements to fulfill the powers of 2 rule.

We remove the series mean before the decomposition. The input is:

```
USE newark
SERIES
    TIME 1964,12
    TPLOT temp
    MEAN temp
    FOURIER temp / LAG=15
```

The output follows:

```
Fourier components of TEMP

Index Frequency     Real    Imaginary   Magnitude     Phase    Periodogram
  1   0.0           0.0       0.0         0.0           .          0.0
  2   0.01563      -0.763    -0.363       0.845       -2.697      14.535
  3   0.03125      -0.803    -0.177       0.822       -2.924      13.760
  4   0.04687      -1.587    -0.779       1.768       -2.685      63.683
  5   0.06250      -1.658    -1.817       2.460       -2.310     123.262
  6   0.07813      -6.248    -7.214       9.544       -2.285    1855.631
  7   0.09375       2.606     3.633       4.471        0.948     407.199
  8   0.10938       1.040     1.786       2.067        1.044      87.038
  9   0.12500       0.592     0.936       1.107        1.007      24.978
 10   0.14063       0.438     0.588       0.733        0.930      10.954
 11   0.15625      -0.127     1.135       1.142        1.682      26.558
 12   0.17188       0.067     0.715       0.718        1.477      10.507
 13   0.18750      -0.255     0.785       0.825        1.885      13.860
 14   0.20313       0.140     0.132       0.192        0.756       0.749
 15   0.21875      -0.071     0.291       0.299        1.811       1.823
```

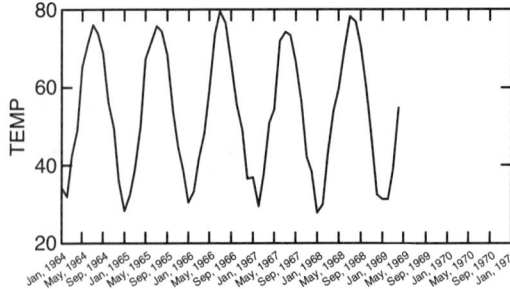

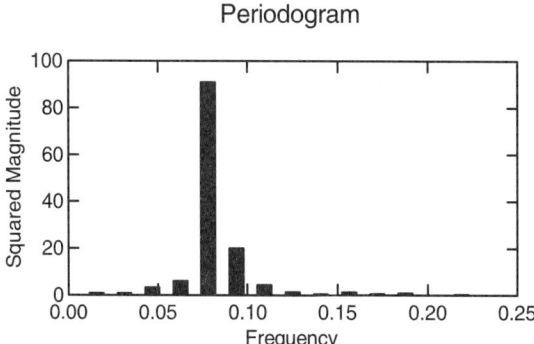

Periodogram

The Quick Graph displays a periodogram—that is, the squared magnitude against frequencies. Notice that our hunch was largely correct. There is one primary peak at a relatively low frequency. This periodogram differs from that produced in earlier versions of SYSTAT. SYSTAT now uses

```
N/pi*(squared magnitude)
```

where N is the number of cases in the file.

Two final points follow. First, some analysts prefer to plot the logs of these values against frequency. We could do this in the following way:

```
SQUARE temp
LOG temp
TPLOT temp
```

Logging, by the way, looks noisier than the plot above but can reveal significant spikes that might be hidden in the raw periodogram.

The second point involves smoothing the periodogram. Often it is best to taper the series first before computing the periodogram. This makes the spikes more pronounced in the log-periodogram plot:

```
MEAN temp
TAPER temp
FOURIER temp
SQUARE temp
LOG temp
TPLOT temp
```

Since we didn't specify a value, split-cosine-bell used its default, 0.5.

Computation

All of the time series smoothers and Fourier routines are computed in single precision. Estimation for ARIMA models is performed in double precision and forecasting is done in single precision.

Algorithms

The LOWESS algorithm for XY and scatterplot smoothing is documented in Cleveland (1979) and Cleveland (1981). The Fast Fourier Transform is due to Gentleman and Sande (1966), and documented further in Bloomfield (1976).

ARIMA models are estimated with a set of algorithms. Residuals and unconditional sums of squares for the seasonal multiplicative model are calculated by an algorithm in McLeod and Sales (1983). The sums of squares are minimized iteratively by a quasi-Newton method due to Fletcher (1972). A penalty function for inadmissible values of the parameters makes this procedure relatively robust when values are near the circumference of the unit circle. Standard errors for the parameter estimates are computed from the inverse of the numeric estimate of the Hessian matrix, following Fisher (1922). Forecasting is performed via the difference equations documented in Chapter 5 of Box and Jenkins (1976).

References

Bloomfield, P. (1976). *Fourier analysis of time series: An introduction.* New York: John Wiley & Sons, Inc.

Box, G. E. P. and Jenkins, G. M. (1976). *Time series analysis: Forecasting and control.* Revised edition. Oakland, Calif.: Holden-Day, Inc.

Brigham, E. O. (1974). *The fast Fourier transform.* New York: Prentice-Hall.

Chambers, J. M., Cleveland, W. S., Kleiner, B., and Tukey, P. (1983). *Graphical methods for data analysis.* Belmont, Calif.: Wadsworth International Group.

Chatterjee and Price. (1977). *Regression analysis by example.* New York: John Wiley & Sons, Inc.

Cleveland, W. S. (1979). Robust locally weight regression and smoothing scatterplots. *Journal of the American Statistical Association,* 74, 829–836.

Cooley, J. W. and Tukey, J. W. (1965). An algorithm for the machine computation of complex Fourier series. *Mathematical Computation,* 19, 297–301.

Gardner, E. S. (1985). Exponential smoothing: The state of the art. *Journal of Forecasting,* 4, 1–28.

Makridakis, W., Wheelwright, S. C., and McGee, U. E. (1983). *Forecasting: Methods and applications.* 2nd ed. New York: John Wiley & Sons, Inc.

McCleary, R. and Hay, R. A., Jr. (1980). *Applied time series analysis for the social sciences.* Beverly Hills: Sage Publications.

Nelson, C. R. (1973). *Applied time series analysis for managerial forecasting.* San Francisco: Holden-Day, Inc.

Tukey, J. W. (1977). *Exploratory data analysis.* Reading: Addison-Wesley.

Vandaele, W. (1983). *Applied time series and Box-Jenkins models.* New York: Academic Press.

Velleman, P. F. and Hoaglin, D. C. (1981). *Applications, basics, and computing of exploratory data analysis.* Belmont: Duxbury Press.

Chapter 17

Two-Stage Least Squares

Dan Steinberg

The TSLS module is designed for estimation of simultaneous equations systems via Two-Stage Least Squares (TSLS) and Two-Stage Instrumental Variables (White, 1984). In the first stage, the independent variables are regressed on the instrumental variables. In the second stage, the dependent variable is regressed on the predicted values of the independent variables (determined from the first stage). TSLS produces heteroskedasticity-consistent standard errors for ordinary least squares (OLS) models and instrumental variables models and provides diagnostic tests for heteroskedasticity and nonlinearity. TSLS also computes regressions with polynomially distributed lag structure in the errors.

Statistical Background

Two-stage least squares was introduced by Theil in the early 1950's in unpublished memoranda and independently by Basmann (1957). Theil's textbook (1971) treats the topic extensively; other textbooks include Johnston (1984), Judge et al. (1986), Maddala (1977), and Mardia et al. (1979).

Two-Stage Least Squares Estimation

Two-Stage Least Squares (TSLS) is the most common example of an instrumental variables (*IV*) estimator. The *IV* estimator is appropriate if we want to fit the statistical model

$$y = Xb + \varepsilon \qquad \text{Equation 17-1}$$

when some of the regressors in **X** are correlated with the errors ε. This can occur if some of the **X**'s are measured with error or when some of the **X**'s are dependent variables in a larger system of equations.

To use the instrumental variables procedure, we must have some variables **Z** in our data set that are uncorrelated with the error terms ε ($E[\mathbf{Z}'\varepsilon] = 0$). These variables, which are called the **instrumental variables**, can include some or all of the variables **X** of the model and any other variables in the data. To estimate a model, there must be at least as many instrumental variables as there are regressors.

Heteroskedasticity

The problem of heteroskedasticity is discussed in Theil (1971) and extensively in Judge et al. (1985), which includes numerous references. The approach to heteroskedasticity taken in this module, which is to produce correct standard errors for the OLS case, was introduced by Eicker (1963, 1967) and Hinkley (1977). It was rediscovered independently by White (1980), who also extended its application to the TSLS context (White, 1982). A technical account of the theory underlying all of the methods used in this module appears in White (1984). The basic statistical model of regression analysis can be written as

$$y = Xb + \varepsilon \qquad \text{Equation 17-2}$$

where y is the dependent variable, X is a vector of independent variables, b is a vector of unknown regression coefficients, and ε is an unobservable random variable. If the regressors are uncorrelated with the random error ($E[X'\varepsilon] = 0$), ordinary least squares (OLS) will generally produce consistent and asymptotically normal estimators. Further, if the errors have constant variance for all of the observations in the data set, the usual t statistics are correct and hypothesis testing can be conducted on the basis of the variance-covariance matrix of the coefficient estimates. These are the assumptions underlying the estimation and hypothesis testing of MGLH and other major regression packages. If either of these assumptions is false, features of TSLS can be used to obtain valid hypothesis tests and consistent parameter estimates.

We estimate heteroskedasticity-consistent standard errors because they are correct asymptotically under a broad set of assumptions. If the random errors in a regression model exhibit heteroskedasticity, the conventional standard errors and covariance matrix are usually inconsistent. The t statistics are erroneous, and any hypothesis tests that employ the covariance matrix estimate will also be incorrect (have the wrong size). The heteroskedasticity-consistent standard errors, by contrast, are correct, whether or not heteroskedasticity is present.

There is no way to tell whether the robust standard errors will be larger or smaller than the OLS results, but they may differ substantially. The classical approach to heteroskedasticity is to postulate an exact functional form for the second moments of the errors. Some analysts assume, for example, that the variance of the error for each observation is proportional to the square of one of the independent variables. (See Judge et al. for further details.) The model is estimated by generalized (or weighted) least squares (GLS) with weights obtained from least-square residuals. Of course, this approach requires that the assumptions of the analyst are correct. If these assumptions are incorrect, the standard errors resulting from GLS will also be incorrect.

The heteroskedasticity-consistent standard errors computed in TSLS are not based on any attempt to correct for, or otherwise model, the heteroskedasticity. Instead, essentially nonparametric estimates of the OLS standard errors are computed. We still get OLS coefficients, but the variances of the coefficients are revised. White (1980) showed that this is possible for virtually any type of heteroskedasticity.

Two-Stage Least Squares in SYSTAT

Two-Stage Least Squares Main Dialog Box

To open the dialog box, from the menus choose:

Statistics
 Regression
  2 Stage Least Squares....

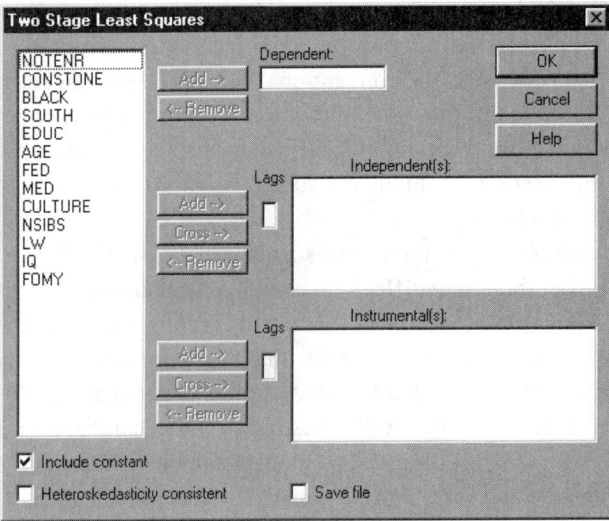

SYSTAT computes Two-Stage Least Squares by first specifying a model and then estimating it.

Dependent. The variable you want to examine. The dependent variable should be continuous and numeric.

Independent(s). Select one or more continuous or categorical variables (grouping variables). To add an interaction to your model, click the Cross button. For example, to add the term *sex*education*, add *sex* to the Independent(s) list and then add *education* by clicking the Cross button.

Instrumental(s). Select the instrumental variable(s) that you want to estimate. Instrumentals may be continuous or categorical. To add an interaction to your model, click the Cross button. For example, to add the term *sex*education*, add *sex* to the Instrumental(s) list and then add *education* by clicking the Cross button. The number of instrumental variables must equal or exceed the number of independent variables.

Lags. Specify the number of lags for variables in the independent or instrumental variable target list. Highlight the variable in the general variable list, enter the number of lags, and click Add. The variable appears in the independent or instrumental variables list with a colon followed by the number of lags.

Include constant. Indicate whether you want the constant turned on or off. In practice, the constant is almost always included.

Heteroskedasticity consistent. Computes heteroskedasticity-consistent standard errors, which are correct whether or not heteroskedasticity is present.

Save file. Saves statistics into *filename.SYD*.

Using Commands

Select a data file with USE filename and continue with:

```
TSLS
    MODEL yvar = CONSTANT +  var + ... + var1*var2 + ...,
                 | ivar + ... + ivar1*ivar2 + ...
    ESTIMATE / HC
```

The CONSTANT term is almost always included. The second block of variables is the set of predictors (regressors). Any predictors can be declared categorical with the CATEGORY statement. This will encode them with dummy variables. After a vertical bar, list the instrumental variables.

Usage Considerations

Types of data. TSLS uses rectangular data.

Print options. PRINT=LONG adds the covariance matrix of the coefficient estimates.

Quick Graphs. No Quick Graphs are produced by TSLS.

Saving files. Predicted values and residuals can be saved to a SYSTAT system file with the SAVE command. The SAVE command must be issued before the ESTIMATE command. The SAVE command works across the BY command. If several BY groups are being analyzed, the predicted values, etc., are saved for each BY group in a single SYSTAT file.

BY groups. TSLS analyzes data by groups. Your file need not be sorted on the BY variable(s).

Bootstrapping. Bootstrapping is not available in this procedure.

Case frequencies. FREQ=<variable> increases the number of cases by the FREQ variable.

Case weights. WEIGHT is not available in TSLS.

Examples

Example 1
Heteroskedasticity-Consistent Standard Errors

An example will illustrate how to use TSLS to diagnose a regression model and obtain correct answers if the classical regression assumptions are violated. The data that we are using were extracted from the National Longitudinal Survey of Young Men, 1979. Information for 38 men is available on natural log of wage (*LW*), highest completed grade (*EDUC*), mother's education (*MED*), father's education (*FED*), race (*BLACK*=1), *AGE*, and several other variables. We want to estimate a model relating wage to education, race, and age. The input for a simple linear model with heteroskedasticity-consistent standard errors is:

```
USE NLS
TSLS
MODEL LW=CONSTANT+EDUC+BLACK+AGE
ESTIMATE / HC
```

The resulting output is:

```
Input records:          200
Records kept for analysis:       200

Ordinary least squares results (OLS)
Dependent variable: LW

N: 200, mean of dependent variable: 6.080000
R-squared: 0.140278
Adjusted R-squared: 0.127119, uncentered R-squared (R0-squared): 0.994372

     Parameter            Estimate      S.E.      t-ratio    p-value
  1  CONSTANT              4.483        0.327     13.726      0.000
  2  EDUC                  0.023        0.013      1.715      0.088
  3  BLACK                -0.207        0.135     -1.530      0.128
  4  AGE                   0.050        0.011      4.605      0.000

F(3,196) = 10.660242, prob= 0.000002

Standard error of regression: 0.462279
Regression sum of squares: 6.834354
Residual sum of squares: 41.885646


Covariance matrix of regression coefficients

              1            2           3           4
  1        0.107
  2       -0.002        0.000
  3       -0.009        0.000       0.018
  4       -0.003       -0.000       0.000       0.000
```

Two-Stage Least Squares

```
Heteroskedastic consistent results
    Parameter              Estimate         S.E.         t-ratio      p-value
 1  CONSTANT                  4.483        0.335          13.386        0.000
 2  EDUC                      0.023        0.014           1.633        0.104
 3  BLACK                    -0.207        0.163          -1.266        0.207
 4  AGE                       0.050        0.012           4.254        0.000

Specification test          statistic       df           p-value
Durbin-Watson                 1.836
White specification           7.907        8.000          0.443
Nonlinearity                  7.710        5.000          0.173


Heteroskedastic consistent covariance matrix of regression coefficients
            1              2              3              4
 1        0.112
 2       -0.002          0.000
 3       -0.015          0.000          0.027
 4       -0.003         -0.000          0.000          0.000
```

Initial TSLS output reports conventional regression output, which could also have been obtained in MGLH. The standard errors reported are obtained from the diagonal of the matrix $s^2(X'X)^{-1}$, where s^2 is the sum of squared residuals divided by the degrees of freedom; the t statistics are the classical ones as well. The one new statistic is the uncentered R^2, reported as $R0$-$squared$ (R_o^2). This statistic has no bearing on the goodness of fit of the regression and should be routinely ignored. It is reported only as a computational convenience for those who want to use the Lagrange multiplier tests discussed by Engle (1984).

In addition to producing what White (1980) called heteroskedasticity-consistent standard errors, the TSLS module calculates three diagnostic statistics for the linear model. The first is the usual Durbin-Watson statistic. This is the same test for autocorrelation that appears in the MGLH module.

The second is the White (1980) specification test, which explicitly checks the residuals for heteroskedasticity. Under the null hypothesis of homoskedasticity, this statistic has an asymptotic chi-square distribution. If this statistic is large, we have evidence of heteroskedasticity. In the example, this statistic is 7.907 with eight degrees of freedom, indicating that we cannot reject the null hypothesis of homoskedasticity. The White test is actually a general test of misspecification (White, 1982) and is sensitive to various departures of the model and data from standard assumptions. A significant statistic is evidence that something is wrong with the model, but it does not identify the source of the problem. It may be heteroskedasticity, but it could also be left-out variables or nonlinearity, for example.

The third is the nonlinearity test, which checks for neglected nonlinearities in the regression function. It is simply a test of the joint hypothesis that all possible interactions, including squared regressors, have zero coefficients in a full model. A

Lagrange multiplier test, it too has an approximate chi-square distribution under the null hypothesis of correct specification. Again, large values for this statistic are evidence for neglected interactions. In our example, there is no evidence of non-linearity on the basis of this broad test.

Each of the latter two tests involves supplementary regressions with a possibly large number of additional independent variables. The White test is computed by regressing the squared OLS residuals on all the squares and cross-products of the **X**'s, and the nonlinearity test regresses residuals on these same cross-products.

Example 2
Two-Stage Least Squares

In this example, we use the extended MODEL statement to construct a TSLS model:

```
USE NLS
TSLS
MODEL LW=CONSTANT+EDUC+BLACK+AGE | CONSTANT+MED+FED+BLACK+AGE
ESTIMATE
```

The first part of the MODEL statement is identical to what we have seen in MGLH. It has a dependent variable and a list of independent variables, characterizing a structural equation. This is the theoretical model we want to estimate. The vertical bar (|) in the middle of the statement signifies the end of the structural equation and indicates that a list of instrumental variables follows. In this example, our structural equation relates the logarithm of the wage, *LW*, to *EDUC, BLACK, AGE*, and a *CONSTANT*. The list of instrumental variables follows, and it consists of *CONSTANT, MED, FED, BLACK*, and *AGE*. At this point, all we need to know is that there are at least as many instrumental variables to the right of the sharp sign as there are regressors to the left. Satisfying this condition means that TSLS will attempt to fit the model.

What exactly does our model mean? In our example, *CONSTANT, BLACK*, and *AGE* appear both in the structural equation and in the list of instrumental variables. By using them in this way, the analyst expresses confidence that these are conventional independent variables, uncorrelated with the error term ε. These exogenous variables can be said to be instruments for themselves. The variable *EDUC*, however, appears only in the structural equation. This is a signal that the analyst wants to consider *EDUC* as an endogenous variable that might be correlated with error term. On the right hand side of the vertical bar, *MED* and *FED* appear as instrumental variables only. They can thus be said to be instruments for *EDUC*.

The total number of instruments is five, which is one greater than the number of regressors. Notice that if the lists before and after the vertical bar are identical, the procedure reduces mathematically to OLS; TSLS, however, will do a lot of extra work to discover this.

Some analysts prefer to think of Two-Stage Least Squares as involving a literal pair of estimated regressions. From this point of view, we have, for example, the following two equations:

```
MODEL LW = CONSTANT + EDUC + BLACK + AGE

MODEL EDUC = CONSTANT + FED + MED
```

The first equation is the structural equation for *LW*, and the second is a possible structural equation for *EDUC*, relating *EDUC* to the education levels of parents. Because *EDUC* is itself seen to be a dependent variable in the larger set of equations, it cannot properly appear as a regressor in a standard regression. The two-stage technique involves estimating the equation for *EDUC* first, forming predicted values for *EDUC*, say *EDUCHAT*, and then estimating the model

```
MODEL LW = CONSTANT + EDUCHAT + BLACK + AGE
```

instead. Notice, however, that to estimate a TSLS model in a literal pair of regressions, the equation for *EDUC* would have to expand to include all of the exogenous independent variables appearing in the equation for *LW*. That is, the correct first-stage regression would actually be

```
MODEL EDUC = CONSTANT + FED + MED + BLACK + AGE
```

although we thought the shorter model was the "true" model. Also, the standard errors obtained from a literal two-stage estimation are not correct, as they must be calculated from actual and not predicted values of the independent variables. Fortunately, these details are taken care of for you by TSLS. Just make sure to partition your variables into exogenous and endogenous groups and list all the exogenous variables to the right of the vertical bar.

Following is the output:

```
Input records:            200
Records kept for analysis:        200

Instrumental variables, OLS results (TSLS)
Dependent variable: LW

N: 200, mean of dependent variable: 6.080000
Instruments:   CONSTANT + MED + FED + BLACK + AGE

      Parameter             Estimate        S.E.      t-ratio     p-value
   1  CONSTANT                 4.695        0.491       9.564       0.000
   2  EDUC                     0.006        0.033       0.177       0.860
   3  BLACK                   -0.223        0.138      -1.610       0.109
   4  AGE                      0.051        0.011       4.614       0.000

Standard error of regression: 0.464223
Residual sum of squares: 42.238554

Covariance matrix of regression coefficients

              1          2          3          4
   1      0.241
   2     -0.013      0.001
   3     -0.020      0.001      0.019
   4     -0.002     -0.000      0.000      0.000
```

Example 3
Two-Stage Instrumental Variables

As in the case of the OLS estimator, the standard errors calculated for the TSLS estimator will be incorrect in the presence of heteroskedasticity. Although we could calculate heteroskedasticity-consistent standard errors, it turns out that sometimes we can do even better. If the number of instrumental variables is strictly greater than the number of regressors in the presence of heteroskedasticity, the two-stage instrumental variables (*TSIV*) estimator is more efficient than TSLS. This means that in *TSIV*, the coefficient estimates as well as the standard errors may differ somewhat from TSLS. Observe, though, that large differences between *TSIV* and TSLS coefficients may indicate model misspecification (for example, the variables assumed to be exogenous are not truly exogenous). As in the case of heteroskedasticity-consistent OLS, computation of the *TSIV* estimator does not require knowledge of the form of heteroskedasticity. See White (1982b, 1984) for more on the *TSIV* estimator.

The following sequence of statements tells TSLS to estimate the model by *TSIV* as well as by TSLS. The only difference from TSLS is that the *HC* option is requested.

```
USE NLS
TSLS
MODEL  LW=CONSTANT+EDUC+BLACK+AGE  |  CONSTANT+MED+FED+BLACK+AGE
ESTIMATE  / HC
```

Two-Stage Least Squares

If the number of instruments is the same as the number of regressors, the *TSIV* and TSLS coefficient estimators are identical. In this cue, only the standard errors printed under the *TSIV* results will differ from TSLS. These are the heteroskedasticity-consistent standard errors for the usual *IV* estimator.

Following is the output:

```
Input records:              200
Records kept for analysis:          200

Instrumental variables, OLS results (TSLS)
Dependent variable: LW

N: 200, mean of dependent variable: 6.080000
Instruments:   CONSTANT + MED + FED + BLACK + AGE
        Parameter              Estimate        S.E.       t-ratio     p-value
    1 CONSTANT                    4.695       0.491         9.564       0.000
    2 EDUC                        0.006       0.033         0.177       0.860
    3 BLACK                      -0.223       0.138        -1.610       0.109
    4 AGE                         0.051       0.011         4.614       0.000

Standard error of regression: 0.464223
Residual sum of squares: 42.238554

Covariance matrix of regression coefficients
                1           2           3           4
    1        0.241
    2       -0.013       0.001
    3       -0.020       0.001       0.019
    4       -0.002      -0.000       0.000       0.000

Instrumental variables, heteroscedastistic consistent results (2SIV)
        Parameter              Estimate        S.E.       t-ratio     p-value
    1 CONSTANT                    4.612       0.514         8.976       0.000
    2 EDUC                        0.020       0.032         0.610       0.542
    3 BLACK                      -0.156       0.169        -0.924       0.357
    4 AGE                         0.046       0.012         3.995       0.000
                1           2           3           4
    1        0.264
    2       -0.014       0.001
    3       -0.031       0.001       0.029
    4       -0.003      -0.000       0.000       0.000
```

Example 4
Polynomially Distributed Lags

In this example, we use the extended MODEL statement to construct an OLS model with polynomially distributed lags. The degree of lag is expressed after the variable name, separated by a colon:

```
USE NLS
TSLS
MODEL LW = CONSTANT + EDUC:3 + BLACK + AGE
EST
```

Following is the output:

```
Input records:                        200
Records kept for analysis:            197
Records deleted for missing incomplete data:    3

Ordinary least squares results (OLS)
Dependent variable: LW

N: 197, mean of dependent variable: 6.086294
R-squared: 0.146857
Adjusted R-squared: 0.119916, uncentered R-squared (R0-squared): 0.994479

  Parameter           Estimate        S.E.      t-ratio    p-value
1 CONSTANT              4.723        0.461      10.250     0.000
2 EDUC                  0.020        0.014       1.445     0.150
3 EDUC<1>               0.010        0.014       0.700     0.485
4 EDUC<2>              -0.013        0.014      -0.968     0.334
5 EDUC<3>              -0.009        0.014      -0.625     0.532
6 BLACK                -0.240        0.136      -1.759     0.080
7 AGE                   0.049        0.011       4.411     0.000

F(6,190) = 5.450993, prob= 0.000032

Standard error of regression: 0.461989
Regression sum of squares: 6.980559
Residual sum of squares: 40.552436


Covariance matrix of regression coefficients
         1           2           3           4           5           6           7
1      0.212
2     -0.002       0.000
3     -0.002      -0.000       0.000
4     -0.002      -0.000      -0.000       0.000
5     -0.003      -0.000      -0.000      -0.000       0.000
6     -0.013       0.000      -0.000       0.000       0.000       0.019
7     -0.004      -0.000       0.000       0.000       0.000       0.000       0.000
```

Computation

All computations are in double precision.

Algorithms

TSLS computes least-squares estimates via standard high-precision algorithms. Specific details are given in the references.

Missing Data

Cases with missing data on any variable in the model are deleted before estimation.

References

Breusch, T. S. and Pagan, A. R., (1979). A simple test for heteroskedasticity and random coefficient variation. *Econometrica,* 47, 1287–1294.

Eicker, F. (1963). Asymptotic normality and consistency of the least squares estimators for families of linear regressions. *Annals of mathematical statistics,* 34, 447–456.

Eicker, F. (1967). Limit theorems for regressions with unequal and dependent errors. In *Proceedings of the fifth Berkeley symposium on mathematical statistics and probability,* Vol. 1. Berkeley: University of California Press.

Engle, R. F. (1984). Wald, likelihood ratio and Lagrange multiplier tests in econometrics. In Griliches, Z. and Intrilligator, M. D. (eds.), *Handbook of econometrics,* Vol. II. New York: Elsevier.

Hinkley, D. D. (1977). Jackknifing in unbalanced situations. *Technometrics,* 19: 285–292.

Johnston, J. (1984). *Econometric methods,* 3rd ed. New York: McGraw-Hill.

Judge, G. G., Griffith, W. E., Hill, R. C., Lutkepohl, H., and Lee, T. C. (1985). *The theory and practice of econometrics,* 2nd ed. New York: John Wiley & Sons, Inc.

MacKinnon, J. G. and White, H. (1985). Some heteroskedasticity-consistent covariance matrix estimators with improved finite sample properties. *Journal of Econometrics,* 29, 305–325.

Maddala, G. S. *Econometrics.* New York: McGraw-Hill, 1977.

Mardia, K. V., Kent, J. T., and Bibby, J. M. (1979). *Multivariate analysis.* New York: Academic Press.

Theil, H. (1971). *Principles of econometrics.* New York: John Wiley & Sons, Inc.

White, H. (1980). A heteroskedasticity-consistent covariance matrix estimator and a direct test for heteroskedasticity. *Econometrica,* 48, 817–838.

White, H. (1982). Maximum likelihood estimation of misspecified models. *Econometrica,* 50, 1–25.

White, H. (1982). Instrumental variables estimation with independent observations. *Econometrica,* 50, 483–500.

White, H. (1984). *Asymptotic theory for econometricians.* New York: Academic Press.

Index

A matrix, I-499
accelerated failure time distribution, II-380
ACF plots, II-484
additive trees, I-62, I-68
AID, I-35, I-37
Akaike Information Criterion, II-215
alternative hypothesis, I-13
analysis of covariance, I-431
  examples, I-462, I-478
  model, I-432
analysis of variance, I-210, I-487
  algorithms, I-485
  ANOVA command, I-438
  assumptions, I-388
  between-group differences, I-394
  bootstrapping, I-438
  compared to loglinear modeling, I-617
  compared to regression trees, I-35
  contrasts, I-390, I-434, I-435, I-436
  data format, I-438
  examples, I-439, I-442, I-447, I-457, I-459, I-461, I-462, I-464, I-470, I-472, I-475, I-478, I-480
  factorial, I-387
  hypothesis tests, I-386, I-434, I-435, I-436
  interactions, I-387
  model, I-432
  multivariate, I-393, I-396
  overview, I-431
  post hoc tests, I-389, I-432
  Quick Graphs, I-438
  repeated measures, I-393, I-436
  residuals, I-432
  unbalanced designs, I-391
  unequal variances, I-388
  usage, I-438
  within-subject differences, I-394
Anderberg dichotomy coefficients, I-120, I-126
angle tolerance, II-338

anisotropy, II-342, II-350
  geometric, II-342
  zonal, II-342
A-optimality, I-246
ARIMA models, II-469, II-479, II-492
  algorithms, II-520
ARMA models, II-474
autocorrelation plots, I-374, II-472, II-475, II-484
Automatic Interaction Detection, I-35
autoregressive models, II-472
axial designs, I-242

backward elimination, I-379
bandwidth, II-302, II-307, II-314, II-338
  optimal values, II-308
  relationship with kernel function, II-308
BASIC, II-378
basic statistics. *See* descriptive statistics
between-group differences
  in analysis of variance, I-394
bias, I-379
binary logit, I-548
  compared to multinomial logit, I-550
binary trees, I-33
biplots, II-226, II-227
Bisquare procedure, II-90
biweight kernel, II-305, II-314, II-315
Bonferroni inequality, I-37
Bonferroni test, I-127, I-389, I-432, I-493, II-433
bootstrap, I-19, I-20
  algorithms, I-28
  bootstrap-t method, I-19
  command, I-20
  data format, I-20

examples, I-21, I-24, I-25, I-26
missing data, I-28
naive bootstrap, I-19
overview, I-17
Quick Graphs, I-20
usage, I-20
box plot, I-210
Box-Behnken designs, I-238, I-264
Box-Hunter designs, I-235, I-256
Bray-Curtis measure, I-119, I-126

C matrix, I-499
candidate sets
 for optimal designs, I-245
canonical correlation analysis, I-487
 bootstrapping, II-259
 data format, II-258, II-259
 examples, II-260, II-263, II-267
 interactions, II-259
 model, II-257
 nominal scales, II-259
 overview, II-249
 partialled variables, II-257
 Quick Graphs, II-259
 rotation, II-258
 usage, II-259
canonical correlations, I-286
canonical rotation, II-227
categorical data, II-127
categorical predictors, I-35
Cauchy kernel, II-305, II-314, II-315
CCF plots, II-485
central composite designs, I-238, I-269
central limit theorem, II-430
centroid designs, I-241
CHAID, I-36, I-37
chi-square, I-160
Chi-square test for independence, I-148
circle model
 in perceptual mapping, II-225
city-block distance, I-126

classical analysis, II-446
classification functions, I-280
classification trees, I-36
 algorithms, I-50
 basic tree model, I-32
 bootstrapping, I-43
 commands, I-42
 compared to discriminant analysis, I-36, I-39
 data format, I-43
 displays, I-40
 examples, I-44, I-46, I-48
 loss functions, I-38, I-40
 missing data, I-50
 mobiles, I-31
 model, I-40
 overview, I-31
 pruning, I-37
 Quick Graphs, I-43
 saving files, I-43
 stopping criteria, I-37, I-42
 usage, I-43
cluster analysis
 additive trees, I-68
 algorithms, I-84
 bootstrapping, I-70
 commands, I-69
 data types, I-70
 distances, I-66
 examples, I-71, I-75, I-78, I-79, I-81, I-82
 exclusive clusters, I-54
 hierarchical clustering, I-64
 k-means clustering, I-67
 missing values, I-84
 overlapping clusters, I-54
 overview, I-53
 Quick Graphs, I-70
 saving files, I-70
 usage, I-70
Cochran's test of linear trend, I-168
coefficient of alienation, II-51, II-71
coefficient of determination. *See* multiple correlation
coefficient of variation, I-211
Cohen's kappa, I-164, I-168
communalities, I-332

Index

compound symmetry, I-394
conditional logistic regression model, I-550
conditional logit model, I-552
confidence curves, II-84
confidence intervals, I-11, I-211
    path analysis, II-213
conjoint analysis
    additive tables, I-88
    algorithms, I-112
    bootstrapping, I-95
    commands, I-95
    compared to logistic regression, I-92
    data format, I-95
    examples, I-96, I-100, I-103, I-107
    missing data, I-113
    model, I-93
    multiplicative tables, I-89
    overview, I-87
    Quick Graphs, I-95
    saving files, I-95
    usage, I-95
constraints
    in mixture designs, I-242
contingency coefficient, I-165, I-168
contour plots, II-348
contrast coefficients, I-393
contrasts
    in analysis of variance, I-390
convex hulls, II-347
Cook's distance, I-375
Cook-Weisberg graphical confidence curves, II-84
coordinate exchange method, I-245, I-270
correlation matrix, II-12
correlations, I-55, I-115
    algorithms, I-145
    binary data, I-126
    bootstrapping, I-129
    canonical, II-249
    commands, I-128
    continuous data, I-125
    data format, I-129
    dissimilarity measures, I-126
    distance measures, I-126

    examples, I-129, I-132, I-134, I-135, I-137, I-140, I-143, I-145
    missing values, I-124, I-146, II-12
    options, I-127
    Quick Graphs, I-129
    rank-order data, I-126
    saving files, I-129
    set, II-249
    usage, I-129
correlograms, II-351
correspondence analysis, II-222, II-226
    algorithms, I-156
    bootstrapping, I-150
    commands, I-150
    data format, I-150
    examples, I-151, I-153
    missing data, I-149, I-156
    model, I-149
    multiple correspondence analysis, I-149
    overview, I-147
    Quick Graphs, I-150
    simple correspondence analysis, I-149
    usage, I-150
covariance matrix, I-125, II-12
covariance paths
    path analysis, II-164
covariograms, II-337
Cramer's V, I-165
critical level, I-13
Cronbach's alpha. *See* descriptive statistics
cross-correlation plots, II-485
crossover designs, I-487
crosstabulation
    bootstrapping, I-171
    commands, I-171
    data format, I-171
    examples, I-173, I-175, I-177, I-178, I-179, I-181, I-186, I-188, I-189, I-192, I-194, I-196, I-197, I-199, I-200
    multiway, I-170
    one-way, I-158, I-160, I-166
    overview, I-157
    Quick Graphs, I-171
    standardizing tables, I-159
    two-way, I-158, I-161, I-167, I-168

usage, I-171
cross-validation, I-37, I-280, I-380

D matrix, I-499
D SUB-A (d_a), II-275
dates, II-378
degrees-of-freedom, II-428
dendrograms, I-57, I-70
dependence paths
    path analysis, II-163
descriptive statistics, I-1
    basic statistics, I-211, I-212
    bootstrapping, I-215
    commands, I-215
    Cronbach's alpha, I-214
    data format, I-215
    overview, I-205
    Quick Graphs, I-215
    stem-and-leaf plots, I-213
    usage, I-215
design of experiments, I-92, I-250, I-251
    axial designs, I-242
    bootstrapping, I-252
    Box-Behnken designs, I-238
    central composite designs, I-238
    centroid designs, I-241
    commands, I-252
    examples, I-253, I-254, I-256, I-258, I-260, I-263, I-264, I-265, I-266, I-269, I-270
    factorial designs, I-231, I-232
    lattice designs, I-241
    mixture designs, I-232, I-239
    optimal designs, I-232, I-244
    overview, I-227
    Quick Graphs, I-252
    response surface designs, I-232, I-236
    screening designs, I-242
    usage, I-252
determinant criterion. *See* D-optimality
dichotomy coefficients
    Anderberg, I-126
    Jaccard, I-126
    positive matching, I-126
    simple matching, I-126
    Tanimoto, I-126
difference contrasts, I-498
difficulty, II-463
discrete choice model, I-552
    compared to polytomous logit, I-553
discrete gaussian convolution, II-312
discriminant analysis, I-487
    bootstrapping, I-288
    commands, I-287
    compared to classification trees, I-36
    data format, I-288
    estimation, I-284
    examples, I-288, I-293, I-298, I-306, I-313, I-315, I-321
    linear discriminant function, I-280
    linear discriminant model, I-276
    model, I-283
    multiple groups, I-282
    options, I-284
    overview, I-275
    prior probabilities, I-282
    Quick Graphs, I-288
    statistics, I-286
    stepwise estimation, I-284
    usage, I-288
discrimination parameter, II-463
dissimilarities
    direct, II-49
    indirect, II-49
distance measures, I-55, I-115
distances
    nearest-neighbor, II-345
distance-weighted least squares (DWLS) smoother, II-312
dit plots, I-15
D-optimality, I-246
dot histogram plots, I-15
D-PRIME (d'), II-274
dummy codes, I-490
Duncan's test, I-390
Dunnett test, I-493
Dunn-Sidak test, I-127, II-433

ECVI, II-215
edge effects, II-347
effects codes, I-383, I-490
efficiency, I-244
eigenvalues, I-286
ellipse model
    in perceptual mapping, II-226
EM algorithm, I-362
EM estimation, II-8
    for correlations, I-127, II-12
    for covariances, II-12
    for SSCP matrix, II-12
endogenous variables
    path analysis, II-164
Epanechnikov kernel, II-305, II-314, II-315
equamax rotation, I-333, I-337
Euclidean distances, II-49
exogenous variables
    path analysis, II-164
expected cross-validation index, II-215
exponential distribution, II-380
exponential model, II-340, II-350
exponential smoothing, II-480
external unfolding, II-224

factor analysis, I-331, II-222
    algorithms, I-362
    bootstrapping, I-339
    commands, I-339
    compared to principal components analysis, I-334
    convergence, I-335
    correlations vs covariances, I-331
    data format, I-339
    eigenvalues, I-335
    eigenvectors, I-338
    examples, I-341, I-344, I-348, I-350, I-353, I-356
    iterated principal axis, I-335
    loadings, I-338
    maximum likelihood, I-335
    missing values, I-362
    number of factors, I-335
    overview, I-327
    principal components, I-335
    Quick Graphs, I-339
    residuals, I-338
    rotation, I-333, I-337
    save, I-338
    scores, I-338
    usage, I-339
factor loadings, II-446
factorial analysis of variance, I-387
factorial designs, I-231, I-232
    analysis of, I-235
    examples, I-253
    fractional factorials, I-234
    full factorial designs, I-234
Fedorov method, I-245
Fieller bounds, I-579
filters, II-482
Fisher's LSD, I-389, I-493
Fisher's exact test, I-164, I-168
Fisher's linear discriminant function, II-222
fixed variance
    path analysis, II-166
fixed-bandwidth method
    compared to KNN method, II-309
    for smoothing, II-307, II-309, II-314
Fletcher-Powell minimization, II-462
forward selection, I-379
Fourier analysis, II-481, II-494
fractional factorial designs, I-487
    Box-Hunter designs, I-235
    examples, I-254, I-256, I-258, I-260, I-263
    homogeneous fractional designs, I-235
    Latin square designs, I-235
    mixed-level fractional designs, I-235
    Plackett-Burman designs, I-235
    Taguchi designs, I-235
Freeman-Tukey deviates, I-620
frequencies, I-20, I-43, I-95, I-129, I-150, I-171, I-215, I-288, I-339, I-403, I-438, I-501, I-563, I-624, II-15, II-55, II-93, II-134, II-151, II-177, II-229, II-243, II-259, II-279, II-317, II-357, II-390, II-434, II-451, II-495, II-527

frequency tables. *See* crosstabulation
Friedman test, II-130

gamma coefficients, I-126
Gaussian kernel, II-305, II-314, II-315
Gaussian model, II-340, II-350
Gauss-Newton method, II-83, II-84
general linear models
   algorithms, I-546
   bootstrapping, I-501
   categorical variables, I-490
   commands, I-501
   contrasts, I-495, I-497, I-498, I-499
   data format, I-501
   examples, I-503, I-510, I-512, I-513, I-515, I-518, I-520, I-523, I-532, I-535, I-536, I-540, I-544, I-545
   hypothesis tests, I-495
   mixture model, I-492
   model estimation, I-488
   overview, I-487
   post hoc tests, I-493
   Quick Graphs, I-501
   repeated measures, I-491
   residuals, I-488
   stepwise regression, I-492
   usage, I-501
generalized least squares, II-175, II-525
generalized variance, II-252
geostatistical models, II-336, II-337
Gini index, I-38, I-40
GLM. *See* general linear models
global criterion. *See* G-optimality
Goodman-Kruskal gamma, I-126, I-165, I-168
Goodman-Kruskal lambda, I-168
G-optimality, I-246
Graeco-Latin square designs, I-235
Greenhouse-Geisser statistic, I-395
Guttman mu2 monotonicity coefficients, I-119, I-126
Guttman's coefficient of alienation, II-51
Guttman's loss function, II-71
Guttman-Rulon coefficient, II-447

Hadi outlier detection, I-123, I-127
Hampel procedure, II-90
Hanning weights, II-468
hazard function
   heterogeneity, II-383
heteroskedasticity, II-524
heteroskedasticity-consistent standard errors, II-525
hierarchical clustering, I-56, I-64
hinge, I-207
histograms
   nearest-neighbor, II-357
hole model, II-341, II-350
Holt's method, II-480
Huber procedure, II-90
Huynh-Feldt statistic, I-395
hyper-Graeco-Latin square designs, I-235
hypothesis
   alternative, I-13
   null, I-13
   testing, I-12, I-371

ID3, I-37
incomplete block designs, I-487
independence, I-161
   in loglinear models, I-616
INDSCAL model, II-47
inertia, I-148
inferential statistics, I-7
instrumental variables, II-523
internal-consistency, II-447
interquartile range, I-207
interval censored data, II-376
inverse-distance smoother, II-312
isotropic, II-337
item-response analysis. *See* test item analysis
item-test correlations, II-446

Jaccard dichotomy coefficients, I-120, I-126
jackknife, I-18, I-20
jackknifed classification matrix, I-280

k nearest-neighbors method
    compared to fixed-bandwidth method, II-309
    for smoothing, II-307, II-314
Kendall's tau-*b* coefficients, I-126, I-165, I-168
kernel functions, II-302, II-304
    biweight, II-305, II-314, II-315
    Cauchy, II-305, II-314, II-315
    Epanechnikov, II-305, II-314, II-315
    Gaussian, II-305, II-314, II-315
    plotting, II-305
    relationship with bandwidth, II-308
    tricube, II-305, II-314, II-315
    triweight, II-305, II-314, II-315
    uniform, II-305, II-314
k-exchange method, I-245
k-means clustering, I-60, I-67
Kolmogorov-Smirnov test, II-128
KR20, II-447
kriging, II-348
    ordinary, II-343, II-354
    simple, II-343, II-354
    trend components, II-343
    universal, II-344
Kruskal's loss function, II-70
Kruskal's STRESS, II-51
Kruskal-Wallis test, II-126, II-127
Kukoc statistic 7
Kulczynski measure, I-126
kurtosis, I-211

lags
    number of lags, II-338
latent trait model, II-446, II-448
Latin square designs, I-235, I-258, I-487

lattice, II-148
lattice designs, I-241
Lawley-Hotelling trace, I-286
least absolute deviations, II-82
Levene test, I-388
leverage, I-376
likelihood ratio chi-square, I-164, I-168, I-618, I-620
    compared to Pearson chi-square, I-618
Lilliefors test, II-145
linear contrasts, I-390
linear discriminant function, I-280
linear discriminant model, I-276
linear models
    analysis of variance, I-431
    general linear models, I-487
    linear regression, I-399
linear regression, I-11, I-371
    bootstrapping, I-403
    commands, I-403
    data format, I-403
    estimation, I-401
    examples, I-404, I-407, I-410, I-413, I-417, I-420,
        I-424, I-426, I-427, I-428, I-429
    model, I-400
    overview, I-399
    Quick Graphs, I-403
    residuals, I-373, I-400
    stepwise, I-379, I-401
    tolerance, I-401
    usage, I-403
    using correlation matrix as input, I-381
    using covariance matrix as input, I-381
    using SSCP matrix as input, I-381
listwise deletion, I-362, II-3
Little MCAR test, II-1, II-11, II-12, II-31
loadings, I-330, I-331
LOESS smoothing, II-312, II-314, II-318, II-319,
    II-322, II-331
logistic item-response analysis, II-462
    one-parameter model, II-448
    two-parameter model, II-448

logistic regression
  algorithms, I-607
  bootstrapping, I-563
  categorical predictors, I-556
  compared to conjoint analysis, I-92
  compared to linear model, I-548
  conditional variables, I-555
  confidence intervals, I-579
  convergence, I-558
  data format, I-563
  deciles of risk, I-559
  discrete choice, I-557
  dummy coding, I-556
  effect coding, I-556
  estimation, I-558
  examples, I-564, I-566, I-567, I-572, I-577, I-580, I-589, I-596, I-598, I-602, I-605
  missing data, I-607
  model, I-555
  options, I-558
  overview, I-547
  post hoc tests, I-561
  prediction table, I-555
  print options, I-563
  quantiles, I-560, I-580
  Quick Graphs, I-563
  simulation, I-561
  stepwise estimation, I-558
  tolerance, I-558
  usage, I-563
  weights, I-563
logit model, I-549
loglinear modeling
  bootstrapping, I-624
  commands, I-623
  compared to analysis of variance, I-617
  compared to Crosstabs, I-623
  convergence, I-619
  data format, I-624
  examples, I-625, I-635, I-638, I-642
  frequency tables, I-623
  model, I-619
  overview, I-615
  parameters, I-620
  Quick Graphs, I-624
  saturated models, I-617
  statistics, I-620
  structural zeros, I-621
  usage, I-624
log-logistic distribution, II-380
log-normal distribution, II-380
loss functions, I-38, II-79
  multidimensional scaling, II-70
LOWESS smoothing, II-469
low-pass filter, II-482
LSD test, I-432, I-493

madograms, II-351
Mahalanobis distances, I-276, I-286
Mann-Whitney test, II-126, II-127
MANOVA. *See* analysis of variance
Mantel-Haenszel test, I-170
MAR, II-9
Marquardt method, II-87
Marron & Nolan canonical kernel width, II-308, II-314
mass, I-148
matrix displays, I-57
maximum likelihood estimates, II-80
maximum likelihood factor analysis, I-334
maximum Wishart likelihood, II-175
MCAR, II-9
MCAR test, II-1, II-12, II-31
McFadden's conditional logit model, I-552
McNemar's test, I-164, I-168
MDPREF, II-226, II-227
MDS. *See* multidimensional scaling
mean, I-3, I-206, I-211
mean smoothing, II-310, II-314, II-316
means coding, I-384
median, I-4, I-206, I-211
median smoothing, II-310
meta-analysis, I-382
MGLH. *See* general linear models
midrange, I-207
minimum spanning trees, II-345

Minkowski metric, II-51
MIS function, II-20
missing value analysis
　algorithms, II-46
　bootstrapping, II-15
　casewise pattern table, II-20
　data format, II-15
　EM algorithm, II-8, II-12, II-25, II-33, II-42
　examples, II-15, II-20, II-25, II-33, II-42
　listwise deletion, II-3, II-25, II-33
　MISSING command, II-14
　missing value patterns, II-15
　model, II-12
　outliers, II-12
　overview, II-1
　pairwise deletion, II-3, II-25, II-33
　pattern variables, II-2, II-42
　Quick Graphs, II-15
　randomness, II-9
　regression imputation, II-6, II-12, II-25, II-42
　saving estimates, II-12, II-15
　unconditional mean imputation, II-4
　usage, II-15
mixture designs, I-232, I-239
　analysis of, I-243
　axial designs, I-242
　centroid designs, I-241
　constraints, I-242
　examples, I-265, I-266
　lattice designs, I-241
　Scheffé model, I-243
　screening designs, I-242
　simplex, I-241
models, I-10
　estimation, I-10
mosaic plots, II-348
moving average, II-307, II-467, II-473
moving-averages smoother, II-312
mu2 monotonicity coefficients, I-126
multidimensional scaling, II-222
　algorithms, II-70
　assumptions, II-48
　bootstrapping, II-55
　commands, II-55
　configuration, II-51, II-54
　confirmatory, II-54
　convergence, II-51
　data format, II-55
　dissimilarities, II-49
　distance metric, II-51
　examples, II-56, II-58, II-60, II-64, II-68
　Guttman method, II-71
　individual differences, II-47
　Kruskal method, II-70
　log function, II-51
　loss functions, II-51
　matrix shape, II-51
　metric, II-51
　missing values, II-72
　nonmetric, II-51
　overview, II-47
　power function, II-51
　Quick Graphs, II-55
　residuals, II-51
　Shepard diagrams, II-51, II-55
　usage, II-55
multinomial logit, I-550
　compared to binary logit, I-550
multiple correlation, I-372
multiple correspondence analysis, I-148
multiple regression, I-376
multivariate analysis of variance, I-396
mutually exclusive, I-160

Nadaraya-Watson smoother, II-312
nesting, I-487
Newman-Keuls test, I-390
Newton-Raphson method, I-615
nodes, I-33
nominal data, II-127
nonlinear modeling
　algorithms, II-122
　estimation, II-83
　loss functions, II-79
　missing data, II-123
　problems in, II-83

nonlinear models, II-75
  bootstrapping, II-93
  commands, II-93
  computation, II-87
  convergence, II-87
  data format, II-93
  examples, II-94, II-97, II-100, II-102, II-105, II-107, II-108, II-110, II-113, II-118, II-120, II-121
  functions of parameters, II-89
  loss functions, II-84, II-91, II-92
  model, II-84
  parameter bounds, II-87
  Quick Graphs, II-93
  recalculation of parameters, II-88
  robust estimation, II-90
  starting values, II-87
  usage, II-93
nonmetric unfolding model, II-47
nonparametric statistics
  algorithms, II-145
  bootstrapping, II-134
  commands, II-129, II-131, II-133
  data format, II-134
  examples, II-134, II-136, II-137, II-139, II-140, II-142, II-144
  Friedman test, II-130
  independent samples tests, II-127, II-128
  Kolmogorov-Smirnov test, II-128, II-131
  Kruskal-Wallis test, II-127
  Mann-Whitney test, II-127
  one-sample tests, II-133
  overview, II-125
  Quick Graphs, II-134
  related variables tests, II-129, II-130
  sign test, II-129
  usage, II-134
  Wald-Wolfowitz runs test, II-133
  Wilcoxon signed-rank test, II-130
  Wilcoxon test, II-127
normal distribution, I-207
NPAR model, II-274
nugget, II-341
null hypothesis, I-12

oblimin rotation, I-333, I-337
observational studies, I-229
Occam's razor, I-91
odds ratio, I-168
omni-directional variograms, II-338
optimal designs, I-232, I-244
  analysis of, I-246
  A-optimality, I-246
  candidate sets, I-245
  coordinate exchange method, I-245, I-270
  D-optimality, I-246
  efficiency criteria, I-246
  Fedorov method, I-245
  G-optimality, I-246
  k-exchange method, I-245
  model, I-247
  optimality criteria, I-246
optimality, I-244
ORDER, II-379
ordinal data, II-126
ordinary least squares, II-175
orthomax rotation, I-333, I-337

PACF plots, II-484
pairwise deletion, I-362, II-3
pairwise mean comparisons, I-389
parameters, I-10
parametric modeling, II-380
partial autocorrelation plots, II-474, II-475, II-484
partialing
  in set correlation, II-253
partially ordered scalogram analysis
    with coordinates
  algorithms, II-160
  bootstrapping, II-151
  commands, II-150
  convergence, II-150
  data format, II-151
  displays, II-149
  examples, II-152, II-153, II-156
  missing data, II-160
  model, II-150

overview, II-147
Quick Graphs, II-151
usage, II-151
path analysis
algorithms, II-212
bootstrapping, II-177
commands, II-177
confidence intervals, II-175, II-213
covariance paths, II-164
covariance relationships, II-173
data format, II-177
dependence paths, II-163
dependence relationships, II-171
endogenous variables, II-164
estimation, II-175
examples, II-178, II-183, II-196, II-202
exogenous variables, II-164
fixed parameters, II-171, II-173
fixed variance, II-166
free parameters, II-171, II-173
latent variables, II-175
manifest variables, II-175
measures of fit, II-213
model, II-169, II-171
overview, II-161
path diagrams, II-161
Quick Graphs, II-177
starting values, II-175
usage, II-177
variance paths, II-164
path diagrams, II-161
Pearson chi-square, I-161, I-166, I-168, I-616, I-620
compared to likelihood ratio chi-square, I-618
Pearson correlation, I-117, I-123, I-125
perceptual mapping
algorithms, II-236
bootstrapping, II-229
commands, II-229
data format, II-229
examples, II-230, II-231, II-232, II-234
methods, II-227
missing data, II-236
model, II-227
overview, II-221
Quick Graphs, II-229
usage, II-229

periodograms, II-481
permutation tests, I-160
phi coefficient, I-38, I-40, I-165, I-168
Pillai trace, I-286
Plackett-Burman designs, I-235, I-263
point processes, II-336, II-344
polynomial contrasts, I-390, I-393, I-498
polynomial smoothing, II-310, II-314, II-316
pooled variances, II-430
populations, I-7
POSET, II-147
positive matching dichotomy coefficients, I-120
power model, II-340, II-350
preference curves, II-224
preference mapping, II-222
PREFMAP, II-227
principal components analysis, I-327, I-328, I-487
coefficents, I-330
compared to factor analysis, I-334
compared to linear regression, I-329
loadings, I-330
prior probabilities, I-282
probability plots, I-15, I-373
probit analysis
algorithms, II-246
bootstrapping, II-243
categorical variables, II-241
commands, II-242
data format, II-243
dummy coding, II-241
effect coding, II-241
examples, II-243, II-245
interpretation, II-240
missing data, II-246
model, II-239, II-240
overview, II-239
Quick Graphs, II-243
saving files, II-243
usage, II-243
Procrustes rotations, II-226, II-227
proportional hazards models, II-381

QSK coefficient, I-126
quadrat counts, II-335, II-347, II-348
quadratic contrasts, I-390
quantile plots, II-382
quantitative symmetric dissimilarity coefficient, I-119
quartimax rotation, I-333, I-337
quasi-independence, I-621
Quasi-Newton method, II-83, II-84

random fields, II-336
random samples, I-8
random variables, I-370
random walk, II-473
randomized block designs, I-487
range, I-207, I-211, II-341
rank-order coefficients, I-126
Rasch model, II-448
receiver operating characteristic curves. *See* signal detection analysis
regression
   linear, I-11, I-399
   logistic, I-547
   two-stage least squares, II-523
regression trees, I-35
   algorithms, I-50
   basic tree model, I-32
   bootstrapping, I-43
   commands, I-42
   compared to analysis of variance, I-35
   compared to stepwise regression, I-36
   data format, I-43
   displays, I-40
   examples, I-44, I-46, I-48
   loss functions, I-38, I-40
   missing data, I-50
   mobiles, I-31
   model, I-40
   overview, I-31
   pruning, I-37
   Quick Graphs, I-43
   saving files, I-43
   stopping criteria, I-37, I-42
   usage, I-43
reliability, II-447, II-449
repeated measures, I-393, I-491
   assumptions, I-394
response surface designs, I-232, I-236
   analysis of, I-239
   Box-Behnken designs, I-238
   central composite designs, I-238
   examples, I-264, I-269
   rotatability, I-237, I-238
response surfaces, I-92, II-84
right censored data, II-376
RMSEA, II-214
robust smoothing, II-310, II-314, II-316
robustness, II-127
ROC curves, II-273, II-274, II-279
root mean square error of approximation, II-214
rotatability
   in response surface designs, I-237
rotatable designs
   in response surface designs, I-238
rotation, I-333
running median smoothers, II-468
running-means smoother, II-312

Sakitt D, II-275
samples, I-8
sampling. *See* bootstrap
saturated models
   loglinear modeling, I-617
scalogram. *See* partially ordered scalogram analysis with coordinates
scatterplot matrix, I-117
Scheffé model
   in mixture designs, I-243
Scheffe test, I-389, I-432, I-493
screening designs, I-242

SD-RATIO, II-275
seasonal decomposition, II-479
second-order stationarity, II-337
semi-variograms, II-351, II-338
set correlations, II-249
    assumptions, II-250
    measures of association, II-251
    missing data, II-271
    partialing. *See* canonical correlation analysis
Shepard diagrams, II-51, II-55
Shepard's smoother, II-312
sign test, II-129
signal detection analysis
    algorithms, II-298
    bootstrapping, II-279
    chi-square model, II-275
    commands, II-278
    convergence, II-275
    data format, II-279
    examples, II-287, II-288, II-289, II-292, II-295, II-296
    exponential model, II-275
    gamma model, II-275
    logistic model, II-275
    missing data, II-299
    nonparametric model, II-275
    normal model, II-275
    overview, II-273
    Poisson model, II-275
    Quick Graphs, II-279
    ROC curves, II-273, II-279
    usage, II-279
    variables, II-275
sill, II-341
similarity measures, I-115
simple matching dichotomy coefficients, I-120
simplex, I-241
Simplex method, II-83, II-84
simulation, II-344
singular value decomposition, I-147, II-226, II-236
skew
    positive, I-4

skewness, I-209, I-211
slope, I-376
smoothing, II-314, II-466
    bandwidth, II-302, II-307, II-314
    biweight kernel, II-305, II-314, II-315
    bootstrapping, II-317, II-319
    Cauchy kernel, II-305, II-314, II-315
    commands, II-316
    confidence intervals, II-319
    data format, II-317
    discontinuities, II-312
    discrete gaussian convolution, II-312
    distance-weighted least squares (DWLS), II-312
    Epanechnikov kernel, II-305, II-314, II-315
    examples, II-318, II-319, II-322, II-331
    fixed-bandwidth method, II-307, II-314
    Gaussian kernel, II-305, II-314, II-315
    grid points, II-313, II-314, II-331
    inverse-distance, II-312
    k nearest-neighbors method, II-307
    kernel functions, II-302, II-304, II-314, II-315
    LOESS smoothing, II-312, II-314, II-318, II-319, II-322, II-331
    Marron & Nolan canonical kernel width, II-308, II-314
    mean smoothing, II-310, II-314, II-316
    median smoothing, II-310
    methods, II-302, II-310, II-316
    model, II-314
    moving-averages, II-312
    Nadaraya-Watson, II-312
    nonparametric vs. parametric, II-302
    overview, II-301
    polynomial smoothing, II-310, II-314, II-316
    Quick Graphs, II-317
    residuals, II-313, II-317
    robust smoothing, II-310, II-314, II-316
    running-means, II-312
    saving results, II-314, II-317, II-318
    Shepard's smoother, II-312
    step, II-312
    tied values, II-313
    tricube kernel, II-305, II-314, II-315
    trimmed mean smoothing, II-314, II-316
    triweight kernel, II-305, II-314, II-315
    uniform kernel, II-305, II-314

usage, II-317
window normalization, II-308, II-314
Somer's *d* coefficients, I-165, I-168
sorting, I-5
Sosa statistic 21, 66, 98
spatial statistics, II-335
   algorithms, II-372
   azimuth, II-351
   bootstrapping, II-357
   commands, II-355
   data, II-357
   dip, II-351
   examples, II-357, II-364, II-365, II-370
   grid, II-353
   kriging, II-343, II-348, II-354
   lags, II-351
   missing data, II-372
   model, II-335
   models, II-350
   nested models, II-342
   nesting structures, II-350
   nugget, II-350
   nugget effect, II-341
   plots, II-348
   point statistics, II-348
   Quick Graphs, II-357
   sill, II-341, II-350
   simulation, II-344, II-348
   trends, II-348
   variograms, II-338, II-348, II-351
Spearman coefficients, I-119, I-126, I-165
Spearman-Brown coefficient, II-447
specificities, I-332
spectral models, II-466
spherical model, II-339, II-350
split plot designs, I-487
split-half reliabilities, II-449
SSCP matrix, II-12
standard deviation, I-3, I-207, I-211
standard error of estimate, I-371
standard error of kurtosis, I-211
standard error of skewness, I-211
standard error of the mean, I-11, I-211

standardization, I-55
standardized alpha, II-447
standardized deviates, I-147, I-620
standardized values, I-6
stationarity, II-337, II-475
statistics
   defined, I-1
   descriptive, I-1
   inferential. *See* descriptive statistics
stem-and-leaf plots. *See* descriptive statistics
step smoother, II-312
stepwise regression, I-379, I-392, I-554
stochastic processes, II-336
stress, II-50, II-70
structural equation models. *See* path analysis
Stuart's tau-*c* coefficients, I-165, I-168
studentized residuals, I-373
subpopulations, I-209
subsampling, I-18
sum of cross-products matrix, I-125
sums of squares
   type I, I-391, I-396
   type II, I-397
   type III, I-392, I-397
   type IV, I-397
surface plots, II-348
survival analysis
   algorithms, II-414
   bootstrapping, II-390
   censoring, II-376, II-383, II-418
   centering, II-415
   coding variables, II-383
   commands, II-389
   convergence, II-420
   Cox regression, II-387
   data format, II-390
   estimation, II-385
   examples, II-391, II-394, II-395, II-399, II-402, II-404, II-409, II-411
   exponential model, II-387
   graphs, II-387
   logistic model, II-387

Index

log-likelihood, II-416
log-normal model, II-387
missing data, II-415
models, II-417, II-383
overview, II-375
parameters, II-415
plots, II-377, II-419
proportional hazards models, II-418
Quick Graphs, II-390
singular Hessian, II-417
stepwise estimation, II-385, II-420
tables, II-387
time varying covariates, II-388
usage, II-390
variances, II-421
Weibull model, II-387
symmetric matrix, I-117

t distributions, II-426
    compared to normal distributions, II-428
t tests
    assumptions, II-430
    Bonferroni adjustment, II-433
    bootstrapping, II-434
    commands, II-434
    confidence intervals, II-433
    data format, II-434
    degrees of freedom, II-428
    Dunn-Sidak adjustment, II-433
    examples, II-435, II-437, II-439, II-441, II-443
    one-sample, II-428, II-432
    overview, II-425
    paired, II-429, II-432
    Quick Graphs, II-434
    separate variances, II-430
    two-sample, II-429, II-431
    usage, II-434
Taguchi designs, I-235, I-260
Tanimoto dichotomy coefficients, I-120, I-126
tau-*b* coefficients, I-126, I-168
tau-*c* coefficients, I-168

test item analysis
    algorithms, II-462
    bootstrapping, II-451
    classical analysis, II-446, II-447, II-449, II-462
    commands, II-451
    data format, II-451
    examples, II-455, II-456, II-459
    logistic item-response analysis, II-448, II-450, II-462
    missing data, II-463
    overview, II-445
    Quick Graphs, II-451
    reliabilities, II-449
    scoring items, II-449, II-450
    statistics, II-451
    usage, II-451
tetrachoric correlation, I-120, I-121, I-126
theory of signal detectability (TSD), II-273
time domain models, II-466
time series, II-465
    algorithms, II-520
    ARIMA models, II-469, II-492
    bootstrapping, II-495
    clear series, II-487
    commands, II-486, II-488, II-491, II-492, II-493, II-495
    data format, II-495
    examples, II-496, II-497, II-498, II-500, II-503, II-504, II-505, II-507, II-508, II-512, II-518
    forecasts, II-490
    Fourier transformations, II-494
    missing values, II-465
    moving average, II-467, II-488
    overview, II-465
    plot labels, II-483
    plots, II-482, II-483, II-484, II-485
    Quick Graphs, II-495
    running means, II-468, II-488
    running medians, II-468, II-488
    seasonal adjustments, II-479, II-491
    smoothing, II-466, II-488, II-489, II-490
    stationarity, II-475
    transformations, II-486, II-487
    trends, II-490
    usage, II-495
tolerance, I-380

Index

T-plots, II-482
trace criterion. *See* A-optimality
transformations, I-209
tree clustering methods, I-37
tree diagrams, I-57
triangle inequality, II-48
tricube kernel, II-305, II-314, II-315
trimmed mean smoothing, II-314, II-316
triweight kernel, II-305, II-314, II-315
Tukey pairwise comparisons test, I-389, I-432, I-493
Tukey's jackknife, I-18
twoing, I-38
two-stage least squares
   algorithms, II-534
   bootstrapping, II-527
   commands, II-527
   data format, II-527
   estimation, II-523
   examples, II-528, II-530, II-533
   heteroskedasticity-consistent standard errors, II-525
   lagged variables, II-525
   missing data, II-534
   model, II-525
   overview, II-523
   Quick Graphs, II-527
   usage, II-527
type I sums of squares, I-391, I-396
type II sums of squares, I-397
type III sums of squares, I-392, I-397
type IV sums of squares, I-397

unbalanced designs
   in analysis of variance, I-391
uncertainty coefficient, I-168
unfolding models, II-223
uniform kernel, II-305, II-314

variance, I-211
   of estimates, I-237
variance of prediction, I-238
variance paths
   path analysis, II-164
varimax rotation, I-333, I-337
variograms, II-338, II-348, II-357
   model, II-339
vector model
   in perceptual mapping, II-225
Voronoi polygons, II-335, II-346, II-348

Wald-Wolfowitz runs test, II-133
wave model, II-341
Weibull distribution, II-380
weight, II-357
weighted running smoothing, II-468
weights, I-20, I-43, I-95, I-129, I-150, I-171, I-215, I-288, I-339, I-403, I-438, I-501, I-563, I-624, II-15, II-55, II-93, II-134, II-151, II-177, II-229, II-243, II-259, II-279, II-317, II-390, II-434, II-451, II-495, II-527
Wilcoxon signed-rank test, II-130
Wilcoxon test, II-127
Wilks' lambda, I-280, I-286
Wilks' trace, I-286
Winter's three-parameter model, II-480
within-subjects differences
   in analysis of variance, I-394

XTAB procedure, I-203

Yates' correction, I-164, I-168
y-intercept, I-376
Young's S-STRESS, II-51
Yule's *Q*, I-165, I-168
Yule's *Y*, I-165, I-168